Microsoft® SQL Server™ 2005 Reporting Services

Brian Larson

McGraw-Hill/Osborne

New York   Chicago   San Francisco
Lisbon   London   Madrid   Mexico City   Milan
New Delhi   San Juan   Seoul   Singapore   Sydney   Toronto

The McGraw·Hill Companies

McGraw-Hill/Osborne
2100 Powell Street, 10th Floor
Emeryville, California 94608
U.S.A.

To arrange bulk purchase discounts for sales promotions, premiums, or fund-raisers, please contact **McGraw-Hill**/Osborne at the above address.

Microsoft® SQL Server™ 2005 Reporting Services

4567890 FGR FGR 01987

ISBN 0-07-226239-7

Acquisitions Editor	Wendy Rinaldi
Project Editor	Patty Mon
Acquisitions Coordinator	Alexander McDonald
Technical Editor	Todd Meister
Copy Editor	Marcia Baker
Proofreader	Paul Tyler
Indexer	Karin Arrigoni
Composition	International Typesetting and Composition
Illustration	International Typesetting and Composition
Series Design	Peter F. Hancik
Cover Series Design	Pattie Lee

This book was composed with Adobe® InDesign® CS.

This book is dedicated to my family. To my children, Jessica and Corey, who gave up many hours of "dad time" during the writing of this book. And especially to my wife, Pam, who, in addition to allowing me to commit to this project, gave countless hours of her own time to make sure things were done right.

About the Author

Brian Larson is a Phi Beta Kappa graduate of Luther College in Decorah, Iowa, with degrees in physics and computer science. Brian has 20 years of experience in the computer industry and 16 years experience as a consultant creating custom database applications. He is currently the Chief of Technology for Superior Consulting Services in Minneapolis, Minnesota, a Microsoft Consulting Partner for Reporting Services. Brian is a Microsoft Certified Solution Developer (MCSD) and a Microsoft Certified Database Administrator (MCDBA).

Brian served as a member of the Reporting Services development team as a consultant to Microsoft. In that role, he contributed to the original code base of Reporting Services.

Brian has presented seminars and provided training and mentoring on Reporting Services across the country. A contributor and columnist for *SQL Server* magazine, Brian is also currently writing the B.I. Powers column appearing on the *SQL Server* magazine website. In addition to this book, Brian is the author of *Delivering Business Intelligence with Microsoft SQL Server 2005*, also from McGraw-Hill/Osborne.

Brian and his wife Pam have been married for 20 years. Pam will tell you that their first date took place at the campus computer center. If that doesn't qualify someone to write a computer book, then I don't know what does. Brian and Pam have two children, Jessica and Corey.

Contents

Foreword

The first time I met Brian Larson was in late 2001. At that time, we had been working on Reporting Services for about a year. We were looking for someone to help write the PDF rendering extension as we were extremely busy with the core reporting processing engine and server infrastructure.

I had known Marty Voegole, Brian's coworker at Superior Consulting, from some previous projects he had worked on for Microsoft. We contacted Marty and asked whether he was interested in doing some work for a new product. The code had to be written in C# using the .NET Framework, both of which had been recently released. The catch was that we were still over a year away from going public with Reporting Services, so they wouldn't be able to talk about any of their work until we had announced the product. They agreed and started working on the extension.

When it was finally complete, Brian and Marty had worked for over six months on the project. It took a lot longer than we initially thought as the rendering APIs were still evolving at the time and we were learning about the PDF format. Also, we had only written the HTML rendering extension, so much of the page-oriented sizing and absolute positioning logic was new. By late 2002, we had finished integrating the code, Brian and Marty moved on to other projects, and we focused on other areas of the product.

Around the same time, we had been quietly showing the product to a small set of partners and customers. While Reporting Services was originally scheduled to be released with SQL Server 2005 (called "Yukon" at the time), feedback from the early demos told us that we had something special on our hands that customers wanted sooner, not later. We decided to package up what we had and release the product as an add-on to SQL Server 2000. In February 2003, we formally announced the existence of SQL Server Reporting Services and began work to deliver the early release.

We released the first beta of the product in April and followed up with a second, public beta in October. Our initial goal for the second beta was 1,000 customers. By the time we had closed the beta, we had over 14,000 customers signed up to participate. The release of the product in January of 2004 capped off three years of hard work and was the highlight of my professional career. I am very proud of our first version and the reaction to the product has exceeded my wildest expectations.

In the first year of release, over 120,000 people tried out the product and there were over 20,000 posts on our public newsgroup.

Brian released the first edition of this book just as we wrapped up the work on the first release and started working on the SQL Server 2005 version. While the core architecture of the product hasn't changed in the new release, there are lots of new features that you will want to take advantage of, especially the new Report Builder end user reporting tool. Brian's in-depth knowledge of the product and his practical approach made the first edition of this book a success and I'm sure that this edition will help you to leverage all of the new features in this release.

Reporting Services wouldn't be the same product without the support of folks like Brian, our early adopters, and the thousands of customers who answer newsgroup posts, write blogs, and generally share their product knowledge with others. It's been very gratifying to meet people who are doing amazing things with the product and pushing it in ways we never dreamed of. I encourage you to use the knowledge and techniques in this book to make it work for you as well.

Enjoy!

Brian Welcker
Group Program Manager
Microsoft SQL Server Reporting Services

Acknowledgments

"A journey of a thousand miles begins with a single step." Perhaps this book project was not a journey of a thousand miles, although it seemed that way in the early hours of the morning with a deadline approaching. Be that as it may, it is possible to identify the first step in this whole process. A coworker of mine at Superior Consulting Services, Marty Voegele, was between assignments, on-the-bench, in consultant-speak. Marty was bored, so he decided to take matters into his own hands. Marty had previously consulted to Microsoft and still had a few contacts in the SQL Server area. He made a few phone calls and before long, Marty was again consulting to Microsoft, this time creating something called Rosetta.

As additional work was added, I had the opportunity to take on part of this assignment as well. It was both challenging and exciting working on code that you knew would be part of a major product from a major software company. What was perhaps most exciting was that Rosetta seemed to be a tool that would fill several needs we had identified while developing custom applications for our own clients.

As the beta version of what was now called Reporting Services was released, a brief introductory article on Reporting Services appeared in *SQL Server* magazine. One of the sales representatives here at Superior Consulting Services, Mike Nelson, decided this would be a nice bit of marketing material to have as we trumpeted our involvement with Reporting Services. One thing led to another and before we knew it, Mike had offered Marty's and my services to write a more in-depth article for *SQL Server* magazine. This article became the cover article for the December 2003 issue and it has become known as the "Delightful" article (you'll have to read the first paragraph of the article to understand why) and it is now available on MSDN.

This was where I grabbed the map and compass, and decided on the next path. Because the magazine article came out fairly well, I decided to write a book on the topic. Marty informed me that writing a 700-page book would probably make his fingers fall off, so I could take this next step on my own. So, here we are today.

All of this is a rather lengthy way of saying that I owe a big thank you to Marty and Mike. Without a shadow of a doubt, this book would not have happened without them. In addition to the contributions already stated, I want to thank Marty for helping to keep me up to speed on Reporting Services information and newsgroup postings.

We have learned a great deal preparing presentations on Reporting Services and providing Reporting Services solutions for clients.

I also want to thank John Miller, the owner of Superior Consulting Services. John hired me as his first employee eight years ago to be Superior's Chief of Technology. He has supported our efforts on Reporting Services and made it a focus area at Superior Consulting. Without John's founding of Superior Consulting Services and his bringing together people such as Marty and Mike, none of this would have come into being.

I need to extend a big thank you to Brian Welcker and the rest of the Reporting Services development team. Their guidance and patience during development is much appreciated. The information they were able to provide during the creation of this book has enhanced the final product you are now holding.

I also want to thank the staff at McGraw-Hill/Osborne, Wendy Rinaldi and Alexander McDonald, along with the technical editor, Todd Meister. Their assistance, guidance, professionalism, and humor have made this project much easier. The attention that Osborne has given this project has been truly overwhelming.

Last, but certainly not least, I want to thank my wife, Pam, for all her efforts and understanding. Not only did she agree to my taking personal time to write this book, but she took it upon herself to proofread every page and work through every sample report. You, as a reader, are greatly benefiting from her efforts.

I also want to thank you, the reader, for purchasing this book. My hope is that it will provide you with an informative overview, steady guide, and quick reference as you use Reporting Services.

Best wishes,
Brian Larson
blarson@teamscs.com
July 17, 2005

Introduction

Microsoft SQL Server 2000 Reporting Services was an exciting product. With the addition of the Report Builder for ad hoc reporting, the Report Viewer control for integration with Windows and web-based applications, and better integration with SQL Server Analysis Services, Microsoft SQL Server 2005 Reporting Services is even more exciting. Never has there been a product with so much potential for sharing business information with such ease of use and at such a reasonable price. Anyone who has ever struggled to find a way to efficiently share database information across an enterprise will see a reason to be delighted with this product.

Now I will admit that I may not be unbiased when expressing this opinion. I did have the opportunity to create a small piece of what has now become Reporting Services. But my excitement goes beyond that.

The main reason I get excited about Reporting Services is because I have been a database application developer for 16 years. I have fought with various reporting tools. I have struggled to find a way to efficiently share data between far-flung sales offices and the corporate headquarters. I have researched enterprise-wide reporting systems and started salivating when I saw the features they offered, only to have my hopes dashed when I looked at the licensing fees. I have shaken my fist at the computer screen and screamed, "There must be a better way!"

With Reporting Services, there is. During the past two years, my colleagues and I at Superior Consulting Services have had the opportunity to incorporate Reporting Services into custom database solutions. We have worked with a number of organizations, helping them get up-to-speed on the product. We have seen how quickly and easily Reporting Services can improve the data analysis and data distribution capabilities within an enterprise.

At one client, we began implementing Reporting Services on Monday morning. By Wednesday afternoon, reports were being e-mailed around the company. Information was being shared as never before. On Thursday morning, the president of the company emerged from his office to see what all the hoopla was about. As he stared at a newly created Reporting Services report, he began saying things like, "So that's why we're having a problem in this area" and "Now I see why our end-of-month's totals went that direction."

At another client, I was working with a manager to mock up a report in Reporting Services. He seemed to be taking a long time going over the layout, so I assumed we did not have things quite right. When I asked what was wrong with the report, he said, "Nothing's wrong. I'm just seeing information about this year's production that I hadn't seen before." Scenarios like these are enough to make even the most cynical data processing professional sit up and take notice!

This book is designed to help you and your organization achieve those same results. As you work through the examples in this book, I hope you have several of those "Aha" moments. Not only moments of discovering new capabilities in Reporting Services, but also moments of discovering how Reporting Services can solve business problems in your organization.

One note about the structure of the book: this book is meant to be a hands-on process. You should never be far from your Reporting Services development installation as you read through these chapters. The book is based on the philosophy that people understand more and remember longer when the learning takes place in an interactive environment. Consequently, the majority of the book is based on business needs, and the reports, code, and configurations you will create to fulfill those needs.

The book is dedicated to offering examples demonstrating complete solutions. I have tried to stay away from code snippets as much as possible. Nothing is worse than seeing five lines of code and knowing they are exactly the solution you need, but being unable to implement them because you do not know what code is supposed to come before or after those five lines to make the whole thing work. With the examples in this book, along with the supporting materials available from the book's website, you should always see a solution from beginning to end, and you should be able to turn around and implement that solution to fulfill your organization's business needs.

I have also tried to have a little fun in the book when appropriate. That is why the business scenarios are based on Galactic Delivery Services (GDS), an interplanetary package delivery service. (You might call it the delivery service to the stars.) While GDS is a bit fanciful with its antimatter transports and robotic employees, the business needs discussed will ring true for most organizations.

I hope you find this book a worthwhile tool for getting up-to-speed on Microsoft's exciting new product. I hope you get a chuckle or two from its GDS examples. Most of all, I hope the book enables you to unlock the potential of Reporting Services for your organization.

Getting Started

Let's Start at the Very Beginning

IN THIS CHAPTER:

Sharing Business Intelligence

Report Authoring Architecture

Report Serving Architecture

Diving In

SQL Server 2000 Reporting Services was Microsoft's entry into the web-based reporting arena. This first version of Reporting Services enabled you to easily share business information—what is commonly known as "business intelligence" these days—with management, coworkers, business partners, and customers throughout the world. In an interconnected workplace, it makes sense that your reporting solution should offer company-wide, nationwide, and even worldwide communication.

SQL Server 2005 Reporting Services builds on the success of the original. Where almost every other aspect of SQL Server 2005 represents a completely new platform, Reporting Services adds to the solid foundation provided by the earlier version to make a great product even better. The 2005 release provides an additional report-authoring environment, improved report-development features, and enhanced capabilities for distributing reports.

Reporting Services was code-named Rosetta during its internal development at Microsoft. This name comes from the Rosetta Stone, a stone slab found in 1799 that contains an inscription in both Egyptian hieroglyphics and Greek. This stone provided the key piece of information necessary to unlock the mystery of Egyptian hieroglyphics for the modern world. Just as the Rosetta Stone brought key information across 1,400 years of history, Rosetta, or Reporting Services, is designed to bring key information across distances to unlock the mystery of success for your business.

The Rosetta project was originally conceived as a feature of SQL Server 2005. However, as Microsoft told prospective customers about the features in Rosetta and demonstrated the first alpha versions, the reaction was strong: "We need this product and we need it now!" Because of this reaction, Microsoft decided that Rosetta would not wait for 2005, but, instead, would be made its own product to work with SQL Server 2000.

Just what are the features of Reporting Services that got everyone so excited? *Reporting Services* provides an environment for creating a number of different types of reports from a number of different data sources. The reports are previewed and refined using this authoring tool. Once completed, the reports are deployed to a *Report Server*, which makes the reports available via the Internet in a structured, secure environment. Last, but not least, the report management and distribution portion of Reporting Services is free of charge to anyone with a SQL Server 2000 or SQL Server 2005 license.

Why did this set of features generate so much excitement? When you put them all together, the result is a product that facilitates the creation, management, and timely use of business intelligence.

Sharing Business Intelligence

Because you are reading this book, you are probably the keeper of some type of information that is important to your organization. You may have information on sales, finance, production, delivery—or one of a hundred other areas. All this information makes up the business intelligence necessary to keep today's corporate, academic, and governmental entities humming along.

The Need to Share

In addition to maintaining this information, you also have a need to share this information with others. This need to share may have come from an important lesson you learned in kindergarten ("The world would be a much happier place if we all learned to share") or, more likely, this need to share your information was probably suggested to you by a manager or executive somewhere higher up the food chain. See if any of these situations sounds familiar.

The Production Manager

Your company's order-entry system automatically updates the inventory database every four hours. In your company's line of business, some orders can require a large quantity of a given product. Because of this, it is important that the Production Manager knows about these changes in the inventory level in a timely manner, so he can adjust production accordingly.

The Production Manager has asked you to provide him with an up-to-date inventory report that is created immediately following each update to the inventory database occurring during business hours. He would like this report to arrive on his PC as quickly as possible, so he can make changes to the production schedule within an hour of the updates. He would also like to be able to print this report, so he can add his own notations to the report as he works out his new production schedule.

One more fact to keep in mind: Your company's inventory system is in Cleveland, but the production facility is in Portland!

The Vice President of Sales

You are responsible for maintaining information on the amount of credit your company will extend to each of its clients. This information is updated daily in the company database. A report containing the credit information for all clients is printed weekly at corporate headquarters and mailed to each sales representative.

The Vice President of Sales has requested that the credit information be made available to the sales staff in a timelier manner. He has asked that this report be accessible over the Internet from anywhere across the country. The sales representatives will print the report when they have access to the Internet, and then carry it with them for those times when they cannot get online. He has also asked that this online version of the report be as up-to-date as possible.

The Chief Executive Officer

The Chief Executive Officer for your company has a hands-on management style. She likes to participate in all facets of the decision-making process and, therefore, needs to stay well informed on all aspects of the company. This includes the corporate balance sheet, inventory and production, and the company's stock price.

The CEO expects all this information to be available on her desktop when she arrives for work each morning at 7 A.M. The information must be in a format that's appropriate to print and share with the corporate vice presidents at their meeting each morning at 9 A.M. As you search for solutions to this one, remember no budget is allocated for this project—and, of course, your job is on the line.

Possible Solutions

These situations, and a thousand others just like them, confront businesses each day. In our world of massive connectivity, these types of requests are not unreasonable. Even if that is the case, it does not mean these requests are easy to fulfill.

An HTML Solution

The first candidate to explore when you're looking to move information across the Internet is, of course, HTML. You could use one of a number of tools for creating data-driven HTML pages. This would include Microsoft's Active Server Pages, Macromedia's ColdFusion, any of a number of Java environments, PHP—the list goes on and on.

Each of these environments is good at creating dynamic web content. However, they all take time and a certain level of programming knowledge. With deadlines looming, you may not have the time to create custom web applications to solve each of these problems. If you are used to manipulating data with Crystal Reports or Access reporting, you may not be ready to jump into full-blown application development and you may not have a desire to do it at any time in the near future.

Even if you did create an application for each of these scenarios, one important requirement in each case is this: the information must be printable. HTML screens can look great in a browser window, but they cause problems when printed. The content can be too wide to fit on the page, and there is no control of page breaks. In fact, the page can break right in the middle of a line of text, with the top half of the characters on one page and the bottom half of the characters on the next! These types of formatting issues could make the output difficult for the sales representatives and the Production Manager to read. Asking the CEO to take this type of a report to the executive meeting could get you fired.

Let's look for another option!

A PDF Solution

Because the capability to control the printed output is important, Adobe PDF should be considered. PDF files look good both on the screen and in print. You can control where the page breaks occur and make sure everything looks great. However, several issues need to be overcome with PDF files.

First of all, you need some type of utility to produce output in a PDF format. This could be Adobe's full version of Acrobat or some other utility. Once this has been obtained, a document must be created that contains the desired database information. This is usually a report created with a reporting tool or development software. After this document is created, it is converted into a PDF document using an export function or a special printer driver.

Once the PDF document has been created, it can be copied to a website for access through the Internet. However, as soon as the PDF document is created, it becomes a static entity. It does not requery the database each time it is requested from the website. To remain up-to-date, the PDF document must be re-created each time the source data is changed. In addition, you may have to return to your programming environment to control access to the PDF documents on the website.

Perhaps there is a better way.

A Third-Party Reporting Environment

Reporting environments from other companies certainly overcome the limitations of our first two options. These third-party products allow reports to be built without requiring large amounts of programming. They can also dynamically generate output in a format such as Adobe PDF that will perform well onscreen and in print.

The problem with third-party reporting environments is the cost. Some products can run into the thousands or tens of thousands of dollars. This can be enough to break the budget—if indeed there is a budget—for reporting projects such as the ones discussed previously.

Microsoft Reporting Services

Now you can begin to see why companies get so excited about Reporting Services. It provides an elegant solution for all three of your demanding users—the Production Manager, the Vice President of Sales, and the Chief Executive Officer. Reporting Services does not have the drawbacks inherent in the possible solutions considered previously.

No Programming Required

Reporting Services provides a simple, drag-and-drop approach to creating reports from database information. You can use two different tools to author reports. The Report Builder enables you to create basic reports even if you do not know much about databases and query languages. The Report Designer lets you truly unlock the power of Reporting Services to convey complex information. The Report Designer is found in the Business Intelligence Development Studio, which comes with SQL Server 2005, and also in Visual Studio 2005, Professional version and above.

Even though these are both development environments, Business Intelligence Development Studio for developing SQL Server Analysis Services and data mining solutions and Visual Studio 2005 for creating software based on the .NET Framework, don't let that scare you. You do not need to be a programmer to create Reporting Services reports. However, if you are comfortable with programming constructs, in Chapters 7 and 8, you learn some simple Visual Basic expressions that can be used to spice up your report's presentation. Note, however, these expressions are not necessary to create useful reports. They are also simple enough that even those who are totally new to Visual Basic can master them with ease.

A Server with a View

Reporting Services includes a report viewer that works with your browser. This *report viewer* provides a high-quality presentation of each report using dynamic HTML. Reports are presented in multiple pages with "VCR-button" controls for navigating between pages.

Because the report viewer uses dynamic HTML, it does not require any additional programs to be downloaded on your PC. There is no ActiveX control to install, no Java applet to download. Any browser that supports HTML 4.0 can view reports.

Plays Well with Printers

In addition to presenting reports in your browser using dynamic HTML, Reporting Services can *render* a report in a number of additional formats. These include Adobe PDF, TIFF, and even a Microsoft Excel spreadsheet. All these formats look great onscreen when they are viewed or on paper when they are printed.

NOTE

When Reporting Services renders a report, it gathers the most recent data from the database, formats the data in the manner the report's author specified, and outputs the report into the selected format (that is, HTML, PDF, TIFF, and so on).

Even when being output in the PDF or TIFF format for printing, a report can be configured to requery the database every time it is accessed. This ensures the report is always up-to-date.

Special Delivery

Reporting Services provides several different ways to deliver reports to end users. The Report Manager website enables users to access reports via the Internet. It also includes security features, which ensure that users access only the reports they should.

Users can also subscribe to reports they would like to receive on a regular basis. Reporting Services will send out a copy of the report as an e-mail attachment to each subscriber on a regularly scheduled basis. Alternatively, a Reporting Services administrator can send out a copy of the report as an e-mail attachment to a number of recipients on a mailing list. If that isn't enough, reports can be embedded right in .NET applications.

The Price Is Right

For anyone who has a licensed copy of SQL Server 2005, the price of Reporting Services is certainly right. Free! As long as the report server is installed on the same computer as the SQL Server database engine, your SQL Server 2005 license covers everything. With this single server architecture, it will not cost you one additional penny to share your reports with others using Reporting Services.

Reporting Services to the Rescue

Let's take one more look at the three scenarios we considered earlier—the Production Manager, the Vice President of Sales, and the Chief Executive Officer. How can you use the features of Reporting Services to fulfill the requests made by each of them?

The Production Manager wants a report showing the current inventory. It is certainly not a problem to query the inventory data from the database and put it into a report. Next, he wants to get a new copy of the report every time the inventory is updated during business hours. The Production Manager can subscribe to your inventory report and, as part of the subscription, ask that a new report be delivered at 8:15 A.M., 12:15 P.M., and 4:15 P.M. Finally, the inventory system is in Cleveland, but the Production Manager is in Portland. Because a subscription to a report can be delivered by e-mail, the Reporting Services server can be set up in Cleveland, produce the report from the local data source, and then e-mail the report to Portland.

The solution for the Vice President of Sales is even more straightforward. He wants a report with credit information for each client. No problem there. Next, he wants the report available to his sales staff, accessible via the Internet. To achieve this, you can publish the report on the Report Manager website. You can even set up security, so only sales representatives with the appropriate user name and password can access the report.

In addition, the Vice President of Sales wants the report to look good when printed. This is achieved with no additional work on the development side. When the sales representatives retrieve the report from the website, it is displayed as HTML. This looks good in the browser, but it may not look good on paper. To have a report that looks good on paper every time, the sales representatives simply need to export the report to either the PDF or TIFF format, and then display and print the exported file. Now they are ready to go knocking on doors!

For the CEO, you can build a report or, perhaps, a series of reports that reflects the state of her company. This will serve to keep her informed on all facets of her business. To have this available on her desktop at 7:00 A.M., you can set up a subscription that will run the reports and e-mail them to her each morning at 6:15 A.M.

Finally, because she wants to print this report and share it with the corporate vice presidents, you can make sure the subscription service delivers the report in either PDF or TIFF format. The best part is that, because you already have a SQL Server 2005 license, the Reporting Services solution costs the company nothing. You have earned a number of bonus points with the big boss, and she will make you the Chief Information Officer before the end of the year!

Report Authoring Architecture

As mentioned previously, Reporting Services reports are created using one of two tools, the Report Builder and the Report Designer. The *Report Builder* is geared toward those power users and analysts who want to do their own ad hoc reporting, without having to learn all the ins and outs of database structure and query creation. The Report Builder presents report authors with a simplified model of your database, so these authors do not need to know the details of querying databases to create reports. Once the Report Builder has created a report, that report can be deployed to the report server and will function exactly like a report created with the Report Designer.

The Report Builder is an outstanding tool for these types of users, but to be easy-to-use, it must remain fairly simple. Therefore, it cannot support all the many wonderful features of Reporting Services reports. Because we want to cover the entirety of the rich capabilities found in Reporting Services, this book focuses on report authoring using the Report Designer, rather than the Report Builder. If you are interested in learning more about the Report Builder, please refer to Appendix D.

The *Report Designer* offers far greater capabilities for creating interesting and highly functional reports used to convey business intelligence to the report users. This book can help you get the most from this incredibly rich report-authoring environment. The Report Designer contains everything necessary to create a wide variety of reports for Reporting Services. Everything you need to select information from data sources, create a report layout, and test your creation is right at your fingertips. Best of all, the Report Designer is found in both the Business Intelligence Development Studio and in Visual Studio 2005.

Both the BI Development Studio and Visual Studio 2005 are a type of program authoring software called an integrated development environment (IDE). (In fact, the BI Development Studio is a special version of Visual Studio 2005 operating under a different name.) *IDE*s came into being when the people who create programming languages thought it would be more convenient if the editor, compiler, and debugger were packaged together. Prior to the advent of integrated development environments, creating and debugging software could be a long and tedious process. With an IDE, however, a programmer can be much more efficient while writing and testing an application.

Even though you will be creating reports rather than writing software, the Report Designer provides you with a friendly working environment. You won't be editing, compiling, and debugging, but you will be selecting data, laying out the report, and previewing the end result. All of this is done quickly and easily within the Report Designer.

The Business Intelligence Project Type

The BI Development Studio and Visual Studio 2005 can be used for a number of business intelligence and software development tasks. The *BI Development Studio* is used to create Integration Services packages for data extract, transform, and load (ETL). It also is used to create Analysis Services multidimensional data structures. Visual Studio 2005 is used to create Windows applications, web applications, and web services.

To facilitate this variety, these IDEs support many different types of projects. These project types organize the multitude of solutions that can be created within the IDE into related groups. Reporting Services reports are created using the Business Intelligence project type.

Project Templates

When you choose to create a new project in the IDE, you will see the New Project dialog box shown in Figure 1-1. The Project Types area of the screen shows the one project type you will be concerned with: Business Intelligence Projects. *Business Intelligence Projects* includes templates for a number of different projects.

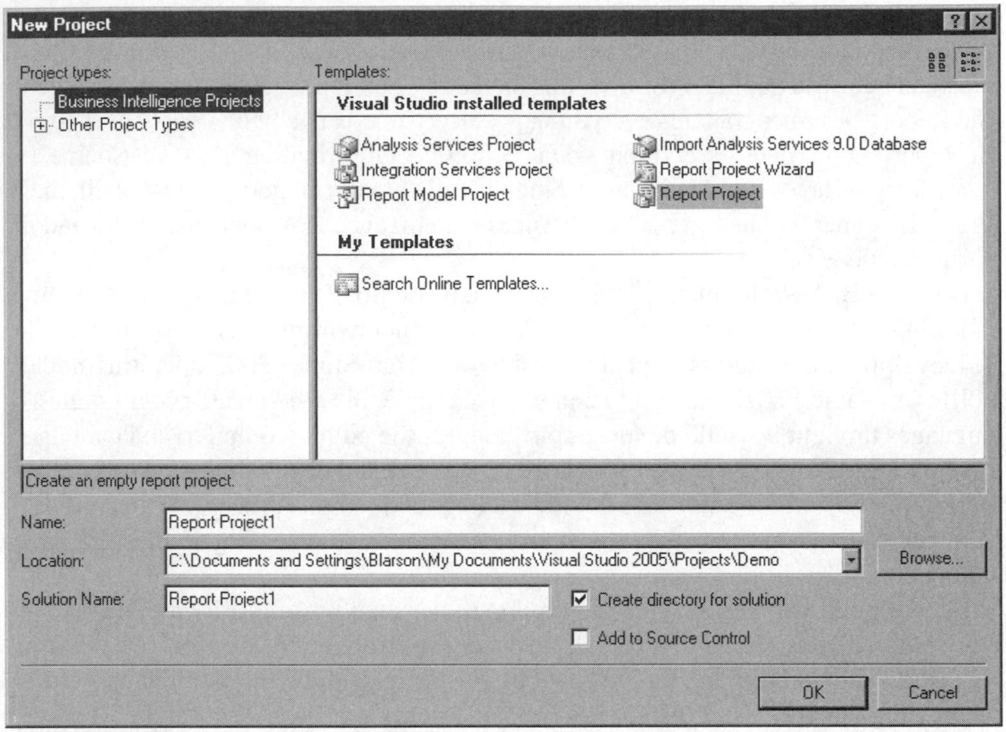

Figure 1-1 *The New Project dialog box*

NOTE

All illustrations of the Report Designer found in the book are created using the BI Development Studio. They will appear almost identical to those screens and dialog boxes in the Report Designer found in Visual Studio 2005.

You will look at three project templates in this book: Report Project Wizard, Report Project, and Report Model Project. Each of the first two templates will, ultimately, create a report project. The *Report Project Wizard* template uses the Report Wizard to guide you through the process of creating the first report in your new report project. The *Report Project* template simply creates an empty report project and turns you loose. The *Report Model Project* creates a data model for use with the Report Builder authoring tool.

Report Structure

A report project can contain a number of reports. Each report contains two distinct sets of instructions that determine what the report will contain. The first is the data definition. The *data definition* controls where the data for the report will come from and what information will be selected from that data. The second set of instructions is the report layout. The *report layout* controls how the information will be presented on the screen or on paper. Both of these sets of instructions are stored using the Report Definition Language.

Figure 1-2 shows this report structure in a little more detail.

Data Definition

The data definition contains two parts: the data source and the dataset. The *data source* is the database server or data file that provides the information for your report. Of course, the data source itself is not included in the report. What is included is the set of instructions the report needs to gain access to that data source. These instructions include the following:

▶ The type of source you will be using for your data (for example, Microsoft SQL Server 2005, Oracle, DB2, Informix, or Microsoft Access). Reporting Services will use this information to determine how to communicate with the data source.

▶ The name of the database server or the path to the data file.

▶ The name of the database.

▶ The login for connecting to this data source, if a login is required.

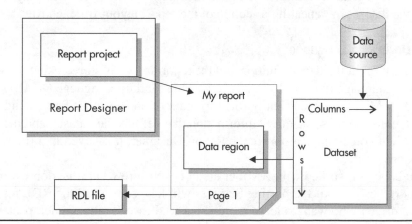

Figure 1-2   *Report structure*

When the report is executing, it uses the data source instructions contained in the report to gain access to the data source. It then extracts information from the data source into a new format that can be used by the report. This new format is called a *dataset*.

The content of the dataset is defined using a tool called the Query Designer. The *Query Designer* helps you build a database query. The database query may be in T-SQL for querying relational data, MDX for querying multidimensional data, or DDX for querying data mining data. The query provides instructions to the data source, telling it what data you want selected for your report. The query is stored in the report as part of the data definition.

The data selected by the query into the dataset consists of rows and columns. The rows correspond to the records the query selects from the data source. The columns correspond to the fields the query selects from the data source. (MDX queries are flattened into a single table of rows and columns.) Information on the fields to be selected into the dataset is stored in the report as part of the data definition. Only the information on what the fields will be called and the type of data they will hold is stored in the report definition. The actual data is not stored in the report definition but, instead, is selected from the data source each time the report is run.

Report Layout

The data that the report has extracted into a dataset is not of much use to you unless you have some way of presenting it to the user. You need to specify which fields go in which locations on the screen or on paper. You also need to add things such as titles, headings, and page numbers. All of this forms the report layout.

In most cases, your report layout will include a special area that interacts with the dataset. This special area is known as a data region. A *data region* displays all the rows in the dataset by repeating a section of the report layout for each row.

Report Definition Language

The information in the data definition and the report layout is stored using the Report Definition Language (RDL). *RDL* is an Extensible Markup Language (XML) standard designed by Microsoft specifically for storing report definitions. This includes the data source instructions, the query information that defines the dataset, and the report layout. When you create a report in the Report Designer, it is saved in a file with an .RDL extension.

If you have not worked with XML or are not even sure what it is, don't worry. The Report Designer and Reporting Services will take care of all the RDL for you. For those of you who want to learn more about RDL, we'll take a quick peek under the hood in Chapter 7. For the more hardcore, a reference to the RDL standard is included in Appendix C.

Report Designer

Figure 1-3 shows the Report Designer in the BI Development Studio environment. This is the tool you will use for creating and editing reports throughout this book. We will look at some features of the Report Designer now and discuss them in more detail in Chapter 5.

Design Window

The Design window, in the center of Figure 1-3, is where you create your report. You create both the data definition and the report layout here. This is also where you get to see your creation come to life!

The Design window has three tabs. On the Data tab, you define the data source for the report. This is also where you use the Query Designer to create datasets.

On the Layout tab, you build the report layout. To do this, you use three of the other windows visible in Figure 1-3: the Datasets window, the Toolbox, and the Properties window. You will learn how this works in the following sections.

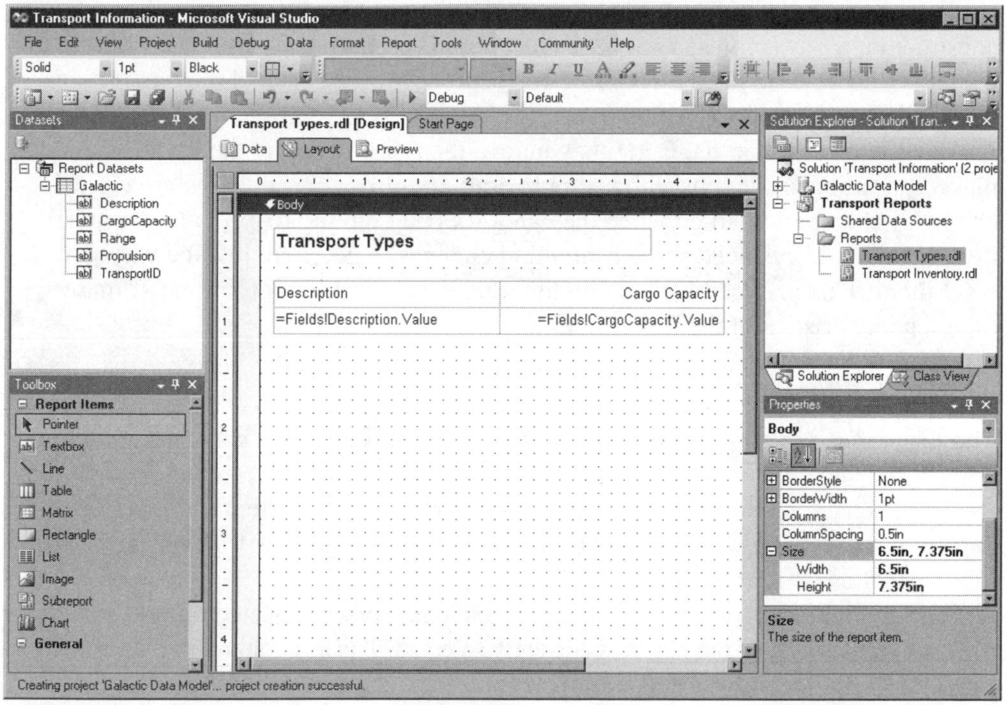

Figure 1-3   *The Report Designer in the Business Intelligence Development Studio*

On the Preview tab, you get to see the report layout and the data combined to create an honest-to-goodness report. The report preview enables you to see what the report will look like as HTML or when it is exported to any of the other data formats.

Datasets

The Datasets window, in the upper-left corner of Figure 1-3, provides a list of the database fields you can use in your report. These are the fields you selected for your dataset using the Query Designer. Once the dataset has been defined in the Query Designer, the selected fields are displayed in the Datasets window.

The Datasets window makes it easy to add database information to your report layout. Simply drag the desired field from the Datasets window and drop it in the appropriate location on your report layout in the Design window. The Report Designer takes care of the rest.

Toolbox

The Toolbox, in the lower-left corner of Figure 1-3, contains all the report items you use to build your reports. These report items, sometimes called *controls*, are responsible for getting the text and graphics to show up in the right place on your reports. As with any construction project, you can only construct reports properly *after* you learn how to use the tools (report items) in the Toolbox. You learn how to use each of the report items in the Toolbox in Chapters 4, 5, and 6.

As with the fields in the Datasets window, the report items in the Toolbox are placed on the report layout with a simple drag-and-drop. However, whereas fields are pretty much ready to go when they are dropped onto the report layout, report items almost always need some formatting changes to get them just the way you want them. This is done by changing the size, the color, the font, or one of many other characteristics of the report item.

Properties Window

The Properties window, in the lower-right corner of Figure 1-3, is the place where you control the characteristics of each report item. The Properties window always shows the characteristics, or *properties*, for the report item currently selected in the Design window. You will see an entry in the Properties window for every aspect of this report item that you can control.

The top of the Properties window shows the name of the selected report item. In Figure 1-3, the body of the report is currently selected. The left column in the Properties window shows the name of each property that can be changed for that report item. The right column shows the current setting for each of those properties. For example, in Figure 1-3, you can see the report body has a size of 6.5 inches by 7.375 inches.

Solution Explorer

The Solution Explorer, in the upper-right corner of Figure 1-3, manages all the objects you are working with in the BI Development Studio or Visual Studio 2005. Objects in the Solution Explorer are displayed in an outline that resembles an upside-down tree. A root entry is at the top of the outline, and branch entries appear further down.

The entries in the outline can be expanded by clicking the plus (+) sign next to each entry. The entries can be contracted by clicking the minus (−) sign next to each entry. An entry in the outline that does not have a plus sign or a minus sign next to it does not have any additional entries beneath it. Expanding and contracting outline entries is useful for hiding portions of a complex outline, so you can concentrate on the area you are currently working on.

In Figure 1-3, the root entry is a solution called "Transport Information." The BI Development Studio and Visual Studio 2005 use solutions to group together a number of projects that all relate to solving the same business problem. Each solution contains one or more projects. This could be a report project, a report model project, or one of the other business intelligence project types shown in Figure 1-1.

In our example, the Transport Information solution contains two projects. The first is a report model project called *Galactic Data Model*, which creates a model for use with the Report Builder. The second project is a report project called *Transport Reports* that creates Reporting Services reports using the Report Designer in the BI Development Studio.

A report project always contains two folders. The *Shared Data Sources* folder contains connections to different sources of data for your reports. As the folder name implies, these data sources can be shared by multiple reports in the report project.

The second folder in the report project is the *Reports folder*, which contains the reports you create in the Report Designer. In Figure 1-3, the Reports folder contains two reports: Transport Types and Transport Inventory.

When you are editing a report project in the Report Designer, the Design window and the Datasets window display information for one report at a time. If your project has multiple reports, you can switch among them by double-clicking a report in the Solution Explorer window.

Report Serving Architecture

Once you finish building your report and have it looking exactly the way you want, it is time to share that report with others. This is the time when your report moves from safe, childhood life inside a report project to its adult life on a Report Server. This is known as *deploying the report*. Let me assure you, reports pass through deployment much easier than you and I passed through adolescence!

Report Server

The Report Server is the piece of the puzzle that makes Reporting Services the product it is. This is the software environment that enables you to share your report with the masses, at least those masses who have rights to your server. Figure 1-4 shows the basic structure of the Report Server.

Report Catalog

When a report is deployed to a Report Server, a copy of the report's RDL definition is put in that server's Report Catalog. The *Report Catalog* is a set of databases used to store the definitions for all the reports available on a particular Report Server. It also stores the configuration, security, and caching information necessary for the operation of that Report Server.

Even though you may use any ODBC- or OLE DB–compliant data source to supply data to your reports, the Report Catalog database can only exist in SQL Server 2000 or SQL Server 2005. The Report Catalog database is created as part of the Reporting Services installation process. Except for creating regular backups of any Report Catalog databases, it is probably a good idea to leave the Report Catalog alone.

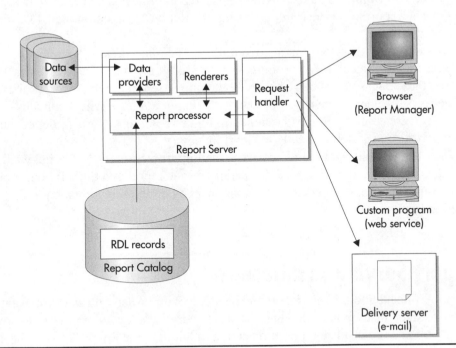

Figure 1-4   *Report serving architecture*

Report Processor

When a report needs to be executed, the report processor component of the Report Server directs the show. The report processor retrieves the RDL for the report from the Report Catalog. It then reads through this RDL to determine what will be needed for the report.

The report processor orchestrates the operation of the other components of the Report Server as the report is produced. It takes the output from each of the other components and combines them together to create the completed report.

Data Providers

As the report processor encounters dataset definitions in the report RDL, it retrieves the data to populate that dataset. It does this by first following the instructions in the report's data source for connecting to the database server or file that contains the data. The report processor selects a data provider that knows how to retrieve information from this type of data source.

The data provider then connects to the source of the data and selects the information required for the report. The data provider returns this information to the report processor, where it is turned into a dataset for use by the report.

Renderers

Once all the data for the report has been collected, the report processor is ready to begin processing the report's layout. To do this, the report processor looks at the format requested. This might be HTML, PDF, TIFF, or one of several other possible formats. The report processor then uses the renderer that knows how to produce that format.

The renderer works with the report processor to read through the report layout. The report layout is combined with the dataset, and any repeating sections of the report are duplicated for each row in the dataset. This expanded report layout is then translated into the requested output format. The result is a report ready to be sent to the user.

Request Handler

The *request handler* is responsible for receiving requests for reports and passing those requests on to the report processor. Once the report processor has created the requested report, the report handler is also responsible for delivering the completed report. In the next section, you learn about the various methods the request handler uses for delivering reports.

Report Delivery

We have discussed how a report is created by the Report Server. What we have not discussed is where that report is going after it is created. The report may be sent to a user through the Report Manager website. It may be sent in response to a web service request that came, not from a user, but from another program. It may also be e-mailed to a user who has a subscription to that report.

Report Manager Website

One way for users to request a report from the Report Server is through the Report Manager website. This website is created for you when you install Reporting Services. Figure 1-5 shows a screen from the Report Manager website.

The Report Manager website organizes reports into folders. Users can browse through these folders to find the report they need. They can also search the report titles and descriptions to locate a report.

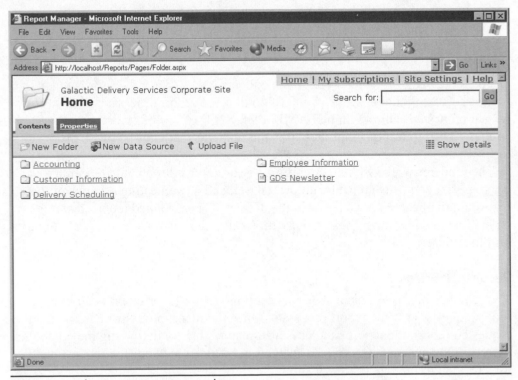

Figure 1-5 *The Report Manager website*

The Report Manager also includes security that can be applied to folders and reports. With this security, the site administrator can create security roles for the users who will be accessing the site. These security roles control which folders and reports a user is allowed to access. You learn about security when we look at the Report Manager in Chapter 10.

In the Report Manager, reports are always displayed using the HTML format. Once a report has been displayed as an HTML page, the user can then export the report into any of the other available formats.

Subscription Delivery

If the users do not want to go to the report, the request handler can make the report go to them. In other words, users do not necessarily need to come to the Report Manager website to receive a report. They can have the report delivered to them through a subscription service. The Report Manager enables users to locate a report on the site, and then subscribe to it, so it will be delivered to them in the future.

When users subscribe to a report, they provide an e-mail address to which the report will be delivered, either as the body of the e-mail or as an e-mail attachment, depending on the requested format. Users can specify the format for the report at the time they create their subscription.

The site administrator can also set up report subscriptions. These function like a mass mailing, using a list of e-mail addresses. Rather than requiring each user to access the Report Manager to create their own subscription, the site administrator can create one subscription that is delivered to every user in the list.

Web Service Interface

In addition to delivering reports to humans, either at their request or on a subscription basis, the request handler can deliver reports to other software applications. This is done through a series of web services. A *web service* is a mechanism that allows programs to communicate with each other over the Internet.

A program calls a web service on the Report Server, requesting a particular report in a particular format. The request handler relays this request to the report processor, just like any other request for a report. The completed report is returned to the program that originated the request as the response to the web service request.

Web services use a standard called the Simple Object Access Protocol (SOAP). SOAP is supported by both Windows and non-Windows environments, so a program running on a non-Windows computer that supports SOAP can receive a report created by Reporting Services.

Diving In

Now that you have been introduced to all the capabilities of Reporting Services, I hope you are ready to dive in and make it work for you. In the next chapter, you learn about the installation and setup of Reporting Services. If Reporting Services has already been installed for you, you can skip ahead to Chapter 3.

In Chapter 3, we make sure you have a firm understanding of database basics before getting to the actual building of reports in Chapter 4. Chapter 3 also introduces you to Galactic Delivery Services (GDS), the company we use as a case study throughout the remainder of the book. Even if your database skills are tip-top, you should spend a few minutes in Chapter 3 to get to know GDS.

Putting the Pieces in Place: Installing Reporting Services

IN THIS CHAPTER:

Before you can begin to enjoy all the benefits of Reporting Services discussed in Chapter 1, you, of course, have to install the Reporting Services software. SQL Server 2000 Reporting Services required its own installation process. Things have gotten a bit simpler with SQL Server 2005 Reporting Services. Reporting Services now installs as part of the SQL Server 2005 installation. Nevertheless, it is important to understand the structure of Reporting Services before completing your installation.

In this chapter, you learn about the components that make up Reporting Services and the three licensed editions of Reporting Services offered by Microsoft. Next, you find out how the components are combined in different types of Reporting Services installations and see how to plan for each installation type. As part of that planning, you learn about the software that must be in place prior to installing Reporting Services. After considering these preliminaries, we walk you through the installation process.

Preparing for the Installation

The most important part of the Reporting Services installation is not what you do as you run the setup program, but what you do before you begin. In this section, we discuss the knowledge you need and the steps you should take to prepare for installation. With the proper plan in place, your Reporting Services installation should go smoothly and you can create reports in no time.

The Parts of the Whole

Reporting Services is not a single program that runs on a computer to produce reports. Instead, it is a series of services, web applications, and databases that work together to create a report management environment. As you plan your Reporting Services installation, it is important that you understand a little bit about each piece of the puzzle and how all these pieces work together to create a complete system.

Figure 2-1 shows all the parts that make up a complete Reporting Services installation. Each part has a specific role to play in the development, management, and delivery of reports or in the management of the Reporting Services environment itself. Not all these items are installed with Reporting Services. Some are prerequisites and must be installed before you can begin the Reporting Services installation process.

Let's take a look at each part and see how it fits into the whole.

NOTE

Not all Reporting Services installations include all the items shown in Figure 2-1. The following sections of this chapter discuss the various types of installations and which components they include.

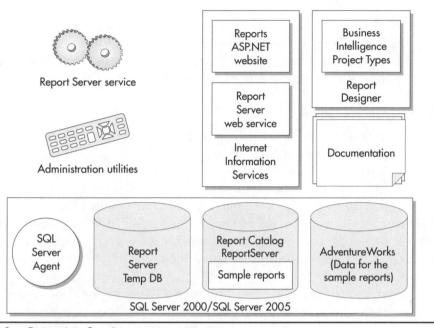

Figure 2-1   *Reporting Services component parts*

The Report Server Service

The Report Server service is the heart of Reporting Services and is, of course, installed as part of the Reporting Services installation. As you saw in Figure 1-4 of Chapter 1, the Report Server is responsible for processing any report requests. This includes fetching the report definition, retrieving the data used in the report, and rendering the report in the desired format.

The Report Server is a Windows service, and it makes its functionality available as web services. This means the Report Server does not directly interact with the user. Instead, the Report Server Windows service runs in the background and handles requests made by other programs through the web services. Like other Windows services, such as SQL Server and Internet Information Services (IIS), the Report Server begins running when the computer starts up and continues running until the computer shuts down.

Because the Report Server service starts up on its own, it needs to have a valid username and password that it can use to log on to the server when it starts up. This login information, along with other information that determines how the Report Server will operate, is stored in the RSReportServer.config file. The content of this configuration file is determined by the choices you make during the setup and configuration process.

NOTE

Most of the information in the RSReportServer.config file is stored as plain text and can be modified using Notepad or a similar text editor. The login information, however, is encrypted when it is stored in this file. It cannot be changed except through the administration utilities.

The Administration Utilities

The administration utilities are tools for managing the Report Server service and for making changes to its configuration. These utilities take care of tasks such as manually starting the Report Server service if it fails to start up automatically. The utilities can also be used to change the login information used by the service when it starts up.

Most of these utility programs are run in a command window. There isn't a user interface with menus, buttons, and text boxes. Instead, the utilities use parameters specified as part of the command line that launches the program. These parameters determine what changes the utility program will make in the Reporting Services configuration.

The one administration utility that does have a Windows user interface is the Report Server Configuration Manager. This program provides a convenient method for examining and modifying the configuration settings of a Reporting Services installation. You learn about the Report Server Configuration Manager in more detail in the section "The Report Server Configuration Manager."

The administration utilities can be run on the computer that is hosting the Report Server service to manage the configuration on that computer. Most of the administrative utilities can also be used to manage a Report Server service that is running on another computer. This is called *remote administration.*

The administration utilities are installed as part of the Reporting Services installation.

SQL Server 2000/SQL Server 2005

SQL Server 2000 or SQL Server 2005 is required to hold the database where Reporting Services stores its Report Catalog database. Reporting Services also uses the SQL Server Agent, which you learn about shortly. In addition, databases in SQL Server can be used as data sources for Reporting Services reports.

SQL Server Agent

SQL Server Agent is part of SQL Server and is created as part of the SQL Server installation process. It is used by SQL Server to execute jobs scheduled to run at a certain time. These jobs might back up a database or transfer information from one database to another. Jobs may be scheduled to run once or they may run on a regular basis, such as once a day or once a week.

Reporting Services also uses the SQL Server Agent to execute scheduled jobs. These jobs are used to run reports and distribute the results. In Chapter 1, you learned about users who subscribe to a report. When users subscribe to a report, they ask for it to be run and delivered to them on a regular basis. When a user creates a subscription, Reporting Services creates a SQL Server Agent job to handle that subscription.

For example, our Production Manager in Chapter 1 wanted an inventory report to be printed every four hours during the workday. He subscribes to the inventory report and creates a delivery schedule of 8:15 A.M., 12:15 P.M., and 4:15 P.M. When this subscription is created, Reporting Services creates a SQL Server Agent job scheduled to run at 8:15 A.M., 12:15 P.M., and 4:15 P.M. each day. The job takes care of running the report and e-mailing it to the Production Manager.

The Report Server and Report Server Temp DB Databases

During the Reporting Services installation process, two databases are created within SQL Server: the Report Server and Report Server Temp DB databases. The Report Server database is used to store the Report Catalog. (Recall from Chapter 1 that the Report Catalog holds the information about all the reports deployed to a Report Server.) The Report Server database also holds information about the Report Manager website. This includes such things as the folder structure of the website and the security settings for each folder and report.

As the name implies, the Report Server Temp DB database is used as temporary storage for Reporting Services operations. Information can be stored here to track the current users on the Report Manager website. Short-term copies of some of the most recently executed reports are also stored here in what is known as the *execution cache*.

Sample Reports and the AdventureWorks Database

As part of the Reporting Services installation process, you can choose to install several sample Reporting Services reports. These reports end up in the Report Catalog within the Report Server database. If you choose to install the sample reports, another database, called AdventureWorks, is installed in SQL Server. The *AdventureWorks* database serves as the data source for the sample reports.

Internet Information Services

Internet Information Services (IIS) is used to host Internet and intranet websites. IIS also serves as the host for web services. A *website,* of course, is used by a person to request information from a computer over the Internet or some other network. A *web service* is used by a computer to request information from another computer over the Internet or some other network.

When Reporting Services is installed, it creates a website and a web service hosted by IIS. Therefore, IIS must be installed before you begin the Reporting Services installation.

The Reports Website

The Reporting Services installation creates a website called Reports. The *Reports website* is what provides the Report Manager interface for Reporting Services. If Reporting Services is installed on a server named www.MyRSServer.com, then when you surf to www.MyRSServer.com/Reports, you will see the Report Manager home page.

The Reports website is built using ASP.NET. This means ASP.NET support has to be enabled on IIS for the website to function. You learn how to do this in the section "Installation Requirements."

Report Server Web Service

A web service called Report Server is also created by the Reporting Services installation. The Report Server web service allows other programs to interact with and even administer Reporting Services. In addition, it allows other programs to request reports without having to go through the Report Manager interface. In short, the Report Server web service allows Reporting Services to be tightly integrated into other applications. Because web services work across an intranet or across the Internet, the web service interface allows Reporting Services to be integrated with applications running in the next room or in the next country.

The Report Server web service is also built using ASP.NET, so once again, ASP.NET support must be enabled on IIS for this feature to function.

Report Designer

As discussed in Chapter 1, Reporting Services reports are created using the Report Designer either in the Business Intelligence Development Studio or in Visual Studio 2005. The Report Designer will function exactly the same in either development tool. There is no difference between a report created in the Business Intelligence Development Studio and in Visual Studio 2005.

If you are going to use the Business Intelligence Development Studio for creating reports, you need to install the Business Intelligence Development Studio as part of the Reporting Services installation process. If you plan to create reports using Visual Studio 2005, you need to purchase it and install it separately. Visual Studio 2005 does not come with Reporting Services.

Documentation

The final piece of Reporting Services is the documentation. The bulk of this documentation is found in the SQL Server Books Online. After Reporting Services is installed, you can view the SQL Server Books Online through your Start menu. You'll find it under Programs | Microsoft SQL Server 2005 | Documentation and Tutorials | SQL Server Books Online. In addition to this is a set of help screens for the Report Manager interface that can be accessed through the Reports website.

Editions of Reporting Services

Reporting Services can be licensed in three different editions: Standard Edition, Enterprise Edition, and Developer Edition. There is also an Evaluation Edition, which does not require a license, but can only be used for a limited time. We won't be discussing the Evaluation Edition in this book, but you can think of it as essentially being a Developer Edition you get to try out for free.

Reporting Services is licensed as part of your SQL Server 2005 license. Therefore, in a production environment, the Reporting Services edition you are licensed to use is the same as the SQL Server 2005 edition you are licensed to use. For example, if you have a Standard Edition of SQL Server 2005, you are only licensed for the Standard Edition of Reporting Services.

The Standard Edition

All editions of Reporting Services provide a rich environment for report authoring, report management, and report delivery. Just a few of the more advanced features of Reporting Services are not included in the Standard Edition. These advanced features are listed in the following section, "The Enterprise Edition."

The Enterprise Edition

The Enterprise Edition of Reporting Services includes the following advanced features:

► **Security Extension API**   Create your own custom security structure, rather than requiring Windows integrated security for the Report Manager web application and the web service. The Security Extension API is discussed in Chapter 12.

► **Data-Driven Subscriptions**   Send a report to a number of users from a predefined mailing list. Data-driven subscriptions are discussed in Chapter 11.

► **Web Farm Configuration**   Configure several IIS servers running the Report Manager web application and the web service to point to a single SQL Server 2000 or 2005 server hosting the report catalog. The web farm configuration is discussed in the section "Types of Reporting Services Installations."

▶ **Advanced Server Support**   Utilize multiple symmetric multiprocessing to support more than four processors and additional memory support to handle more than 2GB of RAM.

▶ **Report Builder**   Develop basic reports based on a model of the underlying database without having a detailed knowledge of database querying or database structure. The Report Builder is discussed in detail in Appendix D.

The Developer Edition

The Developer Edition provides support for all the features of the Enterprise Edition. The Developer Edition does not, however, require that you have an Enterprise Edition license of SQL Server 2005. Of course, the Developer Edition is only for development and testing. It cannot be used in a production environment.

Types of Reporting Services Installations

Now that you are familiar with the components that make up Reporting Services and the ways that Microsoft licenses Reporting Services, you can give some thought to just what your Reporting Services installation will look like. The first decision you need to make is which of the components you want to install. Although you can choose to include or exclude items in any combination you like, in the end, only three combinations make sense: the full installation, the server installation, and the report author installation.

In addition to these are a couple of specialized installation types. These are the distributed installation and the web farm installation. These installations are for high-end, high-volume Reporting Services sites or installations where security concerns prevent IIS and SQL Server from running on the same computer. We will discuss these configurations briefly, so you are familiar with the variety of ways that Reporting Services can be configured.

The Full Installation

The full installation, as the name implies, is the "everything including the kitchen sink" installation. All the items shown in Figure 2-1 and discussed previously are included in this installation. Nothing is left out.

The full installation is most likely to be used in a development environment. This might be on a server used by a group of developers or on a power workstation used by a single developer. In either case, we want to have all the bells and whistles available to us as we figure out how to best use Reporting Services to suit our business needs.

The Server Installation

The server installation is most likely to be used when we're setting up Reporting Services on a production server. On a production server, we only want those items that are going to be used to deliver reports or help us manage Reporting Services. We don't want to include anything that will take up space unnecessarily. Figure 2-2 shows the items included in the server install.

The server installation includes the Report Server service and the administration utilities used to manage it. This type of installation also includes the Reports website and the Report Server web service for managing and delivering reports. In addition, Reporting Services will need the SQL Server Agent, and the Report Server and Report Server Temp DB databases for its operations.

We won't be doing any development work on the production server, so we will not need Visual Studio or the Business Intelligence Project Types. It is possible that you would want the documentation on the production server for questions on managing Reporting Services. Probably a better idea, though, is to have the documentation handy on a development computer and to keep the production installation as uncluttered as possible. The same can be said for the sample reports and the AdventureWorks database. You may want these on your production server for demonstration purposes, but again, it is probably better to do this on a different computer and reserve your production server for reports and data required by your users.

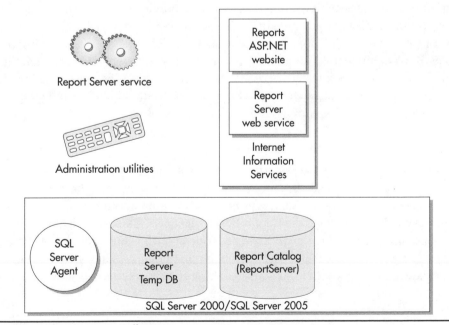

Figure 2-2   *The server installation*

The Report Author Installation

The report author installation is for individuals who are creating Reporting Services reports but not doing heavy-duty development. These report authors may even be creating ad hoc reports and require more capabilities than those available in the Report Builder. Report authors will not be creating full-blown applications that incorporate Reporting Services as part of a larger business system. The items included in the report author installation are shown here.

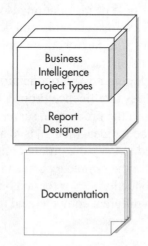

Report authors need the capability to create and preview reports. This capability is found in the Report Designer available in the Business Intelligence Development Studio or in Visual Studio 2005. Report authors may also want access to the Reporting Services Books Online to look up information as they create reports. (Although, in my humble opinion, this book would serve as a better resource.) When report authors have completed their reports and are ready to have others use them, they will deploy the reports to a production Reporting Services server.

The Distributed Installation

In a distributed installation, the Reporting Services items discussed are not installed on a single computer. Instead, they are split between two computers that work together to create a complete Reporting Services system. One computer runs SQL Server 2000 or SQL Server 2005 and hosts the Report Server database. This is the database server. The other computer runs the Report Server service and IIS. This is the report server.

Figure 2-3 shows a distributed installation. Note, Figure 2-3 shows the servers and the report designer workstations. It does not show computers used for viewing reports.

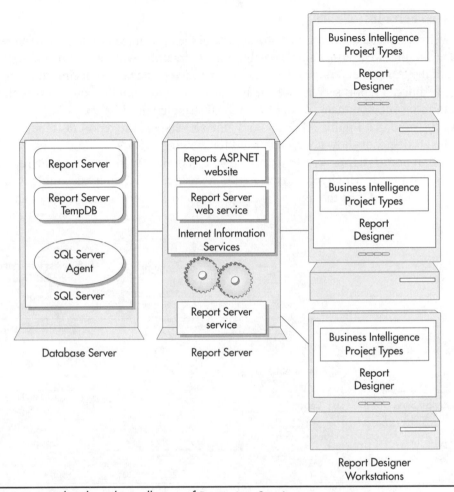

Figure 2-3 *A distributed installation of Reporting Services*

The distributed installation has advantages when it comes to scalability. Because the workload of the three server applications—IIS, SQL Server, and the Report Server—is divided between two servers, it can serve reports to a larger number of simultaneous users. The disadvantage of this type of installation is that it is more complex to install and administer. However, if you need a high-volume solution, it is certainly worth the effort to obtain a solution that will provide satisfactory response times under a heavy workload.

The Web Farm Installation

The web farm installation is a specialized form of the distributed installation, as shown in Figure 2-4. In a web farm, a single database server interacts with several report servers. Each of the Report Servers uses the same Report Server database for its information. By using additional report servers, we can handle even more simultaneous users with the web farm installation than we could with the distributed installation.

Again, note that Figure 2-4 shows only the servers and the report designer workstations. It does not show computers used for viewing reports.

When report designers create reports, they can deploy them to any of the report servers. No matter which server is used, the reports will end up in the single Report Server database. Once the reports are in the Report Server database, they can be

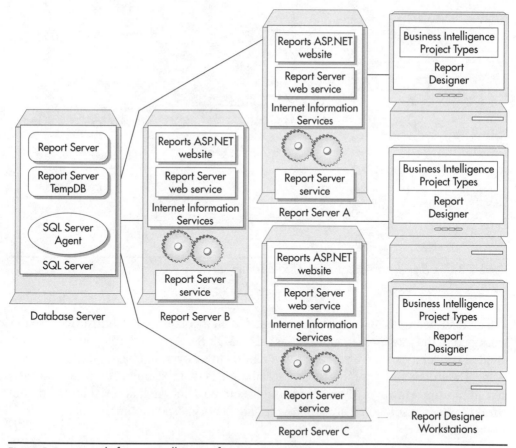

Figure 2-4   *A web farm installation of Reporting Services*

delivered by any of the report servers. In addition, because all the information about the Report Manager is stored in the Report Server database, any changes to the Report Manager configuration made on one server will take effect on all the servers.

For example, suppose an administrator uses the Reports website to access the Report Manager through Report Server A. The administrator creates a new folder in Report Manager called Sales Forecasts 2006, sets the security so the sales staff can access this folder, and places the Sales Forecast report in the folder. Immediately after the administrator is finished, a salesperson brings up Report Manager through Report Server C. The salesperson can browse the contents of the Sales Forecasts 2006 folder and will be able to run the Sales Forecast report.

As with the distributed installation, the web farm installation provides a way to handle a large number of simultaneous requests for reports. Even though the web farm uses a number of servers to deliver reports, it allows the Report Manager interface to be administered without duplication of effort. The web farm installation may take additional effort to get up and running, but once it is ready to go, it provides an efficient means of serving a large number of users.

Installation Requirements

We briefly touched on some of the required software for many of the Reporting Services items. In this section, we itemize these requirements with respect to each of the three installation types just discussed. Before we get to that, however, let's take a look at the hardware requirements for Reporting Services.

Hardware Requirements

The first thing to keep in mind when considering what computer hardware to use for Reporting Services is this: bigger and faster is better. With Reporting Services, we are dealing with a server application that will be handling requests from a number of users at the same time. In most installations, the Report Server service will be sharing processor time and computer memory with IIS and SQL Server 2005. We need to have enough server power, so all three of these systems can happily coexist.

Processor   Microsoft's stated minimum processor is a 500 MHz Pentium II. You should install Reporting Services on this type of computer only if you are a patient person. A more realistic low end is probably a Pentium III at or near 1 GHz. This is true even for the report author installation. The Business Intelligence Development Studio and Visual Studio 2005 demand a fair amount of horsepower to keep them from being sluggish.

Computer Memory   Microsoft's minimum requirement for computer memory is 512MB. This is, indeed, a bare minimum. If you are running Reporting Services on the same server with IIS and SQL Server, that minimum should probably go up to 1GB.

Disk Space   A server installation of Reporting Services requires a minimum of 50MB of disk space. This does not include the space required for SQL Server 2005 or IIS. Consult the Microsoft website for information on the disk space requirements for these items.

   A report author installation requires a minimum of 30MB of disk space. Plan on using an additional 145MB if you are installing the sample reports. Taken all together, you are going to need a minimum of 225MB of disk space for a full installation of Reporting Services.

   Remember, these requirements are minimums. Also, keep in mind that they do not include the space required for reports to be deployed to the server or project files created by the Report Designer. A Reporting Services installation is not useful if there is no room for reports.

Software Requirements

The following software must be installed and running properly on your computer before you can complete a server installation:

▶ The latest service pack for your Windows version. (For Windows 2000, this is SP4. For Windows XP, this is SP2.)

▶ SQL Server 2000 with Service Pack 3a or SQL Server 2005.

▶ Internet Information Services (IIS) 5.0 or higher.

▶ The .NET Framework version 2.0.

▶ ASP.NET support must be enabled in IIS. (See the following section "Other Installation Considerations" for more on this.)

▶ Microsoft Data Access Components (MDAC) 2.6 or higher.

Other Installation Considerations

You need to keep several other tidbits of information in mind as you plan your Reporting Services installation. Many of these items are listed here.

Distributed Installation and Web Farm Installation Considerations

If you create a distributed installation, the report server and the database server must be in the same domain or in domains that have a trust relationship. If you create a web farm installation, all the report servers and the database server must be in the same domain or in domains that have a trust relationship.

Database Server Considerations

The following are a couple of things to keep in mind as you are determining which server will host the Reporting Services databases:

▶ The Report Server and Report Server Temp DB databases must be hosted by SQL Server 2000 or SQL Server 2005. They cannot be hosted by an earlier version of SQL Server, SQL Server Personal Edition, or the Microsoft Data Engine (MSDE).

▶ If you do not want to use the default name for the Reporting Services database (ReportServer), you can specify a different name. The database name you specify must be 117 characters or fewer.

IIS Server Considerations

The following are two things to keep in mind as you are determining which server will host the Reporting Services website and web service:

▶ The Reporting Services installation creates two virtual directories under the default website or another website on the IIS Server. The Reports virtual directory hosts the ASP.NET application that provides the Report Manager interface. The ReportServer virtual directory hosts the Report Server web service.

▶ If you do not want to use the default names for these virtual directories (Reports and ReportServer), you may specify different names. The virtual directory names that you specify must be 50 characters or fewer.

E-mail (SMTP) Server

If you are going to allow users to subscribe to reports and have them e-mailed, you need to specify the address of a Simple Mail Transfer Protocol (SMTP) server during the Reporting Services installation. *SMTP* is the standard for exchanging e-mail across the Internet. You need to specify the address of an e-mail server that will accept e-mail messages from the Report Server service and send them to the appropriate recipients.

In many cases, the address of your e-mail server is the same as the portion of your e-mail address that comes after the @ sign, prefaced by www. For example, if your e-mail address is MyEmail@Galactic.com, your e-mail server's address is probably either www.Galactic.com or smtp.Galactic.com. Be sure to verify the address of your e-mail server with your e-mail administrator. Also, make sure this e-mail server supports the SMTP protocol and that it will accept and forward mail originating from other servers on your network.

Encrypting Reporting Services Information

One of the options you may select during the Reporting Services installation process is to require the use of a Secure Sockets Layer (SSL) connection when accessing the Reports website and the Report Server web service. When an SSL connection is used, all the data transmitted across the network is encrypted, so it cannot be intercepted and read by anyone else. This is important if your reports contain sensitive personal or financial information.

To use SSL on a server, the server must have a server certificate. Server certificates are purchased from a certificate authority and installed on your server. You can find information on certificate authorities on the Internet.

Each server certificate is associated with a specific URL. To use SSL with the Reports website and the Report Server web service, your server certificate must be associated with the URL that corresponds to the default website on the server. If www.MyRSServer.com takes you to the default website on your server, then the server certificate must be associated with www.MyRSServer.com. If you plan to require an SSL connection, you should obtain and install the appropriate server certificate prior to installing Reporting Services.

When you require the use of an SSL connection to access the Reports website and the Report Server web service, your users must specify a slightly different URL to access these locations. For instance, if the users would normally use http:// www.MyRSServer.com/Reports to get to the Reports website, they will now have to use https://www.MyRSServer.com/Reports. The https in place of the http creates the SSL connection.

Microsoft Distributed Transaction Coordinator

The Reporting Services setup program uses the Microsoft Distributed Transaction Coordinator (MS DTC) to help control the setup process. You need to make sure the MS DTC will be available to the setup program. To do this, go to the Control Panel and select Administrative Tools, and then double-click Services. In the list of services, find the entry for Distributed Transaction Coordinator. The entry in the Startup Type column should be Manual or Automatic, as shown in Figure 2-5.

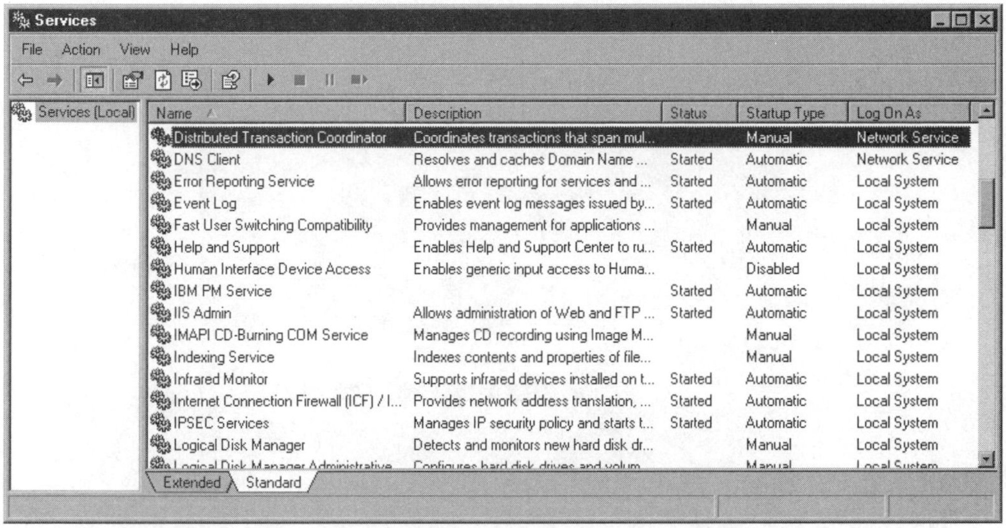

Figure 2-5   *The services entry for the Distributed Transaction Coordinator*

If the Startup Type is Disabled, use the following procedure:

1. Double-click the entry for Distributed Transaction Coordinator in the Services window.
2. Select Manual from the Startup Type drop-down box in the Distributed Transaction Coordinator Properties (Local Computer) dialog box (see Figure 2-6).
3. Click OK.
4. Close the Services window.

Login Accounts

The login account you are logged in as when you run the setup program must have administrative rights on the computer where the installation is being done. If you are doing a distributed or a web farm installation, the login account must have administrative rights on both the computer that will be the report server and the computer that will be the database server.

The login account you are logged in as must also have system administration rights in the SQL Server installation that will contain the Report Catalog. The setup program uses this login to access SQL Server and create the items necessary for the Report Catalog. You may specify a different login, either a SQL login or a Windows login, for the Report Server to use when accessing the Report Catalog after the installation is complete.

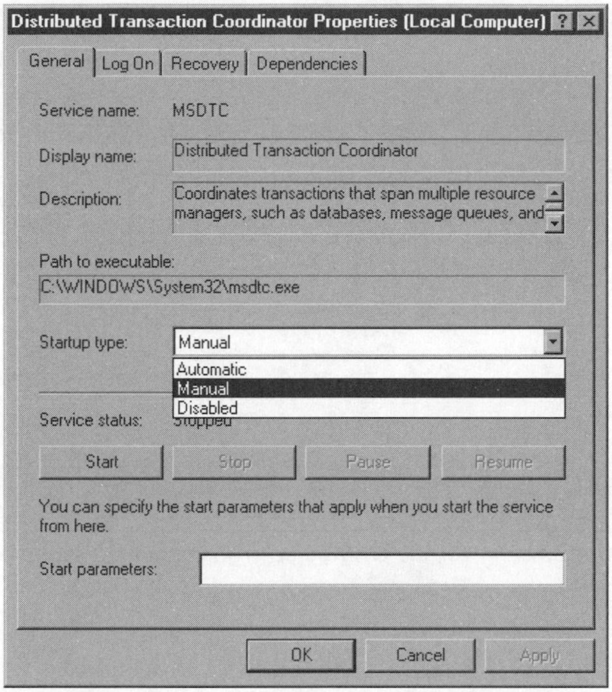

Figure 2-6   *The Distributed Transaction Coordinator Properties (Local Computer) dialog box*

You will be asked to specify several login accounts during the Reporting Services installation. Make your choices ahead of time and track down any passwords you may need before you begin the installation process.

The Report Server Service Login Account for Windows   First, you will be asked to specify the login account used by the Report Server service. You can choose from the following types of accounts:

► **The built-in account NT AUTHORITY\SYSTEM (also called the local system account)**   The local system account has access to almost all resources on the local computer and may or may not have access to resources on other computers in the network.

► **The built-in local service account**   This account exists on Windows 2003 servers for running services. This account cannot access other servers on the network. This choice will only be available if you are installing Reporting Services on Windows 2003.

▶ **The built-in network service account**   This account exists on Windows 2003 servers for running services. This account can access other servers on the network. This choice will only be available if you are installing Reporting Services on Windows 2003.

▶ **A domain user account**   This is a regular user account that exists in the domain in which this server resides.

Microsoft recommends the local system account be used as the login for the Report Server service. Using the local system account ensures the Report Server service has all the rights it needs on the local server.

The Report Server Web Service Login Account for Windows   The second login account required by the Reporting Services installation is used by the Report Server web service. If you are installing on any Windows platform other than Windows 2003, you do not have a choice here. The Report Server web service will be required to use the login account configured for ASP.NET on this computer.

If you are installing Reporting Services on Windows 2003, you can choose between the network service account and the local system account for this login. The network service account is used by services to log on to the local machine. It has the added advantage of being able to log on to other computers in the network. When you're installing on Windows 2003, the network service account is the default for the Report Server web service login.

The Report Server Service Login Account for the Database Server   The third login account required by the Reporting Services installation is used by the Report Server service to log in to SQL Server, and to access the Report Server and Report Server Temp DB databases. As noted earlier, this login account is used after the installation is complete. It is not used to access SQL Server during the installation process.

You have four options:

▶ The login account used by the Report Server service to log in to Windows

▶ The built-in local system account

▶ A domain user account

▶ A SQL Server login

You need to work with the database administrator of your SQL Server to determine which of these options to use.

NOTE

If a SQL Server login other than sa is used, the SQL Server login must be added to the RSExecRole role in the ReportServer, ReportServerTempDB, master, and msdb databases.

Running the SQL Server Installation Program

When you run the SQL Server installation program, you need to run it under a login that is a member of the local system administrators group. In addition, your login needs to have administrator permissions in SQL Server, so you can perform the following tasks:

▶ Create SQL logins

▶ Create SQL roles

▶ Create databases

▶ Assign roles to logins

The Installation Process

Now that you have worked through all the preparation, it is finally time to install Reporting Services. This is done through the SQL Server 2005 setup program, either at the time SQL Server 2005 is originally installed or later, as an addition to an existing SQL Server installation. In this section, you see the portions of the SQL Server 2005 installation dealing with Reporting Services and learn about the option selections necessary for the various types of Reporting Services installations discussed earlier in this chapter.

The SQL Server 2005 Installation

If you are doing a full, server, distributed, or web farm installation of Reporting Services, the setup program must be run on the computer that will serve as the report server. This is the computer that will be running the Report Server Windows service and hosting Report Manager and the Report Server web service in IIS. If you are doing a report author installation, the setup program must be run on the computer you will be using for report authoring.

NOTE

If you are creating reports using Visual Studio 2005, you do not need to run the SQL Server 2005 setup on the computer you are using for report authoring. The Business Intelligence project types are installed as part of the Visual Studio 2005 setup. You need to run the SQL Server 2005 setup on your report authoring computer only if you are using the Business Intelligence Development Environment for report creation.

If you are doing a distributed or web farm installation, you do not need to run the Reporting Services setup program on the database server. You will, of course, need to install SQL Server 2000 or SQL Server 2005 on the database server prior to doing the Reporting Services installation, but you do not need to run the Reporting Services setup program on that computer. The Reporting Services setup program on the report server will access the database server and take care of all the necessary installation and setup remotely.

Begin the installation by inserting the SQL Server 2005 installation CD into the CD or DVD drive. In most cases, the autorun process should take you to the Start screen. If this does not happen automatically, double-click the splash.hta file on the installation CD. Use the Prepare section of the Start screen to insure you have all the necessary hardware and software prerequisites.

When you are ready to begin the actual installation, select Server Components, Tools, Books Online, and Samples from the Start screen.

Preliminaries

The setup process begins with the usual preliminaries. You must read and accept the SQL Server licensing agreement. The setup will also double-check to make sure all the prerequisite software is installed and properly configured. Of course, you also need to enter the product key.

The Components to Install and Feature Selection Pages

Once all this groundwork is complete, you get to the good stuff. On the Components to Install page of the Installation Wizard, you can determine which components of SQL Server to install. Actually, the Components to Install page enables you to begin this process. You need to drill down into the details on the Feature Selection page to select exactly what to install.

The following sections show you which items to select on the Components to Install page and on the Feature Selection page for each type of installation.

Reporting Services Full Installation On the Components to Install page, perform the following for a Reporting Services full installation:

▶ Check SQL Server Database Services if you do not already have a SQL Server 2000 or a SQL Server 2005 server available to host the report catalog.

▶ Check Reporting Services.

 Click Advanced to view the Feature Selection page. On the Feature Selection page:

▶ Locate the Management Tools item under Client Components. Use the dropdown next to this item to select Will Be Installed on Local Hard Drive.

▶ Locate the Business Intelligence Development Studio item under Client Components. Use the dropdown next to this item to select Will Be Installed on Local Hard Drive.

▶ Locate the Software Development Kit item under Client Components. Use the dropdown next to this item to select Will Be Installed on Local Hard Drive.

▶ Locate the Documentation, Samples, and Sample Databases item. Use the dropdown next to this item to select Entire Feature Will Be Installed on Local Hard Drive.

 Once these changes are made, the Client Components section of the Feature Selection page should appear as shown in Figure 2-7. Click Next to continue with the SQL Server Installation Wizard.

NOTE

You may want to select other items on the Components to Install or Feature Selection screen if you are installing other SQL Server components as part of this process. The items documented here represent the minimum for a Reporting Services full installation.

Reporting Services Server Installation On the Components to Install page, perform the following for a Reporting Services server installation:

▶ Check SQL Server Database Services if you do not already have a SQL Server 2000 or SQL Server 2005 server available to host the report catalog.

▶ Check Reporting Services.

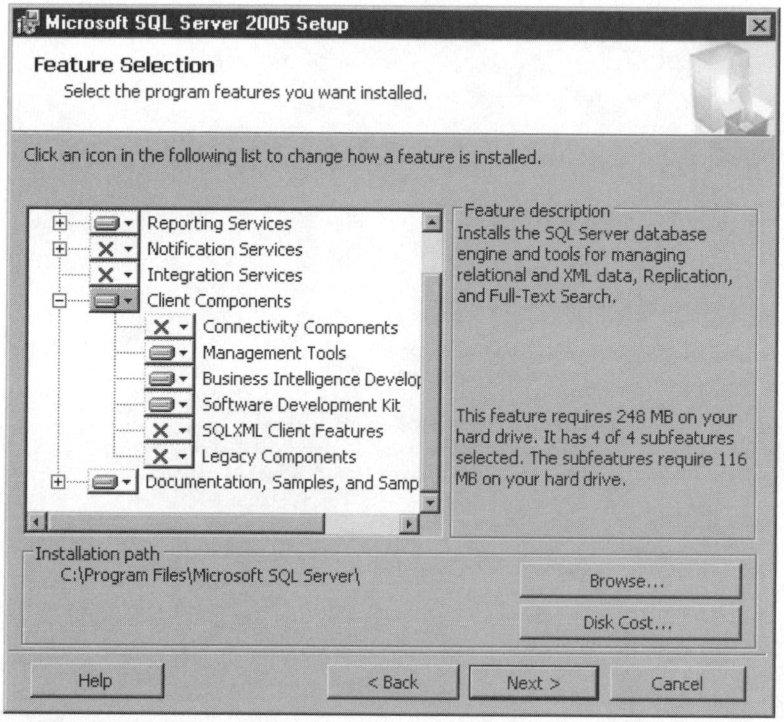

Figure 2-7 *The Feature Selection page for a Reporting Services full installation*

Click Advanced to view the Feature Selection page. On the Feature Selection page:

▶ Locate the Management Tools item under Client Components. Use the dropdown next to this item to select Will Be Installed on Local Hard Drive.

Once these changes are made, the Feature Selection page should appear, as shown in Figure 2-8. Click Next to continue with the SQL Server Installation Wizard.

NOTE

You may want to select other items on the Components to Install or Feature Selection screen if you are installing other SQL Server components as part of this process. The items documented here represent the minimum for a Reporting Services server installation.

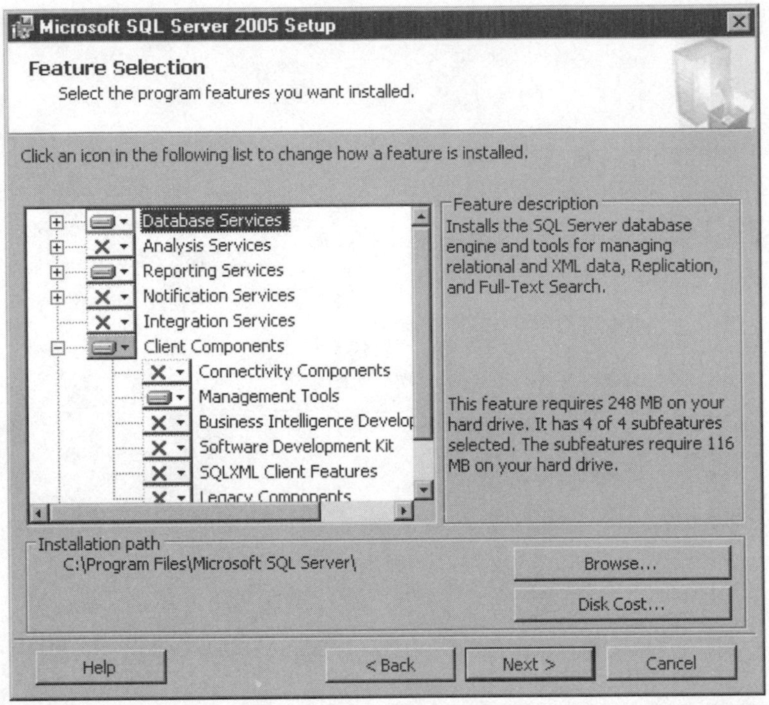

Figure 2-8   *The Feature Selection page for a Reporting Services server installation*

Reporting Services Report Author Installation   On the Components to Install page, leave all the items unchecked. Click Advanced to view the Feature Selection page. On the Feature Selection page:

▶   Locate the Business Intelligence Development Studio item under Client Components. Use the dropdown next to this item to select Will Be Installed on Local Hard Drive.

▶   Locate the Software Development Kit item under Client Components. Use the dropdown next to this item to select Will Be Installed on Local Hard Drive.

▶   Locate the Documentation, Samples, and Sample Databases item. Use the plus sign to expand this item.

▶   Locate the SQL Server Books Online item under Documentation, Samples, and Sample Databases. Use the dropdown next to this item to select Will Be Installed on Local Hard Drive.

▶   Locate the Sample Code and Applications item under Documentation, Samples, and Sample Databases. Use the dropdown next to this item to select Will Be Installed on Local Hard Drive.

Once these changes are made, the Client Components section of the Feature Selection page should appear, as shown in Figure 2-9. Click Next to continue with the SQL Server Installation Wizard.

Reporting Services Distributed Installation and Web Farm Installation   Before completing the Reporting Services portion of a distributed or a web farm installation, you must have either SQL Server 2000 or SQL Server 2005 running on the computer that will serve as the database server. Remember, the Enterprise Edition of Reporting Services is required for a web farm installation. On the Components to Install page, perform the following for a Reporting Services distributed installation or a web farm installation:

▶ Check Reporting Services.

Click Advanced to view the Feature Selection page. On the Feature Selection page:

▶ Locate the Management Tools item under Client Components. Use the dropdown next to this item to select Will Be Installed on Local Hard Drive.

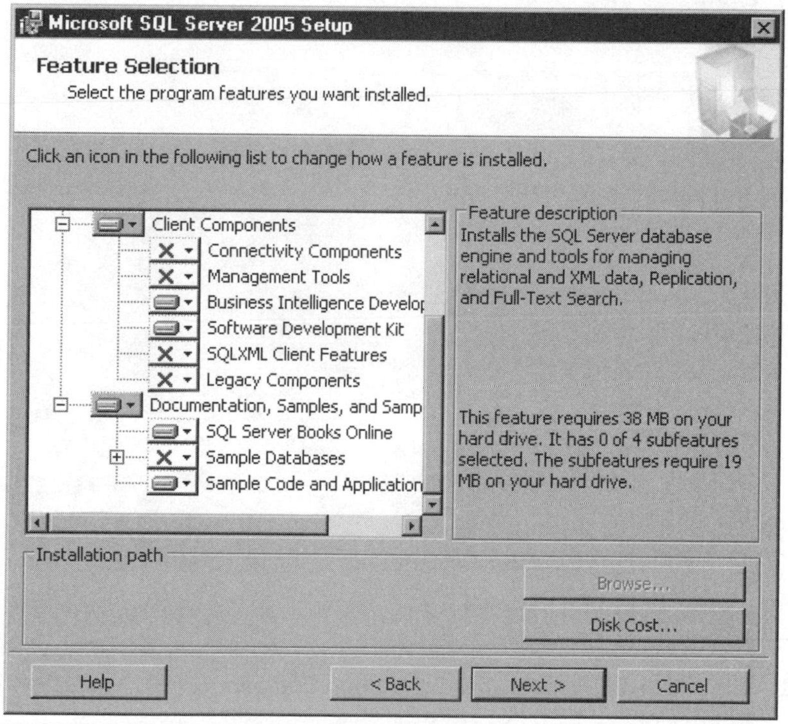

Figure 2-9   *The Feature Selection page for a Reporting Services report author installation*

Once these changes are made, the Feature Selection page should appear as shown in Figure 2-10. Click Next to continue with the SQL Server Installation Wizard.

Instance Name Page

The Instance Name page, shown in Figure 2-11, enables you to choose the name assigned to this instance of the components you are installing, including Reporting Services. The default instance will use Reports as the name of the Report Manager website and ReportServer as the name of the Reporting Services web service. If you specify an instance name, a dollar sign ($) followed by the instance name is appended to the end of the website and web service name. For example, if you specify an instance name of "RS2005," the website will be "Reports$RS2005" and the web service will be "ReportServer$RS2005."

You can click Installed Instances to see all the instances of SQL Server components currently installed on this computer. Of course, your new instance name cannot be

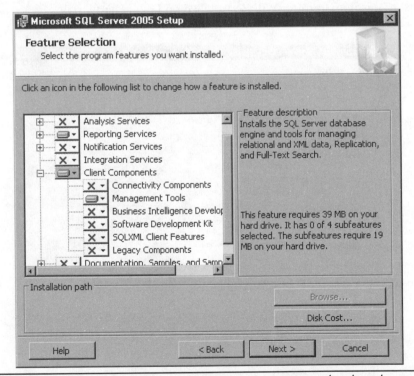

Figure 2-10   *The Feature Selection page for a Reporting Services distributed or web farm installation*

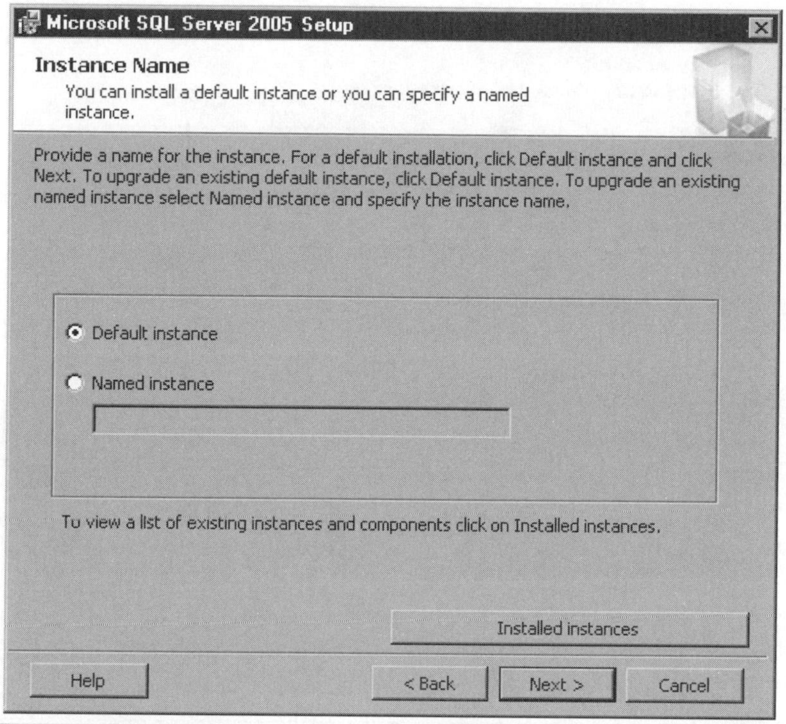

Figure 2-11   *The Instance Name page*

exactly the same name as any existing instance. Unless you have a reason to change the instance name from the default, such as multiple Reporting Services instances on a single server, it is probably a good idea to stick with the default.

After you have entered the Instance Name or if you have decided to use the default instance, click Next to continue with the SQL Server Installation Wizard.

Service Account Page

The Service Account page is shown in Figure 2-12. This page enables you to specify the Windows credentials the Reporting Services Windows service is to run under. The content of this screen will vary, depending on the SQL Server 2005 components you chose to install. The options available here were discussed previously in the "Report Server Service Login Account for Windows" section of this chapter. This page also enables you to select the services that will start at the end of the setup. If SQL Server was included as part of this install, SQL Server Agent should be checked.

After you make your selections on this page, click Next to continue with the SQL Server Installation Wizard.

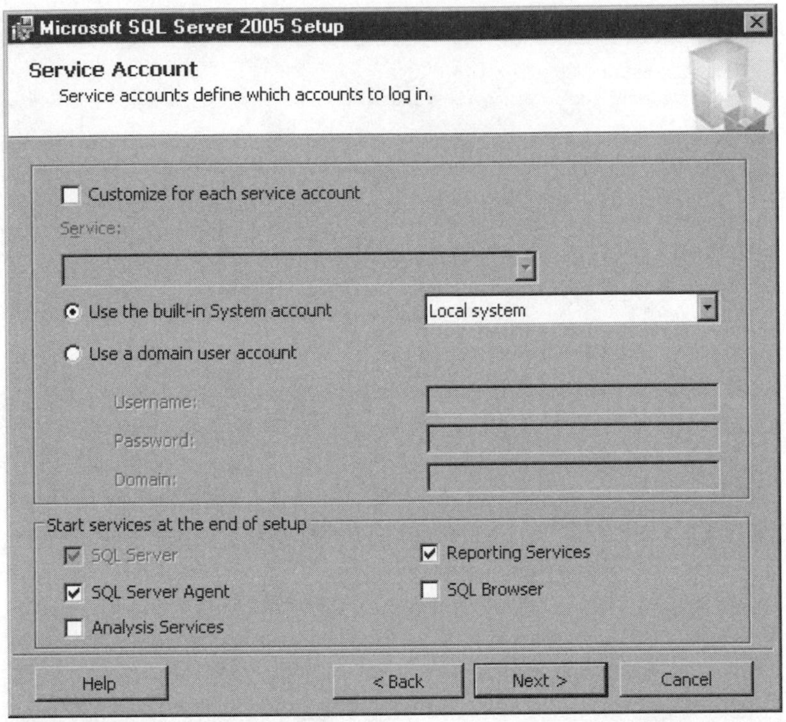

Figure 2-12 *The Service Account page*

The Report Server Installation Options Page

After leaving the Service Account page, you will encounter several pages that deal with the setup of SQL Server itself, if SQL Server was selected on the Components to Install page. Make the appropriate choices for your SQL Server installation. Press Next to move from one page to the following page.

Eventually, you will come to the Report Server Installation Options page, shown in Figure 2-13. If SQL Server was selected on the Components to Install page, this page provides you with two choices for configuring your Reporting Services installation. You can choose to Install the Default Configuration or Install But Do Not Configure the Server. If SQL Server was not selected on the Components to Install page, you will not have a choice; the Install But Do Not Configure the Server option will be selected for you. In either case, if the Install But Do Not Configure the Server option is chosen, your new Reporting Services installation will need to be configured using the Reporting Services Configuration Manager utility program. You learn more about this utility program in the upcoming section "The Report Server Configuration Manager."

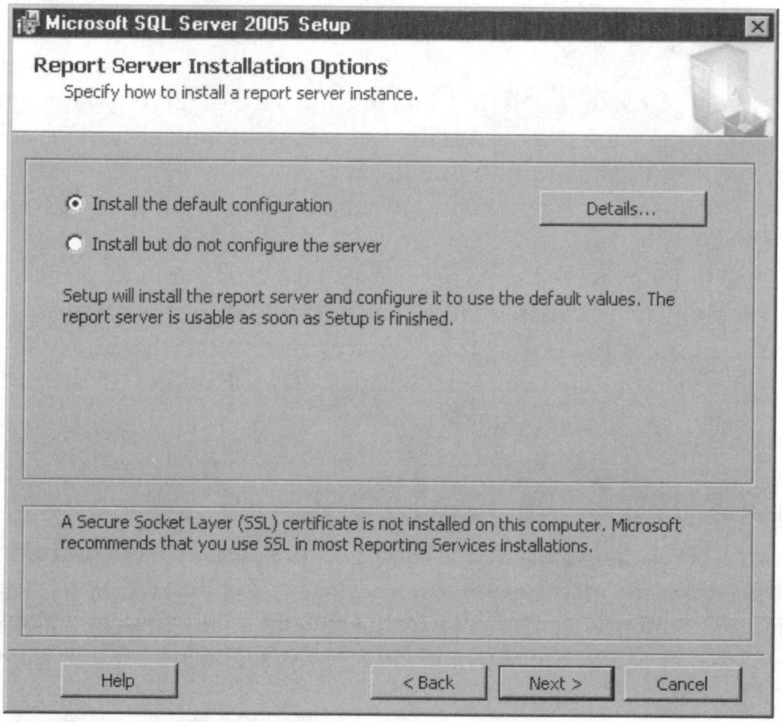

Figure 2-13   *The Report Server Installation Options page*

This may seem like a rather limiting set of choices, sort of an all-or-nothing proposition, but it is not. For the majority of Reporting Services installations, the default choices will do just fine. Only rarely, for distributed or web farm installations, for example, do you need to change the default configuration settings.

The default configuration settings are

► Web service name is ReportServer or ReportServer$ followed by the instance name

► Report Manager website is Reports or Reports$ followed by the instance name

► The local ASPNET user provides the logon credentials for the web service

► The Report Catalog is hosted by the instance of SQL Server 2005 being created by this installation process. (This is why the choice Install the Default Configuration is disabled when you are not installing SQL Server at the same time.)

► The SMTP Server is not specified

After you make your selection on this page, click Next to continue with the SQL Server Installation Wizard.

Completing the SQL Server Installation Wizard

After a summary screen or two, the SQL Server Installation Wizard has all the information it requires to install the components of SQL Server you requested. Complete the wizard to finish the installation process. Remember, if you chose the option to Install But Do Not Configure the Server, you will need to run the Report Server Configuration Manager to complete the final configuration of Reporting Services.

Even if you did use the Reporting Services default configuration, you should run the Report Server Configuration Manager to complete one important task. You should always create a backup of the Reporting Services encryption key as the final step of a Reporting Services installation. See the later section "Backing Up the Encryption Key" for instructions on completing this task.

The Report Server Configuration Manager

As you learned in the previous section of this chapter, the SQL Server Installation Wizard is geared completely toward installing Reporting Services with the default configuration. If you want to deviate from the default configuration, you must use another tool to make these nondefault configuration settings. That tool is the Report Server Configuration Manager.

The Report Server Configuration Manager is found on the Start menu under All Programs | Microsoft SQL Server 2005 | Configuration Tools | Reporting Services Configuration. When this utility starts up, it asks for the name of a server to connect to, as shown in Figure 2-14. Once you enter a server name and click Find, the program

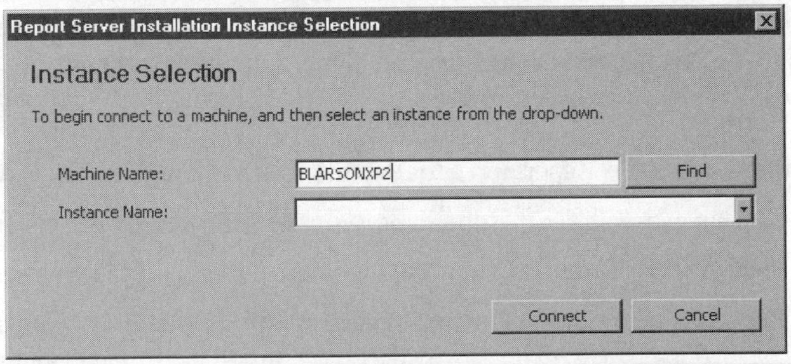

Figure 2-14   *The Report Server Installation Instance Selection dialog box connecting to a server*

finds all instances of Reporting Services 2005 running on that server and displays them in the Instance Name drop-down box, as shown in Figure 2-15. You need to select an instance and click Connect to enter the utility program with the configuration information for that Reporting Services instance loaded.

The Report Server Configuration Manager contains a number of pages, each geared toward configuring a different aspect of Reporting Services. The page names, shown in the page menu on the left side of the screen, each have an icon next to them. If the icon is green with a white check mark, the items on that page are configured correctly. If the icon is red with a white *X*, the items are not configured correctly.

Let's take a look at each of these pages and learn what they are used for.

Server Status Page

The Server Status page displays status information about the Report Server instance you selected. There is no configuration information to change on this page. Instead, it provides an overview of the state of the Report Server.

Report Server Virtual Directory Settings Page

The Report Server Virtual Directory Settings page enables you to view and change the name of the virtual directory used by the Reporting Services web service. This page is shown in Figure 2-16. As mentioned previously, if this is the default instance of Reporting Services on the server, the default name for this virtual directory is ReportServer. If this is not the default instance, the virtual directory name is ReportServer followed by a dollar sign and the instance name.

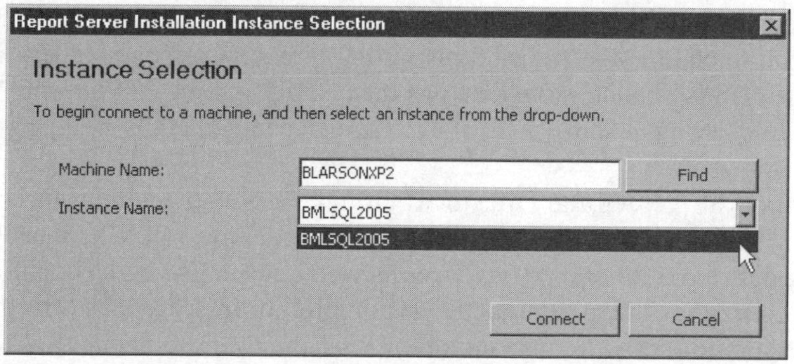

Figure 2-15   *The Report Server Installation Instance Selection dialog box selecting an instance*

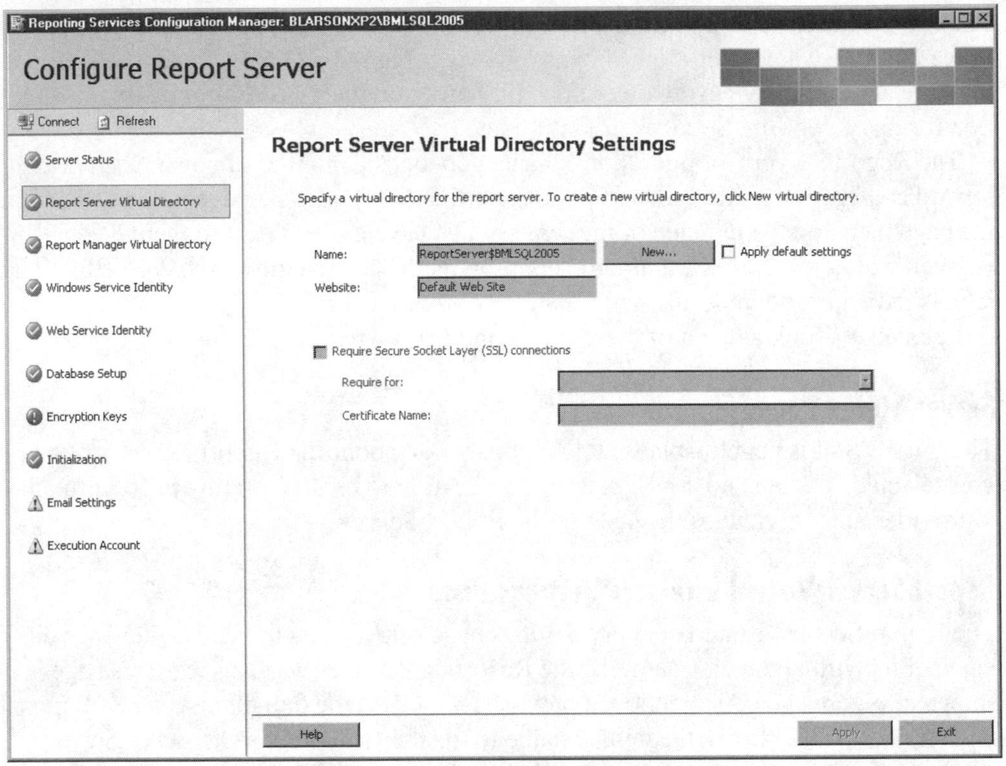

Figure 2-16   *The Report Server Virtual Directory Settings page*

Use the New button to change the name of the virtual directory. This link also enables you to change the website this virtual directory appears under. This is useful when IIS is hosting more than just the default website. If you want to return to the default setting at some point after making a change, click the Apply Default Settings check box.

The Report Server Virtual Directory Settings page also enables you to select whether or not you want to require a Secure Sockets Layer (SSL) connection when retrieving data from the Reporting Services web service. If you have any questions on this option, refer to the section "Encrypting Reporting Services Information." Because a server certificate is required for SSL, the Require Secure Sockets Layer (SSL) Connections check box is disabled if you do not have a server certificate.

Report Manager Virtual Directory Settings Page

The Report Manager Virtual Directory Settings page enables you to view and change the name of the virtual directory used by the Report Manager ASP.NET application.

This page is shown in Figure 2-17. As mentioned previously, if this is the default instance of Reporting Services on the server, the default name for this virtual directory is Reports. If this is not the default instance, the virtual directory name is Reports, followed by a dollar sign and the instance name.

Use the New button to change the name of the virtual directory. This link also enables you to change the website this virtual directory appears under. This is useful when IIS is hosting more than just the default website. If you want to return to the default setting at some point after making a change, click the Apply Default Settings check box.

Windows Service Identity

The Windows Service Identity page enables you to view and change the logon credentials used by the Report Server Windows service. This page is shown in Figure 2-18. See the earlier section "The Report Server Service Login Account for Windows" for more information about the options on this page.

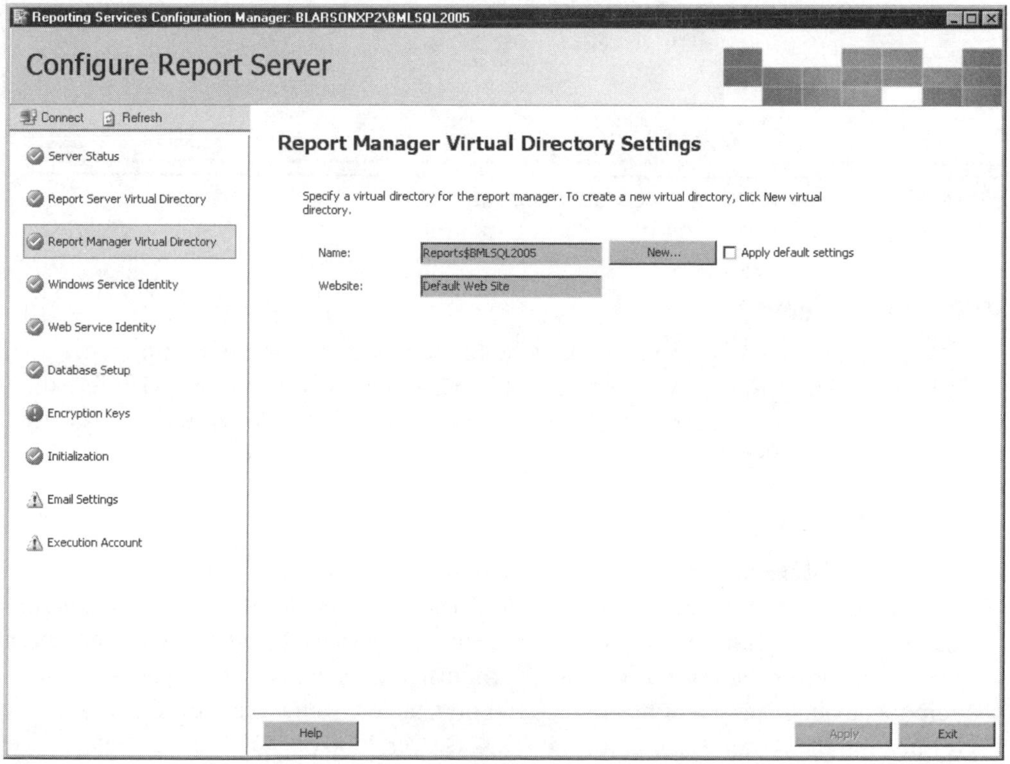

Figure 2-17   *The Report Manager Virtual Directory Settings page*

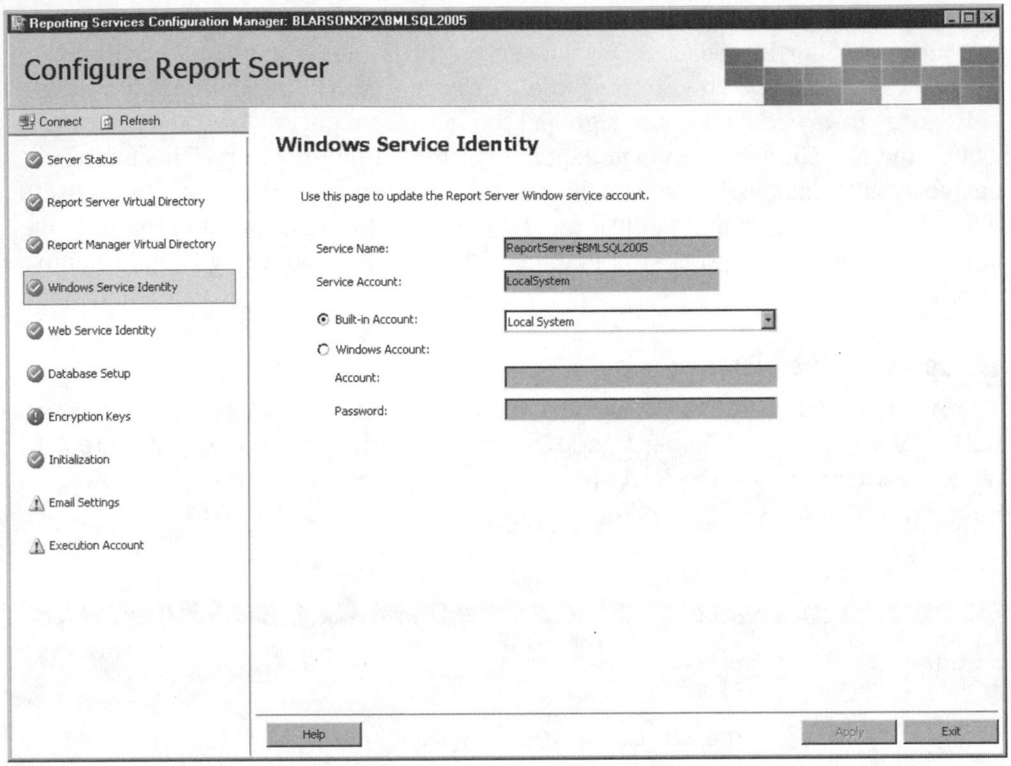

Figure 2-18   *The Windows Service Identity page*

Web Service Identity

The Web Service Identity page enables you to view and change the logon credentials used by the Report Server web service. This page is shown in Figure 2-19. See the section "The Report Server Web Service Login Account for Windows" for more information about the options on this page.

Database Connection

The Database Connection page, shown in Figure 2-20, enables you to select the set of databases that will serve as the Report Catalog. You can select the database server name, the name of the database on that server, and the credentials used to connect to that server. If you are performing a distributed or web farm installation, this is where you will select the remote database server for hosting the Report Catalog. Remember, the database server hosting the Report Catalog must be SQL Server 2000 or SQL Server 2005.

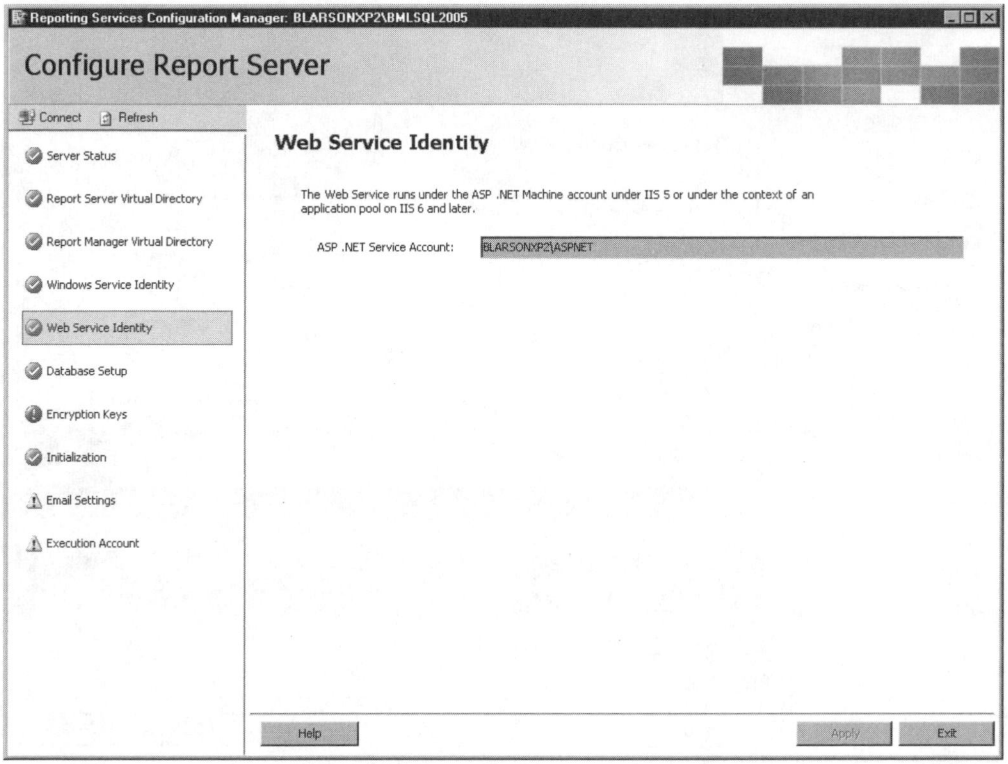

Figure 2-19   *The Web Service Identity page*

Once you enter or select a database server name for Server Name, you can click the Connect link to connect to that server and populate the list of databases available. If you want to create a set of new databases for hosting the Report Catalog, click the New button. Use Credentials Type, Account Name, and Password to specify the credentials used by the Reporting Services Windows service to access the Report Catalog database. See the section "The Report Server Service Login Account for the Database Server" for more information about the options on this page.

It is also possible to generate T-SQL database scripts for creating the Report Catalog databases, for upgrading a database from Reporting Services 2000 to Reporting Services 2005, and for setting the appropriate rights in the Report Catalog databases. This is done using the Script button. Scripts are generated to text files that can then be copied and executed on one or more servers.

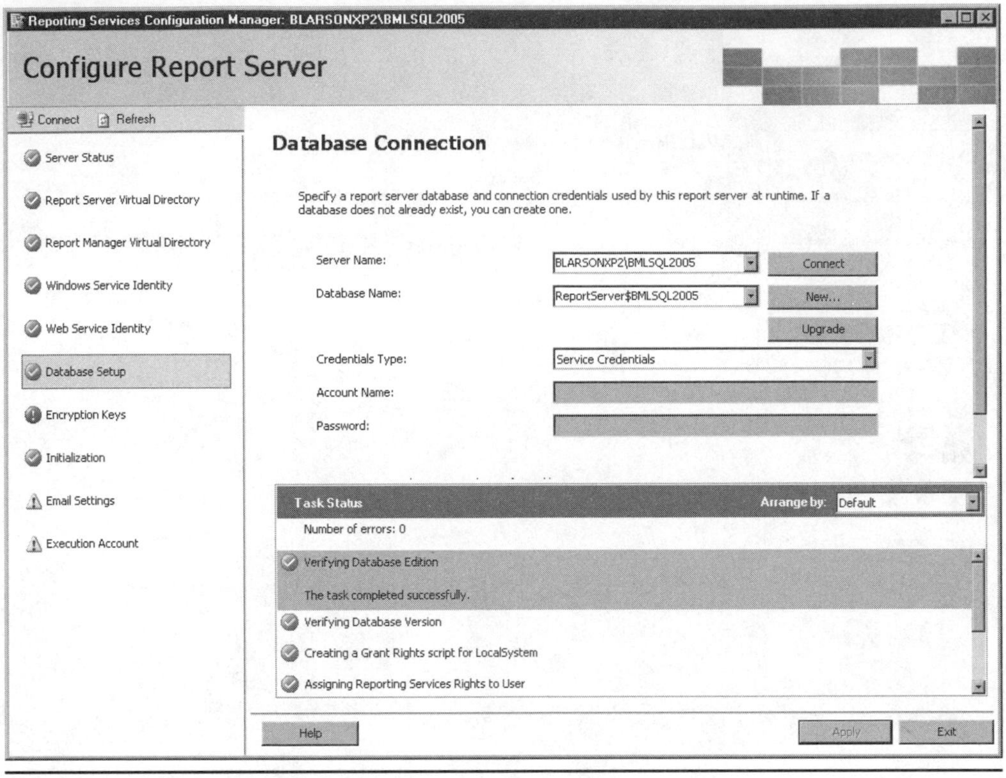

Figure 2-20 *The Database Connection page*

When you click the Apply button the following tasks are performed:

▶ **Verify the Report Server database edition and version** This option will make sure you have specified a Report Catalog of the proper edition and version of Reporting Services.

▶ **Grant access rights to Report Server accounts** This option will set the appropriate rights in the databases for the specified credentials.

▶ **Set the connection information** This option will set this Reporting Services instance to use the specified Report Catalog.

Encryption Keys

As you have seen, Reporting Services uses various sets of credentials for its operation. Whenever a login account and a password are specified, these credentials are stored as encrypted text. In addition, any credentials you specify in a report or shared data source are also encrypted. To encrypt and, more importantly, to decrypt these credentials, Reporting Services needs to use an encryption key. This encryption key is created as part of the Reporting Services installation.

If this encryption key ever becomes corrupt, none of these encrypted credentials can be decrypted. The credentials become useless and Reporting Services becomes inoperable. To remedy this situation, you need to have a backup of the encryption key, which can be restored over the top of the corrupt key. This is the purpose of the Encryption Key page, shown in Figure 2-21.

Use the Backup button to create a backup copy of the encryption key. Use the Restore button to restore a previously created encryption key backup. Use the Change button to create a new encryption key for Reporting Services. This should be done if your current encryption key becomes compromised. The current encryption key must be operable (that is, not corrupt) to use the Change function.

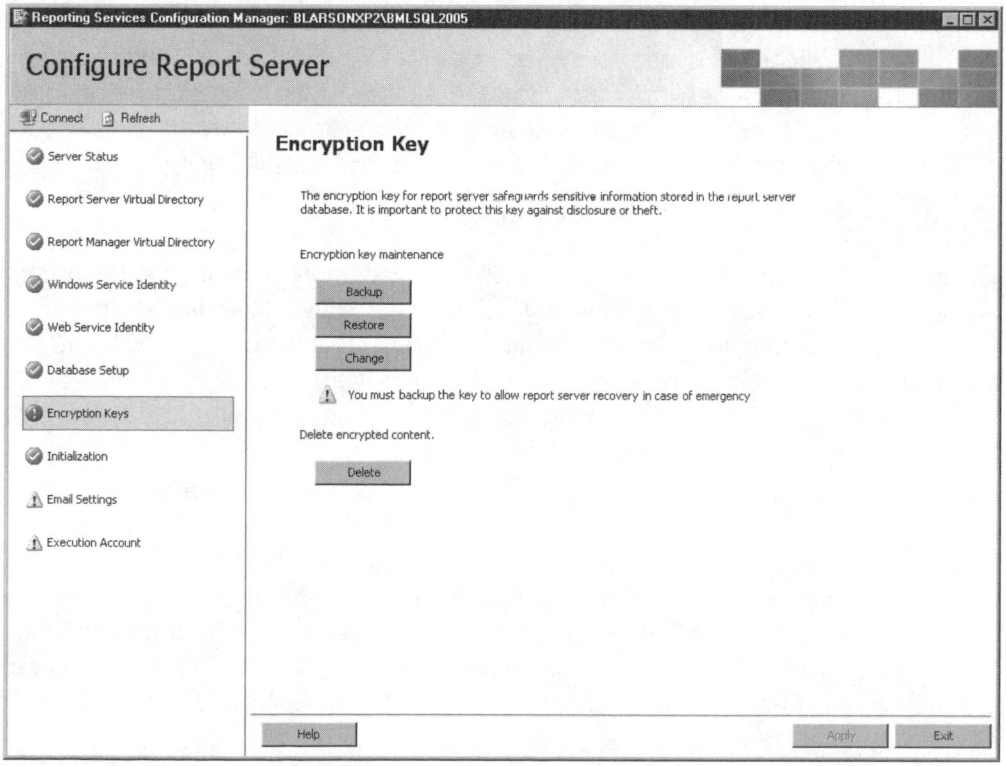

Figure 2-21   *The Encryption Key page*

If your Reporting Services encryption key does become corrupt and you do not have a current backup, use the Delete button. This will remove all the encrypted credentials and create a new encryption key. After using this option, you will need to use the Database Connection page of the Report Server Configuration Manager to reenter the database credentials. When the Delete option is used, Reporting Services will be inoperable until you enter a new set of database credentials. You will also need to reenter the data source credentials for each report and shared data source deployed on the server.

Backing Up the Encryption Key   To create a backup copy of the encryption key, click the Backup button. Enter a password to protect the encryption key, and then enter a path and a filename for storing the key. You may want to put the key backup on a floppy disk or other removable media, so it can be stored in a safe place. Make sure you keep the password in a safe place as well. The password helps protect your encryption key backup and is required by the restore process.

NOTE

The Reporting Services encryption keys have had a bad habit of becoming corrupted in Reporting Services 2000. If the key does become corrupted, Reporting Services ceases to function and all the encrypted credential information on the server must be reentered. Therefore, it is important to maintain a current backup of your Reporting Services encryption key in a secure location.

Initialization

The Initialization page, shown in Figure 2-22, is used to initialize or start up Reporting Services. In some cases, a problem with installation will cause Reporting Services not to initialize at the completion of the installation process. Use the Initialize button to manually activate a Reporting Services instance that is not initialized.

E-mail Settings

The E-mail Settings page, shown in Figure 2-23, enables you to identify an SMTP server that can be used by Reporting Services. The SMTP server is used for delivering report subscriptions via e-mail. If an SMTP server is not specified, the e-mail delivery option will be unavailable when creating report subscriptions.

Enter the name of an SMTP server that will accept mail from Reporting Services. You can also enter an e-mail address for Sender E-mail. This e-mail address will appear in the From line of any report subscriptions e-mailed from Reporting Services.

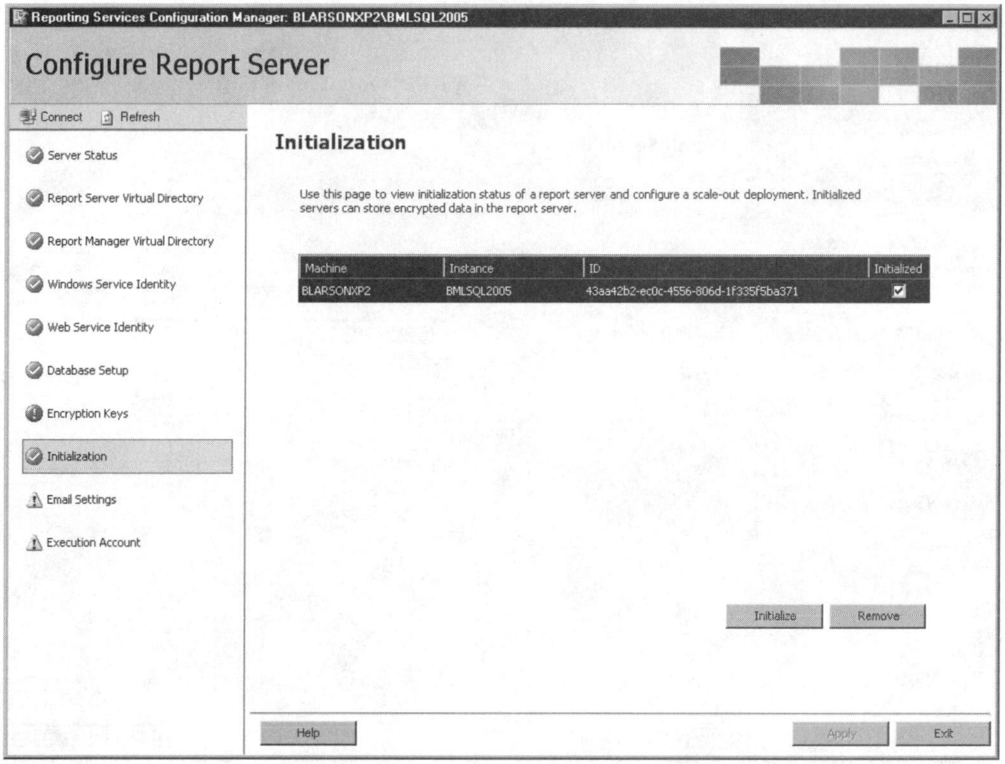

Figure 2-22 *The Initialization page*

Execution Account

The Execution Account page enables you to specify a set of login credentials to be used by Reporting Services when it is doing unattended report rendering. Unattended report rendering occurs when a report is created as the result of a scheduled report subscription or any other time a report is generated when no user is logged on. The Execution Account is required only in situations where the data source does not require login credentials.

For example, suppose you have a report that uses an Access database as its data source and that Access database does not require logon credentials. When a user subscribes to this report, the subscription creates a scheduled process. The scheduled process renders the report without an interactive user being logged in. When it is time for the report to query the data from the Access database, the Execution Account credentials are used to gain rights to the directory containing the Access MDB file.

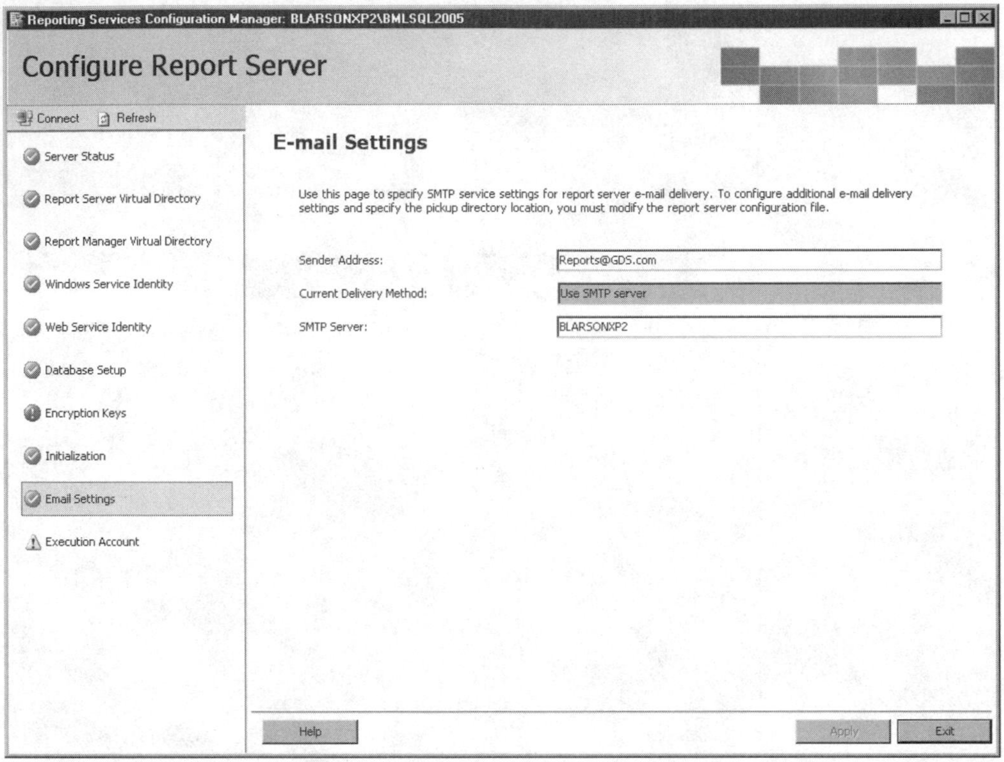

Figure 2-23   *The E-mail Settings page*

Using the Execution Account page, shown in Figure 2-24, you can specify the login account name and the password to be used for unattended report rendering. Make sure this account has the appropriate rights to access any directories that might be hosting data sources. However, this account should have limited rights throughout the network to prevent it from being used in a malicious manner. If you do not anticipate the need to allow unattended report rendering from data sources that do not require credentials, it is best that you not specify an execution account.

Menu Bar

The Connect button on the menu bar lets you connect to a different server, and then select a Reporting Services instance on that server. The Refresh button on the menu bar causes the Report Server Configuration Manager to reread the configuration information from the currently selected instance of Reporting Services.

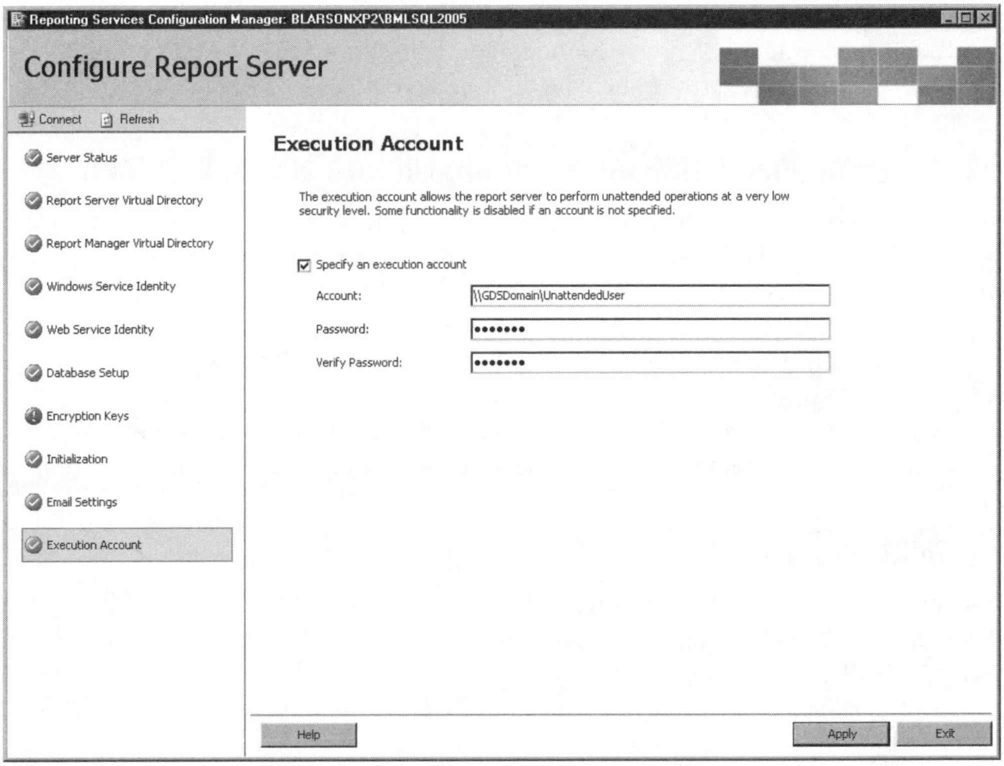

Figure 2-24 *The Execution Account page*

Common Installation Issues

This section lists some of the common problems you may encounter while installing Reporting Services. Suggested solutions are provided to help you resolve these problems.

Administrative Rights

One of the biggest problems with the Reporting Services setup is not using login accounts that have the appropriate rights. If you encounter an error during installation, refer to the earlier section "Login Accounts" and make sure you are using login accounts that have the appropriate rights.

If you discover you received a setup error because one of the login accounts you used was not adequate to the task, try changing that account using the Report Server

Configuration Manager. If this does not work, remove the failed installation of Reporting Services and try again. To remove the failed installation, select Add or Remove Programs from the Control Panel and choose to remove Reporting Services.

Server Components Not Shown on the Feature Selection Screen

If you are performing an installation that requires the server components, but they are not present on the Feature Selection screen, this is probably an indication that you are not up-to-date on your Windows service packs. Reporting Services is finicky about this. As stated earlier, the Reporting Services installation process requires Service Pack 4 if you are using Windows 2000 and Service Pack 1a if you are using Windows XP Professional.

If you encounter this problem, cancel the installation, install the latest service pack for your version of Windows, and then start the installation process again.

Installation Error 1603

You may receive Error 1603 if you are doing a report author installation of Reporting Services on a computer that is not running Internet Information Services. The Reporting Services installation looks for a user called ASPNET. This user is created by the .NET Framework installation on computers running IIS. If IIS is not running, no ASPNET user is created.

This problem is solved by creating a local user called ASPNET on the computer where you are doing the report author installation. This user does not need to have any particular password or any particular rights on the computer. For a report author installation, a user with this name simply needs to exist on the computer.

Installation Error 2755

You may receive Error 2755 if you are installing Reporting Services using a Terminal Server session. This will occur if you are using a mapped drive to access the setup files. The Windows Installer service that performs the setup operation is running in a different Windows session, so it may not have the same drive mappings. The error occurs because certain files needed by the installer cannot be found.

To remedy this problem, use a UNC path to access the setup files, rather than a mapped drive. Alternatively, you may put the installation CD in a drive that is local to the computer on which you are performing the installation or copy the setup files to a drive local to that computer.

The Installation Log File

If none of these suggestions solves your installation issues, you may want to consult the installation log files for more information.

The default location for the log files is

```
C:\Program Files\Microsoft SQL Server\90\Setup Bootstrap\Log\Files
```

Spending Some Time in Basic Training

You now have Reporting Services installed and ready to go. As mentioned at the end of Chapter 1, we will take time to ensure that you understand the basics of database architecture and querying before we begin creating reports. Chapter 3 gives you this database basic training. This basic training won't be as tough as Army boot camp, but it will get you ready to attack all those tough data-reporting challenges.

Chapter 3 also introduces you to Galactic Delivery Services (GDS), what it does, how it is structured, and what its data processing systems look like. We use GDS and its business needs for all our sample reports throughout the book.

Report Authoring

DB 101: Database Basics

IN THIS CHAPTER:

Before you begin creating reports, it is important that you have a good understanding of relational databases. In the first part of this chapter, you will see the tables, rows, and columns that make up relational databases. You also learn about concepts such as normalization and relationships. These are the characteristics that make a relational database . . ., well, relational.

Once you cover the basics, you are introduced to Galactic Delivery Services (GDS). The business needs of GDS serve as the basis for all the sample reports throughout this book. Even though GDS is a unique company in many respects, you will discover its reporting needs and its uses of Reporting Services are typical of most companies in this galaxy.

For the remainder of the chapter, you explore the ins and outs of the *SELECT query*, which is what you use to extract data from your data sources for use in your reports. Even though Reporting Services helps you create SELECT queries through a tool called the Query Designer, it is important that you understand how SELECT queries work and how they can be used to obtain the correct data. A report may look absolutely stunning with charts, graphics, special formatting, and snappy colors, but it is completely useless if it contains the wrong data!

Database Structure

Databases are basically giant containers for storing information. They are the electronic crawlspaces and digital attics of the corporate, academic, and governmental worlds. For example, anything that needs to be saved for later use by payroll, inventory management, or the external auditor is placed in a database.

Just like our crawlspaces and attics at home, the information placed in a database needs to be organized and classified. Figure 3-1 shows my attic in its current state. As you can see, it is going to be pretty hard to find those old kids' clothes for the thrift store clothing drive! I know they are up there somewhere.

Without some type of order placed on it, all the stuff in our home storage spaces becomes impossible to retrieve when we need it. The same is true in the world of electronic storage, as shown in Figure 3-2. Databases, like attics, need structure. Otherwise, we won't be able to find anything!

Getting Organized

The first step in getting organized is to have a place for everything and to have everything in its place. To achieve this, you need to add structure to the storage space, whether this is a space for box storage like my attic or a space for data storage like a database. To maintain this structure, you also need to have discipline of one sort or another as you add items to the storage space.

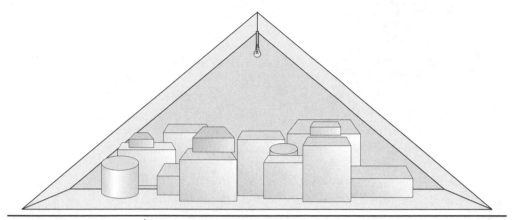

Figure 3-1   *My attic, with no organization*

Tables, Rows, and Columns

To get my attic organized, I need some shelves, a few labels, and some free time, so I can add the much-needed structure to this storage space. To keep my attic organized, I also need the discipline to pay attention to my new signs each time I put another box into storage. Figure 3-3 shows my attic as it exists in my fantasy world, where I have tons of free time and loads of self-discipline.

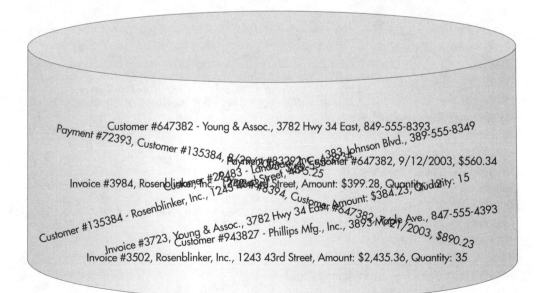

Figure 3-2   *An unorganized database*

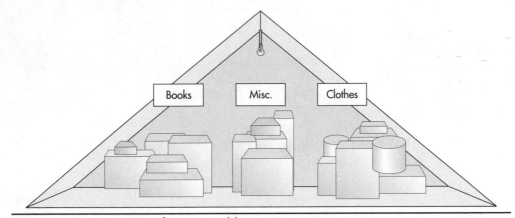

Figure 3-3 *My attic in my fantasy world*

Structure in the database world comes in the form of tables. Each database is divided into a number of tables. These tables store the information. Each table contains only one type of information. Figure 3-4 shows customer information in one table, payment information in another, and invoice header information in a third.

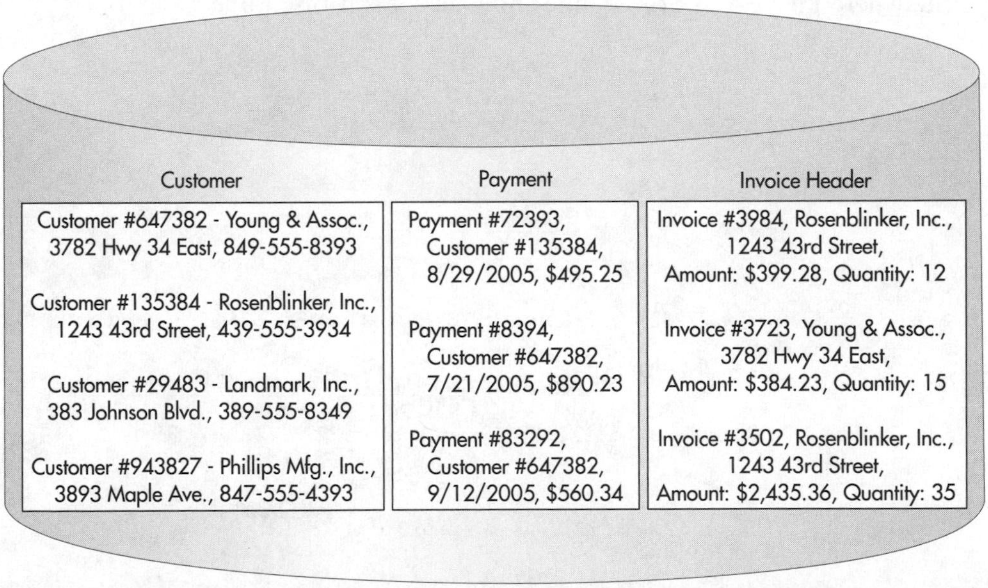

Customer	Payment	Invoice Header
Customer #647382 - Young & Assoc., 3782 Hwy 34 East, 849-555-8393	Payment #72393, Customer #135384, 8/29/2005, $495.25	Invoice #3984, Rosenblinker, Inc., 1243 43rd Street, Amount: $399.28, Quantity: 12
Customer #135384 - Rosenblinker, Inc., 1243 43rd Street, 439-555-3934	Payment #8394, Customer #647382, 7/21/2005, $890.23	Invoice #3723, Young & Assoc., 3782 Hwy 34 East, Amount: $384.23, Quantity: 15
Customer #29483 - Landmark, Inc., 383 Johnson Blvd., 389-555-8349	Payment #83292, Customer #647382, 9/12/2005, $560.34	Invoice #3502, Rosenblinker, Inc., 1243 43rd Street, Amount: $2,435.36, Quantity: 35
Customer #943827 - Phillips Mfg., Inc., 3893 Maple Ave., 847-555-4393		

Figure 3-4 *A database organized by tables*

NOTE

Invoice Header is used as the name of the third table for consistency with the sample database that will be introduced in the section "Galactic Delivery Services" and used throughout the remainder of the book. The Invoice Header name helps to differentiate this table from the Invoice Detail table that stores the detail lines of the invoice. The Invoice Detail table is not discussed here, but it will be present in the sample database.

Dividing each table into rows and columns brings additional structure to the database. Figure 3-5 shows the Customer table divided into several rows—one row for each customer whose information is being stored in the table. In addition, the Customer table is divided into a number of columns. Each column is given a name: Customer Number, Customer Name, Address, and Phone. These names tell you what information is being stored in each column.

With a database structured as tables, rows, and columns, you know exactly where to find a certain piece of information. For example, it is pretty obvious that the customer name for customer number 135384 will be found in the Name column of the second row of the Customer table. We are starting to get this data organized, and it was a lot easier than cleaning out the attic!

NOTE

Rows in a database are also called records. Columns in a database are also called fields. Reporting Services uses the terms "rows" and "records" interchangeably. It also uses the terms "columns" and "fields" interchangeably. Don't be confused by this!

Customer

Customer #	Customer Name	Address	Phone
647382	Young & Assoc.	3782 Hwy 34 East	849-555-8393
135384	Rosenblinker, Inc.	1243 43rd Street	439-555-3934
29483	Landmark, Inc.	383 Johnson Blvd.	389-555-8349
943827	Phillips Mfg., Inc.	3893 Maple Ave.	847-555-4393

Figure 3-5   *A database table organized by rows and columns*

Columns also force some discipline on anyone putting data into the table. Each column has certain characteristics assigned to it. For instance, the Customer Number column in Figure 3-5 may only contain strings of digits (0–9); no letters (A–Z) are allowed. It is also limited to a maximum of six characters. In data design lingo, these are known as *constraints*. Given these constraints, it is impossible to store a customer's name in the Customer Number column. The customer's name is likely too long and contains characters that are not legal in the Customer Number column. Constraints provide the discipline to force organization within a database.

Typically, when you design a database, you create tables for each of the things you want to keep track of. In Figure 3-4, the database designer knew that her company needed to track information for customers, payments, and invoices. Database designers call these things *entities*. The database designer created tables for the customer, payment, and invoice header entities. These tables are named Customer, Payment, and Invoice Header.

Once the entities have been identified, the database designer determines what information needs to be known about each entity. In Figure 3-5, the designer identified the customer number, customer name, address, and phone number as the things that need to be known for each customer. These are *attributes* of the customer entity. The database designer creates a column in the Customer table for each of these attributes.

Primary Key

As entities and attributes are being defined, the database designer needs to identify a special attribute for each entity in the database. This special attribute is known as the primary key. The purpose of the *primary key* is to be able to uniquely identify a single entity or, in the case of a database table, a single row in the table.

Two simple rules exist for primary keys. First, every entity must have a primary key value. Second, no two rows in an entity can have the same primary key value. In Figure 3-5, the Customer Number column can serve as the primary key. Every customer is assigned a customer number and no two customers can be assigned the same customer number.

For most entities, the primary key is a single attribute. However, in some cases, two attributes must be combined to create a unique primary key. This is known as a *composite primary key*. For instance, if you were defining an entity based on Presidents of the United States, the first name would not be a valid primary key. John Adams, John Quincy Adams, and John Kennedy all have the same first name. You would need to create a composite key combining first name, middle name, and last name to have a valid primary key.

Normalization

As the database designer continues to work on identifying entities and attributes, she will notice that two different entities have some of the same attributes. For example, in Figure 3-6, both the customer entity and the invoice header entity have attributes of Customer Name and Address. This duplication of information seems rather wasteful. Not only are the customer's name and address duplicated between the Customer and Invoice Header tables, but they are also duplicated in several rows in the Invoice Header table itself.

Customer

Customer #	Customer Name	Address	Phone
647382	Young & Assoc.	3782 Hwy 34 East	849-555-8393
135384	Rosenblinker, Inc.	1243 43rd Street	439-555-3934
29483	Landmark, Inc.	383 Johnson Blvd.	389-555-8349
943827	Phillips Mfg., Inc.	3893 Maple Ave.	847-555-4393

Invoice Header

Invoice #	Customer Name	Address	Amount	Quantity
3984	Rosenblinker, Inc.	1243 43rd Street	$399.28	12
3723	Young & Assoc.	3782 Hwy 34 East	$384.23	15
3502	Rosenblinker, Inc.	1243 43rd Street	$2,435.36	35

Figure 3-6   *Database tables with duplicate data*

The duplicate data also leads to another problem. Suppose that Rosenblinker, Inc. changes its name to RB, Inc. Then, Ann in the data-processing department changes the name in the Customer table because this is where we store information about the customer entity. However, the customer name has not been changed in the Invoice Header table. Because the customer name in the Invoice Header table no longer matches the customer name in the Customer table, it is no longer possible to determine how many invoices are outstanding for RB, Inc. Believe me, the accounting department will think this is a bad situation.

To avoid these types of problems, database tables are normalized. *Normalization* is a set of rules for defining database tables, so each table contains attributes from only one entity. The rules for creating normalized database tables can be quite complex. You can hear database designers endlessly debating whether a proper database should be in third normal form, fourth normal form, or one hundred and twenty-seventh normal form. Let the database designers debate all they want. All you need to remember is this: a normalized database avoids data duplication.

Relations

A *relation* is a tool the database designer uses to avoid data duplication when creating a normalized database. A relation is simply a way to put the duplicated data in one place, and then point to it from all the other places in the database where it would otherwise occur. The table that contains the data is called the *parent* table. The table that contains a pointer to the data in the parent table is called the *child* table. Just like parents and children of the human variety, the parent table and the child table are said to be *related*.

In our example, the customer name and address are stored in the Customer table. This is the parent table. A pointer is placed in the Invoice Header table in place of the duplicate customer names and addresses it had contained. The Invoice Header table is the child table.

As mentioned previously, each customer is uniquely identified by their customer number. Therefore, the Customer Number column serves as the primary key for the Customer table. In the Invoice Header table, we need a way to point to a particular customer. It makes sense to use the primary key in the parent table, in this case the Customer Number column, as that pointer. This is illustrated in Figure 3-7.

Each row in the Invoice Header table now contains a copy of the primary key of a row in the Customer table. The Customer Number column in the Invoice Header table is called the foreign key. It is called a *foreign key* because it is not one of the native attributes of the invoice header entity. The customer number is a native attribute of the customer entity. The only reason the Customer Number column exists in the Invoice Header table is to create the relationship.

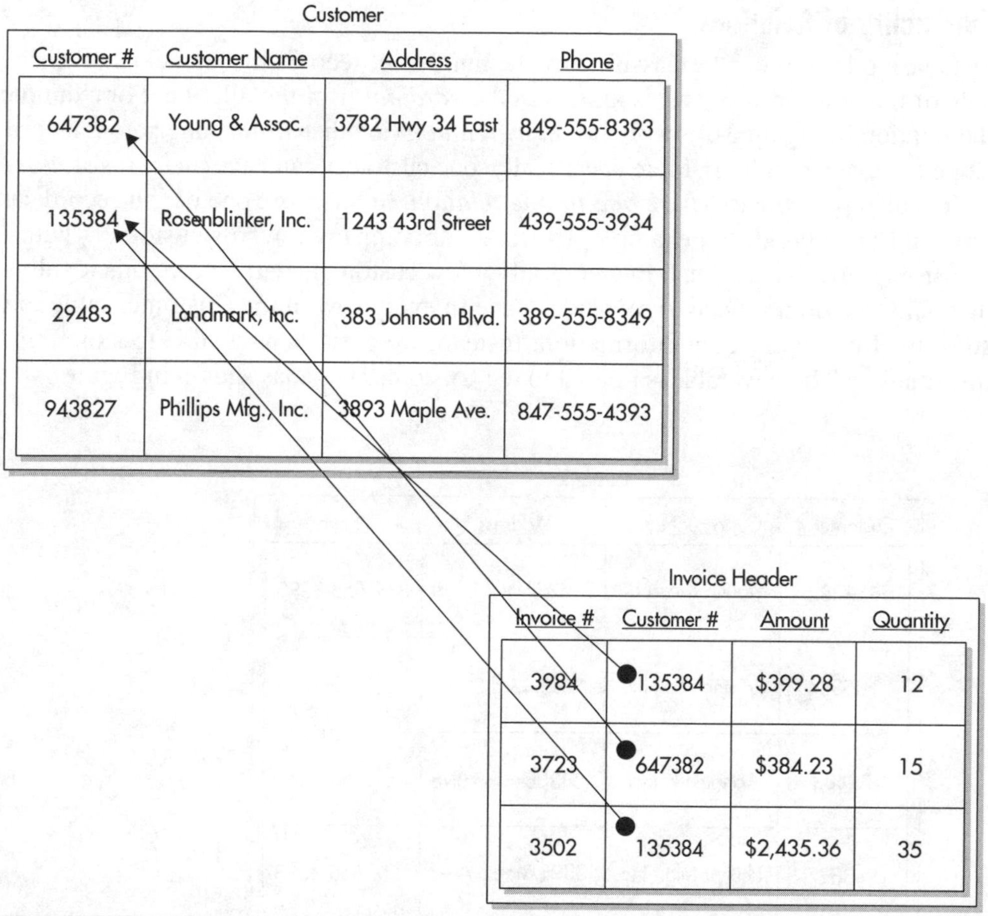

Customer

Customer #	Customer Name	Address	Phone
647382	Young & Assoc.	3782 Hwy 34 East	849-555-8393
135384	Rosenblinker, Inc.	1243 43rd Street	439-555-3934
29483	Landmark, Inc.	383 Johnson Blvd.	389-555-8349
943827	Phillips Mfg., Inc.	3893 Maple Ave.	847-555-4393

Invoice Header

Invoice #	Customer #	Amount	Quantity
3984	135384	$399.28	12
3723	647382	$384.23	15
3502	135384	$2,435.36	35

Figure 3-7   *A database relation*

Let's look back at the name change problem, this time using our new database structure that includes the parent-child relationship. When Rosenblinker, Inc. changes its name to RB, Inc., Ann changes the name in the Customer table as before. In our new structure, however, the customer name is not stored in any other location. Instead, the Invoice Header table rows for RB, Inc. point back to the Customer table row that has the correct name. The accounting department stays happy because it can still figure out how many invoices are outstanding for RB, Inc.

Cardinality of Relations

Database relations can be classified by the number of records that can exist on each side of the relationship. This is known as the *cardinality* of the relation. For example, the relation in Figure 3-7 is a *one-to-many relation* (in other words, one parent record can have many children). More specifically, one customer can have many invoices.

It is also possible to have a *one-to-one relation*. In this case, one parent record can have only one child. For example, let's say our company rewards customers with a customer loyalty discount. Because only a few customers will receive this loyalty discount, we do not want to set aside space in every row in the Customer table to store the loyalty discount information. Instead, we create a new table to store this information. The new table is related to the Customer table, as shown in Figure 3-8.

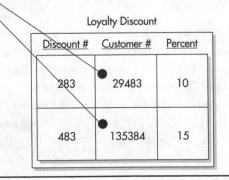

Figure 3-8 *A one-to-one relation*

Our company's business rule says that a given customer can only receive one loyalty discount. Because the Loyalty Discount table has only one Customer Number column, each row can link to just one customer. The combination of the business rule and the table design make this a one-to-one relation.

It is also possible to have a *many-to-many relation*. This relation no longer fits our parent/child analogy. It is better thought of as a brother/sister relationship. One brother can have many sisters, and one sister can have many brothers.

Suppose we need to keep track of the type of business engaged in by each of our customers. We can add a Business Type table to our database with columns for the business type code and the business type description. We can add a column for the business type code to the Customer table. We now have a one-to-many relation, where one business type can be related to many customers. This is shown in Figure 3-9.

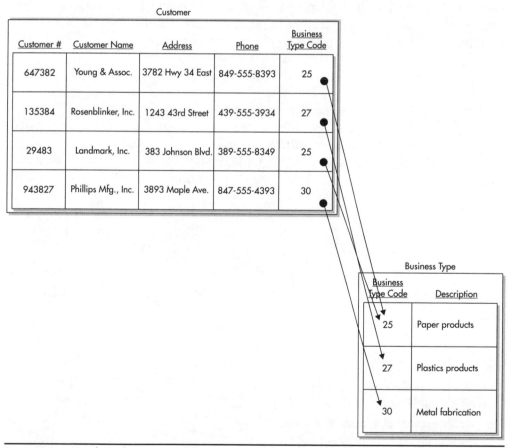

Figure 3-9   *Tracking business type using a one-to-many relation*

The problem with this structure becomes apparent when we have a customer that does multiple things. If Landmark, Inc. only produces paper products, there isn't a problem. We can put the business type code for paper products in the Customer table row for Landmark, Inc. We run into a bit of a snag, however, if Landmark, Inc. also produces plastics. We could add a second business type code column to the Customer table, but this still limits a customer to a maximum of two business types. In today's world of national conglomerates, this is not going to work.

The answer is to add a third table to the mix to create a many-to-many relationship. This additional table is known as a *linking table*. Its only purpose is to link two other tables together in a many-to-many relation. To use a linking table, you create the Business Type table just as before. This time, instead of creating a new column in the Customer table, we'll create a new table called Customer To Business Type Link. The new table has columns for the customer number and the business type code. Figure 3-10 shows how this linking table relates the Customer table to the Business Type table. By using the linking table, we can relate one customer to many business types. In addition, we can relate one business type to many customers.

Retrieving Data

We now have all the tools we need to store our data in an efficient manner. With our data structure set, it is time to determine how we can access that data to use it in our reports. Data that was split into multiple tables must be recombined for reporting. This is done using a database tool called a *join*. In most cases, we will also want the data in the report to appear in a certain order. This is accomplished using a sort.

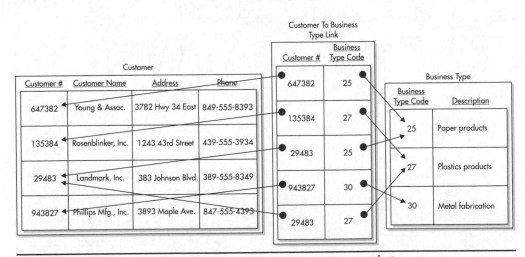

Figure 3-10 *Tracking the business type using a many-to-many relation*

Inner Joins

Suppose we need to know the name and address of the customer associated with each invoice. This is certainly a reasonable request, especially if we want to send invoices to these clients and have those invoices paid. Checking the Invoice Header table, you can see it contains the customer number, but not the name and address. The name and address is stored in the Customer table.

To print our invoices, we need to join the data in the Customer table with the data in the Invoice Header table. This join is done by matching the customer number in each record of the Invoice Header table with the customer number in the Customer table. In the language of database designers, we are joining the Customer table to the Invoice Header table on the Customer Number column.

The result of the join is a new table that contains information from both the Customer table and the Invoice Header table in each row. This new table is known as a *result set*. The result set from the Customer table–to–Invoice Header table join is shown in Figure 3-11. Note, the result set table contains nearly the same information that was in the Invoice Header table before it was normalized. The result set is a *denormalized* form of the data in the database.

It may seem like we are going in circles, first normalizing the data, and then denormalizing it. There is, however, one important difference between the denormalized form of the Invoice Header table that we started with in Figure 3-6 and the result set in Figure 3-11. The denormalized result set is a temporary table: it exists only as long as it is needed; then it is automatically deleted. The result set is re-created each time we execute the join, so the result set is always current.

Customer/Invoice Header Join Result Set

Customer #	Customer Name	Address	Phone	Invoice #	Customer #	Amount	Quantity
135384	Rosenblinker, Inc.	1243 43rd Street	439-555-3934	3984	135384	$399.28	12
647382	Young & Assoc.	3782 Hwy 34 East	849-555-8393	3723	647382	$384.23	15
135384	Rosenblinker, Inc.	1243 43rd Street	439-555-3934	3502	135384	$2,435.36	35

Data from the Customer table   Data from the Invoice Header table

Figure 3-11   *The result set from the Customer table–to–Invoice Header table join*

Let's return once more to Ann, our faithful employee in Data Processing. We will again consider the situation where Rosenblinker, Inc. changes its name to RB, Inc. Ann makes the change in the Customer table, as in the previous example. The next time we execute the join, this change is reflected in the result set. The result set has the new company name because our join gets a new copy of the customer information from the Customer table each time it is executed. The join finds the information in the Customer table based on the primary key, the customer number, which has not changed. Our invoices are linked to the proper companies, so Accounting can determine how many invoices are outstanding for RB, Inc., and everyone is happy!

Outer Joins

In the previous section, we looked at a type of join known as an inner join. When you do an inner join, your result set includes only those records that have a representative on both sides of the join. In Figure 3-11, Landmark, Inc. and Phillips Mfg., Inc. are not represented in the result set, because they do not have any Invoice Header table rows linked to them.

Figure 3-12 shows another way to think about joins. Here, the two tables are shown as sets of customer numbers. The left-hand circle represents the set of customer numbers in the Customer table. It contains one occurrence of every customer number present in the Customer table. The right-hand circle represents the set of customer numbers in the

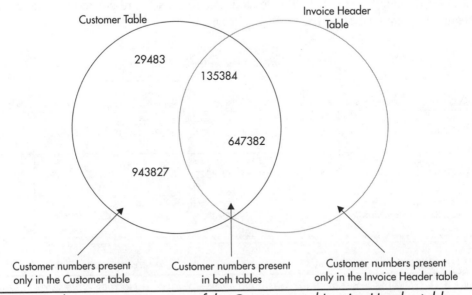

Figure 3-12 *The set representation of the Customer and Invoice Header tables*

Invoice Header table. It contains one occurrence of each customer number present in the Invoice Header table. The center region, where the two sets intersect, contains one occurrence of every customer number present in both the Customer table and the Invoice Header table. Looking at Figure 3-12, you can quickly tell no customer numbers are present in the Invoice Header table, but not in the Customer table. This is as it should be. We should not have any invoice headers assigned to a customer that do not exist in the Customer table.

Figure 3-13 shows a graphical representation of the inner join in Figure 3-11. Only records with customer numbers that appear in the shaded section will be included in the result set. Remember, two rows in the Invoice Header table contain customer number 135384. For this reason, the result set contains three rows—two rows for customer number 135384 and one row for customer number 647382.

The result set in Figure 3-11 enables us to print invoice headers that contain the correct customer name and address. Now let's look at customers and invoice headers from a slightly different angle. Suppose we have been asked for a report showing all customers and the invoice headers that have been sent to them. If we were to print this customers/invoice headers report from the result set in Figure 3-11, it would exclude Landmark, Inc. and Phillips Mfg., Inc. because they do not have any invoices and, therefore, would not fulfill the requirements.

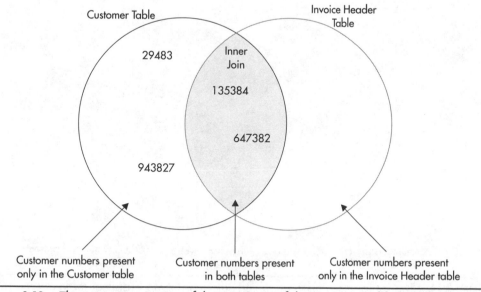

Figure 3-13   *The set representation of the inner join of the Customer table and the Invoice Header table*

What we need is a result set that includes all the customers in the Customer table. This is illustrated graphically in Figure 3-14. This type of join is known as a *left outer join*, so named because this join is not limited to the values in the intersection of both circles. It also includes the values to the left of the inner, overlapping sections of the circles.

We can also perform a right outer join on two tables. In our example, a *right outer join* would return the same number of rows as the inner join. This is because no customer numbers are to the right of the intersection.

The result set produced by a left outer join of the Customer table and the Invoice Header table is shown in Figure 3-15. Notice the columns populated by data from the Invoice Header table are empty in rows for Landmark, Inc. and Phillips Mfg., Inc. The columns are empty because these two customers do not have any Invoice Header rows to provide data on the right side of the join.

Joining Multiple Tables

Joins, whether inner or outer, always involve two tables. However, in Figure 3-10, you were introduced to a many-to-many relation that involved three tables. How do you retrieve data from this type of relation? The answer is to chain together two different joins, each involving two tables.

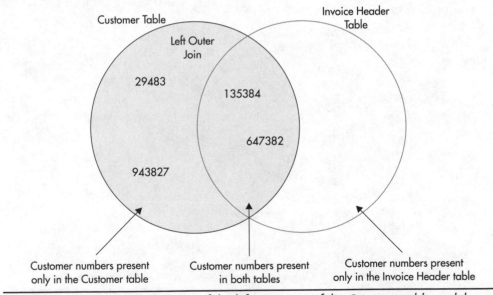

Figure 3-14 *The set representation of the left outer join of the Customer table and the Invoice Header table*

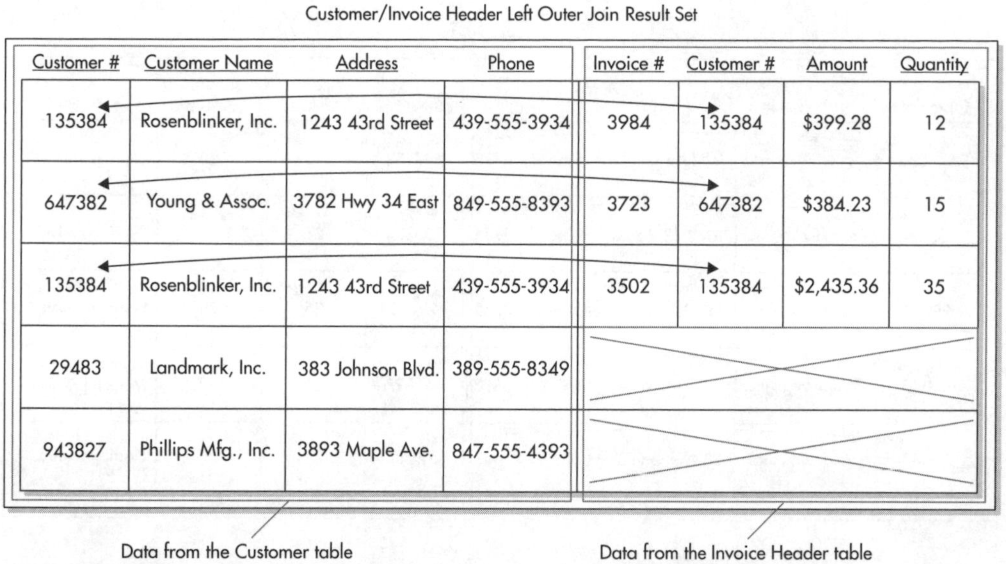

Customer/Invoice Header Left Outer Join Result Set

Customer #	Customer Name	Address	Phone	Invoice #	Customer #	Amount	Quantity
135384	Rosenblinker, Inc.	1243 43rd Street	439-555-3934	3984	135384	$399.28	12
647382	Young & Assoc.	3782 Hwy 34 East	849-555-8393	3723	647382	$384.23	15
135384	Rosenblinker, Inc.	1243 43rd Street	439-555-3934	3502	135384	$2,435.36	35
29483	Landmark, Inc.	383 Johnson Blvd.	389-555-8349				
943827	Phillips Mfg., Inc.	3893 Maple Ave.	847-555-4393				

Data from the Customer table   Data from the Invoice Header table

Figure 3-15 *The result set from the left outer join of the Customer table and the Invoice Header table*

Figure 3-16 illustrates the joins required to reassemble the data from Figure 3-10. Here, the Customer table is joined to the Customer To Business Type Link table using the Customer Number column common to both tables. The Customer To Business Type Link table is then joined to the Business Type table using the Business Type Code column present in both tables. The final result set contains the data from all three tables.

Self-Joins

In our previous example, we needed to join three tables to get the required information. Other joins may only require a single table. For instance, we may have a customer that is a subsidiary of another one of our customers. In some cases, we'll want to treat these two separately, so both appear in our result set. This requires us to keep the two customers as separate rows in our Customer table. In other cases, we may want to combine information from the parent company and the subsidiary into one record. To do this, our database structure must include a mechanism to tie the subsidiary to its parent.

To track a customer's connection to its parent, we need to create a relationship between the customer's row in the Customer table and its parent's row in the Customer table. To do this, we add a Parent Customer Number column to the Customer table,

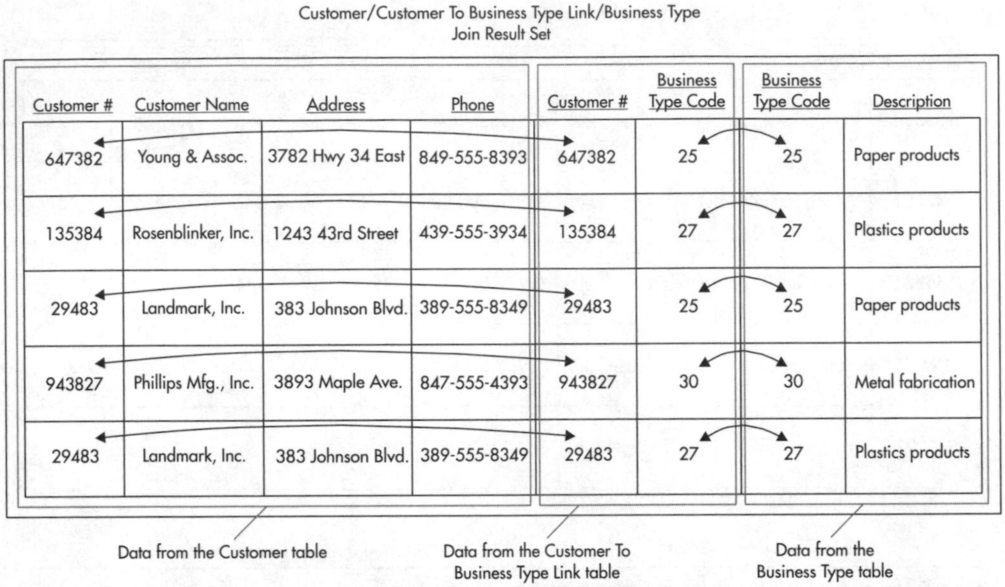

Customer/Customer To Business Type Link/Business Type
Join Result Set

Customer #	Customer Name	Address	Phone	Customer #	Business Type Code	Business Type Code	Description
647382	Young & Assoc.	3782 Hwy 34 East	849-555-8393	647382	25	25	Paper products
135384	Rosenblinker, Inc.	1243 43rd Street	439-555-3934	135384	27	27	Plastics products
29483	Landmark, Inc.	383 Johnson Blvd.	389-555-8349	29483	25	25	Paper products
943827	Phillips Mfg., Inc.	3893 Maple Ave.	847-555-4393	943827	30	30	Metal fabrication
29483	Landmark, Inc.	383 Johnson Blvd.	389-555-8349	29483	27	27	Plastics products

Data from the Customer table   Data from the Customer To Business Type Link table   Data from the Business Type table

Figure 3-16 *The result set from the join of the Customer table, the Customer To Business Type Link table, and the Business Type table*

as shown in Figure 3-17. In the customer's row, the Parent Customer Number column will contain the customer number of the row for the parent. In the row for the parent, and in all the rows for customers that do not have a parent, the Parent Customer Number column is empty.

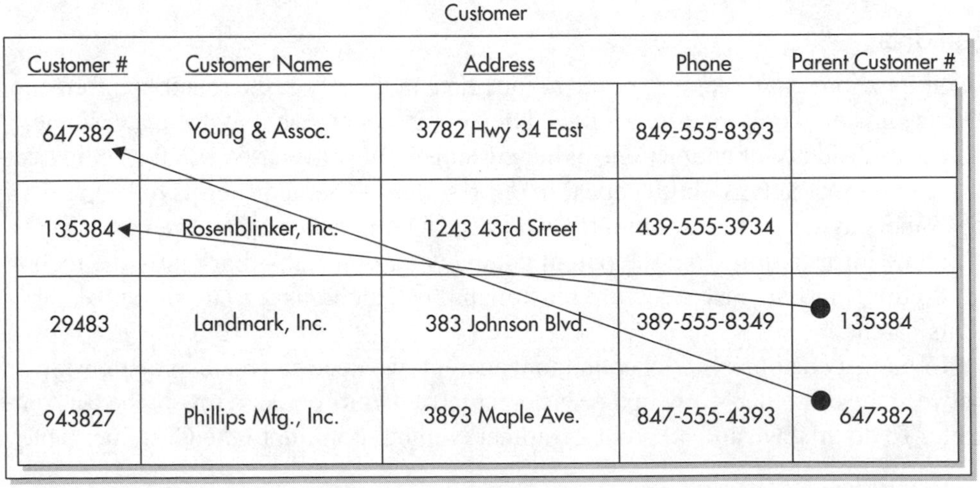

Customer

Customer #	Customer Name	Address	Phone	Parent Customer #
647382	Young & Assoc.	3782 Hwy 34 East	849-555-8393	
135384	Rosenblinker, Inc.	1243 43rd Street	439-555-3934	
29483	Landmark, Inc.	383 Johnson Blvd.	389-555-8349	135384
943827	Phillips Mfg., Inc.	3893 Maple Ave.	847-555-4393	647382

Figure 3-17 *The Customer/Parent Customer relation*

When we want to report from this parent/subsidiary relation, we need to do a join. This may seem like a problem at first because a join requires two tables, and we only have one. The answer is to use the Customer table on one side of the join and a "copy" of the Customer table on the other side of the join. The second occurrence of the Customer table is given a nickname, called an *alias*, so we can tell the two apart. This type of join, which uses the same table on both sides, is known as a *self-join*. Figure 3-18 shows the results of the self-join on the Customer table.

Sorting

In most cases, one final step is required before our result sets can be used for reporting. Let's go back to the result set produced in Figure 3-15 for the customers/invoice headers report. Looking back at this result set, notice the customers do not appear to be in any particular order. In most cases, users do not appreciate reports with information presented in this unsorted manner. This is especially true when two rows for the same customer do not appear consecutively, as is the case here.

We need to sort the result set as it is being created to avoid this situation. This is done by specifying the columns that should be used for the sort. Sorting by Customer Name probably makes the most sense for the customers/invoice headers report. Columns can be sorted either in ascending order, smallest to largest (A–Z), or descending order, largest to smallest (Z–A). An ascending sort on Customer Name would be most appropriate.

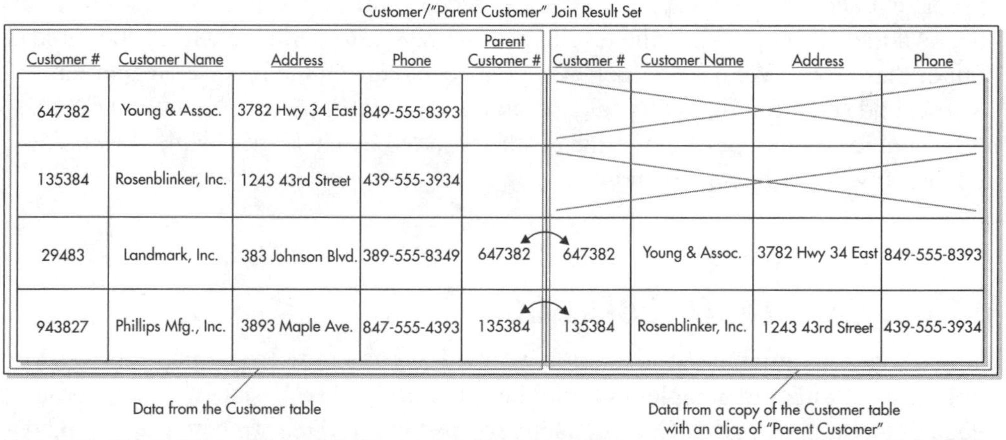

Figure 3-18   *The result set from the Customer table self-join*

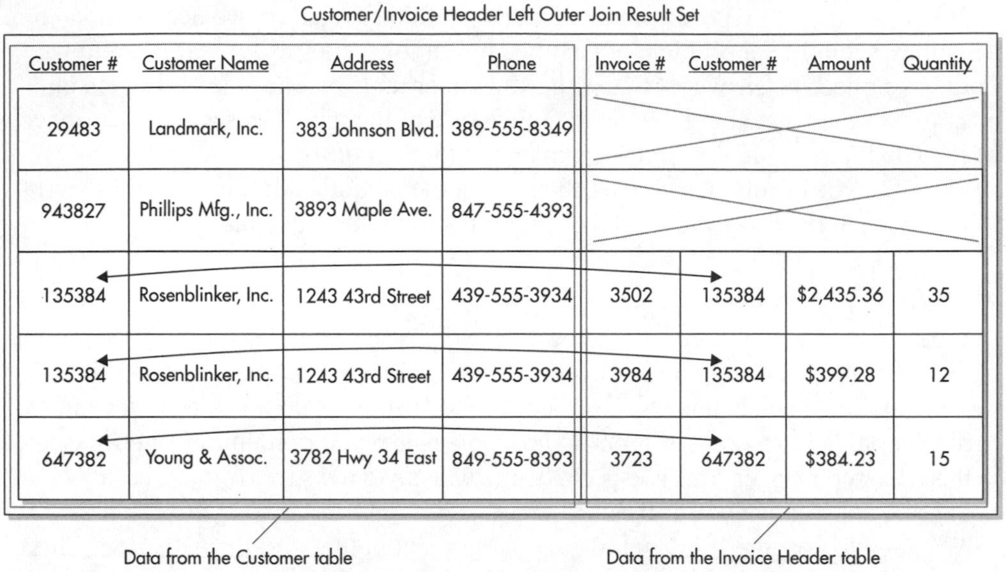

Customer/Invoice Header Left Outer Join Result Set

Customer #	Customer Name	Address	Phone	Invoice #	Customer #	Amount	Quantity
29483	Landmark, Inc.	383 Johnson Blvd.	389-555-8349				
943827	Phillips Mfg., Inc.	3893 Maple Ave.	847-555-4393				
135384	Rosenblinker, Inc.	1243 43rd Street	439-555-3934	3502	135384	$2,435.36	35
135384	Rosenblinker, Inc.	1243 43rd Street	439-555-3934	3984	135384	$399.28	12
647382	Young & Assoc.	3782 Hwy 34 East	849-555-8393	3723	647382	$384.23	15

Data from the Customer table   Data from the Invoice Header table

Figure 3-19   *The sorted result set from the left outer join of the Customer table and the Invoice Header table*

We still have a situation where the order of the rows is left to chance. Because two rows have the same customer name, we do not know which of these two rows will appear first and which will appear second. A second sort field is necessary to break this "tie." All the data copied into the result set from the Customer table will be the same in both of these rows. We need to look at the data copied from the Invoice Header table for a second sort column. In this case, an ascending sort on Invoice Number would be a good choice. Figure 3-19 shows the result set sorted by Customer Name, ascending, and then Invoice Number, ascending.

Galactic Delivery Services

Throughout the remainder of this book, you will get to know Reporting Services by exploring a number of sample reports. These reports will be based on the business needs of a company called Galactic Delivery Services (GDS). To better understand these sample reports, here is some background on GDS.

Company Background

GDS provides package-delivery service between several planetary systems in the near galactic region. It specializes in rapid delivery featuring same-day, next-day, and previous-day delivery. The latter is made possible by its new Photon III transports, which travel faster than the speed of light. This faster-than-light capability allows GDS to exploit the properties of general relativity and deliver a package on the day before it was sent.

Package Tracking

Despite GDS's unique delivery offerings, it has the same data-processing needs as any more conventional package-delivery service. It tracks packages as they are moved from one interplanetary hub to another. This is important not only for the smooth operation of the delivery service, but also to allow customers to check on the status of their delivery at any time.

To remain accountable to its clients and to prevent fraud, GDS investigates every package lost en route. These investigations help to find and eliminate problems throughout the entire delivery system. One such investigation discovered that a leaking antimatter valve on one of the Photon III transports was vaporizing two or three packages on each flight.

GDS stores its data in a database called Galactic. Figure 3-20 shows the portion of the Galactic database that stores the information used for package tracking. The tables and their column names are shown. A key symbol in the gray square next to a column name indicates this column is the primary key for that table. The lines connecting the tables show the relations that have been created between these tables in the database. The key symbol at the end of the line points to the primary key column used to create the relation. The infinity sign, at the opposite end of the line to the key symbol, points to the foreign key column used to complete the relation. (The infinity sign looks like two circles or a sideways number 8.)

Each relation shown in Figure 3-20 is a one-to-many relation. The side of the relation indicated by the key is the "one" side of the relation. The side indicated by the infinity sign is the many side of the relation. For example, if you look at the line between the Customer table and the Delivery table, you can see that one customer may have many deliveries.

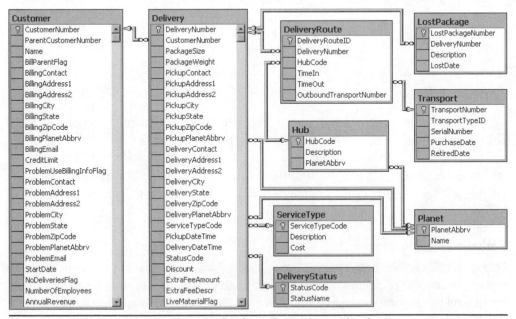

Figure 3-20   *The package tracking tables from the Galactic database*

You may want to refer to these diagrams as we create sample reports from the Galactic database. Don't worry if the diagrams seem a bit complicated right now. They will make more sense as we consider the business practices and reporting needs at GDS. Also, our first report examples will contain only a few tables and the corresponding relations, so we will start simple and work our way up.

Personnel

Every business needs a personnel department to look after its employees. GDS is no different. The GDS personnel department is responsible for the hiring and firing of all the robots employed by GDS. This department is also responsible for tracking the hours put in by the robotic laborers and paying them accordingly. (Yes, robots get paid at GDS. After all, GDS is an equal-opportunity employer.)

The personnel department is also responsible for conducting annual reviews of each employee. At the annual review, goals are set for the employee to attain over the coming year. After a year has passed, several of the employee's coworkers are asked to rate the employee on how well it did in reaching those goals. The employee's manager then uses the ratings to write an overall performance evaluation for the employee and establish new goals for the following year.

Figure 3-21 shows the tables in the Galactic database used by the personnel department. Notice that the Rating table has key symbols next to both the EvaluationID

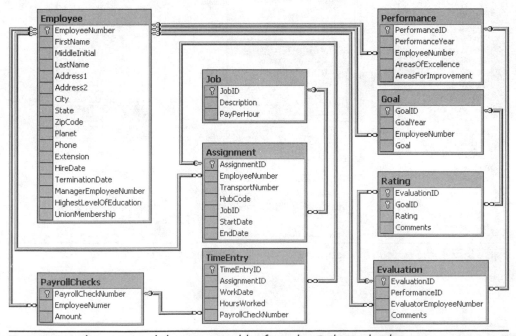

Figure 3-21 *The personnel department tables from the Galactic database*

column name and the GoalID column name. This means the Rating table uses a composite primary key that combines the EvaluationID column and the GoalID column.

Accounting

The GDS accounting department is responsible for seeing that the company is paid for each package it delivers. GDS invoices its customers for each delivery completed. The invoices are sent to the customer and payment is requested within 30 days.

Even though GDS delivers its customers' packages at the speed of light, those same customers pay GDS at a much slower speed. "Molasses at the northern pole of Antares Prime" was the analogy used by the current Chief Financial Droid. Therefore, GDS must track when invoices are paid, how much was paid, and how much is still outstanding.

Figure 3-22 shows the tables in the Galactic database used by the accounting department. Notice the Customer table appears in both Figure 3-20 and Figure 3-22.

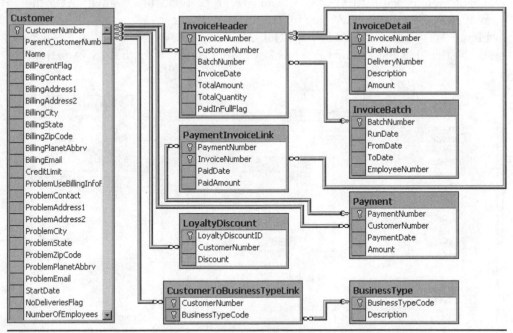

Figure 3-22   *The accounting department tables from the Galactic database*

This is the same table in both diagrams. This table is shown in both, because it is a major part of both the package tracking and the accounting business processes.

Transport Maintenance

In addition to all this, GDS must maintain a fleet of transports. Careful records are kept on the repair and preventative maintenance work done on each transport. GDS also has a record of each flight a transport makes, as well as any accidents and mishaps involved.

Maintenance records are extremely important, not only to GDS itself, but also to the Federation Space Flight Administration (FSFA). Without proper maintenance records on all its transports, GDS would be shut down by the FSFA in a nanosecond. You may think this is an exaggeration, but the bureaucratic androids at the FSFA have extremely high clock rates.

Figure 3-23 shows the transport maintenance tables in the Galactic database.

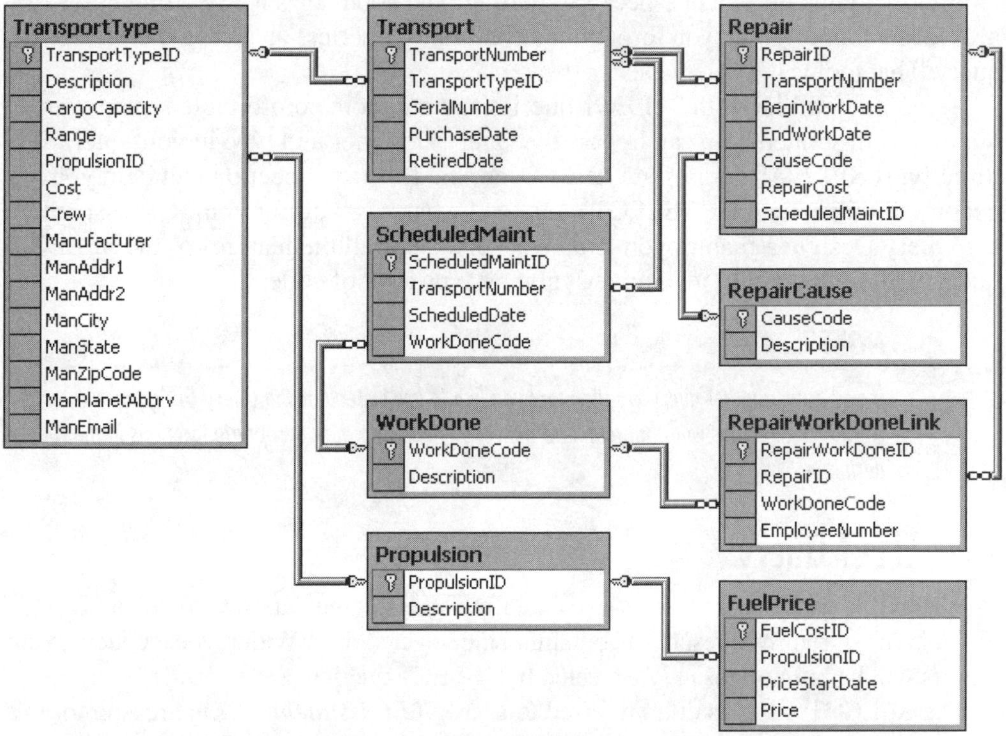

Figure 3-23   *The transport maintenance tables from the Galactic database*

Querying Data

You have now looked at the database concepts of normalization, relations, and joins. You have also been introduced to the Galactic database. We use this relational database throughout the remainder of this book for our examples. Now, it is time to look more specifically at how you retrieve the data from the database into a format you can use for reporting. This is done through the database query.

A *query* is a request for some action on the data in one or more tables. An *INSERT query* adds one or more rows to a database table. An *UPDATE query* modifies the data in one or more existing rows of a table. A *DELETE query* removes one or more rows from a table. Because we are primarily interested in retrieving data for reporting, the query we are going to concern ourselves with is the *SELECT query*, which reads data from one or more tables (it does not add, update, or delete data).

We will look at the various parts of the SELECT query. This is to help you become familiar with this important aspect of reporting. The good news is Reporting Services provides a tool to guide you through the creation of queries, including the SELECT query. That tool is the Query Designer.

If you are familiar with SELECT queries and are more comfortable typing your queries from scratch, you can bypass the Query Designer and type in your queries directly. If SELECT queries are new to you, the following section can help you become familiar with the SELECT query and what it can do for you. Rest assured, the Query Designer enables you to take advantage of all the features of the SELECT query without having to memorize syntax or type a lot of code.

NOTE

If you have another query-creation tool you like to use instead of the Query Designer, you can create your queries with that tool, and then copy them into the appropriate locations in the report definition.

The SELECT Query

The SELECT query is used to retrieve data from tables in the database. When a SELECT query is run, it returns a result set containing the selected data. With few exceptions, your reports will be built on result sets created by SELECT queries.

The SELECT query is often referred to as a *SELECT statement*. One reason for this is because it can be read like an English sentence or statement. As with a sentence in English, a SELECT statement is made up of clauses that modify the meaning of the statement.

The various parts, or clauses, of the SELECT statement enable you to control the data contained in the result set. Use the *FROM clause* to specify which table the data will be selected from. The *FIELD LIST* permits you to choose the columns that will appear in the result set. The *JOIN clause* lets you specify additional tables that will be joined with the table in the FROM clause to contribute data to the result set. The *WHERE clause* enables you to set conditions that determine which rows will be included in the result set. Finally, you can use the *ORDER BY clause* to sort the result set, and the *GROUP BY clause* and the *HAVING clause* to combine detail rows into summary rows.

NOTE

The query statements shown in the remainder of this chapter all use the Galactic database. If you want to try out the various query statements as they are being discussed, open a query window for the Galactic database in the SQL Server Management Studio. If you are not familiar with SQL Server Management Studio, you can try out the queries in the Reporting Services Generic Query Designer. To do this, turn to Chapter 5 and follow the steps for Task 1 of the Transport List Report, but stop after Step 26. You will be in the Generic Query Designer. You can enter the query statements in the upper portion of the Generic Query Designer and execute them by clicking the toolbar button with the exclamation point. When you are finished, close the application without saving your changes.

The FROM Clause

The SELECT statement in its simplest form includes only a FROM clause. Here is a SELECT statement that retrieves all rows and all columns from the Customer table:

```
SELECT *
FROM dbo.Customer
```

The word "SELECT" is required to let the database know this is going to be a SELECT query, as opposed to an INSERT, UPDATE, or DELETE query. The asterisk (*) means all columns will be included in the result set. The remainder of the statement is the FROM clause. It says the data is to be selected from the Customer table. We discuss the meaning of dbo. in a moment.

As stated earlier, the SELECT statement can be read as if it were a sentence. This SELECT statement is read, "Select all columns from the Customer table." If we run this SELECT statement in the Galactic database, the results would appear similar to Figure 3-24. The SELECT query is being run in the Query Designer window of Visual Studio. Note, the scroll bars on the right and on the bottom of the result set area indicate not all the rows and columns returned can fit on the screen.

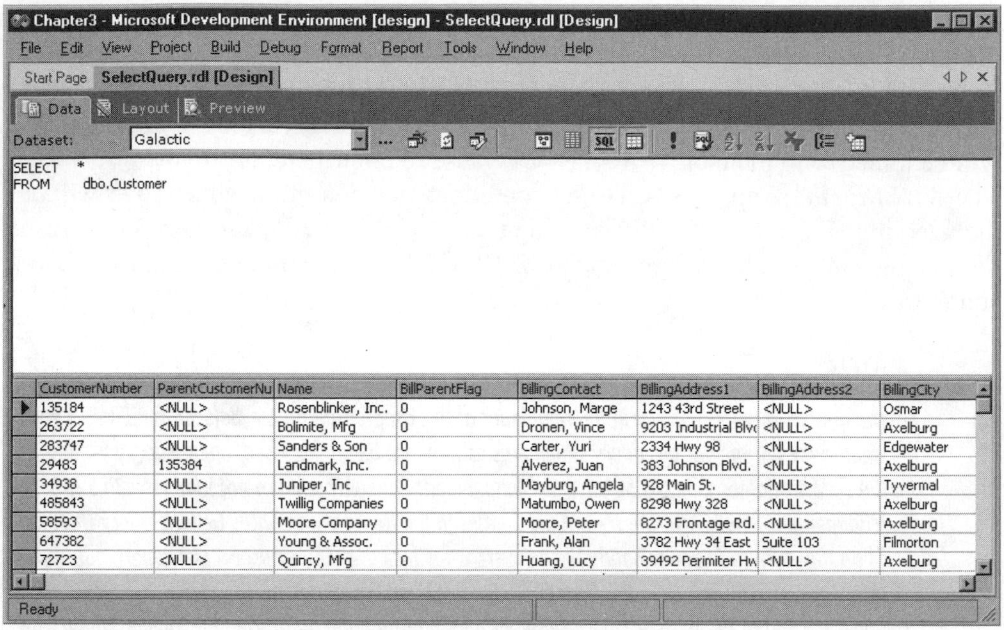

Figure 3-24 *The SELECT statement in its simplest form*

Note, the table name, Customer, has dbo. in front of it. The dbo is the name of the owner of the table. Usually this is the user who created the table. Here, dbo stands for database owner, meaning the user who owns the database is also the user who owns the table. The dbo abbreviation is also another name for the system administrator login. In many cases, an administrative user, logged into the database, will create the database tables. Because of this, the table owner will more than likely be dbo.

In the Galactic database, the dbo.Customer table was created by the system administrator. If another user with a database login of User2 also has rights to create tables in the Galactic database, they could also create a Customer table. This second table would be known as User2.Customer.

This situation, with two tables of the same name in the same database, does not happen often and is probably not a great idea. It can quickly lead to confusion and errors. Even though this is a rare occurrence, the Query Designer needs to account for this situation. The Query Designer uses both the name of the table owner and the name of the table itself in the queries it builds and executes for you.

The FIELD LIST

In the previous example, the result set created by the SELECT statement contained all the columns in the table. In most cases, especially when creating reports, you only need to work with some of the columns of a table in any given result set. Including all the columns in a result set when only a few columns are required wastes computing power and network bandwidth.

A FIELD LIST provides the capability you need to specify which columns to include in the result set. When a FIELD LIST is added to the SELECT statement, it appears similar to the following:

```
SELECT CustomerNumber, Name, BillingCity
FROM dbo.Customer
```

The bold portion of the SELECT statement indicates changes from the previous SELECT statement.

This statement returns only the CustomerNumber, Name, and BillingCity columns from the Customer table. The result set created by this SELECT statement is shown in Figure 3-25.

In addition to the names of the fields to include in the result set, the FIELD LIST can contain a word that influences the number of rows in the result set. Usually, there is one row in the result set for each row in the table from which you are selecting data. However, this can be changed by adding the word "DISTINCT" at the beginning of the FIELD LIST.

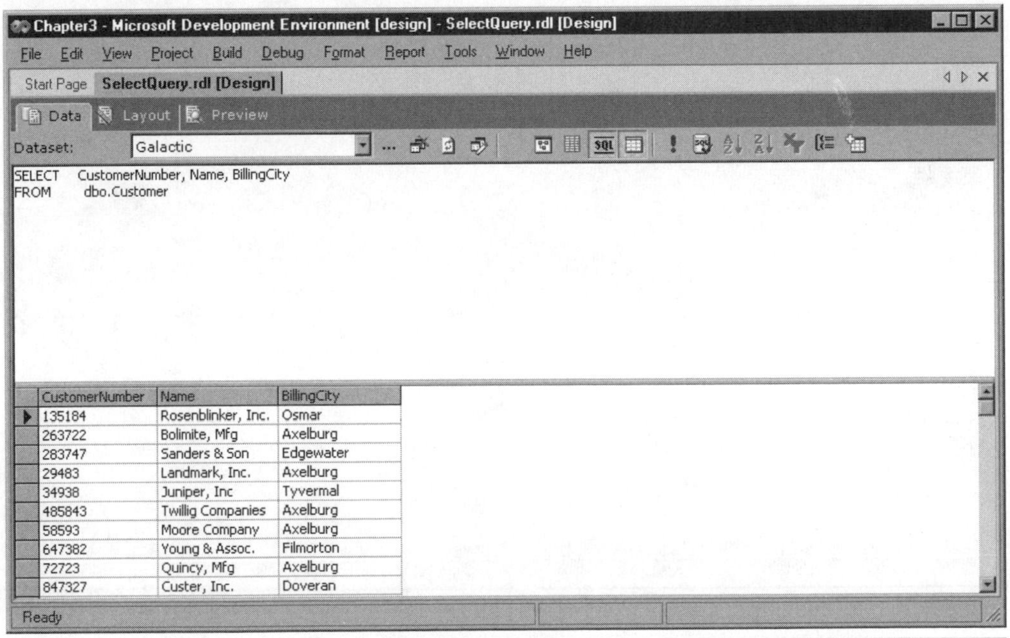

Figure 3-25   *A SELECT statement with a FIELD LIST*

When you use DISTINCT in the FIELD LIST, you are saying that you only want one row in the result set for each distinct set of values. In other words, the result set from a DISTINCT query will not have any two rows that have exactly the same values in every column. Here is an example of a DISTINCT query:

```
SELECT DISTINCT BillingCity
FROM dbo.Customer
```

This query returns a list of all the billing cities in the Customer table. A number of customers have the same billing city, but these duplicates have been removed from the result set, as shown in Figure 3-26.

The JOIN Clause

When your database is properly normalized, you are likely to need data from more than one table to fulfill your reporting requirements. As discussed earlier in this chapter, the way to get information from more than one table is to use a join. The JOIN clause in the SELECT statement enables you to include a join of two or more tables in your result set.

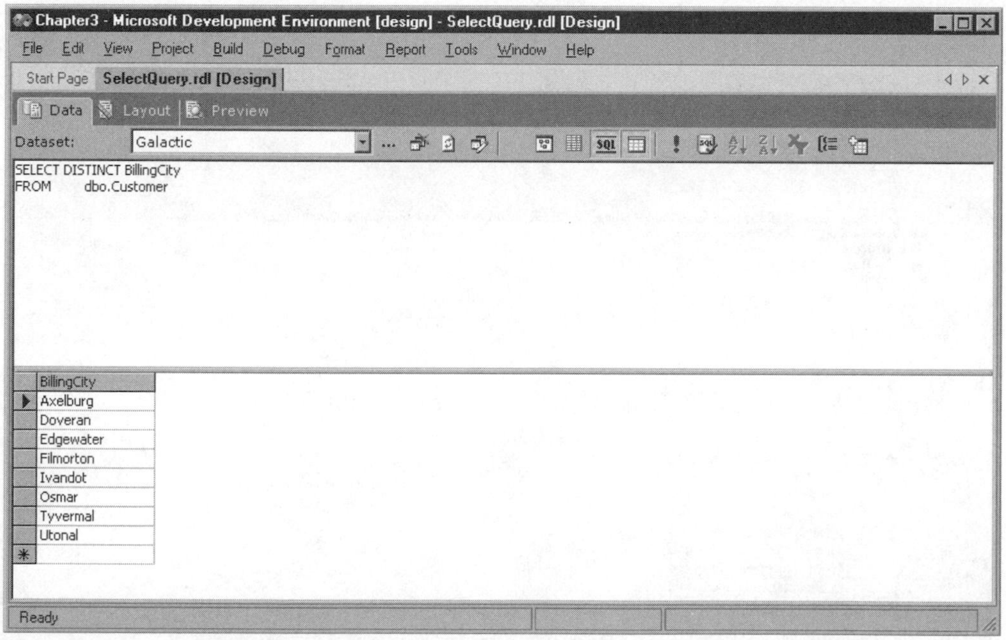

Figure 3-26   *A DISTINCT query*

The first part of the JOIN clause specifies which table is being joined. The second part determines the two columns that are linked to create the join. Joining the Invoice Header table to the Customer table looks like this:

```
SELECT dbo.Customer.CustomerNumber,
    dbo.Customer.Name,
    dbo.Customer.BillingCity,
    dbo.InvoiceHeader.InvoiceNumber,
    dbo.InvoiceHeader.TotalAmount
FROM dbo.Customer
INNER JOIN dbo.InvoiceHeader
 ON dbo.Customer.CustomerNumber = dbo.InvoiceHeader.CustomerNumber
```

With the Customer table and the Invoice Header table joined, you have a situation where some columns in the result set have the same name. For example, a Customer-Number column is in the Customer table and a CustomerNumber column is in the Invoice Header table. When you use the FIELD LIST to tell the database which fields to include in the result set, you need to uniquely identify these fields using both the table name and the column name.

If you do not do this, the query will not run and you will receive an error. Nothing prevents you from using the table name in front of each column name, whether it is a duplicate or not, as in this example. Using the table name in front of each column name makes it immediately obvious where every column in the result set is selected from. The result set created by this SELECT statement is shown in Figure 3-27.

You can add a third table to the query by adding another JOIN clause to the SELECT statement. This additional table can be joined to the table in the FROM clause or to the table in the first JOIN clause. In this statement, we add the Loyalty Discount table and join it to the Customer table:

```
SELECT dbo.Customer.CustomerNumber,
    dbo.Customer.Name,
    dbo.Customer.BillingCity,
    dbo.InvoiceHeader.InvoiceNumber,
    dbo.InvoiceHeader.TotalAmount,
    dbo.LoyaltyDiscount.Discount
FROM dbo.Customer
INNER JOIN dbo.InvoiceHeader
 ON dbo.Customer.CustomerNumber = dbo.InvoiceHeader.CustomerNumber
INNER JOIN dbo.LoyaltyDiscount
 ON dbo.Customer.CustomerNumber = dbo.LoyaltyDiscount.CustomerNumber
```

The screenshot shows the Microsoft Development Environment with the following visible elements:

Window title: Chapter3 - Microsoft Development Environment [design] - SelectQuery.rdl [Design]

Menu bar: File Edit View Project Build Debug Format Report Tools Window Help

Tabs: Start Page | SelectQuery.rdl [Design]

Sub-tabs: Data | Layout | Preview

Dataset: Galactic

```
SELECT    dbo.Customer.CustomerNumber, dbo.Customer.Name, dbo.Customer.BillingCity, dbo.InvoiceHeader.InvoiceNumber,
          dbo.InvoiceHeader.TotalAmount
FROM      dbo.Customer INNER JOIN
          dbo.InvoiceHeader ON dbo.Customer.CustomerNumber = dbo.InvoiceHeader.CustomerNumber
```

CustomerNumber	Name	BillingCity	InvoiceNumber	TotalAmount
135184	Rosenblinker, Inc.	Osmar	73040	938
263722	Bolimite, Mfg	Axelburg	73041	438
283747	Sanders & Son	Edgewater	73042	834
29483	Landmark, Inc.	Axelburg	73043	243
34938	Juniper, Inc	Tyvermal	73044	234
485843	Twillig Companies	Axelburg	73045	732
58593	Moore Company	Axelburg	73046	256
647382	Young & Assoc.	Filmorton	73047	23
72723	Quincy, Mfg	Axelburg	73048	234
847327	Custer, Inc.	Doveran	73049	273

Ready

Figure 3-27   *A SELECT statement with a JOIN clause*

The result set from this SELECT statement is shown in Figure 3-28. Notice that the result set is rather small. This is because Landmark, Inc. is the only customer currently receiving a loyalty discount. Because an INNER JOIN was used to add the Loyalty Discount table, only customers that have a loyalty discount are included in the result set.

To make our result set a little more interesting, let's try joining the Loyalty Discount table with an OUTER JOIN rather than an INNER JOIN. Here is the same statement, except the Customer table is joined to the Loyalty Discount table with a LEFT OUTER JOIN:

```
SELECT dbo.Customer.CustomerNumber,
    dbo.Customer.Name,
    dbo.Customer.BillingCity,
    dbo.InvoiceHeader.InvoiceNumber,
    dbo.InvoiceHeader.TotalAmount,
    dbo.LoyaltyDiscount.Discount
FROM dbo.Customer
INNER JOIN dbo.InvoiceHeader
 ON dbo.Customer.CustomerNumber = dbo.InvoiceHeader.CustomerNumber
LEFT OUTER JOIN dbo.LoyaltyDiscount
 ON dbo.Customer.CustomerNumber = dbo.LoyaltyDiscount.CustomerNumber
```

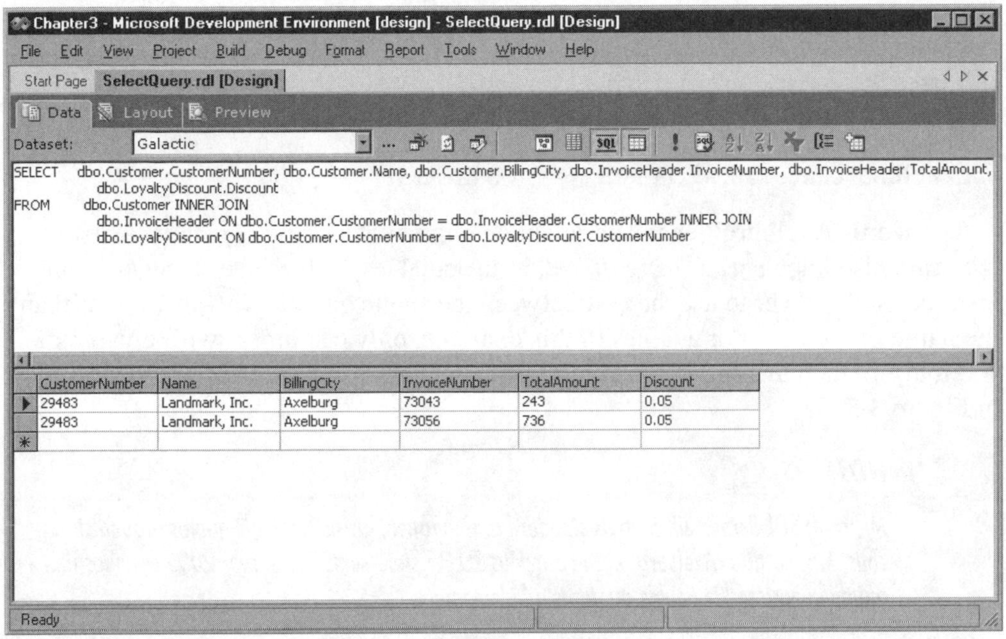

Figure 3-28 *A SELECT statement with two JOIN clauses*

The result set for this SELECT statement is shown in Figure 3-29. Notice that the value for the Discount column is NULL in the rows for all the customers except for Landmark, Inc. This is to be expected because there is no record in the Loyalty Discount table to join with these customers. When no value is in a column, the result set will contain a NULL value.

The WHERE Clause

Up to this point, the result sets have included all the rows in the table or all the rows that result from the joins. The FIELD LIST limits which columns are being returned in the result set. Nothing, however, placed a limit on the rows.

To limit the number of rows in the result set, you need to add a WHERE clause to your SELECT statement. The WHERE clause includes one or more logical expressions that must be true for a row before it can be included in the result set. Here is an example of a SELECT statement with a WHERE clause:

```
SELECT dbo.Customer.CustomerNumber,
    dbo.Customer.Name,
    dbo.Customer.BillingCity,
    dbo.InvoiceHeader.InvoiceNumber,
    dbo.InvoiceHeader.TotalAmount,
    dbo.LoyaltyDiscount.Discount
```

```
FROM dbo.Customer
INNER JOIN dbo.InvoiceHeader
 ON dbo.Customer.CustomerNumber = dbo.InvoiceHeader.CustomerNumber
LEFT OUTER JOIN dbo.LoyaltyDiscount
 ON dbo.Customer.CustomerNumber = dbo.LoyaltyDiscount.CustomerNumber
WHERE (dbo.Customer.BillingCity = 'Axelburg')
```

The word 'Axelburg' (enclosed in single quotes) is a string constant. A *string constant*, also known as a *string literal*, is an actual text value. The string constant instructs SQL Server to use the text between the single quotes as a value rather than the name of a column or a table. In this example, only customers with a value of Axelburg in their BillingCity column will be included in the result set, as shown in Figure 3-30.

NOTE

Microsoft SQL Server 2005, in its standard configuration, insists on single quotes around string constants, such as 'Axelburg' in the previous SELECT statement. SQL Server 2005 assumes that anything enclosed in double quotes is a field name.

To create more complex criteria for your result set, you can have multiple logical expressions in the WHERE clause. The logical expressions are linked together with

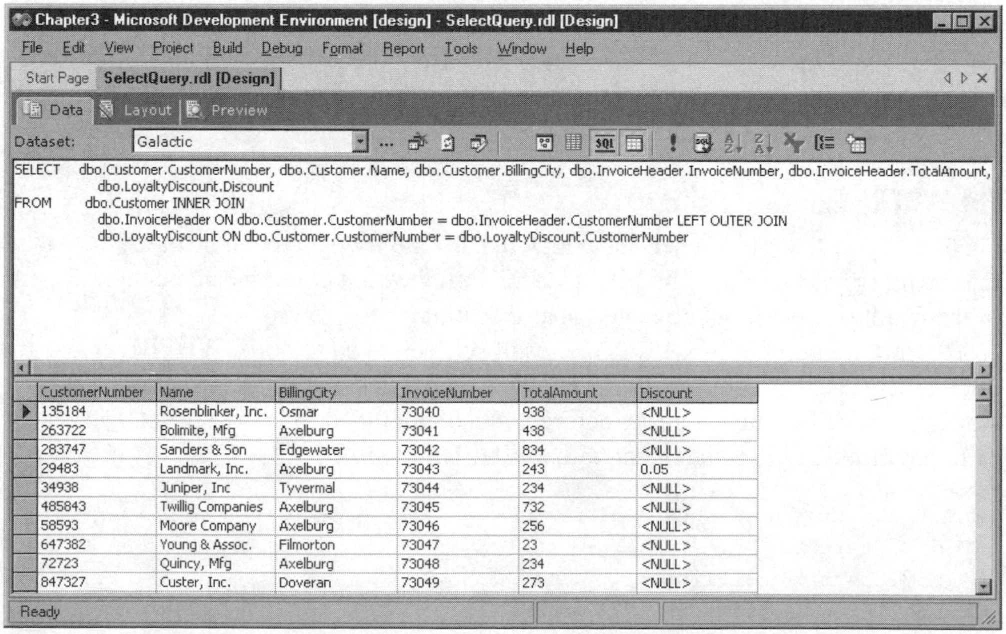

Figure 3-29   *A SELECT statement with an INNER JOIN and an OUTER JOIN*

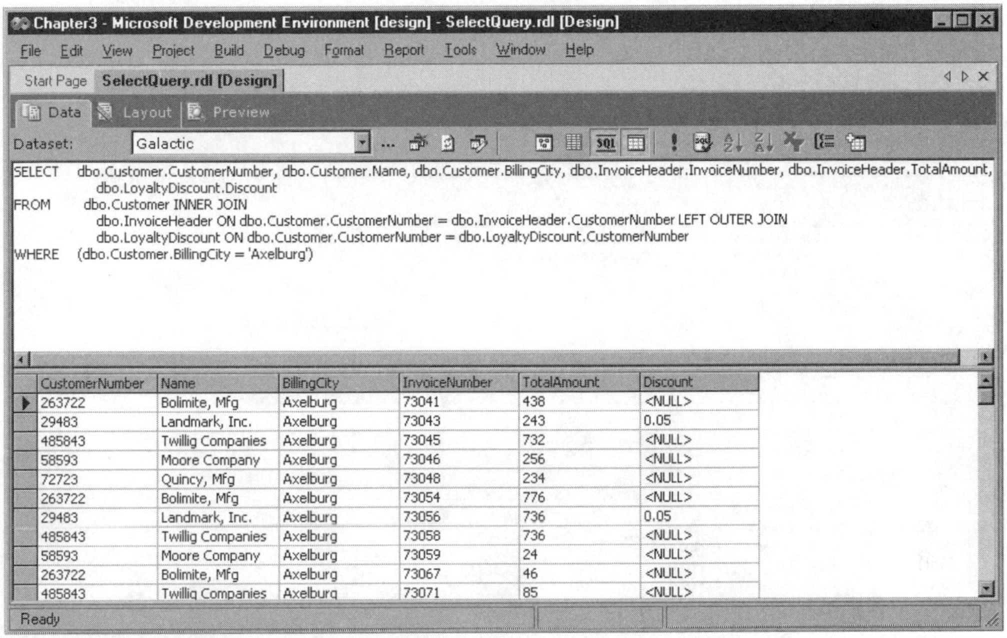

Figure 3-30   *A SELECT statement with a WHERE clause*

an AND or an OR. When an AND is used to link logical expressions, the logical expressions on both sides of the AND must be true for a row in order for that row to be included in the result set. When an OR is used to link two logical expressions, either one or both of the logical expressions must be true for a row in order for that row to be included in the result set.

This SELECT statement has two logical expressions:

```
SELECT dbo.Customer.CustomerNumber,
    dbo.Customer.Name,
    dbo.Customer.BillingCity,
    dbo.InvoiceHeader.InvoiceNumber,
    dbo.InvoiceHeader.TotalAmount,
    dbo.LoyaltyDiscount.Discount
FROM dbo.Customer
INNER JOIN dbo.InvoiceHeader
 ON dbo.Customer.CustomerNumber = dbo.InvoiceHeader.CustomerNumber
LEFT OUTER JOIN dbo.LoyaltyDiscount
 ON dbo.Customer.CustomerNumber = dbo.LoyaltyDiscount.CustomerNumber
WHERE (dbo.Customer.BillingCity = 'Axelburg')
AND (dbo.Customer.Name > 'C')
```

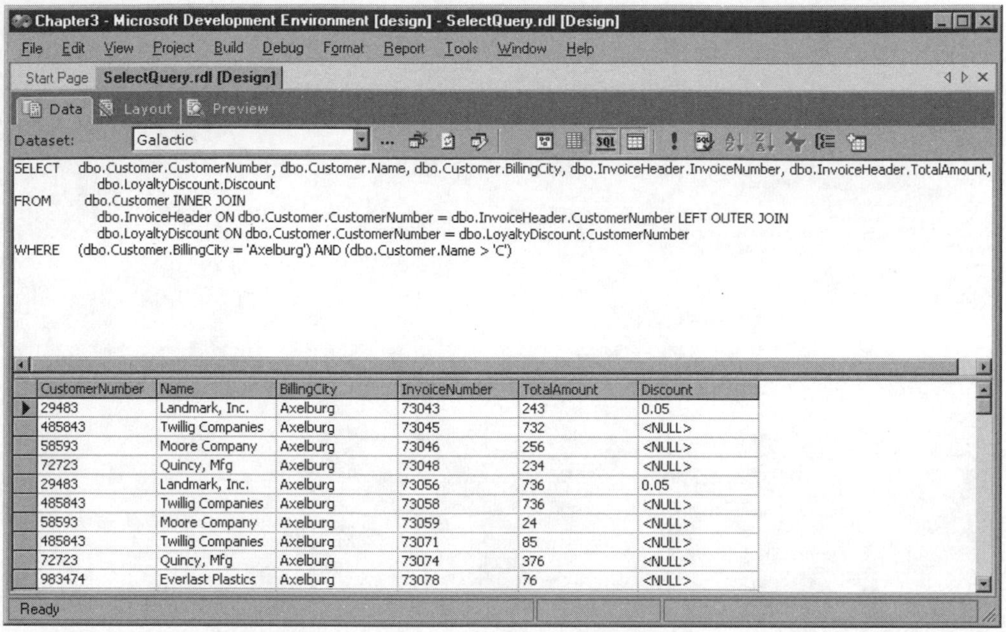

Figure 3-31 *A SELECT statement with two logical expressions in the WHERE clause*

Only customers with a value of Axelburg in their BillingCity column and with a name that comes after *C* will be included in the result set. This result set is shown in Figure 3-31.

The ORDER BY Clause

Up to this point, the data in the result sets has shown up in any order it pleases. As discussed previously, this will probably not be acceptable for most reports. You can add an ORDER BY clause to your SELECT statement to obtain a sorted result set. This statement includes an ORDER BY clause with multiple columns:

```
SELECT dbo.Customer.CustomerNumber,
    dbo.Customer.Name,
    dbo.Customer.BillingCity,
    dbo.InvoiceHeader.InvoiceNumber,
    dbo.InvoiceHeader.TotalAmount,
    dbo.LoyaltyDiscount.Discount
FROM dbo.Customer
INNER JOIN dbo.InvoiceHeader
```

```
ON dbo.Customer.CustomerNumber = dbo.InvoiceHeader.CustomerNumber
LEFT OUTER JOIN dbo.LoyaltyDiscount
ON dbo.Customer.CustomerNumber = dbo.LoyaltyDiscount.CustomerNumber
WHERE (dbo.Customer.BillingCity = 'Axelburg')
AND (dbo.Customer.Name > 'C')
ORDER BY dbo.Customer.Name DESC, dbo.InvoiceHeader.InvoiceNumber
```

The result set created by this SELECT statement, shown in Figure 3-32, is first sorted by the contents of the Name column in the Customer table. The DESC that follows dbo.Customer.Name in the ORDER BY clause specifies the sort order for the customer name sort. DESC means this sort is done in descending order. In other words, the customer names will be sorted from the end of the alphabet to the beginning.

Several rows have the same customer name. For this reason, a second sort column is specified. This second sort is only applied within each group of identical customer names. For example, Twillig Companies has three rows in the result set. These three rows are sorted by the second sort, which is invoice number. No sort order is specified for the invoice number sort, so this defaults to an ascending sort. In other words, the invoice numbers are sorted from lowest to highest.

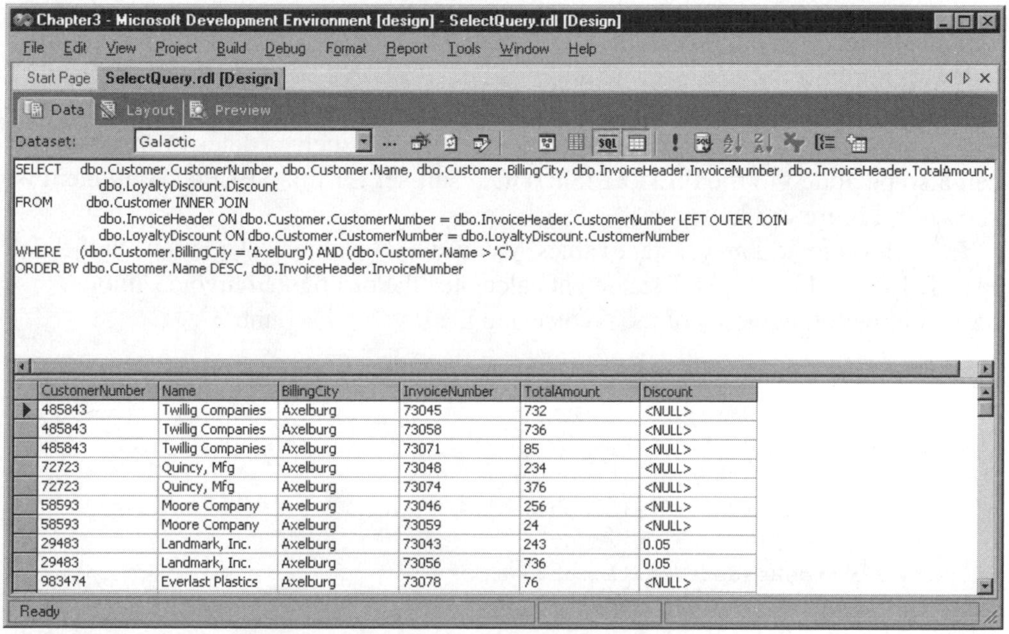

Figure 3-32   *A SELECT statement with an ORDER BY clause*

Constant and Calculated Fields

Our SELECT statement examples thus far have used an asterisk symbol or a FIELD LIST that includes only columns. A FIELD LIST can, in fact, include other things as well. For example, a FIELD LIST can include a constant value, as is shown here:

```
SELECT dbo.Customer.CustomerNumber,
    dbo.Customer.Name,
    dbo.Customer.BillingCity,
    dbo.InvoiceHeader.InvoiceNumber,
    dbo.InvoiceHeader.TotalAmount,
    dbo.LoyaltyDiscount.Discount,
    'AXEL' AS ProcessingCode
FROM dbo.Customer
INNER JOIN dbo.InvoiceHeader
 ON dbo.Customer.CustomerNumber = dbo.InvoiceHeader.CustomerNumber
LEFT OUTER JOIN dbo.LoyaltyDiscount
 ON dbo.Customer.CustomerNumber = dbo.LoyaltyDiscount.CustomerNumber
WHERE (dbo.Customer.BillingCity = 'Axelburg')
AND (dbo.Customer.Name > 'C')
ORDER BY dbo.Customer.Name DESC, dbo.InvoiceHeader.InvoiceNumber
```

The string constant 'AXEL' has been added to the FIELD LIST. This creates a new column in the result set with the value AXEL in each row. By including AS ProcessingCode on this line, we give this result set column a column name of ProcessingCode. Constant values of other data types, such as dates or numbers, can also be added to the FIELD LIST. The result set for this SELECT statement is shown in Figure 3-33.

In addition to adding constant values, you can also include calculations in the FIELD LIST. This SELECT statement calculates the discounted invoice amount based on the total amount of the invoice and the loyalty discount:

```
SELECT dbo.Customer.CustomerNumber,
    dbo.Customer.Name,
    dbo.Customer.BillingCity,
    dbo.InvoiceHeader.InvoiceNumber,
    dbo.InvoiceHeader.TotalAmount,
    dbo.LoyaltyDiscount.Discount,
    dbo.InvoiceHeader.TotalAmount -
      (dbo.InvoiceHeader.TotalAmount *
            dbo.LoyaltyDiscount.Discount)
                AS DiscountedTotalAmount
```

```
FROM dbo.Customer
INNER JOIN dbo.InvoiceHeader
 ON dbo.Customer.CustomerNumber = dbo.InvoiceHeader.CustomerNumber
LEFT OUTER JOIN dbo.LoyaltyDiscount
 ON dbo.Customer.CustomerNumber = dbo.LoyaltyDiscount.CustomerNumber
WHERE (dbo.Customer.BillingCity = 'Axelburg')
AND (dbo.Customer.Name > 'C')
ORDER BY dbo.Customer.Name DESC, dbo.InvoiceHeader.InvoiceNumber
```

The result set for this SELECT statement is shown in Figure 3-34. Notice the value
for the calculated column, DiscountedTotalAmount, is NULL for all the rows that are
not for Landmark, Inc. This is because we are using the value of the Discount column
in our calculation. The Discount column has a value of NULL for every row except for
the Landmark, Inc. rows.

A NULL value cannot be used successfully in any calculation. Any time you try to
add, subtract, multiply, or divide a number by NULL, the result is NULL. The only
way to receive a value in these situations is to give the database a valid value to use in

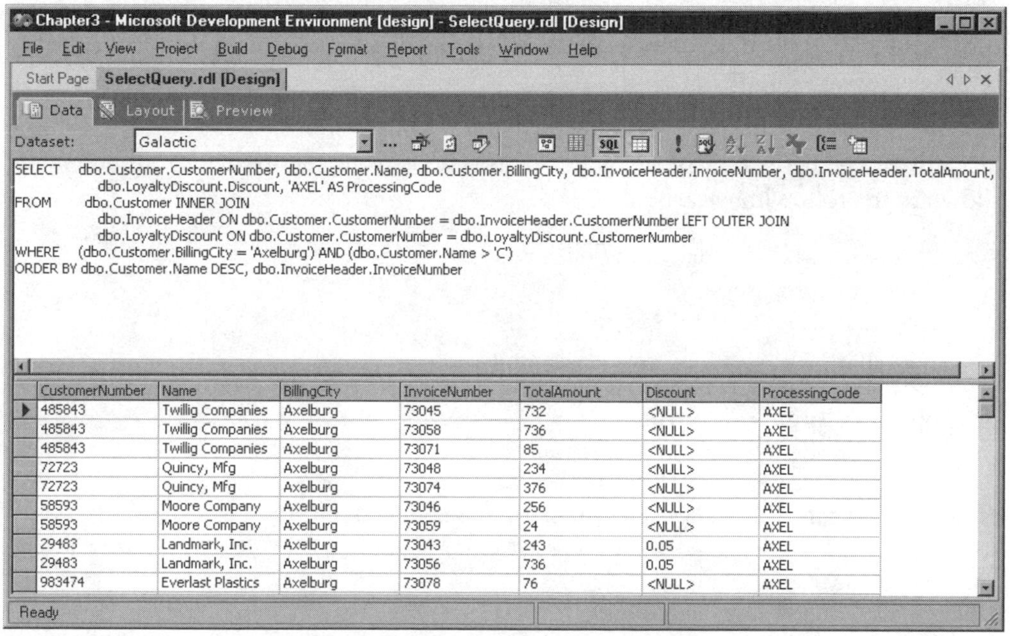

Figure 3-33 *A SELECT statement with a constant in the FIELD LIST*

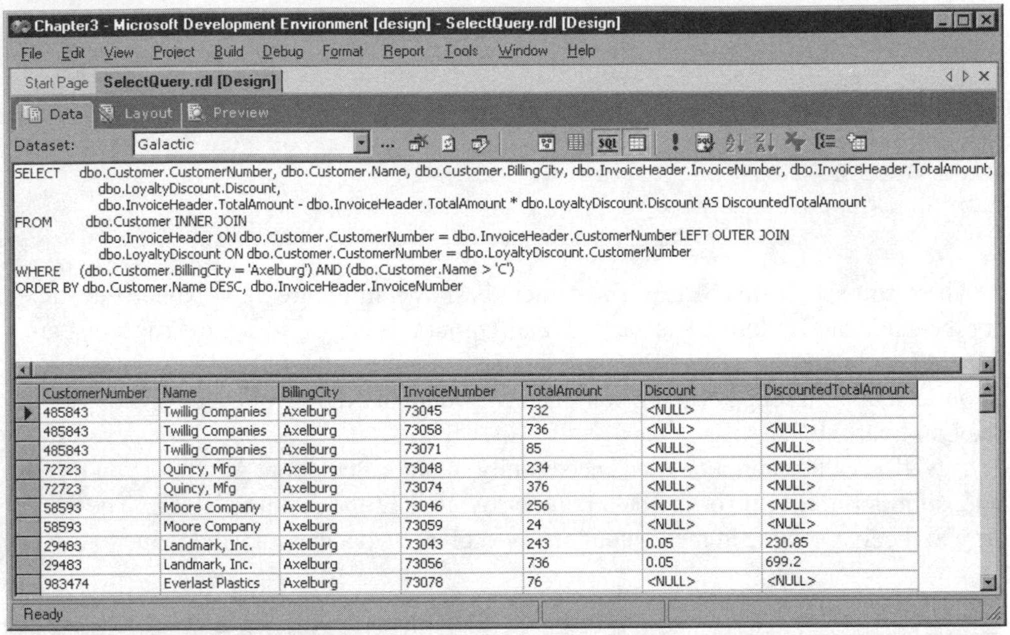

Figure 3-34 *A SELECT statement with a calculated column in the FIELD LIST*

place of any NULLs it might encounter. This is done using the ISNULL( ) function, as shown in the following statement:

```
SELECT dbo.Customer.CustomerNumber,
    dbo.Customer.Name,
    dbo.Customer.BillingCity,
    dbo.InvoiceHeader.InvoiceNumber,
    dbo.InvoiceHeader.TotalAmount,
    dbo.LoyaltyDiscount.Discount,
    dbo.InvoiceHeader.TotalAmount -
      (dbo.InvoiceHeader.TotalAmount *
        ISNULL(dbo.LoyaltyDiscount.Discount,0.00))
                    AS DiscountedTotalAmount
FROM dbo.Customer
INNER JOIN dbo.InvoiceHeader
  ON dbo.Customer.CustomerNumber = dbo.InvoiceHeader.CustomerNumber
```

```
LEFT OUTER JOIN dbo.LoyaltyDiscount
 ON dbo.Customer.CustomerNumber = dbo.LoyaltyDiscount.CustomerNumber
WHERE (dbo.Customer.BillingCity = 'Axelburg')
AND (dbo.Customer.Name > 'C')
ORDER BY dbo.Customer.Name DESC, dbo.InvoiceHeader.InvoiceNumber
```

Now, when the database encounters a NULL value in the Discount column while it is performing the calculation, it substitutes a value of 0.00 and continues with the calculation. The database only performs this substitution when it encounters a NULL value. If any other value is in the Discount column, it uses that value. The result set from this SELECT statement is shown in Figure 3-35.

The GROUP BY Clause

Our sample SELECT statement appears to resemble a run-on sentence. You have seen, however, that each of these clauses is necessary to change the meaning of the statement and to provide the desired result set. We will add just two more clauses to the sample SELECT statement before we are done.

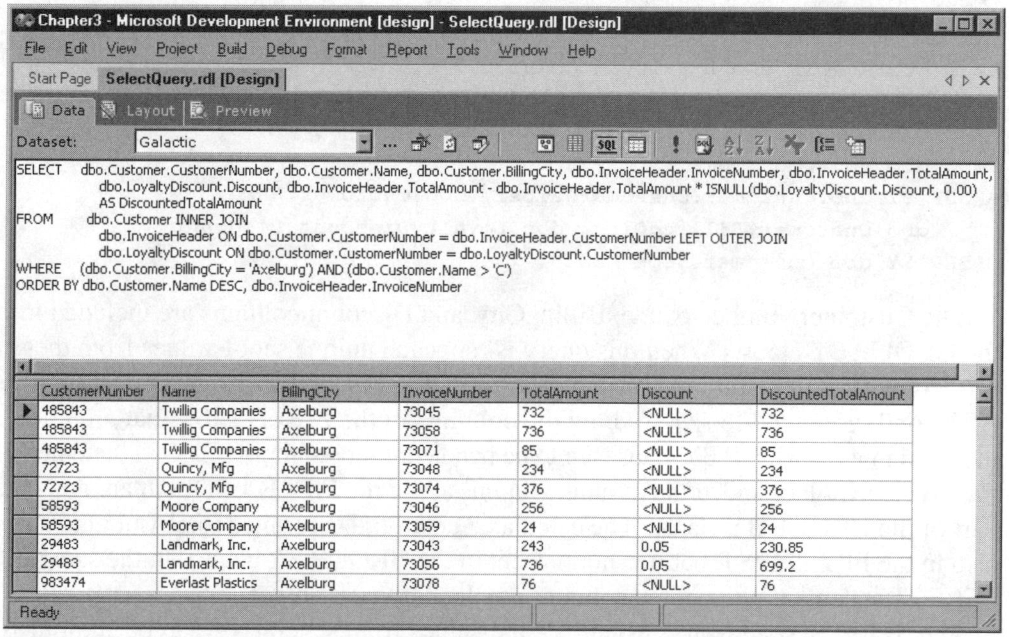

Figure 3-35   *A SELECT statement using the ISNULL() function*

At times, as you are analyzing data, you only want to see information at a summary level, rather than viewing all the detail. In other words, you want the result set to group together the information from several rows to form a summary row. Additional instructions must be added to our SELECT statement in two places for this to happen.

First, you need to specify which columns are going to be used to determine when a summary row will be created. These columns are placed in the GROUP BY clause. Consider the following SELECT statement:

```
SELECT dbo.Customer.CustomerNumber,
    dbo.Customer.Name,
    dbo.Customer.BillingCity,
    COUNT(dbo.InvoiceHeader.InvoiceNumber) AS NumberOfInvoices,
    SUM(dbo.InvoiceHeader.TotalAmount) AS TotalAmount,
    dbo.LoyaltyDiscount.Discount,
    SUM(dbo.InvoiceHeader.TotalAmount -
      (dbo.InvoiceHeader.TotalAmount *
        ISNULL(dbo.LoyaltyDiscount.Discount,0.00)))
                AS DiscountedTotalAmount
FROM dbo.Customer
INNER JOIN dbo.InvoiceHeader
  ON dbo.Customer.CustomerNumber = dbo.InvoiceHeader.CustomerNumber
LEFT OUTER JOIN dbo.LoyaltyDiscount
  ON dbo.Customer.CustomerNumber = dbo.LoyaltyDiscount.CustomerNumber
WHERE (dbo.Customer.BillingCity = 'Axelburg')
AND (dbo.Customer.Name > 'C')
GROUP BY dbo.Customer.CustomerNumber, dbo.Customer.Name,
    dbo.Customer.BillingCity, dbo.LoyaltyDiscount.Discount
ORDER BY dbo.Customer.Name DESC
```

The CustomerNumber, Name, BillingCity, and Discount columns are included in the GROUP BY clause. When this query is run, each unique set of values from these four columns will result in a row in the result set.

Second, you need to specify how the columns in the FIELD LIST that are not included in the GROUP BY clause are to be handled. In the sample SELECT statement, the InvoiceNumber and TotalAmount columns are in the FIELD LIST, but are not part of the GROUP BY clause. The calculated column, DiscountedTotalAmount, is also in the FIELD LIST, but it is not present in the GROUP BY clause. In the sample SELECT statement, these three columns are the non-group-by columns.

The SELECT statement is asking for the values from several rows to be combined into one summary row. The SELECT statement needs to provide a way for this combining to take place. This is done by enclosing each non-group-by column in a special function called an *aggregate function*, which performs a mathematical operation on values from a number of rows and returns a single result. Aggregate functions include:

► **SUM( )**   Returns the sum of the values

► **AVG( )**   Returns the average of the values

► **COUNT( )**   Returns a count of the values

► **MAX( )**   Returns the largest value

► **MIN( )**   Returns the smallest value

The SELECT statement in our group by example uses the SUM( ) aggregate function to return the sum of the invoice amount and the sum of the discounted amount for each customer. It also uses the COUNT( ) aggregate function to return the number of invoices for each customer. The result set from this SELECT statement is shown in Figure 3-36. Note, when an aggregate function is placed around a column name in the FIELD LIST, the SELECT statement can no longer determine what name to use for that column in the result set. You need to supply a column name to use in the result set, as shown in this SELECT statement.

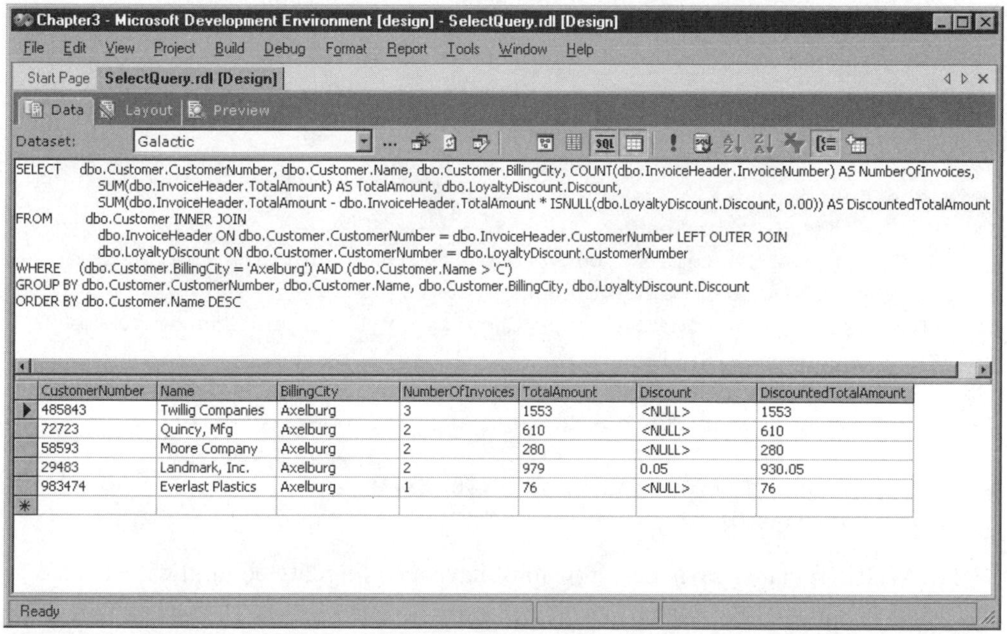

Figure 3-36   *A SELECT statement with a GROUP BY clause*

NOTE

When you're using a GROUP BY clause, all columns in the FIELD LIST must either be included in the GROUP BY clause or be enclosed in an aggregate function. In the sample SELECT statement, the CustomerNumber column is all that is necessary in the GROUP BY clause to provide the desired grouping. However, because the Name, BillingCity, and Discount columns do not lend themselves to being aggregated, they are included in the GROUP BY clause along with the CustomerNumber column.

The HAVING Clause

The GROUP BY clause has a special clause that can be used with it to determine which grouped rows will be included in the result set. This is the HAVING clause. The HAVING clause functions similarly to the WHERE clause. The *WHERE* clause limits the rows in the result set by checking conditions at the row level. The *HAVING* clause limits the rows in the result set by checking conditions at the group level.

Consider the following SELECT statement:

```
SELECT dbo.Customer.CustomerNumber,
    dbo.Customer.Name,
    dbo.Customer.BillingCity,
    COUNT(dbo.InvoiceHeader.InvoiceNumber) AS NumberOfInvoices,
    SUM(dbo.InvoiceHeader.TotalAmount) AS TotalAmount,
    dbo.LoyaltyDiscount.Discount,
    SUM(dbo.InvoiceHeader.TotalAmount -
      (dbo.InvoiceHeader.TotalAmount *
        ISNULL(dbo.LoyaltyDiscount.Discount,0.00)))
                  AS DiscountedTotalAmount
FROM dbo.Customer
INNER JOIN dbo.InvoiceHeader
 ON dbo.Customer.CustomerNumber = dbo.InvoiceHeader.CustomerNumber
LEFT OUTER JOIN dbo.LoyaltyDiscount
 ON dbo.Customer.CustomerNumber = dbo.LoyaltyDiscount.CustomerNumber
WHERE (dbo.Customer.BillingCity = 'Axelburg')
AND (dbo.Customer.Name > 'C')
GROUP BY dbo.Customer.CustomerNumber, dbo.Customer.Name,
    dbo.Customer.BillingCity, dbo.LoyaltyDiscount.Discount
HAVING COUNT(dbo.InvoiceHeader.InvoiceNumber) >= 2
ORDER BY dbo.Customer.Name DESC
```

The WHERE clause says that a row must have a BillingCity column with a value of Axelburg and a Name column with a value greater than *C* before it can be included in the group. The HAVING clause says a group must contain at least two invoices before it can be included in the result set. The result set for this SELECT statement is shown in Figure 3-37.

```
Chapter3 - Microsoft Development Environment [design] - SelectQuery.rdl [Design]

File   Edit   View   Project   Build   Debug   Format   Report   Tools   Window   Help

Start Page   SelectQuery.rdl [Design]

Data     Layout     Preview

Dataset:    Galactic

SELECT    dbo.Customer.CustomerNumber, dbo.Customer.Name, dbo.Customer.BillingCity, COUNT(dbo.InvoiceHeader.InvoiceNumber) AS NumberOfInvoices,
          SUM(dbo.InvoiceHeader.TotalAmount) AS TotalAmount, dbo.LoyaltyDiscount.Discount,
          SUM(dbo.InvoiceHeader.TotalAmount - dbo.InvoiceHeader.TotalAmount * ISNULL(dbo.LoyaltyDiscount.Discount, 0.00)) AS DiscountedTotalAmount
FROM      dbo.Customer INNER JOIN
          dbo.InvoiceHeader ON dbo.Customer.CustomerNumber = dbo.InvoiceHeader.CustomerNumber LEFT OUTER JOIN
          dbo.LoyaltyDiscount ON dbo.Customer.CustomerNumber = dbo.LoyaltyDiscount.CustomerNumber
WHERE     (dbo.Customer.BillingCity = 'Axelburg') AND (dbo.Customer.Name > 'C')
GROUP BY dbo.Customer.CustomerNumber, dbo.Customer.Name, dbo.Customer.BillingCity, dbo.LoyaltyDiscount.Discount
HAVING    (COUNT(dbo.InvoiceHeader.InvoiceNumber) >= 2)
ORDER BY dbo.Customer.Name DESC
```

CustomerNumber	Name	BillingCity	NumberOfInvoices	TotalAmount	Discount	DiscountedTotalAmount
485843	Twillig Companies	Axelburg	3	1553	<NULL>	1553
72723	Quincy, Mfg	Axelburg	2	610	<NULL>	610
58593	Moore Company	Axelburg	2	280	<NULL>	280
29483	Landmark, Inc.	Axelburg	2	979	0.05	930.05

Ready

Figure 3-37   *A SELECT statement with a HAVING clause*

On to the Reports

Good reporting depends more on getting the right data out of the database than it does on creating a clean report design and delivering the report in a timely manner. If you are feeling a little overwhelmed by the workings of relational databases and SELECT queries, don't worry. Refer to this chapter from time to time if you need to.

Also, remember, Reporting Services provides you with the Query Designer tool to assist with the query-creation process. You needn't remember the exact syntax for the LEFT OUTER JOIN or a GROUP BY clause. What you do need to know are the capabilities of the SELECT statement, so you know what to instruct the Query Designer to create.

Finally, when you are creating your queries, use the same method that was used here: in other words, build them one step at a time. Join together the tables you will need for your report, determine what columns are required, and then come up with a WHERE clause that gets you only the rows you are looking for. After that, you can add in the sorting and grouping. Assemble one clause, and then another and another, and pretty soon, you will have a slam-bang query that will give you exactly the data you need!

Now, on to the reports. . . .

A Visit to Emerald City: The Report Wizard

I f the relational database concepts of Chapter 3 were new to you, you may feel like you have been through a twister and are not in Kansas anymore. You can take heart knowing you have completed the preliminaries and are now ready to start building reports. So, without further ado, strap on your ruby slippers and follow the yellow-brick road, because you are off to see the wizard!

That wizard is, of course, the Report Wizard found in the Report Designer. Like the ruler of the Emerald City, the Report Wizard is not all-powerful. For example, the Report Wizard will not let you make use of all the features available in Reporting Services. The wizard is, however, a great place to get a feel for the way reports are constructed.

NOTE

Beginning with this chapter, we will create sample reports using the Galactic database. If you have not done so already, go to http://www.osborne.com, locate the book's page using the ISBN 0072262397, and follow the instructions to download and install the Galactic database.

Your First Report

You are now ready to build your first Reporting Services report. Of course, few people build reports just for the fun of it. Usually there is some business reason for this endeavor. In this book, as stated in the previous chapter, we use the business needs of Galactic Delivery Services (GDS) as the basis for our sample reports.

Each of the sample reports used in this book is presented in a manner similar to what you see in this section. The report is introduced with a list of the Reporting Services features it highlights. This is followed by the business need of our sample company, Galactic Delivery Services, which this report is meant to fill. Next is an overview of the tasks that must be accomplished to create the report.

Finally, there are the steps to walk through for each task, step by step. In addition to the step-by-step description, each task includes a few notes to provide additional information on the steps you just completed. Follow the step-by-step instructions to complete the task, and then read through the task notes to gain additional understanding of the process you have just completed. You can complete the step-by-step instructions using either the Business Intelligence Development Studio or Visual Studio 2005.

The Customer List Report

Here is our first attempt at creating a report: the Customer List Report.

Features Highlighted

- ▶ Creating a data source
- ▶ Using the Query Designer to create a dataset
- ▶ Using the Report Wizard to create a table report

Business Need The accounting department at Galactic Delivery Services would like an e-mail directory containing all the billing contacts for its customers. The directory should be an alphabetical list of all GDS customers. It must include the customer name, along with a billing contact and a billing e-mail address for each customer.

Task Overview

1. Begin a New Project in the Business Intelligence Development Studio or Visual Studio
2. Create a Data Source
3. Create a Dataset
4. Choose the Report Layout

Customer List Report, Task 1: Begin a New Project in the Business Intelligence Development Studio or Visual Studio

1. Run the Business Intelligence Development Studio or Visual Studio 2005. The Start page appears as shown here.

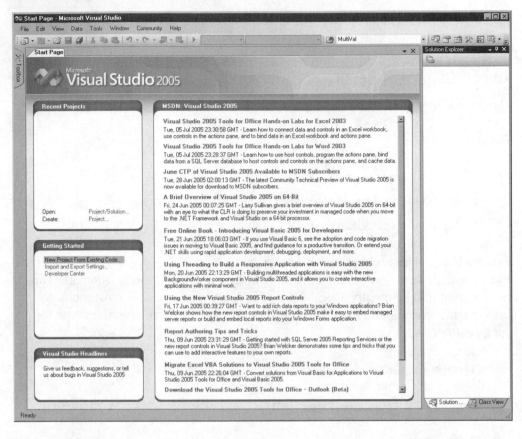

NOTE

The first illustration shows the default configuration of The Business Intelligence Development Studio. Your screen may vary if this configuration has been changed.

2. Click the New Project toolbar button to create a new project. This displays the New Project dialog box, as shown in the following illustration. (You can create a new project in three different ways: Select File | New | Project from the Main menu, click the New Project toolbar button, or click the Create: Project link on the Start page.)

3. Select Business Intelligence Projects in the Project Types area of the dialog box.

4. Select Report Server Project Wizard in the Templates area of the dialog box.

5. Type **Chapter04** for the project name. This project will contain all the reports you create in this chapter.

6. Click Browse to open the Project Location dialog box.

7. Click My Projects to go to the Visual Studio Projects folder.

8. Click the Create New Folder button in the toolbar at the top of the Project Location dialog box. If you have trouble finding the Create New Folder button, look along the top of the dialog box for a picture of a folder with a yellow sparkle.

9. Enter **MSSQLRS** for the name of the new folder. This folder will contain all the projects you create for this book.

10. Click OK in the New Folder dialog box.

11. Click Open in the lower-right corner of the Project Location dialog box. The New Project dialog box should now look like the second illustration.

Task Notes We have now established a name and location for this project. This must be done for every project you create. Because the Business Intelligence Development Studio and Visual Studio 2005 use the project name to create a folder for all the project files, the project name must be a valid Windows folder name. You can use the Browse button to browse to the appropriate location, as we did here, or you can type the path in the Location text box.

NOTE

Valid folder names can contain any character, except the following:
*/ ? : & \ * " < > | # %*
In addition, a folder cannot be named "." or "..".

The project name is appended to the end of the location path to create the full path for the folder that will contain the new project. In our example, a folder called Chapter04 will be created inside the folder MSSQLRS. All the files created as part of the Chapter04 project will be placed in this folder.

Customer List Report, Task 2: Create a Data Source

1. Click OK in the New Project dialog box to start the Report Wizard. The Welcome to the Report Wizard page appears as shown here.

2.   Click Next. The Select the Data Source page appears.

3.   Type **Galactic** for the data source name.

4.   Select Microsoft SQL Server from the Type drop-down list, if it is not already selected.

5.   Click Edit. The Connection Properties dialog box appears.

6.   Type the name of the Microsoft SQL Server database server that is hosting the Galactic database. If the Galactic database is hosted by the computer you are currently working on, you may type (**local**) for the server name.

7.   Click the Use SQL Server Authentication radio button.

8.   Type **GalacticReporting** for the user name.

9.   Type **gds** for the Password.

10. Click the Save My Password check box.

11. Select Galactic from the Select or Enter a Database Name drop-down list. The Connection Properties dialog box should now look like this:

12. Click the Test Connection button. If the message "Test connection succeeded" appears, click OK. If an error message appears, make sure the name of your database server, the user name, the password, and the name of your database were entered properly. If your test connection still does not succeed, make sure you have correctly installed the Galactic database.

13. Click OK to return to the Select the Data Source page of the Report Wizard.

14. Click the Make This a Shared Data Source check box so it is checked. This page should now look like this:

Task Notes As discussed in Chapter 1, the data source is a set of instructions for connecting to the database server or the data file that will provide the information for your report. This set of instructions is also known as a *connection string*. In this sample report, we used the Connection Properties dialog box to build the connection string. Those of you who memorize connection strings can type the appropriate string on the Select the Data Source page without using the Connection Properties dialog box at all. The rest of us will continue to use the Connection Properties dialog box when building future reports to have the connection string created for us.

CAUTION

If you do type in your own connection string, do not include the login and password information. The connection string is stored as plain text in the report definition file, so a password stored as part of the connection string is easy to discover. Instead, use the Credentials button on the Select the Data Source page to enter the login and password, so they are stored in a more secure fashion.

Reporting Services can utilize data from a number of different databases and data files, but you need to tell the wizard what type of database or data file the report will be using. You did this using the Type drop-down list in Step 4 of the previous task. This selection tells Reporting Services which data provider to use when accessing the database or data file. When you select Microsoft SQL Server, Reporting Services uses the .NET Framework Data Provider for SQL Server. This data provider knows how to retrieve information from a SQL Server database.

The Type drop-down list on the Select the Data Source page includes only a few of the possible types of data sources. If you are using data from a data source other than a Microsoft SQL Server database, you need to click the Change button on the Connection Properties dialog box. This displays the Change Data Source dialog box shown in the following illustration.

```
Change Data Source                                    ? X
 ┌─────────────────────────────┐  ┌─────────────────────────┐
 │ Data source:                │  │ ─Description────────────│
 │ Microsoft SQL Server        │  │ Use this data provider  │
 │ Microsoft SQL Server Analysis Services │ to connect to      │
 │ ODBC                        │  │ Microsoft SQL Server 7.0,│
 │ OLE DB                      │  │ 2000 or 2005.           │
 │ Oracle                      │  │                         │
 │                             │  │                         │
 │                             │  │                         │
 │ Data provider:              │  │                         │
 │ .NET Framework Data Provider for SQ ▼ │              │
 │ ☐ Always use this selection │   [ OK ]   [ Cancel ]     │
 └─────────────────────────────┘  └─────────────────────────┘
```

Use this dialog box to select the appropriate data source type.

Each data provider requires slightly different bits of information to create the connection string. The Connection Properties dialog box changes to suit the selected data provider. This means Steps 6 through 11 will vary when you use a data source type other than Microsoft SQL Server. Simply provide the information requested on the Connection Properties dialog box. Be sure to use Test Connection to make sure everything is entered properly before leaving the Connection Properties dialog box.

Checking the Save My Password check box on the Connection Properties page allows the data source credentials to be saved with the data source definition. The *data source credentials* are the user name and password information required to access that data source. The credentials are encrypted before they are saved to help protect them. If you are not comfortable having the credentials stored in this manner, leave both the user name and password blank. You will be prompted for the credentials every time you execute the report or modify the dataset.

NOTE

If you leave the data source credentials blank and your selected data source requires a login, you will be prompted for database credentials when you click Next on the Select the Data Source page. The credentials you enter here are used to create a connection to the data source for the Design the Query page and for the Query Designer. These credentials are not stored with the data source.

A data source can be used by a single report, or it can be shared by several reports in the same project. Checking the Make This a Shared Data Source check box allows this data source to be used by many reports. Shared data sources are stored separately from the reports that use them. Nonshared data sources are stored right in the report definition. If you have a number of reports in the same project that utilize data from the same database or the same data files, you will save time by using a shared data source.

CAUTION

Even though the data source credentials are encrypted, it is never a good idea to use the system administrator account or any other database login with system administrator privileges to access data for reporting. Always create a database login that has only the privileges required for reporting operations and use this login as the reporting credentials.

Some companies require that reports use data from a development database server while they are being developed and a production database server when the reports are completed. Using a shared data source in this type of an environment makes it easier to switch a number of reports from the development database server to the production database server. The change is made once to the shared data source, and all the reports are ready to go.

Customer List Report, Task 3: Create a Dataset

1. Click Next. The Design the Query page of the Report Wizard appears.
2. Click Query Builder. The Query Designer window appears with the Generic Query Designer active. Click the Query Designer toggle button as shown in the following illustration. The Query Designer will switch to the Graphical Query Designer.

3. The Graphical Query Designer is divided into four horizontal sections. The top section is called the *diagram pane*. Right-click in the diagram pane. You see the Context menu as shown here.

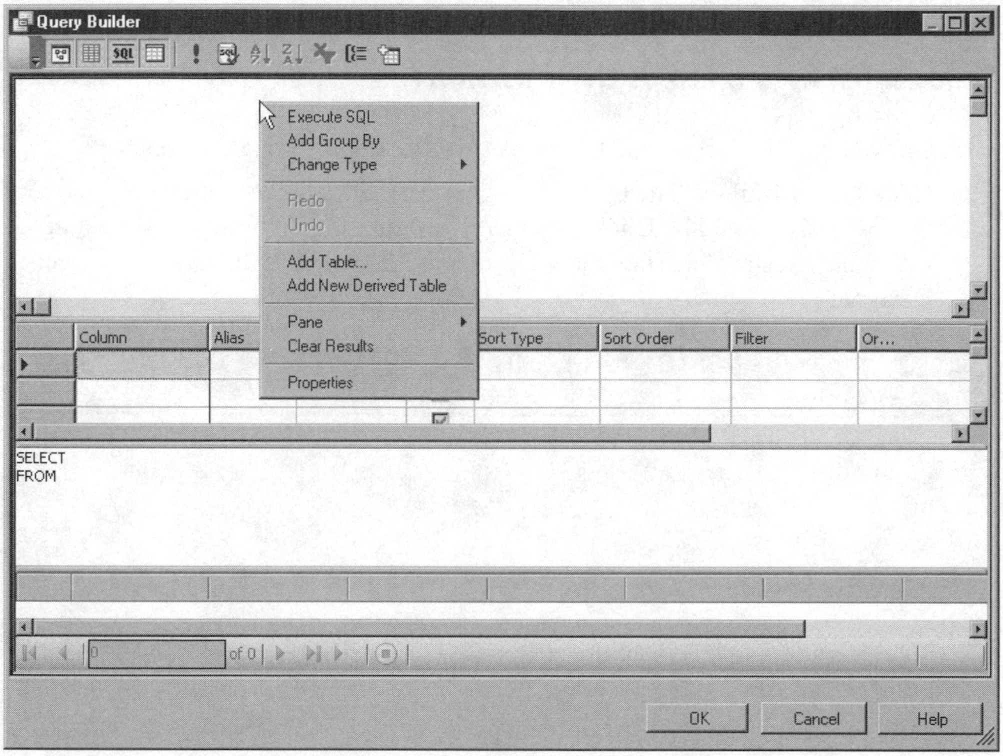

4. Select the Add Table command from the Context menu. This displays the Add Table dialog box shown here. This dialog box contains a list of all the tables, views, and functions that return datasets, which are found in the data source.

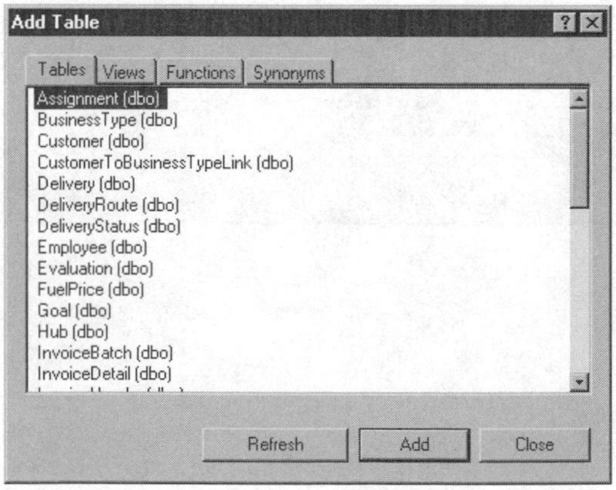

5. Double-click Customer (dbo) in the list of tables. The Customer table is added to the query.

6. Click Close to exit the Add Table dialog box.

7. A list of the fields in the Customer table is displayed. Click the check box next to the Name field.

8. Scroll down the list of fields and check the BillingContact and BillingEmail fields as well.

9. The section of the Query Designer directly below the diagram pane is called the *critieria pane*. In the critieria pane, type **1** in the Sort Order column across from the Name field. Or, you can click in the Sort Order column across from the Name field and select 1 from the drop-down list.

10. The section of the Query Designer directly below the criteria pane is the *SQL pane*. Right-click in the SQL pane. You see the Context menu shown here.

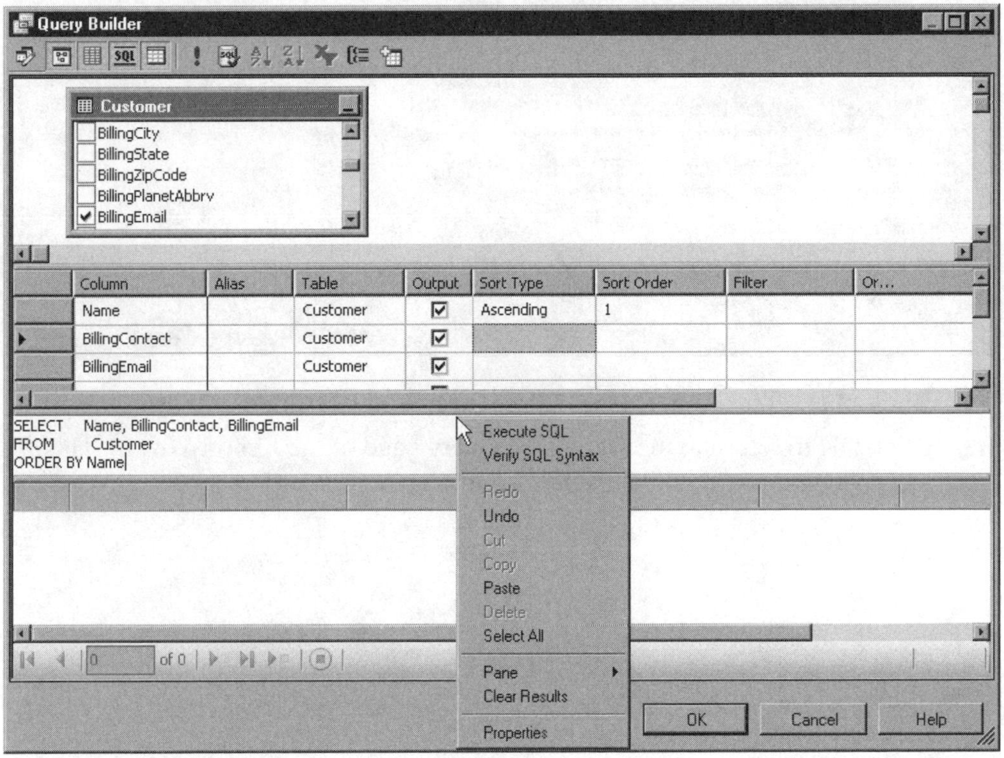

11. Select Execute SQL from the Context menu. This runs the query and displays the results in the bottom section of the Query Designer. This bottom section is called the *results pane*. The Query Designer should now look like this:

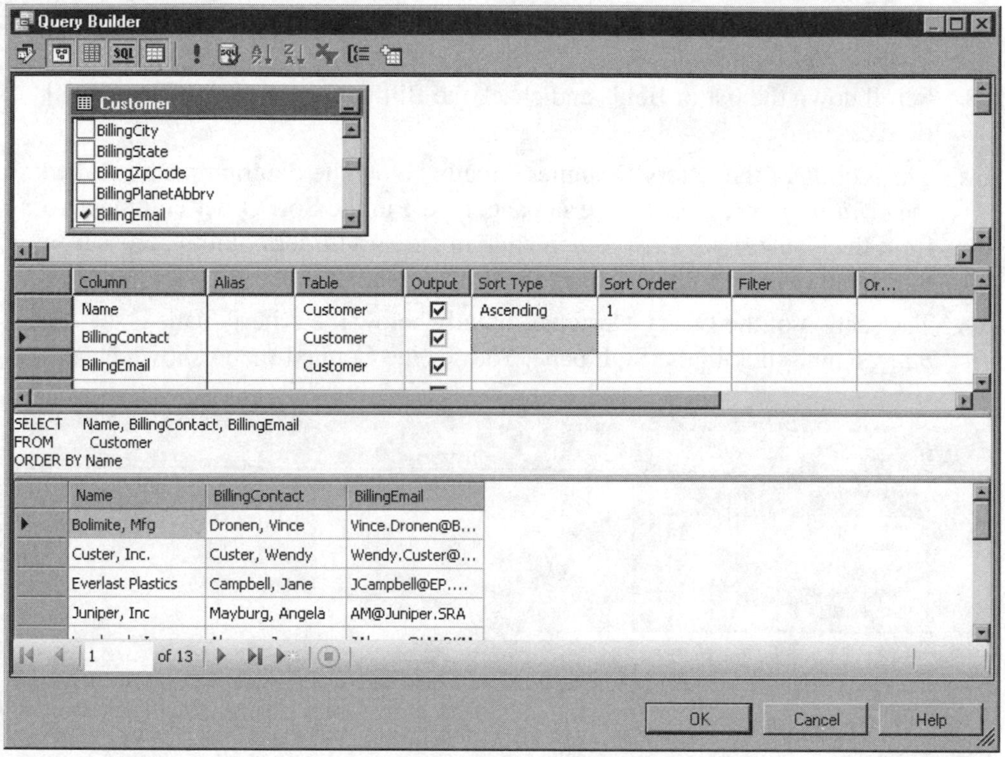

12. Right-click in the results pane. Select Clear Results from the Context menu.

13. Click OK to return to the Design the Query page of the Report Wizard. This page should now look like the following illustration.

Task Notes   The dataset represents the information to be retrieved from the data source and used in your report. The dataset consists of two parts. The first part is the database command used to retrieve data. This is the SELECT statement you created using the Query Designer. This database command is called the *query string*.

The second part is the list of the columns in the result set created by executing the query string. This list of columns is called the *structure* or *schema* of the result set. Visual Studio determines the field list by executing the query string in a special manner, so it returns the structure of the result set, but it does not return any rows in the result set.

Those of you familiar with your data source, and also familiar with the SELECT statement, can type your SELECT statement in the Query String text box on the Design the Query page. This is especially appropriate when you are executing a stored procedure to retrieve data, rather than using a SELECT statement. A *stored procedure* is a program saved inside the database itself that can be used to modify or retrieve data. Using stored procedures in a query string is discussed more in Chapter 7.

It is a good idea to run the query yourself before exiting the Query Designer. We did this in Steps 10 and 11 of this task. This ensures no errors exist in the SQL statement the Query Designer created for you. It also lets you look at the result set in the results pane, so you can make sure you are getting the information you expected.

To display the result set in the results pane, the Query Designer must first load the result set in memory. Keeping result sets in memory can take up valuable resources that might be needed by other programs. This memory is not automatically cleared when you exit the Query Designer. For this reason, you should always clear the result set yourself, as we did in Step 12 of this task. If you do not clear the result set yourself, eventually you will see a dialog box reminding you that the result set is open and asking whether you plan on making any further use of it. If this happens, click No to tell the Query Designer you no longer need the result set.

Customer List Report, Task 4: Choose the Report Layout

1. Click Next. The Select the Report Type page of the Report Wizard appears.

2. Make sure the Tabular radio button is selected and click Next. The Design the Table page of the Report Wizard appears.

3. With the Name field highlighted in the Available Fields list, click Details. The Name field moves to the Displayed Fields list.

4. Do the same thing with the BillingContact and BillingEmail fields. The Design the Table page should now look like the following illustration.

5. Click Next. The Choose the Table Style page of the Report Wizard appears as shown here.

6. Select the Generic style in the style list and click Next. The Choose the
Deployment Location page of the Report Wizard appears.

7. Click Next. The Completing the Wizard page appears.

8. Type **Customer List** for the report name.

9. Click Finish. The Business Intelligence Development Studio or Visual Studio window appears with the Report Designer active.

10. Click the Preview tab located near the middle of the screen just above the report layout. A preview of your report appears.

11. Click the Layout tab.

12. The Report Wizard created columns in our report that seem a bit too narrow. We can improve the report by widening the columns. Click the Name heading ("Name" in a cell by itself).

13. Place your mouse pointer on the line separating the gray box above the Name heading and the gray box above the Billing Contact heading. Your mouse pointer changes to a double-headed arrow, as shown here.

14. Hold down the left mouse button and move the mouse pointer to the right. This makes the Name column wider.

15. Follow the technique described in Step 14 of this task to widen the Billing Contact and Billing Email columns, as well.

16. Click the Preview tab. Your report should appear as shown here.

17. Repeat Steps 11 through 16 until you are satisfied with the appearance of the report.

18. When you are satisfied with the report, click the Save All button in the toolbar. This saves the project, the shared data source, and the report files. The Save All button is highlighted in the following illustration.

Task Notes   As you may have noticed, the Choose the Table Style page offers several table style choices (refer to the illustration in Step 5). You can try these different table styles as you complete the other sample reports in this chapter and as you create your own reports using the Report Wizard. For ease of comparison between sample reports, the figures in this book will continue to use the Generic style.

The report server and deployment folder items on the Choose the Deployment Location page (refer to the illustration in Step 6) are used when the report is moved from the development environment to a report server. These items are saved with the project, not with an individual report. For this reason, the Deployment Location page is only displayed by the Report Wizard for the first report created in a project. We discuss report deployment in Chapter 10.

You probably had to repeat steps 11 through 16 of this task several times to get the report just the way you wanted it to look. This is not a problem. Most reports you create require multiple trips between the Layout and the Preview tabs before everything is laid out as it should be. Knowing you can move between layout and preview with such ease is a real plus of the Report Designer.

Congratulations! You have now completed your first report.

An Interactive Table Report

Now that you have a taste of how the Report Wizard works and what it can do, let's try something a bit more complex. Let's create a table report that implements an interactive feature called drilldown. With the *drilldown* type of report, only the high-level, summary information is initially presented to the viewers. They can then click a special area of the report (in our case, that area is designated by a plus (+) sign) to reveal part of the lower-level, detail information. The viewers drill down through the summary to get to the detail.

The Customer-Invoice Report

Features Highlighted

▶   Using a shared data source

▶   Linking tables in the Graphical Query Designer

▶   Assigning columns for page breaks and grouping

▶   Enabling subtotals and drilldown

Business Need   The accounting department would like a report listing all Galactic Delivery Services (GDS) customers. The customers need to be grouped by Billing City, with each city beginning on a new page. The report allows a viewer to drill down from the customer level to see the invoices for that customer.

Task Overview

1. Reopen the Chapter04 Project
2. Create a New Report in the Chapter04 Project, Select the Shared Data Source, and Create a Dataset
3. Choose the Report Layout

Customer-Invoice Report, Task 1: Reopen the Chapter04 Project

If you have not closed the Chapter04 project since working on the previous section of this chapter, skip to Step 8. Otherwise, follow these steps, starting with Step 1:

1. Run the Business Intelligence Development Studio or Visual Studio 2005.
2. If a link to the Chapter04 project is visible on the Start Page, click this link and the Chapter04 project opens. Proceed to Step 8. If a link to the Chapter04 project is not visible on the Start Page, continue with Step 3.
3. Select File | Open | Project/Solution.
4. Click My Projects.
5. Double-click MSSQLRS.
6. Double-click Chapter04.
7. Double-click Chapter04.sln. (This is the file that contains the solution for Chapter04.)
8. If the CustomerList report is displayed in the center of the screen, click the X button in the upper-right corner of the center section of the screen to close this report.

Task Notes   Opening the Chapter04 solution (Chapter04.sln) and opening the Chapter04 project (Chapter04.rptproj) produce the same end result, so you can do either. Only one project is in the Chapter04 solution, so that project is automatically opened when the solution is opened. When the Chapter04 project is opened, the last report you worked on is displayed in the center of the screen. In this case, it is probably the Customer List Report.

You do not need to close one report before working on another report. In fact, you can have multiple reports open at one time and use the tabs containing the report names to move among them. In most cases, however, I find that a philosophy of "the less clutter, the better" works well when creating reports. For this reason, I recommend you close all unneeded reports as you move from one report to the next.

Customer-Invoice Report, Task 2: Create a New Report in the Chapter04 Project, Select the Shared Data Source, and Create a Dataset

1. In the Solution Explorer on the right side of the screen, right-click the Reports folder. You see the Context menu shown here.

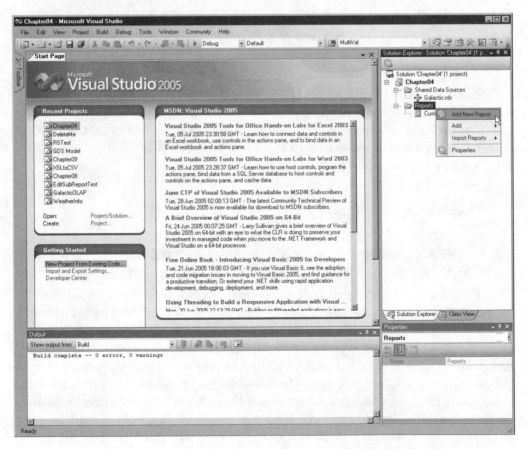

2. Select the Add New Report command from the Context menu. This starts the Report Wizard, enabling you to create another report in the current project.

3. Click Next. The Select the Data Source page appears.

4. Make sure the Shared Data Source radio button is selected and the Galactic data source is selected in the drop-down list, as shown here. Click Next. The Design the Query page appears.

5. Click Query Builder. The Generic Query Designer appears. Click the Query Designer toggle button. The Query Designer switches to the Graphical Query Designer.

6. Right-click in the diagram pane (the upper area) of the Query Designer screen. You see the Diagram Pane Context menu.

7. Select the Add Table command from the Context menu.

8. Double-click Customer (dbo) in the list of tables. The Customer table is added to the query.

9. Double-click InvoiceHeader (dbo) in the list of tables. Make sure you select InvoiceHeader and *not* InvoiceDetail. The InvoiceHeader table is added to the query.

10. Click Close to exit the Add Table dialog box. Notice the Query Designer automatically creates the INNER JOIN between the Customer and the InvoiceHeader tables, as shown in the following illustration.

11. Right-click the gray diamond in the middle of the link joining the Customer
and the InvoiceHeader tables. The Join Context menu is displayed, as shown in
the following illustration.

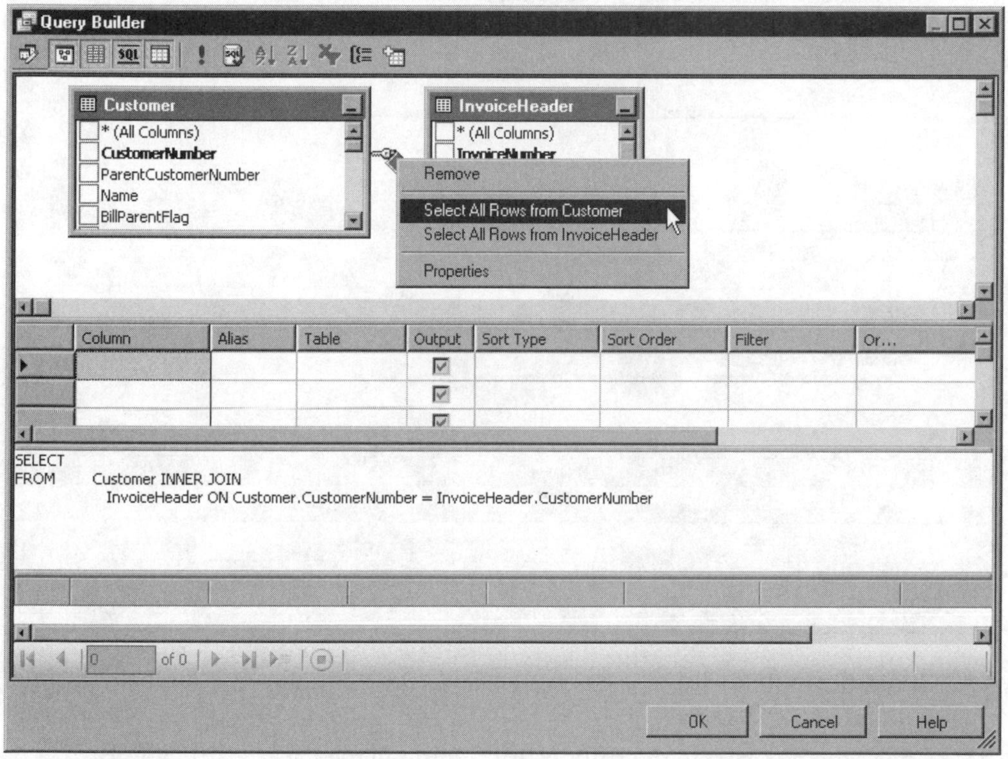

12. Choose the Select All Rows from Customer option from the Context menu.
The diamond symbol changes, as shown in the next illustration.

13. Scroll down in the list of columns for the Customer table until the BillingCity column name is visible.

14. Check the box next to the BillingCity column in the Customer table.

15. Scroll up in the list of columns for the Customer table and check the box next to the Name column. This places the Name field after the BillingCity field in the resulting SQL query.

16. In the list of columns for the InvoiceHeader table, check the boxes next to the InvoiceNumber, InvoiceDate, and TotalAmount columns.

17. Place a **1** in the Sort Order column for the BillingCity field either by typing in the cell or by using the drop-down list.

18. Place a **2** in the Sort Order column for the Name field.

19. Place a **3** in the Sort Order column for the InvoiceNumber field.

20. Right-click in the SQL pane and select Execute SQL from the Context menu. The query executes, and the result set is displayed in the results pane. The Query Designer should appear similar to the following illustration.

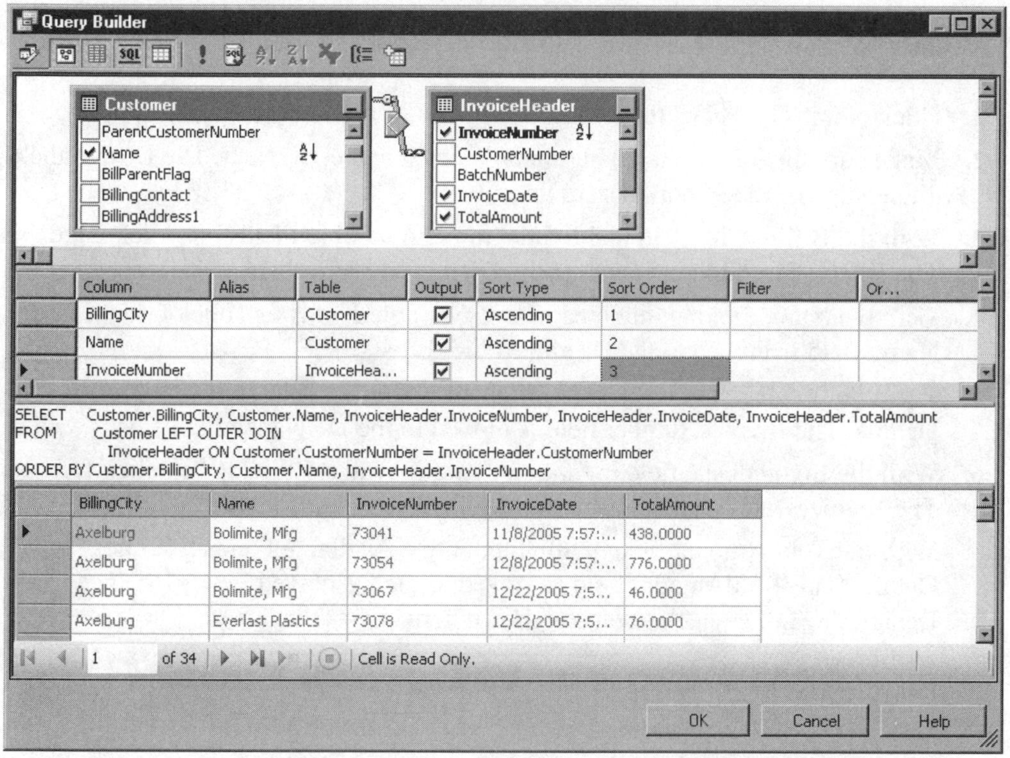

21. Right-click in the results pane. Select Clear Results from the Context menu.

22. Click OK. This returns you to the Design the Query page.

Task Notes   The Galactic data source you created in the first report is a shared data source. As such, the wizard defaults to using this shared data source on the Select the Data Source page any time a new report is created.

In the Query Designer, when a second table is added to the query, the column names from each table are compared. If the Query Designer finds two columns with the same name and data type, it will create a JOIN based on those columns. You saw this in Steps 8 through 10 in this task.

The business need for this report states that the report should include all GDS customers. As you saw in Chapter 3, some customers may not have invoices, so to include all the customers in the report, you need to use a LEFT OUTER JOIN between the Customer table and the InvoiceHeader table. You can accomplish this by choosing Select All Rows from Customer, as you did in Step 12 of this task.

Customer-Invoice Report, Task 3: Choose the Report Layout

1. Click Next. The Select the Report Type page of the Report Wizard appears.
2. Make sure the Tabular radio button is selected and click Next. The Design the Table page of the Report Wizard appears.
3. With the BillingCity field highlighted in the Available Fields list, click Page. The BillingCity field is moved to the Displayed Fields list.
4. With the Name field highlighted in the Available Fields list, click Group. The Name field is moved to the Displayed Fields list.
5. With the InvoiceNumber field highlighted in the Available Fields list, click Details. The InvoiceNumber field is moved to the Displayed Fields list.
6. With the InvoiceDate field highlighted in the Available Fields list, click Details. The InvoiceDate field is moved to the Displayed Fields list.
7. With the TotalAmount field highlighted in the Available Fields list, click Details. The TotalAmount field is moved to the Displayed Fields list. The Design the Table page appears as shown here.

8. Click Next. The Choose the Table Layout page of the Report Wizard appears. This page appears in the Report Wizard because we put fields in the Group area on the Design the Table page.

9. Check the Include Subtotals check box.

10. Check the Enable Drilldown check box. The Choose the Table Layout page appears as shown.

11. Click Next. The Choose the Table Style page of the Report Wizard appears.

12. Select Generic in the style list, and then click Next. The Completing the Wizard page appears.

13. Type **Customer-Invoice Report** for the report name.

14. Click Finish. The Report Designer window appears.

15. Widen the Name column as you did with the previous report.

16. Click the table cell directly under the Invoice heading. This cell is highlighted, as shown in the illustration.

17. Press DELETE on your keyboard to remove the nonsensical totaling of the invoice numbers.

18. Click the Preview tab. A preview of your report appears.

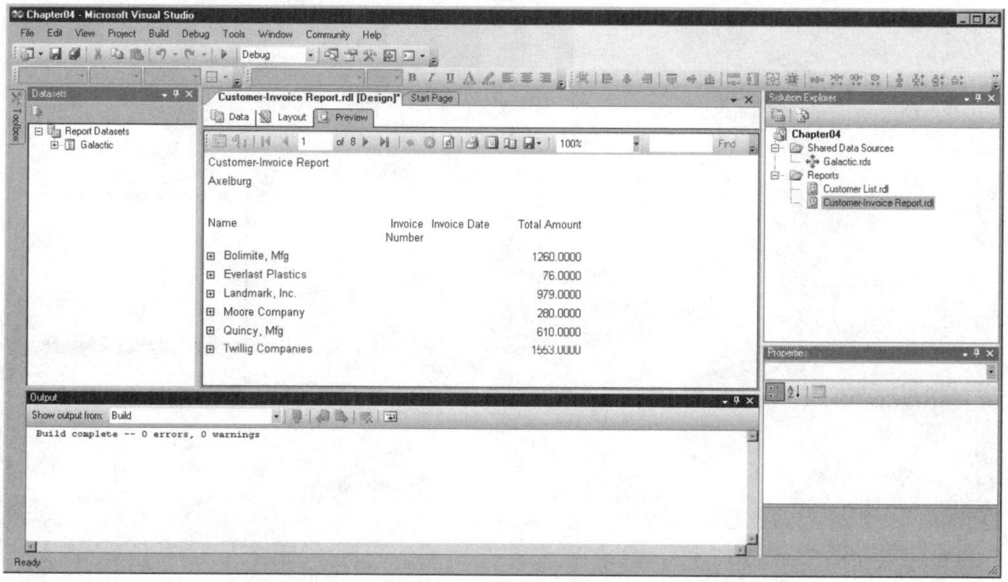

19. Click the plus sign in front of Bolimite, Mfg to view the invoices for this company, as shown here.

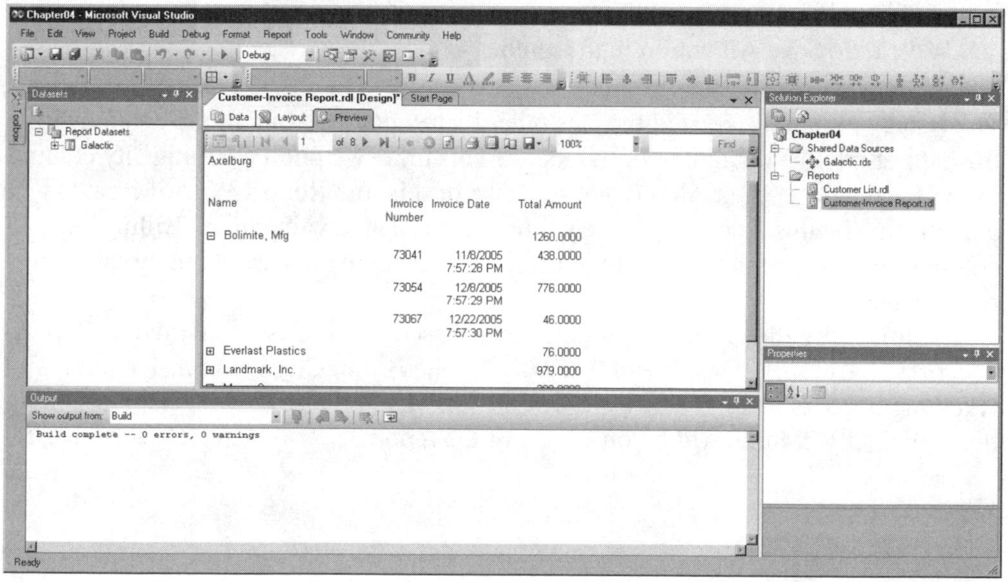

20. Click the Next Page button (the blue triangle just below the Preview tab) to advance to the next page of the report. The Next Page button is highlighted in the following illustration.

21. You can continue to work with the report preview to get a feel for the way report navigation and drilldown works. (For instance, you may want to try clicking the minus (−) sign.)

22. Click the Save All button in the toolbar.

Task Notes When we created the Customer List Report, we put all the columns from the dataset into the detail line of the report. This time, we put the BillingCity column in the Page area of the table layout. Because of this, the Report Wizard created a report that begins a new page every time there is a new value in the BillingCity column. In addition, the value of the BillingCity column appears at the top of each report page.

The following illustration shows the dataset used in the Customer-Invoice Report. The first 13 rows have a value of Axelburg for the BillingCity column. Therefore, Axelburg appears at the top of Page 1 of the report. All the rows with Axelburg in the BillingCity column will be on Page 1 of the report.

Groupings on the Customer-Invoice Report

Page Grouping on BillingCity	Table Grouping on Name		Dataset			
			BillingCity	Name	InvoiceNumber	InvoiceDate	TotalAmount
	Bolimite, Mfg		Axelburg	Bolimite, Mfg	73041	11-08-2005	438.00
			Axelburg	Bolimite, Mfg	73054	12-08-2005	776.00
			Axelburg	Bolimite, Mfg	73067	12-22-2005	46.00
	Everlast Plastics		Axelburg	Everlast Plastics	73078	12-22-2005	76.00
	Landmark, Inc.		Axelburg	Landmark, Inc.	73043	11-08-2005	243.00
Page 1: Axelburg			Axelburg	Landmark, Inc.	73056	12-08-2005	736.00
	Moore Company		Axelburg	Moore Company	73046	11-08-2005	256.00
			Axelburg	Moore Company	73059	12-08-2005	24.00
	Quincy, Mfg		Axelburg	Quincy, Mfg	73048	11-08-2005	234.00
			Axelburg	Quincy, Mfg	73074	12-22-2005	376.00
	Twillig Companies		Axelburg	Twillig Companies	73045	11-08-2005	732.00
			Axelburg	Twillig Companies	73058	12-08-2005	736.00
			Axelburg	Twillig Companies	73071	12-22-2005	85.00
Page 2: Doveran	Custer, Inc.		Doveran	Custer, Inc.	73049	11-08-2005	273.00
			Doveran	Custer, Inc.	73062	12-08-2005	243.00
			Doveran	Custer, Inc.	73075	12-22-2005	368.00
			Edgewater	Sanders & Son	73042	11-08-2005	834.00

Using the Report Wizard, we put the Name column in the Group area of the table layout. This means the report will create a new group each time the value of the Name column changes. Again, looking at the preceding illustration, you can see the first three rows have a value of Bolimite, Mfg in the Name column. Therefore, these three rows will be combined in the first group on Page 1 of the report.

By checking the Enable Drilldown check box, you told the Report Wizard to create a report where the detail lines for each grouping are initially hidden. The detail lines for a group become visible when the plus sign for that group is clicked. By checking the Include Subtotals check box, you told the Report Wizard to total any numeric columns in the detail and to show those totals in the group header for each group.

Let's look again at the first few rows of the dataset shown in the preceding illustration. The first three rows have a value of Bolimite, Mfg in the Name column. Because of this, these three rows are grouped together for the report shown after Step 18 in Task 3. In this report, the number 1260.0000 appears across from Bolimite, Mfg. This is the total of all the invoices in the detail rows for Bolimite, Mfg.

Because the Report Wizard tried to add up any and all numeric columns, it also created an entry in the grouping for a total of the invoice numbers. Adding up the invoice numbers does not result in a meaningful value, so we deleted this grouping entry in Steps 16 and 17 of this task.

Creating Matrix Reports

You have now seen much of what the Report Wizard can do for you when it comes to tabular reports. Now, let's look at the other report type the Report Wizard can produce for you. Prepare yourself. You are going to enter the matrix.

What Reporting Services calls a matrix report is referred to as a *crosstab* or a *pivot table report* elsewhere. In a tabular report, you have columns from a result set across the top and rows from a result set going down the page. In a matrix report, you have row values going across the top and down the page. Matrix reports are much easier to grasp once you have seen one in action, so let's give it a try.

The Invoice-Batch Number Report

Feature Highlighted

▶ Using the matrix report type

Business Need

The accounting department processes invoices in batches. Once a week, the accounting department creates invoices to send to their customers for the deliveries made over the previous week. A batch number is assigned to each invoice as it is created. All the invoices created on the same day are given the same batch number.

The new report requested by the accounting department shows the total amount of the invoices created in each batch. The report also allows batches to be broken down by billing city and by customer. To allow this type of analysis, you need to use a matrix report.

Task Overview

1. Reopen the Chapter04 Project, Create a New Report in the Chapter04 Project, Select the Shared Data Source, and Create a Dataset
2. Choose the Report Layout

Invoice-Batch Number Report, Task 1: Reopen the Chapter04 Project, Create a New Report in the Chapter04 Project, Select the Shared Data Source, and Create a Dataset

1. If you closed the Chapter04 project, reopen it. (If you need assistance with this, see Task 1 of the previous report.)

2. In the Solution Explorer on the right side of the screen, right-click the Reports folder.

3. Select the Add New Report command from the Context menu. This starts the Report Wizard, enabling you to create an additional report in the current project.

4. Click Next. The Select the Data Source page appears.

5. Make sure the Shared Data Source radio button is selected and the Galactic Data Source is selected in the drop-down list. Click Next.

6. Click Query Builder. The Generic Query Designer appears. Switch to the Graphical Query Designer. (If you need assistance with this, see Task 2 of the previous report.)

7. Right-click in the diagram pane (the upper area) of the Query Designer screen. You see the Diagram Pane Context menu.

8. Select the Add Table command from the Context menu.

9. Add the following tables to the query:
Customer (dbo)
InvoiceHeader (dbo)

10. Click Close to exit the Add Table dialog box.

11. Check the following columns in the Customer table in the order shown here:
BillingCity
Name

12. Check the following columns in the InvoiceHeader table in the order shown here:
BatchNumber
InvoiceNumber
TotalAmount

13. Right-click in the SQL pane and select Execute SQL from the Context menu. The query executes, and the result set is displayed in the results pane. The Query Designer should appear similar to the illustration.

14. Right-click in the results pane. Select Clear Results from the Context menu.
15. Click OK. You return to the Design the Query page.

Task Notes   Your dataset contains the columns we need to create the matrix report. Note, we did not specify any sort order for the dataset. The matrix itself takes care of sorting the dataset and displaying things in the correct order. It presents the data in the rows and in the columns in ascending order.

Invoice-Batch Number Report, Task 2: Choose the Report Layout

1. Click Next. The Select the Report Type page of the Report Wizard appears.
2. Select the Matrix radio button.

3. Click Next. The Design the Matrix page of the Report Wizard appears.

4. Use the Columns button to place the following fields in the Displayed Fields list:
BillingCity
Name

5. Use the Rows button to place the following fields in the Displayed Fields list:
BatchNumber
InvoiceNumber

6. Use the Details button to place the following field in the Displayed Fields list:
TotalAmount

7. Check the Enable Drilldown check box at the bottom of the page. The Design the Matrix page should appear as shown.

8. Click Next. The Choose the Matrix Style page of the Report Wizard appears.

9. Select Generic in the style list and click Next. The Completing the Wizard page appears.

10. Type **Invoice-Batch Number Report** for the report name.

11. Click Finish. The Report Designer window appears.

12. Widen the column on the far right of the matrix, as shown in the illustration.

13. Click the Preview tab. A preview of your report appears.

14. Click the Save All button in the toolbar.

Task Notes   The Invoice-Batch Number Report contains a column for each billing city and a row for each batch number. You need to scroll to the right to see all the columns in the report. The numbers in the matrix are the totals for each batch number in each billing city. For example, $1,903 was invoiced to companies in Axelburg in batch number 445.

The column headings are left-justified, whereas the numeric values are right-justified. This makes the report a bit hard to read. We discuss how to correct these types of formatting issues in Chapter 5.

Clicking the plus sign next to a batch number shows you all the invoices in that batch. If you expand batch number 445, you can see that invoice number 73040 included $938 for companies in Osmar and invoice number 73041 included $438 for companies in Axelburg.

Clicking the plus sign next to a billing city shows you all the customers in that city. If you expand Axelburg, you can see that invoice number 73041 included $438 for Bolimite, Mfg. If you click the minus sign next to batch number 445, you can see that batch number 446 included $776 for Bolimite, Mfg.

Report Parameters

From the users' standpoint, all our sample reports up to this point have been "what you see is what you get." These reports each ran a predetermined query to create the dataset. No user input was requested.

In the real world, this is not the way things work. Most reports require the user to specify some criteria that can help determine what information is ultimately in the report. The user may need to enter a start and an end date, or they may need to select the department or sales region to be included in the report. Users like to have control over their reports, so they receive exactly the information they are looking for. Our next report demonstrates how Reporting Services enables you to get user input by using report parameters.

The Parameterized Invoice-Batch Number Report

Feature Highlighted

▶ Using report parameters

Business Need   The accounting department is pleased with the Invoice-Batch Number Report. Like most users, when they are happy with something, they want to change it. No software or report is ever really completed. It only reaches a resting point until users think of another enhancement.

The accounting department would like to be able to view the Invoice-Batch Number Report for one city at a time. And, they would like to pick the city from a list of all the cities where they have customers. They would also like to specify a start date and an end date, and only view batches that were run between those dates.

We can modify the Invoice-Batch Number Report to include these features. We can add a WHERE clause to the SELECT statement that creates the dataset. Then we can send the user's selections for city, start date, and end date to the WHERE clause using report parameters.

Task Overview

1. Reopen the Chapter04 Project, Open the Invoice-Batch Number Report, and Add Parameters to the Query in the Original Dataset
2. Create a Second Dataset Containing a List of Cities
3. Customize the Report Parameters

Parameterized Invoice-Batch Number Report, Task 1: Reopen the Chapter04 Project, Open the Invoice-Batch Number Report, and Add Parameters to the Query in the Original Dataset

1. If you closed the Chapter04 project, reopen it. (If you need assistance with this, see Task 1 of the Customer-Invoice Report.)
2. If the Invoice-Batch Number Report is open, you are ready to go. If it is not open, double-click the entry for the Invoice-Batch Number Report in the Solution Explorer on the right side of the screen.
3. Click the Data tab. You see the Query Designer screen with the query built for this report while running the Report Wizard.

 NOTE

You can change the size of the Solution Explorer window, the Datasets window, and the other windows around the outside of the Visual Studio window to make more room in the center to create your report. Just click the separator between the windows and drag in the desired direction.

4. Right-click in the diagram pane and select Add Table from the Context menu.
5. The accounting department wants to specify a date range based on the date each batch was run. This date is stored in the InvoiceBatch table. We need to join this table with the InvoiceHeader table. Double-click InvoiceBatch (dbo) in the list of tables. The Graphical Query Designer automatically creates the JOIN for us.

6. Click Close to exit the Add Table dialog box.

7. In the InvoiceBatch table, click the check box next to the RunDate field. This adds RunDate to the criteria pane.

8. Now we can create the portion of the WHERE clause involving the billing city. In the criteria pane, click the cell across from BillingCity and under Filter. The cursor moves to that cell. Type **=@City** and press ENTER. The Graphical Query Designer appears as shown in the following illustration. Notice the SQL statement in the SQL pane now includes a WHERE clause.

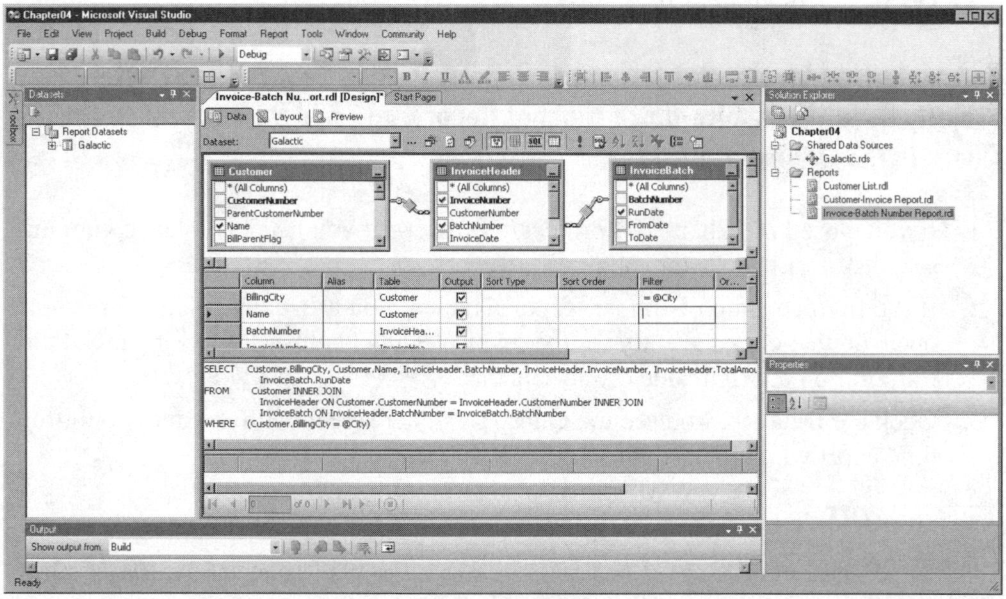

9. Next, we create the portion of the WHERE clause involving the RunDate. Scroll down in the criteria pane until RunDate is visible. Click the cell across from RunDate and under Filter. Type **>= @StartDate AND < @EndDate + 1** and press ENTER. The Query Designer portion of the screen appears as shown in the following illustration. Notice the addition to the WHERE clause in the SQL pane. We discuss why we are using @EndDate + 1 in the task notes.

10. We needed to include RunDate in the WHERE clause, but we do not need to include it in the FIELD LIST of the SELECT statement. Click in the cell across from RunDate and under Output to remove the check mark. The RunDate field is no longer in the FIELD LIST for the SELECT statement in the SQL pane.

11. Right-click in the SQL pane and select Execute SQL from the Context menu.

12. The Query Designer requires values for the three parameters you just created to run the query. You see the Query Parameters dialog box. Enter **Axelburg** for @City, **12/01/2005** for @StartDate, and **12/31/2005** for @EndDate. Click OK.

13. After viewing the result set, right-click in the results pane and select Clear Results from the Context menu.

Task Notes   You have now added three parameters to the WHERE clause of the SELECT statement. Only rows where the City column has a value equal to the value of @City will be displayed in the result set. When you ran the query in the Query Designer just now, you gave the @City parameter a value of Axelburg. Therefore, only rows with Axelburg in the City column were included in the result set.

One of the trickiest things about working with dates in SQL Server is remembering that they consist of both a date and a time. SQL Server does not have columns that are just a date, as in 12/31/2005. SQL Server only has a *datetime* data type, which consists of a date and a time together.

When the invoice batches are run at GDS, the invoicing program assigns both the date and the time the batch was run. For instance, batch 447 was run on 12/31/2005 at 7:54:49 P.M. It has a value of 12/31/2005 7:54:49 PM stored in its RunDate column by the invoicing program.

When a user is asked to enter a date, most of the time they enter the date without a time. When you were asked for a value for @EndDate, you entered 12/31/2005 without any time specified. Because SQL Server only deals with dates and times together, it adds on a time value for you. The default value it uses is 00:00:00 AM or midnight. Remember, midnight is the start of the new day. This means when you're comparing datetime values, midnight is less than any other time occurring on the same day.

Let's think about the comparison created in the WHERE clause involving @EndDate. Assume for a moment that, instead of using RunDate < @EndDate + 1, we used the more obvious RunDate <= @EndDate. When the user enters 12/31/2005 for the end date, they expect the result set to include batches run on 12/31/2005. However, when SQL Server compares the value of RunDate (12/31/2005 7:54:49 PM) with the value of @EndDate (12/31/2005 00:00:00 AM), it finds that RunDate is not less than or equal to @EndDate. This is because 7:54:49 PM, the time portion of RunDate, is greater than 00:00:00 AM, the time portion of @EndDate. Batch 447 would not be included in this result set.

To include batches that occur on the day specified by @EndDate, you need to use RunDate < @EndDate + 1. What this expression does is add one day to the value of @EndDate and check to see if RunDate is less than this calculated value. Let's look at our example with batch 447. This time, SQL Server compares the value of RunDate (12/31/2005 7:54:49 PM) with the calculated value (12/31/2005 00:00:00 AM + 1 day = 1/1/2006 00:00:00 AM). Now it is true that RunDate is less than our calculated value, so batch 447 is included in the result set.

Parameterized Invoice-Batch Number Report, Task 2: Create a Second Dataset Containing a List of Cities

1. The accounting department wants to be able to select a value for the @City parameter from a list of billing cities. You need to create a second dataset in the report that provides that list for the users. Start by selecting <New Dataset...> from the Dataset drop-down list, as shown in the following illustration. The Dataset dialog box appears.

[Screenshot of Microsoft Visual Studio showing the Invoice-Batch Number Report.rdl in Design view with the Data tab selected, showing the Customer, InvoiceHeader, and InvoiceBatch tables, a query grid, and SQL statement.]

2. Type **BillingCities** for the name. The Galactic data source is already selected for you in the Data Source drop-down list, so this does not need to be changed.

NOTE

Make sure you type BillingCities without a space between the two words. Spaces are not allowed in dataset names.

3. Based on what you learned in Chapter 3, we'll compose the query for this dataset without the Query Designer. We want a list of all the billing cities for GDS customers. It also makes sense that each city name should only show up once in the list. Click in the Query string text box and enter the following SQL statement:

```
SELECT DISTINCT BillingCity FROM Customer
```

4. Click OK. You see the Generic Query Designer with the new BillingCities dataset loaded.

Task Notes   Remember, the word DISTINCT means we want SQL Server to remove duplicates for us. To do this, SQL Server automatically sorts the result set. For this reason, you don't need to specify an ORDER BY clause for the SELECT statement.

Parameterized Invoice-Batch Number Report, Task 3: Customize the Report Parameters

1. Click the Layout tab. From the menu, select Report | Report Parameters. The Report Parameters dialog box appears.

2. Make sure City is selected in the Parameters list, then type **Select a City** in the Prompt field. This is the prompt the user sees when running the report.

3. For Available Values, select the From Query radio button. This lets you use the BillingCities dataset to create a drop-down list.

4. From the Dataset drop-down list, select BillingCities.

5. From the Value Field drop-down list, select BillingCity. From the Label Field drop-down list, select BillingCity. The Value Field determines what value is assigned to the parameter. The Label Field determines what the user sees in the drop-down list when selecting a value. In this case, they are one and the same thing.

6. For Default Values, select the Non-Queried radio button.

7. Type **Axelburg** in the text box in the Default Values section. This serves as the default value for the City parameter. The Report Parameters dialog box should now look like this:

8. Click StartDate in the Parameters list.

9. Select DateTime from the Data Type drop-down list.

10. Type **Enter a Start Date** in the Prompt field.

11. Click EndDate in the Parameters list.

12. Select DateTime from the Data Type drop-down list.

13. Type **Enter an End Date** in the Prompt field.

14. Click OK. You will return to the Report Designer.

15. Click the Preview tab.

16. The prompts for the three report parameters appear at the top of the preview area. No report is displayed until a value is entered for each parameter.

17. Axelburg is selected from the Select a City drop-down list because you made this the default. Type or use the date picker to select **12/01/2005** for Enter a Start Date. Type or use the data picker to select **12/31/2005** for Enter an End Date.

18. Click View Report. The report, based on the parameter values you entered, now appears. The report, with all the rows and columns expanded, is shown here.

19. Click the Save All button in the toolbar.

Task Notes   Each time you added a parameter to the query in the dataset, the Report Designer created a corresponding report parameter for you. When the report is viewed, the values entered for the report parameters are automatically passed on to the query parameters before the query is executed. In this way, the user can enter information and have it used in the WHERE clause of the SELECT statement to affect the contents of the report.

The Report Parameters dialog box enables you to control the user's interaction with the report parameters. You can change the prompts the user sees. You can specify the data type of a parameter. You can even determine the default value for a parameter.

One of the most powerful features of the Report Parameters dialog box is the capability to create a drop-down list from which the user can select a value for a parameter. In many cases, the user will not know values, such as department codes, part numbers, and so forth without looking them up. This capability to enable the user to select valid values from a list makes the reports much more user-friendly.

Flying Solo

You have now seen what the Report Wizard can do for you. It can provide you with a great starting place for a number of reports. However, the Report Wizard does have its limitations and, in most cases, you need to make additions to the reports it generates before they are ready for the end user. In the next chapter, you begin learning how to make those enhancements. In addition, you learn how to create reports without the aid of the Report Wizard.

Removing the Training Wheels: Building Basic Reports

In Chapter 4, you built your first reports using the Report Wizard. This is like learning to ride your first two-wheeler with the training wheels on. Now it is time for the training wheels to come off, so you can see what this baby can really do! We are going to begin building reports from scratch. We hope these next few chapters provide the handholding you need, and then you can learn to ride sans training wheels without getting skinned knees.

First, we work with the two types of reports you were introduced to in Chapter 4. We begin by building a table report without the use of the Report Wizard. From there, we do the same with a matrix report. After that, we look at two new report types—the chart report and the list report. We end the chapter by working with some of the basic report items that make up each report—namely, the line control, the text box control, and the rectangle control. Along the way, you learn more about the Report Designer that serves as our development platform.

So, the training wheels are off and the wrenches have been put away. Don your helmets; it's time to ride!

Riding Down Familiar Roads

We cover some familiar territory as we begin building reports without the Report Wizard. In Chapter 4, you used the Report Wizard to create table reports (the Customer List Report and the Customer-Invoice Report) and matrix reports (the Invoice-Batch Number Report). We create these types of reports once more but, this time, without the aid of the wizard.

Again, we look at the business needs of Galactic Delivery Services (GDS) and create reports to satisfy those business needs.

The Transport List Report

Features Highlighted

▶ Building a GROUP BY clause using the Graphical Query Designer

▶ Creating a table report from scratch

Business Need   The transport maintenance department at Galactic Delivery Services needs a list of all the transports currently in service. They want this list to be grouped by transport type. The list includes the serial number, the purchase date, and the date the transport was last in for repairs. The list also includes the cargo capacity and range of each transport type.

Task Overview

1. Create the Chapter05 Project, Create a Shared Data Source, and Create a New Report in the Chapter05 Project
2. Create a Dataset
3. Place a Table Item on the Report and Populate It
4. Add Table Grouping and Other Report Formatting

Transport List Report, Task 1: Create the Chapter05 Project, Create a Shared Data Source, and Create a New Report in the Chapter05 Project

1. Run the Business Intelligence Development Studio or Visual Studio 2005. The Start page is displayed (or select File | Close Project from the menu if a solution is already open).
2. Click New Project to create a new project. This displays the New Project dialog box. (Remember, you can create a new project in three different ways: Select File | New | Project from the Main menu, click the New Project toolbar button, or click the Create Project link on the Start page. All these actions achieve the same result.)
3. Click the Report Server Project icon in the Templates area of the New Project dialog box. (Be sure to click the Report Server Project icon and *not* the Report Server Project Wizard icon.)
4. Type **Chapter05** for the project name. This project will contain all the reports you create in this chapter.
5. Click Browse to open the Project Location dialog box.
6. Click My Projects to go to the Visual Studio Projects folder.

7. In the list of folders, double-click the MSSQLRS folder.

8. Click Open in the lower-right corner of the Project Location dialog box. The New Project dialog box should now look like this:

9. Click OK in the New Project dialog box. A new project is created.

10. In the Solution Explorer on the right side of the screen, right-click the Shared Data Sources folder. Select Add New Data Source from the Context menu, as shown here.

11. Type **Galactic** for Name. Click Edit. The Connection Properties dialog appears.

12. Type the name of the Microsoft SQL Server database server hosting the Galactic database or select it from the drop-down list. If the Galactic database is hosted by the computer you are currently working on, you may type **(local)** for the server name.

13. Click the Use SQL Server Authentication radio button.

14. Type **GalacticReporting** for the user name.

15. Type **gds** for the password.

16. Click the Save My Password check box.

17. Select Galactic from the Select the Database on the Server drop-down list.

18. Click Test Connection. If the message Test Connection Succeeded appears, click OK. If an error message appears, make sure the name of your database server, the user name, the password, and the database are entered properly. If your test connection still does not succeed, make sure you have correctly installed the Galactic database.

19. Click OK to exit the Connection Properties dialog box. Click OK again to exit the Shared Data Source dialog box. A new shared data source called Galactic.rds is created in the Chapter05 project.

20. In the Solution Explorer, right-click the Reports folder.

21. Put your mouse pointer over Add in the Context menu and wait for the submenu to appear. Select the New Item command from the Context menu, as shown here.

22. The Add New Item - Chapter05 dialog box appears. Make sure the Report icon is selected in the Templates area. Enter **TransportList** for the name.

Add New Item - Chapter05	? X

Categories:

.... Report Project

Templates:

Visual Studio installed templates

Report Wizard   Report   Data Source

GDSReport

My Templates

Create a new empty report.

Name: TransportList

Add   Cancel

23. Click Add. A new report called TransportList.rdl is created in the Chapter05 project. You are taken to the Data tab of this new report.

24. Select <New Dataset…> from the Dataset drop-down list. The Dataset dialog box appears.

25. Enter **TransportList** for the dataset's name in the Dataset dialog box.

NOTE

The dataset name must not contain any spaces.

26. Galactic (shared) is selected as the data source by default. Click OK. You return to the Data tab, which now displays the Generic Query Designer. We use the Generic Query Designer in Chapter 6. For now, we switch to the Graphical Query Designer and all the helpful tools it provides.

27. Click the Generic Query Designer button in the Data tab toolbar as shown in the following illustration. This unselects the Generic Query Designer and switches to the Graphical Query Designer.

Task Notes   Because we are creating several reports in the Chapter05 project, all of which select data from the Galactic database, we began by creating a shared data source. This saves us time as we create each of the reports. We continue this practice throughout the remaining chapters.

In Steps 20 and 21, we are adding a report to the project. In Chapter 4, you saw that selecting Add New Report from the Context menu causes the new report to be created with the Report Wizard. In this chapter, we are looking to build our reports from scratch, which is why we used Add New Item in Step 21.

Transport List Report, Task 2: Create a Dataset

1. Right-click in the diagram pane (the upper area) of the Graphical Query Designer screen. Select Add Table from the Context menu.

2. Add the following tables to the query:
   Transport (dbo)
   TransportType (dbo)
   Repair (dbo)

3. Click Close to exit the Add Table dialog box.

4. Right-click the diamond on the connection between the Transport table and the Repair table. Select the Select All Rows from Transport item from the Context menu. You may need to rearrange the TransportType table, the Transport table, and the Repair table to see this diamond.

5. Check the following columns in the TransportType table:
   Description
   CargoCapacity
   Range

6. Check the following columns in the Transport table:
   SerialNumber
   PurchaseDate
   RetiredDate

7. Check the following column in the Repair table:
   BeginWorkDate

8. In the criteria pane (the second area from the top), type **1** in the Sort Order column across from the Description field and type **2** in the Sort Order column across from the SerialNumber field.

9. The business need for this report states it is to include only active transports. That means we only want to include transports that do not have a retired date. Type **IS NULL** in the Filter column across from the RetiredDate field. Remove the check mark under the Output column across from the RetiredDate field.

10. Right-click in the SQL pane (the third area from the top) and select Execute SQL from the Context menu. In the results pane (the bottom area), notice that several records appear for serial number P-348-23-4532-22A.

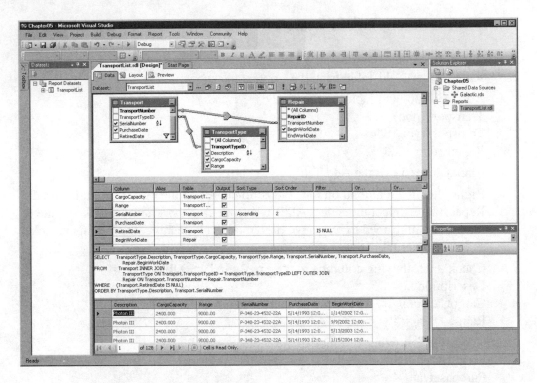

NOTE

You can also run the query by clicking the Run button (the one with a red exclamation point) in the Graphical Query Designer toolbar. The Graphical Query Designer toolbar is directly below the Data, Layout, and Preview tabs.

11. Right-click in the diagram pane of the Graphical Query Designer screen. Select Add Group By from the Context menu. A new column called Group By is added to the criteria pane.

12. In the criteria pane, click in the Group By column across from BeginWorkDate.

13. Use the drop-down list in this cell to select Max, as shown here.

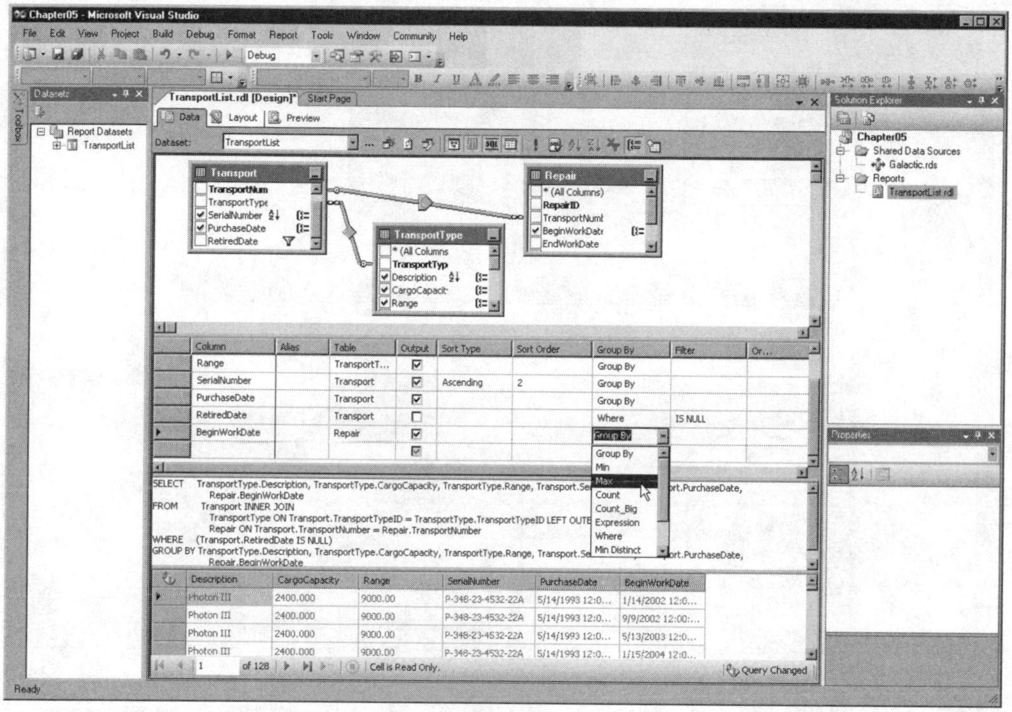

14. When you move your cursor out of the Group By column, Expr1 will be assigned as the alias for BeginWorkDate. Replace Expr1 with LatestRepairDate in the Alias column across from BeginWorkDate.

15. Right-click in the SQL pane and select Execute SQL from the Context menu. Notice that now only one record appears for serial number P-348-23-4532-22A.

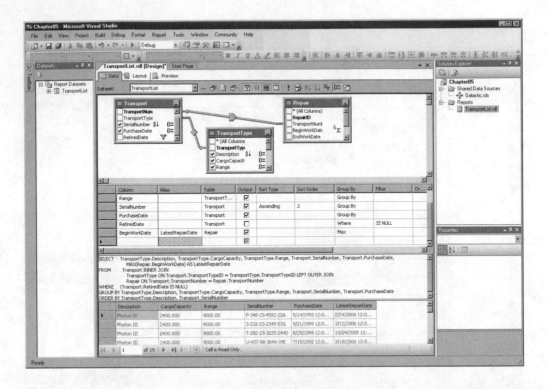

Task Notes   The relationship between the Transport table and the Repair table is a one-to-many relationship. One transport may have many repairs. When you join these two tables, you get one record in the result set for each match between records in the Transport table and the Repair table. Because transport P-348-23-4532-22A has been in for repairs ten times, it generates ten records in the result set.

This is not exactly what the business requirements call for. Instead, we want to have one for transport P-348-23-4532-22A with the latest repair date. To accomplish this, we use the GROUP BY clause. In Step 11, we instruct the Graphical Query Designer to group together records in the result set that have the same value.

When you use the GROUP BY clause, all the fields in the FIELD LIST must fit into one of the following two categories:

▶   The field must be included in the GROUP BY clause.

▶   The field must be enclosed in an aggregate function.

Any fields with the words "Group By" in the Group By column are included in the GROUP BY clause. These fields also have a special Group By symbol next to them in the diagram pane. By selecting Max under the Group By column, as we did in Step 13, we enclose BeginWorkDate in the MAX() aggregate function. This returns the maximum BeginWorkDate (in other words, the latest repair date) for each transport. Note, a special symbol, the Greek letter sigma, next to the BeginWorkDate field in the diagram pane to signify it is enclosed in an aggregate function.

When the BeginWorkDate field is enclosed in the MAX() aggregate function, it becomes a calculated field. It is not simply the value of the BeginWorkDate field that is returned as a column in the result set. Instead, it is a calculation using the value of the BeginWorkDate field that makes up this column of the result set. The Graphical Query Designer needs a name for this calculated column. This is known as the *alias* for the column. By default, the Graphical Query Designer assigns a calculated column an alias of Expr1 or something similar. To better remember what is in this result set column when the time comes to use it in a report, we changed the alias to LatestRepairDate.

Transport List Report, Task 3:
Place a Table Item on the Report and Populate It

1. Click the Layout tab to begin working on the report layout.

NOTE

Your installation of the Report Designer may be using a feature called Auto-Hide with the Toolbox. Auto-Hide is used to provide more screen space for your report layout. When Auto-Hide is active for the Toolbox, the Toolbox is only represented on the screen by a tab containing a tool icon and the word "Toolbox" at the extreme left side of the window. To view the actual Toolbox, place your mouse pointer on top of this tab. After a second or two, the Toolbox appears. Once your mouse pointer moves off the Toolbox, it is automatically hidden again.

2. Click the Table report item in the Toolbox. The mouse pointer changes to a table icon and crosshairs when you move your mouse pointer over the report layout area, as shown in the next illustration.

3. Click-and-drag the mouse over the lower three-quarters of the report layout area, as shown in the following illustration. Note, when you begin dragging, the mouse pointer changes back to the usual arrow icon.

4. When you release the mouse button, after dragging, a table is created to occupy the area you just defined. By default, every cell in the table is occupied by an empty text box. Click in each cell of the table, and note the name and type of report item shown at the top of the Properties window.

5. Let's take a few moments to go over the methods for selecting various parts of the table. You have already seen how to select individual cells. The gray border on top of and to the left of the table item provides handles for selecting other parts of the table. Click any of the gray rectangles in the border above the table item. This action selects the corresponding column, as shown in the following illustration.

6. Click any of the gray rectangles in the border to the left of the table item. This action selects a row, as shown here.

7. Click the gray square in the upper-left corner of the border. This action selects the entire table. When the entire table is selected, the gray border is replaced by the sizing handles (the small white squares) for the table. You must select the entire table before you can move and size the table item.

8. In the Datasets window, expand the TransportList dataset. Drag the SerialNumber field from the Datasets window and drop it on the middle-left table cell. An expression that returns the value of the SerialNumber field is placed in the text box that occupies the middle-left table cell. The name of the field is used to create a column heading. This is placed in the upper-left table cell.

9. Drag the PurchaseDate field from the Datasets window and drop it on the center table cell. Drag the LatestRepairDate field from the Datasets window and drop it on the middle-right table cell. The report layout should now appear, as shown next.

Serial Number	Purchase Date	Latest Repair Date
=Fields!SerialNumber.Value	=Fields!PurchaseDate.Value	=Fields!LatestRepairDate.Value
	Footer	

10. Select the header row (the top row) by clicking the gray rectangle in the border to the left of the row.

11. Make the following changes in the Properties window:

Property	New Value
FontWeight (expand the Font property to find the FontWeight property)	Bold
TextDecoration	Underline

12. In the gray border to the left of the table, click the line between the header row and the detail row. Drag it to reduce the height of the header row.

13. In the gray border to the left of the table, click the line between the detail row and the footer row. Drag it to reduce the height of the detail row.

14. Click the center cell in the table. Hold down SHIFT and click the middle-right cell in the table. Both of these cells are now selected. Make the following changes in the Properties window:

Property	New Value
Format	MM/dd/yyyy
TextAlign	Left

NOTE

Make sure you use uppercase letter Ms in the Format property. MM is the placeholder for month in a format string, whereas mm is the placeholder for milliseconds.

15. Click the Preview tab to preview the report. The report should appear as shown here.

```
Start Page  TransportList.rdl [Design]*                              ▼ ✕
  Data  | Layout | Preview

  [toolbar]  1  of 1         100%                  Find | Next
```

Serial Number	Purchase Date	Latest Repair Date
P-348-23-4532-22A	05/14/1993	02/24/2006
S-232-23-2345-53G	09/21/1999	03/12/2006
T-282-23-3225-244D	08/25/1999	10/24/2005
U-437-98-3849-39E	07/15/2002	03/18/2006
W-283-48-2384-23B	10/23/2004	11/24/2005
X-238-32-3254-24C	04/13/2000	01/19/2006
Y-833-23-6454-35C	11/01/2000	11/17/2005
3809393848	09/23/2003	04/14/2006
8292932983	04/13/2003	12/01/2005
8393939399	04/24/2002	10/11/2005
8439398493	10/17/2001	02/10/2006
8739839848	09/13/2004	02/04/2006
8939874848	12/03/2001	02/02/2006

Task Notes   In the Properties window are several instances where a group of related properties are combined under a summary property. For instance, the FontStyle, FontFamily, FontSize, and FontWeight properties are combined under the Font property. The Font property serves as a summary of the other four.

Initially, only the summary property is visible in the Properties window. A plus (+) sign to the left of a property tells you it is a summary property and has several detail properties beneath it. The summary property has a value that concatenates the values of all the detail properties underneath it.

For example, suppose the FontStyle, FontFamily, FontSize, and FontWeight properties have the following values:

FontStyle:	Normal
FontFamily:	Arial
FontSize:	10pt
FontWeight:	Bold

In that case, the Font property has this value:

Font:	Normal, Arial, 10pt, Bold

You can change the value of a detail property by editing the concatenated values in the summary property, or you can expand the summary property and edit the detail properties directly.

Transport List Report, Task 4: Add Table Grouping and Other Report Formatting

1. Click the Layout tab.
2. Right-click the gray border to the left of the table. You may need to click on the table to get the borders to appear. Select Insert Group from the Context menu. The Grouping and Sorting Properties dialog box appears.
3. Enter **TransportType** for the name (no spaces are allowed in the Name field).
4. Select =Fields!Description.Value from the drop-down list in the first row under Expression. You have to click in this cell to get the drop-down list to appear.
5. Uncheck the Include Group Footer check box.
6. Click OK. A new blank row is added to the table below the header row. This is the grouping row.
7. Click the leftmost cell in the grouping row. Hold down SHIFT, and then click the center and the rightmost cells in the grouping row. Right-click in any of the selected cells and select Merge Cells from the Context menu, as shown here.

Serial Number	Purchase Date	Latest Repair Date
=Fields!SerialNumber.Value	=Fields!PurchaseDate.Value	=Fields!LatestRepairDate.Value

Merge Cells
Select 'table1'
Select 'Body'
Cut
Copy
Paste
Delete
Expression...
Properties

8. Right-click in the newly merged field and select Expression from the Context menu. The Edit Expression dialog box appears.

9. Type the following after the equals sign (=), including the quotation marks and the space after the ampersand, in the Expression area:

```
"Transport Type: " &
```

10. Select the Fields (TransportList) entry in the tree view as shown here. Note, the fields in the TransportList dataset appear in the lower-right list box.

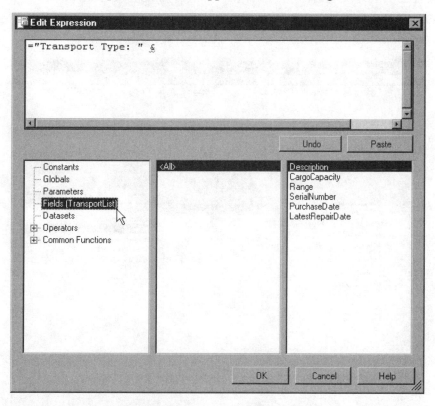

11. Double-click the Description field to append it to the expression in the Expression area.

CAUTION

If you type the field expression, rather than selecting it from the Fields area, it must be typed in the exact case shown in the Fields area. Fields, as well as parameters, are case-sensitive when used in expressions.

12. Type the following at the end of the expression in the Expression area:

```
& vbCrLf & "     Cargo Capacity: " &
```

A space must be before and after each ampersand (&) character.

13. Double-click the CargoCapacity field to append it to the expression in the Expression area.

14. Type the following at the end of the expression in the Expression area:

```
& "  Range: " &
```

A space must be before and after each ampersand (&) character.

15. Double-click the Range field to append it to the expression in the Expression area. The Edit Expression dialog box should appear.

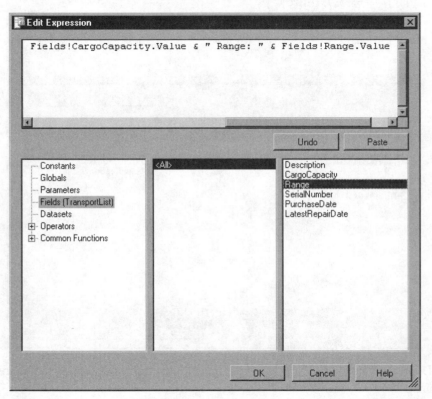

16. Click OK.

17. With the merged field still selected, make the following changes in the Properties window:

Property	New Value
BorderStyle/Bottom (expand the BorderStyle property to find the Bottom property)	Solid
FontWeight	Bold

18. Click the Textbox report item in the Toolbox. The mouse pointer changes to a text box icon and crosshairs when you move your mouse pointer over the report layout area.

19. Click-and-drag the mouse over the entire area above the table on the report layout area. Note, when you begin dragging, the mouse pointer changes back to the usual arrow icon.

20. When you release the mouse button, after dragging, a text box is created to occupy the area you just defined. Click the text box and type the following:

```
Transport List
```

21. With the text box still selected, make the following changes in the Properties window:

Property	New Value
FontSize	16pt
FontWeight	Bold
TextAlign	Center

22. Click the Preview tab. The report should appear as shown here.

Serial Number	Purchase Date	Latest Repair Date
Transport Type: Photon III		
Cargo Capacity: 2400.000 Range: 9000.00		
P-348-23-4532-22A	05/14/1993	02/24/2006
S-232-23-2345-53G	09/21/1999	03/12/2006
T-282-23-3225-244D	08/25/1999	10/24/2005
U-437-98-3849-39E	07/15/2002	03/18/2006
W-283-48-2384-23B	10/23/2004	11/24/2005
X-238-32-3254-24C	04/13/2000	01/19/2006
Y-833-23-6454-35C	11/01/2000	11/17/2005
Transport Type: Star Lifter		
Cargo Capacity: 5000.000 Range: 18000.00		
3809393848	09/23/2003	04/14/2006
8292932983	04/13/2003	12/01/2005
8393939399	04/24/2002	10/11/2005
8439398493	10/17/2001	02/10/2006

Transport List — TransportList.rdl [Design]*

23. Click Save All in the toolbar.

Task Notes When we added the grouping, we specified an expression in Step 4. This group expression determines when a new group header is placed in the report. In the Transport List report, we used the Description field from the TransportType table in the group expression. Because our first sort in the dataset was on the TransportType.Description column, all the Photon III transports came first in the dataset, followed by the StarLifter transports, and, finally, the Warp Hauler transports. Each time the value of the group expression changes, a new group header is added to the report.

Be sure you do not confuse the grouping in the report with the GROUP BY clause we used in SQL SELECT statements. The SQL GROUP BY clause takes a number of records and combines them into a single record in the result set. The grouping in the report takes a number of records in the dataset and surrounds them with a group header and/or group footer when they are output in the report.

In Steps 9–15, we combined all the fields that need to be in the group header into one expression. This was done so we could create a multiline group header, and also to concatenate or combine the labels (Transport Type:, Cargo Capacity:, and Range:) and the contents of the three fields (Description, CargoCapacity, and Range) into one string. The three columns of the group header were merged together to create room for the resulting expression. The Visual Basic concatenation operator (&) is used to combine the values into one long string. The Visual Basic constant vbCrLf is used to put a carriage return and linefeed in the middle of the string. This causes everything following the carriage return and linefeed to be placed on the next line down, giving us a two-line group header.

Remember, table cells are always occupied by a report item. If no other report item has been placed in a cell, the cell is occupied by a text box. When multiple cells are merged, the report item in the leftmost cell expands to fill the merged table cell. The report items in the other cells involved in the merge are automatically deleted.

We created a border on the bottom of the text box in the merged cells to underline our group heading. This is easier and more efficient than adding a Line report item to the report to get the same result. This is especially true when you are trying to underline something in the middle of a table, such as our group header.

When you typed the text in Step 20, it looked like you were entering the text directly into the text box. What you *were* doing is changing the Value property of the text box. You can change the Value property of a text box by typing directly into the text box in the report layout area or by using the Properties window.

In addition, the Edit Expression dialog box can be used to change the Value property of a text box, as well as many other report item properties. In Step 8, we used the Context menu to bring up the Edit Expression dialog box. The Edit Expression dialog box can also be accessed through a drop-down list in the Properties window, as this illustration shows. In addition to the Value property of the text box, the Edit Expression dialog box can be used to change a number of properties of various report items. We discuss this in more detail in Chapter 7.

You probably noticed a red, jagged line that appears occasionally below the expression as you typed it in the Edit Expression dialog box. If you have ever used Microsoft Word, then you know this means something is wrong with the text you have typed. In Word, this red line indicates a spelling error. In the Edit Expression dialog box, this means a problem exists with the syntax of your expression. Hovering over the red line provides you with a brief description of the problem.

Data Regions

The table item is one of four special report items designed specifically for working with datasets. These special report items are called *data regions*. The other data regions are the matrix, the list, and the chart.

Data regions are able to work with multiple records from a dataset. The data region reads a record from the dataset, creates a portion of the report using the data found in that record, and then moves on to the next record. It does this until all the records from the dataset have been processed.

In the report you just completed, you saw how the table data region creates a detail row for each record in the dataset. The matrix data region creates both rows and columns based on the contents of the dataset. You see this demonstrated in our next report. The list data region is not limited to rows and columns. It creates a whole section, perhaps a whole page, for each record in the dataset. We create a report using a list data region later in this chapter. The chart data region creates elements on a graph for each record in a dataset. We create a report using a chart data region in Chapter 6.

Each data region item has a property called DataSetName. This property contains the name of the dataset used by the data region. In the Transport List report you just created, the DataSetName property of the table has the value TransportList (see the following illustration). Visual Basic automatically set this property for you when you placed the first field, the SerialNumber field, in the table. Because the SerialNumber field is from the TransportList dataset and because the table's DataSetName property was empty, Visual Basic put the value TransportList into the DataSetName property.

Now let's move down the road a little further and create a matrix report without the wizard.

The Repair Count By Type Report

Features Highlighted

▶ Creating a matrix report from scratch

▶ Using a specialized property dialog box

Business Need   GDS needs to purchase several new transports to update their delivery fleet. The company must decide which type of transport to purchase. One factor in the decision is the amount of time the new transports will spend in the maintenance hanger for repairs and preventative maintenance.

Upper management has asked the GDS maintenance department to provide a report showing the number of each type of repair required by each type of transport. The report should include statistics from all transports, both active and retired. Also, the report should group the repairs by their cause.

Task Overview

1. Reopen the Chapter05 Project, Create a New Report in the Chapter05 Project, Select the Shared Data Source, and Create a Dataset
2. Place a Matrix Item on the Report and Populate It
3. Add Column Grouping and Other Report Formatting

Repair Count By Type Report, Task 1: Reopen the Chapter05 Project, Create a New Report in the Chapter05 Project, Select the Shared Data Source, and Create a Dataset

1. If you closed the Chapter05 project, reopen it.
2. In the Solution Explorer on the right side of the screen, right-click the Reports folder.
3. Put your mouse pointer over Add in the Context menu and wait for the submenu to appear. Select New Item from the Context menu. This displays the Add New Item Chapter05 dialog box.
4. Make sure the Report icon is selected in the Templates area. Enter **RepairCountByType** for the name.
5. Click Add. A new report called RepairCountByType.rdl is created in the Chapter05 project. You are taken to the Data tab of this new report.
6. Select <New Dateset...> from the Dataset drop-down list. The Dataset dialog box appears.
7. Enter **RepairsByType** for the name in the Dataset dialog box.
8. Galactic (shared) is selected for the data source by default. Click OK. You return to the Data tab, which now displays the Generic Query Designer.
9. Click the Generic Query Designer button to switch to the Graphical Query Designer.
10. Right-click in the diagram pane of the Graphical Query Designer screen. Select Add Table from the Context menu.
11. Add the following tables to the query:
    Repair (dbo)
    Transport (dbo)
    TransportType (dbo)
    RepairWorkDoneLink (dbo)
    WorkDone (dbo)
    RepairCause (dbo)
12. Click Close to exit the Add Table dialog box.

13. Check the following column in the Repair table:
    RepairID

14. Check the following column in the TransportType table:
    Description

15. In the criteria pane, type **TypeOfTransport** in the Alias column in the
    Description row.

16. Check the following column in the WorkDone table:
    Description

17. In the criteria pane, type **TypeOfWork** in the Alias column in the Description
    row for the WorkDone table.

18. Check the following column in the RepairCause table:
    Description

19. In the criteria pane, type **RepairCause** in the Alias column in the Description
    row for the RepairCause table.

20. Type **1** in the Sort Order column for RepairCause. Type **2** in the Sort Order
    column for TypeOfWork.

21. Right-click in the SQL pane and select Execute SQL from the Context menu.
    The Graphical Query Designer should appear similar to this:

Task Notes   Although this report is a pretty straightforward request, we need to link together a number of tables to collect the necessary data. What we are interested in is repairs, so we start with the Repair table. However, none of the fields we need in the result set are in the Repair table. To find the type of transport being repaired, we need to join the Transport table with the Repair table, and then join the TransportType table to the Transport table. To find the type of work done, we need to join the RepairWorkDoneLink table to the Repair table, and then join the WorkDone table to the RepairWorkDoneLink table. Finally, to group by the cause of the repair, we need to join the RepairCause table to the Repair table. If you get confused by all of this, refer to Figure 3-23 in Chapter 3.

Repair Count By Type Report, Task 2: Place a Matrix Item on the Report and Populate It

1. Click the Layout tab to begin working on the report layout.

2. Click the Matrix report item in the Toolbox. The mouse pointer changes to a matrix icon and crosshairs when you move your mouse pointer over the report layout area.

3. Click-and-drag the mouse over the lower three-quarters of the report layout.

4. When you release the mouse button, after dragging, a matrix is created to occupy the area you just defined. By default, every cell in the matrix is occupied by an empty text box.

5. In the Datasets window, expand the RepairsByType dataset. Drag the TypeOfTransport field from the Datasets window and drop it on the cell containing the word "Columns." The values in this column in the dataset determine the columns in the matrix report.

6. Drag the TypeOfWork field from the Datasets window and drop it on the cell containing the word "Rows." The values in this column in the dataset determine the rows in the matrix report.

7. Drag the RepairID field from the Datasets window and drop it on the cell containing the word "Data."

8. In the cell where you just dropped the RepairID field, change Sum to Count, so the contents of the cell appear as follows:

   ```
   =Count(Fields!RepairID.Value)
   ```

9. With this cell still selected, change the following property:

Property	New Value
TextAlign	Center

10. Reduce the width and height of the columns in the matrix. When you finish, your report design should look similar to this:

11. Click the Preview tab. Your report should look similar to the following illustration. The rows and columns in your report may appear in a different order from those shown here.

	Warp Hauler	Star Lifter	Photon III
Repair Control Systems	4	0	1
Replace Hatch	2	2	0
Replace Hatch Seal	2	2	1
Repair Hatch	1	0	1
Repair Plating	0	1	2
Replace Plating	2	2	0
Repair Landing Strut	0	1	1
Replace Landing Strut	1	0	1
Replace Fiber Optic Cable	0	0	1
Replace Viewport	0	2	0
Clean Antimatter Fields	0	32	0
Flush Neutron Emitters	49	0	0
Rotate Injector Heads	0	0	44

Task Notes   Because the matrix report always groups a number of records from the dataset to create the entries in the matrix, the field that supplies the data for the matrix must be enclosed in some type of aggregate function. If the field placed in the data cell is a number, Report Designer encloses the field in the SUM() aggregate function.

The RepairID field, which we placed in the data cell in Step 7, is a number. However, it does not make sense to add up the RepairIDs. Instead, we want to count the number of RepairIDs. For this reason, we changed the SUM() aggregate function to the COUNT() aggregate function.

Repair Count By Type Report, Task 3: Add Column Grouping and Other Report Formatting

1. Click the Layout tab to return to the report layout.

2. Click the cell in the upper-right corner of the matrix and change the following properties:

Property	New Value
FontWeight	Bold
TextDecoration	Underline

3. Click the square in the upper-left corner of the gray border to select the matrix item.

4. In the Properties window, click the Property Pages button shown in the following illustration. The Matrix Properties dialog box appears.

5. Click the Groups tab.

6. In the Rows area, click Add. The Grouping and Sorting Properties dialog box appears.

7. Next you set up your matrix for drilldown. Replace matrix1_RowGroup2 with matrix1_RepairCause for the name. Select Fields!RepairCause.Value from the drop-down list in the first row under Expression. Click OK.

8. In the Rows area, click Up to move matrix1_RepairCause to the top of the list. Click the matrix1_TypeOfWork entry. Click Edit in the Rows area. The Grouping and Sorting Properties dialog box appears.

9. Click the Visibility tab. Set the Initial Visibility to Hidden. Click the Visibility Can Be Toggled by Another Report Item check box. Select textbox2 from the Report Item drop-down list. (If textbox2 is not in the drop-down list, type **textbox2** for the Report item value.)

10. Click OK in the Grouping and Sorting Properties dialog box. Click OK in the Matrix Properties dialog box.

11. Click the cell in the upper-left corner of the matrix and change the following properties:

Property	New Value
FontWeight	Bold
TextDecoration	Underline
Value	Cause/Type of Repair Work

12. Click the Textbox report item in the Toolbox. Click-and-drag the mouse over the area above the matrix on the report layout area. When you release the mouse button, after dragging, a text box is created to occupy the area you just defined. Click the text box and type the following:

```
Repair Count By Type Report
```

13. With the text box still selected, make the following changes in the Properties window:

Property	New Value
FontSize	16pt
FontWeight	Bold
TextAlign	Center

14. Your report layout should appear similar to the illustration.

◆ Body

Repair Count By Type Report

Cause/Type of Repair Work		=Fields!Type
=Fields!RepairCause.Value	=Fields!TypeOfWork.Value	=Count(Fields

15. Click the Preview tab. The report should appear as follows.

NOTE

If the report displays an error message mentioning textbox2 when you preview the report, then textbox2 was not the name assigned to the text box containing the RepairCause group label. Return to the Layout tab and select the text box containing the =Fields!RepairCause.Value expression. Look at the Name property in the Properties window. Return to the drop-down list you populated in Step 9 of this task and replace textbox2 with this name. Click OK to exit the dialog boxes and preview the report again.

RepairCountByType.rdl [Design]*   Start Page   ▼ ✕

📄 Data   📝 Layout   🔍 Preview

⬚ ¶₁ | ◀ ◀ 1   of 1 ▶ ▶ | ← ⊘ 🔄 | 🖨 🔍 🔚▾ | 100%   ▾ | Find | Next

Repair Count By Type Report

Cause/Type of Repair Work	Warp Hauler	Star Lifter	Photon III
⊞ Docking Crash-No Fault	3	2	0
⊞ Docking Crash-Pilot Fault	4	0	3
⊞ Landing Crash-No Fault	2	2	0
⊞ Landing Crash-Pilot Fault	0	0	4
⊞ Midair Collision-No Fault	3	0	1
⊞ Midair Collision-Pilot Fault	0	6	0
⊞ Scheduled Maintenance	49	32	44

16. Click Save All in the toolbar.

Task Notes   The Property Pages button in the Properties window provides an alternative way to change the properties of a report item. This button displays a dialog box that deals specifically with the properties of the selected report item. These specialized property dialog boxes can make it much easier to modify the properties of a report item. You can also access the specialized property dialog boxes by right-clicking a report item and selecting Properties from the Context menu.

New Territory

Now that you have created the table and matrix reports without the aid of the Report Wizard, it is time to venture into new territory. As mentioned previously, the list item is the third type of data region. Just as the table item makes up the main portion of a table report and the matrix item makes up the main portion of a matrix report, the list item is the main part of a list report.

List reports are used when you need to repeat a large area of content—perhaps even an entire page—for each record in the dataset. They are often used to create forms. List reports function similarly to a mail merge in a word processing program such as Microsoft Word.

The Transport Information Sheet

Feature Highlighted

▶   Creating a list report

Business Need   The GDS maintenance department needs an efficient way to look up general information about a particular transport that comes in for repair. The user should be able to select the serial number from a drop-down list and see all the basic information about the transport. This transport information sheet should also include the date of the next scheduled maintenance appointment for this transport.

Task Overview

1.   Reopen the Chapter05 Project, Create a New Report in the Chapter05 Project, Select the Shared Data Source, and Create the TransportSNs Dataset
2.   Create the TransportInfo Dataset
3.   Place a List Item on the Report and Populate It

Transport Information Sheet, Task 1: Reopen the Chapter05 Project, Create a New Report in the Chapter05 Project, Select the Shared Data Source, and Create the TransportSNs Dataset

1. If you closed the Chapter05 project, reopen it.

2. In the Solution Explorer on the right side of the screen, right-click the Reports folder. Select Add | New Item. This displays the Add New Item Chapter05 dialog box.

3. Make sure the Report icon is selected in the Templates area. Enter **TransportInfoSheet** for the name. Click Add.

4. Select <New Dataset…> from the Dataset drop-down list. The Dataset dialog box appears.

5. Enter **TransportSNs** for the name in the Dataset dialog box.

6. The data source should be Galactic (shared).

7. Enter the following for the query string:

```
SELECT SerialNumber FROM Transport WHERE RetiredDate IS NULL ORDER BY
SerialNumber
```

8. Click OK.

9. Click the Generic Query Designer button to switch to the Graphical Query Designer.

10. Right-click in the SQL pane and select Execute SQL from the Context menu. The bottom two panes of the Graphical Query Designer should appear similar to the illustration.

Task Notes   The TransportSNs dataset provides a list of the serial numbers for all the active transports at GDS. This dataset is used to populate the drop-down list from which the user selects the transport for which the Transport Information Sheet will be printed. Because the query for this dataset is relatively straightforward, it is faster to type the query string by hand rather than build it using the Graphical Query Designer.

This is not the case with the query string for the second dataset required by this report, as you shall see in the next task.

Transport Information Sheet, Task 2: Create the TransportInfo Dataset

1. Select <New Dateset…> from the Dataset drop-down list. The Dataset dialog box appears.

2. Enter **TransportInfo** for the name in the Dataset dialog box. The data source should be Galactic. Click OK.

3. Click the Generic Query Designer button to switch to the Graphical Query Designer.

4. Right-click in the diagram pane of the Graphical Query Designer screen. Select Add Table from the Context menu. Add the following tables to the query:
   Transport (dbo)
   TransportType (dbo)
   ScheduledMaint (dbo)
   Repair (dbo)

5. Click Close to exit the Add Table dialog box.

6. Right-click the link between the Transport and the Repair tables, and then select Remove from the Context menu. (You may have to rearrange the tables in the diagram pane to make this visible.)

7. Right-click the diamond in the middle of the link between the Repair table and the ScheduledMaint table. Select the command Select All Rows from ScheduledMaint in the Context menu.

8. Find the diamond in the middle of the link between the Transport and ScheduledMaint tables. (You may have to rearrange the tables in the diagram pane to make this visible.) Right-click this diamond and choose Select All Rows from Transport from the Context menu. With a bit of rearranging, your screen should look similar to the illustration.

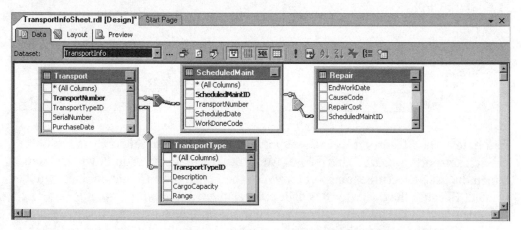

9. Check the following columns in the Transport table:
    SerialNumber
    PurchaseDate

10. Check the following columns in the TransportType table:
    Description
    CargoCapacity
    Range
    Cost
    Crew
    Manufacturer
    ManAddr1
    ManAddr2
    ManCity
    ManState
    ManZipCode
    ManPlanetAbbrv
    ManEmail

11. Check the following column in the ScheduledMaint table:
    ScheduledDate

12. Check the following column in the Repair table:
    RepairID

13. In the criteria pane, type the following in the Filter column for SerialNumber:

    ```
    = @SerialNumber
    ```

14. In the Filter column for RepairID, type this:

    ```
    IS NULL
    ```

15. Right-click in the diagram pane and select Add Group By from the Context menu.

16. In the criteria pane, in the Group By column for ScheduledDate, select Min from the drop-down list.

17. In the Alias column for ScheduledDate, change Expr1 to NextMaintDate.

18. Right-click in the SQL pane and select Execute SQL from the Context menu. Enter **3809393848** for the @SerialNumber parameter and click OK. The Graphical Query Designer should appear similar to the next illustration.

Task Notes The TransportInfo dataset must include all the information about a selected transport. This is not complicated, except for the last item noted in the business need for this report: the date of the next scheduled maintenance for this transport. You need a little background on the way the Galactic database functions regarding scheduled maintenance to understand this query.

Records are added to the ScheduledMaint table for each time a transport needs to come into a maintenance facility for preventative maintenance. These are considered appointments for preventative maintenance. They are scheduled for dates in the future. Transports may have more than one pending preventative maintenance appointment. The ScheduledMaint table records are linked to a transport by the TransportNumber field.

When a transport comes in for preventative maintenance, a record is added to the Repair table. This indicates an appointment for preventative maintenance has been fulfilled. The record in the Repair table is linked to the record in the ScheduledMaint table by the ScheduledMaintID field. If a scheduled appointment is missed, the appointment is rescheduled by changing the value in the ScheduledMaint.Schedule-Date field to a value in the future.

Given these business rules, records in the ScheduledMaint table for a given transport that do not have corresponding records in the Repair table represent pending preventative maintenance appointments. The record that has the minimum value in the ScheduledDate field represents the next appointment. To find this record, we are joining the ScheduledMaint table to the Repair table using a left outer join. Because we require the RepairID to be NULL, our result set only includes the pending appointments (that is, the records in the ScheduledMaint table that do not have a matching record in the Repair table).

Because a transport may have more than one pending appointment, we could end up with more than one record for a given transport. We need to use GROUP BY to consolidate these into one record. The MIN() aggregate function is used to find the ScheduledDate field with the lowest value (that is, the next scheduled appointment).

Transport Information Sheet, Task 3: Place a List Item on the Report and Populate It

1. Click the Layout tab to begin working on the report layout.
2. Select Report | Report Parameters from the menu. The Report Parameters dialog box appears. (The Report menu is only visible when the Report Designer thinks you are making changes to the report. If the Report menu is not visible, click in the body of the report and it reappears.)
3. For the Prompt, change SerialNumber to Serial Number.
4. Select From Query for Available Values.
5. Select TransportSNs from the Dataset drop-down list, if it is not selected by default.
6. Select SerialNumber from the Value Field drop-down list. Select SerialNumber from the Label Field drop-down list as well.
7. Click OK.
8. Move your mouse pointer to the bottom of the white report layout area, so it changes from the regular mouse pointer to the double-headed arrow, as shown in the following illustration. The white report layout area is the body of the report.

9. Drag the bottom of the report body down to create more room to lay out the list report.

10. Select the Toolbox window and click the List report item. The mouse pointer changes to a list icon and crosshairs when you move your mouse pointer over the report layout area.

11. Click-and-drag the mouse over the entire report body.

12. When you release the mouse button, after dragging, a list is created to occupy the area you just defined.

13. Place a text box across the top of the list (inside the list). This will be the title.

14. As an alternative to the Properties window, font and text alignment properties can be set using the items in the Report Formatting toolbar. The Report Formatting toolbar is circled in the following illustration. Use the Report Formatting toolbar to set the properties of the textbox as follows:

Property	Value
FontSize	16pt
FontWeight	Bold
TextAlign	Center

15. Click in the textbox and type **Transport Information Sheet** for the value of the textbox.

16. Place a second text box under the existing title. Type **Serial Number**: in this text box. Size the text box so it just fits this text. This serves as the label for the Serial Number field.

17. In the Datasets window, expand the TransportInfo dataset. Drag the SerialNumber field from the Datasets window and place it to the right of the text box that was added in Step 16. Click the white square to the right-center of the SerialNumber text box and drag it until the text box is approximately twice its original size. Your report layout should appear similar to the illustration.

18. Repeat this operation with each of the following fields, creating a label for the field, and then placing the field to the right of the label. (Hint: you may want to create all the labels first, and then add all the fields, so you are not switching back and forth between the Toolbox window and the Datasets window.)

Label	Field
Purchase Date:	PurchaseDate
Transport Type:	Description
Cargo Capacity:	CargoCapacity
Range:	Range
Cost:	Cost
Crew:	Crew
Next Maint:	NextMaintDate

19. Use either the Report Formatting toolbar or the Properties window to set the properties for these fields as follows (these properties are for the fields themselves, not the labels):

Field	Property	Value
PurchaseDate	Format	MM/dd/yyyy
PurchaseDate	TextAlign	Left
CargoCapacity	TextAlign	Left
Range	TextAlign	Left
Cost	Format	###,###,###.00
Cost	TextAlign	Left
Crew	TextAlign	Left
NextMaintDate	Format	MM/dd/yyyy
NextMaintDate	TextAlign	Left

20. Select the Toolbox window and click on Line. Drag a line across the report layout at the bottom of the Serial Number label and the Serial Number field.

21. Select Rectangle from the Toolbox and drag a rectangle around the unoccupied portion of the report body below the NextMaint fields.

22. Use the Report Borders toolbar, shown here, to set the properties for the border of the Rectangle. Make sure the toolbar items are set to Solid, 1pt, and Black.

Click the Outside Border toolbar button, indicated here by the mouse pointer, to create a solid, 1-point wide, black border on all sides of the rectangle.

23. Select Textbox from the Toolbox and place a text box in the upper-left corner of the rectangle. Type **Manufacturer:** in this text box. This is the manufacturer label.

24. Drag the Manufacturer field from the Datasets window and place it inside the rectangle to the right of the manufacturer label. Size this field until it goes all the way to the right side of the rectangle. If you drag too far to the right, the Report Designer automatically increases the size of the List item and the body of the report. If this happens, simply reduce the size of the rectangle, reduce the width of the List item, and, finally, reduce the width of the body of the report.

25. Place the ManAddr1 and ManAddr2 fields inside the rectangle, below the Manufacturer field. Make these new fields the same size as the Manufacturer field.

26. Place a text box inside the rectangle, directly below the ManAddr2 field. Make this new text box the same size as the ManAddr2 field.

27. Right-click in the text box added in Step 26 and select Expression from the Context menu.

28. Select Fields(TransportInfo).

29. Double-click the ManCity field to add it to the expression at the top of the dialog box.

30. In the Expression area, type the following, including a space before and after each ampersand (&) character after Fields!ManCity.Value:

    & " , " &

31. Double-click the ManState field to add it to the expression.

32. In the Expression area, type the following, including a space before and after each ampersand (&) character after Fields!ManState.Value:

    & " " &

33. Double-click the ManZipCode field.

34. In the Expression area, type the following, including a space before and after each ampersand (&) character after Fields!ManZipCode.Value:

    `& " " &`

35. Double-click the ManPlanetAbbrv field. Make sure no red lines are under any part of your expression indicating a syntax error. Click OK.

36. Drag the ManEmail field from the Datasets window and place it inside the rectangle under the text box added in Step 26. Enlarge this text box. Your report layout should appear similar to this:

37. Click the Preview tab.

38. Select the first serial number from the Serial Number drop-down list and click View Report. Your report should appear similar to the illustration.

```
TransportInfoSheet.rdl [Design]*   Start Page                                    ▾ ✕
  Data    Layout    Preview
Serial Number  3809393848          ▾                                      View Report

       ◄  1    of 1  ►  ◄  ◯  ◢  ◰  ◳  ◳ ▾  100%    ▾              Find | Next
                    Transport Information Sheet

Serial Number:      3809393848
Purchase Date:      09/23/2003
Transport Type:     Star Lifter
Cargo Capacity:     5000.000
Range:              18000.00
Cost:               10,000,000.0
                    0
Crew:               3
Next Maint:         04/14/2007
Manufacturer:       Fly Wright Spaceyards
                    1834 Quay Street
                    Building 7
                    Axelburg, DT 83945 RKM
                    Feedback@FlyWright.RKM
```

39. Click the Save All button in the toolbar.

Task Notes   As you saw in the Transport Information Sheet report, the List item enables you to place information anywhere. Text boxes, lines, and rectangles can be placed anywhere within the List item to create complex forms. This type of report is good for presenting a large amount of information about a single entity, as we did in this report.

As stated earlier, the contents of the List item are repeated for each record in the dataset. The TransportInfo dataset selects only a single record based on the user's selection of a serial number. Therefore, our report only has one page.

The Line report item is used simply to help format the report. It helps separate information on the report to make it easier for the user to understand. When working with the Table report item, we could use the borders of the text boxes in the table cells to create underlines. In the more freeform layout of the List report, the Line report item often works better than using cell borders.

The Rectangle report item serves two purposes. When its border is set to something other than None, it becomes a visible part of the report. Therefore, it can serve to help separate information on the report in the same manner as the Line report item. This is how we are using the Rectangle report item in this report.

The Rectangle report item can also be used to keep together other items in the report. We examine this use of rectangles in Chapter 7.

Getting Graphical

You have now seen three of the four data regions in action. In the next chapter, you learn about the final data region—the chart. We also look at the Image report item and its uses for adding graphics to a report. Finally, in Chapter 6, you learn about ways to control the properties of a report item using Visual Basic expressions.

Graphic Expression: Using Charts and Images in Reports

IN THIS CHAPTER:

Chart Your Course

Image Is Everything

Building Higher

W e live in a world today where image is everything. Color and graphics are used to add interest and convey meaning. This is true not only for TV, newspapers, and magazines, but also for some of the reports you create.

Reports going to managers or executives need to provide the quick, concise communication of charts and graphs. Reports shared with customers need the polish provided by a well-placed image or two. Reporting Services has the tools you need to effectively communicate and impress in each of these situations.

In this chapter, we explore the final data region, the chart, and how it can be used to summarize and express data. We also use the image report item to add graphics to our reports. Finally, we end this chapter by looking at properties that can be used to format the report output and creative ways to control those properties.

Chart Your Course

In many cases, the best way to convey business intelligence is through business graphics. Bar charts, pie charts, and line graphs are useful tools for giving meaning to endless volumes of data. They can quickly reveal trends and patterns to aid in data analysis. They compress lines upon lines of numbers into a format that can be understood in a moment.

In addition, charts can increase the reader's interest in your information. A splash of color excites the reader. Where endless lines of black on white lull people to sleep, bars of red and blue, and pie wedges of purple and green wake people up.

You create charts in Reporting Services using the chart report item. The chart report item is a data region like the table, matrix, and list report items. This means the chart can process multiple records from a dataset. The table, matrix, and list report items enable you to place other report items in a row, a column, or a list area, which is repeated for every record in the dataset. The chart, on the other hand, uses the records in a dataset to create bars, lines, or pie wedges. You cannot place other report items inside a chart item.

In the next sections of this chapter, we explore the many charting possibilities provided by the chart report item.

The Fuel Price Chart

Features Highlighted

- ▶ Creating a report using the chart report item
- ▶ Refining the look of the chart to best present the information

Business Need   Galactic Delivery Services needs to analyze the fluctuations in the price of neutron fuel from month-to-month. The best way to perform this analysis is by creating a chart of the price over time. The user needs to be able to select the year from a drop-down list.

Task Overview

1. Create the Chapter06 Project, a Shared Data Source, a New Report, and Two Datasets
2. Place a Chart Item on the Report and Populate It
3. Refine the Chart

Fuel Price Chart, Task 1: Create the Chapter06 Project, a Shared Data Source, a New Report, and Two Datasets

1. Create a new Reporting Services project called Chapter06 in the MSSQLRS folder. (If you need help with this task, see the section "The Transport List Report" in Chapter 5.)
2. Create a shared data source called Galactic for the Galactic database. (Again, if you need help with this task, see the section "The Transport List Report" in Chapter 5.)
3. Add a blank report called FuelPriceChart to the Chapter06 project. (Do not use the Report Wizard.)
4. Select <New Dataset…> from the Dataset drop-down list. The Dataset dialog box appears.
5. Enter **FuelPrices** for the name in the Dataset dialog box.

6. Galactic will be selected for the data source by default. Click OK. You return to the Data tab, which now displays the Generic Query Designer.

7. Type the following in the SQL pane:

```
SELECT Description AS FuelType,
     PriceStartDate,
     Price
FROM FuelPrice
INNER JOIN Propulsion
     ON FuelPrice.PropulsionID = Propulsion.PropulsionID
WHERE (YEAR(PriceStartDate) = @Year)
AND (Description = 'Neutron')
ORDER BY FuelType, PriceStartDate
```

8. Click the Run button in the Generic Query Designer toolbar to run the query and make sure no errors exist. Correct any typos that may be detected. When the query is correct, the Define Query Parameters dialog box appears. Enter **2005** for the @Year parameter and click OK.

9. The business needs for the report specified the user should select the year from a drop-down list. We need to define a second dataset to populate this drop-down list. Select <New Dataset...> from the Dataset drop-down list. The Dataset dialog box appears.

10. Enter **Years** for the name in the Dataset dialog box.

11. Galactic is selected for the data source by default. Type the following in the Query string area of the dialog box:

```
SELECT DISTINCT YEAR(PriceStartDate) AS Year FROM FuelPrice
```

12. Click OK. The Generic Query Designer now displays the Year dataset. Run the query to make sure it is correct. You see a list of the distinct years from the FuelPrice table.

Task Notes   We created two datasets in the FuelPriceChart report—one to populate the Year drop-down list and the other to provide data for the chart. Only one of these two datasets can be displayed on the Data tab at a time. You use the Dataset drop-down list to switch between the two datasets on the Data tab.

You have undoubtedly noticed that both datasets for this report were created by typing a query, either into the SQL pane of the Generic Query Designer or into the Query string area of the Dataset dialog box. The graphical tools of the Graphical

Query Designer are helpful if you are still learning the syntax of SELECT queries or if you are unfamiliar with the database you are querying. However, it is more efficient to simply type the query into the SQL pane or the Dataset dialog box. In addition, some complex queries must be typed in because they cannot be created through the Graphical Query Designer.

Throughout the remainder of this book, we type our SELECT statements rather than create them using the Graphical Query Designer. This enables us to quickly create the necessary datasets, and then concentrate on the aspects of report creation that are new and different in each report. As you create your own reports, use the interface—Graphical Query Designer or Generic Query Designer—with which you are most comfortable.

Fuel Price Chart, Task 2: Place a Chart Item on the Report and Populate It

1. Switch to the Layout tab.

2. Select Report | Report Parameters from the menu. The Report Parameters dialog box appears.

3. A report parameter called Year has been created to correspond to the @Year parameter from the FuelPrices dataset.

4. Select Available Values: From Query.

5. In the Dataset drop-down list, select Years. Select Year from both the Value Field drop-down list and the Label Field drop-down list. Click OK to exit the Report Parameters dialog box.

6. Click-and-drag the edges of the report layout area, so the layout area fills the available space on the screen.

7. Select the Chart report item in the Toolbox window and place it on the report layout. The chart should cover almost the entire report layout because it will be the only item on the report.

8. The chart has three areas where you can drop fields: Drop Data Fields Here, Drop Series Fields Here, and Drop Category Fields Here. If these areas are not visible, double-click the center of the chart to display them. You may also need to scroll the layout window to see each of the drop areas.

NOTE

If you need to move the chart after you place it in the report layout, click the report layout so the chart is not selected, and then click the chart item so it is selected but the three "Drop fields here" areas are not visible. Now you can click the edge of the chart item to drag it to the appropriate location. Click the chart item one more time to get the three "Drop fields here" areas to reappear.

1. In the Datasets window, expand the FuelPrices dataset entry. Drag the FuelType field and drop it on Drop Series Fields Here.

2. Drag the PriceStartDate field and drop it on Drop Category Fields Here.

3. Drag the Price field and drop it on Drop Data Fields Here.

4. Right-click the chart and select Chart Type | Line | Simple Line from the Context menu. The report layout should appear similar to the following illustration.

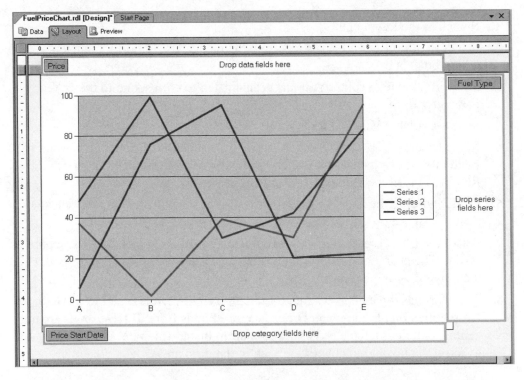

5. Select the Preview tab. Select 2005 from the Year drop-down list, and then click View Report. Your report appears similar to this:

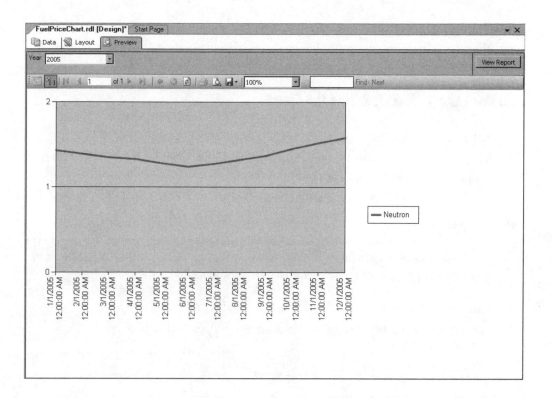

Task Notes   You have now seen how easy it is to create a chart using the chart report item. Simply drag-and-drop the fields from your dataset onto the appropriate locations, select the type of chart you want, and you have a functioning chart. In the next sections, we explore ways to manipulate the properties of the chart to create more complex results.

The field you dropped in the Data Fields area (the Price field in this report) provides the values for the data points. The field you dropped in the Category Fields area (the PriceStartDate field in this report) provides the labels for the x-axis of the chart. This category field also groups the rows from the dataset into multiple categories. One entry is created on the x-axis for each category. In our Fuel Price Chart, we used the PriceStartDate field to create our categories. Because we are looking at data for a single year and because there is one record for each month, we get 12 distinct values for PriceStartDate in our dataset and 12 categories along the x-axis of our chart (one category for each month in the year we are charting).

One series of categories is created for each distinct value in the field you dropped in the Data Series area. Each series is usually charted in its own color: one series in green, one series in blue, and so on. The legend, located to the right in this chart, tells the reader which color has been assigned to each series. Our dataset contains only one fuel type, Neutron. Therefore, we get only one series of data points on our chart.

Now let's use some of the properties of the chart to refine our results.

Fuel Price Chart, Task 3: Refine the Chart

1. Select the Layout tab.
2. Right-click the chart and select Properties from the Context menu. The Chart Properties dialog box will appear.
3. On the General tab, type **Fuel Prices** for Title.

CAUTION

Do not confuse Title with Name. Title contains the text that appears above the chart on the report, whereas Name contains the name of the chart report item itself.

4. Click the Style button (the paint brush and paint pail) next to Title.
5. Set the following properties on the Style Properties dialog box:

Property	Value
Size	14pt
Weight	Bold
Decoration	Underline

6. Click OK.
7. Select the Data tab.
8. Click Edit (next to Values). The Edit Chart Value dialog box appears.
9. Select the Appearance tab. Check the Show Markers check box, and then select Diamond to place a diamond shape at each data point.
10. Click OK to return to the Chart Properties dialog box.
11. Select the *X* Axis tab. Set the following properties:

Property	Value
Title	=Parameters!Year.Value
Format code	MMM
Numeric or time-scale values	(checked)

12. Select the *Y* Axis tab. Set the following properties:

Property	Value
Title	Price in Dollars
Scale, Minimum	0
Scale, Maximum	6

13. Click OK.

14. Select the Preview tab. Select 2005 from the Year drop-down list, and then click View Report. Your report appears similar to the illustration.

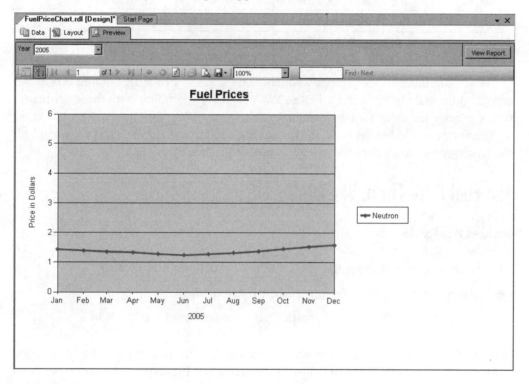

15. Click Save All in the toolbar.

Task Notes   As you have seen, the Chart Properties dialog box provides a great deal of control over the appearance and function of the chart. It is divided into seven different tabs, as shown in the following table, each controlling a different aspect of the chart.

Tab	Charting Aspect Controlled
General	Name of the report item, title, chart type, and color palette. (Chart type can also be selected from the chart item Context menu.)
Data	Dataset fields used to control the data values, categories, and series.
X Axis	Title and scale of the x-axis.
Y Axis	Title and scale of the y-axis.
Legend	If and where a legend containing information on the chart series is included.
3-D Effect	Whether the chart appears as a two-dimensional or three-dimensional object.
Filters	Filtering conditions applied to the data.

We look at more of the settings available on the Chart Properties dialog box as we create additional charts in this chapter. You can also experiment with these settings to get exactly the chart format you need.

The format code MMM is a date-formatting code. It causes the chart to use only the first three characters of the month name for the x-axis labels.

The Fuel Price Chart, Version 2

Features Highlighted

▶ Creating a report using the chart report item with multiple series

▶ Using the union operator in a SELECT statement

▶ Using a WHERE clause to return records of one type or of all types

Business Need   GDS now needs to analyze the fluctuations in the price of all fuel types from month-to-month. Allow the user to select a single fuel type or all fuel types from a drop-down list.

Task Overview

1. Create a New Dataset for the Second Drop-down List and Revise the FuelPrices Dataset to Allow for Multiple Fuel Types

Fuel Price Chart, Version 2, Task 1: Create a New Dataset for the Second Drop-down List and Revise the FuelPrices Dataset to Allow for Multiple Fuel Types

1. Reopen the Chapter06 project if it was closed. Double-click the FuelPriceChart report in the Solution Explorer, if it does not open automatically.

2. Select the Data tab.

3. Choose <New Dataset…> from the Dataset drop-down list. The Dataset dialog box appears.

4. Enter **FuelTypes** for Name in the Dataset dialog box.

5. Galactic is selected for Data Source by default. Click OK. You return to the Generic Query Designer in the Data tab.

6. Type the following in the SQL pane:

```
SELECT 'All' AS FuelType, '_All' AS SortField
UNION
SELECT Description, Description FROM Propulsion ORDER BY SortField
```

7. Run the query to make sure it is correct. You see a list of the distinct fuel types from the FuelPrice table. There is also a record for "All".

8. Choose FuelPrices from the Dataset drop-down list.

9. Change the SELECT statement to the following (the only change is in the second half of the WHERE clause):

```
SELECT Description AS FuelType,
      PriceStartDate,
      Price
FROM FuelPrice
INNER JOIN Propulsion
    ON FuelPrice.PropulsionID = Propulsion.PropulsionID
WHERE (YEAR(PriceStartDate) = @Year)
      AND ((Description = @PropulsionType)
      OR (@PropulsionType = 'All'))
ORDER BY FuelType, PriceStartDate
```

10. Run the query to make sure it is correct. The Define Query Parameters dialog box appears. Enter **2005** for the @Year parameter, **All** for the @PropulsionType parameter, and click OK.

11. Select the Layout tab.

12. Select Report | Report Parameters from the Main menu. The Report Parameters dialog box appears.

13. A report parameter called PropulsionType is created to correspond to the @PropulsionType parameter from the FuelPrices dataset. Select this parameter in the Parameters list box.

14. Select Available Values: From Query.

15. In the Dataset drop-down list, select FuelTypes. In the Value Field drop-down list, select FuelType. In the Label Field drop-down list, select FuelType. Click OK to exit the Report Parameters dialog box.

16. Select the Preview tab. Select 2005 from the Year drop-down list, select All from the PropulsionType drop-down list, and then click View Report. Your report appears similar to the illustration.

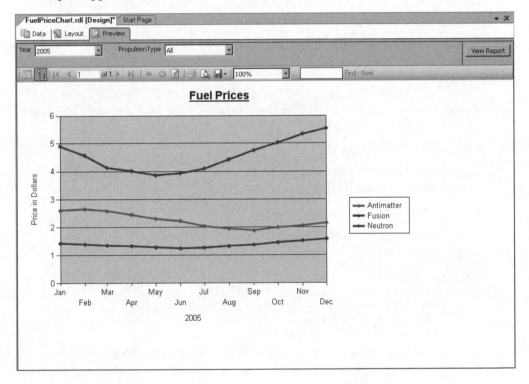

17. Click Save All in the toolbar.

Task Notes The query that creates the FuelTypes dataset is two SELECT statements combined to produce one result set. The first SELECT statement returns a single row with the constant value "All" in the FuelType column and a constant value of "_All" in the SortField. The underscore is placed in front of the word "All" in SortField to make sure it sorts to the top of the list. The second SELECT statement returns a row for each record in the Propulsion table. The two result sets are unified into a single result set by the UNION operator in between the two SELECT statements.

When result sets are *unioned*, the names of the columns in the result set are taken from the first SELECT statement in the union. That is why the FuelTypes dataset has two columns named FuelType and SortField rather than Description. When SELECT statements are unioned, only the last SELECT statement can have an ORDER BY clause. This ORDER BY clause is used to sort the entire result set after it has been unified into a single result set.

The UNION operator can be used with any two SELECT statements as long as the following is true:

▶ The result set from each SELECT statement has the same number of columns.

▶ The corresponding columns in each result set have the same data type.

In fact, the UNION can be used to combine any number of SELECT statements into a unified result set as long as these two conditions hold true for all the SELECT statements in the UNION.

The field we chose for our series field, FuelType, has three distinct values in the dataset when the "All" option is chosen for the PropulsionType report parameter. When this option is selected, the chart contains three series of data points. The legend tells the reader the green series represents the data for antimatter, the blue series represents the data for fusion, and the purple series represents the data for neutron. Each series contains 12 categories. Three series multiplied by 12 categories means we have 36 data points on our chart.

It is important that you understand categories and series as we get into more complex charting. If you are a bit fuzzy on this, review the first part of this chapter before moving on.

The Business Type Distribution Chart

Features Highlighted

▶ Creating a report using a pie chart

▶ Using the Data Label property

▶ Changing the chart palette

▶ Using the 3-D effect

Business Need   The Galactic Delivery Services marketing department needs to analyze what types of businesses are using GDS for their delivery services. This information should be presented as a pie chart.

Task Overview

1. Create a New Report and a Dataset
2. Place a Chart Item on the Report and Populate It

Business Type Distribution Chart, Task I: Create a New Report and a Dataset

1. Reopen the Chapter06 project if it was closed. Close the FuelPriceChart report.
2. Add a blank report called BusinessTypeDistribution to the Chapter06 project. (Do not use the Report Wizard.)
3. Select <New Dataset...> from the Dataset drop-down list. The Dataset dialog box appears.
4. Enter **CustomerBusinessTypes** for the name in the Dataset dialog box.
5. Galactic (shared) is selected for the data source by default. Click OK. You return to the Data tab, which now displays the Generic Query Designer.
6. Type the following in the SQL pane:

    ```
    SELECT Name AS CustomerName,
        Description AS BusinessType
    FROM Customer
    INNER JOIN CustomerToBusinessTypeLink
        ON Customer.CustomerNumber
            = CustomerToBusinessTypeLink.CustomerNumber
    INNER JOIN BusinessType
        ON CustomerToBusinessTypeLink.BusinessTypeCode
            = BusinessType.BusinessTypeCode
    ```

7. Run the query to make sure no errors exist. Correct any typos that may be detected.

Task Notes   The CustomerBusinessTypes dataset simply contains a list of customer names and their corresponding business type. Remember, some customers are linked to more than one business type. That means some of the customers appear in the list more than once.

This dataset is used to populate a pie chart in the next task. The BusinessType field is used to create the categories for the pie chart. The items in the CustomerName field are counted to determine how many customers are in each category.

Business Type Distribution Chart, Task 2:
Place a Chart Item on the Report and Populate It

1. Switch to the Layout tab, and then click-and-drag the edges of the report layout area, so the layout area fills the available space on the screen.

2. Select the Chart report item in the Toolbox window and place it on the report layout. The chart should cover almost the entire report layout because it is the only item on the report.

3. Right-click the chart and select Chart Type | Pie | Simple Pie from the Context menu.

4. In the Datasets window, expand the CustomerBusinessTypes dataset. Drag the CustomerName field from the Datasets window and drop it on Drop Data Fields Here.

5. Drag the BusinessType field and drop it on Drop Category Fields Here.

6. Right-click the chart and select Properties from the Context menu. The Chart Properties dialog box appears.

7. On the General tab, type **Customer Business Types** for the title.

8. Click the Style button (next to the Title). The Style Properties dialog box appears.

9. Set the following properties on the Style Properties dialog box:

Property	Value
Size	14pt
Weight	Bold
Decoration	Underline

10. Click OK to exit the Style Properties dialog box.

11. Select Semi-Transparent from the Palette drop-down list.

12. Select the Data tab.

13. Click Edit (next to Values). The Edit Chart Value dialog box appears.

14. Select the Point Labels tab. Check the Show Point Labels check box.

15. Click the Expression button (the button with *fx* on it) next to the Data Label entry area. The Edit Expression dialog box appears.

16. Type the following in the Expression area:

```
=Fields!BusinessType.Value & vbcrlf &
    "(" & CSTR(Count(Fields!CustomerName.Value)) & ")"
```

17. Click OK to exit the Edit Expression dialog box.

18. Click Label Style. The Style Properties dialog box appears.

19. Select Bold from the Weight drop-down list.

20. Click OK to exit the Style Properties dialog box.

21. Click OK to exit the Edit Chart Value dialog box.

22. Select the Legend tab.

23. Uncheck Show Legend.

24. Select the 3-D Effect tab.

25. Check Display Chart with 3-D Visual Effect.

26. Click OK to exit the Chart Properties dialog box.

27. Select the Preview tab. Your report appears similar to the illustration.

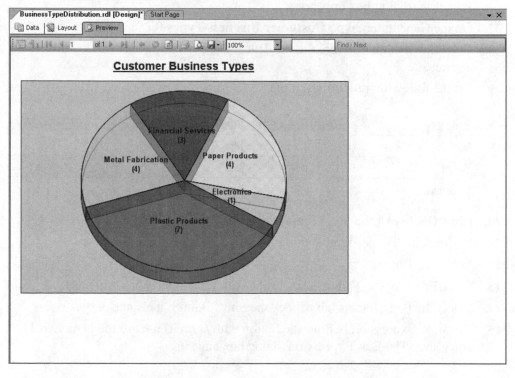

28. Click Save All in the toolbar.

Task Notes   By default, the pie chart uses a legend to the side of the chart to provide labels for each wedge in the pie. In the Business Type Distribution chart, we changed this default behavior. We used the Show Legend check box on the Legend tab to turn off the legend. We used the Data Label entry area on the Point Label tab to put a label for each wedge right on the pie chart itself.

We are using the data label to do double duty for us. It is displaying both the business type for each pie wedge and the number of companies of that business type. This provides the reader with both a graphical representation of the data, in the form of the pie wedge, and the underlying numbers for additional reference. The expression in the Data Label area concatenates the business type and the count of the number of customers with a carriage return/linefeed (vbcrlf) in between. The carriage return/linefeed causes the business type and the count to each appear on its own line.

In this chart, we are also using the 3-D effect. The 3-D effect can help to add interest to a chart by taking a flat graphic and lifting it off the page.

Now let's try one more chart before looking at incorporating images in reports.

The Days in Maintenance Chart

Feature Highlighted

▶   Creating a report using a 3-D, stacked column chart

Business Need   The Galactic Delivery Services transport maintenance department is looking to compare the total maintenance downtime for each year. They would also like to know how that maintenance time is distributed among the different transport types. They would like a graph showing the number of days that each type of transport spent "in for repairs." This information should be presented as a 3-D, stacked column chart. The underlying data should be displayed as a label on each column in the chart.

Task Overview

1. Create a New Report, Create a Dataset, Place a Chart Item on the Report, and Populate It

Days in Maintenance Chart, Task 1: Create a New Report, Create a Dataset, Place a Chart Item on the Report, and Populate It

1. Reopen the Chapter06 project if it was closed. Close the BusinessTypeDistribution report.

2. Add a blank report called DaysInMaint to the Chapter06 project. (Do not use the Report Wizard.)

3. Select <New Dateset…> from the Dataset drop-down list. The Dataset dialog box appears.

4. Enter **DaysInMaint** for the name in the Dataset dialog box.

5. Galactic (shared) is selected for the data source by default. Click OK. You return to the Data tab, which now displays the Generic Query Designer.

6. Type the following in the SQL pane:

```
SELECT Description AS PropulsionType,
     YEAR(BeginWorkDate) AS Year,
     DATEDIFF(dd, BeginWorkDate, EndWorkDate) AS DaysInMaint
FROM Repair
INNER JOIN Transport
     ON Repair.TransportNumber = Transport.TransportNumber
INNER JOIN TransportType
     ON Transport.TransportTypeID = TransportType.TransportTypeID
ORDER BY PropulsionType, Year
```

7. Run the query to make sure there are no errors. Correct any typos that may be detected.

8. Switch to the Layout tab.

9. Set the following properties of the Body:

Property	Value
Size: Width	7.5in
Size: Height	4.375in

10. Select the Chart report item in the Toolbox window and place it on the report layout. The chart should cover almost the entire report layout because it is the only item on the report.

11. In the Datasets window, expand the DaysInMaint dataset. Drag the PropulsionType field from the Datasets window and drop it on Drop Series Fields Here.

12. Drag the Year field and drop it on Drop Category Fields Here.

13. Drag the DaysInMaint field from the Datasets window and drop it on Drop Data Fields Here.

> **NOTE**
>
> *The following uses a more abbreviated format for specifying which items need to be changed for the chart. A table is provided for each dialog box or for each tab within a dialog box. Simply navigate to the appropriate dialog box or tab and change the items specified. Navigation hints are provided with some of the tables for certain dialog boxes and tabs that are a little harder to find.*

14. Right-click the chart and select Properties from the Context menu. The Chart Properties dialog box appears. Set the chart properties, as follows, in the General tab:

Property	Value
Title	Days in Maintenance
Chart sub-type	Stacked column chart

15. Click the Style button (paintbrush and bucket) next to Title on the General tab to access the Style Properties dialog box. Then set the following properties for Report Title:

Property	Value
Size	14pt
Weight	Bold
Decoration	Underline

16. Click the Edit button next to the Values list on the Data tab to access the Edit Chart Value dialog box. Set the following property on the Values tab:

Property	Value
Series label	=Sum(Fields!DaysInMaint.Value)

17. Click the Point Labels tab in the Edit Chart Value dialog box and set these properties:

Property	Value
Show point labels	(checked)
Data label	=Sum(Fields!DaysInMaint.Value)

18. Click the Edit button next to the Category Groups list on the Data tab to access the Grouping and Sorting Properties dialog box. Set the following property for Category Groups:

Property	Value
Label	= "Total Maint. Hours - " & Sum(Fields!DaysInMaint.Value) & vbcrlf & vbcrlf & Fields!Year.Value

19. Click the Edit button next to the Series Groups list on the Data tab to access the Grouping and Sorting Properties dialog box. Set the following property for Series Groups:

Property	Value
Label	= Fields!PropulsionType.Value & " Total Maint. Hours (All Years)"

20. Click the *X* Axis tab and set the following property:

Property	Value
Title	Year

21. Click the Style button (paintbrush and bucket) next to Title on the *X* Axis tab to access the Style Properties dialog box. Set the following properties for *X* Axis Title:

Property	Value
Size	12pt
Weight	Bold

22. Click the *Y* Axis tab and set the following property:

Property	Value
Title	="Days in" & vbcrlf & "Maintenance" & vbcrlf & "Hanger"

23. Click the Style button (paintbrush and bucket) next to Title on the *Y* Axis tab to access the Style Properties dialog box. Set the following properties for *Y* Axis Title:

Property	Value
Size	12pt
Weight	Bold

24. Click the Legend tab and set the following property:

Property	Value
Position	(Select the square in the center of the bottom row of the Position selector.)

25. After you make all these modifications, click OK to exit the Chart Properties dialog box.

26. Select the Preview tab. Your report appears similar to this:

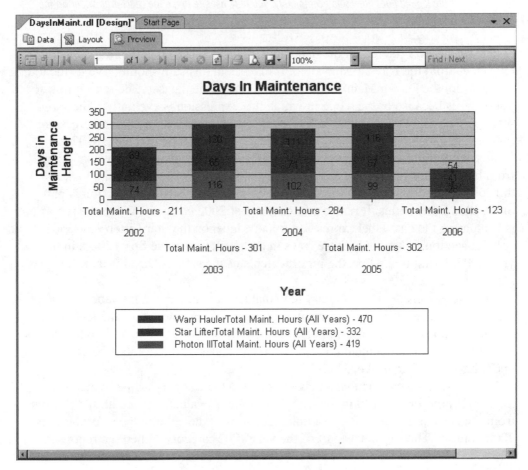

27. Click Save All in the toolbar.

Task Notes   The stacked column chart is a good choice to fulfill the business needs for this report, because it can graphically illustrate two different pieces of information at the same time. Each colored section of the graph shows the number of maintenance days for a given propulsion type. In addition, the combined height of the three sections of the column shows the fluctuations in the total maintenance days from year to year.

Above and beyond the graphical information provided in the chart, several additional pieces of information are provided numerically on the chart. This includes the category labels along the x-axis, the legend at the bottom of the graph, and the detail data displayed right on the column sections themselves. The values on the columns are the result of the expression entered for the data label on the Point Labels tab.

TIP

If the legend does not display completely, you may need to make the chart area wider on the Layout tab.

The expression entered for the data label uses the SUM() function to add up the values from the DaysInMaint field. It may seem this sum should give us the total values from the DaysInMaint field for every row in the dataset. The reason this does not occur is because of the scope in which this expression is evaluated. The *scope* sets boundaries on which rows from the dataset are used with a given expression.

The data label expression operates at the innermost scope in the chart. This means expressions in the data label are evaluated using only those rows that come from both the current category and the current series. For example, let's look at the column section for Star Lifters for the year 2002. This column section is part of the Star Lifter series. It is also part of the year 2002 category. When the report is evaluating the data label expression to put a label on the Star Lifter/year 2002 column section, it uses only those rows in the result set for the Star Lifters in the year 2002. Using this scope, the report calculates the sum of DaysInMaint for Star Lifters in the year 2002 as 68 days.

Next, let's consider the summary data that appears in the column labels along the x-axis. These entries are the result of the expression entered for the label in the category groups. This expression also uses the SUM() function to add up the values from the DaysInMaint column. However, it calculates different totals because it is operating in a different scope.

In this case, the calculations are being done in the category scope, which means the expression for the label in the category group is evaluated using all the records from the current category. For example, let's look at the column label for the year 2002 column. This column is part of the year 2002 category. When the report is evaluating the label expression to put a label below this column, it uses all the rows in the result set for the year 2002. The propulsion type of each row does not make a difference, because it is not part of this scope. Using the year 2002 category scope, the report calculates the sum of DaysInMaint for the year 2002 as 211 days.

Finally, we come to the summary data that appears in the legend below the chart. These entries are the result of two expressions that are concatenated when the report is created. The first expression comes from the label in the series groups. The second expression comes from the Series label on the Values tab. If you leave the label in the series group empty, a generic series label (Series 1, Series 2, and so on) is created by default. If the Series label on the Values tab is left blank, it is ignored. When both the label in the series group and the Series label on the Values tab contain expressions, the results of the two expressions are concatenated with a dash in between.

The expression in the Series label on the Values tab of our current chart also uses the SUM() function to add up the values from the DaysInMaint column. Once again, it is working in a different scope, so it comes up with different results. Here, the calculations are being done in the series scope. That means the expressions for both the Series label on the Values tab and the label in the series group are evaluated using all the records from the current series. For example, let's look at the entry in the legend for the Star Lifter series. When the report is evaluating the Series label expression from the Values tab and the label expression from the series group to put a label in the legend, it uses all the rows in the result set for Star Lifters. The year of each row does not make a difference, because it is not part of this scope. Using the Star Lifter series scope, the report calculates the sum of DaysInMaint for the Star Lifters as 332 days.

In a number of the expressions used in this chart, we are concatenating together several strings to create the labels we need. This is being done using the Visual Basic string concatenation operator (&). You may notice several of the fields being concatenated are numeric rather than string fields. The reason these concatenations work is the & operator automatically converts numeric values to strings. In this way, we can take "Total Maint. Hours -" and concatenate it with 211 to get the first line of the year 2002 column label. The 211 is converted to "211", and then concatenated with the rest of the string.

The final noteworthy item on this report is the expression used to create the label on the y-axis. To have this label fit nicely along the y-axis, we used our old friend the carriage return/linefeed to split the label onto three lines. Because the text is rotated 90 degrees, the first line of the label is farthest from the y-axis, the next line is to the right of the first line, and the last line is to the right of the other two.

Image Is Everything

Now that we have charted up a storm, it is time to turn our attention to two other methods for adding color to a report. One way is through the use of borders and background colors. Almost all report items have properties you can use to specify borders and background colors.

The other way to add color to your reports is through the use of images. Images can be placed on a report using the image report object. They can serve as a background for other report objects. They can even serve as the background to the main body of the report itself.

In addition to determining where an image is placed on the report, you also have to determine where the image will come from. Images can be stored in the report project, embedded in the report itself, pulled from a binary field in a database, or obtained from the Web using a URL. Each image location has its own benefits and drawbacks.

Images stored in the report project are, of course, saved as separate files. They are not stored as part of the report definition. This means when the report is rendered, the renderer must find each of these image files to render the report correctly.

Images stored in the report project are easier to update if they have to be changed in the future. You can simply modify the image file because it is not embedded in a report definition file. They can also be shared among several reports. However, because the report and its required images exist as separate files, some care has to be taken to ensure that the renderer can always locate the images when it is rendering the report.

Embedded images are stored right in the report definition file. With embedded images, only one file is required for rendering the report. There is no risk of the renderer being unable to find a required image. The downside of embedded images is it is more difficult to update an image. To change an embedded image, you need to modify the source image, re-embed the modified image, and redeploy the report. Also, it is impossible to share an embedded image between reports. It can only be used by the report in which it is embedded.

Images stored in a database file can be shared among reports and are easy to track down when a report is rendered. In addition, when images are stored with the data in the database, it is possible to use a different image in your report for each row in the dataset. This is more difficult to do with project or embedded images.

Images in the database do pose two concerns. First, retrieving images from the database puts an additional load on your database server. Care must be taken to make sure your server can handle this additional load without degradation in response time. And, second, managing large binary objects, such as images, in database records is not always a trivial task.

Images obtained through the Internet have a number of advantages. They can be easily shared among tens or even hundreds of reports; all the reports simply reference the same URL. They can be easily updated; just post a new image to the web server and all the reports are referencing this new version. In addition, web servers are designed for serving images, so there should not be an issue with additional load on the web server, unless it is extremely busy already.

The downside to obtaining images from a web server is this: the renderer must take the time to make an HTTP request for each image it needs to put in the report. If the image's URL points to the report server itself or if it points to another server on the same internal network, this may not be a big deal. If, on the other hand, the URL points to a server across the Internet from the report server, the time required for rendering will increase. You also need to insure that the report server can always connect to the web server hosting the image.

As a rule of thumb, images to be shared among many reports, such as company logos, should be kept either in the report project or accessed through a URL. These shared images should be put in one central location, so they can be accessed by the reports when they are needed. Images that have a strong association with data in a particular record in a database table should be stored in the database itself. For example, a picture of a particular employee has a strong association with that employee's record in the Employee table. We are only interested in displaying the picture of a particular employee when the row in the dataset for that employee is being processed. Any images that do not fall into these two categories should be embedded in the report to ease deployment issues.

Conference Nametags

Features Highlighted

▶   Using background colors on report objects

▶   Using borders on report objects

▶   Placing an image on a report

Business Need   Galactic Delivery Services is preparing for its annual customer conference. The billing contact for each customer has been invited to the conference. As part of the preparations, the GDS art department must create nametags for the conference attendees. Because the names of all the billing contacts are available in the Galactic database, and this database can easily be accessed from Reporting Services, the art department has decided to use Reporting Services to create the nametags.

The conference nametags should include the name of the attendee and also the name of the company they work for. The art department would like the nametags to be bright and colorful. They should include the GDS logo.

Task Overview

1. Create a New Report, Create a Dataset, and Place the Report Items on the Report

Conference Nametags, Task 1: Create a New Report, Create a Dataset, and Place the Report Items on the Report

1. Reopen the Chapter06 project if it was closed. Close the DaysInMaint report.
2. Add a blank report called Nametags to the Chapter06 project. (Do not use the Report Wizard.)
3. Select <New Dateset...> from the Dataset drop-down list. The Dataset dialog box appears.
4. Enter **BillingContacts** for the name in the Dataset dialog box.
5. Galactic (shared) is selected for the data source by default. Click OK. You return to the Data tab, which now displays the Generic Query Designer.
6. Type the following in the SQL pane:

```
SELECT BillingContact, Name
FROM Customer
ORDER BY BillingContact
```

7. Run the query to make sure no errors exist. Correct any typos that may be detected.
8. Switch to the Layout tab.
9. Select the List report item in the Toolbox window and drop it onto the report layout. Modify the following properties of the list:

Property	Value
BackgroundColor	DarkOrange
Location: Left	0.125in
Location: Top	0.125in
Size: Width	4.75in
Size: Height	2.125in

We are using a list here because this report is going to have a freeform layout, rather than the rows and columns of a table or matrix.

10. In the Datasets window, expand the BillingContact dataset. Drag the BillingContact field from the Datasets window and drop it onto the list. Modify the following properties of the text box that results:

Property	Value
BackgroundColor	Gold
BorderColor	DarkBlue
BorderStyle	Solid
BorderWidth	4pt
Color	DarkBlue
Font: FontSize	20pt
Font: FontWeight	Bold
Location: Left	0.125in
Location: Top	0.125in
Size: Width	4.5in
Size: Height	0.5in
TextAlign	Center
VerticalAlign	Middle

11. Drag the Name field from the Datasets window and drop it onto the list. Modify the following properties of the text box that results:

Property	Value
BackgroundColor	Gold
BorderColor	DarkBlue
BorderStyle	Solid
BorderWidth	4pt
Color	DarkBlue
Font: FontSize	16pt
Font: FontWeight	Bold
Location: Left	0.125in
Location: Top	0.875in
Size: Width	4.5in
Size: Height	0.375in
TextAlign	Center
VerticalAlign	Middle

12. Drag a text box from the Toolbox and drop it onto the list. Modify the following properties of this text box:

Property	Value
Font: FontSize	23pt
Location: Left	1in
Location: Top	1.375in
Size: Width	3.625in
Size: Height	0.625in
TextAlign	Center
Value	GDS Conference 2006
VerticalAlign	Middle

13. Drag a line from the Toolbox and drop it onto the list. Modify the following properties of the line:

Property	Value
EndPoint: Horizontal	4.75in
EndPoint: Vertical	2.125in
LineColor	DarkBlue
LineWidth	10pt
Location: Left	0in
Location: Top	2.125in

14. Drag an image report item from the Toolbox and drop it onto the list. The Image Wizard appears. Click Next.

15. Click the Project radio button. This will be an external image. The Image Wizard places it in the Chapter06 project for us. Click Next.

16. Click New Image. The Import Image dialog box appears.

17. Navigate to the GDS.gif image file and select it. Click Open.

> **NOTE**
>
> *The image files used in the reports in this chapter are available on the website for this book. If you have not done so already, go to http://www.osborne.com, locate the book's page using the ISBN 0072262397, and follow the instructions to download the image files.*

18. Click Next, and then click Finish.

19. Modify the following properties of the image in the Properties window:

Property	Value
Location: Left	0.125in
Location: Top	1.375in
Sizing	AutoSize

20. Check to make sure the list is still the correct size. Change the dimensions to match the following, if necessary:

Property	Value
Size: Width	4.75in
Size: Height	2.125in

21. Click in the report layout area. This causes the report body to be selected in the Properties window. Modify the following properties of the report body:

Property	Value
BackgroundColor	DarkBlue
Size: Width	5in
Size: Height	2.25in

22. Click the Preview tab. The nametags are ready to be printed, cut apart, and placed in nametag holders, as shown here.

23. Click Save All in the toolbar.

Task Notes   We used several properties of the report objects in our Conference Nametags report to add color. The BackgroundColor property controls the color in the background of the report item. This defaults to Transparent, meaning that whatever is behind the item shows through. When the BackgroundColor property is set to a color rather than Transparent, that color fills in and covers up everything behind the item.

The BorderColor property controls the color of the border around the outside of the report item. BorderColor works in cooperation with two other properties: BorderStyle and BorderWidth. The BorderStyle property defaults to None. When BorderStyle is None, the border is invisible. No matter what color you set for BorderColor, it does not show up when the BorderStyle is set to None.

To have a visible border around an object, you must change the BorderSyle property to a solid line (Solid), a dotted line (Dotted), a dashed line (Dashed), a double line (Double), or one of the other settings in the BorderStyle drop-down list. Once you select one of these visible settings for the BorderStyle property, you can set the color of the border using the BorderColor property and the thickness of the border using the BorderWidth property.

The border settings for each side of a report item can be controlled separately or altogether. If you expand any of the three border properties, you can see they have separate entries for Default, Left, Right, Top, and Bottom. The Default property is, as it says, the default value for all four sides of the report item. When the Left, Right, Top, or Bottom property is blank, the setting for that particular side is taken from the Default property. For example, if the BorderStyle: Default property is set to None, and BorderStyle: Left, BorderStyle: Right, BorderStyle: Top, and BorderStyle: Bottom are all blank, then there is no border around the report item. If the BorderStyle: Bottom property is set to Double, this overrides the default setting and a double line appears across the bottom of the item. The border on the other three sides of the item (left, right, and top) continues to use the default setting.

The Color property controls the color of the text created by a report item. You find the Color property on a text box, which is expected, because the main purpose of a text box is to create text. You also find the Color property on each of the data regions, tables, matrixes, lists, and charts. A data region can create a text message when no rows are in the dataset attached to it. The Color property specifies the color of the text in this special "no rows" message when it is displayed. (We discuss the "no rows" message more in Chapter 7.)

The final color property we used in the Conference Nametags report is the LineColor property. This property exists only for line report items. It should come as no surprise that this property controls the color of the line.

One thing you quickly notice when you begin using background colors is this: a report item with a BackgroundColor property set to Transparent is only transparent when the report is rendered. The report item is not transparent on the Layout tab. Report items that have a BackgroundColor property set to Transparent have a white background on the Layout tab. This makes it easier to select a report item as you are moving things around or changing properties in the report layout.

We used the TextAlign property to adjust the way text is placed horizontally inside a text box (left, center, or right). In this report, we also used the VerticalAlign property to adjust the way text is placed vertically inside a text box (top, middle, or bottom).

The vertical alignment of text in a text box is not usually an issue unless the border of the text box is visible and you can see where the text is being placed relative to the top and bottom of the text box.

Conference Place Cards

Features Highlighted

▶   Using background images on report objects

▶   Using embedded images

▶   Using the WritingMode property of a text box

Business Need   Galactic Delivery Services is continuing its preparations for the annual customer conference. In addition to the nametags, the GDS art department must also create place cards for the conference attendees. The place cards are going to be put on the table in front of each attendee during roundtable discussions. As with the nametags, place cards should be created for all the billing contacts.

   The conference place cards should include the name of the attendee and also the name of the company they work for. The art department would like the place cards to continue the color scheme set by the nametags, but with a more intricate pattern. They should include the GDS logo.

Task Overview

1.   Create a New Report, Create a Dataset, and Place the Report Items on the Report

Conference Place Cards, Task 1: Create a New Report, Create a Dataset, and Place the Report Items on the Report

1.   Reopen the Chapter06 project if it was closed. Close the Nametags report.
2.   Add a blank report called PlaceCards to the Chapter06 project. (Do not use the Report Wizard.)
3.   Select <New Dateset...> from the Dataset drop-down list. The Dataset dialog box appears.
4.   Enter **BillingContacts** for the name in the Dataset dialog box.
5.   Galactic (shared) is selected for the data source by default. Click OK. You return to the Data tab, which now displays the Generic Query Designer.

6. Type the following in the SQL pane:

```
SELECT BillingContact, Name
FROM Customer
ORDER BY BillingContact
```

7. Run the query to make sure no errors exist. Correct any typos that may be detected.

8. Switch to the Layout tab.

9. Select Report | Embedded Images from the Main menu. The Embedded Images dialog box appears.

10. Click New Image. The Import Image dialog box appears.

11. Navigate to the GDSBackRect.gif image file and select it. Click Open.

12. Click New Image. The Import Image dialog box appears.

13. Navigate to the GDSBackOval.gif image file and select it. Click Open.

14. Click New Image. The Import Image dialog box appears.

15. Navigate to the GDSBig.gif image file and select it. Click Open.

16. Click OK to exit the Embedded Images dialog box.

17. Click in the report layout area. This causes the report body to be selected in the Properties window. Modify the following properties of the report body:

Property	Value
BackgroundColor	DarkOrange
BackgroundImage: Source	Embedded
BackgroundImage: Value	gdsbackrect (The drop-down list shows all the images embedded in the report.)
Size: Width	8.875in
Size: Height	3.2in

18. Drag a List from the Toolbox and drop it onto the report layout. Modify the following properties of the list:

Property	Value
Location: Left	0in
Location: Top	0in
Size: Width	8.75in
Size: Height	3.2in

19. In the Datasets window, expand the BillingContact dataset. Drag the BillingContact field from the Datasets window and drop it onto the list. Modify the following properties of the text box that results:

Property	Value
BackgroundImage: Source	Embedded
BackgroundImage: Value	gdsbackoval
Font: FontSize	30pt
Font: FontWeight	Bold
Location: Left	2.5in
Location: Top	1.75in
Size: Width	6.125in
Size: Height	0.625in
TextAlign	Center
VerticalAlign	Middle

20. Drag the Name field from the Datasets window and drop it onto the list. Modify the following properties of the text box that results:

Property	Value
BackgroundImage: Source	Embedded
BackgroundImage: Value	gdsbackoval
Color	DarkBlue
Font: FontSize	30pt
Font: FontWeight	Bold
Location: Left	2.5in
Location: Top	2.5in
Size: Width	6.125in
Size: Height	0.625in
TextAlign	Center
VerticalAlign	Middle

21. Drag an Image report item from the Toolbox, and drop it onto the list. The Image Wizard appears.

22. Click Next.

23. Make sure Embedded is selected. Click Next.

24. Select the gdsbig image. Click Next.

25. Click Finish to exit the Image Wizard.

26. Modify the following properties of the image:

Property	Value
BorderStyle	Double
BorderWidth	3pt
Location: Left	0.3in
Location: Top	1.715in
Size: Width	1.625in
Size: Height	1.375in
Sizing	Fit

27. Drag a text box from the Toolbox and drop it onto the list. Modify the following properties of this text box:

Property	Value
Font: FontSize	9pt
Font: FontWeight	Bold
Location: Left	0.05in
Location: Top	1.715in
Size: Width	0.25in
Size: Height	1.375in
TextAlign	Center
Value	GDS Conference 2006
WritingMode	tb-rl

28. This text box looks strange on the Layout tab. Have faith; it will look fine in the Preview tab.

29. Drag a text box from the Toolbox and drop it onto the list. Modify the following properties of this text box:

Property	Value
Font: FontSize	9pt
Font: FontWeight	Bold
Location: Left	1.925in
Location: Top	1.715in
Size: Width	0.25in
Size: Height	1.375in
TextAlign	Center
Value	GDS Conference 2006
VerticalAlign	Bottom
WritingMode	tb-rl

30. This text box also looks strange on the Layout tab.

31. Click the Preview tab. The place cards are ready to be printed, cut apart, folded, and placed on the tables, as shown here.

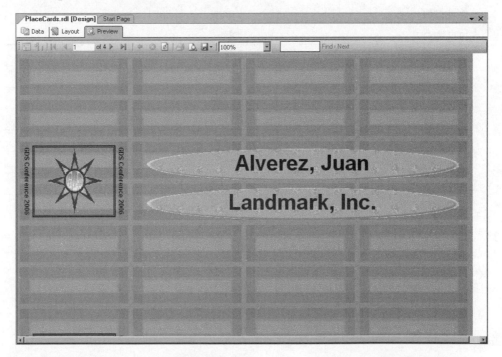

32. Click Save All in the toolbar.

Task Notes In this report, we used embedded images instead of using external images, as we did in the previous report. Remember, the method of storing the image has nothing to do with the way the image is used in the report. External images can be used as background images. Embedded images can be used in image report items.

The Embedded Images dialog box enables you to manage the images embedded in the report. Remember, an embedded image remains in the report even if no report item is referencing it. The only way to remove an embedded image from a report is to use the Delete button in the Embedded Images dialog box. Always remove embedded images from the report if they are not being used. This way, the report definition does not become any larger than it needs to be.

Also, in this report, we used the WritingMode property to rotate the contents of two text boxes by 90 degrees. The normal writing mode for English text in a text box is left-to-right, top-to-bottom (lr-tb). We changed this default writing mode and told these two text boxes to output our text top-to-bottom, right-to-left (tb-rl). The WritingMode property was implemented to allow Reporting Services to work with languages written from top to bottom and right to left. However, that does not prevent us from using the WritingMode property to produce a fancy effect with our English text.

The Rate Sheet Report

Features Highlighted

- ► Using database images
- ► Using rectangle report items within table cells

Business Need The Galactic Delivery Services marketing department needs to produce a new rate sheet. The rate sheet needs to include a description of each type of delivery service provided by GDS. Each type has its own image to help customers remember the three types of service. The rate sheet also includes the name of each service type with a longer description below it and the cost of each service type off to the right side of the page.

Because all the information on the three types of service is available in the database, the marketing department wants to produce the rate sheet from a report, rather than creating or updating a document each time the rates change.

Task Overview

1. Create a New Report, Create a Dataset, and Place the Report Items on the Report
2. Refine the Report Layout

Rate Sheet Report, Task 1: Create a New Report, Create a Dataset, and Place the Report Items on the Report

1. Reopen the Chapter06 project if it was closed. Close the PlaceCards report.

2. Add a blank report called RateSheet to the Chapter06 project. (Do not use the Report Wizard.)

3. Select <New Dataset…> from the Dataset drop-down list. The Dataset dialog box appears.

4. Enter **ServiceTypes** for the name in the Dataset dialog box.

5. Galactic (shared) is selected for the data source by default. Click OK. You return to the Data tab, which now displays the Generic Query Designer.

6. Type the following in the SQL pane:

```
SELECT Description, LongDescription, Cost, PriceSheetImage
FROM ServiceType
ORDER BY Cost
```

7. Run the query to make sure no errors exist. Correct any typos that may be detected.

8. Switch to the Layout tab.

9. Drag an image report item from the Toolbox and drop it onto the report layout. The Image Wizard appears.

10. Click Next.

11. Select Project, and then click Next.

12. Select the gds image, and then click Next.

13. Click Finish to exit the Image Wizard.

14. Modify the following properties of the image:

Property	Value
Location: Left	0in
Location: Top	0in

15. Drag a text box from the Toolbox and drop it onto the report layout. Modify the following properties of this text box:

Property	Value
Color	DarkBlue
Font: FontSize	30pt
Font: FontWeight	Bold
Location: Left	0.875in
Location: Top	0in
Size: Width	6in
Size: Height	0.625in
Value	Galactic Delivery Services
VerticalAlign	Middle

16. Drag a text box from the Toolbox and drop it onto the report layout. Modify the following properties of this text box:

Property	Value
Color	DarkOrange
Font: FontSize	25pt
Font: FontWeight	Bold
Location: Left	0.875in
Location: Top	0.625in
Size: Width	6in
Size: Height	0.5in
Value	Types of Service
VerticalAlign	Middle

17. Drag a text box from the Toolbox and drop it onto the report layout. Modify the following properties of this text box:

Property	Value
Color	Gold
Font: FontSize	20pt
Font: FontWeight	Bold
Format	MMMM d, yyyy
Location: Left	0.875in
Location: Top	1.125in
Size: Width	6in
Size: Height	0.5in
TextAlign	Left
VerticalAlign	Middle

18. Right-click the last text box added to the report and select Expression from the Context menu. The Edit Expression dialog box appears.

19. Click Globals in the Fields area.

20. Double-click ExecutionTime.

21. Click OK to exit the Edit Expression dialog box.

22. Drag a table from the Toolbox and place it on the report layout.

23. Right-click in the gray rectangle to the left of the header row. Select Table Header to unselect it on the Context menu. This removes the header row.

24. Right-click in the gray rectangle to the left of the footer row. Select Table Footer to unselect it on the Context menu. This removes the footer row.

25. Click the gray square in the upper-left corner of the table. This selects the table. Modify the following properties of the table:

Property	Value
DataSetName	ServiceTypes
Location: Left	0.875in
Location: Top	1.75in
Size: Width	6.25in
Size: Height	2.125in

26. Drag an image report item from the Toolbox and drop it onto the leftmost table cell. The Image Wizard appears.

27. Click Next.

28. Select Database. Click Next.

29. Select PriceSheetImage from the Image Field drop-down list.

30. Select image/gif from the MIME Type drop-down list.

31. Click Next.

32. Click Finish to exit the Image Wizard.

33. Click the center table cell. Click the gray rectangle above the center table cell. Modify the following property of the table column:

Property	Value
Width	2.45in

34. In the Datasets window, expand the ServiceTypes dataset. Drag the Description field from the Datasets window and drop it onto the center table cell. Modify the following properties of the text box that results:

Property	Values
Color	DarkBlue
Font: FontSize	14pt
Font: FontWeight	Bold

35. Drag the Cost field from the Datasets window and drop it onto the rightmost table cell. Modify the following properties of the text box that results:

Property	Values
Font: FontSize	14pt
Format	$###,###.00
VerticalAlign	Middle

36. Click the Preview tab. Your report appears similar to the illustration.

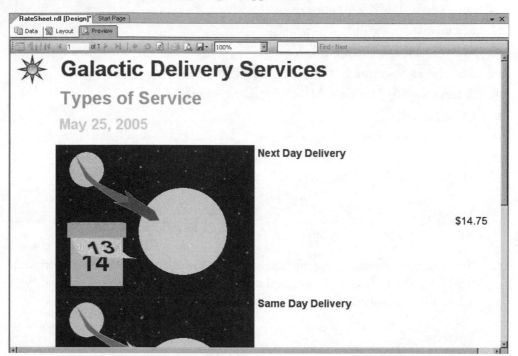

Task Notes   In the Rate Sheet Report, we used image data stored in a database table. As we discussed earlier in the chapter, this allows the report to have a different image for each row in the table report object. The Next Day Delivery row, the Same Day Delivery row, and the Previous Day Delivery row each have their own unique image on the report.

Although the image data appears correctly on the report, the formatting leaves something to be desired. The images are all run together. The bottom of one image touches the top of the next. Also, the business needs specified that the long description of the service type should come below the name of that service type.

Let's reformat our report a bit to see if we can improve the look of the images and include the long description in the report.

Rate Sheet Report, Task 2: Refine the Report Layout

1. Click on the Layout tab.

2. Click the leftmost table cell containing the image. This selects the image report item.

3. Press DELETE to remove the image report item. The image report item has been removed from the table cell and, by default, a text box is created and put in its place.

4. Drag a rectangle from the Toolbox and drop it on the leftmost table cell. A rectangle report item is now in the leftmost table cell.

5. Drag an image from the Toolbox and drop it on the rectangle you just created. The Image Wizard appears.

6. Click Next.

7. Select Database, and then click Next.

8. Select PriceSheetImage from the Image Field drop-down list.

9. Select image/gif from the MIME Type drop-down list.

10. Click Next.

11. Click Finish to exit the Image Wizard.

12. Modify the following properties of the image:

Property	Value
BorderColor	DarkBlue
BorderStyle	Double
BorderWidth	4pt
Location: Left	0.125in
Location: Top	0.125in
Size: Width	1.75in
Size: Height	1.375in
Sizing	Fit

13. Click the center table cell. This selects the text box in the cell.

14. Press DELETE to remove the text box.

15. Drag a rectangle from the Toolbox and drop it on the center table cell. A rectangle report item is now in the center table cell.

16. Drag the Description field from the Datasets window and drop it on the rectangle you just created.

17. Modify the following properties of the text box that results:

Property	Value
Color	DarkBlue
Font: FontSize	14pt
Font: FontWeight	Bold
Location: Left	0.125in
Location: Top	0.125in
Size: Width	2.3in
Size: Height	0.375in

18. Drag the LongDescription field from the Datasets window and drop it onto the same rectangle that contains the text box for the Description field. Modify the following properties of the text box that results:

Property	Value
Location: Left	0.125in
Location: Top	0.625in
Size: Width	2.3in
Size: Height	0.875in

19. Click the Preview tab. Your report appears similar to the illustration.

20. Click Save All in the toolbar.

Task Notes   Looking at our second attempt, you can see the rectangle saved the day. It solved both of our formatting problems. Having a rectangle in the leftmost cell allowed us to size the image so it did not fill the entire cell. We were able to adjust the size of the image because the Sizing property of the image was set to Fit. This, in turn, created some white space between the images, making them look much nicer. We even took advantage of that white space by adding a border to the image object.

The rectangle solved our second problem as well. The business needs specified the long description of the service type should appear below the name of the service type. We could accomplish this by putting a rectangle in the center table cell, and then putting two text boxes inside the rectangle.

The Rate Sheet Report is ready to go.

Building Higher

We have now covered all the basic aspects of creating reports in Reporting Services. In the next two chapters, we continue to look at report creation, but we move to the intermediate and advanced level. Building on what you have learned so far, we create more complex reports with more interactivity.

With each new feature you encounter, you gain new tools for turning data into business intelligence.

Kicking It Up a Notch: Intermediate Reporting

B asic training is at an end. Boot camp is over. You now know the basics of building reports in Reporting Services. You should be able to create reports both with the Report Wizard and from scratch. When needed, you can spice up your reports with color, images, and charts.

In the last chapter, you learned how to add punch to your reports with color and graphics. In this chapter, you learn how to add value to your reports through summarizing and totaling, and added interactivity. All this enhances the users' experience and allows them to more readily turn information into business intelligence.

We begin the chapter, however, by looking for a way to enhance your experience as a report developer. In the first section, we create a report template that can be used to standardize the look of your reports. The report template can also take care of some of the basic formatting tasks, so they do not need to be repeated for each report.

Never Having to Say "I'm Sorry"

Users can be particular about the way their reports are laid out. In many cases, you will be creating new reports to replace existing ones. It may be that the user was getting a report from a legacy system, from an Access report or a spreadsheet, or from a ledger book. Whatever the case, the user is used to seeing the data presented in a certain way with everything arranged just so.

Now you come along with Microsoft SQL Server 2005 Reporting Services, telling the user that the new reporting system is infinitely better than the old way—more efficient, more timely, with more delivery options. That is all well and good with the user but, invariably, the question will arise, "Can you make the report look the same as what I have now?" No matter how antiquated or inefficient the current reporting system might be, it is familiar, perhaps even comforting, to your users. Change is difficult. The irony of the human race is this: on a large scale we like change, but on an individual level, we mainly want things to stay the same.

Even if Reporting Services is well established and you are not converting reports from an existing system, users still have preconceived notions. They have a vision for the way a new report should be laid out. These visions need to be respected. After all, the report developer is not the one who has to look at the report every day, week, or month—the user is! The user is the one who probably knows how to best turn the data into something useful.

What the users don't want to hear is, "I'm sorry, but we can't do it that way in Reporting Services." You will be miles ahead if you spend your time fulfilling your users' vision, rather than trying to convince them that Reporting Services is a great tool, despite the fact that it cannot do what they want it to do. The techniques in this section, and also in parts of Chapter 8, can help you to make Reporting Services reports do exactly what your users want them to do. After all, if your users ain't happy, ain't nobody happy!

Successful report development means never having to say, "I'm sorry."

The Report Template

Features Highlighted

- ► Creating a reusable template for reports
- ► Using values from the Globals collection

Business Need   Galactic Delivery Services is looking to increase the efficiency of its report developers. GDS would like a template that can be used for each new report created. The report template is to include the GDS logo and the company name in a header across the top of each page. The template is also to include a footer across the bottom of each page showing the date and time the report was printed, who printed the report, the current page number, and the total number of pages in the report.

Task Overview

1. Create the Template Project and the Template Report with a Page Header
2. Create the Page Footer on the Template Report
3. Copy the Template to the Report Project Directory

Report Template, Task 1: Create the Template Project and the Template Report with a Page Header

1. Create a new Reporting Services project called Template in the MSSQLRS folder. (If you need help with this task, see the section "The Transport List Report" in Chapter 5.)
2. Add a blank report called GDSReport to the Template project. (Do not use the Report Wizard.)
3. Select the Layout tab.

4. From the Main menu, select Report | Page Header. A space for the page header layout appears above the layout area for the body of the report. (If Report is not showing on the Main menu, click anywhere on the report layout. The Format and Report menu choices appear.) Drag the gray bar separating the page header and the body down, so the page header area is larger.

5. From the Toolbox, place an image item in the layout area for the page header. The Image Wizard appears.

6. Click Next.

7. The Embedded choice should be selected. Click Next.

8. Click New Image. Browse to the GDS.gif image file and select it. Click Open.

9. Click Next.

10. Click Finish to exit the Image Wizard. The image is placed in the page header.

11. Modify the following properties of the image:

Property	Value
Location: Left	0in
Location: Top	0in
Name	tmpl_Logo
Size: Width	0.75in
Size: Height	0.625in

12. Place a text box in the layout area for the page header. Modify the following properties of the text box:

Property	Value
Color	DarkBlue
Font: FontSize	30pt
Font: FontWeight	Bold
Location: Left	0.75in
Location: Top	0in
Name	tmpl_Name
Size: Width	5.75in
Size: Height	0.625in
Value	Galactic Delivery Services
VerticalAlign	Middle

13. Click in the page header layout area outside the text box and image. Page Header is selected in the drop-down list at the top of the Properties window.

14. Modify the following property for the page header:

Property	Value
Size: Height	0.75in

Task Notes   Reporting Services reports have a page header layout area that can be used to create a page heading for the report. The page header has properties, so it can be turned off on the first page or the last page of the report. Aside from these options, if the page header is turned on in the Report menu, it appears on each report page.

The page header can be populated with images, text boxes, lines, and rectangles. You cannot, however, place any data regions, tables, matrixes, lists, or charts in a page header. In fact, you cannot directly reference fields from a dataset in the page header.

Each report item placed in the report layout is given a name. Up to this point, we have been letting the Report Designer provide a default name for each item (textbox1, image2, and so on). In most cases, these default names will work just fine. The only time you need to provide a more meaningful name is when you need to reference one report item from another, such as when one item toggles the visibility of another, or when you are creating a template.

The reason we need to provide nondefault names for our report template is to avoid any naming collisions when we create reports using our template. When you add the first text box to a report created with our template, it is automatically called textbox1. This causes a problem if we already have a text box called textbox1 that came from our template.

To avoid these naming collisions, we need to provide names for the report items in our template that are unlikely to be duplicated in a report. For this reason, we put the prefix tmpl_ in front of the name of each item. These names should be unique enough to prevent naming collisions when we put our template to use.

In the previous task, you chose to make the logo image in the report header an embedded image. This was done for reasons of convenience for these exercises. In an actual template created for your company, retrieving images from the Internet is probably a good idea. As discussed previously, this allows for the image to be used in a multitude of reports while being stored in a single location. This also makes it easy to update the image the next time the marketing department gives it a makeover.

Report Template, Task 2: Create the Page Footer on the Template Report

1. Click in the report layout area.
2. From the Main menu, select Report | Page Footer. A space for the page footer layout appears below the layout area for the body of the report.
3. Page Footer is selected in the Properties window. Modify the following property for the page footer:

Property	Value
Size: Height	0.375in

4. Place a text box in the layout area for the page footer. Modify the following properties of the text box:

Property	Value
Font: FontSize	8pt
Location: Left	0in
Location: Top	0.125in
Name	tmpl_ReportName
Size: Width	2.25in
Size: Height	0.25in

5. Right-click the text box and select Expression from the Context menu, or select <Expression...> from the drop-down list for the Value property in the Property window. The Edit Expression dialog box appears.
6. Select Globals.
7. Double-click ReportName. The expression to return ReportName from the Globals collection is placed in the Expression area.
8. Click OK to exit the Edit Expression dialog box.
9. Place a second text box in the layout area for the page footer. Modify the following properties of the text box:

Property	Value
Font: FontSize	8pt
Location: Left	2.75in
Location: Top	0.125in

Property	Value
Name	tmpl_PageNumber
Size: Width	1in
Size: Height	0.25in

10. Right-click this text box and select Expression from the Context menu. The Edit Expression dialog box appears.

11. Type the following in the Expression area after the equals (=) sign:

    ```
    "Page " &
    ```

    A space should be typed both before and after the ampersand character (&).

12. Select Globals.

13. Double-click PageNumber to append it. The expression to return PageNumber from the Globals collection is added to the Expression area.

14. After the PageNumber expression, type the following:

    ```
    & " of " &
    ```

    A space should be typed both before and after each ampersand.

15. Double-click TotalPages. The expression to return TotalPages from the Globals collection is added to the Expression area.

16. Click OK to exit the Edit Expression dialog box.

17. Place a third text box in the layout area for the page footer. Modify the following properties of the text box:

Property	Value
Font: FontSize	8pt
Location: Left	4.25in
Location: Top	0.125in
Name	tmpl_DateTime
Size: Width	2.25in
Size: Height	0.25in
TextAlign	Right

18. Right-click this text box and select Expression from the Context menu. The Edit Expression dialog box appears.

19. Select Globals.

20. Double-click ExecutionTime. The expression to return ExecutionTime from the Globals collection is added to the Expression area.

21. Click OK to exit the Edit Expression dialog box. Your report layout should appear similar to Figure 7-1.

22. Select the Preview tab. Your report should appear similar to Figure 7-2.

23. For a better look at what the header and footer will look like on a printed report, click the Print Layout button, as shown in Figure 7-3.

24. Let's put the page header closer to the top of the page and the page footer closer to the bottom of the page. Select the Layout tab.

25. In the Main menu, select Report | Report Properties. The Report Properties dialog box appears.

26. Select the Layout tab.

27. Modify the following values:

Property	Value
Top margin	0.5in
Bottom margin	0.5in

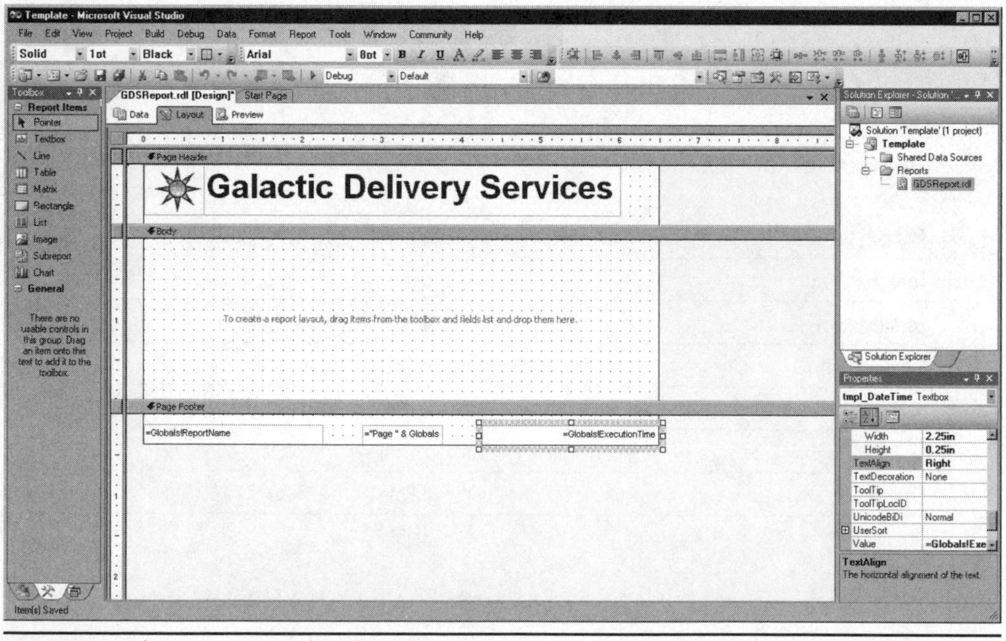

Figure 7-1 *The report template layout*

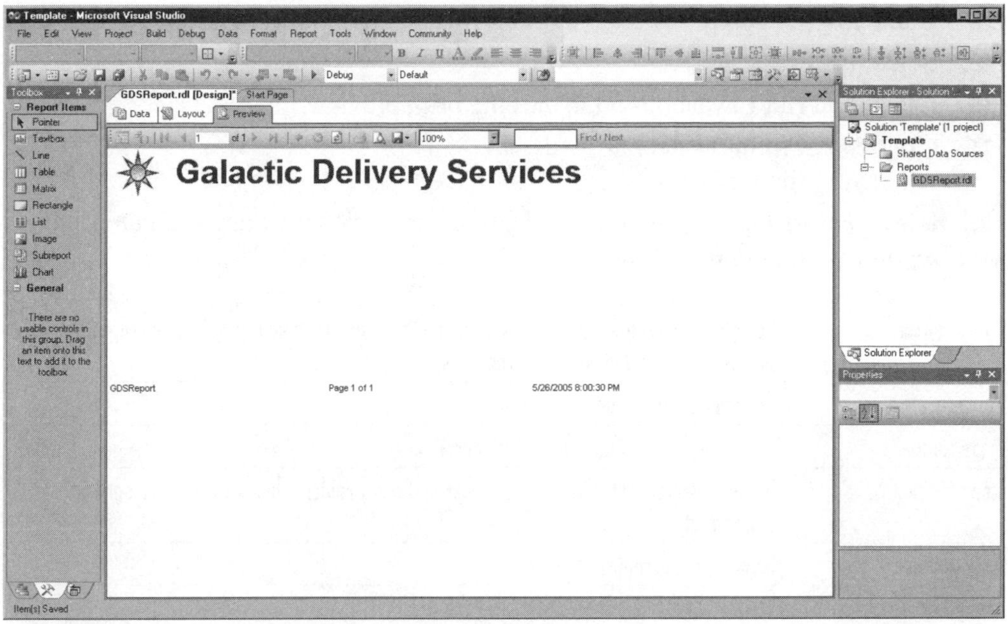

Figure 7-2   *The report template on the Preview tab*

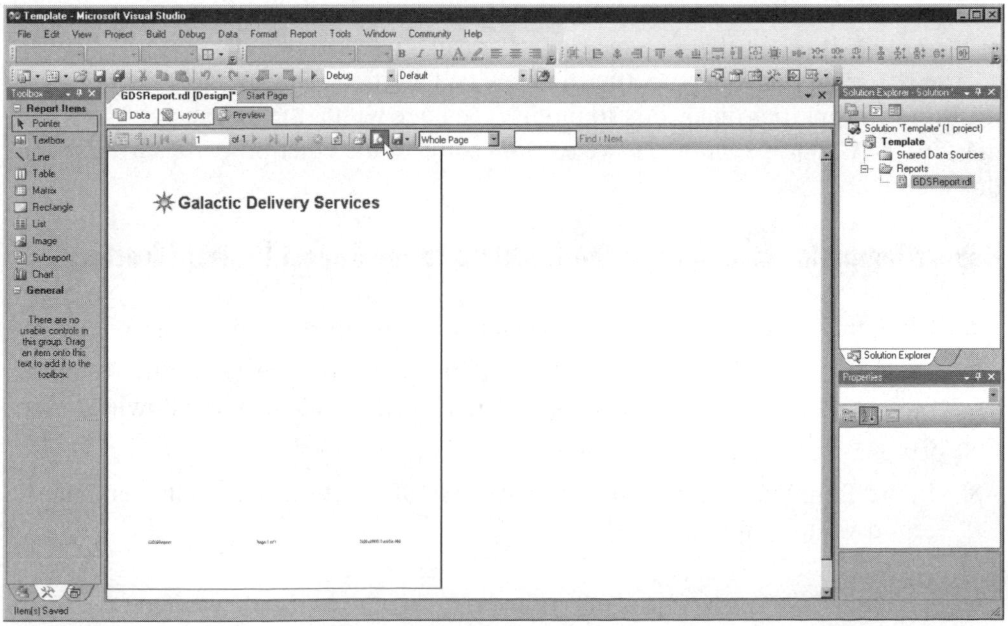

Figure 7-3   *The report template in Print Preview mode*

   28. Click OK.

   29. Select the Preview tab.

   30. Click the Print Layout button to exit the print preview.

   31. Click Save All in the toolbar.

Task Notes Reporting Services provides a number of global values you can use in your reports, including the following:

ExecutionTime	The date and time the report was executed. (This is not the time it takes for the report to run but, rather, the time at which the report was run.)
Language	The language the report is output in.
PageNumber	The current page number within the report.
ReportFolder	The report server folder the report resides in. Report Folder is blank in the development environment.
ReportName	The name of the report.
ReportServerUrl	The URL of the Internet server hosting the report.
TotalPages	The total number of pages in the report.
UserID	The network user name of the person executing the report.

These global values are commonly used in the page header and page footer areas of the report. It is possible, however, to use them anywhere in the report.

The report has its own properties that can be modified. You are most likely to use the Report Properties dialog box to modify the page width, the page height, and the margins. In Chapter 8, however, we explore some of the other properties available in this dialog box.

Report Template, Task 3: Copy the Template to the Report Project Directory

   1. From the Main menu, select File | Close Property to close the solution.

   2. Open Windows Explorer and navigate to the folder you created for the Template project. From the My Documents folder, the path should be the following:

```
Visual Studio 2005\Projects\MSSQLRS\Template
```

   3. In the Template folder, highlight the file GDSReport.rdl. This is the template report we just created.

4. Press CTRL-C to copy this file.

5. Navigate to the directory where the Report Designer stores its templates. In a default installation this is

```
C:\Program Files\Microsoft Visual Studio 8\Common7\IDE\
              PrivateAssemblies\ProjectItems\ReportProject
```

6. Select the ReportProject folder.

7. Press CTRL-V to paste the copied file in this directory.

8. Close Windows Explorer.

Task Notes   When we add a new item to a report project, the Report Designer looks in the ProjectItems\ReportProjects folder. Any report files (.rdl) it finds in this folder are included in the Templates area of the Add New Item dialog box. This is shown in Figure 7-4.

In the remainder of this chapter, we use our new template to create reports.

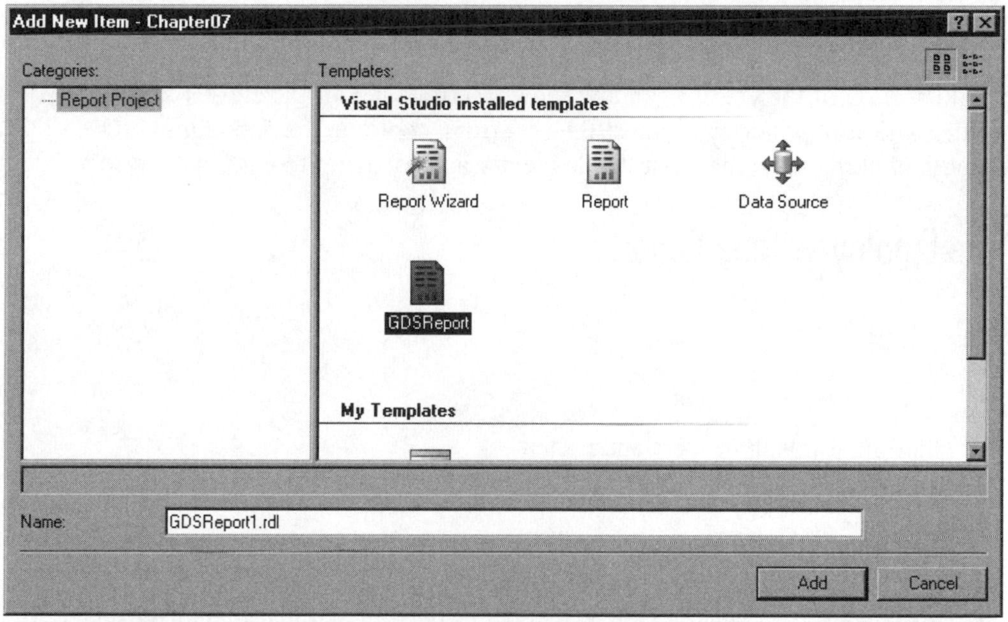

Figure 7-4   *The Add New Item dialog box with a custom template*

Handling Errors in Reports

As you create more complex reports and use more intricate expressions in those reports, you increase the chance of introducing errors. The Report Designer lets you know you have an error when you try to preview a report. You receive a message in the Preview tab saying, "There are compilation errors. See Task List for details."

Fortunately, the Report Designer also provides tools for dealing with errors. A list of detailed error messages is displayed in both the Build section of the Output window and in the Task List window. In most cases, these error messages provide a pretty good description of the problem. In many cases, the problem is a syntax error in an expression you constructed in a property of a report item.

If you double-click an error entry in the Task List window, you return to the Layout tab (if you are not already there) and the report item that contains the offending expression is selected. You can then use the error message to determine which property contains the error and you can fix the problem. In some cases, if you open the Properties dialog box for the report item, the property containing the error has an exclamation mark surrounded by a red circle placed next to it.

Once you make changes to remedy each error listed in the Task List window, you can click the Preview tab to run the report. If all the errors have been corrected, the Build section of the Output window shows 0 errors and all the entries are cleared out of the Task List window. If you still have errors, continue the debugging process by double-clicking on a Task List window entry and try again to correct the error.

The Employee Time Report

Features Highlighted

- ▶ Using a report template
- ▶ Putting totals in headers and footers
- ▶ Using the scope parameter in an aggregate function
- ▶ Toggling visibility

Business Need   The Galactic Delivery Services personnel department needs a report showing the amount of time entered by its employees on their weekly timesheets. The report should group the time by job, employee, and week, with totals presented for each grouping. The groups should be collapsed initially, and the user should be able to drill down into the desired group. Group totals should be visible even when the group is collapsed.

Task Overview

1. Create the Chapter07 Project, a Shared Data Source, a New Report, and a Dataset
2. Populate the Report Layout
3. Add Drilldown Capability
4. Add Totaling

Employee Time Report, Task 1: Create the Chapter07 Project, a Shared Data Source, a New Report, and a Dataset

1. Create a new Reporting Services project called Chapter07 in the MSSQLRS folder. (If you need help with this task, see the section "The Transport List Report" in Chapter 5.)

2. Create a shared data source called Galactic for the Galactic database. (Again, if you need help with this task, see the section "The Transport List Report" in Chapter 5.)

3. Right-click Reports in the Solution Explorer. Select Add | New Item from the Context menu. The Add New Item dialog box appears.

4. Single-click GDSReport in the Templates area to select it. Change the Name to EmployeeTime and click Add.

5. Select <New Dateset...> from the Dataset drop-down list. The Dataset dialog box appears.

6. Enter **EmployeeTime** for the name in the Dataset dialog box.

7. Galactic (shared) is selected for the data source by default. Click OK. You return to the Data tab, which now displays the Generic Query Designer.

8. Type the following in the SQL pane:

```
SELECT Description AS Job,
    Employee.EmployeeNumber,
    FirstName,
    LastName,
    CONVERT(char(4),DATEPART(yy, WorkDate))+'-'+
        CONVERT(char(2),DATEPART(wk, WorkDate)) AS Week,
    WorkDate,
    HoursWorked
FROM TimeEntry
INNER JOIN Assignment
    ON TimeEntry.AssignmentID = Assignment.AssignmentID
INNER JOIN Employee
    ON Assignment.EmployeeNumber = Employee.EmployeeNumber
```

```
INNER JOIN Job
    ON Assignment.JobID = Job.JobID
ORDER BY Job, Employee.EmployeeNumber, Week, WorkDate
```

9. Run the query to make sure no errors exist.

10. Select the Layout tab.

Task Notes   If you need to, refer to the database diagram for the personnel department in Chapter 3 to see how the TimeEntry, Assignment, Employee, and Job tables are related. Our query joins these four tables to determine what work hours were entered for each employee and what job they held.

We are using a combination of the CONVERT() and DATEPART() functions to create a string containing the year and the week number for each time entry. This enables us to group the time into workweeks. Note, the year comes first in this string, so it sorts correctly across years.

When you selected the Layout tab, content was already in the page header and page footer of the report. This, of course, is because we used our new GDSReport template to create the report. By using our report template, we have a consistent header and footer on our reports without having to work at it.

Employee Time Report, Task 2: Populate the Report Layout

1. Place a text box onto the body of the report. Modify the following properties of this text box:

Property	Value
Font: FontSize	25pt
Font: FontWeight	Bold
Location: Left	0in
Location: Top	0in
Size: Width	2.875in
Size: Height	0.5in
Value	Employee Time

2. Place a table onto the body of the report immediately below the text box you just added.

3. In the Datasets window, expand the EmployeeTime dataset. Drag the WorkDate field into the detail row in the center column of the table.

4. Drag the HoursWorked field into the detail row in the right-hand column of the table.

5. Select the entire header row in the table. Modify the following property:

Property	Value
TextDecoration	Underline

6. Right-click in the gray square to the upper-left of the table. Select Properties from the Context menu. The Table Properties dialog box appears. Select the Groups tab.

7. Click Add. The Grouping and Sorting Properties dialog box appears.

8. Type **JobGroup** for the name. (No spaces are allowed in group names.)

9. In the Expression area, select =Fields!Job.Value from the drop-down list.

10. Click OK to exit the Grouping and Sorting Properties dialog box.

11. Click Add again. The Grouping and Sorting Properties dialog box appears.

12. Type **EmpNumGroup** for the name.

13. In the Expression area, select =Fields!EmployeeNumber.Value from the drop-down list.

14. Click OK to exit the Grouping and Sorting Properties dialog box.

15. Click Add a third time. The Grouping and Sorting Properties dialog box appears.

16. Type **WeekGroup** for the name.

17. In the Expression area, select =Fields!Week.Value from the drop-down list.

18. Click OK to exit the Grouping and Sorting Properties dialog box.

19. Click OK to exit the Table Properties dialog box.

20. Click in any cell in the table. Notice how three group header rows and three group footer rows have been added to the table. The gray boxes to the left of the table identify the group rows as 1, 2, and 3. Drag the Job field into the leftmost cell in the Group 1 header row.

21. Right-click the gray rectangle above the leftmost column in the table. Select Insert Column to the Right from the Context menu.

22. Drag the EmployeeNumber field into the cell in the column you just created and in the Group 2 header row.

23. Drag the width of the leftmost column in the table until the column is just wide enough for the word "Job" in the table header cell.

24. Select the two leftmost cells in the row for the Group 1 header, right-click them, and select Merge Cells from the Context menu. (Click-and-drag or hold down SHIFT while clicking to select multiple cells at the same time.)

25. Right-click the gray rectangle above the second-from-the-left column in the table. Select Insert Column to the Right from the Context menu.

26. Drag the Week field into the cell in the column you just created in the Group 3 header row.

27. Drag the width of the second column from the left until it is just wide enough for the words "Employee Number" in the table header cell.

28. Drag the width of the third column from the left until it is just wide enough for the =Fields!Week.Value expression in the Group 3 header cell.

29. Select the three group header rows at the same time. Modify the following property in the Property window:

Property	Value
Font: FontWeight	Bold

30. Select the three cells in the center of the Group 2 header row, right-click them, and select Merge Cells from the Context menu.

31. Modify the following properties for the merged cell that results from Step 30:

Property	Value
TextAlign	Left
Value (Select <Expression...> from the drop-down list to make editing easier. You can select the field expressions from the Fields area and double-click to add them to the Expression area. Remember, the Globals, Parameters, and Fields expressions are case-sensitive!)	=Fields!EmployeeNumber.Value & "-" & Fields!FirstName.Value & " " & Fields!LastName.Value

32. Your report layout should appear similar to Figure 7-5.

33. Select the Preview tab. Your report should appear similar to Figure 7-6.

Task Notes   We placed a table on our report to contain the employee time information. We created three groups within the table to contain the groups required by the business needs for this report. The detail information is grouped into weeks (WeekGroup). The week groups are grouped into employees (EmpNumGroup). The employee groups are grouped into jobs (JobGroup). By merging cells in the grouping rows, we can give the report a stepped look, yet keep the width of our steps small, so it has enough room for the detail information.

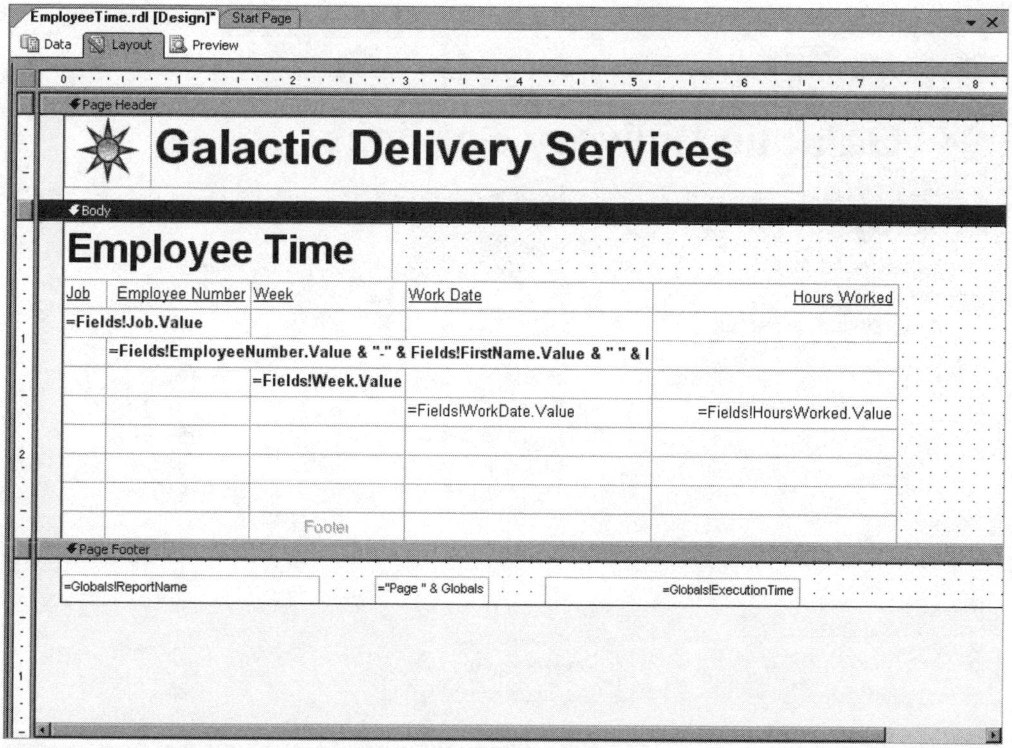

Figure 7-5   *Employee Time Report layout after Task 2*

Employee Time Report, Task 3: Add Drilldown Capability

1. Select the Layout tab.

2. Select the entire table and bring up the Table Properties dialog box as we did in Step 6 of Task 2. Select the Groups tab.

3. Select EmpNumGroup and click Edit. The Grouping and Sorting Properties dialog box appears.

4. Select the Visibility tab.

5. Select Hidden for the Initial Visibility setting.

6. Check the box labeled Visibility Can Be Toggled by Another Report Item.

7. Select Job from the Report Item drop-down list.

8. Click OK to exit the Grouping and Sorting Properties dialog box.

9. Select WeekGroup and click Edit. The Grouping and Sorting Properties dialog box appears.

10. Select the Visibility tab.

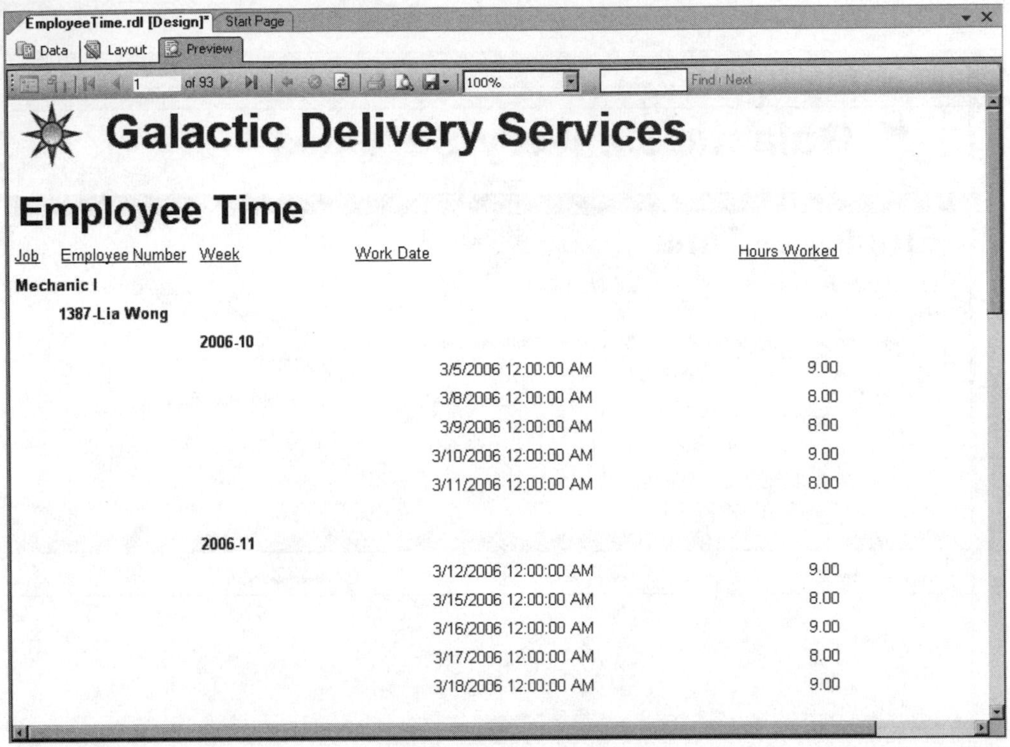

Figure 7-6 *Employee Time Report preview after Task 2*

11. Select Hidden for the Initial Visibility setting.

12. Check the box labeled Visibility Can Be Toggled by Another Report Item.

13. Select EmployeeNumber from the Report Item drop-down list.

14. Click OK to exit the Grouping and Sorting Properties dialog box.

15. Click Details Grouping. The Details Grouping dialog box appears.

16. Select the Visibility tab.

17. Select Hidden for the Initial Visibility setting.

18. Check the box which is labeled Visibility Can Be Toggled by Another Report Item.

19. Select Week from the Report Item drop-down list. (This is at the bottom of the list.)

20. Click OK to exit the Details Grouping dialog box.

21. Click OK to exit the Table Properties dialog box.

22. Select the Preview tab. Your report should appear similar to Figure 7-7 after expanding the top few groups.

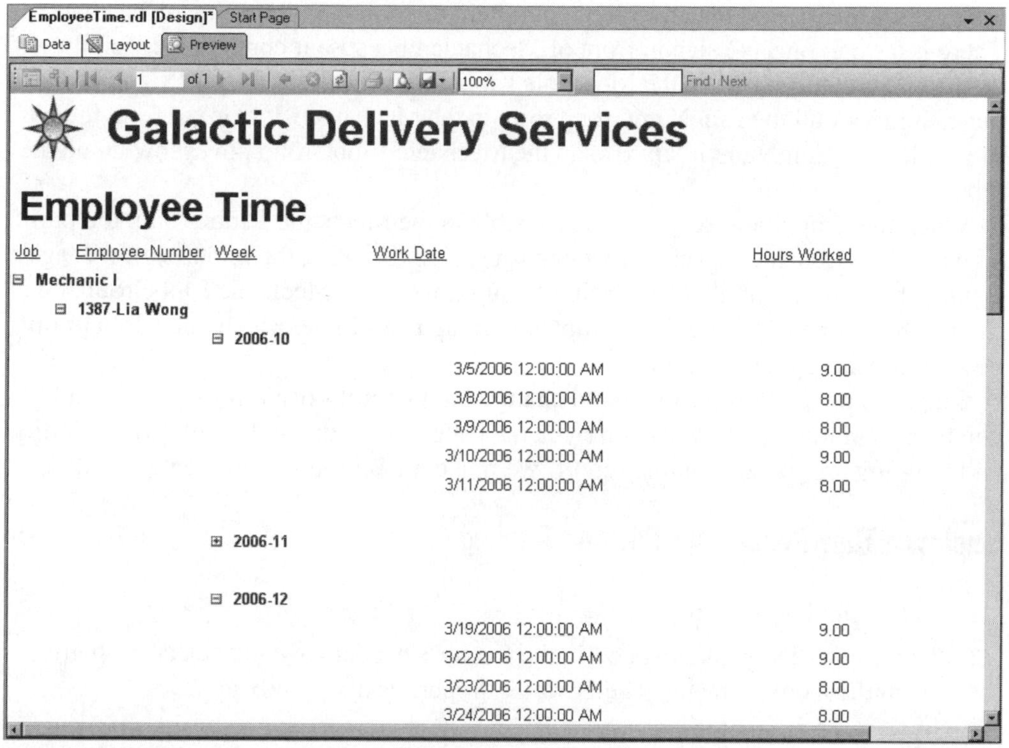

Figure 7-7   *Employee Time Report preview*

Task Notes   We now have the drilldown capability working as required for this report. This was done by using the visibility and toggling properties of the groupings in the table. The visibility of each group is set to be toggled by a report item in the group above it. Therefore, EmpNumGroup is set to be toggled by the Job report item in JobGroup, and WeekGroup is set to be toggled by the EmployeeNumber report item in EmpNumGroup.

For the purposes of visibility, the detail row of the table is treated as a group and is called the *details grouping*. The details grouping is set to be toggled by the Week report item, which is part of WeekGroup.

EmpNumGroup, WeekGroup, and the details grouping all have their initial visibility set to Hidden. This means when you run the report in the Preview tab, you do not see any of these groups. Only the top group, JobGroup, is visible.

Remember, in data regions, the items are repeated according to the rows in the dataset. Therefore, the report contains a number of JobGroup rows, one for each distinct job contained in the dataset. Each JobGroup contains sets of EmpNumGroup rows, WeekGroup rows, and the details grouping rows.

The first JobGroup contains a Job report item (text box) with a value of Mechanic I. There is a small plus (+) sign in front of Mechanic I because it controls the visibility of the EmpNumGroup rows in the Mechanic I JobGroup. Clicking the plus sign changes the visibility of all the EmpNumGroup rows in the Mechanic I JobGroup from hidden to visible. The EmpNumGroup rows in the Mechanic I JobGroup now show up on the report.

When the EmpNumGroup rows are visible in the Mechanic I JobGroup, the plus sign next to Mechanic I changes to a minus (−) sign. Clicking the minus sign will again change the visibility of all the EmpNumGroup rows in the Mechanic I JobGroup, this time from visible to hidden. The EmpNumGroup rows in the Mechanic I JobGroup now disappear from the report.

Click the plus and minus signs to change the visibility of various groups and detail rows in the report. Make sure you have a good understanding of how visibility and toggling are working in the report. We make it a bit more complicated in Task 4.

Employee Time Report, Task 4: Add Totaling

1. Select the Layout tab.
2. Right-click the rightmost cell in the Group 1 header row and select Properties from the Context menu. The Textbox Properties dialog box appears.
3. Type the following for Value:

   ```
   =Sum(Fields!HoursWorked.Value)
   ```

NOTE

To save some typing, you can select =Fields!HoursWorked.Value from the Value drop-down list, and then add in the additional text.

4. Select the Visibility tab.
5. Check the box which is labeled Visibility Can Be Toggled by Another Report Item.
6. Select Job from the Report Item drop-down list. (We are leaving Initial Visibility set to Visible.)
7. Click OK to exit the Textbox Properties dialog box.
8. Right-click the rightmost cell in the Group 2 header row and select Properties from the Context menu. The Textbox Properties dialog box appears.
9. Type the following for Value:

   ```
   =Sum(Fields!HoursWorked.Value)
   ```

10. Select the Visibility tab.

11. Check the box labeled Visibility Can Be Toggled by Another Report Item.

12. Select EmployeeNumber from the Report Item drop-down list. (We are leaving Initial Visibility set to Visible.)

13. Click OK to exit the Textbox Properties dialog box.

14. Right-click the rightmost cell in the Group 3 header row and select Properties from the Context menu. The Textbox Properties dialog box appears.

15. Type the following for Value:

    ```
    =Sum(Fields!HoursWorked.Value)
    ```

16. Select the Visibility tab.

17. Check the box labeled Visibility Can Be Toggled by Another Report Item.

18. Select Week from the Report Item drop-down list. (We are leaving Initial Visibility set to Visible.)

19. Click OK to exit the Textbox Properties dialog box.

20. Click the gray square for the Group 1 footer row. Modify the following properties for this footer row using the Properties window (the drop-down list at the top of the Properties window calls this TableRow8):

Property	Value
Visibility: Hidden	True
Visibility: ToggleItem	Job

21. Click the gray square for the Group 2 footer row. Modify the following properties for this footer row using the Properties window:

Property	Value
Visibility: Hidden	True
Visibility: ToggleItem	EmployeeNumber

22. Click the gray square for the Group 3 footer row. Modify the following properties for this footer row using the Properties window:

Property	Value
Visibility: Hidden	True
Visibility: ToggleItem	Week

23. Select the rightmost cell in the Group 3 footer row. Modify the following properties for this text box using the Properties window:

Property	Value
BorderStyle: Top	Solid
Font: FontWeight	Bold
Value (Select <Expression...> from the drop-down list to make it easier to enter this value.)	=Sum(Fields!HoursWorked.Value)

NOTE

You can accomplish Steps 24 and 25 by copying the text box whose properties you modified in Step 23, and then pasting it into the cells specified in Steps 24 and 25. Make sure you have the text box selected without the flashing text edit cursor inside of it, before you try to copy it.

24. Repeat Step 23 for the rightmost cell in the Group 2 footer row.
25. Repeat Step 23 for the rightmost cell in the Group 1 footer row.
26. Select the rightmost cell in the table footer row. Modify the following properties for this text box using the Properties window:

Property	Value
BorderStyle: Top	Double
BorderWidth: Top	3pt
Font: FontWeight	Bold
Value (Select <Expression...> from the drop-down list to make it easier to enter this value.)	=Sum(Fields!HoursWorked.Value)

27. Your report layout should appear similar to Figure 7-8.
28. Select the Preview tab. Your report should appear similar to Figure 7-9 when the top few groups are expanded.
29. Click Save All in the toolbar.

Task Notes   Now we not only have a report with group totals, we have a report that keeps its group totals where they ought to be. When the group is collapsed, the group total is on the same line with the group header. When the group is expanded, the group total moves from the group header to the group footer.

When you think about it, this is how you would expect things to work. When the group is collapsed, we expect it to collapse down to one line. Therefore, the group total

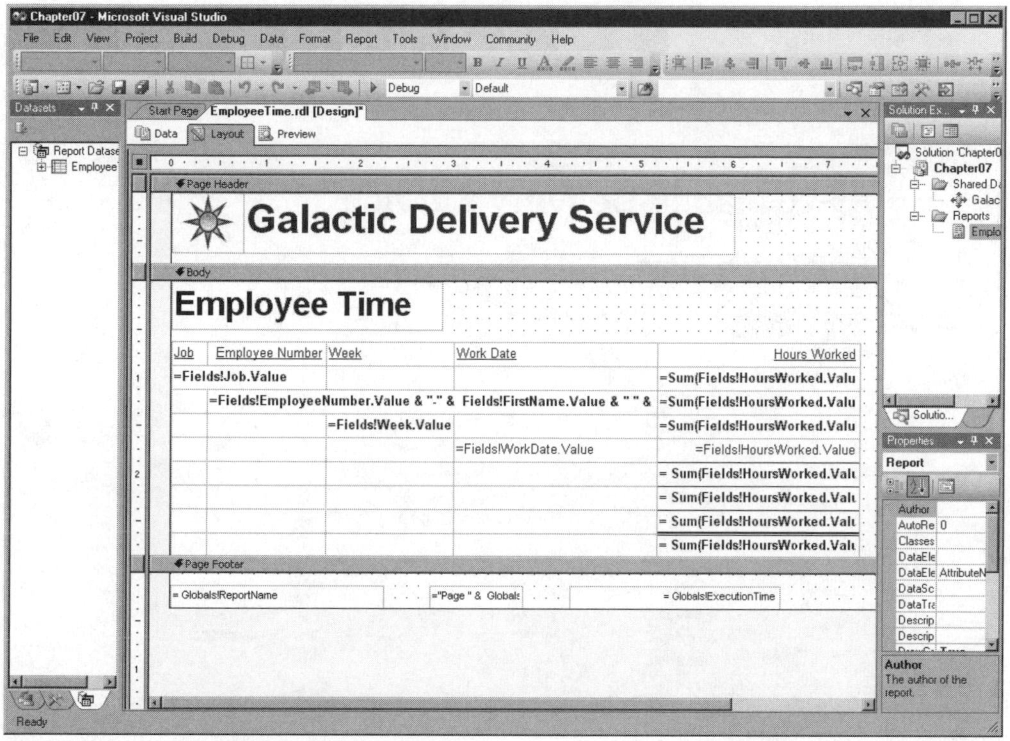

Figure 7-8   *The Employee Time Report layout after Task 4*

should be on the line with the group header. When the group is expanded, a column of numbers is in the group. We would naturally expect the total for that column of numbers to be below it. Therefore, the group total should move to the group footer.

We achieved this functionality by using our toggle items to control the visibility of three other items at the same time. In the previous section, we discussed the fact that Mechanic I controls the visibility of the EmpNumGroup rows in the Mechanic I JobGroup. Now, Mechanic I also controls the visibility of the Hours Worked total in the group header and the Hours Worked total in the group footer. The Hours Worked total in the group header is initially set to Visible. The Hours Worked total in the group footer is initially set to Hidden.

When the plus sign next to Mechanic I is clicked, three things occur:

▶ The EmpNumGroup rows are set to Visible.

▶ The Hours Worked total in the group header is set to Hidden.

▶ The Hours Worked total in the group footer is set to Visible.

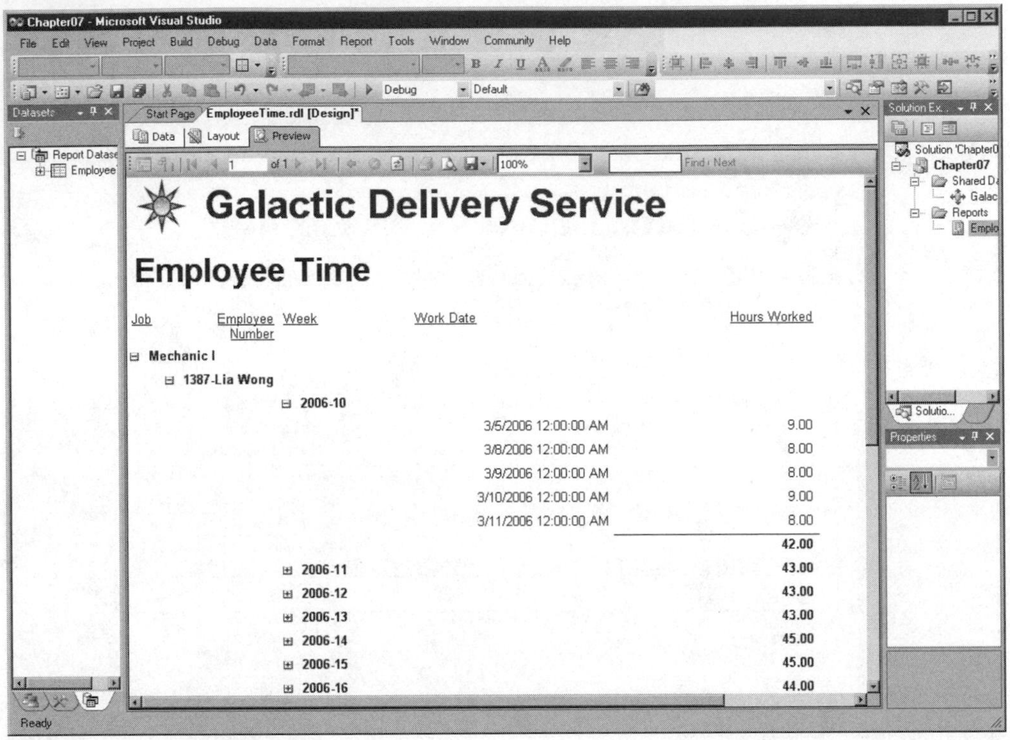

Figure 7-9   *The Employee Time Report preview after Task 4*

When the minus sign next to Mechanic I is clicked, the reverse takes place. This same behavior occurs at each level. Again, you can click the plus and minus signs to change the visibility of various groups and detail rows in the report. Make sure you understand how the visibility and toggle items interrelate.

The other feature of note used in this task is the Sum() aggregate function. If you were paying attention, you noticed we used the following expression in a number of different locations:

```
= Sum(Fields!HoursWorked.Value)
```

If you were paying close attention, you also noticed this expression yields a number of different results. How does this happen? It happens through the magic of scope.

Scope is the data grouping in which the aggregate function is placed. For example, the Sum() function placed in the JobGroup header row (the Group 1 header row) uses the current JobGroup as its scope. It sums hours worked only for those records in the current JobGroup data grouping. The Sum() function placed in the EmpNumGroup header row (the Group 2 header row) uses the current EmpNumGroup as its scope.

It sums the hours worked only for those records in the current EmpNumGroup data grouping. The Sum() function placed in the table footer row is not within any data grouping, so it sums the hours worked in the entire dataset.

As you have seen in this report, it does not make a difference whether the aggregate function is placed in the group header or the group footer. Either way, the aggregate function acts on all the values in the current data grouping. At first, this may seem a bit counterintuitive. It is easy to think of the report being processed sequentially from the top of the page to the bottom. In this scenario, the total for a group would only be available in the group footer after the contents of that group are processed. Fortunately, this is not the way Reporting Services works. The calculation of aggregates is separate from the rendering of the report. Therefore, aggregates can be placed anywhere in the report.

Finally, it is important not to confuse the aggregate functions within Reporting Services with the aggregate functions that exist within the environs of SQL Server. Many of the Reporting Services aggregate functions have the same names as SQL Server aggregate functions. Despite this, Reporting Services aggregate functions and SQL Server aggregate functions work in different locations.

SQL Server aggregate functions work within a SQL Server query. They are executed by SQL Server as the dataset is being created by the database server. SQL Server aggregate functions do not have a concept of scope. They simply act on all the data that satisfies the WHERE clause of the query. As just discussed, Reporting Services aggregate functions are executed after the dataset is created, as the report is executing and are dependent on scope.

Here is a list of the Reporting Services aggregate functions:

Avg()	Calculates the average of the values in a scope.
Count()	Counts the number of values in a scope.
CountDistinct()	Counts the number of unique values in a scope.
CountRows()	Counts the number of rows in a scope.
First()	Returns the first value in the scope.
Last()	Returns the last value in the scope.
Max()	Returns the maximum value in the scope.
Min()	Returns the minimum value in the scope.
StDev()	Calculates the standard deviation of the values in the scope.
StDevP()	Calculates the population standard deviation of the values in the scope.
Sum()	Calculates the sum of the values in the scope.
Var()	Calculates the variance of the values in the scope.
VarP()	Calculates the population variance of the values in the scope.

Each of the aggregate functions in the previous table returns a single result for the entire scope. The following two functions are known as running aggregates. The *running aggregates* return a result for each record in the scope. That result is based on a value in the current row and all of the previous rows in the scope.

The running aggregate functions are:

RowNumber()	Returns the number of the current row, starting at 1 and counting upward.
RunningValue()	Returns the running sum of the values.

Data Caching During Preview

You switched between layout and preview a number of times during the development of this report. If you were to look on your SQL Server, however, you would find the rather complex query that provides the data for this report was only executed once. This is because the data returned for the dataset the first time the report was run is stored in a cache file. Any time after that, when the same report is run in the Report Designer with the same query, same parameters, and same data access credentials, the cached data is used.

This data caching helps to make your report development sessions more efficient. Even if you have a report based on a query that takes a fair amount of time to run, you only have to wait for it once. Any time you preview the report after that, the data is pulled from the cache file with no delay. This caching process also substantially decreases the load on your SQL Server. This can be important if you are following the frowned-upon practice of developing reports against a production database server.

The drawback to the data-caching process comes when you are making changes to the data at the same time as you are developing a report. If you insert new records or update existing records after the first time you preview the report, and then expect to see those changes in your report the next time you preview it, you are going to be confused, disappointed, or perhaps both. The report is rendered from the cached data that does not include the changes.

To remedy this situation, you need to delete the cache file. Once the cached file is deleted, the Report Designer is forced to rerun the queries in the report and create a new cache file. The cache file is in the same folder as the report definition file and has the same name with a .data on the end. For example, MyReport.rdl has a cache file located in the same folder called MyReport.rdl.data.

Remember, this data-caching process is only used by the Report Designer during report development. A different data-caching scheme operates on the report server after the report has been put into production. We discuss that caching scheme in Chapter 11.

The Employee List Report

Features Highlighted

- ▶ Implementing user-selectable grouping
- ▶ Implementing interactive sorting
- ▶ Using explicit page breaks
- ▶ Using a floating header

Business Need   The Galactic Delivery Services personnel department wants a flexible report for listing employee information. Rather than having a number of reports for each of their separate grouping and sorting needs, they want a single report where they can choose the grouping and sort order each time the report is run. The report should be able to group on job, hub, or city of residence. The report should be able to sort by employee number, last name, or hire date. Also, each new group should start on a new page. The header information should remain visible even when the user scrolls down the report page.

Task Overview

1. Create a New Report and a Dataset
2. Create the Report Layout
3. Add Interactive Sorting and a Floating Header

Employee List Report, Task 1: Create a New Report and a Dataset

1. Reopen the Chapter07 project if it was closed. Close the Employee Time Report if it is still open.
2. Right-click Reports in the Solution Explorer and select Add | New Item from the Context menu. The Add New Item dialog box appears.
3. Single-click GDSReport in the Templates area to select it. Change the name to EmployeeList and click Add.
4. Choose <New Dataset…> from the Dataset drop-down list. The Dataset dialog box appears.
5. Enter **Employees** for the name in the Dataset dialog box.
6. Galactic (shared) is selected for the data source by default. Click OK. You return to the Generic Query Designer in the Data tab.

7. Type the following in the SQL pane:

```
SELECT Job.Description AS Job,
    Hub.Description AS Hub,
    Employee.EmployeeNumber,
    FirstName,
    LastName,
    Address1,
    City,
    State,
    ZipCode,
    HireDate,
    HighestLevelOfEducation,
    UnionMembership
FROM Employee
INNER JOIN Assignment
    ON Employee.EmployeeNumber = Assignment.EmployeeNumber
INNER JOIN Job
    ON Assignment.JobID = Job.JobID
INNER JOIN Hub
    ON Assignment.HubCode = Hub.HubCode
```

8. Run the query to make sure it is correct.

Task Notes Notice no ORDER BY clause is in our SELECT statement. In most cases, this would cause a problem. Users like to have their information show up in something other than a random sort order. In this case it is fine, because we are sorting the data within the report itself according to what the user selects as report parameters.

Employee List Report, Task 2: Create the Report Layout

1. Select the Layout tab.
2. Place a text box onto the body of the report. Modify the following properties of this text box:

Property	Value
Font: FontSize	25pt
Font: FontWeight	Bold
Location: Left	0in
Location: Top	0in
Size: Width	2.875in
Size: Height	0.5in
Value	Employee List

3. Place a table onto the body of the report immediately below the text box you just added.

4. In the Datasets window, expand the Employees dataset. Drag the EmployeeNumber field into the leftmost cell in the detail row of the table.

5. Drag the FirstName field into the middle cell in the detail row of the table.

6. Drag the LastName field into the rightmost cell in the detail row of the table.

7. Right-click the gray rectangle above the rightmost column in the table and select Insert Column to the Right from the Context menu.

8. Drag the Address1 field into the detail row of the newly created column.

9. Repeat Steps 7 and 8 for the City, State, ZipCode, HireDate, HighestLevel-OfEducation, and UnionMembership fields.

10. Right-click the cell in the detail row containing the HireDate expression and select Properties from the Context menu. The Textbox Properties dialog box appears.

11. Select the Format tab.

12. Click the ellipsis button (…) next to the Format Code text box. The Choose Format dialog box appears.

13. Select Date from the list on the left. Select the bottom-most date format from the list on the right.

14. Click OK to exit the Choose Format dialog box. Note, the Visual Basic formatting code that corresponds to the date format you selected is now placed in the Format Code text box.

15. Click OK to exit the Textbox Properties dialog box.

16. Size each column appropriately. Use the Preview tab to check your work. Continue switching between the Layout tab and the Preview tab until you have the table columns sized correctly.

17. Drag the right edge of the report body layout area until it is just touching the right side of the table.

18. Click the gray square for the table header row. Modify the following property:

Property	Value
TextDecoration	Underline

19. Click in the report layout area. From the Main menu, select Report | Report Parameters. The Report Parameters dialog box appears.

20. Click Add.

21. Type **GroupOrder** for Name and **Group By** for Prompt.

22. Uncheck the Allow Blank Value option.

23. Fill in the Available Values grid as follows:

Label	Value
Job	Job
Hub	Hub
City	City

 NOTE

Use the arrow keys rather than the Tab key to move between the cells in the Available Values grid.

24. Select Non-queried for Default Values.

25. Type **Job** in the text box for Default Values.

26. Click OK to exit the Report Parameters dialog box.

27. Select the entire table and bring up the Table Properties dialog box.

28. Check the box labeled Repeat Header Rows on Each Page.

29. Select the Groups tab.

30. Click Add. The Grouping and Sorting Properties dialog box appears.

31. Select <Expression...> from the Expression drop-down list. The Edit Expression dialog box appears.

32. Type the following in the Expression area:

```
= IIF( Parameters!GroupOrder.Value = "Job", Fields!Job.Value,
       IIF(Parameters!GroupOrder.Value = "Hub", Fields!Hub.Value,
           Fields!City.Value))
```

NOTE

Use the Parameters and Fields entries in the Edit Expression dialog box to help build expressions, such as the previous one. Double-click the desired parameter or field to add it to the expression you are building.

33. Highlight the entire expression you just entered and press CTRL-C to copy this text.

34. Click OK to exit the Edit Expression dialog box.

35. Check the box labeled Page Break at End.

36. Uncheck the box labeled Include Group Footer.

37. Select the Sorting tab.

38. Select <Expression...> from the Expression drop-down list. The Edit Expression dialog box appears.

39. Delete the equals sign from the Expression area and press CTRL-V to paste the expression into the Expression area. This should be the same expression you entered in Step 32.

40. Click OK to exit the Edit Expression dialog box.

41. Leave the sort direction as Ascending. Click OK to exit the Grouping and Sorting Properties dialog box.

42. Select the Sorting tab.

43. In the Expression area, select =Fields!EmployeeNumber.Value from the drop-down list.

44. Leave the sort direction as Ascending. Click OK to exit the Table Properties dialog box.

45. Select the three leftmost cells in the Group 1 header row. Right-click these cells and select Merge Cells from the Context menu.

46. Right-click these cells again and select Expression from the Context menu.

47. Delete the equals sign from the Expression area and press CTRL-V to paste the expression into the Expression area. This should be the same expression you entered in Step 32.

48. Click OK to exit the Edit Expression dialog box.

49. Modify the following property of the merged cells:

Property	Value
Font: Weight	Bold

50. Your report layout should appear similar to Figure 7-10.

51. Select the Preview tab. Select a grouping, and then click View Report. Your report should appear similar to Figure 7-11. Experiment with changing the grouping. Remember to click View Report each time to refresh the report.

52. Click Save All in the toolbar.

Task Notes   In this report, the report parameter is used to control properties within the report rather than as a parameter to a SQL query. Because of this, we needed to create these report parameters manually, rather than having them created automatically from the dataset query. We also manually constructed a list of valid values and provided a default value. We were then able to use the values selected for this parameter to change the grouping and the group sorting of the table in the report.

Figure 7-10 *The Employee List Report layout after Task 2*

We are able to change the grouping and group sorting of the table because of the IIF() function. This function has three parameters. The first parameter is a Boolean expression (in other words, an expression that results in either a true or false value). The second parameter is the value returned if the Boolean expression is true. The third parameter is the value returned if the Boolean expression is false.

Let's take a look at one of our expressions using the IIF() function:

```
= IIF( Parameters!GroupOrder.Value = "Job", Fields!Job.Value,
       IIF(Parameters!GroupOrder.Value = "Hub", Fields!Hub.Value,
            Fields!City.Value))
```

Figure 7-11   *The Employee List Report preview after Task 2*

This expression uses two IIF() functions, one nested inside the other. The first parameter of the outer IIF() function is

```
Parameters!GroupOrder.Value = "Job"
```

If Job is selected for the grouping, the value of the second parameter is returned by the function. In this case, the second parameter is

```
Fields!Job.Value
```

Therefore, if Job is selected for the grouping, the value of the Job field is used.

If Job is not selected for the grouping, the value of the third parameter is returned. The value of this third parameter is another complete IIF() function:

```
IIF(Parameters!GroupOrder.Value = "Hub", Fields!Hub.Value,
          Fields!City.Value)
```

In this second IIF() function, if Hub is selected for the grouping, the second parameter of this IIF() function is returned. Here, the second parameter is

```
Fields!Hub.Value
```

Therefore, if Hub is selected for the grouping, the value of the Hub field is used.

Finally, if Hub is not selected for the grouping, the value of the third parameter of this IIF() function is returned. Here, the third parameter is

```
Fields!City.Value
```

Therefore, if Hub is not selected for the grouping, the value of the City field is used.

We used the same expression for both the grouping and the group sorting. The group sorting property sorts the groups themselves, so they come out in the proper order. We also used the Sorting tab in the Table Properties dialog box. This provided a default sort order for the rows within each group.

In many cases, a report needs to start each new group on a new page. We used the Page Break at End option in the grouping properties to force the report to start a new page after each grouping. Page break options can be set before or after new groupings. Page breaks can also be set before or after a report item. For instance, you can force a page break before the beginning of a table or after the end of a table.

Employee List Report, Task 3: Add Interactive Sorting and a Floating Header

1. Select the Layout tab.
2. Select the entire table and bring up the Table Properties dialog box.
3. Check the box labeled Header Should Remain Visible While Scrolling.
4. Click OK to exit the Table Properties dialog box.
5. Click the gray square for the table header row. Modify the following property:

Property	Value
BackgroundColor	White

6. Right-click the Employee Number text box in the table header row and select Properties from the Context menu. The Textbox Properties dialog box appears.
7. Select the Interactive Sort tab.

8. Check the box labeled Add an Interactive Sort Action to This Textbox.

9. Select =Fields!EmployeeNumber.Value from the Sort Expression drop-down list.

10. Click OK to exit the Textbox Properties dialog box.

11. Right-click the Last Name text box in the table header row and select Properties from the Context menu. The Textbox Properties dialog box appears.

12. Select the Interactive Sort tab.

13. Check the box labeled Add an Interactive Sort Action to This Textbox.

14. Click the Expression button (the button with *fx* on it) next to the Sort Expression text box. The Edit Expression dialog box appears.

15. Type the following in the Expression area:

    ```
    =Fields!LastName.Value & Fields!FirstName.Value
    ```

16. Click OK to exit the Edit Expression dialog box.

17. Click OK to exit the Textbox Properties dialog box.

18. Right-click the Hire Date text box in the table header row and select Properties from the Context menu. The Textbox Properties dialog box appears.

19. Select the Interactive Sort tab.

20. Check the box labeled Add an Interactive Sort Action to This Textbox.

21. Select =Fields!HireDate.Value from the Sort Expression drop-down list.

22. Click OK to exit the Textbox Properties dialog box.

23. Select the Preview tab.

24. Click the Interactive Sort button next to the Last Name column as shown in Figure 7-12.

25. Page through the report and note the rows are now sorted by last name in ascending order.

26. Click the Interactive Sort button next to the Last Name column again. You return to the first page of the report. Again, page through the report and note that the rows are now sorted by last name in descending order.

27. Click the Interactive Sort button next to the Hire Date column heading. You return to the first page of the report.

28. Page through the report once more. The rows are now sorted by hire date in ascending order.

29. Go to Page 5 of the report.

30. Scroll the page up and down, and notice the table headers always remain visible at the top of the page.

31. Click Save All in the toolbar.

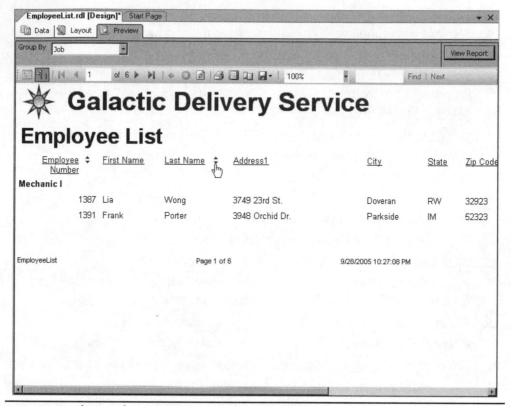

Figure 7-12   *The Employee List Report with interactive sorting*

Task Notes   The interactive sort feature enables the user viewing the report to choose the sort order they would like to see. This could also be done using a report parameter passed as part of the query that creates the dataset. This scheme requires the query to be rerun every time the sort order is changed. Interactive sorting, on the other hand, redisplays the report in the newly selected sort order without rerunning the dataset query. The sorting is all done within the report renderer using the data already collected from the data source.

In our example, the Last Name text box in the table header row has interactive sort enabled. Therefore, when the Interactive Sort button is clicked for this item, the content of the entire table is resorted. In our example, the column header text boxes we used for interactive sorting were in the table header. Therefore, their scope was the entire table. Clicking an interactive sort button resorts the rows within all of the groups in the table. When interactive sorting is applied to column headings in a group header, you can choose whether to apply the sort to all of the groups in the table or to the current group only.

In addition to choosing the scope affected by the interactive sort, you can also choose the scope to be used when evaluating the sort expression. In most cases, you want the sort expression evaluated in the scope of the detail rows, because the detail rows are being sorted. Occasionally, you may want to evaluate the sort expression within the scope of a particular grouping, if the grouping value figures into the sort expression. Note that interactive sorting only works when applied to a text box that is serving as a group header or a data region header.

The floating header does, indeed, seem to float over the columns of the report as you scroll down the page. For this reason, the background of a floating header row should be set to something other than transparent. If this is not done, the column data shows right through the header, making it rather difficult to read.

The Employee Mailing Labels Report

Features Highlighted

- ▶ Enable multiple columns
- ▶ Put information from the database into the report header

Business Need   The Galactic Delivery Services personnel department has a new version of the employee manual. The personnel department needs mailing labels to send the new manual out to each employee. The mailing labels are to be printed on a 2½-inches wide and 1-inch high label. The label sheet has three labels across the sheet and ten labels down the sheet with no margin between each label.

The labels should be sorted in ZIP code, and then last name order. It would also be helpful if the total number of labels is printed in the top margin of the first page printed. Finally, a sequence number should be printed in the lower-right corner of each label.

Task Overview

1. Create the Mailing Label Content
2. Add the Report Header and Multiple Columns

Employee Mailing Labels Report, Task 1: Create the Mailing Label Content

1. Reopen the Chapter07 project if it has been closed. Close the Employee List Report if it is still open.

2. Right-click Reports in the Solution Explorer and select Add | New Item from the Context menu. The Add New Item dialog box appears.

3. Single-click Report in the Templates area to select it. Change the name to EmployeeMailingLabels and click Add.

4. Choose <New Dataset…> from the Dataset drop-down list. The Dataset dialog box appears.

5. Enter **Employees** for the name in the Dataset dialog box.

6. Galactic (shared) is selected for the data source by default. Click OK. You return to the Generic Query Designer in the Data tab.

7. Type the following in the SQL pane:

```
SELECT FirstName + ' ' + LastName AS Name,
    Address1,
    City + ', ' + State + ' ' + ZipCode AS CSZ
FROM Employee
WHERE TerminationDate IS NULL
ORDER BY ZipCode, LastName, FirstName
```

8. Run the query to make sure it is correct.

9. Choose <New Dataset…> from the Dataset drop-down list. The Dataset dialog box appears.

10. Enter **EmployeeCount** for the name in the Dataset dialog box.

11. Galactic is selected for the data source by default. Click OK. You return to the Generic Query Designer in the Data tab.

12. Type the following in the SQL pane:

```
SELECT 'Total Employees: ' + CONVERT(varchar(4), COUNT(*))
            AS EmpCount
FROM Employee
WHERE TerminationDate IS NULL
```

13. Run the query to make sure it is correct.

14. Select the Layout tab.

15. Place a List onto the body of the report. Modify the following properties of the list:

Property	Value
Location: Left	0in
Location: Top	0in
Size:Width	2.5in
Size:Height	1in

16. Select the Datasets window and expand the Employees dataset. Drag the Name field onto the list and set the following properties:

Property	Value
Location: Left	0in
Location: Top	0in
Size:Width	2.25in
Size:Height	0.25in

17. Drag the Address1 field onto the list and set the following properties:

Property	Value
Location: Left	0in
Location: Top	0.25in
Size:Width	2.25in
Size:Height	0.25in

18. Drag the CSZ field onto the list and set the following properties:

Property	Value
Location: Left	0in
Location: Top	0.5in
Size:Width	2.25in
Size:Height	0.25in

19. Drag a text box onto the list, and set the following properties of the text box:

Property	Value
Font: FontSize	8 pt
Location: Left	1.125in
Location: Top	0.75in
Size:Width	1.375in
Size:Height	0.25in
TextAlign	Right
VerticalAlign	Bottom

20. Right-click the text box you just added and select Expression from the Context menu. The Edit Expression dialog box appears.

21. Expand the Common Functions item in the list on the left and select Miscellaneous. The list in the center contains the miscellaneous functions available in Reporting Services.

22. Double-click RowNumber in the center list to add the RowNumber aggregate to the expression.

23. Type (after RowNumber in the expression. The parameter information for the RowNumber aggregate function appears as shown in Figure 7-13.

24. The parameter information tells you there are two different forms of the RowNumber aggregate function. Click the up and down arrows to switch between these two definitions. (The down arrow is indicated by the mouse pointer in Figure 7-13.) The first form has one parameter that specifies the scope of the aggregation. The second form has two parameters: one for the scope and a second for the name of a group to count.

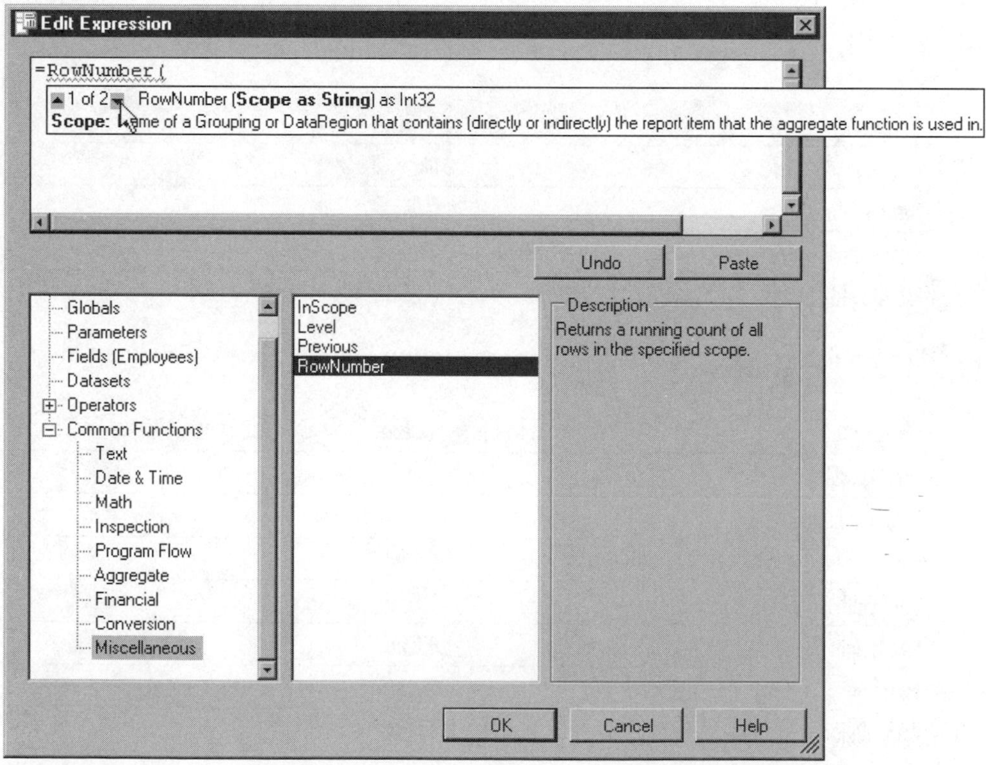

Figure 7-13 *The Edit Expression dialog box with parameter information*

25. In this report, you use the first form of the RowNumber aggregate function. To complete the expression, type **"list1")** after the (.

26. Click OK to exit the Edit Expression dialog box.

27. Adjust the report body so it is exactly the same size as the list report item.

28. Select the Preview tab. Your report should appear similar to Figure 7-14.

29. Click Save All in the toolbar.

Task Notes   The Edit Expression dialog box provides assistance in building expressions. Earlier, we talked about the syntax checking done as you type an expression and the jagged red line that indicates an error. The Edit Expression dialog box enables you to add

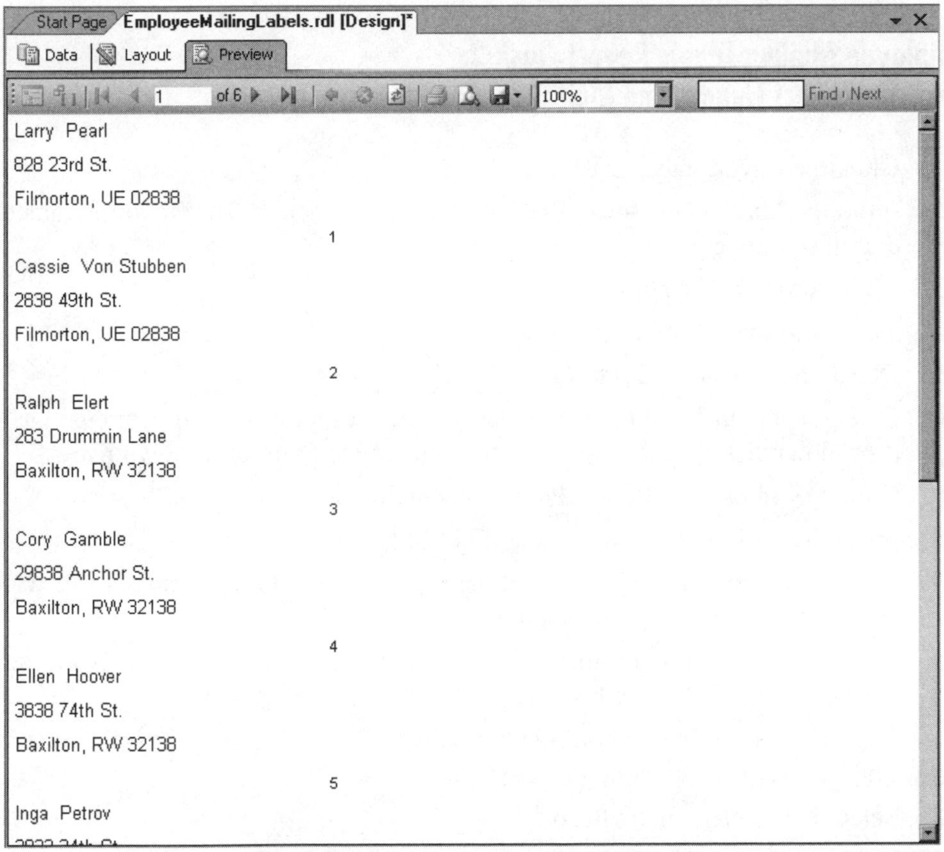

Figure 7-14   *The Employee Mailing Labels Report preview after Task 1*

global variables, parameters, fields, and even common functions to an expression with a double-click. Finally, we saw in Steps 23 and 24 how the Edit Expression dialog box provides information on the parameters expected by a function.

The business requirements call for a sequence number on each label. To do this, we look to the functions available in Reporting Services. The RowNumber function provides just what is needed.

In the next section, you finalize the formatting of the mailing labels. One of the things the business requirements asked for was the count of the number of employees at the top of the first page of labels. The EmployeeCount dataset returns the employee count, so we have the information we need. The only place we can put this employee count without messing up the label layout is in the page header. The problem is, the page header cannot contain information from datasets. In the next task, you employ a little sleight-of-hand using a report parameter to get the job done.

Employee Mailing Labels Report, Task 2: Add the Report Header and Multiple Columns

1. Click the Layout tab.
2. From the Main menu, select Report | Report Parameters. The Report Parameters dialog box appears.
3. Click Add to add a report parameter.
4. Type **EmployeeCount** for Name.
5. Check the box labeled Internal.
6. Change Default Values to From Query. Select EmployeeCount from the Dataset drop-down list. Select EmpCount from the Value Field drop-down list.
7. Click OK to exit the Report Parameters dialog box.
8. From the Main menu, select Report | Page Header.
9. Place a text box on the left side of the page header. Make the text box as wide as the text box holding the Name field.
10. Right-click the text box in the page header and select Properties from the Context menu. The Textbox Properties dialog box appears.
11. Click the Expression button (the button with *fx* on it) next to the Value text box. The Edit Expression dialog box appears.
12. Select Parameters in the list on the left.
13. Double-click EmployeeCount in the list on the right to add it to the expression.

14. Click OK to exit the Edit Expression dialog box and return to the Textbox Properties dialog box.

15. Select the Visibility tab.

16. Change Initial Visibility from Visible to Expression.

17. Click the Expression button for Initial Visibility.

18. Expand Common Functions and select Program Flow in the list on the left.

19. Double-click IIf in the center list.

20. Type (after IIf in the expression.

21. Click Globals in the list on the left.

22. Double-click PageNumber in the center list.

23. Type **> 1, true, false)** at the end of the expression.

24. Click OK to exit the Edit Expression dialog box.

25. Click OK to exit the Textbox Properties.

26. From the Main menu, select Report | Report Properties. The Report Properties dialog box appears.

27. Select the Layout tab.

28. Change Columns to 3.

29. Type **0in** for Spacing.

30. Type **0.5in** for each of the following: Left Margin, Right Margin, and Bottom Margin.

31. Type **0.25in** for the Top Margin.

32. Click OK to exit the Report Properties dialog box. Your report layout should appear similar to Figure 7-15.

33. Select the Preview tab, and then click the Print Layout toolbar button. The report appears similar to Figure 7-16.

34. Click Save All in the toolbar.

Task Notes   You cannot place information from a dataset in the page header . . . directly! You can, however, put the value of a parameter in the page header. You can also use a dataset to specify the default value of a parameter. Therefore, using this two-step approach, we can put the count of employees from the EmployeeCount dataset into the page header.

When we created the EmployeeCount parameter, we specified it was an internal parameter. This means this parameter is only used inside the report. The user should never be prompted for this value. Furthermore, the user should not be able to specify

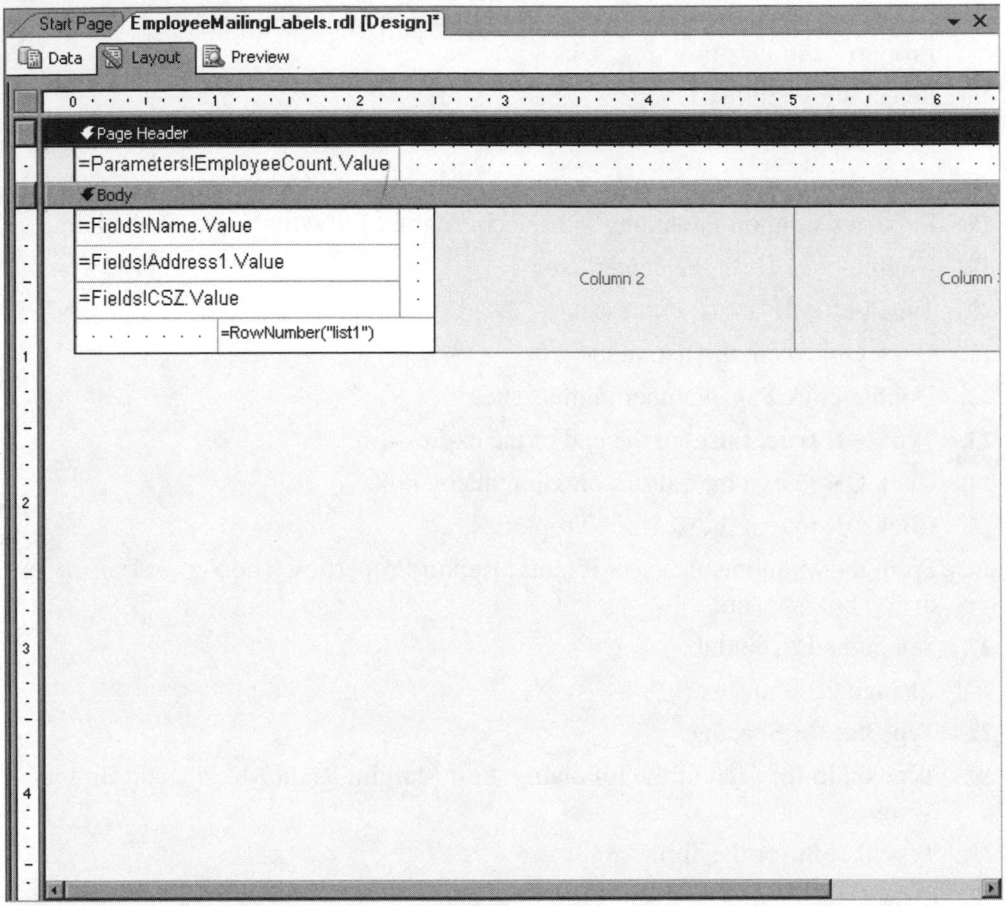

Figure 7-15 *The Employee Mailing Labels Report layout after Task 2*

a value for this parameter through any other means either. Because of this restricted access, the parameter must have a default value specified by either a query or a non-queried (constant) source. This is the only way to set a value for an internal parameter.

The business requirements also specify that the employee count should only be displayed on the first page. The page header has properties that hide it on the first page or the last page. There is no option to have it display only on the first page. To accomplish this, you created an expression to control the visibility of the text box that contains the employee count. If the page number is less than or equal to 1, the employee count is visible. If the page number is greater than 1, the employee count is hidden.

```
Start Page  EmployeeMailingLabels.rdl [Design]*                              ▼ ✕
  🗐 Data  🗐 Layout  🗐 Preview
  ⊞ ⯗ |◀ ◀  1    of 2 ▶  ▶| | ⟵ ⊗ 🗐 | 🖨 🗋 🖫▼ |100%        ▼ |         | Find · Next

    Total Employees: 56
    Larry  Pearl              Fritz  Morris              Sarah  Anthony
    828 23rd St.              4273 5th Ave.              2838 Poplar Ct.
    Filmorton, UE 02838       Orbeck, RW 32483           Axion, RE 37487
                                   1                         10
    Cassie  Von Stubben       Ramona  Carson             Petra  Dragich
    2838 49th St.             2384 Juniper Ln.           2838 Mayfair Ln.
    Filmorton, UE 02838       Doveran, RW 32923          Axion, RE 37487
                                   2                         11
    Ralph  Elert             Stanley  Roosevelt          Walter  Hederson
    283 Drummin Lane         2839 32nd Ave.              135 Small Street
    Baxilton, RW 32138       Doveran, RW 32923           Axion, RE 37487
                                   3                         12
    Cory  Gamble             Winifred  Stanton           Greg  Perkins
    29838 Anchor St.         2839 Overton Dr.            8283 58th Ave.
    Baxilton, RW 32138       Doveran, RW 32923           Axion, RE 37487
                                   4                         13
    Ellen  Hoover            Hilda  Von Brocken          Daniel  Taylor
    3838 74th St.            2983 45th St.               8232 Baker Ave.
```

Figure 7-16   *The Employee Mailing Labels Report preview after Task 2*

Finally, you need to set up the report layout to match the label sheet. This is done on the Layout tab of the Report Properties dialog box. The Columns property, of course, specifies the number of columns in the report. The Spacing property specifies the amount of space in between each column. In addition, the margins need to be set appropriately. Because the labels are three across with 2 ½ inches per label, the labels take up 7 ½ inches. Therefore, the left and right margins must be set to ½ inch each to get a total of 8 ½ inches in width. A similar set of calculations tells us that the top and bottom margins must also be ½ inch each, but ¼ inch must be subtracted from the top margin to accommodate the page header.

The Overtime Report

Features Highlighted

- ▶ Implementing cascading parameters
- ▶ Using SQL stored procedures
- ▶ Using table filters
- ▶ Using the NoRows property

Business Need   The Galactic Delivery Services personnel department needs to monitor the amount of overtime put in at each of its repair and distribution hubs to determine when additional personnel must be hired. The personnel department needs a report that lists the employees with over 45 hours worked in a given week at a given hub. The report should have two sections. The first section should list employees with more than 45 hours and less than 55 hours worked for the selected week. The second section should list employees with more than 55 hours worked for the selected week.

The user should be able to select a workweek from a drop-down list, and then see a second drop-down list showing the hubs that have one or more employees with more than 45 hours for the selected week. The user selects a hub from this second list, and then sees the report for that hub.

Two stored procedures in the Galactic database should be used for retrieving data. The stp_HubsOver45 stored procedure returns a list of hubs with one or more employees who have over 45 hours worked for the selected week. The stp_EmployeesOver45 stored procedure returns a list of employees who have over 45 hours worked for the selected week at the selected hub. We discuss stored procedures in the task notes.

Task Overview

1. Create a New Report and Three Datasets
2. Create the Report Layout

Overtime Report, Task 1: Create a New Report and Three Datasets

1. Reopen the Chapter07 project if it was closed. Close the Employee Mailing Labels Report if it is open.
2. Right-click Reports in the Solution Explorer and select Add | New Item from the Context menu. The Add New Item dialog box appears.

3. Single-click GDSReport in the Templates area to select it. Change the name to **Overtime** and click Add.

4. Choose <New Dataset...> from the Dataset drop-down list. The Dataset dialog box appears.

5. Enter **Weeks** for the name in the Dataset dialog box.

6. Galactic (shared) is selected for the data source by default. Click OK. You return to the Generic Query Designer in the Data tab.

7. Type the following in the SQL pane:

```
SELECT DISTINCT CONVERT(char(4), DATEPART(yy,WorkDate))+'-'+
   RIGHT('0'+CONVERT(varchar(2), DATEPART(wk,WorkDate)),2) as Week
FROM TimeEntry
ORDER BY Week
```

8. Run the query to make sure it is correct.

9. Choose <New Dataset...> from the Dataset drop-down list. The Dataset dialog box appears.

10. Enter **HubsOver45** for the name in the Dataset dialog box.

11. Galactic is selected for the data source by default.

12. Select StoredProcedure from the Command Type drop-down list.

13. Click OK. You return to the stored procedure version of the Generic Query Builder in the Data tab.

14. Select **stp_HubsOver45** from the Stored Procedure drop-down list in the Data tab toolbar.

15. Run the stored procedure to make sure it is functioning properly. When you run the stored procedure, the Report Designer determines what parameters are required. Type **2006-15** for the @Week parameter in the Define Query Parameters dialog box and click OK.

16. Choose <New Dataset...> from the Dataset drop-down list. The Dataset dialog box appears.

17. Enter **EmployeesOver45** for the name in the Dataset dialog box.

18. Galactic is selected for the data source by default.

19. Select StoredProcedure from the Command Type drop-down list.

20. Type **stp_EmployeesOver45** for the query string.

NOTE

You can select the stored procedure from the Stored Procedure drop-down list in the Data tab toolbar or you can type in the name of the stored procedure yourself; whichever is most convenient.

21. Click OK. You return to the stored procedure version of the Generic Query Designer in the Data tab.

22. Run the stored procedure to make sure it is functioning properly. Type **2006-15** for the @Week parameter and **BLNR** for the @HubCode parameter in the Define Query Parameters dialog box, and then click OK.

Task Notes   For two of our three datasets, we used stored procedures rather than queries. A *stored procedure* is a query or a set of queries given a name and stored in the database itself. You can think of a stored procedure as a data-manipulation program created and kept right inside the database.

Stored procedures have several advantages over queries:

▶ **Speed**   A certain amount of preprocessing must be done on any query before it can be run in the database. Stored procedures are preprocessed when they are created, and this preprocessing information is saved with them. This means when you execute a stored procedure, you do not need to wait for the preprocessing. The result is faster execution time.

▶ **Simplicity**   A developer or database administrator can create a stored procedure that uses a number of intricate queries. When you execute the stored procedure, you do not need to understand, or even see, this complexity. All you need to do is execute the stored procedure to get the result set you need.

▶ **Security**   When you query a set of tables, you must be given rights to see any and all data in each of the tables. However, when a stored procedure is used, you only need rights to execute the stored procedure. You do not need rights to any of the tables being queried by the stored procedure. The stored procedure can then control which rows and which columns can be seen by each user.

▶ **Reusability**   A single stored procedure can be used by a number of reports. Therefore, complex queries do not have to be created over and over again when a number of reports need to use the same data.

▶ **Maintainability**   When changes are made to the database structure, the developer or database administrator can make the corresponding changes in the stored procedure, so the stored procedure continues to return the same result set. Without stored procedures, a change in the database structure could result in a number of reports needing to be edited.

For these reasons, it is often advantageous to use stored procedures rather than queries for your datasets.

When you are using a stored procedure for your dataset, all you need to do is set Command Type to StoredProcedure and enter the name of the stored procedure. The Report Designer can figure out the parameters required by the stored procedure and add them to the report. Can't get much simpler than that!

Overtime Report, Task 2: Create the Report Layout

1. Select the Layout tab.
2. From the Main menu, select Report | Report Parameters. The Report Parameters dialog box appears.
3. With Week selected in the Parameters list, change Available Values to From Query. The Dataset drop-down list should be set to Weeks. Select Week from the Value Field drop-down list. Select Week from the Label Field drop-down list.
4. Select HubCode from the Parameters list.
5. Change Prompt to Hub.
6. Change Available Values to From Query.
7. Select HubsOver45 from the Dataset drop-down list. Select HubCode from the Value Field drop-down list. Select Hub from the Label Field drop-down list.
8. Click OK to exit the Report Parameters dialog box.
9. Place a text box onto the body of the report. Modify the following properties of this text box:

Property	Value
Font: FontSize	25pt
Font: FontWeight	Bold
Location: Left	0in
Location: Top	0in
Size: Width	2in
Size: Height	0.5in
Value	Overtime

10. Place a second text box onto the body of the report. Modify the following properties of this text box:

Property	Value
Font: FontSize	16pt
Location: Left	0in
Location: Top	0.5in
Size: Width	5.25in
Size: Height	0.375in

11. Right-click this text box and select Expression from the Context menu.

12. Type the following in the Expression area:

```
= "Week: " & Parameters!Week.Value &
"      Hub: " & Parameters!HubCode.Value
```

13. Click OK to exit the Edit Expression dialog box.

14. Place a third text box onto the body of the report. Modify the following properties of this text box:

Property	Value
Font: FontSize	16pt
Font: FontWeight	Bold
Location: Left	0in
Location: Top	1.125in
Size: Width	5.25in
Size: Height	0.375in
Value	Employees with 45 to 55 hours for this week

15. Place a table onto the body of the report immediately below the third text box.

16. Select the Dataset window and expand the EmployeesOver45 dataset.

17. Drag the EmployeeNumber field into the leftmost cell in the detail row of the table.

18. Drag the FirstName field into the center cell in the detail row of the table.

19. Drag the LastName field into the rightmost cell in the detail row of the table.

20. Right-click the gray bar above the rightmost column and select Insert Column to the Right from the Context menu.

21. Drag the HoursWorked field into the cell in the detail row in the column you just added.

22. Right-click the gray square to the left of the footer row. Select Table Footer from the Context menu to toggle off the table footer.

23. Select the table header row. Modify the following property:

Property	Value
TextDecoration	Underline

24. Select the leftmost table column. Modify the following property:

Property	Value
TextAlign	Left

NOTE

Remember, you can use the items in the Report Formatting toolbar to do things such as turning on underlining and changing the text alignment.

25. Select the entire table and bring up the Table Properties dialog box.

26. Select the Filters tab.

27. Type **=CStr(Fields!HoursWorked.Value)** for the expression.

28. From the Operat… drop-down list, select <=.

29. Type **55.00** for the value.

30. Click OK to exit the Table Properties dialog box.

31. Modify the following property for the table using the Properties window:

Property	Value
NoRows	No Employees

32. Select both the table and the text box with the string Employees with 45 to 55 Hours for This Week. Press CTRL-C to copy these two report items. We are going to paste a copy of these two items and use them to create the layout for the Employees over 55 Hours.

33. Drag the bar between the report body and the page footer, so the report body is larger.

34. Press CTRL-V to paste a copy of the two report items. Drag the two new items so they are below the originals.

35. Select the new text box by itself. Change the value of the text box to Employees with Over 55 Hours for This Week. (You can edit it right in the text box itself.)

36. Select the new table and bring up the Table Properties dialog box.

37. Select the Filters tab.

38. From the Operat… drop-down list, select >.

39. Click OK to exit the Table Properties dialog box. Your report layout should appear similar to Figure 7-17.

40. Select the Preview tab.

41. Notice the Week drop-down list is enabled, but the Hub drop-down list is disabled. Select 2006–15 from the Week drop-down list.

42. Once a week is selected, the Hub drop-down list is enabled. Select Borlaron Repair Base from the Hub drop-down list. Click the View Report button. Your report should appear similar to Figure 7-18.

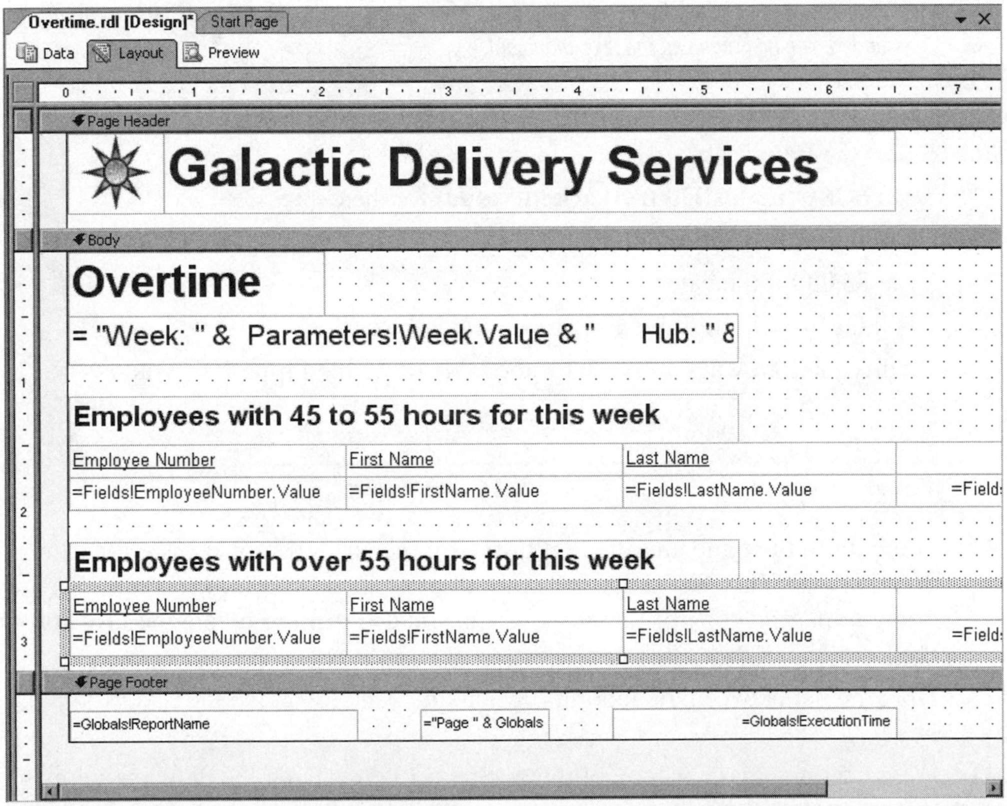

Figure 7-17 *The Overtime Report layout*

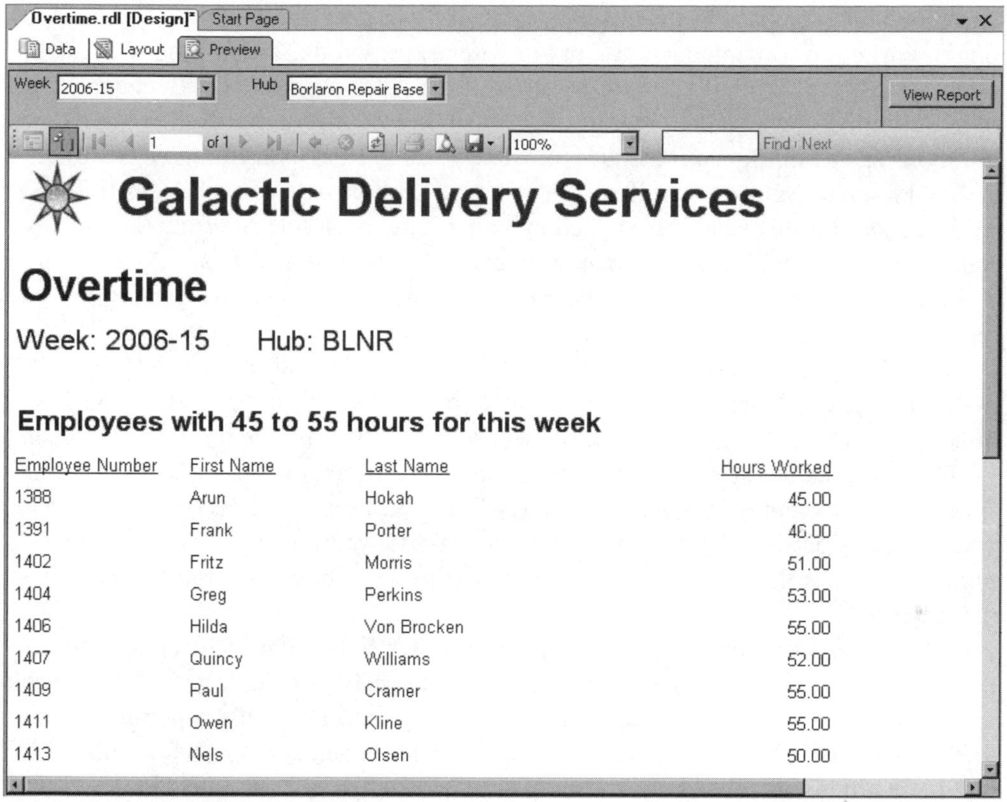

Figure 7-18 *The Overtime Report preview*

43. Select 2006–10 from the Week drop-down list. Borlaron Repair Base is still selected in the Hub drop-down list. Click the View Report button. Note the text under the Employees with Over 55 Hours for This Week heading.

44. Click Save All in the toolbar.

Task Notes In this report, we used the same dataset to populate two tables. We got different information in the two tables by applying different filters on each table. The filter for the upper table on the report says we only want records in this table where the number of hours worked is less than or equal to 55. The filter for the lower table on the report says we only want records in this table where the number of hours worked is greater than 55. In this way, we can divide the data in the dataset to fulfill the business requirements of the report.

You may have noted that we used the Visual Basic function CStr() to convert the hours worked to a string data type in our filter expressions. This is due to a quirk (some might call it a bug) in the operation of the filter expressions. Because of this quirk, filters deal much better with strings than they do with other data types. To get around this, we simply convert our numbers to strings, and everything works fine.

In addition to what you saw here, filters can be applied to data in other locations as well. A dataset can have a filter applied to it after it has been selected from the database. Individual groups within a table, matrix, or chart can also utilize filters.

Filters work well in situations like the one in this report where we want to use one dataset to provide a slightly different set of records to multiple data regions. They can also be useful for taking data from a stored procedure that provides almost, but not quite, the result set you need. It is usually best, however, to have your filtering done by your select query or stored procedure, rather than by the report. The reason is, in most cases, it is considerably faster and more efficient if the database does the filtering as it executes the query or stored procedure. It does not make sense to have your query select 1,000 records from the database if your report is going to filter out all but ten of these records. Filters are a good tool to have; just remember to use them wisely.

In the Overtime Report, we used two drop-down lists to let the user select the parameters for our report. The Week drop-down list enables the user to select the week of the year for which the report should be run. This drop-down list is populated by the Week dataset. The Hub drop-down list lets the user select the hub for which the report should be run. This drop-down list is populated by the HubsOver45 dataset. The HubsOver45 dataset requires a value from the Week drop-down list before it can return a list of the hubs with employees working over 45 hours for that week. In this way, the data that populates the Hub drop-down list is dependent on the value selected in the Week drop-down list.

Reporting Services is smart enough to recognize this dependency and act accordingly. If no value is selected in the Week drop-down list, the Hub drop-down list cannot be populated, so it is disabled. Every time the selected value in the Week drop-down list changes, the Hub drop-down list is repopulated.

Finally, in this report we used the NoRows property of each of the tables. This property enables you to define a string that is output when there are no rows to populate the table. When the filter on the lower table in the report filters out all the rows in the dataset, the content of the NoRows property is displayed. This is more helpful to the user than simply having a blank space where a table should be. The NoRows property is available on any of the data region report items.

Under the Hood

In Chapter 1, we talked about the fact that the report definitions are stored using the Report Definition Language (RDL). RDL was created by Microsoft specifically for Reporting Services. Two things set this file structure apart from other Microsoft file structures, such as a Word document or an Excel spreadsheet. First, RDL is a published standard. Second, RDL is an Extensible Markup Language (XML) document.

Microsoft has gone public with the specifications for RDL. Third parties can create their own authoring environments for creating report definitions. If the RDL from these third-party tools conforms to the RDL standard, the reports created by these tools can be managed and distributed by Reporting Services.

Because RDL is an XML document, you can look at a report definition in its raw form. If you try that with a Word document or an Excel spreadsheet, you will see nothing but gibberish. If you were so inclined, you could use Notepad to open an RDL file and look at its contents. In fact, you don't even need Notepad. You can look at the contents of an RDL file right in the Report Designer.

Viewing the RDL

Right-click the entry for Overtime.rdl in the Solution Explorer, and then select View Code from the Context menu. You see a new tab in the layout area called Overtime.rdl [XML]. This tab contains the actual RDL of the report, as shown in Figure 7-19.

XML Structure

Because the RDL is an XML document, it is made up of pairs of tags. A begin tag is at the beginning of an item and an end tag at the end of the item. A *begin tag* is simply a string of text, the tag name, with < at the front and > at the back. An *end tag* is the same string of text with </ at the front and > at the back. This pair of tags creates an XML element. The information in between the two tags is the value for that element. In the following example, the Height element has a value of 0.625in:

```
<Height>0.625in</Height>
```

There can never be a begin tag without an end tag, and vice versa. In fact, it can be said that XML is the Noah's Ark of data structures, because everything must go two by two.

```
Overtime.rdl [XML]   Overtime.rdl [Design]   Start Page                            ▾ ×
   <?xml version="1.0" encoding="utf-8"?>
   <Report xmlns="http://schemas.microsoft.com/sqlserver/reporting/2005/01/reportdefinition
     <DataSources>
       <DataSource Name="Galactic">
         <rd:DataSourceID>59f9ac05-ccc7-4915-87ed-9df29916a225</rd:DataSourceID>
         <DataSourceReference>Galactic</DataSourceReference>
       </DataSource>
     </DataSources>
     <InteractiveHeight>11in</InteractiveHeight>
     <ReportParameters>
       <ReportParameter Name="Week">
         <DataType>String</DataType>
         <Prompt>Week</Prompt>
         <ValidValues>
           <DataSetReference>
             <DataSetName>Weeks</DataSetName>
             <ValueField>Week</ValueField>
             <LabelField>Week</LabelField>
           </DataSetReference>
         </ValidValues>
       </ReportParameter>
       <ReportParameter Name="HubCode">
         <DataType>String</DataType>
         <Prompt>Hub</Prompt>
         <ValidValues>
           <DataSetReference>
             <DataSetName>HubsOver45</DataSetName>
             <ValueField>HubCode</ValueField>
             <LabelField>Hub</LabelField>
           </DataSetReference>
         </ValidValues>
       </ReportParameter>
     </ReportParameters>
```

Figure 7-19   *The RDL for the Overtime Report*

In addition to simple strings of text, XML elements can contain other elements. In fact, a number of elements can nest one inside the other to form complex structures. Here's an example:

```
<Textbox>
  <Style>
    <Color>DarkBlue</Color>
  </Style>
</Textbox>
```

In some cases, begin tags contain additional information as attributes. An *attribute* comes in the form of an attribute name, immediately following the tag name, followed by an equal sign (=) and the value of the attribute. In this example, the Textbox element has an attribute called Name with a value of "tmpl_Name":

```
<Textbox Name="tmpl_Name">…</Textbox>
```

The RDL contains several sections: the page header, the body, the data sources, the datasets, the embedded images, the page footer, and the report parameters. Each section starts with a begin tag and is terminated by an end tag. For example, the page header section of the RDL starts with <PageHeader> and is terminated by </PageHeader>.

In Figure 7-19, you can see the entire XML structure for the Week report parameter. The begin tag of the report parameter includes a Name attribute. This corresponds to the Name property of the report parameter. In between the begin and end tags of the report parameter element are additional elements, such as DataType, Prompt, and ValidValues. These elements correspond to the other properties of this report parameter. Only those properties that have been changed from their default values are stored in the RDL.

Editing the RDL

One other interesting thing about viewing the RDL in the Report Designer is you can make changes to the RDL and have them affect the report design. Find the Prompt element within the Week report parameter element, as shown in Figure 7-20.

```
Overtime.rdl [XML]   Overtime.rdl [Design]   Start Page                                        ▾ ✕
    <?xml version="1.0" encoding="utf-8"?>
    <Report xmlns="http://schemas.microsoft.com/sqlserver/reporting/2005/01/reportdefinition
      <DataSources>
        <DataSource Name="Galactic">
          <rd:DataSourceID>59f9ac05-ccc7-4915-87ed-9df29916a225</rd:DataSourceID>
          <DataSourceReference>Galactic</DataSourceReference>
        </DataSource>
      </DataSources>
      <InteractiveHeight>11in</InteractiveHeight>
      <ReportParameters>
        <ReportParameter Name="Week">
          <DataType>String</DataType>
          <Prompt>Week</Prompt>
          <ValidValues>
            <DataSetReference>
              <DataSetName>Weeks</DataSetName>
              <ValueField>Week</ValueField>
              <LabelField>Week</LabelField>
            </DataSetReference>
          </ValidValues>
        </ReportParameter>
        <ReportParameter Name="HubCode">
          <DataType>String</DataType>
          <Prompt>Hub</Prompt>
          <ValidValues>
            <DataSetReference>
              <DataSetName>HubsOver45</DataSetName>
              <ValueField>HubCode</ValueField>
              <LabelField>Hub</LabelField>
            </DataSetReference>
          </ValidValues>
        </ReportParameter>
      </ReportParameters>
```

Figure 7-20   *The Prompt element of the Week report parameter*

Replace Week with Work Week and click Save All in the toolbar. Right-click the entry for Overtime.rdl in the Solution Explorer, and then select View Designer from the Context menu. Select the Preview tab. You notice the prompt has been changed to Work Week.

If you do find a reason to make modifications directly to the RDL, do so with care. If you break up a begin/end pair or enter an invalid value for a property element (such as puce for a color), you can end up with a report that will not load in the Report Designer. Save your work immediately before making changes directly to the RDL. In just about every case, however, the designer works better for making changes to a report layout, so do your editing there.

Practicing Safe Source

The Report Designer works with another software tool called Visual SourceSafe (VSS). VSS controls access to source code, such as report definitions. This can prevent two report designers from trying to modify the same report at the same time. Even if you do not have multiple report designers, VSS can provide a consistent location where all your reporting projects can be found. VSS stores all the source code entrusted to its safekeeping in its own library database. If this VSS library database is located on a network, you have a central location where all the source code can be backed up regularly.

VSS has one more valuable feature. It keeps multiple versions of your source code. When you check in your source code, VSS does not write over the previous version. Instead, it keeps both the older version and the new version. You continue to work with the newest version of the source code unless there is a problem and you ask to go back to an earlier version. This can be a lifesaver when you make those massive formatting changes to a report, and then you or your users decide it was better the way it was.

Using Visual SourceSafe

VSS is tightly integrated with the Report Designer. Once VSS is installed and configured on your PC, you can probably do almost all your interaction with VSS through the Report Designer menus. We look at adding a reporting project to VSS control, checking reports into and out of VSS, and reverting to an older version of a report.

Adding a Reporting Project to Visual SourceSafe Control

Once VSS is set up on your PC, adding a reporting project to VSS control is simple. Right-click the solution or the project in the Solution Explorer and select Add Solution to Source Control. You are prompted to log in to VSS and to specify the VSS database you want to use. Provide this login information and click OK.

You see the Add to SourceSafe Project dialog box displaying the project folder hierarchy in your VSS database. Modify the project name at the top of the dialog box if desired, and then browse to the appropriate location in the project folder hierarchy and click OK.

Check In, Check Out, and Get Latest Version

Once the solution has been added to VSS control, a small lock icon appears next to each entry in the Solution Explorer. This indicates each file is checked into VSS. The local copy of each of these files is marked as read-only. The file cannot be modified until it has been checked out.

To check out a report definition file, right-click the entry for that report in the Solution Explorer and select Check Out from the Context menu. If you choose, you can enter a comment stating why the report is being checked out. The most recent version of the report is then copied from the VSS database to your PC. It is no longer read-only but, instead, is ready to accept changes. The lock icon is replaced by a small check mark in the Solution Explorer to indicate the report is checked out. Only one person may have a report checked out at any given time.

Once you complete your changes to the report definition, you need to check the report back into VSS. Right-click the entry for the report in the Solution Explorer and select Check In from the Context menu. Again, you can enter a comment summarizing the changes you made. This is helpful if you ever have to revert to an older version of a report.

If you want to get the latest version of a report someone else is working on, without checking out the report, you can use the Get Latest Version feature of VSS. Right-click the entry for the report in the Solution Explorer, and then select Get Latest Version from the Context menu. A read-only copy of the latest version of the report is then copied to your PC.

Getting a Previous Version

Retrieving an earlier version of a report from VSS is straightforward. Select the report in the Solution Explorer, and then select File | Source Control | History. The History Options dialog box appears. You can enter a range of dates to see the history of the report within that date range. You can also enter a user to see the versions checked in by that user. To see the entire history of the report, leave everything blank and click OK.

The History Of dialog box appears. Here, you can scroll through the previous versions of the report. Click Get to retrieve a copy of a previous version. This previous version then becomes your current copy of the report. Any previous versions of the report checked in after the version you just retrieved continue to reside in the VSS database. Click Rollback to retrieve a copy of a previous version and to delete any versions of the report that were checked in after the version you just retrieved.

Advance, Never Retreat

In this chapter, we continued to unlock additional features of Reporting Services. We're always working toward the goal of giving you the tools you need to meet your reporting needs. You should now be well on your way to being able to say, "Yes, I can do that!"

In the next chapter, we look at some of the advanced features of Reporting Services. After that, we take a brief look at the different formats for rendering reports, and then we move on to report serving.

Beyond Wow: Advanced Reporting

In this chapter, we explore some of the flashy features of Reporting Services. These are the features that get us techies excited. If you do not say "Wow!" after seeing at least one of these features in the reports created in this chapter, then we (the developers at Microsoft and I) are not doing our jobs. Just to clarify, the "Wow!" does not need to be said out loud. Simply thinking "Wow!" in your head counts just as much.

Getting you to say, or think, "Wow!" is not ultimately the goal of the Microsoft developers who created Reporting Services or the goal of this author as he writes this chapter. The developers who create games for Microsoft can be satisfied with eliciting a "Wow!" from their clientele and consider it a job well done. The developers who create business intelligence tools for Microsoft have to aim a bit higher.

If you develop business intelligence tools, you need to go beyond the "Wow!" to the "Ah ha!" The "Wow!" comes when you see a feature of a software product and think, "Wow! That is really cool!" The "Ah ha!" comes when you see a feature of a software product and say, "Ah ha! That is how we can make that report work just the way we need it to," or "Ah ha! That is how we can turn that bit of data into meaningful business intelligence." Only when we hear the "Ah ha!" can we be satisfied.

So, don't be shy when that moment comes along. When you get to that "Ah ha!" feature you have been searching for, say it nice and loud. I want to hear it, so I can go home happy.

Speaking in Code

One of the features of Reporting Services that gives it a tremendous amount of power and flexibility is its capability to speak in code—Visual Basic .NET code, that is. Valid Visual Basic .NET expressions can be used to control many of the properties of report items. They can even be used to control the query you are using to create your dataset.

For more complex tasks, you can embed whole Visual Basic .NET functions in your report. If that isn't enough, you can access methods from .NET assemblies. These assemblies are not limited to Visual Basic .NET. They can be written in any .NET language, such as C#.

Let's write some

-.-. --- -.. .

and have some

..-. ..- -.

NOTE

For those of you who may not be familiar with it, the previous sentence contains two words in Morse Code. If you want to know what it says, do what I did: Look it up on the Internet.

The Delivery Status Report

Features Highlighted

- ▶ Using the Label property of a parameter
- ▶ Using multiline headers and footers
- ▶ Using Visual Basic .NET expressions to control properties
- ▶ Specifying scope in aggregate functions

Business Need   The customer service department at Galactic Delivery Services would like a report to check on the status of deliveries for a customer. The customer service representative should be able to select a customer and a year, and then see all the deliveries for that customer in that year. The hubs each package went through as it was in transit should be listed.

   The status for packages that have been delivered should show up in green. The status for packages still en route should be blue. The status for packages that have been lost should be red. In case of a problem, the name and e-mail address of the person to be contacted at that customer site should appear below the entry for each lost package.

Task Overview

1. Create the Chapter08 Project, a Shared Data Source, a New Report, and Two Datasets
2. Set Up the Report Parameters and Place the Titles on the Report Layout
3. Add a Table to the Report
4. Add the Expressions

Delivery Status Report, Task 1: Create the Chapter08 Project, a Shared Data Source, a New Report, and Two Datasets

1. Create a new Reporting Services project called Chapter08 in the MSSQLRS folder.
2. Create a shared data source called Galactic for the Galactic database.
3. Create a new report called DeliveryStatus using the GDSReport template.

4. Create a new dataset called DeliveryStatus that calls the stp_DeliveryStatus stored procedure.

5. Run the stored procedure using **263722** for @CustomerNumber and **2005** for @Year.

6. Create a second dataset called Customers that uses the following query:

```
SELECT CustomerNumber, Name FROM Customer ORDER BY Name
```

Task Notes   You probably noticed the instructions are a bit sketchy here. Now that you have reached the level of advanced report authoring, you can handle these basic tasks on your own. If you have any trouble with these steps, refer to the previous chapters for a refresher.

Delivery Status Report, Task 2: Set Up the Report Parameters and Place the Titles on the Report Layout

1. Select the Layout tab.

2. Use the Main menu to open the Report Parameters dialog box.

3. Configure the report parameters as follows:

Property	Value
For the CustomerNumber parameter:	
Prompt	Customer
Available values	From query
Dataset	Customers
Value field	CustomerNumber
Label field	Name
For the Year parameter:	
Available values	(Enter the values from the following table)
Default values	Nonqueried
Default values text area	2005

Set the Available Values property for the Year parameter as follows:

Label	Value
2003	2003
2004	2004
2005	2005

4. Click OK to exit the Report Parameters dialog box.

5. Place a text box onto the body of the report. Modify the following properties of this text box:

Property	Value
Font: FontSize	16pt
Font: FontWeight	Bold
Location: Left	0in
Location: Top	0in
Size: Width	3.5in
Size: Height	0.375in
Value	="Delivery Status for " & Parameters!Year.Value

6. Place a second text box onto the body of the report. Modify the following properties of this text box:

Property	Value
Font: FontSize	16pt
Font: FontWeight	Bold
Location: Left	0in
Location: Top	0.375in
Size: Width	4.75in
Size: Height	0.375in

7. Right-click this text box and select Expression from the Context menu. The Expression Edit dialog box appears.

8. Select Parameters in the list on the left and double-click CustomerNumber in the list on the right.

9. Delete the word "Value" at the end of the expression. (Do not delete the period.) You see a Context menu showing you the available properties of the CustomerNumber parameter.

10. Double-click Label in the Context menu.

11. Click OK to exit the Expression Edit dialog box.

Task Notes   We have two parameters for this report. The CustomerNumber parameter is selected from a drop-down list created by a dataset. The customer names are displayed in the drop-down list because Name was chosen as the Label field. However, the customer number is the value assigned to this parameter because CustomerNumber is chosen as the Value field. The Year parameter is selected from a drop-down list created by a static list of values we entered. The Label and Value are the same for each entry in this list.

The items placed on the report thus far were put there to provide a heading for the report and to indicate which parameters were selected to create the report. This is pretty straightforward for the Year parameter. All we need is a text box that displays the value of this parameter, with a little explanatory text thrown in for good measure.

The CustomerNumber parameter presents a bit of a problem, though. When we select a parameter in an expression, the value property of the parameter is selected by default. The value property of the CustomerNumber parameter contains the customer number of the selected customer. However, it makes more sense to the user if the customer's name is displayed at the top of the report. To accomplish this, we use the label property rather than the value property. The label property contains the text that appears in the parameter drop-down list for the selected item. In this case, the label property contains the customer's name.

Delivery Status Report, Task 3: Add a Table to the Report

1. Add a table to the body of the report immediately below the text boxes.
2. Expand the DeliveryStatus dataset in the Datasets window and drag the Hub field onto the leftmost cell in the details row of the table.
3. Drag the TimeIn and TimeOut fields onto each of the two remaining cells in the details row of the table.
4. Right-click the gray square to the left of the details row and select Insert Group from the Context menu. The Grouping and Sorting Properties dialog box appears.
5. Select =Fields!DeliveryNumber.Value from the Expression drop-down list. We are now grouping the information in the table by the values in the DeliveryNumber field.
6. Select the Sorting tab.
7. Select =Fields!DeliveryNumber.Value from the Expression drop-down list.
8. Click OK to exit the Grouping and Sorting Properties dialog box.
9. We need to move the labels in the table header row to the group header row. Select the text box that contains the word "Hub." Do this by clicking once in this text box. If you can see a text-editing cursor blinking in this cell, you clicked too many times. If you see the blinking cursor, click elsewhere, and then try again.

10. Press CTRL-X to cut the text box from this table header cell. Click in the group header cell immediately below it and press CTRL-V to paste the text box there.

11. Repeat this for the text boxes containing Time In and Time Out.

12. Right-click any gray square to the left of the table and select Table Header from the Context menu. This turns off the table header option for this table. The table header row disappears. Do the same for the table footer.

13. Right-click the gray square to the left of the group header row and select Insert Row Above from the Context menu. An additional group header row appears. This is not a new grouping, but rather an additional row for the current grouping.

14. Drag the ServiceType field to the leftmost cell in the new group header row.

15. Drag the StatusName field to the next cell in the new group header row.

16. Right-click the gray square to the left of the new group header row and select Insert Row Above from the Context menu. Another new group header row appears.

17. Right-click the gray rectangle at the top of the first column in the table and select Insert Column to the Left from the Context menu. A new column is added to the table.

18. Drag the DeliveryNumber field to the leftmost cell in the new group header row. Modify the following property of the text box in this cell:

Property	Value
TextAlign	Left

19. Double-click the next cell in the new group header row and type **Pickup:**.

20. Drag the PickupPlanet field to the next cell in the new group header row.

21. Drag the PickupDateTime field to the rightmost cell in the new group header row.

22. Double-click in the group footer cell below =Fields!Hub.Value and type **Delivery:**.

23. Drag the DeliveryPlanet field to the next cell in the group footer row.

24. Drag the DeliveryDateTime field to the rightmost cell in the group footer row.

25. Right-click the gray square to the left of the group footer row and select Insert Row Below from the Context menu. A new group footer row appears.

26. Double-click in the group footer cell below Delivery and type **Problem Contact:**.

27. Drag the ProblemContact field to the next cell in the new group footer row.

28. Drag the ProblemEMail field to the rightmost cell in the new group footer row.

29. Right-click the gray square to the left of the new group footer row and select Insert Row Below from the Context menu. A new group footer row appears. This row is left blank.

30. Click in the leftmost cell of the top group header row and hold down the mouse button. Drag the mouse to the rightmost cell of the bottom group header row and release the mouse button. You have selected all the cells in the group header.

31. Modify the following property for these cells:

Property	Value
Font: FontWeight	Bold

32. Repeat Steps 30 and 31 for all the cells in the group footer. Your report layout should appear similar to Figure 8-1.

33. Select the Preview tab. Select Bolimite, Mfg from the Customer drop-down list. Select 2005 from the Year drop-down list. Click View Report. Your report should appear similar to Figure 8-2.

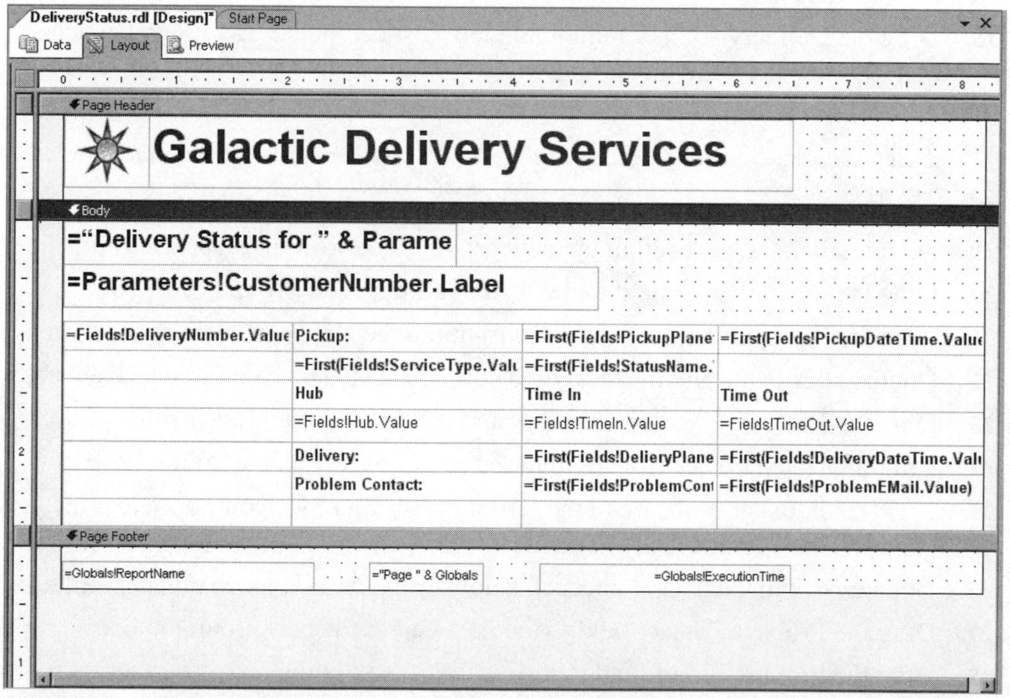

Figure 8-1   *The Delivery Status Report layout after Task 3*

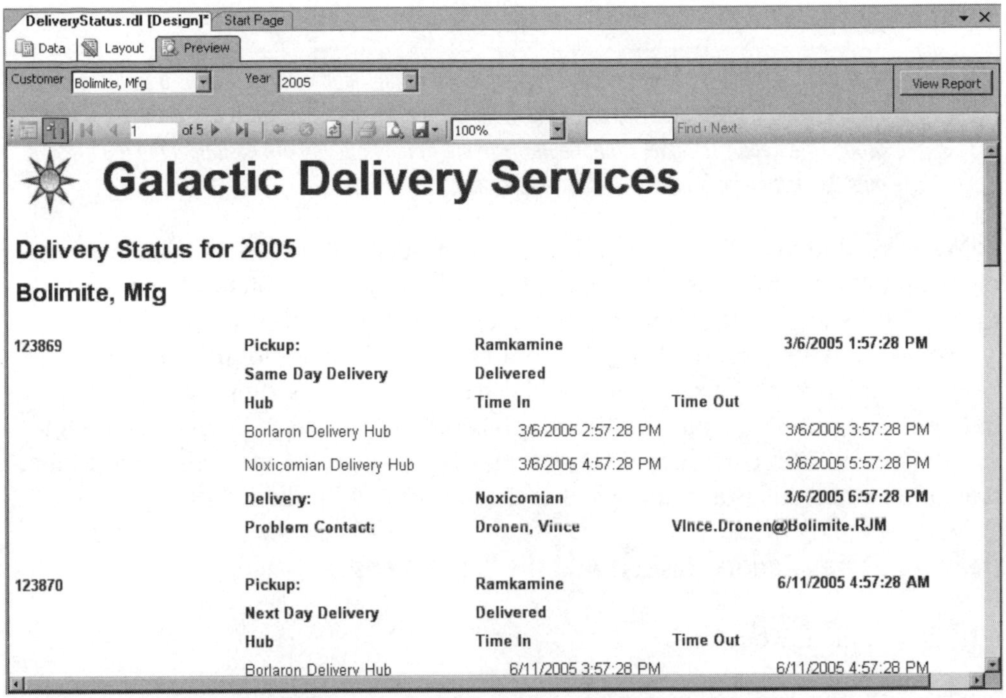

Figure 8-2   *The Delivery Status Report preview after Task 3*

Task Notes   If you are observant, you will notice the expressions created for all but one of the fields placed in the group header and footer rows include the First() aggregate function. Only the expression for the DeliveryNumber field does not include this function. This aggregate function must be used because there are many records in each group. Somehow, we need to specify which of these records should be used to supply the values for these fields. By default, the first record in the group is used by including the First() aggregate function with each field expression. However, you could replace the First() aggregate function with any of the other Reporting Services aggregate functions that work with a text or datetime data type, if you desired.

Why is there no aggregate function included in the DeliveryNumber field expression? In Step 5, we selected the DeliveryNumber field as the grouping field. Because the table is grouped on this field, the value of the DeliveryNumber field must be the same for each record in the group. In short, it does not make a difference which record the DeliveryNumber field comes from because it will be the same value for each record in the group.

NOTE

As it turns out, each of the fields we placed in the group header and footer is directly related to the DeliveryNumber field. Therefore, all these fields have the same value for all the records in the group. The Report Designer cannot determine this at the time you are designing the report, so it puts the aggregate functions in these expressions.

We were able to add rows to both the group header and footer. This let us create more complex group header and footer layouts. In the same fashion, you can add rows to the table header, table footer, or detail line, as needed.

We now have the proper layout for our report, but we do not have the proper behavior of some of the report items. The delivery status is supposed to appear in color. The problem contact information is only supposed to be displayed with lost deliveries. Some additional formatting lines would also make the report more readable. All of this is accomplished in the next task with the aid of expressions.

Delivery Status Report, Task 4: Add the Expressions

1. Select the Layout tab.
2. Enter the following expression for the Color property of the cell containing the StatusName field:

```
= IIF(Fields!StatusName.Value = "Delivered", "Green",
      IIF(Fields!StatusName.Value = "In Route", "Blue", "Red"))
```

NOTE

When entering each of the expressions, you probably want to select <Expression...> from the drop-down list for the property and enter this expression in the Edit Expression dialog box. Also, remember, the Edit Expression dialog box offers help for finding the correct function, and for inserting fields and parameters. Note, expressions involving the Globals, Parameters, and Fields collections are case-sensitive.

3. Click the gray square to the left of the top group header row, so the entire row is selected.
4. Enter the following expression for the BorderStyle: Top property:

```
= IIF(Fields!DeliveryNumber.Value =
   FIRST(Fields!DeliveryNumber.Value, "DeliveryStatus")
                                  , "Solid", "None")
```

NOTE

"DeliveryStatus" is case-sensitive in this expression.

5. Click and hold down the left mouse button in the cell containing the word "Hub." Continue to hold down the left mouse button and drag the cursor through the Time In cell to the Time Out cell. All three cells should now be selected. Modify the following property for these cells:

Property	Value
BorderStyle: Bottom	Solid

6. Select the following three cells using the same method as in Step 5: "Delivery:", "=First(Fields!DeliveryPlanet.Value)", "=First(Fields!DeliveryDateTime.Value)". Modify the following property for these cells:

Property	Value
BorderStyle: Top	Solid

7. Click the gray square to the left of the top group footer row, so the entire row is selected. Enter the following expression for the BorderStyle: Bottom property for this row:

    ```
    = IIF(Fields!StatusName.Value = "Lost", "None", "Solid")
    ```

8. Click the gray square to the left of the middle group footer row, so the entire row is selected. Enter the following expression for the BorderStyle: Bottom property:

    ```
    = IIF(Fields!StatusName.Value <> "Lost", "Solid", "None")
    ```

9. Enter the following expression for the Visibility: Hidden property for this same row:

    ```
    = IIF(Fields!StatusName.Value = "Lost", false, true)
    ```

10. Select the Preview tab. Select Bolimite, Mfg from the Customer drop-down list and 2005 from the Year drop-down list, if they are not already selected. Click View Report if the report does not appear. Your report should appear similar to Figure 8-3.

11. Select Save All in the toolbar.

Task Notes   If you scroll through the pages of the report, you see the report now meets the business needs specified. Let's look at what each expression is doing. The expression entered in Step 2 returns green when the status is Delivered, and blue when the status is In Route. Otherwise, it returns red.

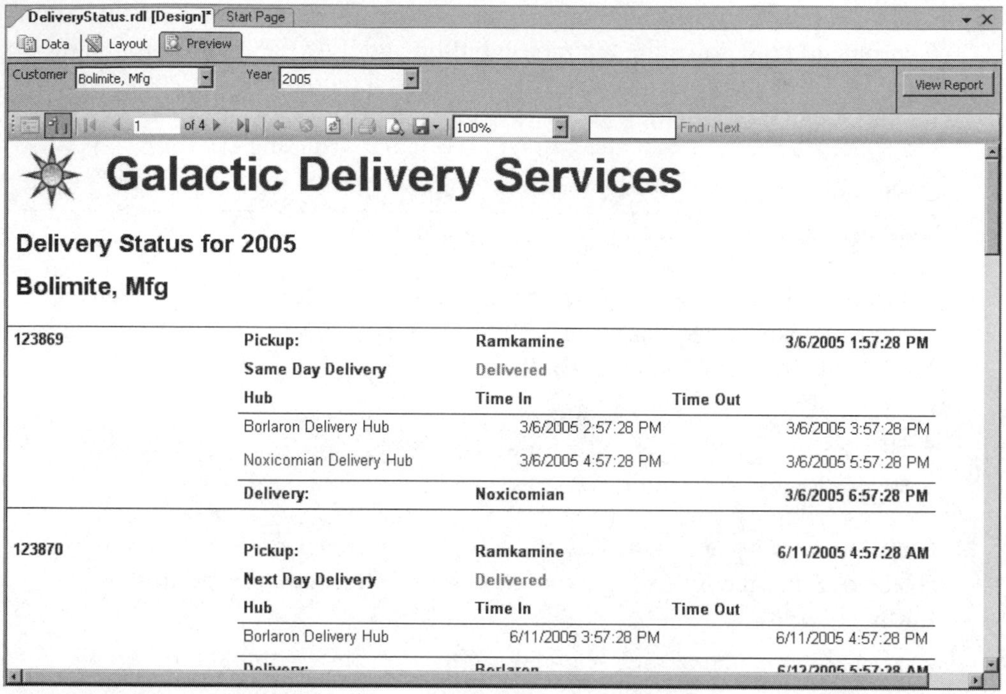

Figure 8-3 *The Delivery Status Report preview after Task 4*

The expression in Step 4 is a bit more complex. It checks whether the current value of the DeliveryNumber field is equal to the first value of the DeliveryNumber field in the DeliveryStatus dataset. As you saw in Chapter 7, aggregate functions act within a scope. By default, the First() aggregate function would return the value for the first record in the current scope. Because this expression is in the group header, by default it would return the value for the first record in each group.

However, in this expression, the First() aggregate function includes a second parameter that specifies the scope it should use. This parameter specifies that the First() aggregate function should use the scope of the entire DeliveryStatus dataset rather than just the current group. Therefore, it returns the first record in the dataset. When the current delivery number is equal to the first delivery number in the dataset, a solid border is created across the top of these text boxes. When the current delivery number is not equal to the first delivery number in the dataset, no border is created.

The expressions in Step 7 and Step 8 use the value of the StatusName field to control the border across the bottom of each grouping. If the row with the problem contact is displayed, the border should appear across the bottom of this row. However, if the row with the problem contact is not displayed, the border should appear across the bottom of the row above it. The expression in Step 9 controls whether the grouping row containing the problem contact is displayed. This is also based on the value of the StatusName field.

As you can see, expressions can be useful when the formatting or even the visibility of a report item needs to change depending on some condition in the report. Expressions can also be used to calculate the values to appear in a text box, as you see in the next report.

The Lost Delivery Report

Features Highlighted

▶ Using Visual Basic .NET expressions to calculate values in a text box

▶ Adding static columns to a matrix

▶ Adding totals to a matrix

▶ Formatting total cells in a matrix

Business Need   The quality assurance department at Galactic Delivery Services would like a report to help them analyze the packages lost during delivery. The report should show the number of packages lost each year at each processing hub. It should break down these numbers by the cause for each loss. It should also show the number of losses by cause as a percentage of the total number of packages lost for each hub.

Task Overview

1. Create a New Report, Create a Dataset, and Add a Matrix to the Report
2. Add a Calculated Column to the Matrix
3. Add Totals to the Matrix

Lost Delivery Report, Task 1: Create a New Report, Create a Dataset, and Add a Matrix to the Report

1. Reopen the Chapter08 project if it was closed.
2. Create a new report called LostDelivery using the GDSReport template.
3. Create a new dataset called LostDelivery that calls the stp_LostDeliveries stored procedure.

4. Place a matrix onto the body of the report. Drag the DeliveryNumber field into the Data cell. Edit the aggregate function in the resulting expression to change it from Sum to Count.

5. Drag the Cause field into the Rows cell. Drag the Hub field into the Columns cell.

6. Open the Matrix Properties dialog box and select the Groups tab.

7. Click Add in the Columns area. The Grouping and Sorting Properties dialog box appears.

8. Type the following for Expression to group the values by year:

   `=Year(Fields!PickupDateTime.Value)`

9. Click OK to exit the Grouping and Sorting Properties dialog box.

10. Click Up in the Columns area.

11. Click OK to exit the Matrix Properties dialog box.

12. Modify the following properties of the text box in the upper-left corner of the matrix:

Property	Value
BackgroundColor	Gainsboro (A light gray, near the top of the list)
Font: FontSize	18pt
Font: FontWeight	Bold
Size: Width	2in
Value	Lost Deliveries by Cause

13. Modify the following property of the text box in the lower-left corner of the matrix:

Property	Value
BackgroundColor	Gainsboro

14. Modify the following properties of the text box in the upper-right corner of the matrix:

Property	Value
BackgroundColor	Gainsboro
BorderStyle: Left	Solid
Font: FontSize	14pt

Property	Value
Font: FontWeight	Bold
TextAlign	Center

15. Modify the following properties of the text box in the center of the right-hand column of the matrix:

Property	Value
BackgroundColor	Gainsboro
BorderStyle: Left	Solid
BorderStyle: Bottom	Solid
Font: FontWeight	Bold
TextAlign	Center

16. Modify the following property of the text box in the lower-right corner of the matrix:

Property	Value
BorderStyle: Left	Solid

Task Notes   So far, we have a fairly straightforward matrix report. Let's see what happens when we add another column and totals to the matrix.

Lost Delivery Report, Task 2: Add a Calculated Column to the Matrix

1. Right-click the text box in the lower-right corner of the matrix and select Add Column from the Context menu. A new column and a new set of column headings appear.

2. Modify the following properties of the new text box in the lower-right corner of the matrix:

Property	Value
BorderStyle: Left	Solid
Format	###.00%
TextAlign	Right
Value	=Count(Fields!DeliveryNumber.Value)/ Count(Fields!DeliveryNumber.Value,"matrix1_Hub")

3. Modify the following properties of the text box immediately above the text box modified in Step 2:

Property	Value
BackgroundColor	Transparent
BorderStyle: Left	Solid
BorderStyle: Bottom	None
Font: FontWeight	Normal
TextAlign	Right
TextDecoration	Underline
Value	% of Column

4. Modify the following properties of the text box immediately to the left of the text box modified in Step 3:

Property	Value
BackgroundColor	Transparent
BorderStyle: Left	Solid
BorderStyle: Bottom	None
Font: FontWeight	Normal
TextAlign	Right
TextDecoration	Underline
Value	# Lost

5. Your report layout should appear similar to Figure 8-4.

6. Select the Preview tab. Your report should appear similar to Figure 8-5.

Task Notes   In the previous report, we created a multirow group header and a multirow group footer in a table. In this report, we created a multicolumn detail section in a matrix. When we add the second column, a new set of headers is added, so we can identify the contents of each column.

Our new column takes the count from the current row and calculates it as a percentage of the total for the column. This is done, once again, through the magic of scope. The first Count() aggregate function does not have a scope parameter, so it defaults to the scope of the current cell. In other words, it counts the number of lost deliveries in the current cell.

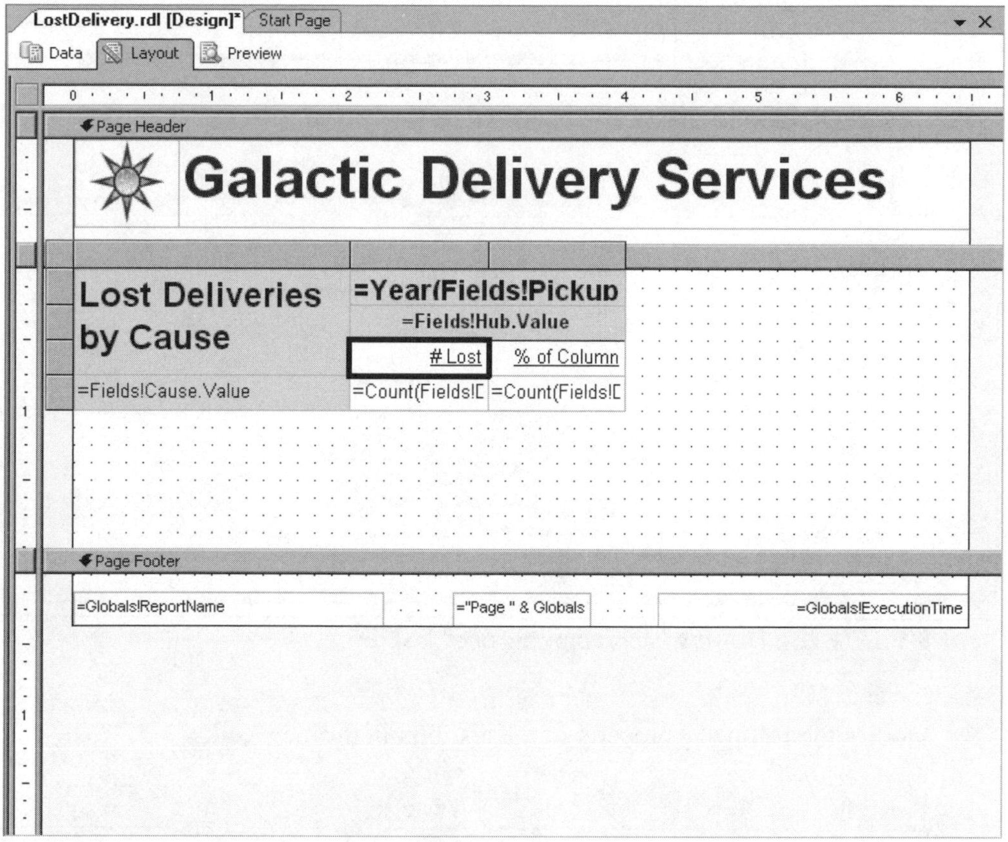

```
LostDelivery.rdl [Design]*  Start Page                                    ▾ ✕
  Data    Layout    Preview
```

Galactic Delivery Services

Lost Deliveries by Cause

=Year(Fields!Pickup
=Fields!Hub.Value

Lost   % of Column

=Fields!Cause.Value   =Count(Fields!C   =Count(Fields!C

=Globals!ReportName   ="Page " & Globals   =Globals!ExecutionTime

Figure 8-4   *The Lost Delivery Report layout after Task 2*

The second Count() aggregate function has a scope parameter of matrix1_Hub. This is the name of the column group that creates the column for each hub. Therefore, this aggregate function counts the number of lost deliveries in the entire column. We then divide and use the ##.00% format string to create a percentage.

Lost Delivery Report, Task 3: Add Totals to the Matrix

1. Select the Layout tab.
2. Right-click the text box in the lower-left corner of the matrix and select Subtotal from the Context menu. A Total cell is added to the bottom of the matrix.

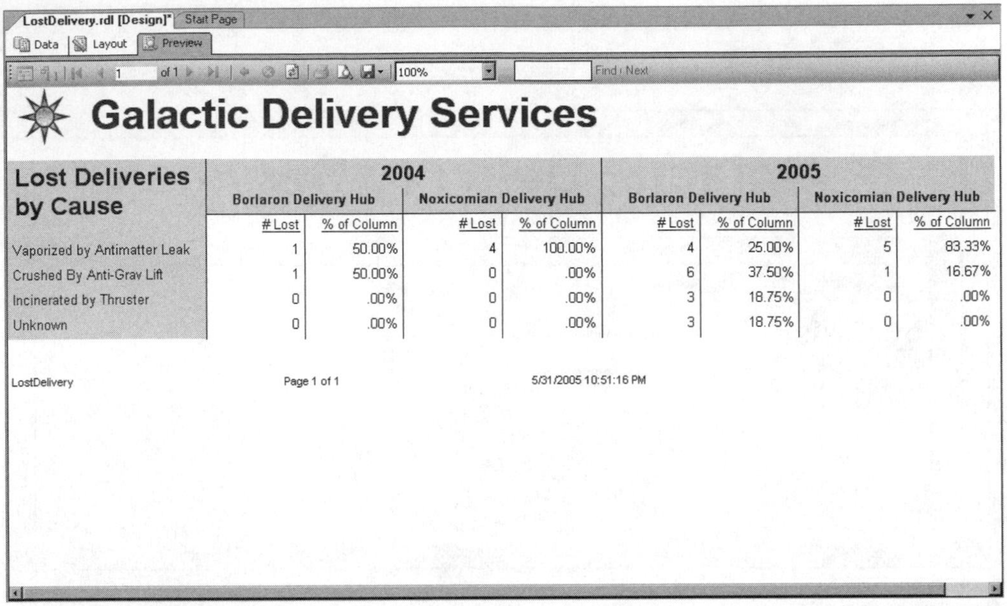

Figure 8-5 *The Lost Delivery Report preview after Task 2*

3. Modify the following property of the text box in this new cell:

Property	Value
BorderStyle: Top	Solid
BorderWidth	2pt

4. Select the Preview tab. Notice the border we added to the top of the text box only affects the text box with the word "Total" in it. It did not affect any of the text boxes that contain the actual totals.

5. Select the Layout tab.

6. Click the green triangle in the upper-right corner of the text box with the word "Total" in it. It may take a few tries to click the green triangle and not the Total cell text box. When you have done it correctly, the drop-down list at the top of the Properties window changes to Subtotal. Modify the following properties:

Property	Value
BorderStyle: Left	Solid
BorderStyle: Top	Solid

7. Select the Preview tab. We now have the desired format, with the border at the top of each text box that contains a total.

8. Select the Layout tab.

9. Right-click the text box in the upper-right corner of the matrix. Select Subtotal from the Context menu. A Total cell is added to the right of the matrix.

10. Modify the following properties of the text box in this new cell:

Property	Value
BorderStyle: Left	Solid
BorderStyle: Bottom	Solid

11. Your report layout should appear similar to Figure 8-6.

12. Select the Preview tab. Your report should appear similar to Figure 8-7.

13. Select Save All in the toolbar.

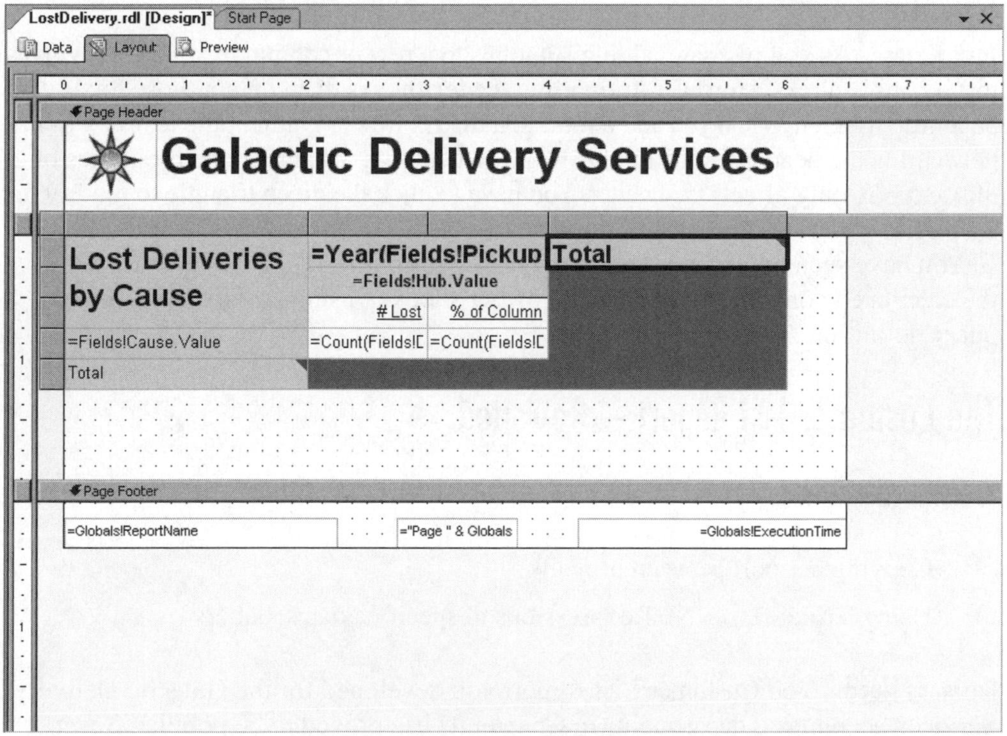

Figure 8-6 *The Lost Delivery Report layout after Task 3*

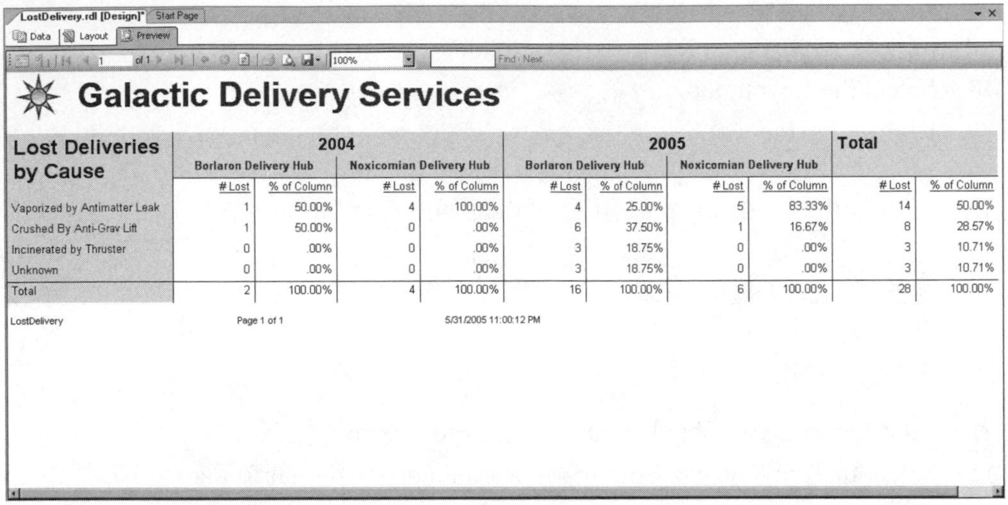

Galactic Delivery Services

Lost Deliveries by Cause	2004				2005				Total	
	Borlaron Delivery Hub		Noxicomian Delivery Hub		Borlaron Delivery Hub		Noxicomian Delivery Hub			
	# Lost	% of Column	# Lost	% of Column	# Lost	% of Column	# Lost	% of Column	# Lost	% of Column
Vaporized by Antimatter Leak	1	50.00%	4	100.00%	4	25.00%	5	83.33%	14	50.00%
Crushed By Anti-Grav Lift	1	50.00%	0	.00%	6	37.50%	1	16.67%	8	28.57%
Incinerated by Thruster	0	.00%	0	.00%	3	18.75%	0	.00%	3	10.71%
Unknown	0	.00%	0	.00%	3	18.75%	0	.00%	3	10.71%
Total	2	100.00%	4	100.00%	16	100.00%	6	100.00%	28	100.00%

LostDelivery Page 1 of 1 5/31/2005 11:00:12 PM

Figure 8-7 *The Lost Delivery Report preview after Task 3*

Task Notes As you just saw, adding subtotals to a row or column in a matrix involves just a couple clicks. However, formatting the text boxes that contain those totals can be a little trickier. When you add a total to a matrix row or column, the text box in the new cell is the header for the total row or total column. Changing the properties of this text box only affects the header. You have to click the green triangle to modify the properties for the text boxes that contain the totals.

You have seen how expressions can be used to control properties and to provide the calculated contents of a text box. Now let's look at using an expression in the query definition for a dataset.

The Customer List Report—Revisited

Features Highlighted

- Copying a report between projects
- Using Visual Basic .NET expressions to specify a dataset query

Business Need The Customer List Report you developed for the Galactic Delivery Services accounting department (in Chapter 4) has proved to be popular. Several other departments would like similar reports to help them track their own lists of e-mail contacts. Rather than create separate reports for each department, which would be hard to maintain, the IT Manager has asked for one report that enables the user to select which type of contact they want to view.

Task Overview

1. Copy the Report from the Chapter04 Project and Add It to the Chapter08 Project
2. Add a Report Parameter and Modify the Dataset to Use the Report Parameter

Customer List Report—Revisited, Task 1: Copy the Report from the Chapter04 Project and Add It to the Chapter08 Project

1. Use Windows Explorer to copy the report definition file for the Customer List Report (Customer List.rdl) from the Chapter04 project folder and paste it in the Chapter08 project folder. Both of these folders should be found under My Documents in the Visual Studio 2005\Projects\MSSQLRS folder.
2. In Report Designer, reopen the Chapter08 project if it was closed.
3. Right-click the Reports folder in the Solution Explorer and select Add | Existing Item from the Context menu. The Add Existing Item—Chapter08 dialog box appears.
4. Make sure you are looking at the Chapter08 folder in the dialog box and select the CustomerList.rdl file. Click Add to exit the Add Existing Item—Chapter08 dialog box.
5. Double-click the CustomerList.rdl entry in the Solution Explorer to open the report definition.
6. Select the Preview tab to show this report is functioning properly in the Chapter08 project.

Task Notes   Because the entire definition of a report is contained within a single RDL file, it is easy to copy reports to different locations. As you saw here, we can even add them to a project other than the project within which they were originally created. The Customer List Report uses a shared data source called Galactic. We did not need to copy the shared data source because we already have a shared data source with the same name and the same properties in the Chapter08 project. If this was not the case, we could have copied the shared data source file (Galactic.rds) along with the report file and added that to our new project as well.

Customer List Report—Revisited, Task 2: Add a Report Parameter and Modify the Dataset to Use the Report Parameter

1. Select the Data tab. Make sure you are in the Generic Query Designer and *not* the Graphical Query Designer.
2. Open the Report Parameters dialog box.
3. Add a new report parameter and modify the properties for this new parameter as follows:

Property	Value
Name	ListType
Prompt	Select a List
Allow blank value	unchecked
Available Values	(See the following table)

Set the Available Values property for the ListType parameter as follows:

Label	Value
Billing Contacts	B
Manufacturer Contacts	M
Problem Contacts	P

4. Click OK to exit the Report Parameters dialog box.
5. Replace the entire select statement with the following expression:

```
=IIF(Parameters!ListType.Value="B", "EXEC stp_BillingContacts",
    IIF(Parameters!ListType.Value="M",
        "EXEC stp_ManufacturerContacts",
        "EXEC stp_ProblemContacts"))
```

6. Click the . . . button in the Generic Query Designer toolbar. The Dataset dialog box appears. You may receive an error message indicating the query cannot be parsed. Ignore this error message.
7. Select the Fields tab.
8. Change the Fields table to match the following:

Field Name	Type	Value
Name	Database Field	Name
Email	Database Field	Email
Contact	Database Field	Contact

9. Click OK to exit the Dataset dialog box.

10. Select the Layout tab.

11. Drag the Contact field and drop it on the text box that currently contains the expression for the BillingContact field.

12. Double-click the table header cell directly above the text box from Step 11 and change the text to Contact.

13. Drag the Email field and drop it on the text box that currently contains the expression for the BillingEmail field.

14. Double-click the table header cell directly above the text box from Step 13 and change the text to Email.

15. Select Save All in the toolbar.

16. Select the Preview tab. Try selecting each of the list types. Remember to click View Report.

NOTE

The database does not contain a contact name for each manufacturer, so no contact names are in the manufacturer list.

Task Notes   Rather than specifying the query in the Generic Query Designer, we used an expression to choose among three possible queries (in this case, three stored procedure calls). This is known as a *dynamic query*. The name comes from the fact that the query that is run depends on input from the user at the time the report is run.

Because the content of the query is not known until run time, the Report Designer cannot "pre-run" the query to determine the fields that will result. Instead, we need to manually specify the fields that will result from our dynamic query. All the possible queries that could be run should return result sets with the same field names for your report to work properly.

At this point, you may be ready to suggest two or three alternative approaches to creating this report. It is certainly not unusual to come up with a number of possible ways to meet the business needs of a report. When this happens, use the following criteria to evaluate the possible solutions:

▶ Efficiency of operation

▶ Your comfort with implementing and debugging a given solution in a reasonable amount of time

▶ Maintainability

▶ Your need to illustrate a certain point in a book chapter

Well, maybe that last point won't apply to you, but it was, in fact, the overriding reason for choosing this approach for this particular report.

Payroll Checks

Features Highlighted

▶ Using Visual Basic .NET functions embedded in the report to create reusable code

▶ Using a stored procedure that updates data

▶ Grouping in the details row of a data region

▶ Using nested data regions

Business Need The Galactic Delivery Services accounting department needs a report to print payroll checks for its hourly employees. The checks should have the check portion in the top one-third of the page and the check register in the bottom two-thirds of the page. The check register should list the work hours included in this check. The user should be able to select a week for which unpaid time is entered and receive the payroll checks for that week. The planetary system tax amount (25 percent) and state tax amount (5 percent) must be deducted from the amount being paid.

Task Overview

1. Create a New Report, Create Two Datasets, Add a List to the Report Layout, and Populate It
2. Add a Table to the Report Layout and Populate It
3. Configure the Report Parameter and Add Embedded Code to the Report

Payroll Checks, Task 1: Create a New Report, Create Two Datasets, Add a List to the Report Layout, and Populate It

1. Reopen the Chapter08 project if it was closed.
2. Create a new report called PayrollChecks. Do *not* use the GDSReport template.
3. Create a new dataset called PayrollChecks that calls the stp_PayrollChecks stored procedure. Do *not* run the stored procedure in the Query Designer. This marks records as having been paid.

4. Create a new dataset called WeekNumbers that calls the stp_WeekNumbers stored procedure.

5. Select the Layout tab.

6. Place a list onto the body of the report. Modify the following properties of this list in the Properties window:

Property	Value
BackgroundColor	LightGreen
BorderStyle	Solid
DataSetName	PayrollChecks
PageBreakAtStart	True

7. Open the List Properties dialog box. Click Edit Details Group. The Details Grouping dialog box appears.

8. Select =Fields!PayrollCheckNumber.Value from the Expression drop-down list.

9. Click OK to exit the Details Grouping dialog box. Click OK to exit the List Properties dialog box.

10. Add text boxes to the list to get the layout shown in Figure 8-8. You can create text boxes containing fields by dragging the fields from the Datasets window. You can create a text box containing a constant string by dragging a text box from the Toolbox and typing the constant string in the new text box. Enlarge the report body and the list report item, if necessary.

11. Right-click the text box containing the LineAmount field and select Properties from the Context menu. The Textbox Properties dialog box appears.

12. Select the Format tab.

13. Click the ellipsis button (...) next to Format code. The Choose Format dialog box appears.

14. Select Currency in the list on the left.

15. Click OK to exit the Choose Format dialog box.

16. Click OK to exit the Textbox Properties dialog box.

Task Notes   Our payroll check has two separate parts: the check itself and the check register. The check register contains a line showing the amount paid for each day worked during the selected workweek. The *check* is essentially a summary of the information in the check register. The *check amount* is the sum of the amount to be paid for all the days worked.

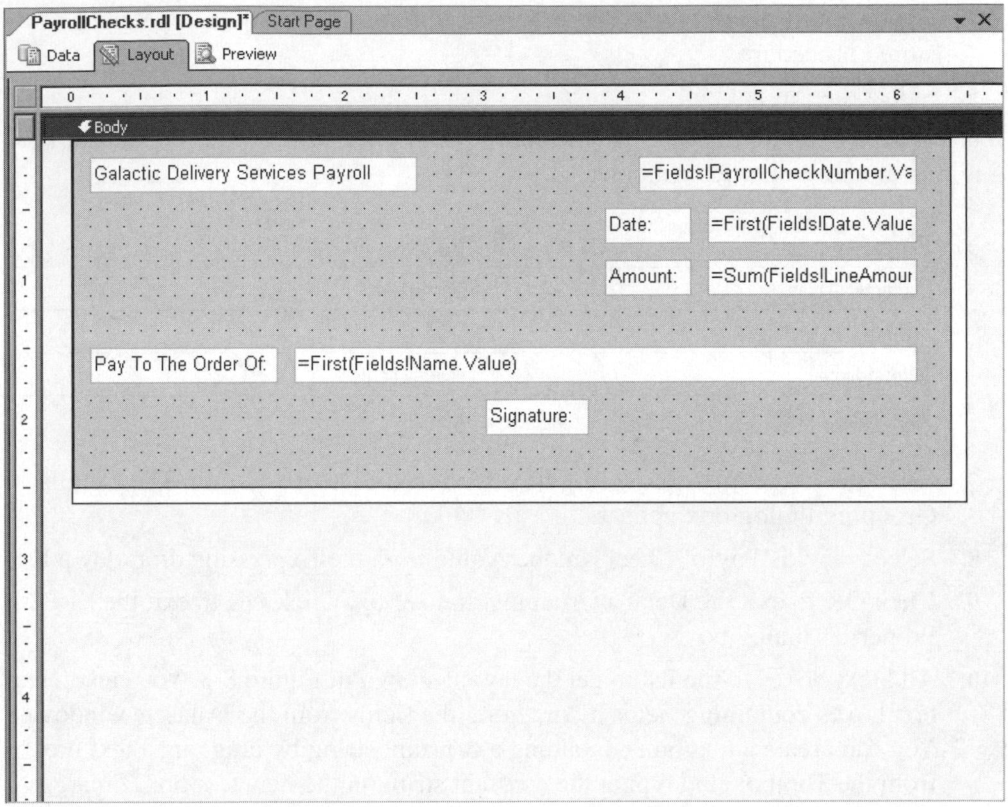

Figure 8-8 *The payroll check layout after Task 1*

We could use two different datasets to provide data to these two areas. To be a little more efficient with our database resources, however, we are going to use a single dataset. The dataset includes all the detail information required by the check register. It is going to have one row for each date worked. However, we do not want to create a check for each date worked. We only want one check for all the days worked by a given employee in the week.

To accomplish this, we need to group the detail data to print the check. We did this by adding the details grouping in Steps 7 through 9. Because we want one check per check number, the PayrollCheckNumber field seems an obvious choice for grouping. (The number in the PayrollCheckNumber field is generated by the stored procedure.) With this details grouping, our list receives one record for each check number; therefore, we get one check per check number.

Payroll Checks, Task 2: Add a Table to the Report Layout and Populate It

1. Increase the height of the report body and the list.

2. Place a table *inside* the list below the signature text box.

3. Drag the WorkDate, HoursWorked, and LineAmount fields from the Datasets window into the cells in the details row of the table.

4. Drag the LineAmount field from the Datasets window into the rightmost table footer cell and set the following properties for this new text box:

Property	Value
BorderStyle: Top	Solid
Format	C

5. Set the following property for the text box in the rightmost details row cell:

Property	Value
Format	C

> **NOTE**
>
> Entering C for the Format property is the same as selecting Currency on the Choose Format dialog box.

6. Set the following properties for the table:

Property	Value
BackgroundColor	White
PageBreakAtEnd	True

7. Drag the bottom of the list and the bottom of the report body up, so they are the same as the bottom of the table. Your report layout appears similar to Figure 8-9.

Task Notes   In Task 1, we created a list with a detail grouping to create the check portion of our payroll checks. In Task 2, we created a table to provide the detail information for the check register. The table data region must be nested inside of the list data region so that we get one set of detail information for each check. If the table was placed below the list, we would get all the checks first and then all the check register information at the end.

The PageBreakAtEnd property was set on the table so there is a page break immediately after the table. This keeps our output to one check per page.

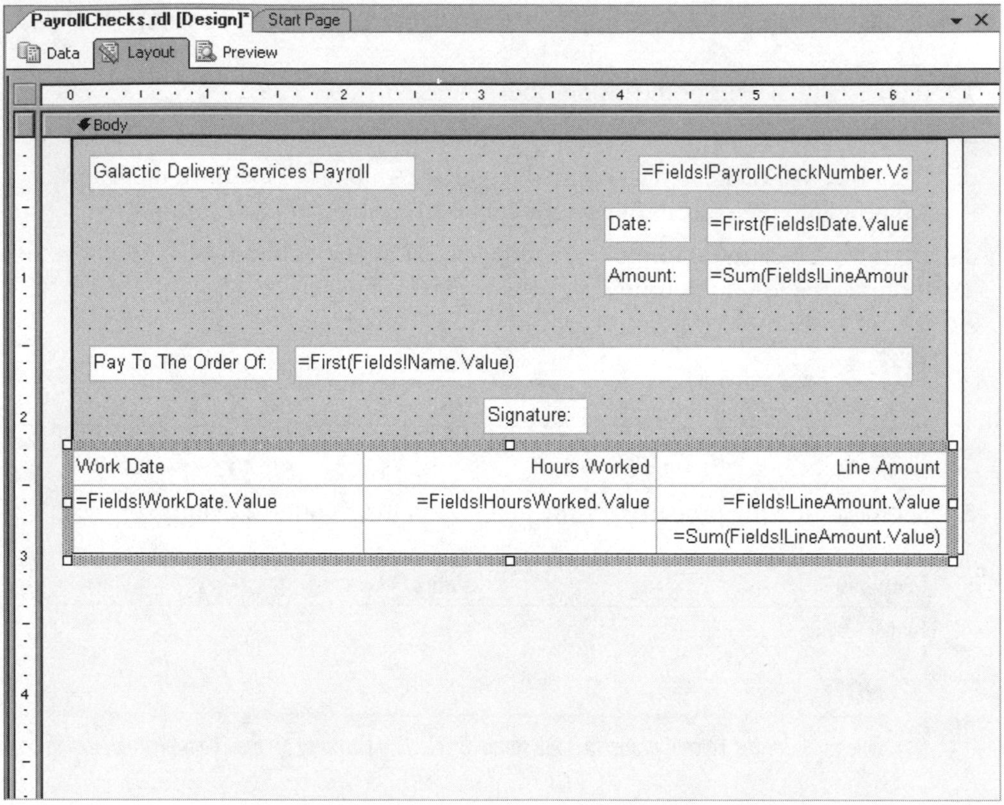

Figure 8-9 *The payroll check layout after Task 2*

Payroll Checks, Task 3: Configure the Report Parameter and Add Embedded Code to the Report

1. Open the Report Parameters dialog box.
2. Modify the following properties for the WeekNumber parameter:

Property	Value
Prompt	Week Number
Available values	From query
Dataset	WeekNumbers
Value field	WeekNumber
Label field	WeekNumber

3. Click OK to exit the Report Parameters dialog box.

4. Open the Report Properties dialog box.

5. Select the Code tab.

6. Enter the following in the Custom Code area:

```
' State and Planetary System Tax Deductions
Public Function TaxDeductions(ByVal Amount As Double) As Double
        ' Planetary System Tax = 25%
        ' State Tax = 5%
        TaxDeductions = Amount * .25 + Amount * .05
End Function
```

7. Click OK to exit the Report Properties dialog box.

8. Right-click the text box in the list, but not in the table, containing the sum of the LineAmount values and select Expression from the Context menu. The Edit Expression dialog box appears.

9. Replace the contents of the Expression area with the following:

```
=Sum(Fields!LineAmount.Value) -
        Code.TaxDeductions(Sum(Fields!LineAmount.Value))
```

10. Click OK to exit the Edit Expression dialog box.

11. Repeat Steps 8 through 10 with the text box in the table containing the sum of the LineAmount values.

12. Right-click the text box in the details row of the table containing the LineAmount value and select Expression from the Context menu. The Edit Expression dialog box appears.

13. Replace the contents of the Expression area with the following:

```
=Fields!LineAmount.Value - Code.TaxDeductions(Fields!LineAmount.Value)
```

14. Click OK to exit the Edit Expression dialog box.

15. Select the Preview tab.

16. Select 09-2006 from the Week Number drop-down list and click View Report. Your report should appear similar to Figure 8-10. Remember, once checks have been run for a given week, you cannot produce checks for that week again. Each time you enter the report, the Week Number drop-down list only contains entries for weeks that have not been run. (The check number you see on the first page in your preview may be different from the check number shown in the figure. This is normal.)

17. Select Save All from the toolbar.

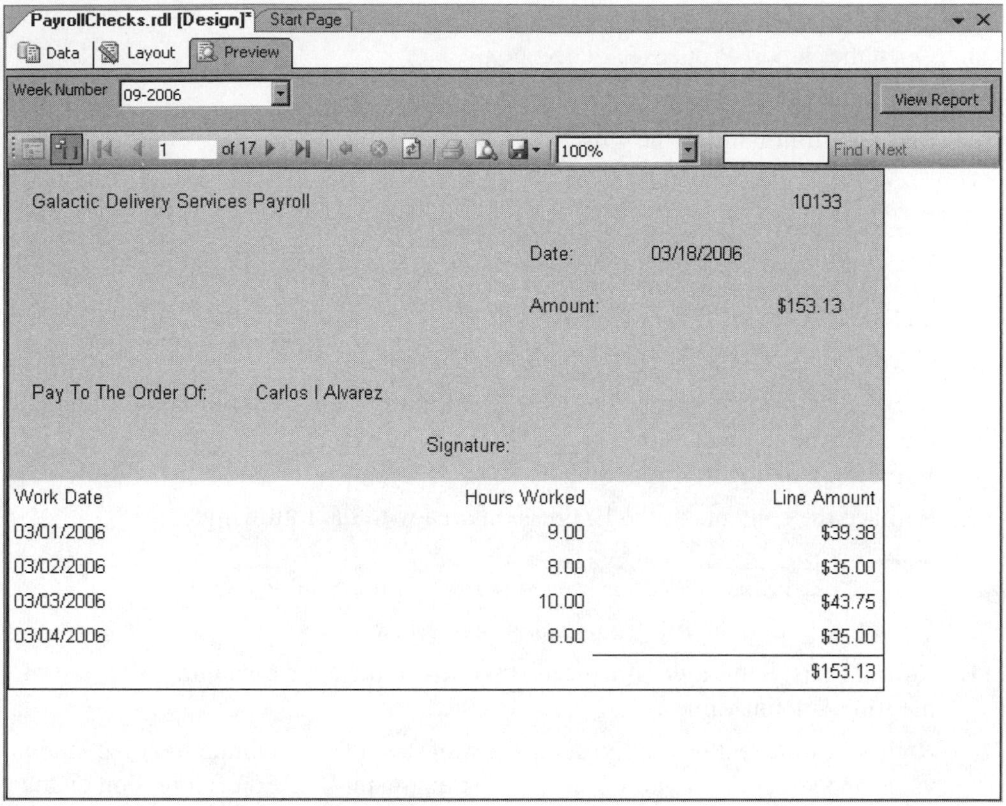

Figure 8-10 *The payroll check preview*

Task Notes   Payroll tax calculations are straightforward on the planets where Galactic Delivery Services operates. Everyone pays 25 percent of their pay to the planetary system government and 5 percent of their pay to the state government. Even though this is a simple formula, we need to use it in three different places. Using the embedded code feature of Reporting Services, we are able to put this formula in one location and use it in several locations. This also makes things easier to change when one or the other of these tax amounts is increased.

We created a function called TaxDeductions on the Code tab in the Report Properties dialog box. This is simply a valid Visual Basic .NET function definition. We access this function by using the key word "Code" followed by a period and the name of the function. You can see this in the expression we entered in Step 9.

The Weather Report

Features Highlighted

▶ Referencing .NET assemblies in the report

▶ Using a multivalued parameter

Business Need   The Galactic Delivery Services flight control department needs a way to quickly list the current weather conditions at selected planets served by GDS. (After all, space transports have to go through the atmosphere to take off and land.) One of the GDS programmers has created a .NET assembly that uses a web service to get the weather from various locations. The user should be able to select one or more planets from a list and see the weather for all selected planets. A call must be made to a method of the .NET assembly for each of the selected planets and the results must be incorporated into the report.

Task Overview

1. Copy the .NET Assembly into the Appropriate Location, Create a New Report, and Create a Reference to the Assembly

2. Create a Dataset, Add a Table to the Report Layout, and Populate It

Weather Report, Task 1: Copy the .NET Assembly into the Appropriate Location, Create a New Report, and Create a Reference to the Assembly

1. If you have not already done so, download the WeatherInfo.dll assembly from the website for this book.

2. Copy this file to the Report Designer folder. The default path for the Report Designer folder is

   ```
   C:\Program Files\Microsoft Visual Studio 8\Common7\IDE\PublicAssemblies
   ```

3. Launch the Microsoft .NET Framework 2.0 Configuration program from the Administrative Tools section of your Control Panel.

4. Click the Configure Code Access Security Policy link.

5. Click the Increase Assembly Trust link.

6. Select Make Changes to This Computer and click Next.

7. Click Browse and go to the PublicAssemblies folder. Select WeatherInfo.dll, click Open, and then click Next.

8. Select This One Assembly and click Next.

9. Change the Trust Level slider to Full Trust, and then click Next.

10. Click Finish.

11. Close the Microsoft .NET Configuration 2.0 program.

12. Reopen the Chapter08 project in the Report Designer if it was closed.

13. Create a new report called WeatherReport using the GDSReport template.

14. Open the Report Properties dialog box and select the References tab.

15. Click . . . next to the References area. The Add Reference dialog box appears.

16. Scroll down to the entry for the WeatherInfo assembly and select it. Click Add to add this file to the Selected Projects and Components list.

17. Click OK to exit the Add Reference dialog box. Click OK to exit the Report Properties dialog box.

Task Notes   For a custom assembly to be used in our reports, the assembly must be in a location where it can be found by the Report Designer. When you are designing reports, the assembly must be either in the Public Assemblies folder or in the Global Assembly Cache. We placed the WeatherInfo.dll assembly in the Public Assemblies folder in Step 2. Consult your .NET documentation for information on placing an assembly in the Global Assembly Cache.

We are using a class from the WeatherInfo assembly called PlanetaryWeather and a method from that class called GetWeather. The GetWeather method is a shared method. This means you do not need to create an instance of the PlanetaryWeather class to use the GetWeather method.

To use a method that is not a shared method, you need to use the Classes area of the Report Properties dialog box. First, create a reference in the References area, as we did in Steps 15 and 16. Then, under Class name, specify the name of the class within that assembly you want to instantiate. Finally, provide a name for the instance of that class. Reporting Services creates an instance of the class with the name you provide when the report is run.

Once the assembly is in the correct location and you have created a reference to that assembly, you can use the methods of this assembly in your reports. When referencing a shared method in an assembly, use the following syntax:

```
Namespace.ClassName.MethodName(Parameters…)
```

For the WeatherInfo assembly, the syntax is

```
WeatherInfo.PlanetaryWeather.GetWeather(PlanetAbbrv)
```

To use a nonshared method from a class you instantiated, use the syntax

```
Code.InstanceName.MethodName(Parameters…)
```

Weather Report, Task 2: Create a Dataset, Add a Table to the Report Layout, and Populate It

1. Create a new dataset called Planets. Use the following for the query string:

   ```
   SELECT Name, PlanetAbbrv FROM Planet ORDER BY Name
   ```

2. Select the Layout tab.

3. Place two text boxes and a table onto the body of the report. Complete your report layout so it is similar to Figure 8-11.

4. Open the Report Parameters dialog box.

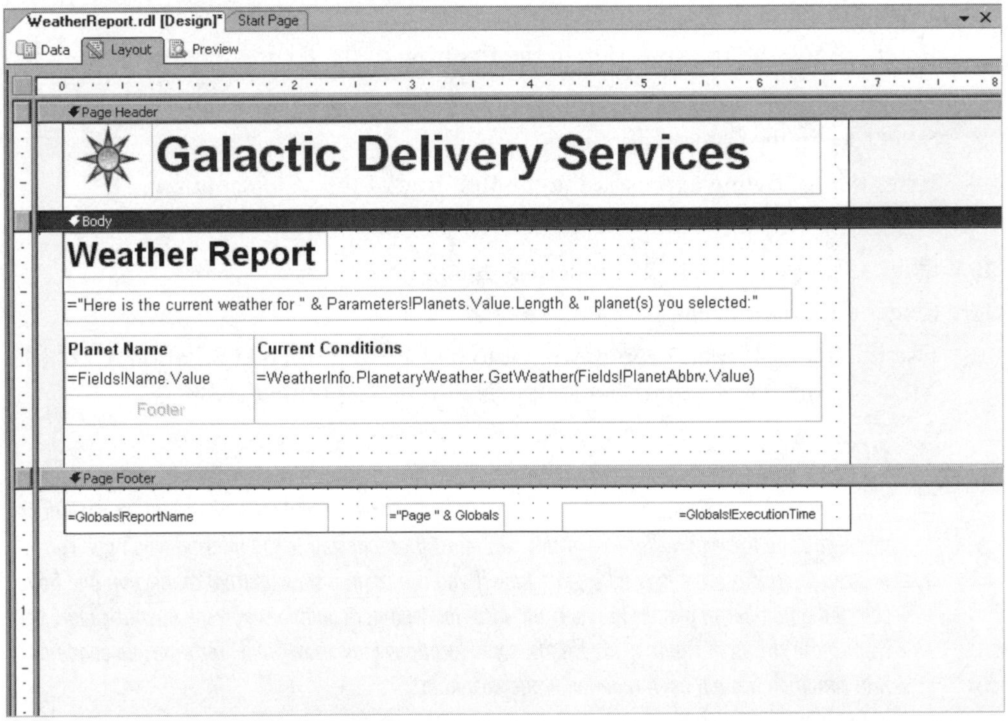

Figure 8-11   *Weather Report layout*

5. Click Add to create a new report parameter. Set the properties of this new parameter as follows:

Property	Value
Name	Planets
Prompt	Select Planets
Multivalue	checked
Allow blank value	unchecked
Available values	From query
Dataset	Planets
Value field	PlanetAbbrv
Label field	Name

Click OK to exit the Report Parameters dialog box.

6. Open the Table Properties dialog box. Select the Filters tab.

7. Enter the following expression in the first row of the Expression column:

```
=Array.IndexOf(Parameters!Planets.Value, Fields!PlanetAbbrv.Value)
```

8. Select >= in the Operator column.

9. Enter the following expression in the first row of the Value column:

```
=CInt(0)
```

10. Click OK to exit the Table Properties dialog box.

11. Select the Preview tab.

12. Use the Select Planets drop-down list to check Borlaron and Stilation. Click View Report. Your report should appear similar to Figure 8-12.

NOTE

Remember, the GetWeather method is going out to the Internet and retrieving weather conditions when you run the report. Because of this, you must be connected to the Internet when you run this report. This process may take some time if you are using a slow Internet connection and have selected a number of planets to report on. Also, the weather conditions you see in your report vary from those shown in Figure 8-12. Finally, some locations may show "null" for a certain condition if that condition has not been reported in the past hour.

13. Select Save All from the toolbar.

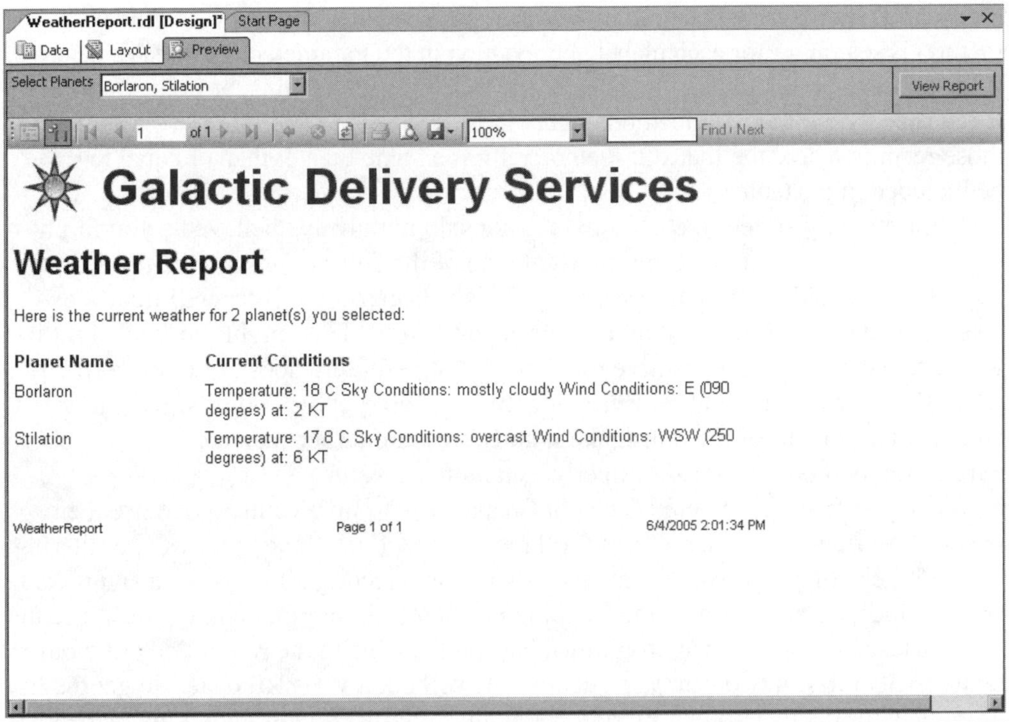

Figure 8-12   *Weather Report preview*

Task Notes   The Weather Report makes use of a special type of parameter that allows for more than one value to be selected. Rather than requiring the user to select a single value from the Available Values drop-down list, a multivalued parameter enables the user to check off a number of values to be used when creating the report. Then, it is up to the Report Designer to figure out how to use those multiple values to return a report with the desired information.

The properties of the report parameter change when that parameter becomes multivalued. Instead of containing single values, the Value and Label properties become arrays. The arrays have one element for each of the items selected by the user. If the user checks three items in the drop-down list, the Value and Label arrays each have three elements. (These are zero-based arrays, so they are elements 0, 1, and 2 in this case.) The Length property of each array contains the number of elements in that array.

In this report, we used the multivalue parameter in a table filter to determine which records would be output. (In the Transport Monitor report, we use a multivalue parameter to create a WHERE clause in a query.) We are using a shared method of the Array class called IndexOf, which searches an array for a value. In this case, the IndexOf method is searching for each planet abbreviation in the Parameters!Planets.Value array. If the abbreviation is found, the index of the element that contains the abbreviation is returned by the IndexOf method; otherwise, it returns −1. Therefore, we want only those records where the IndexOf method returns a value greater than or equal to 0 to be included in the table.

As previously stated, the filter expressions do not always behave as you might expect. If we simply put a 0 on the right side of the filter expression (Step 9), the expression would not function properly. This is because the filter will treat it as a string value of "0" rather than a numeric value of 0. This might work all right if we were only comparing positive numbers, but it definitely does not work correctly when the IndexOf method returns a negative one. To get around this, we put an equals sign in front of the 0 to make it an expression rather than a constant. The expression is then evaluated correctly as a numeric value.

When you first encountered filters in Chapter 7, you were cautioned to use them wisely. The filter makes sense here for three reasons. First, the dataset we are filtering is small. Selecting just two or three records versus selecting all six is not a significant time savings. Second, as with the example in Chapter 7, the filter enables us to use the same dataset to populate the drop-down list and the table in the report body. It would be inefficient to run two database queries, one without a WHERE clause to get the list of planets for the drop-down list and one with a WHERE clause to get the planets selected for the table in the report. Finally, the most time-consuming part of the report is not the database interaction, but the calls to the web service over the Internet. Because our filter is applied before we step through the table and make the web service call, we are in good shape.

The Delivery Analysis Report

Features Highlighted

▶ Using an Analysis Services cube as a data source via an MDX query

▶ Parameterizing an MDX query

▶ Localizing the label strings in a report

Business Need   The Galactic Delivery Services long-range planning committee is working on forecasting the equipment and work force needs necessary for future growth. They need a report showing the number of deliveries and the average weight of those deliveries grouped by customer by quarter. They would also like to select whether the data includes next day deliveries, same day deliveries, previous day deliveries, or some combination of the three. The data for this report should come from the GalacticDeliveriesDataMart cube hosted by Microsoft SQL Server Analysis Services.

There are committee members from a number of planets. Most speak English, but the committee does include several Spanish-speaking members. (I know it is rather strange that people in a galaxy far, far away should speak English and Spanish, but work with me here!)

Task Overview

1. Copy the .NET Assembly into the Appropriate Location, Create a New Report, Create a Reference to the Assembly, and Create a Dataset Using the MDX Query Designer
2. Add a Table to the Report Layout, Populate It, and Localize the Report Strings

Delivery Analysis Report, Task 1: Copy the .NET Assembly into the Appropriate Location, Create a New Report, Create a Reference to the Assembly, and Create a Dataset Using the MDX Query Designer

NOTE

You need to download the GalacticOLAP project from the website for this book and deploy it to a SQL Server Analysis Services server before you can complete this report. If you do not have access to Analysis Services, skip this report and continue with the "Reports within Reports" section of this chapter.

1. If you have not already done so, download the ReportUtil.dll assembly from the website for this book.
2. Copy this file to the Report Designer folder. The default path for the Report Designer folder is

   ```
   C:\Program Files\Microsoft Visual Studio 8\Common7\IDE\PublicAssemblies
   ```
3. Launch the Microsoft .NET Framework 2.0 Configuration program from the Administrative Tools section of your Control Panel.
4. Click the Configure Code Access Security Policy link.
5. Click the Increase Assembly Trust link.
6. Select Make Changes for This Computer and click Next.

7. Click Browse. Browse to the PublicAssemblies folder and select ReportUtil.dll. Click Open, and then click Next.

8. Select This One Assembly and click Next.

9. Change the Trust Level slider to Full Trust and click Next.

10. Click Finish.

11. Close the .NET Framework 2.0 Configuration program.

12. Reopen the Chapter08 project in the Report Designer if it was closed.

13. Create a new report called DeliveryAnalysis using the GDSReport template.

14. Open the Report Properties dialog box. Select the References tab.

15. Click . . . next to the References area. The Add Reference dialog box appears.

16. Scroll down to the entry for ReportUtil Assembly and select it. Click Add to add this file to the Selected Projects and Components list.

17. Click OK to exit the Add Reference dialog box. Click OK to exit the Report Properties dialog box.

18. Create a new dataset called DeliveryInfo. Select New Data Source from the Data Source drop-down list. The Data Source dialog box appears.

19. Enter **GalacticDM** for the Name. Select Microsoft SQL Server Analysis Services from the Type drop-down list.

20. Click Edit next to the Connection String text box. The Connection Properties dialog box appears.

21. Enter the name of the SQL Server Analysis Services server for Server name.

22. Select GalacticOLAP from the Select or Enter a Database Name drop-down list. You can test the connection if you like, but if GalacticOLAP shows up in the drop-down list, the connection has already been tested.

23. Click OK to exit the Connection Properties dialog box. Click OK to exit the Data Source dialog box. Click OK one more time to exit the Dataset dialog box. The MDX Query Designer appears as shown in Figure 8-13.

24. Expand the Measures in the Metadata pane. Expand the Delivery measure group and then expand the Delivery entry within it.

25. Drag the Delivery Count measure onto the Results pane (the pane with the words "Drag levels or measures here to add to the query" in the center). The total count of all deliveries currently in the GalacticDeliveriesDataMart cube is shown in the Results pane.

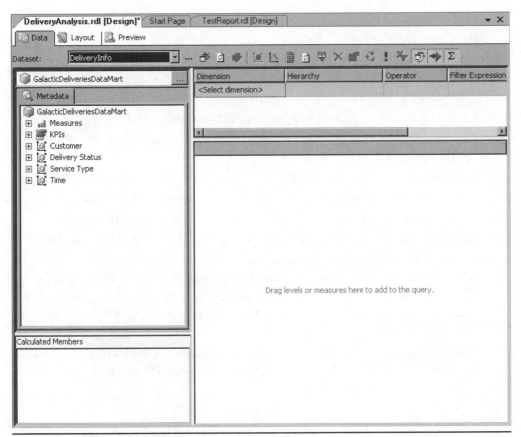

Figure 8-13   *The MDX Query Designer*

26. Expand the Customer dimension in the Metadata pane. Drag the CustomerName attribute onto the Results pane to the left of the Delivery Count. The Results pane now shows the total count of all deliveries for each customer.

27. Expand the Time dimension in the Metadata pane. Drag the Delivery-Quarter attribute onto the Results pane to the left of the CustomerName column. The Results pane now shows the total count of all deliveries for each customer for each quarter.

28. Right-click in the Calculated Members pane and select New Calculated Member from the Context menu. The Calculated Member Builder dialog box appears.

29. Enter **AvgWeight** for the Name.

30. In the Expression area, enter **ROUND(**. Expand the Measures in the Metadata area, expand the Delivery measure group, and then expand the Delivery entry within it. Double-click Package Weight to add it to the expression.

31. Enter **/** at the end of the expression. Double-click Delivery Count to add it to the expression.

32. Enter **,2)** at the end of the expression and click Check to check the syntax of the expression. Click OK to close the Check Syntax dialog box. Make any corrections to the expression, if a syntax error is encountered.

33. Click OK to exit the Calculated Member Builder dialog box.

34. Drag the AvgWeight calculated member onto the Results pane to the right of the Delivery Count.

35. In the Filter pane (the pane in the upper-right corner of the MDX Query Designer), select Service Type from the drop-down list in the Dimension column.

36. Select Description from the drop-down list in the Hierarchy column.

37. Equal should be selected from the drop-down list in the Operator column.

38. Examine the values in the drop-down window in the Filter Expression column, but do not make a selection. The Filter Expression column enables us to select one or more values for the right side of our filter expression. Instead of doing this at design time, we let our users make the selection at run time. Click Cancel to exit the drop-down window.

39. Check the box in the Parameters column. This selection enables the user to select the values of the filter expression at run time. The MDX Query Designer should appear as shown in Figure 8-14.

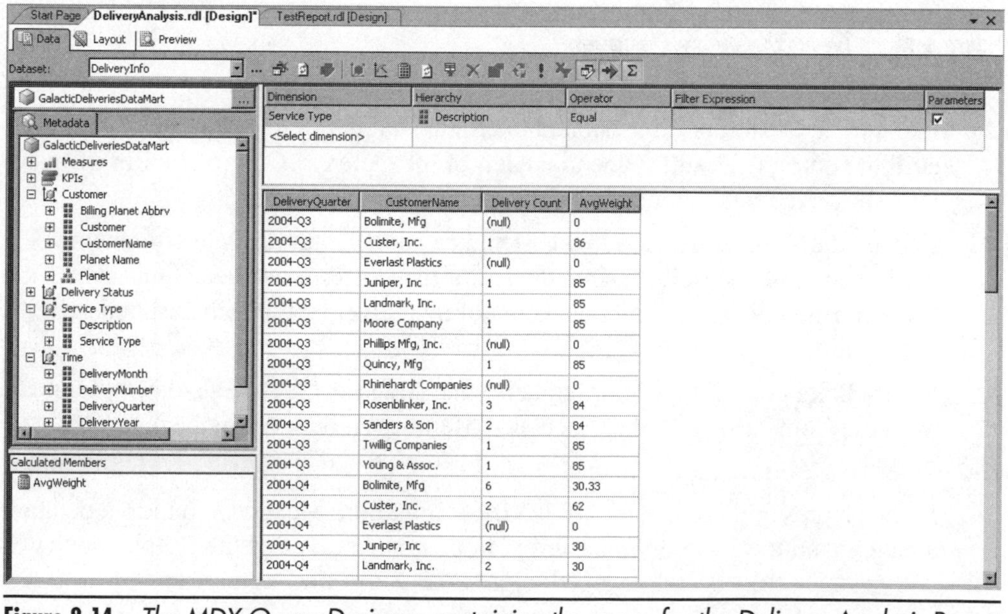

Figure 8-14   *The MDX Query Designer containing the query for the Delivery Analysis Report*

Task Notes   The MDX Query Designer works almost entirely through drag-and-drop. We drag measures, dimensions, and hierarchies from the Metadata Browser pane and place them in the Results pane to create our query. We can define calculated members and add them to the results pane as well.

At the top of the Metadata pane is the name of the cube being queried. To select a different cube, click the . . . button and make a selection from the Cube Selection dialog box that appears.

Notice two refresh buttons are in the toolbar for the designer. The refresh button on the left refreshes the fields for this dataset in the Datasets window. The refresh button on the right refreshes the metadata from the cube. The toolbar button with the pickaxe switches from the MDX Query Designer to the DMX Query Designer. The toolbar button with the x-axis and y-axis switches back to the MDX Query Designer. Where the MDX Query Designer is used to query cubes in an Analysis Services database, the DMX Query Designer is used to query data mining models in an Analysis Services database. Because the same Analysis Services database may contain both cubes and data mining models, the Report Designer may not be able to tell which query designer you need simply by examining the database. Therefore, it is necessary to have a way to switch between the two.

The Show Empty Cells toolbar button toggles between showing and hiding empty cells in the Results pane. An empty cell is a combination of dimension and hierarchy members that have a null value for every measure, calculated or otherwise, in the Results pane. If empty cells are hidden in the Results pane, they are also hidden in the final report query. The Design Mode toolbar button enables you to toggle between the design view and the query view of the MDX query. If you are comfortable with MDX query syntax, you may want to type your queries into the query view rather than creating them through the drag-and-drop programming method of the design view. The Auto Execute toolbar button toggles autoexecute mode in the Query Designer. When autoexecute mode is on, the cube is requeried and the Results pane is updated every time an item is added to or removed from the Results pane.

The Filter pane enables us either to hardcode filter expressions at design time or use report parameters for the user to make selections at run time. When the Parameters check box is checked, a parameterized filter is created. Several things happen when we move from the Data tab to the Layout tab for the first time after a parameterized filter has been added to the query. When this occurs, the Report Designer creates a new dataset for each item being used in a parameterized filter. This dataset includes all the valid members of that item.

In addition to the datasets, new report parameters are created for each parameterized filter. The datasets are used to populate the available values for these report parameters. The report parameters are multivalued. Using this mechanism, the user is allowed to select one or more valid members to be used in the parameterized filters at the time the report is executed.

Delivery Analysis Report, Task 2: Add a Table to the Report Layout, Populate It, and Localize the Report Strings

1. Select the Layout tab.
2. Place a text box onto the body of the report and set its properties as follows:

Property	Value
Font:FontSize	20pt
Font: FontWeight	Bold
Location: Left	0in
Location: Top	0in
Size: Width	5.875in
Size: Height	0.375in

3. Set the content of the text box to the following expression:

   `=ReportUtil.Localization.LocalizedString("DeliveryReportTitle",User!Language)`

4. Place a matrix onto the report body.
5. Expand the DeliveryInfo dataset and drag DeliveryQuarter into the Columns cell. Click the Bold button and the Center button in the toolbar.
6. Drag CustomerName into the Rows cell. Click the Bold button in the toolbar.
7. Drag Delivery_Count into the Data cell.
8. Drag AvgWeight into the same cell where Delivery_Count was placed. Drag to the right side of the cell. This creates a second data column to the right of the first.
9. Enter the following expression in the text box that contains Delivery:

   `=ReportUtil.Localization.LocalizedString("DeliveryCountColHead",User!Language)`

10. Enter the following expression in the text box that contains avg weight:

    `=ReportUtil.Localization.LocalizedString("AvgWeightColHead",User!Language)`

11. Open the Report Parameters dialog box. You can see the ServiceTypeDescription report parameter, which was created to work with the parameterized filter.
12. Enter **Select Service Types** for the Prompt.
13. Click OK to exit the Report Parameters dialog box.

14. Select the Preview tab. Check All in the Select Service Types drop-down list and click View Report.

15. Select Save All from the toolbar.

Task Notes   You may have noticed we did not type text strings for the report title and the two column headings on the report. Instead, we used expressions that call the LocalizedString method of the Localization class in the ReportUtil assembly. (*Localization* refers to the process of making a report or computer program appear in the language of a certain location.) This method requires two parameters: the name of the string to localize and the language it should be localized into. The string name is hardcoded in each expression. The language comes from the User!Language global variable. This global variable is populated with the language of the client application requesting the report.

The ReportUtil assembly uses multiple resource files to manage the localization. There is one resource file for each language it must support. In the demonstration code supplied for this example, the ReportUtil only has two resource files: one for English and one for Spanish. To support another language, you simply need to add another resource file and rebuild the project.

We used the LocalizedString method to get localized versions of the report title and the two column headers. The remainder of the report content is either proper names or numeric. Neither of these needs to be translated. If you are sharp, you will notice the report parameter prompt and the items in the report parameter drop-down list have not been localized. We cannot use expressions for either of these items, so we cannot use our nifty LocalizedString method.

The drop-down list content is selected from the database, so some localization of the data could be done as part of the query. The report parameter is a bigger problem. In fact, the current version of Reporting Services does not have a nice way to deal with this.

Reports Within Reports

Thus far, we have placed report items within report items and data regions within data regions. In this section, we look at putting whole reports inside one another. This is done using the subreport report item; the only item in the Toolbox that we have not yet used.

The *subreport item* is simply a placeholder in a report. It sits in the parent report and shows the space to be occupied by another report when the parent report is run. Nothing is special about a report placed in a subreport item. Any report can be used as a subreport.

The report placed in the subreport can even contain parameters. These parameter values can be passed from the parent report to the subreport. Any field value, parameter value, or expression in the parent report can be used as a parameter in the subreport.

Subreports are used for many reasons. They can provide an easy way to reuse a complex report layout within a parent report. They can also be used to implement a more complex form of drilldown.

The following subreports are anything but subpar!

The Employee Evaluation Report

Features Highlighted

- ▶ Using a subreport as reusable code
- ▶ Using the page width and page height properties for a landscape report
- ▶ Using a rectangle for grouping

Business Need   The Galactic Delivery Services personnel department has created an application for employees to conduct peer reviews as part of each employee's annual review process. They are also collecting a review and comments from each employee's manager. They need a report that can be used to present the results of the peer review at the employee's meeting with their supervisor.

The manager's review and comments should be noted as coming from the manager. The peer reviews, however, should be presented anonymously.

Task Overview

1. Create a New Report, Create a Dataset, Add a Table to the Report Layout, and Populate It
2. Create a New Report, Create a Dataset, and Populate the Report Layout
3. Add a Rectangle

Employee Evaluation Report, Task 1: Create a New Report, Create a Dataset, Add a Table to the Report Layout, and Populate It

1. Reopen the Chapter08 project if it was closed.
2. Create a new report called EvalDetail. Do *not* use the GDSReport template.

3. Create a new dataset called EvalRatings that calls the stp_EvalRatings stored procedure.

4. Select the Layout tab.

5. Place a table onto the body of the report.

6. Place the Goal, Rating, and GoalComment fields in the details row of the table.

7. Add a group to the table using EvaluatorEmployeeNumber as the grouping expression.

8. Complete your report layout so it is similar to Figure 8-15. The top row has the BorderStyle: Top property set to Solid. The bottom row has the BorderStyle: Bottom property set to Solid and the BorderWidth: Bottom property set to 5pt. Also note that the table header and table footer have been turned off.

9. Select Save All from the toolbar.

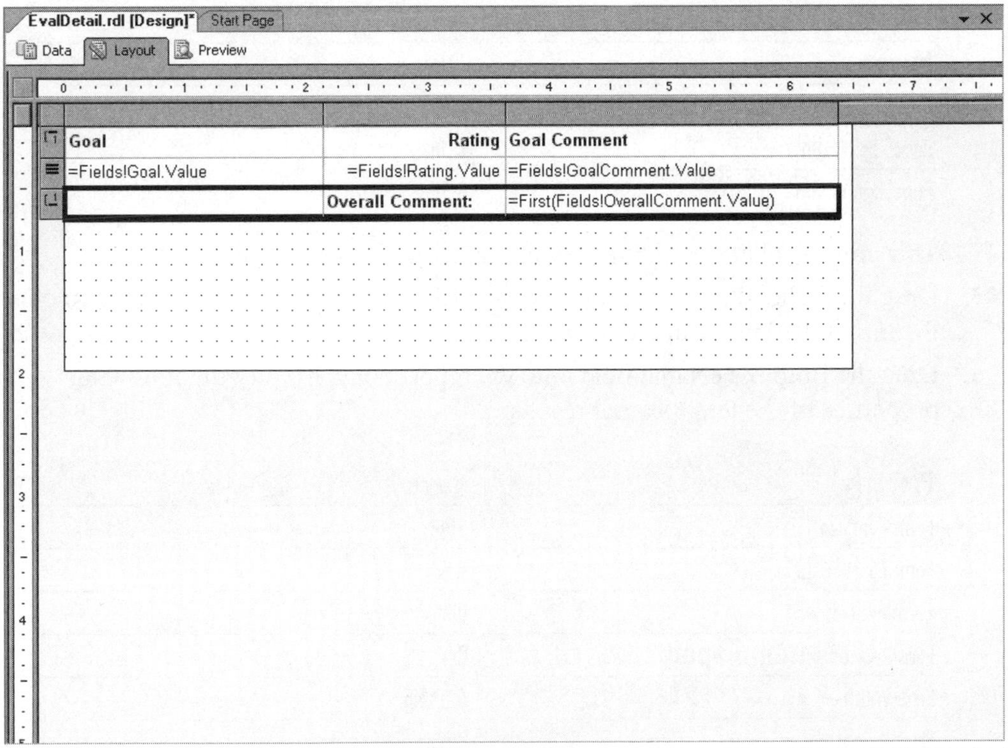

Figure 8-15 *The Employee Evaluation Detail Report layout*

Task Notes   The EvalDetail report is going to be used in two subreports in our parent report. It is going to be used in one location to display the peer reviews and in another location to display the manager review. We can create this layout for displaying review information, and then use it in multiple places.

Employee Evaluation Report, Task 2: Create a New Report, Create a Dataset, and Populate the Report Layout

1. Create a new report called EmployeeEval using the GDSReport template.
2. Create a new dataset called EvalPerformance that calls the stp_EvalPerformance stored procedure.
3. Select the Layout tab.
4. Modify the following properties of the report:

Property	Value
InteractiveSize: Width	11in
InteractiveSize: Height	8.5in
PageSize: Width	11in
PageSize: Height	8.5in

This creates a landscape page layout, rather than a portrait page layout.

5. Drag the right edge of the report body until it is 10 inches wide. Use the ruler at the top of the layout area as a guide.
6. Drag the EmployeeName field onto the report body. Modify the following properties of the text box that results:

Property	Value
Font: FontSize	20pt
Font: FontWeight	Bold
Location: Left	0in
Location: Top	0in
Size: Width	6.875in
Size: Height	0.5in

7. Place a text box onto the report body. Modify the following properties of this text box:

Property	Value
Font: FontSize	20pt
Font: FontWeight	Bold
Location: Left	8.25in
Location: Top	0in
Size: Width	1.625in
Size: Height	0.5in
Value	=Parameters!Year.Value

8. Place a text box onto the report body. Modify the following properties of this text box:

Property	Value
Font: FontSize	16pt
Font: FontWeight	Bold
Location: Left	0in
Location: Top	0.625in
Size: Width	2in
Size: Height	0.375in
Value	Peer Evaluations

9. Place a subreport onto the report body immediately below the text box. Modify the following properties of this subreport:

Property	Value
Location: Left	0in
Location: Top	1in
Size: Width	6.875in
Size: Height	1.125in

10. Right-click the subreport and select Properties from the Context menu. The Subreport Properties dialog box appears.

11. Select EvalDetail from the Subreport drop-down list.

12. Select the Parameters tab.

13. Configure the parameters as shown here:

Parameter Name	Parameter Value
EmpNum	=Parameters!EmpNum.Value
Year	=Parameters!Year.Value
MgrFlag	=0

Remember to use the Edit Expression dialog box to select the parameter values.

14. Click OK to exit the Subreport Properties dialog box.

15. Select the Peer Evaluations text box and the subreport. Press CTRL-C to copy these two items. Press CTRL-V to paste a copy of these items on the report body. Drag the two copied items, so they are immediately below the original subreport.

16. Modify the new text box to read "Manager Evaluation." Adjust the width of the text box as needed.

17. Open the Subreport Properties dialog box for the new subreport and select the Parameters tab.

18. Change the parameter value for MgrFlag from =0 to =1. This causes the second subreport to contain the manager's evaluation rather than the peer evaluations.

19. Click OK to exit the Subreport Properties dialog box.

20. Place a text box onto the report body. Modify the following properties of this text box:

Property	Value
Font: FontWeight	Bold
Location: Left	7.125in
Location: Top	1in
Size: Width	2in
Size: Height	0.25in
Value	Areas of Excellence

21. Drag the AreasOfExcellence field onto the report body. Modify the following properties of the text box that results:

Property	Value
Location: Left	7.125in
Location: Top	1.375in
Size: Width	2.75in
Size: Height	0.25in

22. Place a text box onto the report body. Modify the following properties of this text box:

Property	Value
Font: FontWeight	Bold
Location: Left	7.125in
Location: Top	1.875in
Size: Width	2in
Size: Height	0.25in
Value	Areas for Improvement

23. Drag the AreasForImprovement field onto the report body. Modify the following properties of the text box that results:

Property	Value
Location: Left	7.125in
Location: Top	2.25in
Size: Width	2.75in
Size: Height	0.25in

24. Select the Preview tab. Enter **1394** for EmpNum and **2005** for Year, and then click View Report. Your report should appear similar to Figure 8-16.

Task Notes   We used the InteractiveSize and PageSize properties of this report to change its orientation from portrait to landscape. When you are creating your report templates, you may want to create one template for portrait reports with the default InteractiveSize and PageSize values, and another report template for landscape reports with the InteractiveSize and PageSize values used in this report. The InteractiveSize parameter controls the dimensions of the report when it is viewed interactively. The PageSize parameter controls the dimensions of the report when it is printed.

Two steps are required to get each subreport item ready to use. First, you have to specify which report is going to be used within the subreport item. Once this is done,

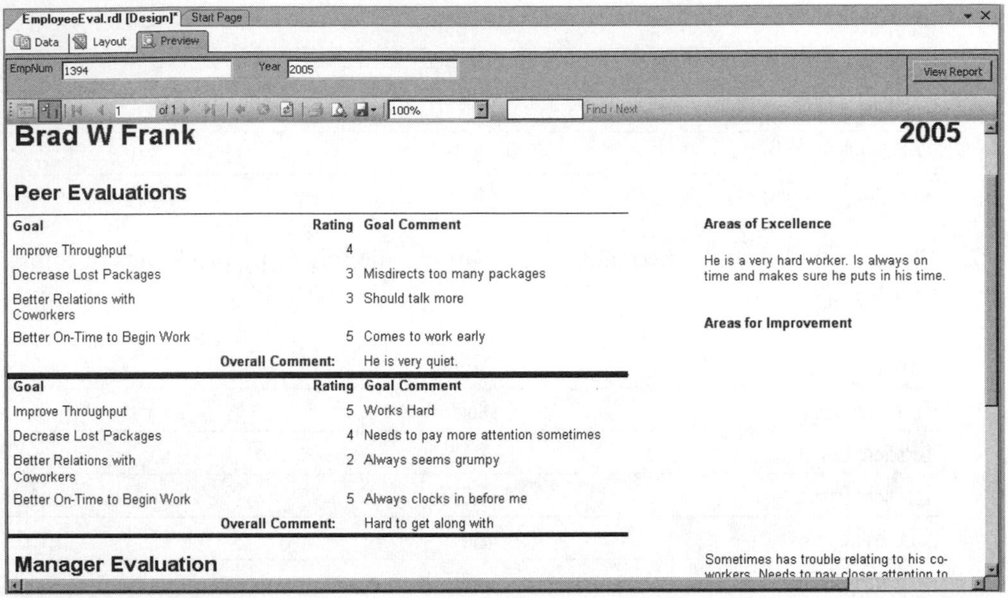

Figure 8-16 *The Employee Evaluation Report preview after Task 2*

you need to specify a value for each of the parameters in the selected report. With these two tasks completed, your subreports are ready to go.

In this report, we are using several fields outside of a data region: the EmployeeName field, the AreasOfExcellence field, and the AreasForImprovement field. Remember, data regions are set up to repeat a portion of their content for each record in the result set. When a field value occurs outside of a data region, it is not repeated; it occurs only once. Therefore, the field value must be put inside an aggregate function to determine how to get one value from the many records in the result set. The First() aggregate function is chosen by default.

In this particular report, the EvalPerformance dataset has only one record. Of course, the Report Designer does not know at design time how many records the dataset will have at run time. (Even if the dataset has only one record at design time, it could have 100 records at run time.) Therefore, the Report Designer insists on the aggregate function for this field value.

Finally, you may have noticed a little problem with the text box that contains the contents of the AreasForImprovement field. It seems to be sliding down the page. In actuality, it was pushed down the page when the subreport grew.

The text boxes that contain the Areas of Excellence title, the AreasOfExcellence field value, and the Areas for Improvement title are all even with the first subreport. However, the text box containing the value of the AreasForImprovement field starts below the bottom of the first subreport. When the subreport grows because of its content, the text box is pushed further down the report, so it remains below the bottom of the subreport.

In Task 3, you see a way to prevent this problem.

Employee Evaluation Report, Task 3: Add a Rectangle

1. Select the Layout tab.
2. Select the Areas of Excellence text box, the AreasOfExcellence field value text box, the Areas for Improvement text box, and the AreasForImprovement field value text box. Press CTRL-X to cut these four text boxes.
3. Select a rectangle from the Toolbox and place it in the area just vacated by these four text boxes.
4. With the rectangle still selected, press CTRL-V to paste the four text boxes into the rectangle.
5. Arrange the rectangle and the four text boxes as needed. Your layout should appear similar to Figure 8-17.

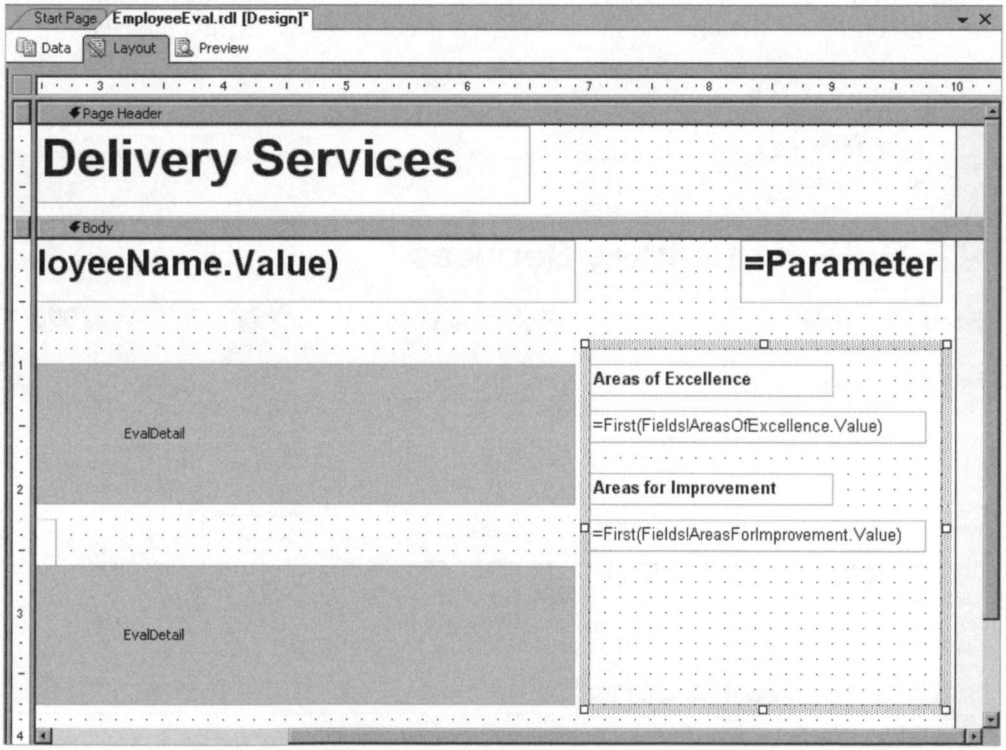

Figure 8-17   *The Employee Evaluation Report layout with a rectangle*

6. Select the Preview tab. Enter **1394** for EmpNum and **2005** for Year, and then click View Report. Your report should appear similar to Figure 8-18.

7. Select Save All from the toolbar.

Task Notes   The rectangle report item comes to your rescue here. Once the four text boxes are inside the rectangle, they remain together no matter how much the subreport grows. As your report designs become more complex, rectangles are often necessary to keep things right where you want them.

The Invoice Report

Features Highlighted

▶ Using a subreport in a table

▶ Using a subreport to facilitate drilldown

Business Need   The Galactic Delivery Services accounting department wants an interactive Invoice Report. The Invoice Report needs to show the invoice header

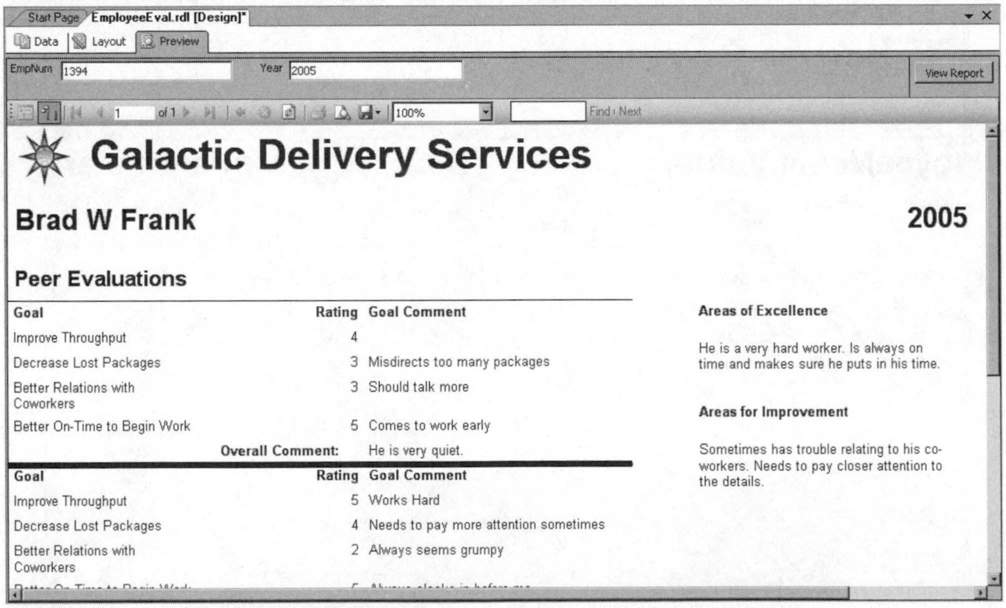

Figure 8-18   *The Employee Evaluation Report preview with a rectangle*

and invoice detail information. The user can then expand an invoice detail entry to view information on the delivery that created that invoice detail.

Task Overview

1. Create a New Report, Create a Dataset, and Copy the Layout from the DeliveryStatus Report
2. Create a New Report, Create a Dataset, and Populate the Report Layout

Invoice Report, Task 1: Create a New Report, Create a Dataset, and Copy the Layout from the DeliveryStatus Report

1. Reopen the Chapter08 project if it was closed.
2. Create a new report called DeliveryDetail. Do *not* use the GDSReport template.
3. Create a new dataset called DeliveryStatus that calls the stp_DeliveryDetail stored procedure.
4. Select the Layout tab.
5. Double-click the entry for the DeliveryStatus report in the Solution Explorer to open the DeliveryStatus report.
6. Select the table in the DeliveryStatus report and press CTRL-C to copy it. (Make sure you have the entire table selected and not just a single cell in the table.)
7. Close the DeliveryStatus report and return to the DeliveryDetail report.
8. Press CTRL-V to paste the table into the report body.
9. Move the table to the upper-left corner of the report body. Size the report body, so it exactly contains the table.

Task Notes   Instead of re-creating a layout for the delivery detail, we borrowed a layout created previously in another report. This works because the stp_DeliveryDetail stored procedure returns the same columns as the stp_DeliveryStatus stored procedure used for the previous report. The other requirement needed to make this cut-and-paste operation successful was to use the same name for the dataset in both reports.

When you have a layout that is nice and clean, reusing it whenever possible is always a good idea. Even better would be to modify the DeliveryStatus report to use our new DeliveryDetail report in a subreport. That way, we would only need to maintain this layout in one location.

Consider that an extra credit project.

Invoice Report, Task 2: Create a New Report, Create a Dataset, and Populate the Report Layout

1. Create a new report called Invoice using the GDSReport template.
2. Create a new dataset called InvoiceHeader that calls the stp_InvoiceHeader stored procedure.
3. Create a second dataset called InvoiceDetail that calls the stp_InvoiceDetail stored procedure.
4. Select the Layout tab.
5. Place a list onto the report body.
6. Size the list and add fields and text boxes to create the layout shown in Figure 8-19. The fields come from the InvoiceHeader dataset. The black line across the bottom is a solid bottom border on the list item with a border width of 10 points.
7. Drag the report body to make it larger.
8. Place a table onto the report body immediately below the list.

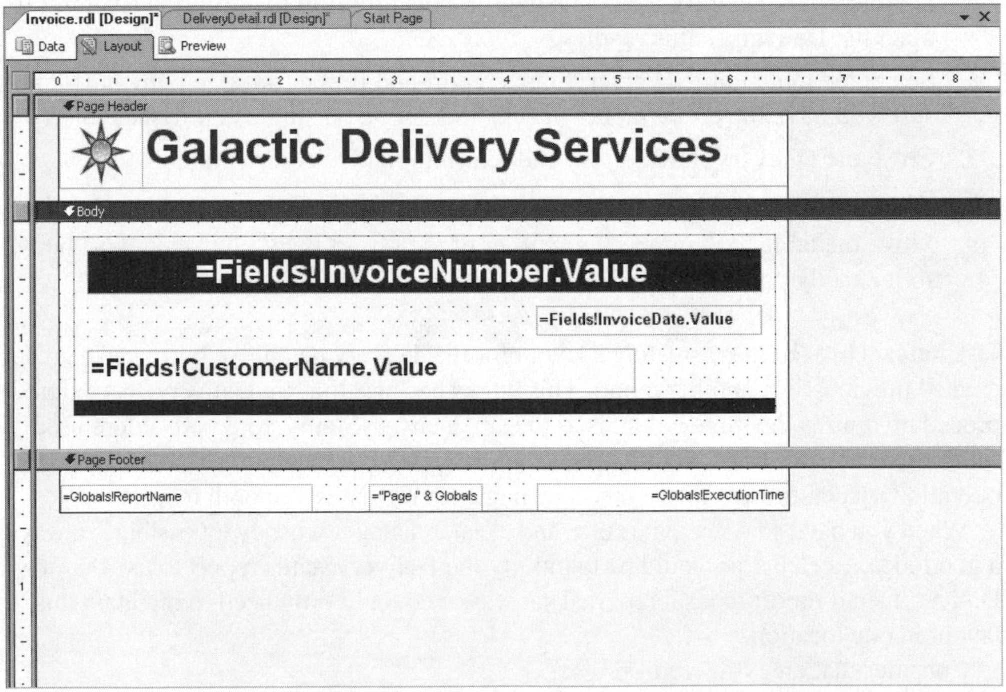

Figure 8-19   *The Invoice Report layout with an invoice header*

9. Drag the LineNumber, Description, and Amount fields from the InvoiceDetail dataset into the details row of the table.

10. Size the table columns appropriately. Type the letter **C** for the Format property of the text box containing the Amount field value.

11. Turn off the table header and table footer.

12. Add a second details row below the existing details row.

13. Merge the three cells in this new details row.

14. Place a subreport in the merged cell.

15. Open the Subreport Properties dialog box. Set the subreport to DeliveryDetail.

16. Select the Parameters tab and configure it as follows:

Parameter Name	Parameter Value
DeliveryNumber	=Fields!DeliveryNumber.Value

17. Click OK to exit the Subreport Parameters dialog box.

18. Click the gray box to the left of the row containing the subreport. Modify the following properties for this table row using the Properties window:

Property	Value
Visibility: Hidden	True
Visibility: ToggleItem	LineNumber

19. Select the Preview tab. Type **73054** for InvoiceNumber and click View Report.

20. Expand one of the invoice detail entries and observe how the subreport appears.

21. You can widen the report body, list, and table so the report layout does not expand when the subreport appears. Your report should appear as shown in Figure 8-20.

22. Select Save All from the toolbar.

Task Notes   In the Invoice Report, we placed our subreport right in a table cell. A field from the table's dataset is used as the parameter for the subreport. Because of this, the subreport is different for each details row in the table.

We chose to have the subreport initially hidden in our report. The reason for this is the subreport contains a large amount of detail information. This detail would overwhelm the users if it were displayed all at once. Instead, the users can selectively drill down to the detail they need.

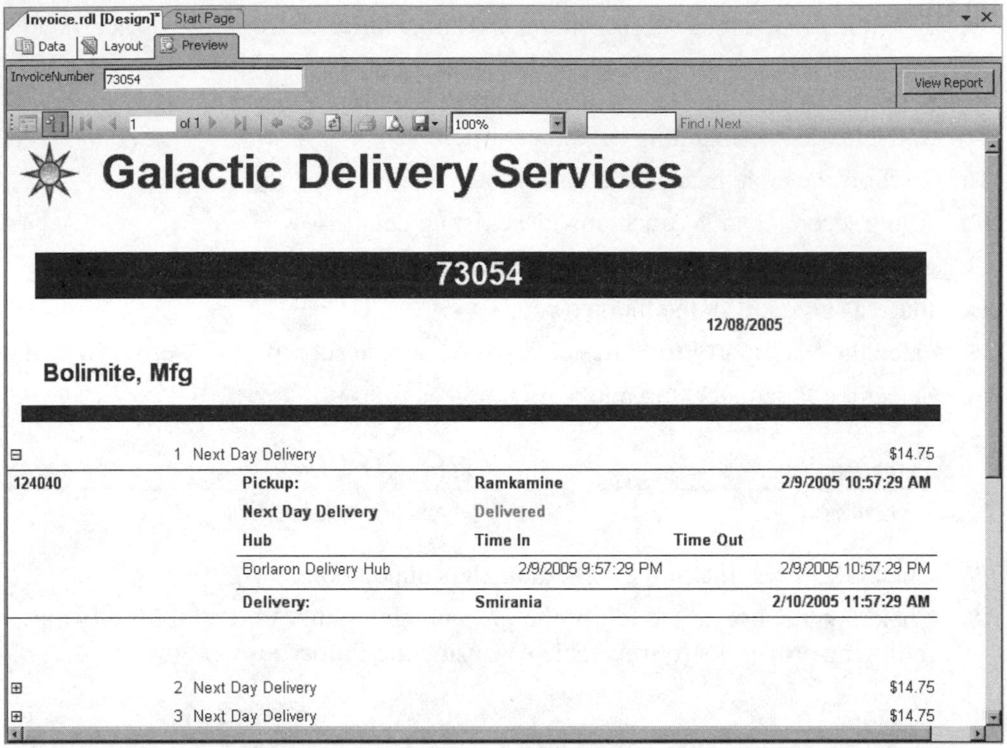

Figure 8-20 *The Invoice Report preview*

In our next report, you look at another way to manage large amounts of detail by using the drill-through feature of Reporting Services.

Interacting with Reports

In many cases, your reports can be much more effective when users can view them electronically. Reporting Services offers a number of options for enabling the user to interact with the reports when viewed electronically. You have already seen several examples of drill-down interactivity. This type of interactivity hides detail information until it is needed by the user.

In this section, you learn additional methods for navigating within reports and even moving between reports. You also see how to link a report to other Internet content. Finally, you look at a way for your report to interact with you by always keeping its data current.

So don't be shy: interact!

The Invoice Front-End Report

Features Highlighted

- ▶ Using drill-through navigation to move between reports
- ▶ Using the document map to navigate within a report
- ▶ Using bookmarks to navigate within a report
- ▶ Using links to navigate to Internet content

Business Need   The Galactic Delivery Services accounting department is pleased with the Invoice Report. They would now like a front end to make the Invoice Report easier to use. The front-end report should list all invoices by customer and let the user click an invoice to see the complete Invoice Report. The front end should have each customer start on a new page. In addition, the front end should provide a quick way to navigate to the page for a particular customer, and a way to move from a customer to the page for its parent company. Finally, the front end should include a link to the customer's website for further information on the customer.

Task Overview

1. Create a New Report, Create a Dataset, and Populate the Report Layout
2. Add the Navigation

Invoice Front-End Report, Task 1: Create a New Report, Create a Dataset, and Populate the Report Layout

1. Reopen the Chapter08 project if it was closed.
2. Create a new report called FrontEnd using the GDSReport template.
3. Create a new dataset called CustomerInvoices that calls the stp_CustomerInvoices stored procedure.
4. Select the Layout tab.
5. Place a table onto the report body.
6. Drag the InvoiceNumber, InvoiceDate, and TotalAmount fields into the details row of the table.
7. Type the letter **C** for the Format property for the text box containing the TotalAmount field value.

8. Turn off the table header and table footer.

9. Add a group to the table using the CustomerName as the grouping expression. The group should have a group header, but not a group footer. There should be a page break at the start of each new group.

10. Drag the CustomerName field into the leftmost cell in the group header row. Set the FontWeight property to Bold for this text box.

11. Drag the ParentName field into the center cell in the group header row.

Task Notes   We have the layout for the Invoice Front-End Report. However, it is not really a front end because it does not lead anywhere yet. Let's continue to the good stuff.

Invoice Front-End Report, Task 2: Add the Navigation

1. Right-click the leftmost cell in the details row (the cell containing the invoice number) and select Properties from the Context menu. The Textbox Properties dialog box appears.

2. Select the Navigation tab.

3. Select the Jump to Report option for the Hyperlink action.

4. Select Invoice from the Jump to Report drop-down list.

5. Click Parameters. The Parameters dialog box appears.

6. Select InvoiceNumber from the Parameter Name drop-down list.

7. Select =Fields!InvoiceNumber.Value from the Parameter Value drop-down list.

8. Click OK to exit the Parameters dialog box.

9. Click OK to exit the Textbox Properties dialog box.

10. Right-click the leftmost cell in the group header row (the cell containing the customer name) and select Properties from the Context menu. The Textbox Properties dialog box appears.

11. Select the Navigation tab.

12. Select =Fields!CustomerName.Value from the Document Map Label drop-down list.

13. Select =Fields!CustomerName.Value from the Bookmark ID drop-down list.

14. Click OK to exit the Textbox Properties dialog box.

15. Right-click the center cell in the group header row (the cell containing the parent name) and select Properties from the Context menu. The Textbox Properties dialog box appears.

16. Select the Navigation tab.
17. Select the Jump to Bookmark option for the Hyperlink action.
18. Select =Fields!ParentName.Value from the Jump to Bookmark drop-down list.
19. Click OK to exit the Textbox Properties dialog box.
20. Right-click the rightmost cell in the group header row and select Properties from the Context menu. The Textbox Properties dialog box appears.
21. Type **Website Link** for Value.
22. Select the Navigation tab.
23. Select the Jump to URL option for the Hyperlink action.
24. Select =Fields!CustomerWebsite.Value from the Jump to URL drop-down list.
25. Click OK to exit the Textbox Properties dialog box.
26. Select the Preview tab.
27. Select Save All from the toolbar.

Task Notes   When you look at the report preview, you notice a new feature to the left of the report. This is the *document map*, which functions like a table of contents for your report. We created entries in the document map when we placed an expression in the Document Map Label drop-down list in Step 12.

Because you used the customer name as the document map label, when you expand the FrontEnd entry in the document map, you see a list of all the customer names. (FrontEnd is the name of the report. That is why it is the top entry in the document map.) When you click a customer name in the document map, you are taken directly to the page for that customer.

If you are not using the document map, you can hide it by clicking the Document Map button in the report viewer toolbar. The Document Map button is the leftmost button in the toolbar. Clicking this button a second time causes the document map to return.

In addition to creating document map entries for each customer name, we also created bookmarks for each customer name. This was done in Step 13. We are using these bookmarks to link child companies to their parent company. We are creating a Jump to Bookmark using the value of the ParentName field. This was done in Steps 17 and 18.

When a customer has a value in the ParentName field, a Jump to Bookmark link is created on that parent name (the center cell in the group header row). The bookmark link jumps to the page for the customer with the matching name. To try this out, use the document map to jump to the page for Everlast Plastics. Everlast's parent company is Young & Assoc. Click the link for Young & Assoc., and you will jump to the page for Young & Assoc.

We also created a Jump to URL link for each customer. This link was placed in the cell that reads Website Link and was created in Steps 23 and 24. Clicking this cell is supposed to take you to the website for each customer. However, we are unable to connect to the Inter-galactic-net used by GDS and its customers. Instead, clicking this link opens a browser and takes you to the Osborne website.

Earlier in the process, we created a Jump to Report. This was done in Steps 3 through 7. Clicking an invoice number jumps you to the Invoice Report and passes the invoice number as a parameter. This enables you to see the detail information for the invoice. When you finish looking at the invoice, you can return to the Invoice Front-End Report by clicking the Back button in the report viewer toolbar.

The Transport Monitor Report

Features Highlighted

▶ Using a chart as the data section of a matrix

▶ Indicating values over a set maximum on a chart

▶ Using the autorefresh report property

▶ Using a multivalued parameter with a WHERE clause

Business Need   The Galactic Delivery Services maintenance department needs a report to assist in monitoring transport operations. Each transport feeds real-time sensor data back to the central database. The maintenance department needs a report to display this information for a selected set of transports. Because the sensor data is updated every minute, the report should refresh every minute. The sensor data should be displayed in a graphical form with a highlight of any values that are above the normal maximums.

Task Overview

1. Create a New Report, Create a Dataset, Populate the Report Layout, and Set Report Properties

Transport Monitor Report, Task 1: Create a New Report, Create a Dataset, Populate the Report Layout, and Set Report Properties

1. Reopen the Chapter08 project if it was closed.
2. Create a new report called TransportMonitor. Do *not* use the GDSReport template.
3. Create a new dataset called TransportMonitor that calls the stp_TransportMonitor stored procedure.

4. Create a second dataset called TransportList that calls the stp_TransportList stored procedure.

5. Select the Layout tab.

6. Configure the TransportNumber Report Parameter as follows:

Property	Value
Prompt	Transports
Multivalue	Checked
Available values	From query
Dataset	TransportList
Value field	TransportNumber
Label field	TransportNumber

7. Click OK to exit the Report Parameters dialog box.

8. Place a text box on the report body and set its properties as follows:

Property	Value
Font: FontSize	20pt
Font: FontWeight	Bold
Location: Left	0in
Location: Top	0in
Size: Width	3in
Size: Height	0.375in
Value	Transport Monitor

9. Place a matrix onto the report body. Set the properties of the matrix as follows:

Property	Value
Location: Left	0in
Location: Top	0.5in

10. Drag the TransportNumber field from the TransportMonitor dataset into the Rows cell. Set the following properties of the text box created in that cell:

Property	Value
BackgroundColor	White

Property	Value
Font: FontWeight	Bold
VerticalAlign	Middle

11. Drag the Item field into the Columns cell. Set the following properties of the text box created in that cell:

Property	Value
BackgroundColor	White
Font: FontWeight	Bold
TextAlign	Center

12. Open the Matrix Properties dialog box and select the Groups tab.

13. Click Edit in the Rows area. The Grouping and Sorting Properties dialog box appears.

14. Check the Grouping Header Should Remain Visible While Scrolling option.

15. Click OK to exit the Grouping and Sorting Properties dialog box.

16. Click Edit in the Columns area. The Grouping and Sorting Properties dialog box appears.

17. Check the Grouping Header Should Remain Visible While Scrolling option.

18. Click OK to exit the Grouping and Sorting Properties dialog box. Click OK to exit the Matrix Properties dialog box.

19. Click the gray rectangle to select the top row of the matrix. Set its Height property to 0.25in.

20. Click the gray rectangle to select the bottom row of the matrix. Set its Height property to 1.625in.

21. Click the gray rectangle to select the left-hand column of the matrix. Set its Width property to 1in.

22. Click the gray rectangle to select the right-hand column of the matrix. Set its Width property to 2.25in.

23. Expand the TransportMonitor dataset in the Datasets window.

24. Place a chart in the Data cell.

25. Drag the Value field and drop it on Drop Data Fields Here. (This may be a little tricky. You might have to drag the fields over the chart to reactivate the drop areas before you can drop the field in the appropriate location.)

26. Drag the Reading field and drop it on Drop Category Fields Here. Drag the ReadingPortion field and drop it on the Drop Series Fields Here.

27. Set the following properties of the chart using the Chart Properties dialog box:

Property	Value
On the General tab:	
Palette	Excel
Chart subtype	Stacked column chart
On the Y Axis tab:	
Maximum	100
On the Legend tab:	
Show legend	Unchecked

28. Click OK to exit the Chart Properties dialog box.
29. Open the Report Properties dialog box.
30. Check Autorefresh and set the autorefresh rate to 60 (seconds).
31. Click OK to exit the Report Properties dialog box.
32. Select the Preview tab.
33. Select several transport numbers from the drop-down list and click View Report. (Autorefresh is not supported in the report preview.) Your report appears similar to Figure 8-21.
34. Select Save All from the toolbar.

Task Notes   A number of interesting things are going on in this report. First, a multi-valued parameter is being sent to SQL Server for use in a stored procedure. The stored procedure uses the contents of this multivalued parameter to build a query string on the fly. The SELECT statement in the stored procedure is a bit complicated because it is using some random number generation to simulate the Transport telemetry. Here is a more straightforward version of the content of the stored procedure:

```
DECLARE @DynamicQuery    varchar(8000)

SET @DynamicQuery = 'SELECT TransportNumber, Item, Reading, Value '
SET @DynamicQuery = @DynamicQuery + 'FROM transMonitor '
SET @DynamicQuery = @DynamicQuery + 'WHERE TransportNumber IN
                          ('+@TransportNumber+') '

EXEC (@DynamicQuery)
```

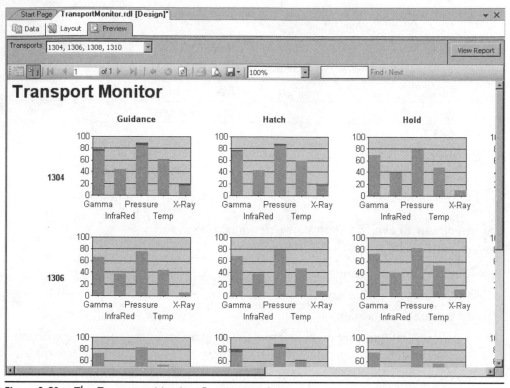

Figure 8-21 *The Transport Monitor Report preview*

This stored procedure code builds the SELECT statement in the @DynamicQuery variable. It uses the IN operator to look for the content of the TransportNumber field in a list of values. The values must be comma-separated and enclosed in parentheses to be used with the IN operator. The values in the multivalued parameter are being passed to the @TransportNumber stored procedure parameter. Because these values are already comma-separated, all you have to do is place them inside the parentheses to use them with the IN operator.

We placed a chart in the data portion of the matrix data region. Because the data portion of a matrix is an aggregate, the chart has a set of values to use for charting. When the report is rendered, the chart is repeated in each data cell in the matrix. Each chart then acts within the scope of its data cell and charts the data in that scope.

The chart contains two series. The first series is a value up to the maximum normal value for that reading. The second series is the amount of the reading above the maximum normal value. The second series value is 0 if the reading is below or at its maximum normal value. The stacked column chart puts these two series one on top of the other. The result is any readings that are above their maximum normal value have a maroon section at the top of the column. This should be enough to get the attention of any technician monitoring the readings.

Finally, we used autorefresh to meet the business requirements of the report. When the Autorefresh property is set, the report is automatically rerun on the schedule you specify. Unfortunately, autorefresh is only supported in the Report Manager. You can see autorefresh in action if you deploy this report to the Report Manager after reading Chapter 11.

A Conversion Experience

Reporting Services is not the first report-authoring environment to come along. Hundreds of thousands of reports have been created using other tools. If you have legacy reports and are looking to switch to Reporting Services, these legacy reports need to be re-created—that is, unless your legacy reports were written in Microsoft Access. If that is the case, you are in luck.

The Report Designer includes an import tool for taking Access reports and making them into Reporting Services reports. Not everything in your Access reports imports directly into Reporting Services. Even so, this import tool gives you a leg up on having to rebuild each entire report from scratch.

We now go through a sample report import to give you an introduction to the import tool. You can consult the Reporting Services Books Online for more information on exactly which features the Access report import will and won't import.

The Paid Invoices Report

Feature Highlighted

- ► Importing an Access report

Business Need   The Galactic Delivery Services accounting department has an Access report that lists paid invoices. The accounting department would like to convert this report to Reporting Services and eliminate the InvoiceInfo.mdb file. The MDB file uses linked tables to pull data from the SQL Server database.

NOTE

The Access import can only be done if you have Microsoft Access installed on the PC where you are running Reporting Services.

Task Overview

1. Import the Access Report and Change the Data Source

Paid Invoices Report, Task 1: Import the Access Report and Change the Data Source

1. If you have not already done so, download the InvoiceInfo.mdb file from the website for this book.

2. Create a System ODBC data source called Galactic that points to the Galactic database. Use GalacticReporting for the SQL login and gds for the password. This ODBC data source is used by the linked tables in InvoiceInfo.mdb to access the Galactic database in SQL Server. This ODBC data source must be in place for the conversion to function properly.

CAUTION

This is a Windows ODBC data source, not a Reporting Services data source. Use the ODBC Data Source Administrator under Administrative Tools in the Control Panel to create this data source.

3. Reopen the Chapter08 project if it was closed.

4. Right-click the Reports folder in the Solution Explorer and select Import Reports | Microsoft Access from the Context menu. The Open dialog box appears.

5. Browse to the InvoiceInfo.mdb file, select it, and click Open.

6. The Report Designer imports any reports it finds in the selected MDB file.

7. When the import is complete, you have a new report called PaidInvoices.rdl in your Solution Explorer. Double-click this report to open it.

8. Select the Data tab.

9. Click the . . . button in the Query Builder toolbar. The Dataset dialog box appears.

10. Click the . . . button next to the Data Source drop-down box. The Data Source dialog box appears.

11. If you examine the connection string, you see that the data source is going back to the MDB file to get its data. Because the MDB file was using linked tables and pulling data from the SQL Server database, it makes sense to now go to the SQL Server database directly.

12. Click Cancel to exit the Data Source dialog box.

13. Select Galactic (shared) from the Data Source drop-down list.

14. Click OK to exit the Dataset dialog box.

15. Change the query in the SQL Panel to the following:

```
SELECT InvoiceHeader.CustomerNumber, InvoiceHeader.InvoiceNumber,
       InvoiceHeader.TotalAmount, PaymentInvoiceLink.PaidDate,
       PaymentInvoiceLink.PaidAmount
FROM   InvoiceHeader
INNER JOIN PaymentInvoiceLink
       ON InvoiceHeader.InvoiceNumber = PaymentInvoiceLink.InvoiceNumber
INNER JOIN Payment
       ON PaymentInvoiceLink.PaymentNumber = Payment.PaymentNumber
WHERE (InvoiceHeader.PaidInFullFlag = 1)
ORDER BY InvoiceHeader.CustomerNumber, InvoiceHeader.InvoiceNumber,
         PaymentInvoiceLink.PaidDate
```

16. Run the query to verify it now works properly with the SQL tables.

17. Clear your query results.

18. Select the Preview tab.

19. Make any additional formatting changes necessary to get the report looking as it should.

20. Select Save All from the toolbar when the report is completed.

Task Notes   You can see the column headings from the Access report were placed in the page header in the Reporting Services report. This looks rather strange, but it is nothing a minute or two of additional formatting couldn't fix. The import does not create a perfect replica of your Access report in Reporting Services. It does, however, save you a lot of time over rebuilding each report from scratch.

What's Next

We have now touched on almost all the report-authoring features for Reporting Services. It is time to move on from report development to report deployment and delivery. We take a quick look at the various formats available for Reporting Services reports, and then move on into the world of the Report Manager.

CHAPTER

9
A Leading Exporter: Exporting Reports to Other Rendering Formats

A Report in Any Other Format Would Look as Good
Presentation Formats
Data Exchange Formats
Call the Manager

U p to this point, we have been viewing reports in the preview format. The preview format works great during report development for checking out your report layout and interactivity. However, when you want to present your report to users who do not have the Report Designer, you need something other than the preview format to do the job.

In place of the preview format, Reporting Services lets you export your report to other rendering formats so it can be presented to a user. These *presentation rendering formats* retain the layout, fonts, colors, and graphics of the report. The presentation rendering formats are as follows:

- ▶ TIFF Image
- ▶ Adobe PDF
- ▶ MHTML (web archive)
- ▶ Excel
- ▶ Print
- ▶ HTML

Reporting Services also lets you export your report to two additional formats, which are used primarily for rendering report data into a form that can be used by other computer programs. These *data exchange rendering formats* contain the data portion of the report along with a minimal amount of formatting. Here are the data exchange rendering formats:

- ▶ Comma-Separated Values (CSV)
- ▶ XML

Most of these rendering formats can be generated from the Preview tab in the Report Designer using the Export toolbar button. This enables you to render a report to a file or to a printer and manually distribute it to your users. It also lets you verify what the report will look like when your users choose to receive your report rendered in one of these formats.

In this chapter, we look at each of these rendering formats, which report features they support, and how they can best be used. To demonstrate each rendering format, we use a report project that contains a set of reports with many of the layout and interactivity characteristics discussed in the previous chapters. If you want to "play along at home," you can download the Chapter09 report project from the website for this book and try exporting the report to each rendering format yourself.

A Report in Any Other Format Would Look as Good

If Reporting Services only enabled you to view reports in the preview format when using the Report Designer and in a browser when using the Report Manager, it would be an interesting tool. The fact that reports can be delivered in a number of other presentation formats while maintaining their basic look and feel makes Reporting Services a powerful tool. Adding the capability to transfer information using a pair of data exchange formats further enhances the flexibility of Reporting Services.

Exporting and Printing a Report

We look at each of the export formats in detail in the "Presentation Formats" and "Data Exchange Formats" sections. First, let's look at how the export process works in the Report Designer. We try exporting a report, and then displaying it with the appropriate viewer. Then, we print the report from the Report Designer.

Exporting a Report

Follow these steps to export a report.

1. If you have downloaded the Chapter09 project, open this project, double-click the RenderingTest report, and select the Preview tab. (You may need to re-enter the password in the shared data source in this project before you can preview the report.) If you have not downloaded the Chapter09 project, open your favorite report project from one of the previous chapters, double-click a report, and select the Preview tab. The report is displayed in the preview format.

2. Expand the Bolimite row and the 2004 column in the matrix.

3. Click the Export button in the Report Designer toolbar. You see a drop-down list showing all the available export formats, as shown in Figure 9-1.

4. Select any of the available formats. (Choose one of the presentation formats to make this a more interesting example.) The Exporting dialog box appears.

5. After a few moments, the Save As dialog box appears over the top of the Exporting dialog box. Select the folder where you want the export file to be created. Modify the filename if you would like. Click Save.

6. The Export dialog box disappears after the export file is created. The report has now been exported or rendered in the selected format.

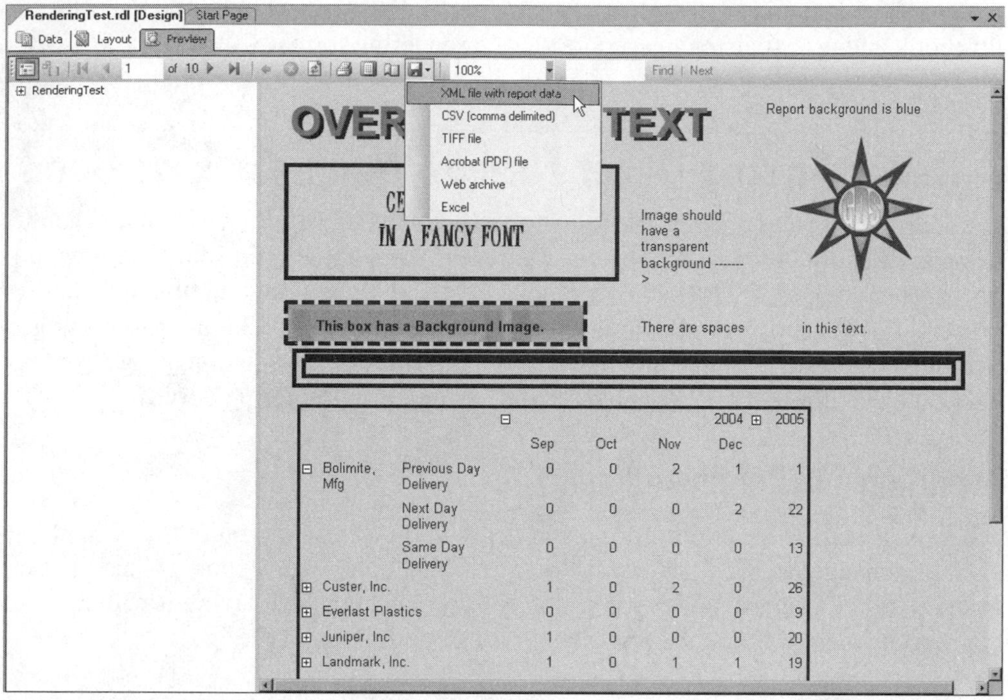

Figure 9-1 *The Export menu on the Preview tab*

Viewing the Exported Report

Follow these steps to view the report.

1. To view the export file, open Windows Explorer.
2. Navigate to the folder where the export file was created.
3. Double-click the export file. Windows opens the export file using the appropriate application for viewing this type of file. (We cover viewer requirements as we discuss each export format in the "Presentation Formats" and "Data Exchange Formats" sections.)

Printing a Report

Follow these steps to print the report.

1. Return to the Preview tab in the Report Designer.
2. Click the Print Layout button on the toolbar below the Preview tab. The contents of the Preview tab are replaced by the print layout, as shown in Figure 9-2.

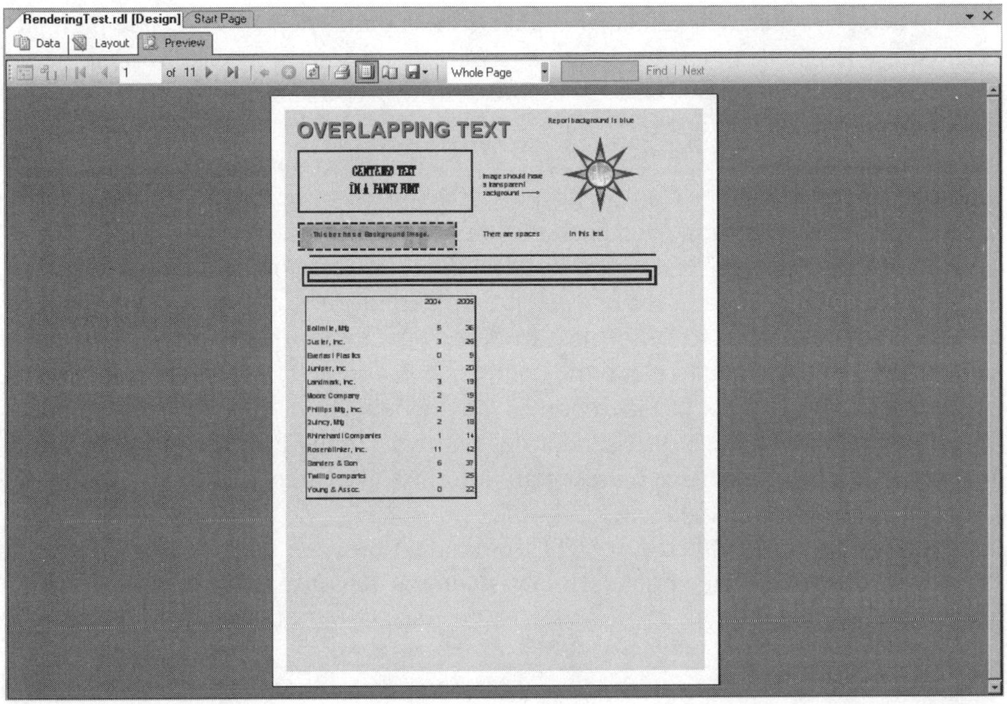

RenderingTest.rdl [Design] Start Page

Data Layout Preview

| 1 of 11 | Whole Page | Find | Next |

OVERLAPPING TEXT   Report background is blue

CENTERED TEXT
IN A FANCY FONT

Image should have
a transparent
background ➔

This box has a background image.   There are spaces   in this text.

	2004	2005
Bellmire, Mfg	5	36
Custer, Inc.	3	26
Bertelli Plastics	0	5
Juniper, Inc	1	20
Landmark, Inc.	3	19
Moore Company	2	15
Phillips Mfg, Inc.	2	29
Quincy, Mfg	2	18
Rhinehard Companies	1	14
Rosenwinkel, Inc.	11	62
Sanders & Son	6	37
Twillig Companies	3	25
Young & Assoc.	0	22

Figure 9-2   *The Print Layout*

3. Use the drop-down list in the toolbar below the Preview tab to zoom in or zoom out, as needed.

4. Click the Print button just to the left of the Print Layout button. The Print dialog box appears.

NOTE

You must be in Print Layout mode for the Print button to be active.

5. Select the appropriate printer, set the necessary printer properties, and then click OK. Your report is printed.

Presentation Formats

Most of the export or rendering formats provided by Reporting Services are presentation formats. They are intended to reproduce, as faithfully as possible, the format and the interactivity of your report as it appears in the preview format. The degree to which each presentation format can duplicate these things depends, in large part, on the features available in and the limitations of the viewer used by each format. For instance, a TIFF image viewer does not provide any hyperlinks, so the TIFF export does not support the navigation features.

In this section, we look at the viewer required to display each format. Also, the features supported and the features not supported by each presentation format are listed. We also discuss how each presentation format can best be utilized.

We use the RenderingTest report from the Chapter09 report project to examine some of the features supported by each presentation format. As mentioned earlier, you may download this report project from the website for this book if you want to perform the exports and make the comparisons yourself. Our standard is the appearance and behavior of this report in the Preview tab in the Report Designer. The top of the first page of the RenderingTest report in the Preview tab is shown in Figure 9-3. As we look at each presentation format, we can compare it to the way the report looks in this figure.

Note, I used a font called Juice ITC for the text box containing the words "Centered Text in a Fancy Font." This was done to demonstrate the behavior of

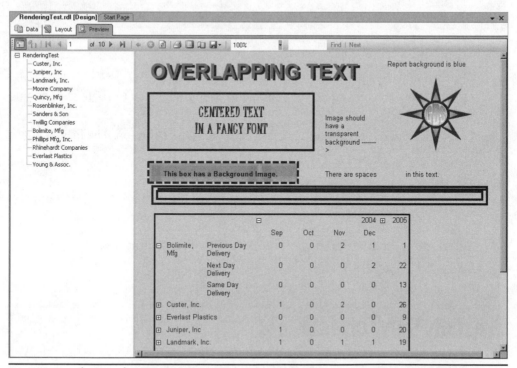

Figure 9-3 *The RenderingTest report in the Preview tab*

a font that may not be available on other computers. However, because of this, you may not actually see a fancy font in this text box. Instead, you see the font the Report Designer chooses to substitute for the requested font, which is unavailable. If this is the case, you have to trust the text and the figures to show you the behavior of this text box.

Note, too, the preview format does not pay strict attention to the physical page size specified for the report. The preview format allows a page to grow wider than a report page. The preview format does create page breaks based on the length of the page, but it does this only as an approximation. It does not strictly adhere to the page size specified for the report. Therefore, the page breaks found in the preview format differ from the page breaks found in formats that exactly follow the size properties of the report.

TIFF Image Presentation Format

TIFF is an acronym for Tagged Image File Format. *TIFF* is a file standard for storing images on personal computers, similar to the BMP and PCX formats. Unlike these formats, a TIFF file can store a number of images as multiple pages of a single document. This feature makes TIFF a popular format for storing fax documents.

When a report is rendered to a TIFF file, each page of the report is converted to a bitmap image. When we view the image, we see letters and numbers. However, the TIFF file itself contains only a series of dots. Because the entire report is stored as a bitmap image, TIFF files tend to be rather large.

Viewing TIFF Documents

On most Windows systems, TIFF files can be viewed using the Windows Picture and Fax Viewer. The Windows Picture and Fax Viewer has features for moving between pages, printing, and zooming in and out. This viewer also enables you to add annotations, including highlighting, drawing, text, and "sticky notes," as shown in Figure 9-4. These annotations can be helpful if reports are distributed electronically while they are being analyzed.

If you do not have the Windows Picture and Fax Viewer available, TIFF viewers are available for nearly any personal computer platform. In many cases, a TIFF viewer can be obtained for a minimal charge as shareware or freeware. Note, not all TIFF viewers include the annotation features found in the Windows Picture and Fax Viewer.

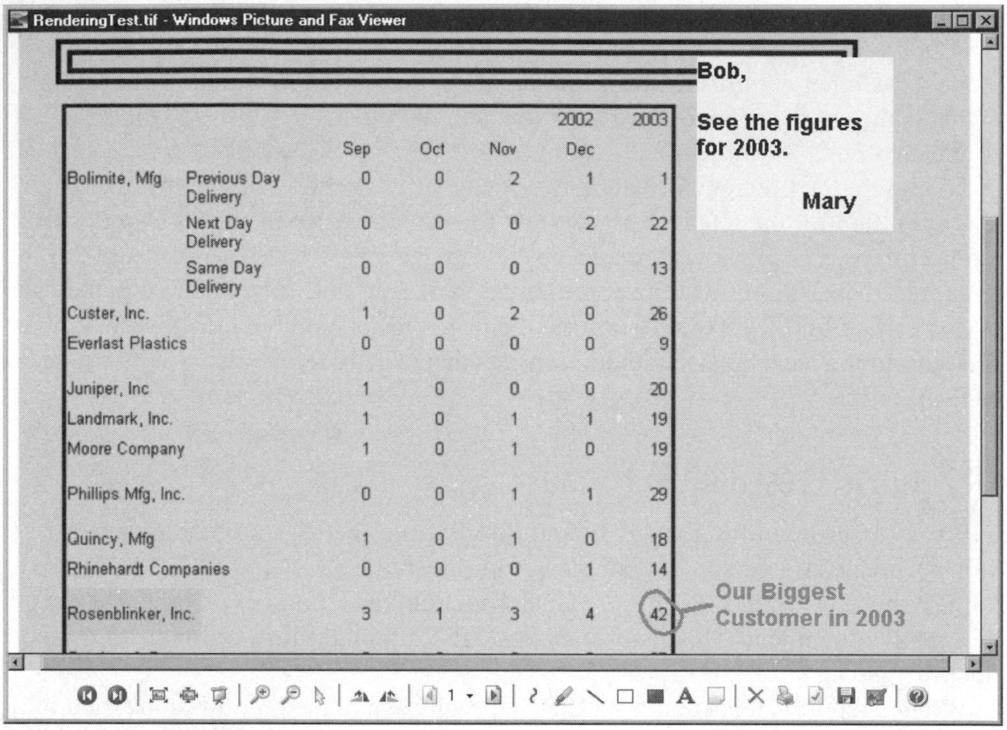

Figure 9-4   *The Windows Picture and Fax Viewer with an annotated report*

Features Supported by the TIFF Format

The top of the first page of the RenderingTest report exported to a TIFF file is shown in Figure 9-5. As you can see, the TIFF image provides a faithful representation of the report as it is seen in the preview layout. It includes colors, images (including background images), and charts. It preserves strings of text, including embedded new lines and multiple spaces in a row. (You soon see this causes a problem in another file format.)

The TIFF format preserves the font for all text rendered in the report. This is true even if a font used in the report is not present on the computer being used to view the report. This is the only presentation format that possesses this characteristic. Also, the TIFF format preserves the exact location of each report item relative to other report items. This is true even if report items overlap one another.

Physical pages are supported by the TIFF format. This means when a report is exported to a TIFF file, the renderer pays attention to the physical page size specified for the report and does not let a page grow beyond that size. When a report page is taller or wider than the physical page size, the TIFF renderer splits it into multiple pages.

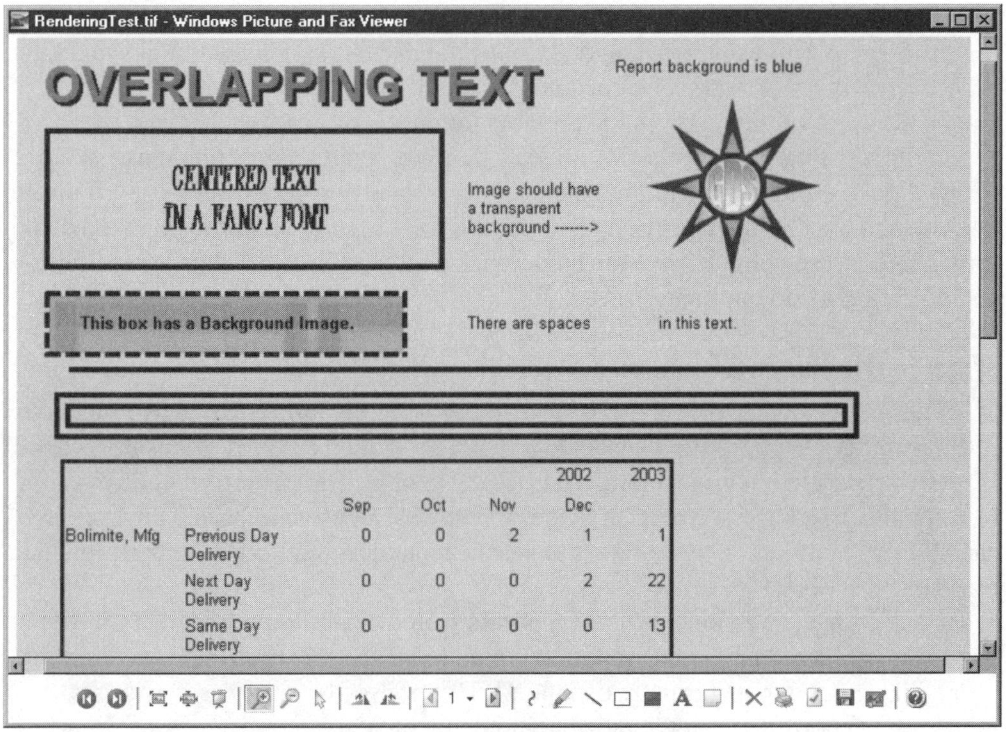

![RenderingTest.tif screenshot in Windows Picture and Fax Viewer showing OVERLAPPING TEXT report]

Figure 9-5 *The RenderingTest report exported to a TIFF file*

Because physical pages are supported, the TIFF format can be printed with the assurance that the printed report is going to match the report on the screen in both layout and pagination.

NOTE

When you're exporting a report to TIFF or any of the other formats that support physical pages, it is important that your report is not wider than the report page. Be sure to include the page margins when you are calculating how wide the body of your report can be.

Features Not Supported by the TIFF Format

The TIFF format does not support any of the interactive features of a report. You cannot use drill-down functionality to expand rows in a table or rows and columns in a matrix. The rows and columns that were expanded when the report was exported are also expanded in the resulting TIFF file. The rows and columns that were hidden when the report was exported are not included in the resulting TIFF file.

In addition, the TIFF format does not support navigation within a report, between reports, or to a web page. Bookmarks, drill-through functionality, and links to a URL do not work in a TIFF file. The document map does not show up in the TIFF file, even if it is part of the report in the preview format.

Finally, as stated earlier, the TIFF file is simply a series of dots that make up an image. Because of this, it is impossible to copy text and numbers from the TIFF image to paste into another document. Therefore, the TIFF format does not work as a method for passing information to someone who wants to cut-and-paste it into a spreadsheet and do their own ad hoc analysis.

When to Use the TIFF Format

TIFF format files work well for smaller reports that do not utilize interactive functions. The capability of some TIFF viewers to provide annotation features makes this a good choice for sharing analysis among a number of people. The TIFF format also works well for situations where reports are viewed both onscreen and in print. However, users cannot copy numbers from the report to paste into another application to perform their own analysis.

Because the entire content of the report is stored as a bitmap image, TIFF files become very large very fast. A report exported to a TIFF file is as much as ten times as large as other export formats. Use the TIFF export with care so as not to create monstrous export files that are unwieldy to deliver and use.

Adobe PDF Presentation Format

PDF is an acronym for Portable Document Format, which was developed by Adobe Systems, Inc. *PDF* was designed so a document could be moved from one computer to another—even between computers with different operating systems—and appear exactly the same on both computers.

When a report is rendered to a PDF file, its formatting is stored using a language similar to the PostScript description language. Images that appear in the report are stored right within the PDF file. Text entries in the report remain text; they are not converted to images as they are with the TIFF format.

Viewing PDF Documents

PDF files are viewed using the Adobe Acrobat Reader. The Acrobat Reader is available as a free download from the Adobe website at www.adobe.com. Versions of the Acrobat Reader are available for Windows, Mac, Solaris Sun, Linux, several flavors of UNIX, and even for handheld devices. The Acrobat Reader has features for moving between pages, printing, and zooming in and out.

Features Supported by the PDF Format

The top of the first page of the RenderingTest report exported to a PDF file is shown in Figure 9-6. (Other versions of Adobe Acrobat Reader may appear slightly different.) As with the TIFF format, the PDF format provides a faithful representation of the report as it is seen in the preview layout. It includes colors, images (including background images), and charts. It also preserves strings of text, including embedded new lines and multiple spaces in a row. PDF also enables report items to overlap.

Just as in the TIFF format, physical pages are supported by the PDF format. When a report page is taller or wider than the physical page size, the PDF renderer splits it into multiple pages. Because physical pages are supported, the PDF format can be printed with the assurance that the printed report will match the report on the screen in both layout and pagination.

The PDF format supports some of the navigation features available in Reporting Services reports. The report's document map entries become PDF bookmarks. In addition, links to URLs are supported. Also, because the PDF format does retain text and numbers as text and numbers, you can copy these items. Therefore, users can copy-and-paste information from the PDF format into a spreadsheet and do their own ad hoc analysis.

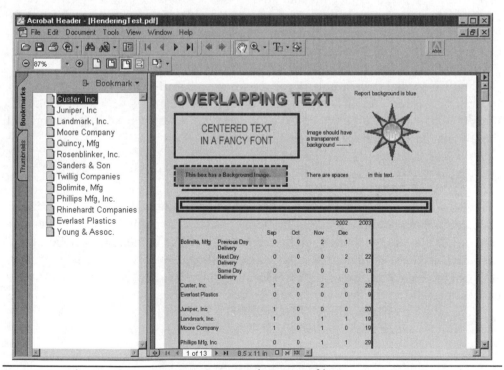

Figure 9-6   *The RenderingTest report exported to a PDF file*

Features Not Supported by the PDF Format

The PDF format preserves the font for almost all text rendered in the report. The exception to this is the situation where a font used in the report is not present on the computer being used to view the report. As you can see in Figure 9-6, the text CENTERED TEXT IN A FANCY FONT did not appear in a fancy font when viewed on a computer that did not have that font loaded.

Although the PDF format supports the document map and a link to a URL, it does not support any of the other interactive features of a report. You cannot use drill-down functionality to expand rows in a table or rows and columns in a matrix. The rows and columns expanded when the report was exported are expanded in the resulting PDF file. The rows and columns hidden when the report was exported are not included in the resulting PDF file. The PDF format does not support Reporting Services bookmarks (not to be confused with the PDF bookmarks that act as a document map) and drill-through functionality.

When to Use the PDF Format

The PDF format works well for reports that need to be distributed across a variety of platforms where maintaining the report layout and pagination are required. If an investment is made in Adobe Standard or Adobe Professional, the PDF format can be used when annotation features are required. The PDF format works well for both large and small reports, and in situations where reports are viewed both on the screen and in print. The PDF format does enable users to copy numbers from a report and paste them into another application to do ad hoc analysis.

The PDF format does not work for reports where drill-down or drill-through functionality is required. It is also not appropriate for situations where one or more fonts that may not be available on the end user's computer are used in the report and these fonts must be preserved in the report output.

Web Archive Presentation Format

The web archive is a special form of web page. In addition to the HTML formatting code, the web archive file contains all the supporting files required by the page. The supporting files are the images referenced by the HTML. As the name implies, the *web archive* can be used to gather all the necessary parts of a web page in one place, so it can be easily moved to a different location and archived. This also makes it an excellent candidate for distributing reports in an HTML format.

The extension on web archive files is .mhtml.

Viewing Web Archive Documents

Because web archive documents are self-contained web pages, they are viewed using a web browser. Having a web browser available on a computer is usually not an issue these days, so web archive documents can be distributed across multiple computer platforms. Web archive documents can also be displayed in many e-mail programs that support HTML e-mail messages.

Features Supported by the Web Archive Format

The top of the first page of the RenderingTest report exported to a web archive file is shown in Figure 9-7. The web archive format provides a somewhat faithful representation of the report as it is seen in the preview layout. It includes colors, images (including background images), and charts.

The web archive format retains only one of the navigation features in Reporting Services reports. It allows for links to URLs to be embedded in the report. Also, because the web archive format retains text and numbers as text and numbers, you can copy these items. Therefore, users can copy-and-paste information from the web format into a spreadsheet and do their own ad hoc analysis.

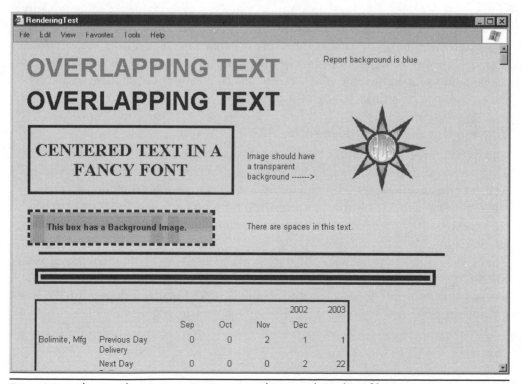

Figure 9-7   *The RenderingTest report exported to a web archive file*

Features Not Supported by the Web Archive Format

In the web archive format, physical pages are not supported. Instead, the report is presented as one continuous web page. Horizontal lines are added to the report to indicate where the page breaks would occur in other formats. Because of this, the web archive format does not work well when printing a report.

You can see in Figure 9-7, the web archive format does not preserve strings of text, including embedded new lines and multiple spaces in a row. (The text "CENTERED TEXT IN A FANCY FONT" should have a new line after the word "TEXT." The sentence "There are spaces in this text," located below the GDS graphic, should have a gap between the word "spaces" and the word "in".) This is a characteristic of HTML rendering that compresses white space (such as multiple spaces) and ignores new lines. Another HTML limitation is the inability to support overlapping report items as shown by the top line of the report.

Like the PDF format, the web archive format preserves the font for almost all text rendered in the report. The exception, again, is the situation where a font used in the report is not present on the computer being used to view the report. In Figure 9-7, the text "CENTERED TEXT IN A FANCY FONT" is no longer in a fancy font.

Although the web archive format supports a link to a URL, it does not support any of the other interactive features of a report. You cannot use drill-down functionality to expand rows in a table or rows and columns in a matrix. The rows and columns expanded when the report was exported are expanded in the resulting web archive file. The rows and columns hidden when the report was exported are not included in the resulting web archive file. The web archive format does not support document maps, bookmarks, or drill-through functionality.

When to Use the Web Archive Format

The web archive format works well for reports that need to be distributed across a variety of platforms, where pagination and printing are not required. It also works well for situations where the content of the report is to be embedded in an e-mail message. The web archive format works well for both large and small reports. The web archive format does let users copy numbers from a report and paste them into another application for ad hoc analysis.

The web archive format does not work well in situations where the report's exact formatting must be preserved. Its limitations also make it a bad choice in situations where pagination and printing capabilities are needed. Finally, it does not work when drill-down, drill-through, or other navigation features are required.

Excel Presentation Format

Excel, of course, is Microsoft's spreadsheet application. The Excel presentation format is simply an Excel workbook file. The workbooks created from Reporting Services reports have multiple tabs or spreadsheets to represent the document map and the logical pages in the report.

Viewing Excel Documents

Excel documents are, of course, viewed using Microsoft Excel. The initial version of SQL Server 2000 Reporting Services required Excel 2002 (version 10) or Excel 2003 (version 11) to display reports exported in the Excel format. SQL Server 2000 Reporting Services SP2 and SQL Server 2005 Reporting Services, however, work with earlier versions of Excel.

Features Supported by the Excel Format

The document map portion of the RenderingTest report as it appears in the Excel file is shown in Figure 9-8. The top of the first page of the RenderingTest report as

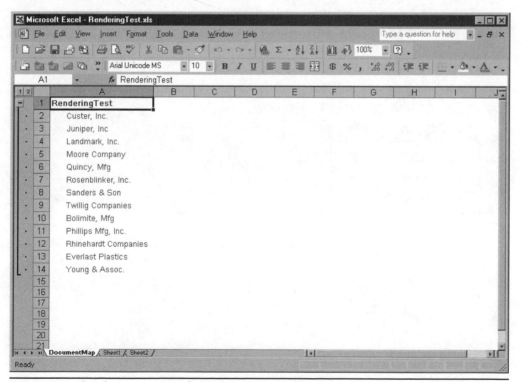

Figure 9-8   *The document map from the RenderingTest report exported to an Excel file*

it appears in the Excel file is shown in Figure 9-9. The Excel format provides as faithful a representation of the report as it can within the confines of spreadsheet rows and columns. It includes colors, foreground images, and charts. Note, if your report contains any charts, they are exported as images by the Excel export. They are not exported as chart objects, so they cannot be modified in Excel.

The Excel format does not create page breaks based on the page size of the report. It does split the report up into separate tabs at locations where your report logic says there should be page breaks. For example, if a grouping on your report has the PageBreakAtStart property set to True, each new instance of this grouping would begin on a new tab in Excel.

The Excel format does include several of the navigation features in Reporting Services reports. It supports the document map as well as bookmarks. It also allows for links to URLs to be embedded in the report. The Excel format does preserve strings of text, including embedded new lines and multiple spaces in a row.

The Excel format is a series of spreadsheets, so naturally it allows for ad hoc analysis to be done on its contents. The contents of most cells are represented as text or numeric constants. However, in some cases, the cell may contain a formula.

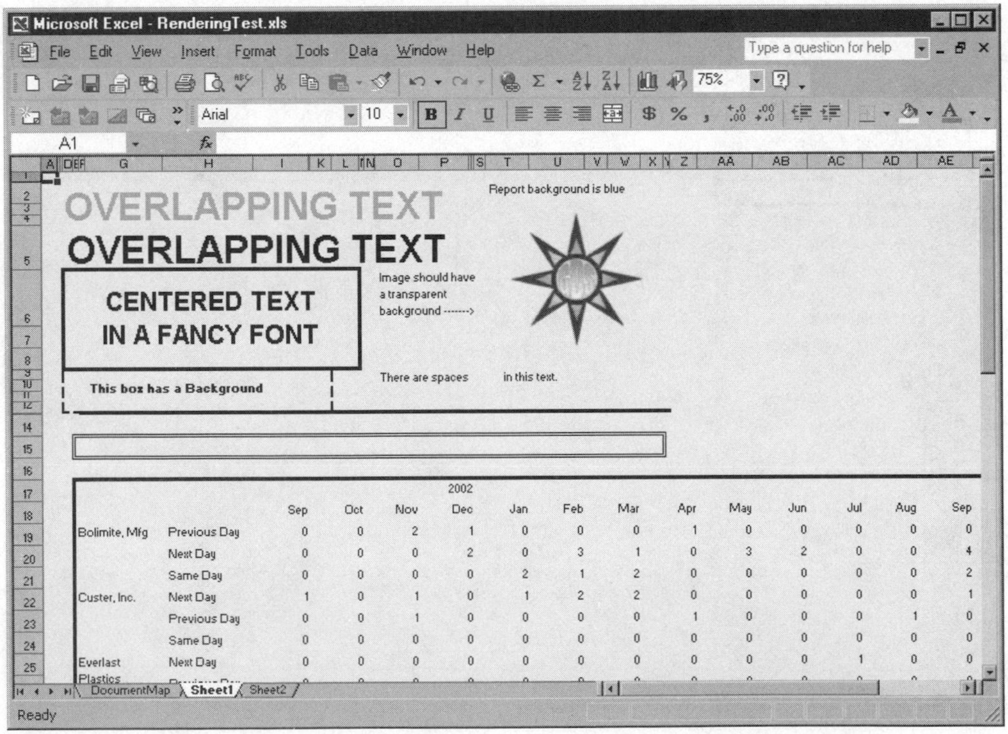

Figure 9-9 *The RenderingTest report exported to an Excel file*

This results if the value of one report item is a calculation utilizing the value of another report item.

Features Not Supported by the Excel Format

In the Excel format, physical pages are not supported. Only logical page breaks are supported, as mentioned previously. Because of this, the Excel format does not work well when printing a report. As with several of the previous formats, the Excel format preserves the font, except when a font used in the report is not present on the computer being used to view the report. Even though the Excel format supports foreground images, it does not support background images.

Although the Excel format supports several navigation features, it does not support drill-down functionality. The rows and columns in a table or matrix are completely expanded in the Excel format, so all the rows and columns are included. The Excel format does not support drill-through functionality.

When to Use the Excel Format

The Excel format works well for situations when the end user wants to perform some ad hoc analysis after they receive the report. The Excel format should only be used for small and medium-size reports. It should not be used for large reports because the resulting files can become very large. The Excel format does not work well in situations where the report's exact formatting must be preserved. Also, the Excel format is inappropriate in situations where pagination and printing are required. Finally, it does not work when drill-down or drill-through functionality is needed.

Printed Presentation Format

At first, it may not seem like printing the report on paper belongs in the same category as the other presentation formats. But, if you think about it, rendering the report to hard copy and delivering that printed paper to your users is a valid way to deliver a report. In fact, it was the first way and, for many years, the only way to deliver a report. It seems only fitting, if for no other reason than to give a nod to history, that we include this format along with all the others.

Viewing Printed Documents

Printed documents are viewed on paper. Enough said.

Features Supported by the Printed Format

The printed format faithfully captures all the report formatting, along with both physical and logical page breaks.

Features Not Supported by the Printed Format

The only navigation supported by the printed format requires a thumb and forefinger.

When to Use the Printed Format

The printed format should only be used when your end user requires information to be on paper and is not interested in any of the navigation features or ad hoc analysis made available by the other formats.

HTML Presentation Format

HTML is not listed in the export drop-down list in the Report Designer. It is a choice when you are exporting a report from the Report Manager. It is, in fact, the native mode for report viewing in the Report Manager. (We begin looking at reports in the Report Manager in Chapter 10.)

The HTML format is similar to the web archive format in the way it handles most formatting. This is not too surprising because both use HTML as their document formatting language. Whereas all the other formats are meant to provide a standalone representation of the report, the HTML format uses the report viewer and the Reporting Services web service to present a connected representation of the report. This connection to Reporting Services allows the HTML format to implement all the navigational features.

Viewing HTML Documents

The HTML format is, of course, viewed using a browser. To use features such as document maps, drill-down, and bookmarks, you must have Microsoft Internet Explorer 6.0 with Service Pack 1 or Microsoft Internet Explorer 5.5 with Service Pack 2. In either case, scripting must be enabled in the browser. Drill-through functionality requires Microsoft Internet Explorer 5.01 or above with Service Pack 2 and does not require scripting.

Features Supported by the HTML Format

The HTML format supports almost all the formatting and navigational features of Reporting Services reports. It supports logical page breaks and physical page breaks, after a fashion. The first page of the RenderingTest report in HTML format is shown in Figure 9-10.

The HTML format does not pay attention to page width. A page can be as wide as it wants. However, the HTML format does create page breaks when a page gets too long. These page breaks do not correspond exactly with the physical size of

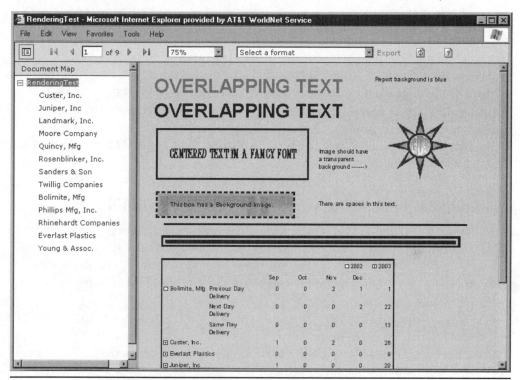

Figure 9-10   *The RenderingTest report exported to an HTML file*

the page but, rather, are only an approximation. If you print the HTML document, the page breaks created by the HTML format do not correspond to the page breaks required by the printer.

Features Not Supported by the HTML Format

The HTML format does not support overlapping report items. It has the same short-coming with embedded white space and new lines as described in the web archive section. Given these exceptions and the quirks with pagination described previously, the HTML format supports all other Reporting Services report features.

When to Use the HTML Format

The HTML format works well when your user can view the report while connected to the report server. HTML is the essential format for the occasions when all the navigation features of Reporting Services are required from a single format.

The HTML format does not work well when the report needs to be printed.

Data Exchange Formats

The two remaining export or rendering formats provided by Reporting Services are data exchange formats. They are intended to take the data in a report and put it into a format that can be used by another computer program. In this section, we look at the basic structure of each of these formats. We also discuss the customization that can be done with each format.

We continue to use the RenderingTest report from the Chapter09 report project to examine the data output by each format.

Comma-Separated Values (CSV) Data Exchange Format

The Comma-Separated Values (CSV) format has been around for a number of years. The CSV format is used to represent tabular data. Each line in the file represents one row in the table. Each value between two commas represents a column in the table. If a column value contains a comma (for example, "Bolimite, Mfg"), the value is enclosed in quotation marks.

CSV exports include the data contained within tables, matrixes, and lists in your report. All the data from the table, matrix, or list is included in the CSV export, even if a column or a row is hidden. CSV exports do not contain values from charts or text boxes that are not within a table, matrix, or list.

Reports to be exported using the CSV format should be kept simple. Only one table, matrix, or list should be placed on the report. When reports with more than one table, matrix, or list are exported using the CSV format, the resulting file can be complex and confusing.

If you open the CSV file that results from the RenderingTest report in Notepad, it appears as follows. (A CSV file opens in Excel by default.) This represents the values from the matrix near the top of the report.

```
"Bolimite, Mfg",Previous Day Delivery,0,0,2,1,…
"Bolimite, Mfg",Next Day Delivery,0,0,0,2,…
"Bolimite, Mfg",Same Day Delivery,0,0,0,0,…
"Custer, Inc.",Next Day Delivery,1,0,1,0,…
"Custer, Inc.",Previous Day Delivery,0,0,1,0,…
"Custer, Inc.",Same Day Delivery,0,0,0,0,…
```

XML Data Exchange Format

In Chapter 7, we discussed XML and the fact that reports are stored in an XML format called Report Definition Language (RDL). Here, we are looking at XML as a means of exchanging data between programs. In both cases, the XML files are simply text files with information organized between XML tags.

By default, XML exports include the data contained within tables, matrixes, lists, and charts in your report. All the data from the table, matrix, list, or chart is included in the XML export, even if a column or a row is hidden. XML exports do not contain values from text boxes that are not with a table, matrix, or list.

Because each item in the XML export is labeled with an XML tag, reports to be exported using the XML format can be more complex than those exported using the CSV format. Because of this, reports to be exported using the XML format may have more than one table, matrix, list, or chart.

The following is a section of the XML file that results from the RenderingTest report:

```
<Report xmlns="RenderingTest" …>
<matrix1>
  <matrix1_CustomerName_Collection>
    <matrix1_CustomerName CustomerName="Bolimite, Mfg">
      <matrix1_RowGroup2_Collection>
        <matrix1_RowGroup2 textbox6="Previous Day Delivery">
              <matrix1_Year_Collection>
          <matrix1_Year Year="2002">
                    <matrix1_ColumnGroup2_Collection>
                      <matrix1_ColumnGroup2 textbox5="Sep">
            <Cell DeliveryNumber="0" />
          </matrix1_ColumnGroup2>
                      <matrix1_ColumnGroup2 textbox5="Oct">
            <Cell DeliveryNumber="0" />
          </matrix1_ColumnGroup2>
```

You can quickly see how the XML structure follows the report layout. The Report tag provides information about the report as a whole. After that tag is a series of tags containing the data in the matrix near the top of the report. Again, note, by default, the text boxes at the top of the report are not included in the XML export.

Customizing the XML Data Exchange Format

You can customize the XML export to fit your needs. Let's change the XML export to include the contents of the text box that reads CENTERED TEXT IN A FANCY FONT. We can also change the matrix1_RowGroup2_Collection tag to DeliveryTypes and the matrix1_RowGroup2 tag to DeliveryType. Finally, we remove the DeliveryNumber altogether.

If you have downloaded the Chapter09 project, open the project and try this procedure:

1.   Open the RenderingTest report.

2.   Select the Layout tab.

3.   Right-click the text box containing CENTERED TEXT IN A FANCY FONT. Select Properties from the Context menu. The Textbox Properties dialog box appears.

4.   Select the Font tab.

5.   Look in the Family drop-down list for Juice ITC. If it is not there, select a font present in the list. (You are unable to save the changes made in this dialog box unless a valid font is selected.)

6.   Select the Data Output tab.

7.   Type **FancyFont** for Element Name. (This specifies the name to use for this element.)

8.   Select Yes for Output. (This forces this item to be output in the XML.)

9.   Select Element for Render As. (This causes the item to be output as an element rather than as an attribute.)

10.   Click OK to exit the Textbox Properties dialog box.

11.   Select matrix1 from the drop-down list at the top of the Properties window.

12.   Click the Property Pages button in the Properties window to display the Matrix Properties dialog box.

13.   Select the Groups tab.

14.   Select matrix1_RowGroup2 and click Edit next to the Rows area. The Grouping and Sorting Properties dialog box appears.

15.   Select the Data Output tab.

16.   Enter **DeliveryType** for Element name.

17.   Enter **DeliveryTypes** for Collection.

18.   Click OK to exit the Grouping and Sorting Properties dialog box.

19.   Click OK to exit the Matrix Properties dialog box.

20.   Right-click the text box in the lower-right corner of the matrix. Select Properties from the Context menu. The Textbox Properties dialog box appears.

21. Select the Data Output tab.

22. Select No for Output. (This causes this item not to be output in the XML.)

23. Click OK to exit the Textbox Properties dialog box.

24. Click the Preview tab.

25. Select XML File with Report Data from the Export drop-down list.

26. Select a location to store this export, enter a filename, and then click Save.

27. Use the Windows Explorer to find the file you just created, and then double-click the file to open it.

28. The first few lines of the XML file appear similar to the following:

```
<Report xmlns="RenderingTest"... >
  <FancyFont>CENTERED TEXT IN A FANCY FONT</FancyFont>
  <matrix1>
    <matrix1_CustomerName_Collection>
      <matrix1_CustomerName CustomerName="Bolimite, Mfg">
        <DeliveryTypes>
          <DeliveryType textbox6="Previous Day Delivery">
        <matrix1_Year_Collection>
          <matrix1_Year Year="2002">
            <matrix1_ColumnGroup2_Collection>
              <matrix1_ColumnGroup2 textbox5="Sep">
                <Cell />
              </matrix1_ColumnGroup2>
              <matrix1_ColumnGroup2 textbox5="Oct">
                <Cell />
              </matrix1_ColumnGroup2>
```

The values on the Data Output tab for each item in your report can be used in this way to completely customize the XML output generated by the report.

Call the Manager

Now, it is time to move on to the Report Manager. In the next chapters in this book, we look at ways to put your reports into the Report Manager and ways to administer those reports once they are there.

PART
III

Report Serving

CHAPTER
10

How Did We Ever Manage Without You? The Report Manager

IN THIS CHAPTER:

Folders

Moving Reports and Supporting Files to the Report Server

Managing Items in Folders

Seek and Ye Shall Find: Search and Find Functions

Printing from Report Manager

Managing Reports on the Report Server

Linked Reports

Delivering the Goods

I n Part II of this book, we focused on report authoring. You learned fancy techniques for creating whiz-bang reports. However, the fact is, even the whiz-bangiest of reports are not much good if you cannot easily share them with end users.

In this chapter, you learn how to do just that. We move from authoring to managing reports and delivering them to the end users. This is done through the Report Server and its Report Manager web interface.

We took a brief look at the Report Server and the Report Manager in Chapter 1. Now, we take a more detailed look. Much of our examination focuses on the Report Manager, and how it is used to access and control the Report Server.

The first step is moving your report definitions and supporting files from the development environment to the Report Catalog. Recall that the Report Catalog is the SQL Server 2005 database where the Report Server keeps all its information. This information includes the definitions of the reports it is managing. We look at several ways to accomplish this report deployment.

Once your reports are available through the Report Server, you need to control how they are executed. We use the Report Server's security features to control who can access each report, and we use the caching and report history to control how a report is executed each time it is requested by a user. Finally, we control all these Report Server features using the Report Manager.

In short, in this chapter, we take your reports from a single-user development environment to a secure, managed environment where they can be executed by a number of users.

Folders

Before you deploy reports to the Report Server, you need to have an understanding of the way the Report Server organizes reports in the Report Catalog. In the Report Catalog, reports are arranged into a system of folders similar to the Windows or Mac file system. Folders can contain reports, supporting files such as external images and shared data sources, and even other folders. The easiest way to create, view, and maintain these folders is through the Report Manager.

Although the Report Catalog folders look and act like Windows file system folders, they are not actual file system folders. You cannot find them anywhere in the file system on the computer running the Report Server. *Report Catalog folders* are screen representations of records in the Report Catalog database.

Each folder is assigned a name. Folder names can include just about any character, including spaces. However, folder names cannot include any of the following characters:

```
; ? : @ & , \ * < > | " /
```

In addition to a name, folders can also be assigned a description. The description can contain a long explanation of the contents of the folder. The description can help users determine what type of reports are in a folder without having to open that folder and look at the contents. Both the folder name and the description can be searched by a user to help them find a report.

The Report Manager

The Report Manager web application provides a straightforward method for creating and navigating folders in the Report Catalog. When you initially install Reporting Services, the Home folder is created by default. This is the only folder that exists at first.

Use the following URL to access the Report Manager site on the computer running Reporting Services:

```
http://ComputerName/reports
```

In this case, ComputerName is the name of the computer where Reporting Services was installed. If you are using a secure connection to access the Report Manager site, replace http: with https:. If you are on the same computer where Reporting Services is running, you can use the following URL:

```
http://localhost/reports
```

No matter how you get there, when you initially access the Report Manager, it appears similar to Figure 10-1.

Notice the URL shown in Figure 10-1 is a bit different from the URLs given previously. This is because the Report Manager web application redirects you to the Pages/Folder.aspx web page. The Folder.aspx page is used to display folder contents.

NOTE

Figure 10-1 shows the Report Manager as it appears for a user with content manager privileges. If you do not see the New Folder, New Data Source, Upload File, and Report Builder buttons in the toolbar on the Contents tab, you do not have content manager privileges and will be unable to complete the exercises in this section of the chapter. If possible, log out and log in with a Windows login that has local administration privileges on the computer running the Report Server.

To use the Report Manager, you must be using Microsoft Internet Explorer 6.0 with Service Pack 1 (SP1) or Internet Explorer 5.5 with Service Pack 2 (SP2). In either case, you must have scripting enabled.

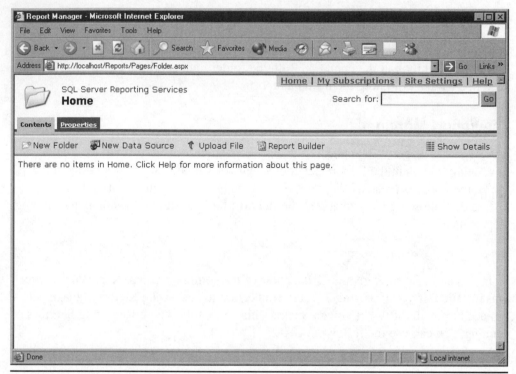

Figure 10-1   *The Report Manager with no folders defined*

Adding a New Folder Using the Report Manager

Let's create a new folder into which we will deploy some of the Galactic Delivery Services reports from the previous chapters. Here are the steps to follow:

> **NOTE**
>
> *Examples showing report deployment throughout this chapter assume the Galactic Delivery Services folder is created in the Home folder. If you already have other folders created in your Report Catalog, be sure you are in the Home folder when you complete the following steps.*

1. Click the New Folder button in the toolbar on the Contents tab. The New Folder page appears, as shown in Figure 10-2.

2. Type **Galactic Delivery Services** for Name and **Reports created while learning to use Reporting Services** for Description.

3. Click OK to create the new folder and return to the Home folder.

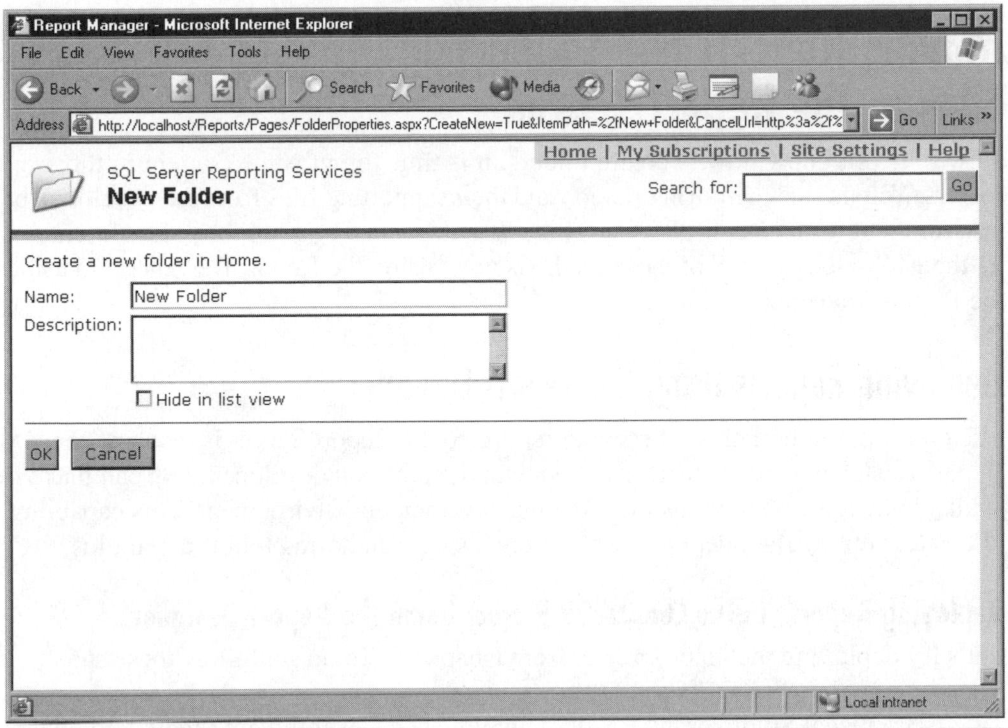

Figure 10-2 *The New Folder page*

You see an entry for your new folder with its name and description on the Contents tab of the Home folder. The text !NEW next to the folder name remains there for 48 hours. This helps to notify users of new content added to your Report Server.

If you were observant, you noticed one item on the New Folder page we did not use. (If you missed it, look at Figure 10-2.) This is the Hide in List View check box. When the Hide in List View check box is checked, the new folder does not appear on the Contents tab. This is useful when you want to make the reports in a folder available through a custom interface, but unavailable through the Report Manager. We discuss this in detail in Chapter 12.

To view the contents of the new folder, click the folder name. The name of the current folder appears in bold text near the top of the page. Immediately above the name of the current folder is the path from the Home folder to the current folder. Because the Galactic Delivery Services folder is in the Home folder, the path only contains Home >. You can return to any folder in the current path by clicking that folder name in the path shown near the top of the page. You can return to the Home folder by clicking Home at the beginning of the current path or by clicking Home in the upper-right corner of the page.

Moving Reports and Supporting Files to the Report Server

Now that you know how to create folders, it is time to put some content in those folders. You do this by moving reports and their supporting files from the development environment to the Report Server. This can be done using a number of different methods. We look at two of those methods now: using the Report Designer and using the Report Manager.

Deploying Reports Using the Report Designer

The most common method of moving reports to the Report Server is by using the Report Designer. Once you are satisfied with a report you developed, you can make it available to your users without leaving the development environment. This capability to create, preview, and deploy a report from a single authoring tool is a real plus.

Deploying Reports in the Chapter09 Project Using the Report Designer

Let's try deploying the report project from Chapter 9. To do so, follow these steps:

1. Start Visual Studio or the Business Intelligence Development Studio and open the Chapter09 project.
2. Select Project | Chapter09 Properties from the Main menu. The Chapter09 Property Pages dialog box appears.
3. Type **Galactic Delivery Services/Chapter 09** for TargetReportFolder. This is the folder into which the report is going to be deployed.
4. Type **http://ComputerName/ReportServer** for TargetServerURL, where ComputerName is the name of the computer where the Report Server is installed. You should replace http: with https: if you are using a secure connection. You can use localhost in place of the computer name if the Report Server is installed on the same computer you are using to run Visual Studio (see Figure 10-3).
5. Click OK to exit the Chapter09 Property Pages dialog box.
6. Right-click the Chapter09 project entry in the Solution Explorer and select Deploy from the Context menu.
7. The Report Designer builds all the reports in the project, and then deploys all the reports, along with their supporting files, to the Report Server. (During the build process, the Report Designer checks each report for any errors that would prevent it from executing properly on the Report Server.) The results of the build and deploy are shown in the Output window.

Chapter09 Property Pages   ? X

Configuration: Active(Debug) ▼   Platform: N/A ▼   Configuration Manager...

⊟ Configuration Properties   ⊟ **Debug**
  └ General   StartItem   **RenderingTest.rdl**
                                     ⊟ **Deployment**
                                       OverwriteDataSources   False
                                       TargetDataSourceFolder
                                       TargetReportFolder   **Galactic Delivery Services/Chapter 09**
                                       TargetServerURL   **http://localhost/ReportServer**

                                     Deployment

                                                   OK   Cancel   Apply

Figure 10-3   *The Chapter09 Property Pages dialog box*

8. Open the Report Manager in your browser. Click the Galactic Delivery Services folder to view its content. You see that Visual Studio created a new folder in the Galactic Delivery Services folder called Chapter 09.

9. Click the Chapter 09 folder to view its content. All the items in the Chapter09 project—three reports and a shared data source—were deployed.

10. Click the RenderingTest report. You see the HTML version of the RenderingTest report.

NOTE

You can also deploy the contents of a project by selecting Build | Deploy Solution or Build | Deploy {Project Name} from the Main menu.

Working Through the Web Service

When the Report Designer deploys reports, it works through the Reporting Services web service. The Report Manager web application provides a human interface to Reporting Services. The web service provides an interface for other programs to communicate with Reporting Services. Because the Report Designer falls into the latter of these two categories, it uses the web service to deploy reports.

The web service has a different URL than the Report Manager. You must enter the URL for the web service and not the Report Manager in the Properties Pages dialog box for the deployment to work properly. The default URL for the web service is shown in Step 4 in the previous section.

Creating Folders While Deploying

In Steps 2 through 5, you entered information into properties of the Chapter09 project. These values tell the Report Designer where to put the reports and supporting items when the project is deployed. In this case, you instructed the Report Designer to put our reports and shared data source in the Chapter 09 folder within the Galactic Delivery Services folder.

You created the Galactic Delivery Services folder in the previous section. You did not create the Chapter 09 folder. Instead, the Report Designer created that folder for us as it deployed the items in the project. In fact, the Report Designer creates folders for any path you specify.

Deploying a Single Report

In Step 6, you used the project's Context menu to deploy all the items in the project. Alternatively, you could have right-clicked a report and selected Deploy from the report's Context menu. However, this would have deployed only this report, not the entire project.

On some occasions, you might want to deploy a single report rather than the entire project. At times, one report is going to be completed and ready for deployment, while the other reports in the project are still under construction. At other times, one report will be revised after the entire project has already been deployed. In these situations, it is only necessary to redeploy the single revised report.

Deploying Shared Data Sources

Even when a single report is deployed, any shared data sources used by that report are automatically deployed along with it. This only makes sense. A report that requires shared data sources does not do much if those shared data sources are not present.

If you look back at Figure 10-3, you notice an OverwriteDataSources item in the dialog box. This controls whether a shared data source that has been deployed to the Report Server is overwritten by subsequent deployments. In most cases, shared data sources do not change, so they do not need to be overwritten. For this reason, OverwriteDataSources is set to False, meaning do not overwrite existing data sources.

Aside from saving unnecessary effort, not overwriting data sources also helps out in another way. Consider the environment shown in Figure 10-4. In this environment,

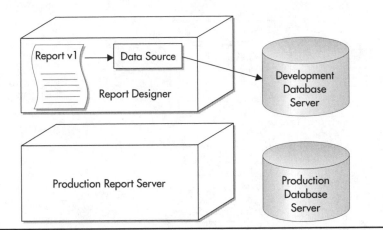

Figure 10-4   *A report and a shared data source ready to deploy*

reports are developed in Visual Studio using a shared data source that points to a development database server. Once the first version of the report is completed, it is deployed to a production Report Server, as shown in Figure 10-5. As soon as the deployment is complete, the shared data source on the production Report Server needs to be changed to point to the production database server. This is shown in Figure 10-6.

Now, as time has passed, a new version of the report (version 2) is created in the development environment. This time, when version 2 of the report is deployed to the production Report Server, the shared data source already exists there.

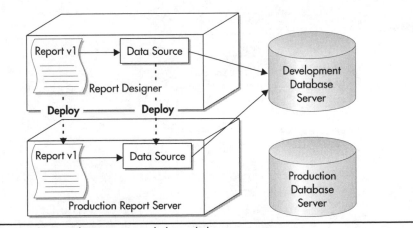

Figure 10-5   *Deploying the report and shared data source*

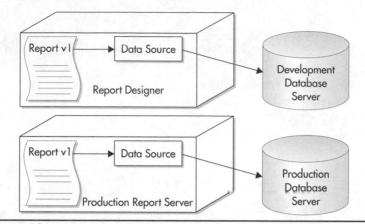

Figure 10-6   *Modifying the shared data source to point to the production database server*

If OverwriteDataSources is set to True, the data source from the development environment would overwrite the data source in the production environment, and we would be back to the situation in Figure 10-5. With this setting, we would have to redirect the shared data source each time a report is deployed.

To avoid this, OverwriteDataSources is set to False. Now when version 2 of the report (and subsequent versions) is deployed to the production Report Server, the shared data source is not overwritten. It remains pointing to the production database server. This is shown in Figure 10-7. We have saved a bit of extra effort with each deployment.

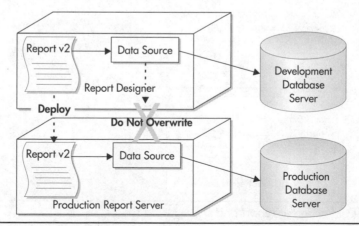

Figure 10-7   *A subsequent deployment with OverwriteDataSources set to False*

As you will see throughout this chapter, folders are used to organize reports on the Report Server and help manage security for those reports. You can, if you are managing your Report Server properly, have reports deployed in a number of different folders. A number of these reports use the same database as the source for their data. Rather than having a number of shared data sources scattered throughout the folders on your Report Server, it makes more sense to have the reports all reference a single data source or set of data sources stored in one central folder. This is accomplished through the use of the TargetDataSourceFolder.

Just as the TargetReportFolder property enables you to specify a path to a Report Server folder where a report is to be deployed, the TargetDataSourceFolder property, on the Property Pages dialog box, lets you specify a path to a Report Server folder where the shared data source should be deployed or found, if it already exists there. If no folder path is specified, the TargetDataSourceFolder defaults to the TargetReportFolder. The OverwriteDataSources flag applies whether the shared data source is being deployed to the TargetReportFolder or the TargetDataSourceFolder.

Additional Properties in the Property Pages Dialog Box

If you look back at Figure 10-3, you can see a couple additional items in the Property Pages dialog box that we have not discussed. We look at those two items now.

Maintaining Multiple Configurations   At the top of the dialog box is the Configuration drop-down list. This drop-down list enables you to maintain several different deployment configurations for the same project. Each configuration has its own values for TargetDataSourceFolder, TargetReportFolder, TargetServerURL, and the other settings in the dialog box.

This is useful if you need to deploy the reports in a project to more than one Report Server. Perhaps you have the Report Server loaded on your own PC for your own testing, a development Report Server where the report undergoes quality assurance testing, and a production Report Server where the report is to be made available to the end users. You can enter the properties for deploying to the Report Server on your PC in the DebugLocal configuration, the properties for deploying to the development Report Server in the Debug configuration, and the properties for deploying to the production Report Server in the Production configuration.

You can then easily switch between deploying to each of these Report Servers as new versions of your reports go from your own testing to quality assurance testing and are then made available to the users. You can change the configuration you are using for deployment through the Solution Configuration drop-down list in the Report Designer toolbar, as shown in Figure 10-8.

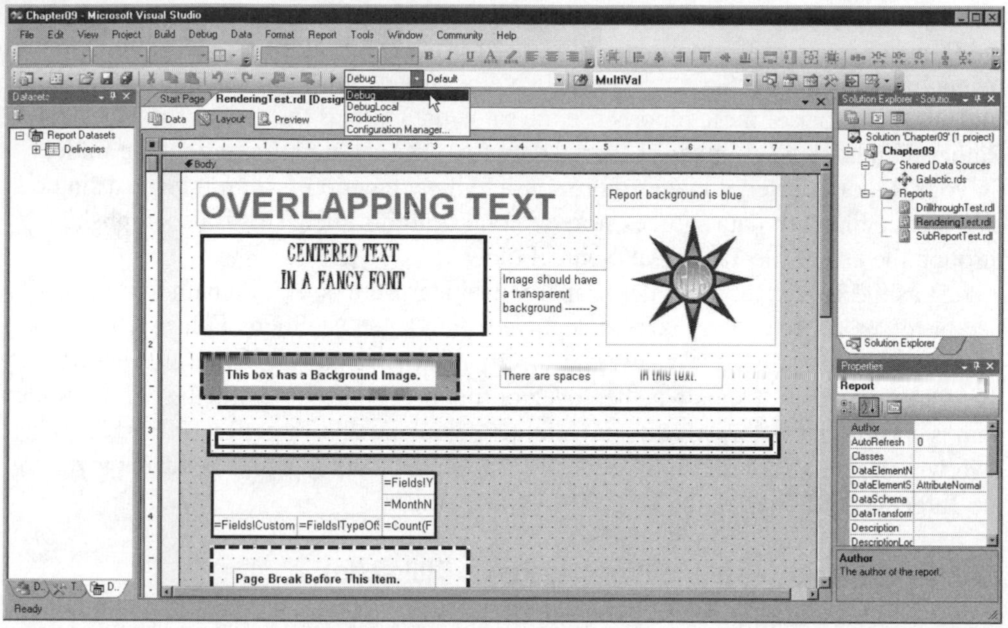

Figure 10-8 *The Solution Configuration drop-down list*

NOTE

Active(Debug) in the Configuration drop-down list simply refers to the Debug configuration that is currently the selected or active configuration.

Running a Report Project The final item we want to look at in the Project Property Pages dialog box is StartItem, which is used when running your report project. Use the StartItem drop-down list to select which report from your project should be executed when you run the project. The report selected as the start item is displayed in a browser window in HTML format.

When you run a report project, you deploy all the reports, shared data sources, and other supporting information in the project to the target server and target folders in your active configuration. Once the deployment is complete, the report specified as the start item is executed in a browser window. You can then debug this report, making sure it looks correct and functions properly in HTML format. You can run the project by clicking the Start button on the toolbar (to the left of the Solution Configuration drop-down list) or by selecting any of the following items from the Debug menu (or by pressing any of the shortcut keys that correspond to these menu items):

▶ Start Debugging

▶ Start Without Debugging

▶ Step Into

▶ Step Over

There is no such thing as stepping into or over a report. These menu items simply run the project. The report selected as the start item is executed in a browser window from start to finish.

Uploading Reports Using Report Manager

Another common method of moving a report to the Report Server is by using the Report Manager. This is known as *uploading* the report. Deploying reports from the Report Designer can be thought of as pushing the reports from the development environment to the Report Server, whereas uploading reports from the Report Manager can be thought of as pulling the reports from the development environment to the Report Server.

You may need to use the Report Manager upload in situations where your report authors do not have rights to deploy reports on the Report Server. The report authors create their reports and test them within the Report Designer. When a report is completed, the report author can place the RDL file for the report in a shared directory or send it as an e-mail attachment to the Report Server administrator. The Report Server administrator can upload the RDL file to a quality assurance Report Server and test the report for clarity, accuracy, and proper use of database resources. Once the report has passed this review, the Report Server administrator can upload the report to the production Report Server.

Uploading Reports in the Chapter06 Project Using the Report Manager

Let's try uploading some of the reports from the Chapter06 report project:

1. Open the Report Manager in your browser. Click the Galactic Delivery Services folder to view its content.
2. Create a new folder called **Chapter 06**.
3. Select the new folder to view its contents.
4. Click the Upload File button in the toolbar on the Contents tab. The Upload File page appears, as shown in Figure 10-9.

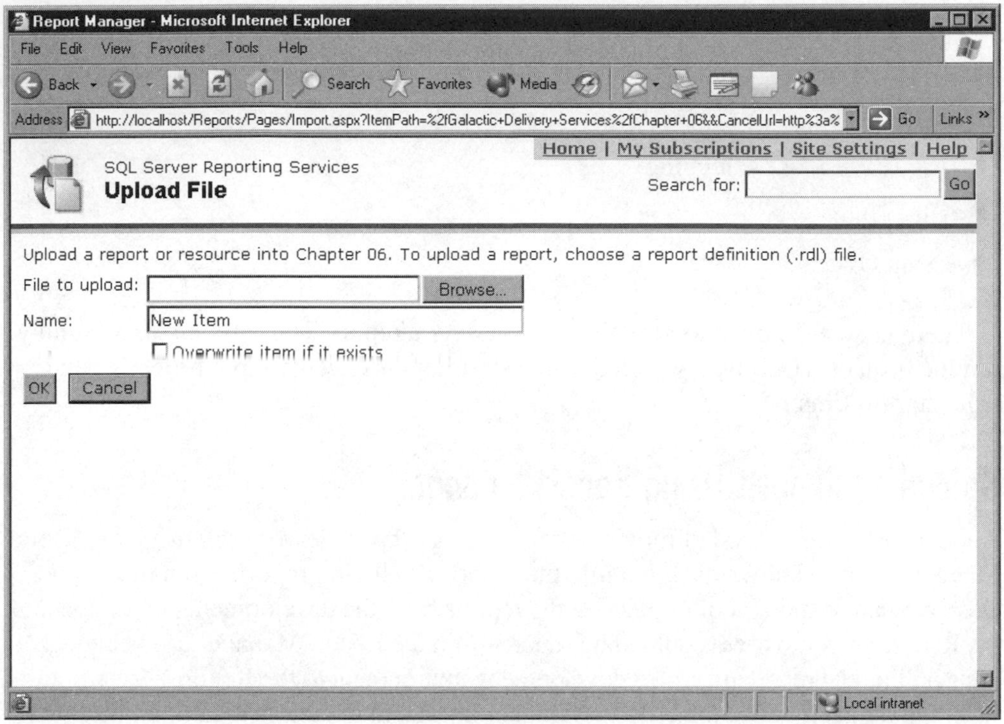

Figure 10-9 *The Upload File page*

5. Click Browse. The Choose file dialog box appears.

6. Navigate to the folder where you created your solution for Chapter 6. If this folder is in the default location, you can find it under the following path:

```
My Documents\Visual Studio 2005\Projects\MSSQLRS\Chapter06
```

7. Select the Nametags report (Nametags.rdl) and click Open to exit the Choose file dialog box.

8. Click OK to upload the file.

9. The Nametags report has been uploaded to the Chapter 06 folder.

10. Click the Nametags report to execute it. You see an error similar to the one in Figure 10-10. You received this because, unlike the deployment from the Report Designer, the upload in Report Manager did not bring the shared data source along with the report.

11. Click the link to the Chapter 06 folder at the top of the page.

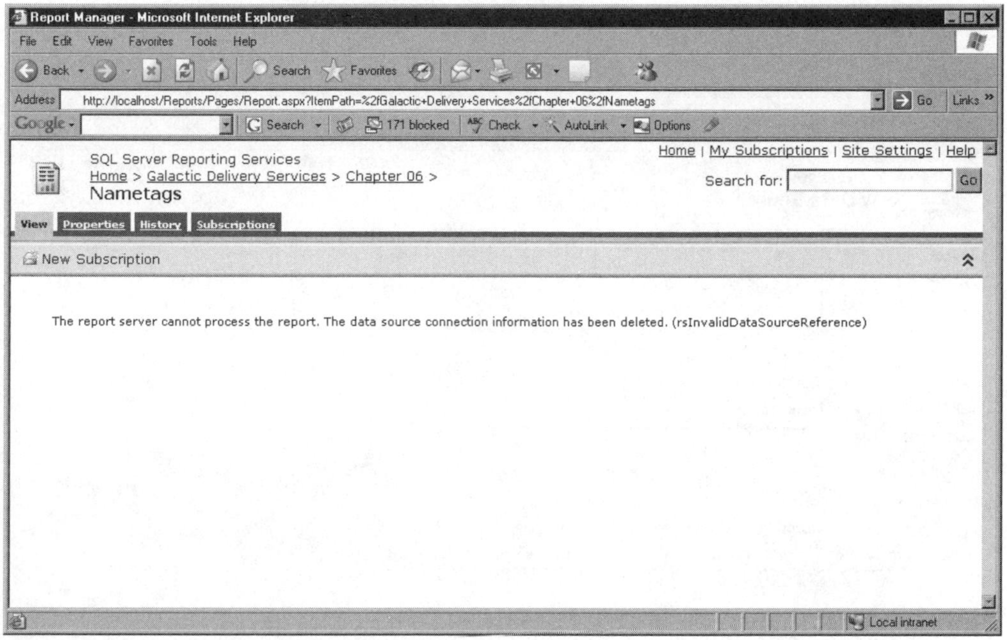

Figure 10-10   *The Reporting Services Error page*

Creating a Shared Data Source in the Report Manager

To get the Nametags report functioning, you need to provide it with a shared data source. One way to do this is to create a new shared data source using the Report Manager. Follow these steps:

1. Click the New Data Source button in the toolbar on the Contents tab. The New Data Source page for a shared data source appears, as shown in Figure 10-11.

2. Type **Galactic** for Name.

3. Type **Connection to the Galactic Database** for Description.

4. Make sure Microsoft SQL Server is selected in Connection type. Other options here are OLE DB, Microsoft SQL Server Analysis Services, Oracle, ODBC, and XML.

5. Type **data source=(local);initial catalog=Galactic** for Connection String. If the Galactic database is not on the Report Server, but is on a different computer, put the name of that computer in place of (local) in the connection string.

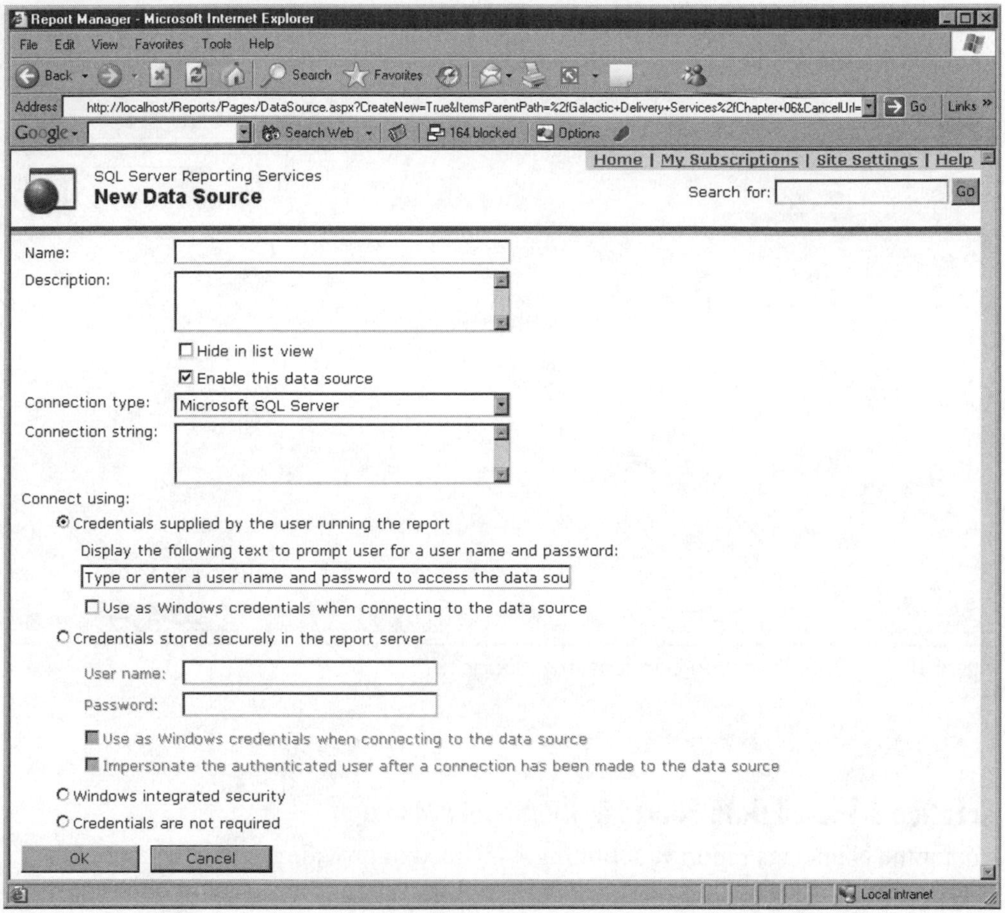

Figure 10-11 *The New Data Source page*

NOTE

Do not include the parentheses if you use a computer name in place of (local).

6. Select the option Credentials Stored Securely in the Report Server.

7. Type **GalacticReporting** for User Name.

8. Type **gds** for Password.

9. Click OK to save the data source and return to the Chapter 06 folder.

10. Click the Nametags report to execute it. You receive the same error message page because we have not yet told the report to use our new data source.

11. Select the Properties tab. The properties page for the Nametags report appears.

12. Click the Data Sources link on the left side of the screen. The Data Sources page for an individual report appears.

13. A shared data source should be selected. Click Browse. The Select a Shared Data Source page appears.

14. Expand each folder in the tree view under Location until you can see the Galactic shared data source in the Chapter 06 folder. Click the Galactic shared data source. The path to the Galactic shared data source is filled in Location. (You can also type this path into Location if you do not want to use the tree view.)

15. Click OK to exit the Select a Shared Data Source page.

16. Click Apply at the bottom of the page.

NOTE

It is easy to forget to click Apply when making changes to a report's data sources. If you do not click Apply, none of your changes are saved. This can lead to confusion, frustration, and wasted troubleshooting time. At least, that is what I have been told.

17. Select the View tab to view the report. The report now generates using the new shared data source. (A red *X* is where the GDS logo should be. We deal with this in the section "Uploading External Report Images.")

18. Once the report has completed generating, click the Chapter 06 link at the top of the page.

Hiding an Item

Figure 10-12 shows the list view of the Chapter 06 folder. The Galactic shared data source appears in the left column. Shared data sources have a cylinder and four arrows icon. The Nametags report appears in the right column. Reports have an icon showing a piece of paper with a bulleted list.

When users are browsing through folders to find a report, you may not want other items, such as shared data sources, cluttering things up. It makes more sense to have the shared data sources where the reports can use them, but out of sight of the users. Fortunately, Report Manager provides a way to do just that:

1. Click the Galactic data source. The Data Source Properties page appears.

2. Check the Hide in List View check box.

3. Click Apply to save this change.

4. Click the Chapter 06 link at the top of the page.

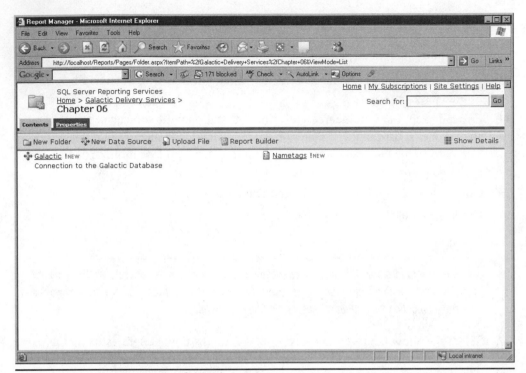

Figure 10-12 *The Chapter 06 folder list view*

The Galactic data source is no longer visible in the list view. You can use this same technique to hide reports you do not want to have generally available to users browsing through the folders.

If you do need to edit the Galactic data source, you can view it by using the detail view of the folder. Follow these steps:

1. Click the Show Details button in the toolbar on the Contents tab. The Galactic data source is now visible in this detail view, as shown in Figure 10-13. By default, the detail view is in alphabetical order by name.

2. Click the Type column heading. The detail view is now sorted by type in ascending order. (In an ascending sort by type, the reports are at the top of the list, with supporting items, such as shared data sources, at the bottom.) Note, the downward, black arrow is now next to the Type column heading on your screen.

3. Click the Type column heading again. The detail view is now sorted by type in descending order. Now the black arrow is pointing upward next to the column heading.

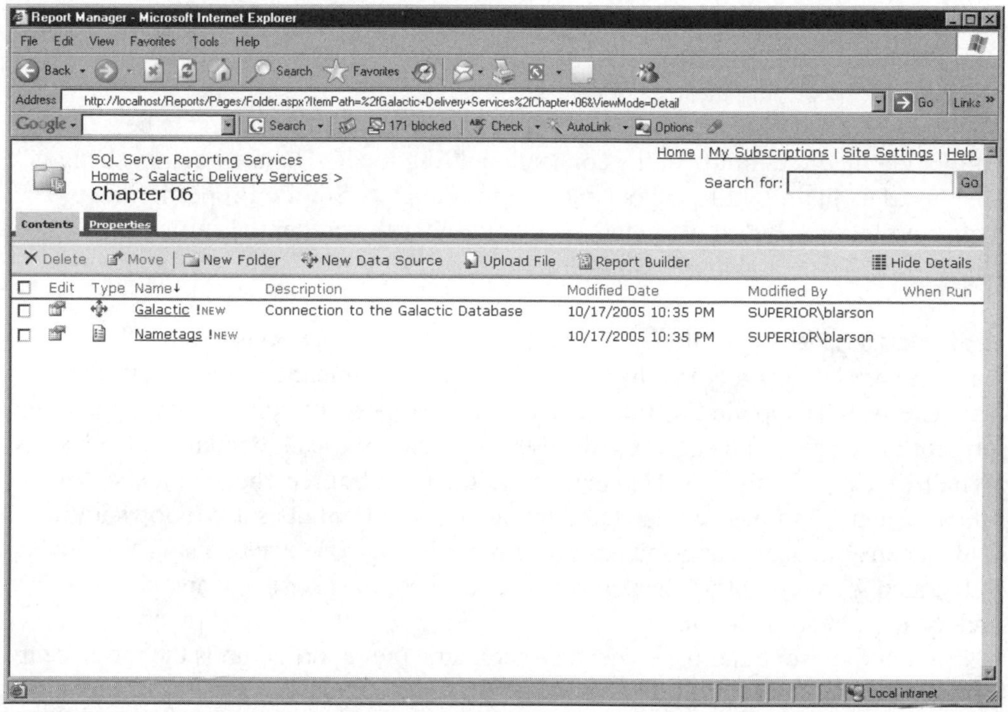

Figure 10-13   *The Chapter 06 folder detail view*

NOTE

The name of the sort order (ascending or descending) and the direction of the black arrow may seem opposite to one another. Remember this: in an ascending sort, you move from smaller values (A, B, C . . .) to larger values (. . . X, Y, Z). When you move through the list in the direction of the arrow, you also move from smaller values to larger values.

4. Click the Modified Date column heading. The detail view is sorted by modified date in ascending order. You can sort the detail view by Type, Name, Description, Modified Date, Modified By, or When Run, in either ascending or descending order.

5. Click the Hide Details button in the toolbar on the Contents tab. You are back to the list view.

Connect Using Options

When you are accessing data from a server-based database, such as SQL Server or Oracle, you need to provide some type of credentials, usually a user name and password, to show you have rights to access the data. Keeping these credentials secure is an important concern. The shared data sources created on the Report Server provide several methods for specifying these credentials.

When entering the connection string into a shared data source, it is best not to include the credentials in the connection string itself. The connection string is displayed as plain text to anyone who views the Data Source Properties page. To better protect password information, always enter the credential information under one of the Connect Using options described here.

Credentials Supplied by the User   The first Connect Using option is to have the user enter the credentials required by the data source each time the report is run. This is the "Credentials supplied by the user running the report" option. You can specify the prompt to be presented each time the user must enter these credentials. If the Use as Windows Credentials When Connecting to the Data Source check box is checked, the user name and password entered by the user are treated as a Windows login. This means the user name and password provide database access using Windows Integrated security. If this check box is not checked, the user name and password are treated as a database login.

Having the user enter the credentials each time the report is run is the most secure option. No login information is stored with the data source, but most users are not pleased with a system where they must enter login information each time they run a report. This option may be appropriate when your organization's security policy forbids storing login information in any way. In most other cases, the other Connect Using options provide a better solution.

Credentials Stored in the Report Server   The next option enables you to have the user name and password stored in the Report Catalog on the Report Server. This is the "Credentials stored securely in the report server" option. The user name and password entered with this option are encrypted when they are stored in the Report Catalog. Also, the password is not displayed to the user in the Data Source Properties page.

This Connect Using option is convenient for the user because they do not need to remember and enter credentials to run reports using this data source. It also provides the required security for most situations through the measures noted in the previous paragraph.

As with the first Connect Using option, there is a Use as Windows Credentials When Connecting to the Data Source check box here as well. If this check box is checked, the user name and password stored in the Report Catalog are treated as a Windows login. If this check box is not checked, the user name and password are treated as a database login.

The second check box under this Connect Using option is Impersonate the Authenticated User After a Connection Has Been Made to the Data Source. If this check box is checked, the data source can use these credentials to impersonate this user. Not all database servers support this type of delegation of credentials. Consult the documentation for your specific database server for more information.

Integrated Security   If you are not comfortable with storing credentials in the Report Catalog, but you do not want your users entering credentials every time a report is run, integrated security may be the solution for you. The Windows integrated security option does not require the user to enter credentials. Instead, it takes the Windows login credentials that let the user access the Report Manager and passes them along to the database server. Your database server, of course, needs to be set up to accept these credentials.

Integrated security always works when the data source exists on the same server as the Report Server. It may run into problems, however, if the data source is on another server. The problems are caused by the way integrated security works between servers.

For a better understanding of the problems with integrated security, let's look at an example of the way integrated security works. The user logs in to their computer. This computer knows everything about this user because the original authentication occurred here.

When the user accesses the Report Manager application, the user's credentials are passed from the original computer to the computer hosting the Report Server. However, using standard Windows security, not everything about this login is passed to the Report Server computer—only enough to authenticate the user is passed. Some sensitive information does not make this hop across the network.

When the user runs a report with a data source using integrated security, the Report Server must pass on the credentials to the database server. However, the Report Server does not have the complete credentials to pass along. In fact, it does not know enough about the user to successfully authenticate them on the database server. The authentication on the database server fails. Using standard Windows security, integrated security only works across one hop, from the original authenticating computer to a second computer. In the case of the Report Manager, this is the hop from the user's computer to the Report Server.

To get integrated security to work across more than one hop, your Windows domain must use a special kind of security known as Kerberos, which allows authentication across multiple hops. Using Kerberos security, integrated security works across any number of servers in the network.

Credentials Not Required The final Connect Using option is for data sources that do not require any authentication. This option would be used for connection to some Access databases, FoxPro databases, and others that do not require any login or password. This option could also be used if you insist, despite prior warnings here, on putting your credentials right in the connection string.

Uploading Other Items Using Report Manager

In addition to reports and shared data sources, other items can be uploaded to Report Server folders. External images needed as part of the reports can be uploaded, for example, as well as documentation and other supporting materials.

Uploading External Report Images

If you look closely at the Nametags report when it comes up in Report Manager, you notice this report has a problem. The GDS logo that should appear in the lower-left corner of each nametag is missing. You see the broken-link *X* symbol instead of the GDS logo.

This image was stored as an external image in the Chapter06 project. We need to upload this image to the Report Server. Once the image is uploaded into the same folder as the report, the report can find it. Here are the steps to follow to do this:

1. Return to the Chapter 06 folder in the Report Manager.
2. Click Upload File in the Contents tab toolbar. The Upload File page appears.
3. Click Browse. The Choose File dialog box appears.
4. Navigate to the folder containing the Chapter06 project. Select the gds.gif file and click Open to exit the Choose File dialog box.
5. Leave the name as gds.gif. The image needs to keep this name, so it can be found by the report. Click OK to upload this file.
6. Click the Nametags report to execute it. If the broken-link *X* is still visible, click the Refresh Report button in the Report Viewer toolbar, as shown in Figure 10-14.

NOTE

When you need to have Report Manager refresh a report, always use the Refresh Report button in the Report Viewer toolbar. Do not use the browser's Refresh button. The browser's Refresh button causes the page to be refreshed, but it does not cause the report to be reexecuted.

7. Click the link for the Chapter 06 folder.

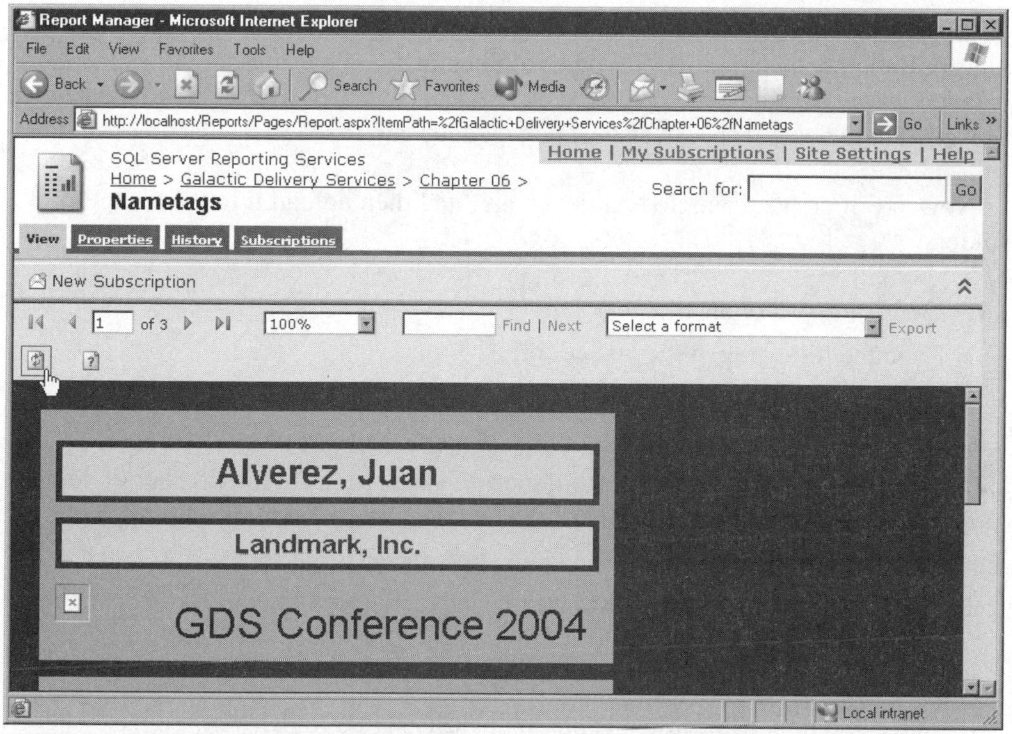

Figure 10-14   *The Refresh Report button in the Report Viewer toolbar*

8. The entry for the gds.gif image shows in the list view of the Chapter 06 folder. As with the Galactic shared data source, you probably don't want entries for supporting resources cluttering up your list view. Click the entry for gds.gif. The gds.gif image is displayed.

9. Click the Properties tab.

10. Check the Hide in List View check box.

11. Click Apply.

12. Click the link for the Chapter 06 folder.

Uploading Supporting Materials

In some cases, you need to provide your users with documentation on one or more reports in the form of either a text file, or a Word or HTML document. Supporting materials may also be created in other applications. For example, you may have a PowerPoint presentation or a Visio diagram that aids in the interpretation and understanding of a set of reports. These materials can be uploaded as a folder item just like report files.

A text file or an HTML document can be displayed right in the browser without any additional software. For other types of documents, if the appropriate application is installed on the user's computer, the documents can be viewed right in the browser as well. These documents can also be downloaded and saved to the user's computer, if desired.

Now, we'll create a simple text document, and then upload it to the Chapter 06 folder:

1. Open Notepad or another text editor.

2. Type the following in the text editor:

   ```
   The items in this folder are for the GDS Conference.
   ```

3. Save this as ReportReadMe.txt in a temporary location on your computer.

4. Return to your browser with the Report Manager viewing the Chapter 06 folder. Click Upload File in the Contents tab toolbar. The Upload File page appears.

5. Click Browse. The Choose File dialog box appears.

6. Navigate to the ReportReadMe.txt file and click Open to exit the Choose File dialog box.

7. Click OK to upload this file.

8. Select the ReportReadMe.txt entry in the Chapter 06 folder. You see the contents of the text file displayed within the Report Manager.

9. Click the link for the Chapter 06 folder.

10. Let's add a second line to our text file. Open the ReportReadMe.txt file in your text editor and add the following as a second line:

    ```
    These items were created for the GDS Art Department.
    ```

11. Save the changes and close your text editor.

12. Return to your browser with the Report Manager viewing the Chapter 06 folder. Click Upload File in the Contents tab toolbar. The Upload File page appears.

13. Click Browse. The Choose File dialog box appears.

14. Navigate to the ReportReadMe.txt file and click Open to exit the Choose File dialog box.

15. Check the Overwrite Item If It Exists check box. If you fail to check this check box, the new version of the text file does not overwrite the older version on the Report Server.

16. Click OK to upload this file.

17. Select the ReportReadMe.txt entry in the Chapter 06 folder. You see the new version of the text file.

18. Click the Properties tab.

19. Type **The purpose of these reports** . . . for the description.

20. Click Apply to save your changes.

21. Click the link for the Chapter 06 folder. The description shows up under the entry for ReportReadMe.txt.

22. Let's make another change to our text file and look at another way to overwrite an entry on the Report Server. Open the ReportReadMe.txt file in your text editor and add the following as a third line:

```
These items were created for all billing contacts.
```

23. Save the changes and close your text editor.

24. Return to your browser with the Report Manager viewing the Chapter 06 folder. Select the ReportReadMe.txt entry.

25. Click the Properties tab.

26. Click Replace.

27. Click Browse. The Choose File dialog box appears.

28. Navigate to the ReportReadMe.txt file and click Open to exit the Choose File dialog box.

29. Click OK to upload this file.

30. Click the View tab. You see the latest version of the text file.

31. Click the link for the Chapter 06 folder.

32. Delete the ReportReadMe.txt file on your computer.

Uploading Reports Using .NET Assemblies

In addition to external images, reports can also reference .NET assemblies. You saw this in the Weather Report and the Delivery Analysis Report created in Chapter 8. Let's look at the steps necessary to move these reports to the Report Server.

Copying the .NET Assembly to the Report Server

For a report to access a .NET assembly, it must be in the application folder of the Report Server. No fancy deployment, upload, or installation routine is required here. Simply copy the assembly's DLL file to the appropriate directory. We can give this a try using the Weather Report and its .NET assembly, WeatherInfo.dll, as well as the

Delivery Analysis Report and its .NET assembly, ReportUtil.dll. Here are the steps to follow:

1. Locate the WeatherInfo.dll and ReportUtil.dll files. You also need the ES folder that contains the Spanish version of the ReportUtil.dll. This Spanish version is called ReportUtil.resources.dll. (The folder name, ES, is the two-letter code for Español.) If you do not have them anywhere else, they should be in the Public Assemblies folder on your development computer. The default path for the Public Assemblies folder is

```
C:\Program Files\Microsoft Visual Studio 8\Common7\IDE\PublicAssemblies
```

2. Copy these files and the ES folder.

3. Paste the files and the ES folder into the Report Server application folder on the computer acting as your Report Server computer. You may receive a warning because a folder called ES already exists. Click Yes to continue. The default path for the Report Server application folder is

```
C:\Program Files\Microsoft SQL Server\MSSQL.3\Reporting Services\
                                              ReportServer\bin
```

Code Access Security

Because Reporting Services is a .NET application, it uses *code access security* to determine what execution permissions are possessed by each assembly. A *code access* group associates assemblies with specific permissions. The criteria for membership in a code access group are determined by a *security class*, and the permissions are determined by *named permission sets*.

Figure 10-15 provides an illustration of code access security. A .NET assembly or web service can gain entry into a code access group only if it matches the criteria specified by the security class. Once the .NET assembly or web service is allowed into a code access group, it can use the named permission set associated with that code access group to gain rights. These rights allow the .NET assembly or web service to perform tasks on a computer. Full trust rights and execution rights are the two types of rights we use with the Weather report. A number of different types of rights, however, can be included in a named permission set.

Code access groups can be nested one inside another. A .NET assembly or web service can be allowed into a parent group and gain its permissions; then it can try to gain membership in child code access groups to accumulate additional rights. A code access group can be a *first match code group*, where a .NET assembly or web service can only gain membership in one code access group—the first one it matches. Or, a code access group can be a *union code group*, where a .NET assembly or web service is allowed to gain membership in a number of code access groups, joining together the permissions from each group.

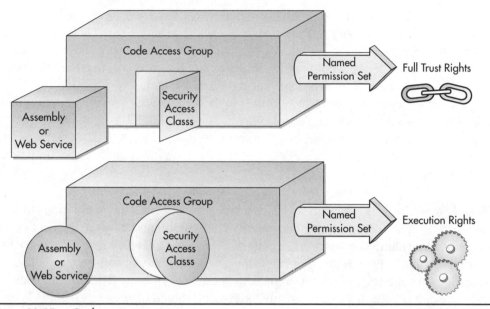

Figure 10-15   *Code access security*

For our Weather report to execute properly, we will have to create a code access group that provides permissions to the WeatherInfo.dll assembly. Also, we will have to create a second code access group to provide permissions to the web service that we are using to get our weather information. Even though this web service is not executing on our server, our WeatherInfo.dll assembly is executing some of its methods, so it needs to have permission to execute.

Security Classes   A security class describes the conditions a .NET assembly or web service needs to meet to get into a code access group. We use two different types of security classes with the Weather report. The UrlMembershipCondition security class is used with the web service, and the StrongNameMembershipCondition security class is used with the WeatherInfo.dll and ReportUtil.dll assemblies.

The UrlMembershipCondition security class says that any assembly or web service being executed from a specified URL is to be included in a particular code access group. The URL that must be matched is listed in each code access group using the UrlMembershipCondition security class. For example, the GDSServer code access group may use UrlMembershipCondition and give http://GDSServer/* as the URL that must be matched. Any web service running on the GDSServer would be included in this code access group.

The StrongNameMembershipCondition security class uses the strong name associated with an assembly to identify it. The *strong name*, which is a long string of hexadecimal digits that uniquely identifies an assembly, is assigned to the assembly when it is created. The StrongNameMembershipCondition security class is a good way to ensure that only the intended assembly is allowed into your code access group.

You see a couple of other security classes in the Report Server security configuration. The AllMembershipCondition security class allows in all .NET assemblies and web services. The ZoneMembershipCondition security class allows in .NET assemblies and web services that originate in a particular zone. Some sample zones are MyComputer, intranet, and Internet.

Named Permission Sets   Named permission sets group together the permissions to be assigned by code access groups. The security configuration used by the Report Server contains three named permission sets. The *Nothing permission*, which grants no rights, is used to initially take away all rights from a .NET assembly or web service before specific rights are added back by subsequent code access groups. This ensures each .NET assembly or web service has only the rights it should have.

The *Execution permission* grants execution rights to a .NET assembly or web service. This means the .NET assembly or web service can be run. The .NET assembly or web service does not, however, have rights to access any protected resources, such as the file system, the registry, or the Internet.

The *FullTrust permission* grants the .NET assembly or web service access to everything. This includes access to all the protected resources. FullTrust permission should only be granted to .NET assemblies and web services that you trust not to mess up your computer!

Modifying the Report Server's Security Configuration

Now that you have a basic understanding of code access security, we can modify the Report Server's security configuration to allow the WeatherInfo.dll and the ReportUtil.dll to run.

 CAUTION

Consult with your Reporting Services or network administrator before making any changes to server security.

We need to make some additions to the Report Server's security configuration to provide our custom assemblies with the rights they need to execute. The security configuration for the Report Server is in the rssrvpolicy.config file. The default path for this file is

```
C:\Program Files\Microsoft SQL Server\MSSQL.3\Reporting Services\
                                              ReportServer
```

This file contains the code-access security information in an XML structure.

CAUTION

Make a backup copy of the rssrvpolicy.config file before making any modifications to it. If you accidentally create an invalid XML structure or otherwise cause a problem with the security configuration, the Report Server cannot execute any reports.

The XML structure in the rssrvpolicy.config file can be divided into three sections: Security Classes, Named Permission Sets, and Code Groups. We only need to make changes to the Code Groups section of the document. Here are the steps to follow:

1. Open the rssrvpolicy.config file in Notepad or another text editor.
2. Scroll down until you locate the Code Group portion of the document. The Code Group portion of the document starts on the line after the closing XML tag for the named permission sets:

```
</NamedPermissionSets>
```

3. The first code group is the parent code group, which makes use of the AllMembershipCondition to assign the Nothing permission to all .NET assemblies and web services. We add a new child code group right beneath this. Insert this new code group as shown here (add the lines shown in bold):

```
.
.
.
<CodeGroup
      class="FirstMatchCodeGroup"
      version="1"
      PermissionSetName="Nothing">
   <IMembershipCondition
         class="AllMembershipCondition"
         version="1"
   />
   <CodeGroup
         class="UnionCodeGroup"
         version="1"
         PermissionSetName="Execution"
         Name="WeatherWebServiceCodeGroup"
         Description="Code group for the Weather Web Service">
      <IMembershipCondition class="UrlMembershipCondition"
```

```
                    version="1"
                    Url="http://live.capescience.com/*"
        />
    </CodeGroup>
    <CodeGroup
            class="UnionCodeGroup"
            version="1"
            PermissionSetName="Execution"
            Name="Report_Expressions_Default_Permissions"
            Description="This code group grants default permissions for
                            code in report expressions and Code element. ">
```

4. Another parent code group uses ZoneMembershipCondition to assign Execution permissions to all .NET assemblies and web services in the MyComputer zone. We add a new child code group right beneath this. Insert this new code group as shown here (add the lines shown in bold). Note, the Description and PublicKeyBlob should each be entered on one line.

```
    <CodeGroup
            class="FirstMatchCodeGroup"
            version="1"
            PermissionSetName="Execution"
            Description="This code group grants MyComputer code
                                        Execution permission. ">
        <IMembershipCondition
                class="ZoneMembershipCondition"
                version="1"
                Zone="MyComputer" />
        <CodeGroup
                class="UnionCodeGroup"
                version="1"
                PermissionSetName="FullTrust"
                Name="MSSQLRSCodeGroup"
                Description="Code group for the MS SQL RS Book Custom
                                            Assemblies">
            <IMembershipCondition
                    class="StrongNameMembershipCondition"
                    version="1"
                    PublicKeyBlob="0024000004800000940000000602000000
                            240000525341310004000001000100B9F7
                            4F2D5B0AAD33AA619B00D7BB8B0F767839
                            3A0F4CD586C9036D72455F8D1E85BF635C
                            9FB1DA9817DD0F751DCEE77D9A47959E87
                            28028B9B6CC7C25EB1E59CB3DE01BB516D
                            46FC6AC6AF27AA6E71B65F6AB91B957688
                            6F2EF39417F17B567AD200E151FC744C6D
                            A72FF5882461E6CA786EB2997FA968302B
                            7B2F24BDBFF7A5"
            />
```

```
</CodeGroup>
<CodeGroup
        class="UnionCodeGroup"
        version="1"
        PermissionSetName="FullTrust"
        Name="Microsoft_Strong_Name"
        Description="This code group grants code signed with the
                          Microsoft strong name full trust. ">
    <IMembershipCondition
            class="StrongNameMembershipCondition"
            version="1"
            PublicKeyBlob="0024000004800000940000000602000000
                          2400005253413100040000010001007D1
                          FA57C4AED9F0A32E84AA0FAEFD0DE9E8FD
                          6AEC8F87FB03766C834C99921EB23BE79A
                          D9D5DCC1DD9AD236132102900B723CF980
                          957FC4E177108FC607774F29E8320E92EA
                          05ECE4E821C0A5EFE8F1645C4C0C93C1AB
                          99285D622CAA652C1DFAD63D745D6F2DE5
                          F17E5EAF0FC4963D261C8A12436518206D
                          C093344D5AD293"
    />
</CodeGroup>
```

.
.
.

5. Save the modified file and exit your text editor.

NOTE

Looking at the rssrvpolicy.config file, you can see that expressions written within a report are granted Execute permissions. Because the WeatherInfo.GetWeather method is called from a report expression, by default, it should only be able to get Execute permissions. .NET Security says a process cannot get rights that exceed the rights granted to processes further up the stack. The GetWeather method needs FullTrust rights to make the web service call. The GetWeather method uses a special process to assert that it needs to exceed the rights of the calling process and gain FullTrust rights. If you downloaded the source code for the WeatherInfo.dll, you can look to see how the assert is accomplished.

Uploading the Report

You are now ready to upload the Weather report. Complete the following steps using the Report Manager:

1. Create a folder called **Chapter 08** in the Galactic Delivery Services folder.

2. Open the Chapter 08 folder and upload the WeatherReport.rdl file from the Chapter08 project folder.

3. Click the report WeatherReport to execute it. The report produces an error because the shared data source does not exist.

4. Click the Properties tab. The properties page for WeatherReport appears.

5. Click the Data Sources link on the left side of the screen. The Data Sources page for an individual report appears.

6. A shared data source should be selected. Click Browse. The Select a Shared Data Source page appears.

7. Rather than create another shared data source, we are going to use the existing shared data source in the Chapter 06 folder. Click Browse. Expand each folder in the tree view under Location until you can see the Galactic shared data source in the Chapter 06 folder. Click the Galactic shared data source.

8. Click OK to exit the Select a Shared Data Source page.

9. Click Apply at the bottom of the page.

10. Select the View tab to view the report. Select one or more planets and click View Report. The report now generates. (Remember, the .NET assembly calls a web service, so it requires an Internet connection.)

Try the Deploy One More Time

This last report upload required us to manually point the report to a shared data source in a different folder. This is because we do not want to have a shared data source in every report folder. If we had numerous shared data sources spread across a number of report folders, this would defeat much of the purpose of having shared data sources. When the database server name changes or the login credentials need to be updated, we would still have a major headache.

Instead, we want to have just one shared data source for each unique connection needed by our reports. This small group of shared data sources should be placed in one central location. That still leaves us with the task of manually pointing each report at the central group of shared data sources after each report upload.

You may recall there was a property on the report project's Property Pages dialog box specifying the folder path where the shared data source is to be deployed. Let's try deploying the Delivery Analysis Report from the Report Designer and see if this property can help us avoid all of the manual updating. Try the following:

1. Open the Chapter08 project in Visual Studio or the Business Intelligence Development Studio.

2. From the Main menu, select Project | Chapter08 Properties. The Chapter08 Property Pages dialog box appears.

3. Enter **/Galactic Delivery Services/Chapter 06/** for TargetDataSourceFolder.

4. Enter **/Galactic Delivery Services/Chapter 08/** for TargetReportFolder.

5. Enter **http://ComputerName/ReportServer** for TargetServerURL. Substitute the appropriate value for ComputerName as you did earlier in this chapter.

6. Click OK to close the Chapter08 Property Pages dialog box.

7. Select Save All from the toolbar.

8. Right-click the entry for the DeliveryAnalysis report in the Solution Explorer window and select Deploy from the Context menu.

9. Notice in the Output window that the Report Designer attempted to deploy the shared data source from this project along with the report. This did not work because there is already a shared data source with the same name in the Chapter 06 folder and the OverwriteDataSources property is set to False. What, you may ask, did we accomplish by putting a path in TargetDataSourceFolder? In addition to trying to deploy the shared data source to a specific folder, this process also instructs the deployed report to look in that same folder for the data sources it needs.

10. Switch to the browser and navigate to the Chapter 08 folder.

11. Execute the DeliveryAnalysis report.

12. Select a number of service types from the drop-down list and click View Report. The report displays using the shared data source found in the Chapter 06 folder.

A Look at Localization

You may recall we used the ReportUtil.dll assembly to present the report labels in both English and Spanish. (If you do not recall this, look at the instructions for this report in Chapter 8.) We passed the User!Language parameter to the LocalizedString method to retrieve a report label in the appropriate language. The User!Language parameter contains the language setting for the application requesting the report. When we are using the Report Manager, the browser is that application.

Let's try changing the language setting of the browser and see if our localization works the way it should. (The following directions apply to Internet Explorer.)

1. Select Tools | Internet Options from Internet Explorer's Main menu. The Internet Options dialog box appears.

2. Click Languages. The Language Preference dialog box appears.

3. If an entry for Spanish (Mexico) [es-mx] is not in the Language list, click Add. The Add Language dialog box appears.

4. Highlight Spanish (Mexico) [es-mx] in the Language list and click OK to exit the Add Language dialog box.

5. Highlight Spanish (Mexico) [es-mx] in the Language list and click Move Up as many times as necessary to move the Spanish entry to the top of the list.

6. Click OK to exit the Language Preference dialog box. Click OK to exit the Internet Options dialog box.

7. Click the link for the Chapter 08 folder, and then re-execute the Delivery Analysis report. The User!Language parameter now has a value of es-mx because you set the primary language of your browser to Spanish (Mexico). Because of this, the title of the report and the column headings are now Spanish.

8. Use the Language Preference dialog box to remove the Spanish entry, if you created it in Steps 3 and 4. Make sure you return the correct language to the top of the Language list.

The ReportUtil.dll assembly has resource files for English and Spanish. English is the default language. If the parameter passed to the LocalizedString method is any of the cultural variations of Spanish, the method uses the Spanish resource file to look up the text for the report title or a column heading. If anything else is passed to the LocalizedString method, the English resource file is used.

Modifying Reports from the Report Server

In addition to uploading a report definition to the Report Server, it is also possible to download a report definition, modify it, and send your modifications back to the Report Server as an update. You only need to do this if you do not have a copy of the RDL file for a report that is on the Report Server and needs to be modified. If you already have the report in a report project, you can edit that report using the Report Designer, and then redeploy it.

Downloading a Report Definition

For this example, imagine we do not have the RDL file for the SubReportTest report and need to make a change to the report. The first task we need to complete is to download this report's RDL file from the Report Server to our local computer. Follow these steps:

1. Open the Report Manager in your browser and navigate to the Chapter 09 folder.

2. In the previous section, when we wanted to view the Properties tab for a report, we first executed that report. Now, we use the Show Details button to get at the Properties tab another way. Click the Show Details button in the Contents tab toolbar. The detail view of the folder's contents appears.

3. Click the icon in the Edit column next to the SubReportTest report. The Properties tab for the SubReportTest report appears.

4. There is a Report Definition section on this page just above the buttons at the bottom. Click the Edit link in the Report Definition section. This causes the Report Manager to download a copy of the SubReportTest.rdl file, so you can edit it. The File Download dialog box appears.

5. Click Save. The Save As dialog box appears.

6. Browse to an appropriate temporary location on your computer. Leave the filename as SubReportTest.rdl. Click Save to exit the Save As dialog box. The file is downloaded and saved in the specified location.

NOTE

If you have logon credentials stored in one or more data source definitions in the report, for security purposes, these are not saved in the resulting report definition file.

Editing the Report Definition

We now have the report definition file for the SubReportTest report moved from the Report Server to our local computer. However, an RDL file by itself is not useful. To edit it, we have to place it in a report project. Again, remember, for this example, we are imagining we do not already have the SubReportTest report in a report project. Here are the steps to follow:

1. Start Visual Studio or the Business Intelligence Development Studio.

2. Create a new report project in the MSSQLRS folder called EditSubReportTest. (Do not use the Report Wizard.)

3. Create a shared data source called Galactic for the Galactic database using GalacticReporting for the user name and gds for the password.

4. Right-click the Reports entry in the Solution Explorer and select Add | Add Existing Item from the Context menu. The Add Existing Item dialog box appears.

5. Navigate to the location where you stored the SubReportTest.rdl file in the previous section. Select the SubReportTest.rdl file and click Open to exit the Add Existing Item dialog box.

6. Double-click the SubReportTest report to open it for editing. (If you encounter an error while trying to edit this report, save the project, close the Report Designer, restart it again, and reopen the EditSubReportTest project.)

7. On the Data tab, add the PurchaseDate to the output.

8. On the Layout tab, put the PurchaseDate in a text box to the right of the SerialNumber. Set the Format property for this text box to MM/dd/yyyy.

9. Use the Preview tab to make sure your changes were made properly.

10. Click Save All in the toolbar.

11. Close the Report Designer.

Uploading the Modified Report Definition

Now that the report definition changes are completed, we are ready to upload the modified report:

1. Return to the Report Manager. If you are not already there, navigate to the Properties tab for the SubReportTest report.

2. Click the Update link in the Report Definition section of the page. The Import Report page appears.

3. Click Browse. The Choose File dialog box appears.

4. Navigate to the EditSubReportTest folder to find the updated version of the SubReportTest.rdl file.

NOTE

Do not select the copy of SubReportTest.rdl you originally downloaded. The modified version is in the folder with the EditSubReportTest report project.

5. Select SubReportTest.rdl and click Open to exit the Choose File dialog box.

6. Click OK to upload the file.

7. Click the View tab to view the report, and then click the Report Refresh button in the Report Viewer toolbar. The purchase date is now shown for each transport.

Managing Items in Folders

You now know how to load items into folders on the Report Server. Of course, we live in a dynamic world, so things seldom stay where they are originally put. We need to be able to move items around as we come up with better ways of organizing them. We also need to be able to delete items as they are replaced by something better or are simply not needed anymore. Fortunately, the Report Manager provides ways for us to do this housekeeping in an efficient manner.

Moving Items Between Folders

As an example, let's create a more descriptive folder for our Nametags report and its supporting items. We begin by moving a single item to this new folder. Then, we look at a method for moving multiple items at the same time.

Moving a Single Item

Here are the steps to follow to move a single item:

1. Open the Report Manager in your browser and navigate to the Galactic Delivery Services folder.
2. Click New Folder. The New Folder page appears.
3. Type **2006 Conference** for Name and type **Materials for the 2006 User Conference** for Description.
4. Click OK to create the new folder.
5. Click Chapter 06 to view the contents of this folder.
6. Click Show Details.
7. Click the icon in the Edit column for the Nametags report. The Nametags report Properties tab appears.
8. Click Move. The Move Item page appears.
9. Select the 2006 Conference folder in the tree view.
10. Click OK to move the report to this folder.
11. Click the 2006 Conference link at the top of the page to view the contents of this folder.

Moving Multiple Items

You can see the Nametags report has been moved to the 2006 Conference folder. However, the report cannot function until the supporting items are also moved to this folder. Moving each item individually, as we did with the report, is rather time-consuming. Fortunately, there is another way:

1. Click the Galactic Delivery Services link at the top of the page.
2. Click Chapter 06 to view the contents of this folder.
3. In the Detail view, you see check boxes next to each item in the folder. These check boxes work with the Delete and Move buttons in the Contents tab toolbar. When you click Delete, any checked items are deleted. Likewise, when you click Move, any checked items are moved.

4. Click the uppermost check box (the check box to the left of the word "Edit"). Checking this check box checks all items in the folder. Unchecking this check box unchecks all items in the folder. Because we are moving all the items in the folder, we want all the items to be checked.

5. Click Move in the Contents tab toolbar. The Move Multiple Items page appears.

6. Select the 2006 Conference folder in the tree view.

7. Click OK to move these items to this folder.

This method works for moving a single item, multiple items, or the entire contents of a folder. Just check the items you want to move and click the Move button. Remember, you need to be in the Detail view when using this method.

This section demonstrated moving reports and supporting items. You can also move whole folders using the same techniques.

Deleting a Folder

The Chapter 06 folder is now empty and ready to be deleted. As with the Move function, you can accomplish this in two ways. The first way is to view the Properties tab for the folder you want to delete, and then click the Delete button. Just for fun, we'll try the second method.

Deleting a Folder Using the Check Boxes and Toolbar

1. Click the Galactic Delivery Services link at the top of the page to view the contents of this folder.

2. Check the Chapter 06 folder.

3. Click Delete. The confirmation dialog box appears.

4. Click OK to confirm your deletion. The Chapter 06 folder is deleted.

Folders do not need to be emptied before they are deleted. If the Chapter 06 folder had contained reports, supporting items, or even other folders, these would have been deleted along with the folder.

Renaming a Folder

In addition to moving and deleting items, we may also want to rename items. Let's give the Chapter 09 folder a more descriptive name:

1. Click the icon in the Edit column for the Chapter 09 folder. The Chapter 09 Properties tab appears.

2. Replace the contents of Name by typing **Rendering Test Reports**. Then type **Reports for testing the performance of various rendering types** for Description.

3. Click Apply.

4. Click the Galactic Delivery Services link at the top of the page.

5. Click Hide Details.

This same technique makes it just as easy to change the names and descriptions for reports and other items. Just because it is easy to make these changes does not mean you should do it often. Once users become familiar with a folder name, a report name, or a report's location within the folder structure, you should change it only if you have a good reason to do so.

You may have noted that we could have changed the name of the Chapter 06 folder rather than going through the move-and-delete processes of the previous sections. This is true; we could have simply changed the folder name. If we had done that, though, you would not know how to do moves and deletes!

Seek and Ye Shall Find: Search and Find Functions

The Report Manager provides two features to help users find information. The Search function helps the user locate a report within the Report Server folder structure, and the Find function enables the user to jump to a certain piece of information while viewing a report.

Searching for a Report

First, we look at the Search function. This function lets the user enter a portion of a word, a complete word, or a phrase. The Report Manager then searches the names and descriptions of items in the Report Server folder structure for occurrences of this text. The Report Manager does not search the contents of a report or supporting files.

For example, searching for "GDS Report" would find "The GDS Report" and "GDS Reporting." It would not find "Report GDS Income" or "GDS Accounting Report." This is strictly a search for the text exactly as it is entered—no Boolean logic, proximity searching, or other features you find in Internet search engines. Also, the search is not case-sensitive.

Follow these steps to use the Search function:

1. Open the Report Manager in your browser and navigate to the Home folder.

2. Type **report** for Search For in the upper-right corner of the screen, and then click Go. The Search page is displayed with the search results.

3. The Report Manager finds five items: two folders, a text document, and two reports. No weighting or relevance is assigned to each result. They are simply displayed in alphabetical order. Click the Galactic Delivery Services folder. You see the contents of that folder.

4. Click your browser's Back button to return to the search results.

5. Click ReportReadMe.txt. You see the contents of this file.

6. Click your browser's Back button.

7. Click the SubReportTest report to execute this report. (Keep your browser on this report. We use it in the Find feature.)

Finding Text Within a Report

Next, we look at the Find function. This function also enables the user to enter a portion of a word, a complete word, or a phrase. The Report Manager then searches the contents of the current report for occurrences of this text. Next, it highlights the first occurrence and moves it to the top of the view. The user can use the Next button to move to the next occurrence.

As with the Search function, Find locates text just as it is entered—no Boolean logic or proximity searching. Also, Find is not case-sensitive.

We use the SubReportTest report to demonstrate the Find function. This report should be open in your browser. The SubReportTest report lists all the transports used by GDS. They are listed in transport number order. Suppose we want to look at just the Warp Hauler–type transports sprinkled throughout the report. Rather than skimming through the entire report looking for what we are interested in, here is a better way:

1. Type **warp haul** in the entry area to the left of the words "Find | Next" in the Report Viewer toolbar.

2. Click Find. The first Warp Hauler transport (#1303) is brought to the top of the viewing area and the Warp Haul portion of the transport type is highlighted.

3. Click Next. (Make sure you do not click Find. Clicking Find simply starts the find operation again from the top of the page.) The next Warp Hauler transport (#1307) is brought to the top of the viewing area.

4. Click Next. The report jumps to the next Warp Hauler transport (#1310). Click Next once more and the report jumps to the next Warp Hauler transport (#1311) on Page 2 of the report.

Printing from Report Manager

No matter how convenient you make it for your users to access reports in a browser, and no matter how many interactive drill-down and drill-through features you provide, your users always want to print their reports on paper. You can explain all the wonders of the multiple, cascading parameters you have created until you are blue in the face, but some users always need to touch and feel the numbers on paper. They need to be able to put something in a briefcase and take it home with them at night. It doesn't matter that they could receive up-to-date numbers through their VPN at home. They want ink on paper.

Printing Options

Reporting Services provides several options for printing a report from Report Manager. Each provides some advantages and disadvantages for the user.

HTML Printing

These users could just press the Print button in their browser and get whatever type of printout HTML printing provides. As you are probably aware, HTML printing is not a good choice when formatting is important as it usually is for reports. Lines of text can wrap in unusual ways or simply be cut off. A line of text at the bottom of the page can even be cut right in half, with the top-half on one page and the bottom-half on the next page.

Fortunately, the Report Manager provides a couple of alternatives to HTML printing.

Printing from a PDF Document or TIFF File

As discussed previously, a PDF document or a TIFF file does an excellent job of maintaining report format when a report is printed. Therefore, when users want to have a high-quality report printout, they can export the report to a PDF document or a TIFF file. Once this is complete, they can view the exported report using the appropriate viewer: Adobe Acrobat Reader for the PDF document and the Windows Picture and Fax Viewer for a TIFF file. The report can then be printed using the view.

This process provides the user with a quality printout. However, not all users are comfortable with saving a file to a local disk, finding that file and opening it in the appropriate viewer, and then printing the report. There is another printing alternative, which is even more straightforward.

Client-Side Printing

You may have noticed a button with a printer icon on the report toolbar. This button is for the client-side printing feature of Reporting Services. *Client-side printing* works through an ActiveX object downloaded to the user's computer. From then on, whenever the Client-Side Printing button is clicked, this ActiveX object provides the user interface and controls the printing.

The first time a user activates the client-side printing feature, they may be prompted with a security warning about the ActiveX download. After taking the appropriate precautions, such as making sure the ActiveX object is signed by Microsoft, the user should approve the download to enable client-side printing. Once the ActiveX has been downloaded by this first use, it does not need to be downloaded again.

If a user has trouble downloading the ActiveX control, they may need to set the Report Manager as a trusted site in their browser. This is done on the Security tab of the Internet Options dialog box. The user should not lower their security setting for all sites in general to accomplish the ActiveX download.

Once downloaded, client-slide printing enables users to set various report attributes. These include margins, page size, and even page orientation. Users can also preview a report before putting it on paper.

Managing Reports on the Report Server

Now that you have moved some of your reports to the Report Server, you may be thinking your job is about done, but it is just beginning. Now you need to manage the reports and supporting materials to ensure the reports can be utilized properly by your users.

Two of the biggest concerns when it comes to managing reports are security and performance. Reports containing sensitive data must be secured, so they are only accessed by the appropriate people. Reports must return information to users in a reasonable amount of time without putting undo stress on database resources. Fortunately, Reporting Services provides tools for managing both of these concerns. Security roles and item-level security give you extremely fine control over just who has access to each report and resource. Caching, snapshots, and history let you control how and when reports are executed.

Security

In Reporting Services, security was designed with both flexibility and ease of management in mind. Flexibility is provided by the fact that individual access rights can be assigned to each folder and to each item within a folder. An item is either a report or a resource. You can specify exactly who has rights to each item and exactly what those rights are. Ease of management is provided by security inheritance, security roles, and integration with Windows security. We begin our discussion with the last entry in this list.

NOTE

Remember, although we are creating and maintaining these role assignments using the Report Manager, the security rights apply to Reporting Services as a whole. No matter how you access folders and items—through the Report Manager or through the web service—these security rights are enforced.

Integration with Windows Security

Reporting Services does not maintain its own list of users and passwords. Instead, it depends entirely on integration with Windows security. When a user accesses either the Report Manager web application or the web service, that user must authenticate with the Report Server. In other words, the user must have a valid domain user name and password, or a local user name and password, to log on to the Report Server. Both the Report Manager web application and the web service are set up requiring integrated Windows authentication to ensure this logon takes place.

NOTE

If it is impossible for each report user to have their own credentials on the Report Server, it is possible to create your own custom security. You can create a security scheme such as forms-based security to enable the users to authenticate and access reports. This is discussed in detail in Chapter 12.

Once this logon occurs, Reporting Services utilizes the user name and the user's group memberships to determine what rights the user possesses. The user can access only those folders and items they have rights to. In Report Manager, users do not even see the folders they cannot browse and reports they cannot run. There is no temptation for the user to try and figure out how to get into places they are not supposed to go, because they do not even know these places exist.

Local Administrator Privileges

In most cases, rights must be explicitly assigned to folders and items. One exception to this rule, however, is local administrator privileges. Any user who is a member of the local administrators group on the computer hosting the Report Server has content manager rights to all folders and all items. These automatic rights cannot be modified or removed.

Let's look at the security page:

1. Open the Report Manager in your browser and navigate to the Home folder.
2. Select the Properties tab. You see the security page for the Home folder, as shown in Figure 10-16.

The Report Server maintains a security page for each item in the Report Catalog—every folder, every report, and every supporting item. The security page lists all the role assignments for an item. Each role assignment is made up of two things: a Windows user or group and a security role. The rights associated with the security role are assigned to the Windows user or group.

Initially, one role assignment is on the security page for each item. This entry assigns the Content Manager security role to the BUILTIN\Administrators group. This entry is a reminder that any user who is a member of the local administrators group has rights to manage the contents of this folder.

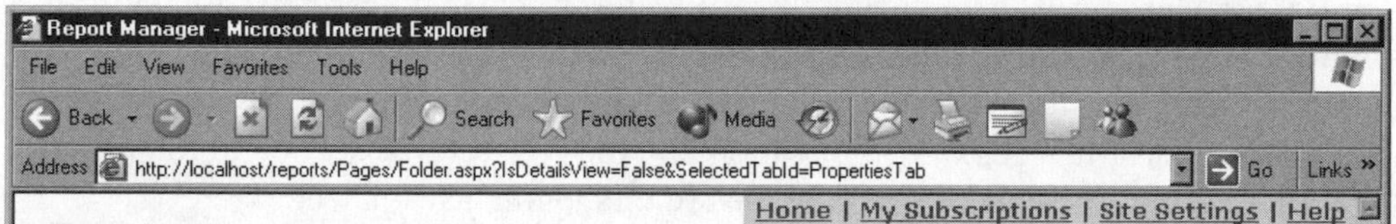

Figure 10-16   *The security page for the Home folder*

NOTE

You could delete the role assignment for BUILTIN\Administrators, and the members of the local administrators group would still have rights to manage the contents of this folder. These rights are hardwired into Reporting Services. The BUILTIN\Administrators assignment on the security page is, in most cases, just a reminder of the rights held by anyone in the local administrators group.

Tasks and Rights

You can perform a number of tasks in Reporting Services. Each task has a corresponding right to perform that task. For example, you can view reports. Therefore, a corresponding right exists to view reports. The tasks within Reporting Services are shown in Table 10-1.

You are probably not familiar with some of these tasks. We discuss linked reports in the section "Linked Reports," and we discuss report history snapshots and subscriptions

Task	Description
Consume reports	Read report definitions.
Create linked reports	Create linked reports and publish them to a folder.
Manage all subscriptions	View, modify, and delete any subscription, regardless of who owns the subscription.
Manage data sources	Create, modify, and delete shared data sources.
Manage folders	Create, view, and delete folders. View and modify folder properties.
Manage individual subscriptions	Create, view, modify, and delete your own subscriptions.
Manage models	Create, view, and delete models. Modify model properties.
Manage report history	Create, view, and delete report history snapshots. Modify report history properties.
Manage reports	Create, view, and delete reports. Modify report properties.
Manage resources	Create, modify, and delete resources. View and modify resource properties.
Set security for individual items	View and modify security settings for reports, folders, resources, and shared data sources.
View data sources	View shared data sources and their properties.
View folders	View folders and their properties.
View models	View models. Use models as report data sources. Query models for data.
View reports	View reports and linked reports along with their report history snapshots and properties.
View resources	View resources and their properties.

Table 10-1   *Security Tasks within Reporting Services*

in Chapter 11. For now, you simply need to know these are tasks with associated rights within Reporting Services.

In addition to the tasks listed in Table 10-1, there are system-wide tasks with associated rights. These system-wide tasks deal with the management and operation of Reporting Services as a whole. The system-wide tasks within Reporting Services are shown in Table 10-2.

Again, you may not be familiar with all the tasks in this list. We discuss jobs and shared schedules in Chapter 11.

Roles

The rights to perform tasks are grouped together to create *roles*. Reporting Services includes several predefined roles to help you with security management. In addition, you can create your own custom roles, grouping together any combination of rights that you like. The predefined roles and their corresponding rights are listed here.

The Browser Role   The *Browser* role is the basic role assigned to users who are going to view reports, but who are not going to create folders or upload new reports. The Browser role has rights to perform the following tasks:

▶   Manage individual subscriptions

▶   View folders

Task	Description
Execute Report Definitions	Start execution of a report from a report definition without deploying it to the Report Server.
Generate events	Provide an application with the capability to generate events within the Report Server.
Manage jobs	View and cancel running Report Server jobs.
Manage Report Server properties	View and modify configuration properties for the Report Server.
Manage Report Server security	View and modify system-wide role assignments.
Manage roles	Create, view, modify, and delete role definitions.
Manage shared schedules	Create, view, modify, and delete shared schedules used for snapshots and subscriptions.
View Report Server properties	View properties that apply to the Report Server.
View shared schedules	View a shared schedule.

Table 10-2   *System-Wide Security Tasks within Reporting Services*

- ▶ View models
- ▶ View reports
- ▶ View resources

The Publisher Role   The *Publisher* role is assigned to users who are going to create folders and upload reports. The Publisher role does not have rights to change security settings or manage subscriptions and report history. The Publisher role has rights to perform the following tasks:

- ▶ Create linked reports
- ▶ Manage data sources
- ▶ Manage folders
- ▶ Manage models
- ▶ Manage reports
- ▶ Manage resources

The My Reports Role   The *My Reports* role is designed to be used only with a special folder called the My Reports folder. Within this folder, the My Reports role gives the user rights to do everything except change security settings. The My Reports role has rights to perform the following tasks:

- ▶ Create linked reports
- ▶ Manage data sources
- ▶ Manage folders
- ▶ Manage individual subscriptions
- ▶ Manage report history
- ▶ Manage reports
- ▶ Manage resources
- ▶ View data source
- ▶ View folders
- ▶ View reports
- ▶ View resources

The Content Manager Role The *Content Manager* role is assigned to users who are managing the folders, reports, and resources. All members of the Windows local administrators group on the computer hosting the Report Server are automatically members of the Content Manager role for all folders, reports, and resources. The Content Manager has rights to perform all tasks, excluding system-wide tasks.

The System User Role The system-wide security tasks have two predefined roles. The *System User* role has rights to perform the following system-wide tasks:

► Execute Report Definitions

► View report server properties

► View shared schedules

The System Administrator Role The *System Administrator* role provides the user with rights to complete any of the tasks necessary to manage the Report Server. All members of the Windows local administrators group on the computer hosting the Report Server are automatically members of the System Administrator role. This role has rights to perform the following system-wide tasks:

► Execute Report Definitions

► Manage jobs

► Manage report server properties

► Manage report server security

► Manage roles

► Manage shared schedules

Creating Role Assignments

As stated previously, role assignments are created when a Windows user or a Windows group is assigned a role for a folder, a report, or a resource. Role assignments are created on the security page for the folder, report, or resource. These role assignments control what the user can see within a folder and what tasks the user can perform on the folder, report, or resource.

Let's try creating role assignments for some of our folders and reports.

 NOTE

To complete the next set of activities, you need a user who has rights to log on to the Report Server, but who is not a member of the local administrators group on that computer. You should know the password for this user, so you can log on as that user and view the results of your security settings.

Creating a Role Assignment for a Folder   Let's try creating a new role assignment for the Home folder:

1. Open the Report Manager in your browser. You should be viewing the contents of the Home folder.

2. Select the Properties tab. You see the security page for this folder.

3. Click New Role Assignment. The New Role Assignment page appears, as shown in Figure 10-17.

4. Type the name of a valid user for Group or User Name. If you are using a domain user or domain group, this must be in the format DomainName\UserName or DomainName\GroupName. If you are using a local user or local group, this must be in the format ComputerName\UserName or ComputerName\GroupName.

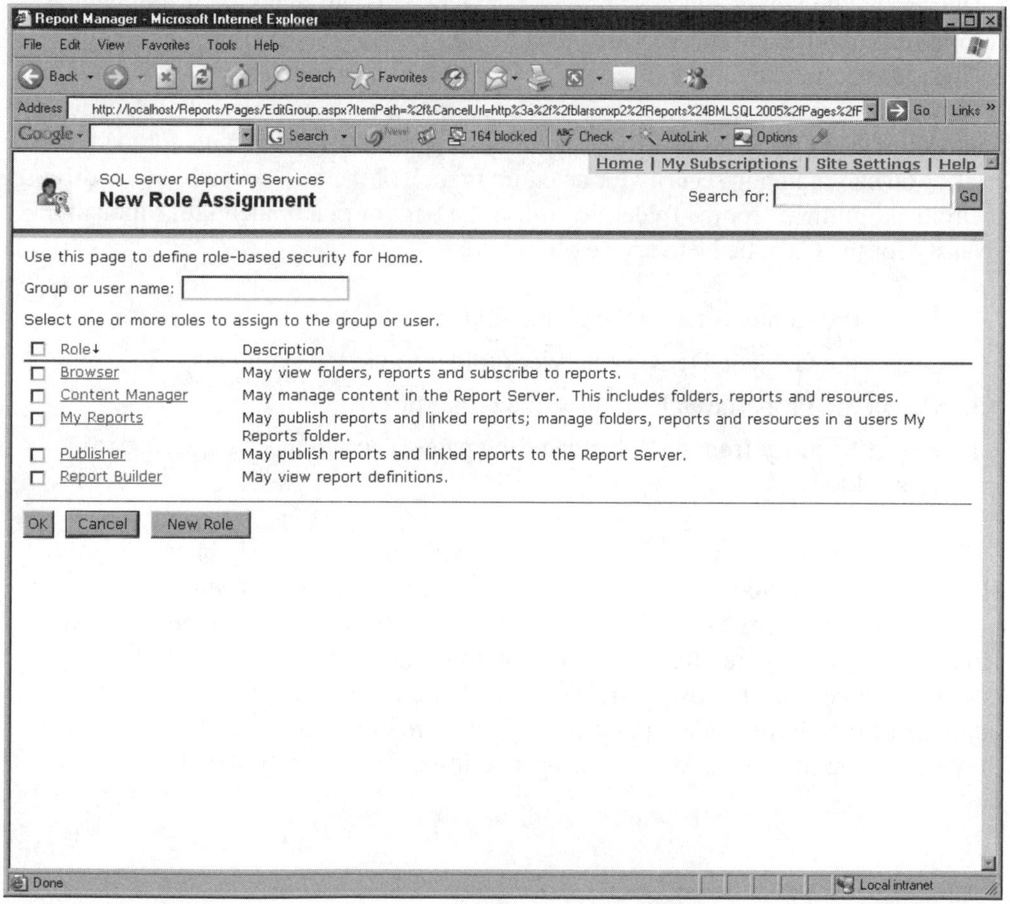

Figure 10-17   *The New Role Assignment page*

5. Check the check box for the Browser role.

6. Click OK to save your role assignment and return to the security page. Reporting Services checks to ensure you entered a valid user or group for the role assignment. If this is not a valid user or group, you receive an error message and your role assignment is not saved.

NOTE

A user needs to have at least viewing rights in the Home folder to view other folders and navigate to them.

Inherited Role Assignments   By default, folders (other than the Home folder), reports, and resources inherit their role assignments from the folder that contains them. You can think of the nested folders as branches of a tree, with the reports and resources as the leaves. *Inherited security* means you can make security changes to one folder and have those changes take effect for all the branches and leaves further along the tree.

This makes managing security easy. You can maintain security for all the reports and resources within a folder simply by modifying the role assignments for the folder itself. You can maintain security for an entire branch of the tree structure by modifying the role assignments for the folder that forms the base of that branch. Let's look at the security for the Galactic Delivery Services folder:

1. Select the Contents tab of the Home folder.

2. Select the Galactic Delivery Services folder to view its contents.

3. Select the Properties tab. You see the properties page for this folder.

4. Select Security from the left side of the page. You see the security page for this folder.

The Galactic Delivery Services folder is inheriting its role assignments from the Home folder. You did not add a role assignment giving Browser rights to your user in this folder and, yet, there it is! As soon as you added the role assignment to the Home folder, it appeared for all the items within the Home folder.

You gave your user Browser rights in the Home folder, so they could view the contents of the Home folder, and then navigate into other folders to find the reports they need. You may want to give this user additional rights in folders further along in the tree. Perhaps the user can manage the content of certain folders that belong to their department, but can only browse when in the Home folder.

To accomplish this task, you must first break the inherited security for the Galactic Delivery Services folder:

1. Click Edit Item Security. A dialog box with an inherited security message appears. The Report Manager is confirming you want to break that inheritance by creating your own role assignments for this folder.
2. Click OK to confirm you want to break the inherited security.

Now that you have broken the inherited security, you have new buttons on the toolbar for adding a new role assignment, deleting existing role assignments, and reverting to inherited security.

Now you can edit the role assignment for your user:

1. Click the Edit link next to the role assignment giving your user Browser rights. The Edit Role Assignment page appears.
2. Uncheck the check box for the Browser role.
3. Check the check box for the Content Manager role.
4. Click Apply to save the changes to your role assignment and return to the security page. The user now has Content Manager rights in the Galactic Delivery Services folder.
5. Click the Contents tab.
6. Select the Rendering Test Reports folder to view its content.
7. Select the Properties tab. You see the properties page for this folder.
8. Select Security from the left side of the page. You see the security page for this folder.

You can see the Rendering Test Reports folder is inheriting its role assignments from the Galactic Delivery Services folder.

 NOTE

Although we do not do so in these exercises, you can check more than one role when creating or editing a role assignment. The user's rights are then the sum of the rights granted by each role.

Managing Role Assignments for Reports Now, let's try managing role assignments for reports:

1. Select the Contents tab.
2. Click Show Details.
3. Click the icon in the Edit column for the RenderingTest report. The properties page for this report appears.
4. Click Security on the left side of the page. The security page for this report appears.

Again, you can see this report is inheriting its role assignments from the folder that contains it—in this case, the Rendering Test Reports folder. Because the user has Content Manager rights for the folder, the user also has Content Manager rights for the report. This means the user can change any and all properties of this report and even delete the report altogether.

To continue our security example, we are going to suppose it is alright for the user to have Content Manager rights for the Rendering Test Reports folder, but not for the RenderingTest report. We need to edit the role assignment for your user. However, before we can do this, we must break the inheritance, as explained in the following steps.

1. Click Edit Item Security. The confirmation dialog box appears.
2. Click OK to confirm.
3. Click the Edit link next to the role assignment giving your user Content Manager rights. The Edit Role Assignment page appears.
4. Uncheck the check box for the Content Manager role.
5. Check the check box for the Browser role.
6. Click Apply to save the changes to your role assignment and return to the security page.
7. Click the Rendering Test Reports link at the top of the page.

Now we modify the rights granted to this user for the SubReportTest report. In our example, because this is a subreport, we assume the user should have limited rights to this report. In fact, they should only be able to review the report. In this case, the predefined Browser role has too many rights. We have to define our own custom role. To do so, follow these steps:

1. Click the icon in the Edit column for the SubReportTest report. The properties page for this report appears.
2. Click Security on the left side of the page. The security page for this report appears.
3. Click Edit Item Security. Click OK to confirm.
4. Click the Edit link next to the role assignment giving your user Content Manager rights. The Edit Role Assignment page appears.
5. Click New Role.
6. Type **View Report** for Name.
7. Type **View Report Only** for Description.
8. Check View Reports.
9. Click OK to save this new role and return to the Edit Role Assignment page.
10. Uncheck the check box for the Content Manager role.
11. Check the check box for the View Report role.
12. Click Apply to save the changes to your role assignment and return to the security page. The user has rights to view the SubReportTest report, but no other rights with that report.

We make one more change to test security. We remove all rights assigned to this user for the DrillthroughTest report:

1. Navigate to the Rendering Test Reports folder.
2. Click the icon in the Edit column for the DrillthroughTest report. The properties page for this report appears.
3. Click Security on the left side of the page. The security page for this report appears.
4. Click Edit Item Security. Click OK to confirm.
5. Check the check box next to the role assignment giving your user Content Manager rights.
6. Click Delete. The confirmation dialog box appears.
7. Click OK to confirm the deletion.

You can now close your browser, log out of Windows, and log on with the user name you have been using in the role assignments. Let's test our security changes:

1. Open the Report Manager in your browser. You should be viewing the contents of the Home folder. Notice no buttons are in the Contents tab toolbar for creating folders and data sources or uploading files, as shown in Figure 10-18. That is because the user you are now logged on as has only Browser rights in this folder.

2. Select the Galactic Delivery Services folder to view its contents. When you are in this folder, the New Folder, New Data Source, Upload File, and Report Builder buttons have returned, as shown in Figure 10-19. In this folder, your user has Content Manager rights.

3. Select the Rendering Test Reports folder to view its contents.

4. Click Show Details.

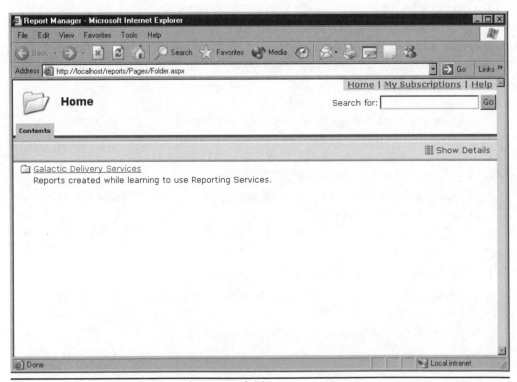

Figure 10-18   *Browser rights in the Home folder*

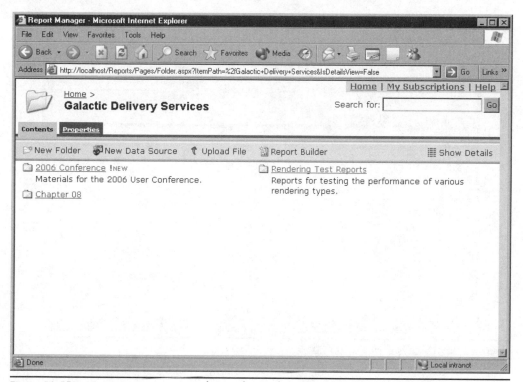

Figure 10-19   *Content Manager rights in the Galactic Delivery Services folder*

5. Click the icon in the Edit column for the RenderingTest report. The properties page for this report appears. Note that Security doesn't appear on the left side of the page, as shown in Figure 10-20. Your user has Browser rights to this report, so you can view the report and its history and create subscriptions, but you cannot change its security. (Don't worry about what subscriptions are right now; we discuss them in Chapter 11.)

6. Click the link for the Rendering Test Reports folder at the top of the page.

7. Click the icon in the Edit column for the SubReportTest report. The properties page for this report appears. Now, the Subscriptions tab is gone, as shown in Figure 10-21. Your user has the rights from our custom View Report role for this report. You can view the report and its history, but you cannot create subscriptions.

8. Click the link for the Rendering Test Reports folder at the top of the page. Notice the DrillthroughTest report is nowhere to be seen because your user does not have any rights for this report, not even the rights to view it.

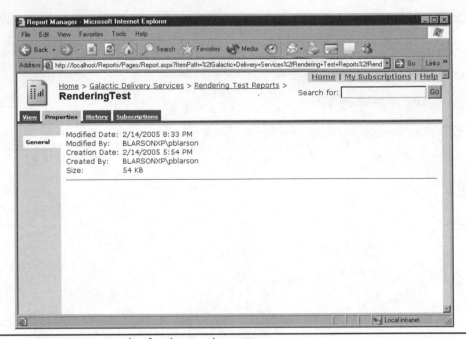

Figure 10-20 *Browser rights for the RenderingTest report*

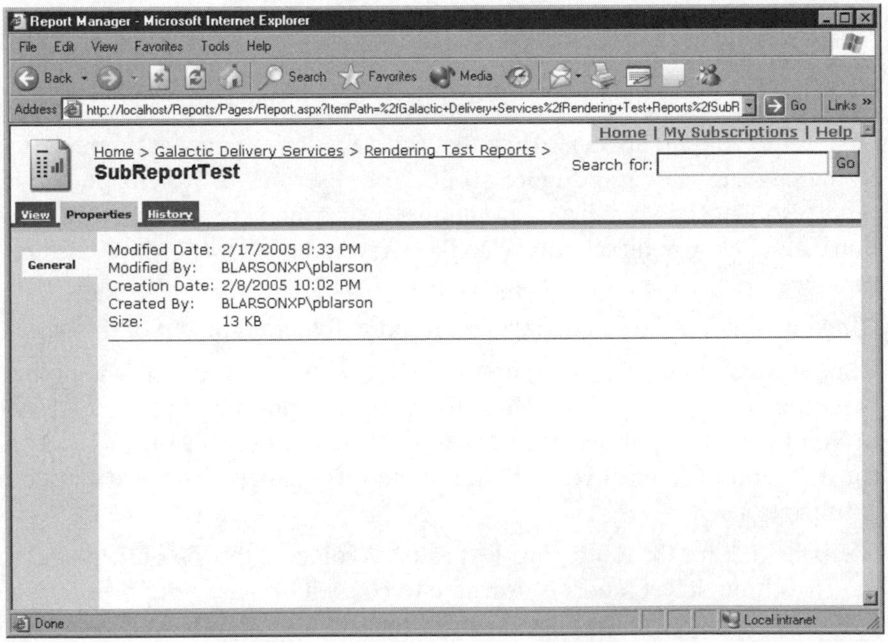

Figure 10-21 *View Report rights for the SubReportTest report*

9. Click the RenderingTest report to execute it.

10. Go to Page 2 of the report. Scroll down to the table below the graph where you see Custer, Inc.

11. The heading Custer, Inc. is a link to the DrillthroughTest report. The problem is, your user does not have any rights to the DrillthroughTest report. Clicking this link results in an insufficient rights error message, as shown in Figure 10-22.

Giving users only the rights they need is important. This prevents users from viewing data they should not see or from making modifications or deletions they should not be allowed to make. On the other hand, providing users with enough rights is important, so their reports function properly. We don't want users to end up with an error message like the one shown in Figure 10-22 when they are trying to do legitimate work.

Role Assignments Using Windows Groups

As mentioned previously, role assignments can be made to Windows users or to Windows groups. If you create your role assignments using Windows users, you need to create a new set of role assignments every time a new user needs to access Reporting Services. This can be extremely tedious if you have a complex set of role assignments for various folders, reports, and resources.

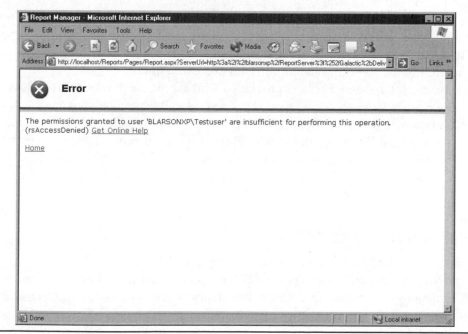

Figure 10-22   *Insufficient rights error*

In most cases, creating role assignments using Windows groups is better. Then, as new users come along, you simply need to add them to the Windows group that has the appropriate rights in Reporting Services. This is much easier!

CAUTION

In some cases, Internet Information Services (IIS) and, therefore, Reporting Services do not immediately recognize changes to group membership. This is because IIS caches some Windows security information, and then works from that cache. Stopping and starting the IIS service causes the IIS security cache to be reloaded with the latest and greatest group membership information.

Linked Reports

In many cases, the security set up within Reporting Services restricts the folders a user can access. The sales department may be allowed to access one set of folders. The personnel department may be allowed to access another set of folders. The personnel department doesn't want to see sales reports and, certainly, some personnel reports should not be seen by everyone in the sales department.

This works well—a place for everything and everything in its place—until you come to the report that needs to be used by both the sales department and the personnel department. You could put a copy of the report in both places, but this gets to be a nightmare as new versions of reports need to be deployed to multiple locations on the Report Server. You could put the report in a third folder accessed by both the sales department and the personnel department, but that can make navigation in the Report Manager difficult and confusing.

Fortunately, Reporting Services provides a third alternative: the linked report. With a *linked report*, your report is deployed to one folder. It is then pointed to by links placed elsewhere within the Report Catalog, as shown in Figure 10-23. To the user, the links look just like a report. Because of these links, the report appears to be in many places. The sales department sees it in their folder. The personnel department sees it in their folder. The fact of the matter is the report is only deployed to one location, so it is easy to administer and maintain.

Creating a Linked Report

To demonstrate a linked report, we are going to make use of the Invoice-Batch Number Report from Chapter 4. This report shows the invoice amounts for companies in various cities. Galactic Delivery Services has sales offices in each of these cities and each sales office has its own folder within the GDS Report Catalog.

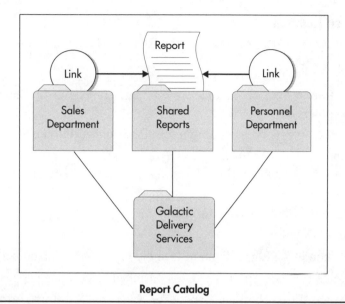

Report Catalog

Figure 10-23   *A linked report*

A sales office should be able to access the Invoice-Batch Number Report in their own folder and see the invoices for customers in their city.

Deploying the Report to a Common Folder

We begin by deploying the report to a common folder. Here are the steps to follow:

1. Log in with a user name and password that has Content Manager rights in Reporting Services.
2. Start Visual Studio or the Business Intelligence Development Studio and open the Chapter04 project.
3. Modify the properties of the Chapter04 project as follows:

Property	Value
TargetDataSourceFolder	GalacticDeliveryServices/DataSources
TargetServerURL	http://ServerName/ReportServer
TargetReportFolder	Galactic Delivery Services/Shared Reports

Replace ServerName with the appropriate server name or with localhost.

4. Deploy the Invoice-Batch Number Report.
5. Close the development environment.

Creating Linked Reports

Now that the report has been deployed to the Report Catalog, it is time to create our linked reports:

1. Open the Report Manager in your browser and navigate to the Galactic Delivery Services folder.

2. Create a new folder. Type **Axelburg** for Name and **Axelburg Sales Office** for Description.

3. Create another new folder. Type **Utonal** for Name and **Utonal Sales Office** for Description.

4. Navigate to the Shared Reports folder.

5. Click Show Details.

6. Click the icon in the Edit column next to the Invoice-Batch Number Report.

7. Click Create Linked Report. The Create Linked Report page appears.

8. Type **Invoice-Batch Number Report** for Name and **Axelburg invoices in each batch** for Description.

9. Click Change Location. The Folder Location page appears.

10. Select the Axelburg folder and click OK to return to the Create Linked Report page.

11. Click OK to create and execute this linked report in the Axelburg folder.

12. Type **01/01/2005** for Enter a Start Date and **12/31/2005** for Enter an End Date. Click View Report.

13. Click the link for the Axelburg folder at the top of the page.

14. Click Hide Details. You can see the linked report we just created looks like a regular report.

15. Navigate back to the Shared Reports folder.

16. Click Show Details.

17. Click the icon in the Edit column next to the Invoice-Batch Number Report.

18. Click Create Linked Report. The Create Linked Report page appears.

19. Type **Invoice-Batch Number Report** for Name and **Utonal invoices in each batch** for Description.

20. Click Change Location. The Folder Location page appears.

21. Select the Utonal folder and click OK to return to the Create Linked Report page.

22. Click OK to create and execute this linked report in the Utonal folder.

23. Select Utonal from the Select a City drop-down list. Type **01/01/2005** for Enter a Start Date and **12/31/2005** for Enter an End Date. Click View Report.

We have now successfully created and tested our two linked reports.

Managing Report Parameters in Report Manager

We have our linked reports, but we have not quite fulfilled all the business needs stated for these linked reports. The Axelburg sales office is supposed to be able to see only their own invoice data. The same is true for the Utonal sales office. We can meet these business needs by managing the report parameters right in the Report Manager. Here are the steps to follow:

1. Navigate to the Axelburg folder. Note the small chain links on the icon for the Invoice-Batch Number Report. This indicates it is a linked report.

2. Click the icon in the Edit column next to the Invoice-Batch Number Report.

3. Click Parameters on the left side of the screen. The Parameter Management page appears. Note, the City parameter has a default of Axelburg. Because this is the Axelburg folder, we leave that default alone. What we modify is the user's ability to change this default value.

4. Uncheck the Prompt User check box in the City row. The user is no longer prompted for a city. Instead, the report always uses the default value. As you may have guessed, you can have a default value, you can prompt the user for the value, or you can do both. You must do at least one of these.

5. Check the Has Default check box in the StartDate row. Type **01/01/2005** for the default value for this row.

6. Check the Has Default check box in the EndDate row. Type **12/31/2005** for the default value for this row.

7. Click Apply to save your changes.

8. Select the View tab.

9. Notice you can no longer select a city. It is always Axelburg. Also, notice we now have default values for the date. Also worth noting is these default values are much easier to modify than the default values that are part of the report, because we can make changes without having to redeploy the report.

10. Navigate to the Utonal folder.

11. Click the icon in the Edit column next to the Invoice-Batch Number Report.

12. Click Parameters on the left side of the screen.

13. Change the City field's default parameter to Utonal.

14. Uncheck the Prompt User check box in the City row.

15. Check the Has Default check box in the StartDate row. Type **01/01/2005** for the default value for this row.

16. Check the Has Default check box in the EndDate row. Type **12/31/2005** for the default value for this row.

17. Click Apply to save your changes.

18. Select the View tab.

Now we have the linked reports working just the way we need them. Not only did we simplify things by not deploying the report in multiple places, but we also were able to hardcode parameter values for each linked report.

Delivering the Goods

In this chapter, you learned how to put the reports where your users could come and get them. Your users were set up to pull the reports off the Report Server. In the next chapter, you learn how to deliver the goods right to the users. In Chapter 11, the Report Server pushes the reports out to the users. The pull-and-push capabilities combine to give Reporting Services some powerful tools for putting information in the hands of the users, right where it needs to be.

Delivering the Goods: Report Delivery

I n the previous chapter, we moved from the development environment to the Report Server. The Report Server enables us to make our reports available to end users. We reviewed the various ways reports and their supporting resources can be moved from the development environment to the Report Server. We also reviewed the security features the Report Server provides.

In addition to all this, we looked at the Report Manager interface, which provides users with one method of accessing reports on the Report Server. In this chapter, you learn about additional ways to take reports from the Report Server to the users. You also learn ways to manage how and when reports are executed. These features can be used to level out server load and to increase user response time.

Caching In

One of the best features of Reporting Services is that the data is requeried each time the report is executed. This is shown in Figure 11-1. The user is not viewing information from a static web page that is weeks or months old. Reporting Services reports include data accurate up to the second the report was run.

This feature can also be the source of one of the drawbacks of Reporting Services. The user is required to wait for the data to be requeried each time a report is run.

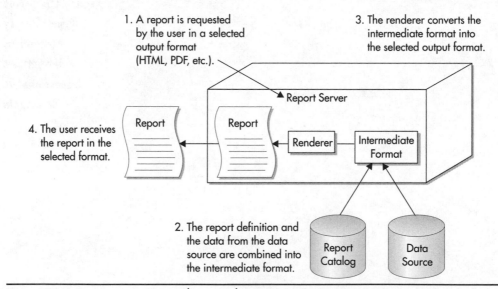

Figure 11-1 *Serving a report without caching*

If your query or stored procedure runs quickly, this may not be a problem. However, even fairly quick queries can slow down a server if enough of them are running at the same time.

Fortunately, Reporting Services has a solution to this problem. The solution is report caching.

Report Caching

With many reports, it is not essential to have up-to-the-second data. You may be reporting from a data source that is only updated once or twice a day. The business needs of your users may only require data that is accurate as of the end of the previous business period, perhaps a month or a quarter. In these types of situations, it does not make sense to have the data requeried every time a user requests a report. Report caching is the answer.

Report caching is an option that can be turned on individually for each report on the Report Server. When this option is turned on, the Report Server saves a copy, or *instance*, of the report in a temporary location the first time the report is executed, as shown in Figure 11-2.

On subsequent executions, with the same parameter values chosen, the Report Server pulls the information necessary to render the report from the report cache, rather than requerying data from the database, as shown in Figure 11-3. Because these subsequent executions do not need to requery data, they are, in most cases, faster than the report execution without caching.

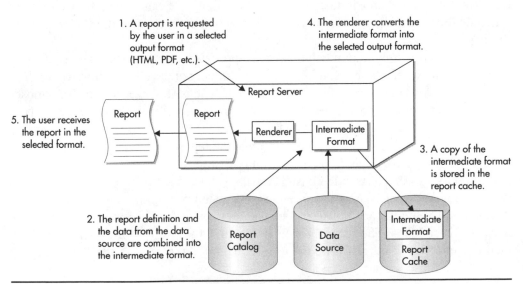

Figure 11-2   *Serving a report with caching, the first time*

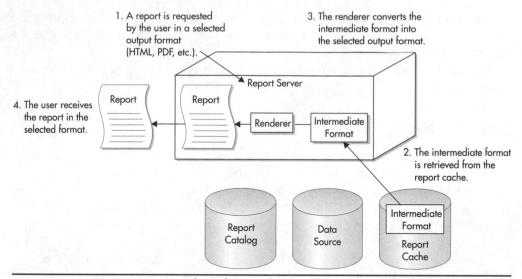

1. A report is requested by the user in a selected output format (HTML, PDF, etc.).

3. The renderer converts the intermediate format into the selected output format.

Report Server

4. The user receives the report in the selected format.

Report

Report

Renderer

Intermediate Format

2. The intermediate format is retrieved from the report cache.

Report Catalog

Data Source

Intermediate Format

Report Cache

Figure 11-3   *Serving a report with caching, subsequent times*

Cached Report Expiration

Once an instance of the report is stored in the report cache, it is assigned an expiration date and time. The expiration date and time can be calculated in one of two ways. The expiration date can be calculated based on a certain number of minutes after the creation of the cached instance. For example, the cached instance of the report exists for 30 minutes, and then it is deleted. Or, the expiration date can be determined by a set schedule. For example, the cached instance of the report is deleted at 2:00 A.M. every Sunday morning.

The first type of expiration calculation is appropriate for a report that requires a large amount of database resources and is run often, but does not require up-to-the-second data. We can decrease the workload on the database server by fulfilling most of the requests for the report from the report cache. Every 30 minutes, we throw the cached report away. The next person who requests the report causes a new instance of the report, with updated data, to be placed in the report cache.

The second type of expiration calculation is appropriate for reports run against data that changes on a scheduled basis. Perhaps you have a report being run from your data warehouse. The data warehouse is updated from your transactional database each Sunday at 12:30 A.M. The data in the warehouse remains static in between these loads. The cached report is scheduled to expire right after the data load is completed. The next time the user requests the report after the expiration, a new instance of the report, with the updated data, is placed in the cache. This cached report contains up-to-date data until the next data load.

Cached Reports and Data Source Credentials

To create a cached instance of a report, the report must be using stored credentials. These can be credentials for either a Windows logon or a database logon, but they must be stored with the data source. If you think about this from a security standpoint, this is how it has to be.

Suppose for a minute that Reporting Services allowed a cached report to be created with Windows Integrated Security. The Windows credentials of the first person to run the report would be used to create a cached instance of the report. Subsequent users who request this report would receive this cached instance. However, this would mean the subsequent users are receiving data in the report created using the credentials from another user.

If the results of the database query or stored procedure that populates this report vary based on the rights of the database login, we have the potential for a big problem. If the vice president of sales is the first person to run the report and create the cached instance, all subsequent users would receive information meant only for the VP! Conversely, if a sales representative is the first person to run the report and create the cached instance, when the VP comes along later and requests the report, he will not receive all the information he needs.

The same problem exists if the report prompts for credentials. The first person who runs the report and creates the cached instance is the one who supplies the credentials. Everyone who views the cached instance is essentially using someone else's logon to see this data.

The only way that caching works without creating the potential for a security problem is with credentials stored with the report. In this situation, the same credentials are used to access the database—whether it is the VP or a lowly sales representative running the report. There is no risk that the cached instance of the report will create a breach in database security.

Caching and Report Formats

As you can see in Figure 11-2, the intermediate format of the report, and not the final format of the report, is stored in the report cache. The intermediate format is a combination of the report definition and the data from the datasets. It is not formatted as an HTML page, a PDF document, or other type of rendering format. It is an internal format ready for rendering.

Because the intermediate format is stored in the report cache, the cached report can be delivered in any rendering format. The user who first requested the report and, thus, caused the cache instance to be created, may have received the report as an HTML document. The next user may receive the cached instance of the report and export it to a PDF document. A third user may receive the cached instance of the report and export it to an Excel file. Caching the intermediate format gives the report cache the maximum amount of flexibility.

Enabling Report Caching

Let's try enabling caching for one of our deployed reports. We have a report that is a good candidate for caching. The Weather report takes a long time to execute because of the calls to the web service. Also, the weather conditions returned by the web service are not going to change from minute-to-minute, so it is not essential to retrieve new information every time the report is executed. The Weather report works just fine if it is retrieved from the cache, as long as we expire the cached instance fairly often, say, every 45 minutes.

Enabling Report Caching for the Weather Report

Let's try enabling caching for the Weather report.

1. Open the Report Manager and navigate to the Chapter 08 folder.
2. Click Show Details.
3. Click the icon in the Edit column for the Weather report. The Properties page for the Weather report appears.
4. Select Execution from the left side of the screen. The Execution Properties page appears, as shown in Figure 11-4.
5. Select the option "Cache a temporary copy of the report. Expire copy of report after a number of minutes."
6. Set the number of minutes to 45.
7. Click Apply.
8. Select the View tab. Check (Select All) in the Select Planets drop-down list and click View Report. The Weather report runs.

The first time the Weather report runs after caching is turned on, the report needs to perform its regular execution process to gather the data for the intermediate format. This intermediate format is then copied to the report cache before it is rendered for you in the browser. Because the report goes through its regular execution process, it still takes a while to appear.

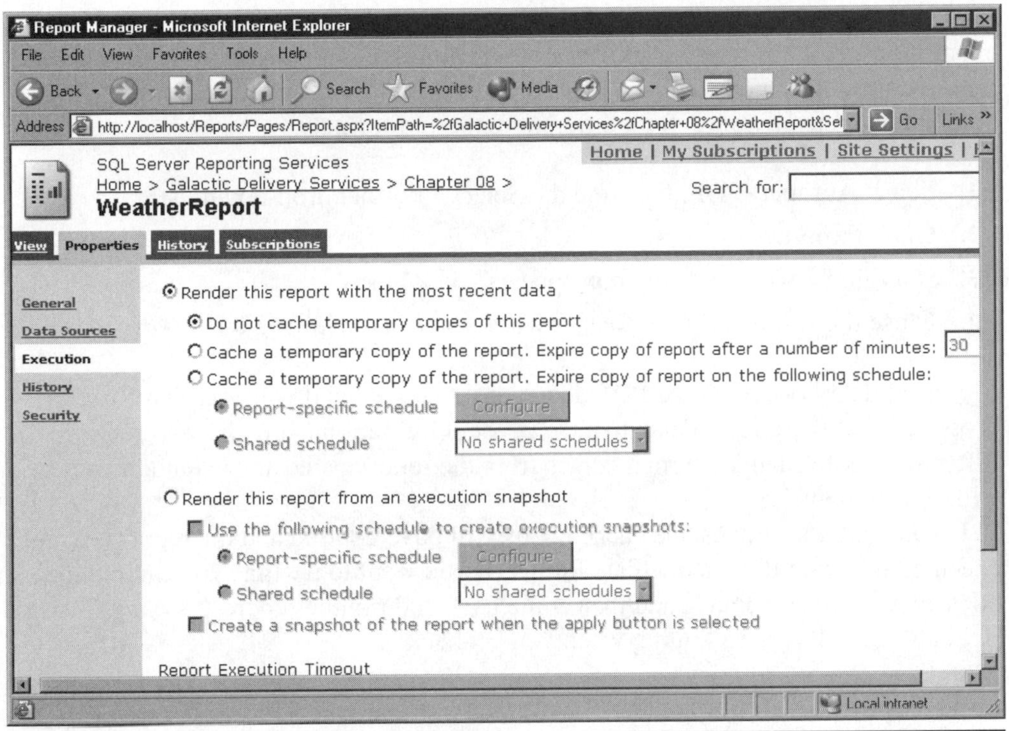

Figure 11-4   *The Execution Properties page*

Viewing the Report from the Report Cache

Now let's run the report again. Because a cached copy of the report has not expired, the report is rendered from the cached copy.

1. Click the Refresh Report button in the toolbar. The report appears almost immediately. That happened so fast, I bet you don't even believe it retrieved the report. Let's try it again another way.

2. Click the Chapter 08 link at the top of the page.

3. Click the WeatherReport link in the Name column to run this report.

4. Check (Select All) in the Select Planets drop-down list and click View Report.

NOTE

Be sure to make the same parameter selection each time you run this test. We discuss how report parameters affect caching in the section "Report Caching and Report Parameters."

Pretty slick! The Report Server doesn't need to retrieve any data, execute any expressions, call any assemblies, or create the intermediate format. All it needs to do is convert the intermediate format into the rendered format (in this case, HTML).

What happens if we ask for a different rendering format?

1. Select Acrobat (PDF) file from the Select a Format drop-down list.
2. Click Export.
3. If a File Download dialog box appears, click Open.
4. Close the Adobe Acrobat Reader when you finish viewing the report.

A brief delay occurs as the PDF document is created and your Acrobat Reader is opened, but there is no delay to retrieve the information using the web service. Instead, the intermediate format comes from the report cache and is rendered into a PDF document.

If you wait 45 minutes, the cached copy will have expired and the report is again executed to create the intermediate format. If you want to try this, you can put the book down, go have lunch, and then come back and run the report. It's okay. You go right ahead. I'll be here waiting when you get back.

Cache Expiration on a Schedule

You have just learned the weather web service we are using for our Weather report is updated every hour on the hour. It makes sense for us to set our cached copy of this report to expire on this same schedule. The cached copy should expire at five minutes past the hour, so a new copy of the weather information shows up the next time the report is run after the web service information is updated.

1. Navigate to the Weather report in the Report Manager, if you are not already there.
2. Select the Properties tab. The Properties page appears.
3. Select Execution from the left side of the screen. The Execution Properties page appears.
4. Select "Cache a temporary copy of the report. Expire copy of report on the following schedule."
5. Report-Specific Schedule is selected by default. Click Configure next to Report-Specific Schedule. The Schedule page appears, as shown in Figure 11-5.
6. You can specify hourly, daily, weekly, monthly, or one-time schedules. Select Hour.

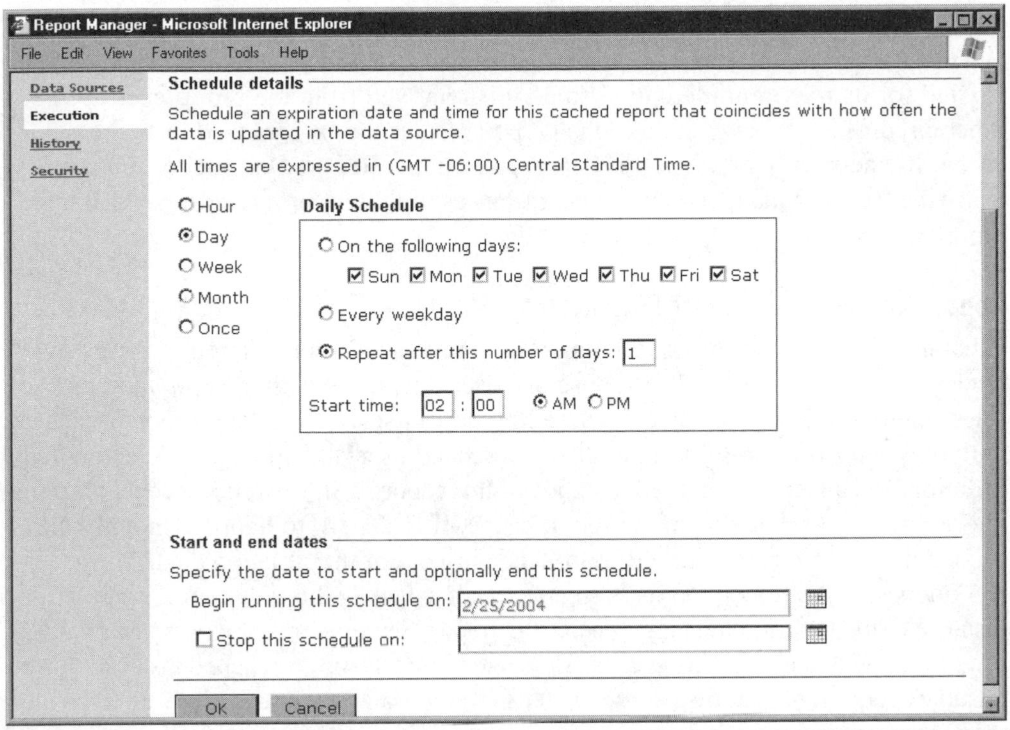

Figure 11-5   *The Schedule page*

7. Leave the Hourly Schedule set to run every 1 hours 00 minutes. Set Start Time to five minutes after the next hour. (If it is 2:30 P.M. now, set Start Time to 3:05 P.M.)

8. Today's date should be selected for Begin Running This Schedule On. Leave the field Stop This Schedule On blank. (You change these dates by clicking the calendar icon to the right of the entry area. You cannot type in the date directly.)

9. Click OK to return to the Execution Properties page. Note the description of the schedule you just created under Report-Specific Schedule.

10. Click Apply to save your changes to the report cache settings.

11. Select the View tab. Check (Select All) in the Select Planets drop-down list and click View Report. The Weather report runs.

Again, the report takes longer to execute the first time as the intermediate format is created and put into the report cache. This cached instance of the report remains there until five minutes past the hour.

Report Cache and Deploying

When a cached report instance expires, either because of a schedule or because it has existed for its maximum length of time, it is removed from the report cache. One other circumstance can cause a cached report instance to be removed from the report cache. If a new copy of a report is deployed from the Report Designer or uploaded using the Report Manager, any cached instances of that report are removed from the report cache.

Report Caching and Report Parameters

What happens with our report caching if different users enter different parameters when the report is executed? Suppose one user runs the Weather Report and only selects Borlaron from the Select Planets drop-down list. The Weather Report is cached with only the Borlaron information. Now a second user runs the report selecting only Stilation. Because a nonexpired instance of this report is in the report cache, it seems the report should come from the report cache. If this were to happen, though, the second user would receive the Borlaron data instead of the Stilation data.

   Fortunately, the Report Server is smart enough to handle this situation. As part of the instance of the report in the report cache, the Report Server stores any parameter values used to create that cached instance, as shown in Figure 11-6. The cached instance is used to satisfy requests made by a subsequent user only if all the parameters used to create the cached instance match the parameters entered by the subsequent user.

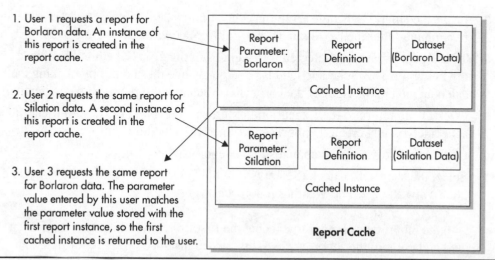

Figure 11-6   *Report caching with parameters*

Report Caching and Security

Not all users can change report-caching properties. To change the report caching properties for a report, you must have rights to the Manage Reports task. Of the four predefined security roles, the Content Manager, My Reports, and Publisher roles have rights to this task.

Execution Snapshots

Report caching is a great tool for improving the performance of reports with long execution times, but one problem still exists. The first user who requests the report after the cached instance has expired must wait for the report to be created from the underlying data. It would be nice if there were a way to have cached report instances created automatically, so no user has to endure these wait times. Fortunately, Reporting Services can do this as well.

An *execution snapshot* is another way to create a cached report instance. Up to this point, we have discussed situations where cached report instances are created as the result of a user action. A user requests a report, and a copy of that report's intermediate format is placed in the report cache. With execution snapshots, a cached report instance is created automatically.

Execution snapshots can create cached report instances on a scheduled basis or they can be created as soon as this feature is turned on for a particular report. If a schedule is used, each time the schedule is run, it replaces the current cached instance with a new one. Cached report instances created by an execution snapshot are used to satisfy user report requests the same as any other cached report instance.

Enabling Execution Snapshots

You can enable the creation of execution snapshots using two methods. Let's look at the manual method first.

Manually Creating an Execution Snapshot

Let's try enabling execution snapshots for the Weather report:

1. Navigate to the Weather report in the Report Manager, if you are not already there.
2. Select the Properties tab. The Properties page appears.

3. Select Execution from the left side of the screen. The Execution Properties page appears.

4. Select the option Render This Report from a Report Execution Snapshot.

5. Check the Create a Report Snapshot When You Click the Apply Button on This Page check box.

6. Click Apply. Note the error message that appears next to the execution snapshot option. When an execution snapshot is created, it is done as a background process, so no one will be available to select a value for the report parameter. Because this parameter has no default value, the Report Server does not know what value to use for the report parameter when the report is run by the schedule. Let's provide a default value for the parameter so we can proceed.

7. Select Parameters from the left side of the screen. The Parameters page appears.

8. Check the box in the Has Default column.

9. Enter the following in the Default Value drop-down edit area:

    AFU
    BLN
    NOX
    RKM
    SLN
    SRA

    (We need to enter the values passed to the parameter, in this case, the planet abbreviations, not the planet names that are displayed in the drop-down list. Each value should be entered on a separate line.)

10. Click Apply to save the default value.

11. Let's try to set up snapshot execution again. Select Execution from the left side of the screen. The Execution Properties page appears.

12. Select the option Render This Report from a Report Execution Snapshot.

13. Check the Create a Report Snapshot When You Click the Apply Button on This Page check box.

14. Click Apply. As soon as you click Apply, the Report Server executes the report and places an instance of the report in the report cache. Allow time for this process to complete.

15. Select the View tab.

The report is rendered from the cached report instance created by the execution snapshot.

Creating Execution Snapshots on a Schedule

Now let's try the scheduled approach to creating execution snapshots:

1. Select the Properties tab. The Execution Properties page should appear. If not, select Execution from the left side of the page.

2. Check the Use the Following Schedule to Create Report Execution Snapshots check box.

3. Report-Specific Schedule is selected by default. Click Configure next to Report-Specific Schedule. The Schedule page appears.

4. You can specify hourly, daily, weekly, monthly, or one-time schedules. The Day option should be selected by default. Leave this option selected.

5. Select On the Following Days.

6. Uncheck all the days except for today. (If you are reading this on Monday, for example, leave only Monday checked.)

7. Set the start time to five minutes from now.

8. Select today's date for Begin Running This Schedule On.

9. Check the box Stop This Schedule On, and then select tomorrow's date.

NOTE

I know this schedule does not fit the stated business requirements of refreshing the report at five minutes past the hour. However, you probably don't want to waste computer resources generating an execution snapshot of the Weather report hour after hour, day after day, so we use this schedule for the demonstration.

10. Click OK to return to the Execution Properties page. Note the description of the schedule you just created under Report-Specific Schedule.

11. Click Apply to save your changes to the execution snapshot settings. After five minutes, the scheduled execution snapshot will create a cached instance of the report.

12. Select the View tab after five minutes. (Go grab some caffeine while you are waiting. You wouldn't want to fall asleep while you are working through all this good stuff!) The Weather report runs and is rendered from the cached report instance created by your scheduled execution snapshot.

This type of execution snapshot schedule would be appropriate for a report whose underlying data is changed only periodically (again, think of a data warehouse updated from a transactional system). The execution snapshot would be scheduled to create a new cached instance of the report right after the new data is available in the warehouse.

Execution Snapshots and Security

Not all users can change execution snapshots. To change the execution snapshot properties for a report, you must have rights to the Manage Reports task. Of the four predefined security roles, the Content Manager, My Reports, and Publisher roles have rights to this task.

Report History

The *report history* feature of the Report Manager enables you to keep copies of a report's past execution. This lets you save the state of your data without having to save copies of the data itself. You can keep documentation of inventory levels, production schedules, or financial records. You can look back in time, using the report history to do trend analysis or to verify past information.

Enabling Report History

To demonstrate the report history feature of Reporting Services, we need a report whose results change often. It just so happens we have such a report in our Chapter08 solution. The TransportMonitor report provides different values every time the report is run. We can move that report to the Report Server, and then enable the report history.

1. Open the Report Manager and navigate to the Chapter 08 folder.
2. Use the Upload File button to upload the TransportMonitor report from the Chapter 08 solution.
3. Select Show Details, if it is available in the report viewer toolbar. If it is unavailable, you are already in Show Details mode.
4. Click the icon in the Edit column for the TransportMonitor report. The Properties page appears.
5. Click Parameters on the left side of the page. The Parameters page appears.
6. Click the Has Default check box and type **1304** for Default Value.
7. Click Apply.
8. Click Data Sources on the left side of the page. The Data Sources page appears.
9. Click Browse. The Data Source page appears.
10. Use the tree view to find the 2006 Conference folder in the tree structure. The 2006 Conference folder is inside thc Galactic Delivery Services folder.
11. Select the Galactic shared data source and click OK.

12. Click Apply.

13. Click History on the left side of the page. The History Properties page appears, as shown in Figure 11-7.

14. Make sure the Allow History to Be Created Manually check box is checked. If it is not, check it and click Apply.

15. Click the View tab at the top of the page. Remember, this report has autorefresh set. After a few seconds, the report refreshes and new data is displayed.

Manually Creating a Report History Snapshot

One way to create a report history is to do so manually. We can give this a try in the following example:

1. Select the History tab. (This is the History tab along the top, not the History link on the left side of the page.) The Create/View History page appears.

2. Click the New Snapshot button in the report viewer toolbar. An entry for a report history snapshot appears.

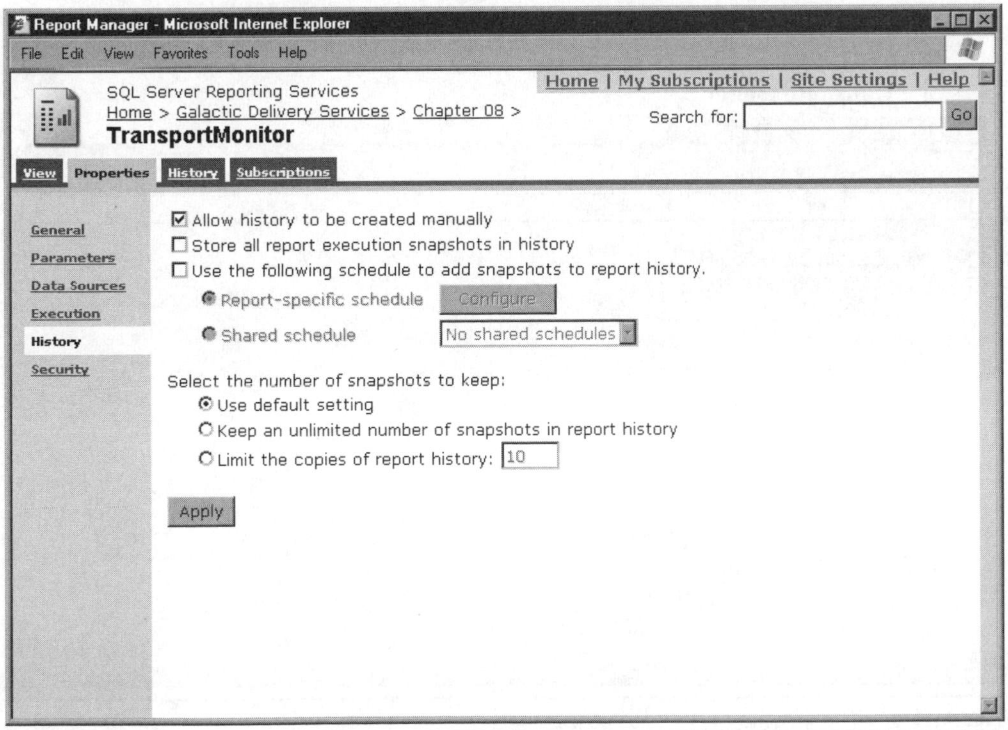

Figure 11-7   *The History Properties page*

3. Click the New Snapshot button two more times to create two more report history snapshots, as shown in Figure 11-8.

4. Click the link in the When Run column to the first report history snapshot you created. This report should appear in a new browser window.

5. Open the other two report history snapshots and compare all three.

   As with the cached report instances, the report history snapshots store the intermediate format of the report. Because of this, you can export this report to any of the rendering formats.

1. Select one of your browser windows containing a report history snapshot.

2. Export the snapshot to the Acrobat (PDF) file format and open it in Adobe Acrobat Reader.

3. Close Acrobat Reader and the browser windows containing your report history snapshots.

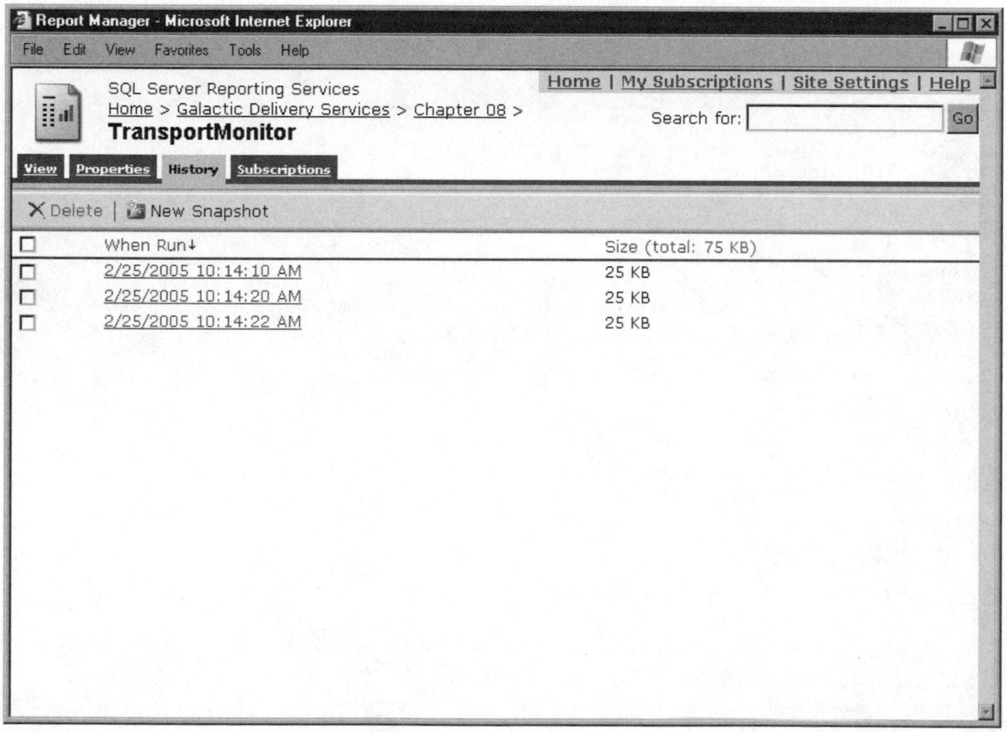

Figure 11-8 *The Create/View History page*

Report History Snapshots and Report Parameters

To make our TransportMonitor report work with report history snapshots, we had to provide a default value for the transport number parameter. These parameters cannot be changed when each snapshot is created. (They can be changed, however, if the report is run normally through the Report Manager.)

Essentially, we are saving report history snapshots for only one transport. To save report history snapshots for other transports, we need to create linked reports with parameters defaulted to the other transport numbers.

1. Select the Properties tab.
2. Click General on the left side of the page.
3. Click Create Linked Report.
4. Type **Transport 1305 Monitor** for Name and **The Transport Monitor Report for Transport 1305** for Description.
5. Click OK. The linked report executes.
6. Select the Properties tab.
7. Click Parameters on the left side of the page.
8. Change Default Value to **1305**.
9. Click Apply.
10. Click the History tab.
11. Click New Snapshot.
12. Click the entry for the new snapshot to view it. You can see this is a snapshot for transport number 1305.
13. Close the browser window containing your report history snapshot.

We can create as many linked reports as we need to collect report history snapshots for the different possible parameter values. Remember, linked reports all point back to a single report definition. If the TransportMonitor report is ever updated, it only needs to be deployed in one location, and all the linked reports will have the updated report definition.

Additional Methods for Creating Report History Snapshots

You can create report history snapshots in two other ways, in addition to the manual method just described. You can instruct the Report Server to create a report history snapshot each time it creates an execution snapshot. With this setting turned on, any time the Report Server creates an execution snapshot—either manually or on a scheduled basis—a copy of that execution snapshot is saved as a report history snapshot.

You can also set up a schedule to create your report history snapshots. Let's give that a try:

1. Click the Chapter 08 link at the top of the page.

2. Click the icon in the Edit column for the TransportMonitor report. (The original report, not the linked copy.) The Properties page appears.

3. Click History on the left side of the page.

4. Check the Use the Following Schedule to Add Snapshots to Report History check box.

5. Report-Specific Schedule is selected by default. Click Configure next to Report-Specific Schedule. The Schedule page appears.

6. Select Hour.

7. Change the Hourly Schedule to run every 0 hours 1 minutes. Set Start Time to five minutes from now.

8. Today's date should be selected for Begin Running This Schedule On.

9. Check the Stop This Schedule On check box and set it to tomorrow's date.

10. Click OK to return to the History Properties page. Note the description of the schedule you just created under Report-Specific Schedule.

11. Click Apply to save your changes to the history snapshot settings.

12. Select the History tab.

As each minute passes beyond the time you chose for the schedule to start, a new report history snapshot is created. You need to refresh your browser to see the new history snapshots in the list.

Report History Snapshots and Security

Not all users can change report history snapshot properties. To change the report history snapshot properties for a report, you must have rights to the Manage Report History task. Of the four predefined security roles, the Content Manager and My Reports roles have rights to this task.

Managing Report History Snapshots

You will not usually have a report that requires a new report history snapshot every minute of the day, as we set up in our example. Even so, report history snapshots can start to pile up if you let them. Making business decisions about the number of history snapshots to save for each report is important. Even more important, then, is to implement those business decisions and manage the number of history snapshots being saved on the Report Server.

Setting Limits on the Number of Report History Snapshots

Reporting Services provides a way to limit the number of history snapshots saved for any given report. Let's take a look and put a limit on our TransportMonitor report snapshots at the same time.

1. Select the Properties tab.
2. In the Select the Number of Snapshots to Keep section of the page, select the Limit the Copies of Report History option.
3. Set the limit to 5.
4. Click Apply to save your changes to the history snapshot settings.
5. Click OK in response to the warning dialog box.
6. Select the History tab.

If you waited long enough to accumulate more than five report history snapshots, you see the list was reduced to the five most recent history snapshots. The older history snapshots were automatically deleted. As each new history snapshot is created, the oldest history snapshot is deleted, so the total always remains at five. Again, remember, you need to refresh your browser to see these changes as each minute passes.

We chose to set a limit on the number of history snapshots saved for this report. In addition to this option, you have two others to choose from (see Figure 11-7). You can keep an unlimited number of history snapshots, or you can use the default setting for history snapshot retention. You see how to change this default setting in the section "Configuration Options and Default Values."

Manually Deleting Report History Snapshots

In addition to using the history snapshot limit on the History Properties page, you can also manually delete unwanted history snapshots.

1. Refresh your browser.

CAUTION

If you reached the limit of five history snapshots, the Report Server is automatically deleting old history snapshots as new ones are created. If your Create/View History page is not current, you could try to delete a history snapshot that has already been removed by the Report Server. This results in an error.

2. Check the check box in the Delete column for three of the snapshot history entries.

3. Click Delete in the History tab toolbar.

4. Click OK to confirm the deletion.

The Report Server again accumulates history snapshots for this report until it has reached our five snapshot limit. At that point, it again deletes the oldest history snapshot as each new one is created.

Disabling Report History Snapshot Creation

We can now disable the creation of report history snapshots for this report, so we are not wasting valuable execution cycles.

1. Select the Properties tab.

2. Uncheck the Use the Following Schedule to Add Snapshots to Report History check box.

3. Click Apply.

4. Select the History tab.

New history snapshots are no longer created for this report on a scheduled basis. Note, however, that the existing history snapshots were not deleted. These history snapshots are still available for viewing, even though the schedule that created them was disabled.

Updating Report Definitions and Report History Snapshots

One of the best features of report history snapshots is this: they are not lost if the definition of the underlying report is changed. Let's see this in action.

1. Start Visual Studio or the Business Intelligence Development Studio and open the Chapter 08 solution.

2. Open the TransportMonitor report layout.

3. Select the Data tab. Select the TransportMonitor dataset.

4. Click the ellipsis button (. . .) to view the Dataset dialog box.

5. Select the Filters tab.

6. Select =Fields!Item.Value from the Expression column drop-down list. Select != from the Operator column drop-down list. Enter **Thruster** in the Value column. This filter removes the thruster data from the report.

7. Click OK to exit the Dataset dialog box.

8. Select the Preview tab. Check 1304 in the Transports drop-down list and click View Report. Note the Thruster graph is missing.

9. Click Save All in the toolbar.

10. Right-click the TransportMonitor report in the Solution Explorer and select Deploy from the Context menu.

11. After the deployment has succeeded, close Visual Studio or the Business Intelligence Development Studio.

12. Return to the Report Manager in your browser.

13. Select the View tab for the TransportMonitor report. Note, the report now includes our change, eliminating the thruster data from the report.

14. Select the History tab. We still have some report history snapshots based on the old report definition.

15. Click New Snapshot to manually create a report history snapshot based on the new report definition. Our five history-snapshot limit is still in effect, so one of the old history snapshots may have to be deleted to make room for the new one.

16. Click the most recent history snapshot to view it. It does not contain thruster data because it is based on the new report definition.

17. Close this browser window.

18. Click the oldest history snapshot to view it. It does contain thruster data because it is based on the old report definition.

19. Close this browser window.

Just like the cached report instance, the report history snapshot contains both the report definition and the dataset. Therefore, it is unaffected by subsequent changes to the report definition.

Subscriptions

Up to this point, we have discussed only one way for users to receive reports. They log on to the Report Manager site, find the report they want, and execute it, which is known as *pull* technology. The user pulls the information out of Reporting Services by initiating the execution of the report.

Reporting Services also supports push technology for delivering reports. In a *push* technology scenario, Reporting Services initiates the execution of the report, and then sends the report to the user. This is done through the report subscription.

Standard Subscriptions

Reporting Services supports several types of *subscriptions*. The first is the *standard* subscription, which is a request to push a particular report to a particular user or set of users. The standard subscription is usually a self-serve operation. A user logs on to the Report Manager site and finds the report they want. The user then creates the subscription by specifying the schedule for the push delivery and the delivery options.

Standard subscriptions have two delivery options: e-mail and file share. The *e-mail delivery* option, of course, sends an e-mail to the specified e-mail addresses with a link to the report or with the report itself either embedded as HTML or as an attached document. The *file share* option creates a file containing the report in a specified folder on a file share. The file share option can be used to place the report into a document store managed and/or indexed by another application, such as Microsoft's SharePoint Portal Services.

Creating a Standard E-Mail Subscription with an Embedded Report

You have been hired as the traffic manager for Galactic Delivery Services and are responsible for routing transport traffic. As part of your job, it is important to know what the weather is like at all the hubs. Rather than taking the time to go look at the Weather report on the Report Manager website, you want to have the report e-mailed to you hourly.

1. Open the Report Manager and navigate to the Chapter 08 folder.
2. Click the entry for the Weather report.
3. Select the Subscriptions tab. The Create/View Subscriptions page appears.
4. Click New Subscription. The Subscription Properties page appears, as shown in Figure 11-9.
5. The Delivered By drop-down list defaults to Report Server E-Mail. Leave this set to the default setting.
6. Type your e-mail address for To. Note, you can enter multiple e-mail addresses, separated by a semicolon (;), and you can also enter e-mail addresses for Cc and Bcc.
7. Enter an e-mail address for Reply-To. This can be your own e-mail address, someone else's, or a dummy e-mail address that does not even exist.
8. By default, the subject of the e-mail is the name of the report, followed by the time the report was executed. Change Subject to @**ReportName**.
9. Leave the Include Report check box checked. This includes the report in the e-mail. Uncheck the Include Link check box.

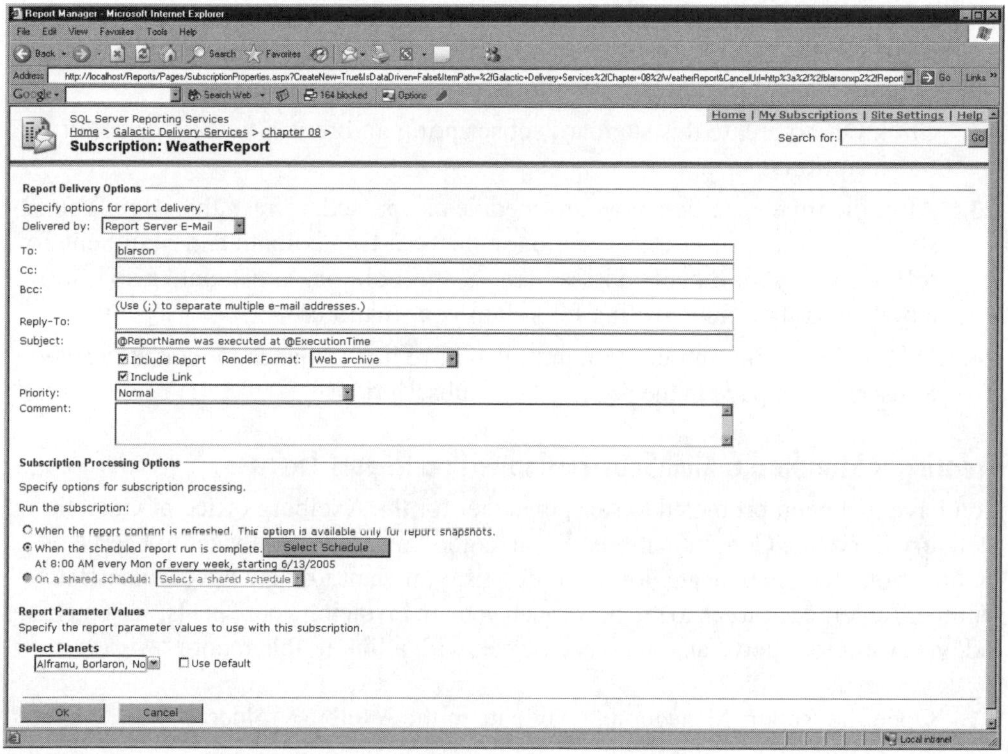

Figure 11-9   *The Subscription Properties page*

10.   The Render Format drop-down list defaults to Web Archive. Leave this selected.

11.   Select High from the Priority drop-down list.

12.   For Comment, type **This e-mail was sent from Reporting Services**.

13.   For Run the Subscription, select the option When the Scheduled Report Run Is Complete.

14.   Click Select Schedule. The Schedule page appears.

15.   Select Hour.

16.   Leave the schedule to run every 1 hour and 00 minutes. Set the start time to five minutes from now.

17.   Today's date should be selected for Begin Running This Schedule On.

18.   Check Stop This Schedule On and select tomorrow's date.

19.   Click OK to return to the Schedule Properties page.

20. Note the default parameter values for this report appear in the Report Parameter Values section of this report. If necessary, you can specify parameters to use when running this subscription. Leave the parameter set to its default.

21. Click OK to create this standard subscription and return to the View/Edit Subscriptions page.

23. After the time specified by your schedule has passed, refresh this page. You should see the time of the execution in the Last Run column and Mail Sent To followed by your e-mail address in the Status column. You should also have a high-priority e-mail waiting for you in your mailbox.

24. Do not delete this subscription until you have had a chance to look at the My Subscriptions page in the section "My Subscriptions."

Creating a Standard E-Mail Subscription with a Report Link

You have just been promoted to sales manager for the Axelburg office of Galactic Delivery Services. Congratulations! Being a good manager, you want to keep tabs on how your salespeople are doing. To do this, you want to view the Invoice-Batch Number Report each week to see how much you are invoicing your clients. As a memory aid, you want to receive an e-mail each week with a link to this report.

1. Open the Report Manager and navigate to the Axelburg folder.

2. Click the Invoice-Batch Number Report to execute it.

3. Click New Subscription in the toolbar for the View tab. The Subscription Properties page appears.

4. Delivered By defaults to Report Server E-Mail. Leave this as the default setting.

5. Type your e-mail address for To.

6. Enter an e-mail address for Reply-To.

7. Change Subject to @**ReportName**.

8. Uncheck the Include Report check box. Leave the Include Link check box checked.

9. Render Format is not used because we are just embedding a link to the report.

10. Select High from the Priority drop-down list.

11. For Comment, type **Remember to check the invoice amounts**.

12. For Run the Subscription, select the option When the Scheduled Report Run Is Complete.

13. Click Select Schedule. The Schedule page appears.

14. Select Week.

15. Leave Repeat After This Number of Weeks set to 1.

16. Check Today for On day(s). For example, Check Mon if today is Monday. Uncheck all the other days.

17. Set the start time to five minutes from now.

18. Today's date should be selected for Begin Running This Schedule On.

19. Check Stop This Schedule On and select tomorrow's date.

20. Click OK to return to the Schedule Properties page.

21. At the bottom of the Schedule Properties page, you see a list of the parameters for the selected report. Leave the default values for the parameters.

22. Click OK to create this standard subscription and return to the Report Viewer page.

When the scheduled time has passed, you will receive an e-mail with a link to this report.

Standard Subscriptions and Execution Snapshots

In addition to creating your own schedule for your standard subscriptions, you can also synchronize your subscriptions with scheduled execution snapshots. For example, the Weather report is set to create an execution snapshot every hour. We want to receive an e-mail with the new version of the report after each new execution snapshot has been created.

One way to do this is to keep the schedule for the execution snapshot synchronized with the schedule for the subscription. The execution snapshot runs, and then the subscription runs one minute later. This can cause problems if the execution snapshot occasionally takes more than one minute to create or if one of the schedules is edited.

A better solution is to let the creation of the execution snapshot drive the delivery of the subscription. The When the Report Content Is Refreshed option does just that (refer to Figure 11-9). When this option is selected for a subscription, the subscription is sent out every time a new execution snapshot is created. Of course, this option is only available for reports that have execution snapshots enabled.

Multiple Subscriptions for One Report

Nothing prevents a user from creating more than one subscription for the same report. Perhaps you want a report delivered every Friday and on the last day of the month. You can't do this with one subscription, but you can certainly do it with two—a weekly subscription for the Friday delivery and a monthly subscription for delivery on the last day of the month.

Another reason for multiple subscriptions is to receive a report run for multiple sets of parameters. You saw it is possible to specify parameter values as part of the subscription properties. Using this feature, you could have one subscription send you a report with one set of parameters and another subscription send you the same report with a different set of parameters.

Embedded Report versus Attached Report

When you choose to include the report along with the subscription e-mail, the report can show up either embedded in an HTML e-mail or as an attached document. If you select the Web Archive format, the report is embedded. If you select any of the other render formats, the report is sent as an attached document.

Having the report embedded in the e-mail makes it convenient for the user to view the report: it is simply part of the body of your e-mail. However, not all e-mail packages support HTML e-mail, so some users might be unable to view an embedded report. If a user is unsure of the capabilities of their e-mail package, they should choose the Acrobat (PDF) file format. This format is sent as an attachment and can be viewed by just about anyone.

Standard Subscriptions and Security

Not all users can create standard subscriptions. In fact, it is possible to view a report, but not be able to subscribe to it. To subscribe to a report or create a subscription for delivery to others, you must have rights to the Manage Individual Subscriptions task. Of the four predefined security roles, the Browser, Content Manager, and My Reports roles have rights to manage individual subscriptions.

Managing Your Subscriptions

An active user may subscribe to a number of reports scattered throughout a number of folders. Just remembering all the reports you subscribed to can be a big challenge. Managing all those subscriptions can be even tougher. Fortunately, the Report Manager provides a way to view all your subscriptions in one place.

My Subscriptions

The My Subscriptions page consolidates all your standard subscriptions in one place.

1. Click the My Subscriptions link at the top of the page. The My Subscriptions page appears, as shown in Figure 11-10.
2. You can click on any heading to sort your list of subscriptions.

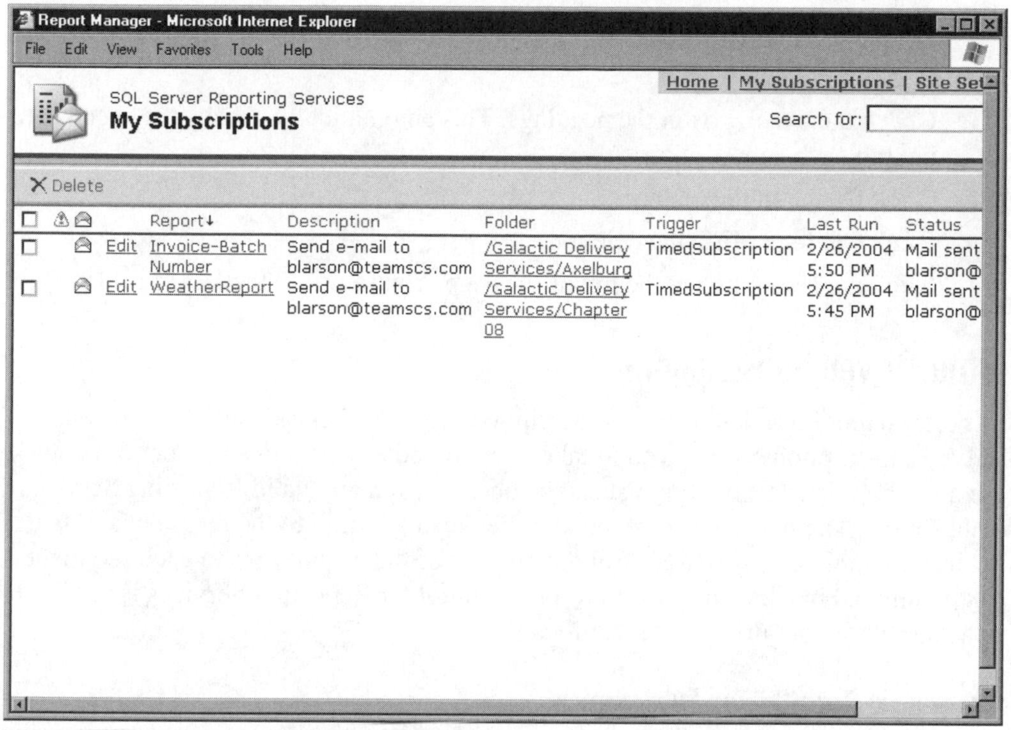

Figure 11-10   *The My Subscriptions page*

3. Click the Edit link next to WeatherReport. The Subscription Properties page appears.

4. You can make changes to this subscription, if you desire. Click Cancel to return to the My Subscriptions page.

5. Click the WeatherReport link in the Report column. You jump to the Weather report.

6. Click your browser's Back button.

7. Click the text in the Folder column for the Invoice-Batch Number Report. You jump to the Axelburg folder.

8. Click your browser's Back button.

The My Subscriptions page lists all the standard subscriptions you created on this Report Server. This makes the subscriptions much easier to manage. You can sort the list several different ways to help you find and manage the subscriptions. You can also use the My Subscriptions page to delete unwanted subscriptions.

Let's delete these subscriptions, so you do not waste computing power e-mailing reports.

1. Check the check box in the headings. This automatically checks the check box next to each subscription.
2. Click Delete in the toolbar.
3. Click OK to confirm the deletion.
4. Click the Home link at the top of the page. You return to the Home folder.

Data-Driven Subscriptions

A better name for a data-driven subscription might be "mass mailing." The data-driven subscription enables you to take a report and e-mail it to a number of people on a mailing list. The mailing list can be queried from any valid Reporting Services data source. The mailing list can contain fields, in addition to the recipient's e-mail address, which are used to control the content of the e-mail sent to each recipient. As mentioned in Chapter 2, the Enterprise Edition of Reporting Services is required for you to use data-driven subscriptions.

Creating a Data-Driven Subscription

Transport 1305 has been acting up. GDS wants all its mechanics to have a good background on the types of problems this transport is having. To facilitate this, the results from the Transport 1305 Monitor report should be e-mailed to all mechanics every four hours. Employees holding the position of Mechanic I should receive the report as a high-priority e-mail. Employees holding the position of Mechanic II should receive the report as a normal-priority e-mail.

1. Open the Report Manager and navigate to the Chapter 08 folder.
2. Click Show Detail.
3. Click the icon in the Edit column for the Transport 1305 Monitor report.
4. Select the Subscriptions tab.
5. Click the New Data-Driven Subscription button. The first page of the Data-Driven Subscription process appears, as shown in Figure 11-11.
6. Type **Maintenance Watch on Transport 1305** for Description.
7. Select Report Server E-Mail from the Specify How Recipients Are Notified drop-down list.
8. Select the Specify a Shared Data Source option.

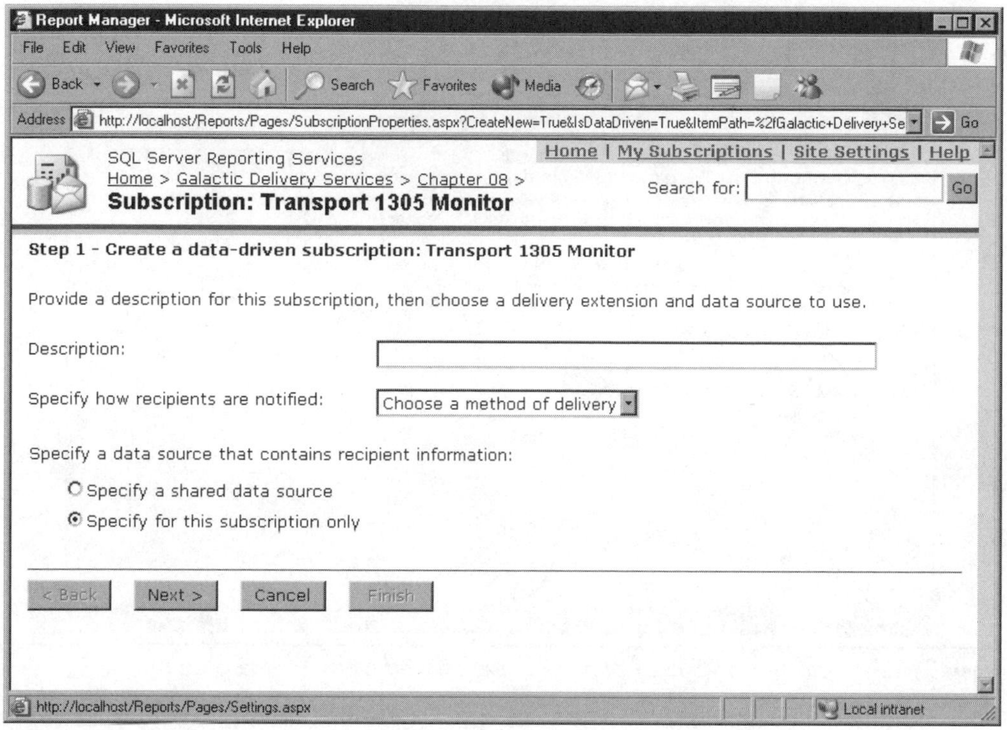

Figure 11-11   *Data-Driven Subscription process, first page*

9. Click the Next button. The Shared Data Source page appears, as shown in Figure 11-12.

10. Use the tree view to find the 2006 Conference folder in the Galactic Delivery Services folder.

11. Select the Galactic shared data source in the 2006 Conference folder.

12. Click the Next button. The Query page appears, as shown in Figure 11-13.

13. Type the following for the query:

    ```
    EXEC stp_MechanicMailingList
    ```

14. Click Validate to make sure you don't have any typos or other problems.

15. If the query does not validate successfully, look for the error in the query you typed. Otherwise, click Next. The Data Association page appears as shown in Figure 11-14. Here, you can associate columns in the result set with fields in the subscription e-mail.

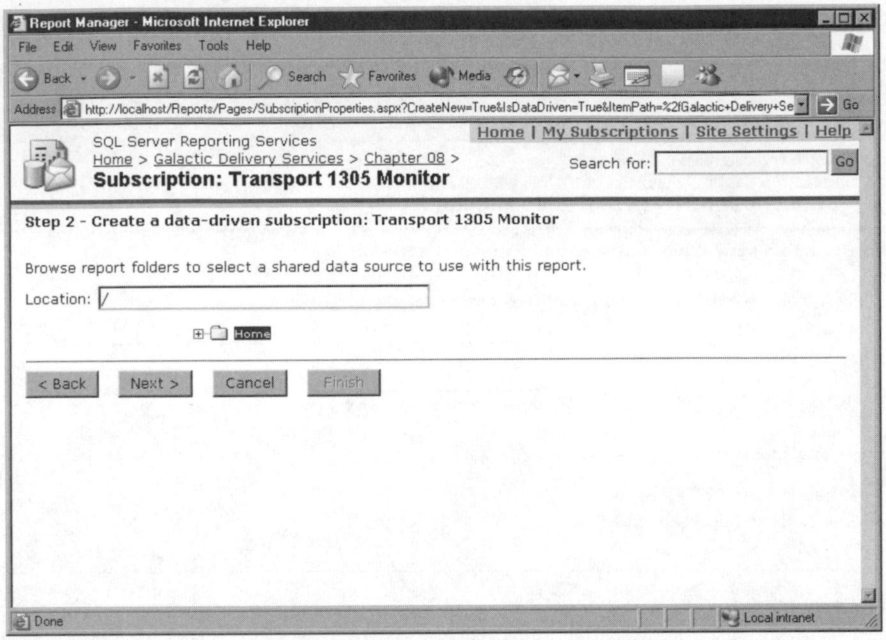

Figure 11-12 *Data-Driven Subscription process, Shared Data Source page*

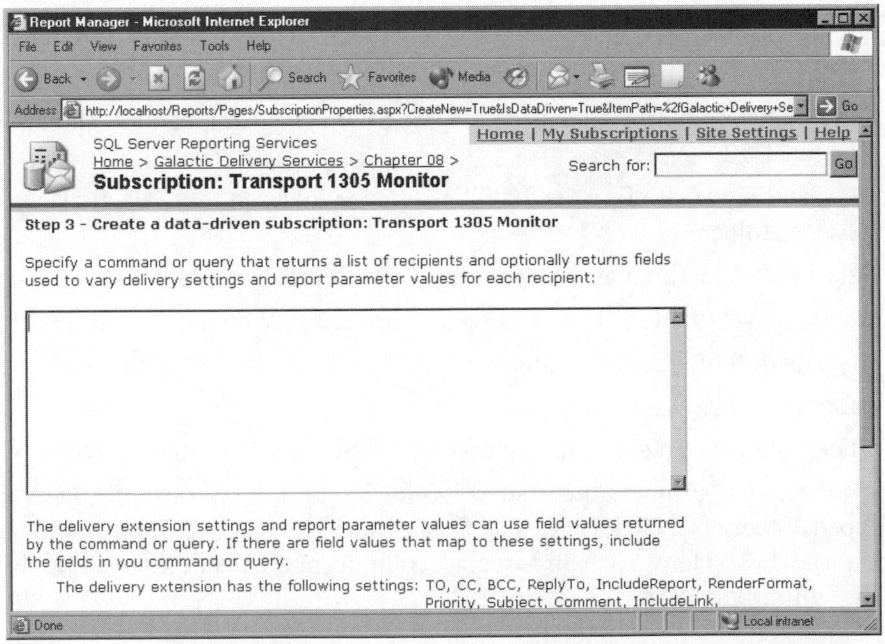

Figure 11-13 *Data-Driven Subscription process, Query page*

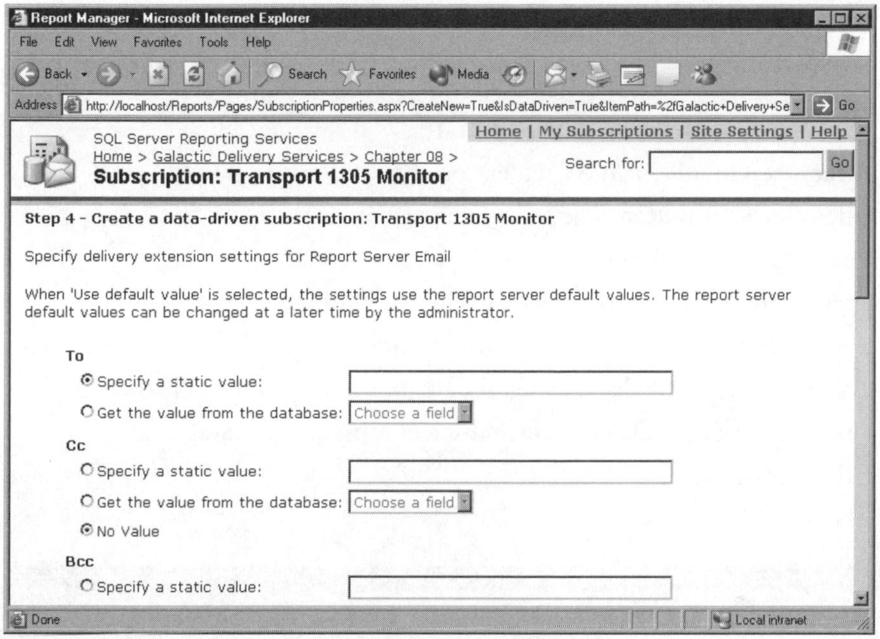

Figure 11-14   *Data-Driven Subscription, Data Association page*

16. Set the following properties on this page:

Property	Value
To	Specify a static value
Specify a static value (For To)	(Type your e-mail address here. Normally, you would select the e-mail address from a database field, but we want to have a valid e-mail address for our example. Because your system cannot send interplanetary e-mail, we have to use your e-mail address.)
Reply-To	Specify a static value
Specify a static value (Reply-To)	Reports@Galactic.SRA
Render Format	Specify a static value
Specify a static value (Render Format)	Acrobat (PDF) file
Priority	Get the value from the database
Get the value from the database (Priority)	Priority
Subject	Get the value from the database
Get the value from the database (Subject)	Subject
Include Link	Specify a static value
Specify a static value (Include Link)	False

17. Click the Next button. The Parameter Values page appears, as shown in Figure 11-15.

18. Leave this page set to the defaults. Click the Next button. The Notify Recipients page appears, as shown in Figure 11-16.

19. Select the On a Schedule Created for This Subscription option.

20. Click the Next button. The Schedule page appears.

21. Select the Hour option.

22. Change the schedule to run every 4 hours 00 minutes.

23. Set the start time to five minutes from now.

24. Today's date should be selected for Begin Running This Schedule On.

25. Check Stop This Schedule On and select tomorrow's date.

26. Click Finish.

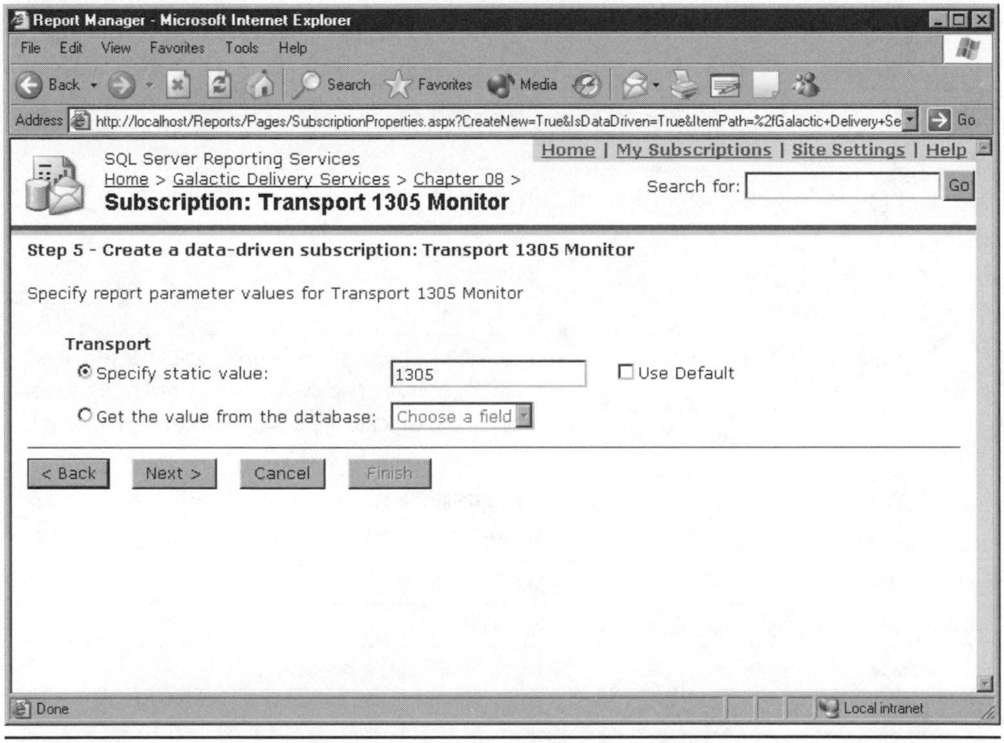

Figure 11-15 *Data-Driven Subscription, Parameter Values page*

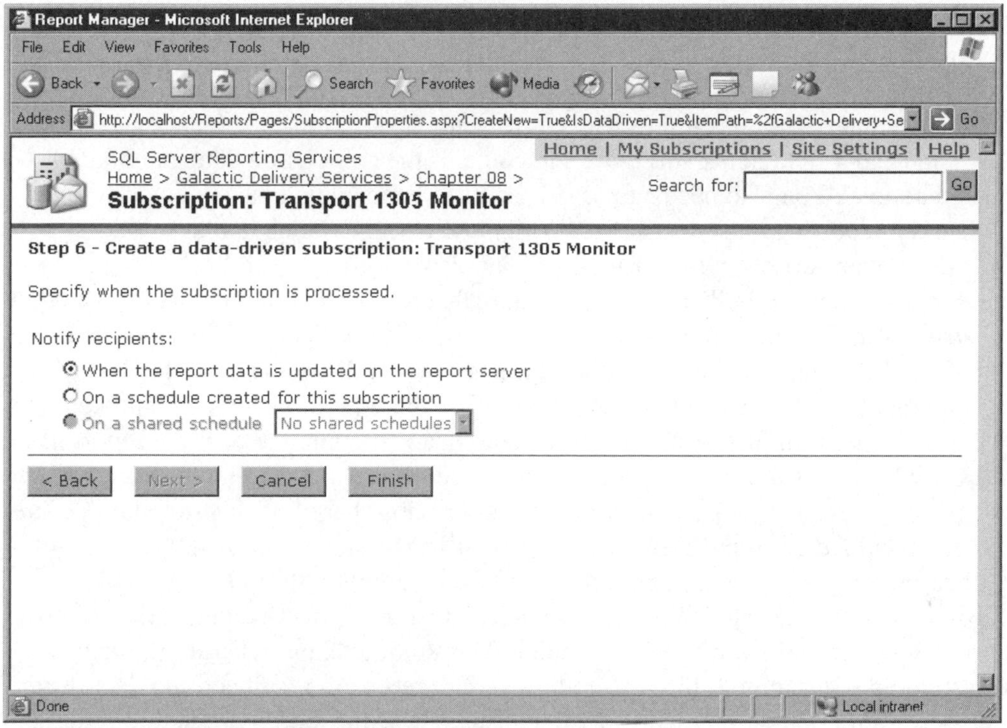

Figure 11-16 *Data-Driven Subscription, Notify Recipients page*

27. Once the scheduled time for your subscription has passed, refresh this page.
     You should see the time of the execution in the Last Run column and Done:
     8 processed of 8 total; 0 errors in the Status column. You should also receive eight
     e-mails (eight mechanics are in the database, and we sent an e-mail to each one)
     with the Transport 1305 Monitor report attached.

28. If you do not want to receive eight e-mails every four hours for the next day,
     you can delete this subscription.

Data-Driven Subscriptions and Security

Not all users can create data-driven subscriptions. To create a data-driven subscription
for a report, you must have rights to the Manage All Subscriptions task. Of the four
predefined security roles, only the Content Manager role has rights to this task.

Data-Driven Subscriptions and Event-Driven Behavior

You can do a couple of tricks with data-driven subscriptions that make them even more
powerful. For instance, at times, you might not want a subscription sent out until after

a certain event has occurred. For instance, you may want to e-mail a report to a number of recipients after a specific data update process has completed. While a data-driven subscription is a scheduled process, rather than triggered by a particular event, we can make it behave almost as if it were event-driven.

You need a field in a status table that contains the completion date and time of the last data load. You also need a field in a status table that contains the date and time when the report was last distributed. With these two flag fields in place, you can simulate event-driven behavior for your data-driven subscription.

First, you need to build a stored procedure that returns the mailing list for the report distribution. To this stored procedure, add logic that checks the date and time of the last data load, and the date and time of the last report distribution. If the data load is complete and the report has not yet been distributed today, the stored procedure returns the mailing list result set. If the data load is incomplete or if the report has already been distributed today, the stored procedure returns an empty result set.

Now you create a series of data-driven subscriptions based on this stored procedure. If the data load completes sometime between 1:00 A.M. and 3:00 A.M., you might schedule one data driven to execute at 1:00 A.M., another at 1:30 A.M., another at 2:00 A.M., and so on. When each data-driven subscription executes, the stored procedure determines whether the data load is complete and whether the report was already distributed. If the stored procedure returns a result set, the data-driven subscription e-mails the report to the mailing list. If the stored procedure returns an empty result set, the data-driven subscription terminates without sending any e-mails.

This same approach can be used to e-mail reports only when the report data has changed. You create a stored procedure that only returns a mailing list result set if the data has changed since the last time the report was e-mailed. This stored procedure is used to create a data-driven subscription. Now the data-driven subscription only sends out reports when the data has changed; otherwise, it sends nothing.

Data-Driven Subscriptions and Report Caching

If you looked closely, you may have noticed that the Specify How Recipients Are Notified drop-down list included the entry Null Delivery Provider. This doesn't seem to make much sense—why would you create a subscription and then not send it anywhere? This Null Delivery Provider is used to support report caching.

Suppose you have a report with a number of possible report parameter combinations that would benefit from caching. As you have seen, report parameter values must match for a report to be pulled from cache. How do we create cached copies of the report with all the possible parameter combinations? The answer is a data-driven subscription using the Null Delivery Provider.

The first step is to create a query that returns all the possible report parameter combinations (or at least the most popular ones) for this report. You then use this query to create a data-driven subscription to execute the report with each of these parameter combinations. If report caching is enabled, the data-driven subscription would cause a copy of the report to be cached with each of these parameter combinations. This is true even if the Null Delivery Provider is used and the report is never delivered anywhere by the subscription. Because the subscription created all these cached copies with the various parameter value combinations, no matter what combination of parameters a user enters the following day, the report is rendered from a cached copy.

Site Settings

When setting the limit for the number of report history snapshots kept for a given report, we encountered a setting that referred to using a default value. Each time you have the opportunity to specify a schedule for an execution snapshot, a subscription, or other feature, you have an option to select a shared schedule. The report history snapshot default value, the shared schedules, and several other site-wide settings are managed on the Site Settings page.

Configuration Options and Default Values

The main Site Settings page enables you to set several default values and configuration options. This page also acts as a front end for other configuration screens. You can access the Site Settings page by clicking the Site Settings link at the top of the page. The main Site Settings page is shown in Figure 11-17.

We begin our examination of the site settings by looking at the configuration items and default values on the main Site Settings page.

Name

The value in the Name field appears at the top of each page in the Report Manager. You can change this to the name of your company or some other phrase that can help users identify this report server.

Report History Default

The report history default setting lets you specify a default value for the maximum number of report history snapshots to keep. This can be set to a specific number or set to allow an unlimited number of snapshots. Each report utilizing report history snapshots can either specify its own maximum number or use this default value.

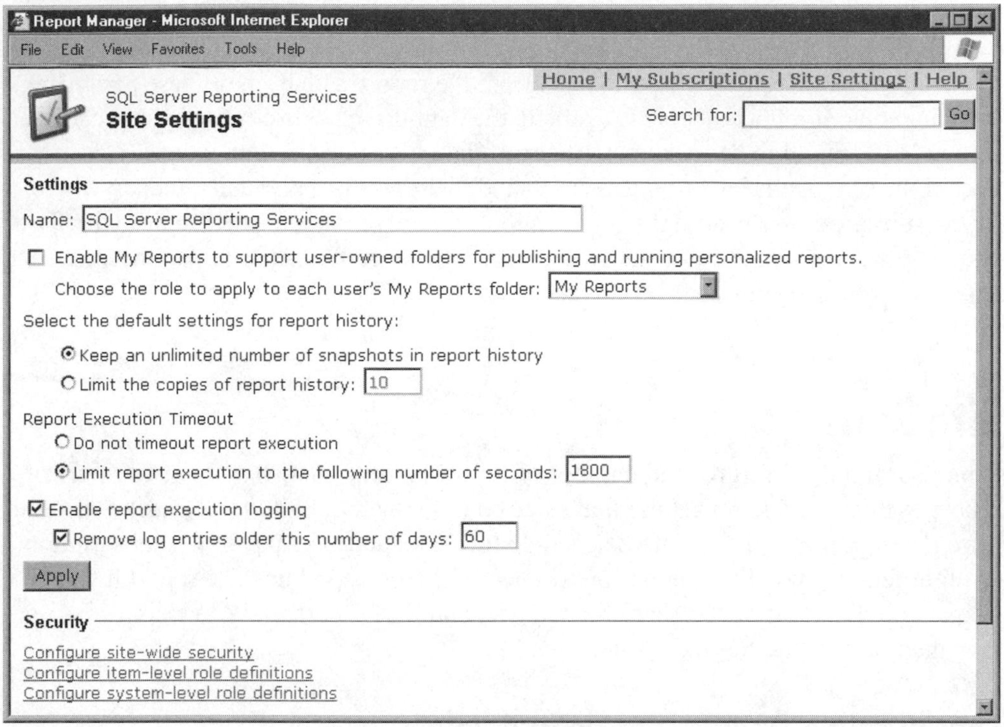

Figure 11-17   *The main Site Settings page*

Report Execution Timeout

The default for Report Execution Timeout enables you to specify a default value for the maximum amount of time a report may run before it times out. This can be a specific number of seconds or set to no timeout (unlimited execution time). Each report can either specify its own timeout value or use this default value.

NOTE

The report execution timeout is specified on the Execution Properties page for each report.

Report Execution Logging

The Enable Report Execution Logging option determines whether information about each report execution is placed in the execution log. The execution log this option refers to is the ExecutionLog table in the ReportServer database. This is not referring to any of the log text files created by the Report Server application. Along with turning logging off and on, you can specify how long the Report Server should keep these log entries.

Your Reporting Services installation includes a DTS package you can use to copy the contents of the ExecutionLog into a set of user-defined tables. You can then use these user-defined tables as a data source and create reports showing the activity occurring on your Report Server. The DTS package is located in

```
C:\Program Files\Microsoft SQL Server\80\Tools\
                                Reporting Service\ExecutionLog
```

For instructions on using this DTS package, search on "Querying and Reporting on Report Execution Log Data" on www.Microsoft.com.

Additional Settings

In addition to the configuration items on the Site Settings page, you can modify the functionality of the Report Server in other ways. In Chapter 12, we look at settings that can be changed using system properties. The system properties can be set through the Reporting Services Configuration Tool and through the SctSystemProperties method of the Reporting Services web service. See Chapter 12 for more details.

My Reports

The Enable My Reports option turns on a feature giving each user their own private folder on the Report Server. When this option is enabled, a special folder called Users Folders is created in the Home folder. Only users assigned the System Administrator role can see this folder.

CAUTION

You should enable the My Reports option only if you intend to use it. Getting rid of the Users Folders folder and its content once it is created is a bit tricky. If you do create the folder, and then need to delete this folder, turn off the My Reports option, go into each folder in the Users Folders folder, and give yourself Content Manager rights. Now you can delete the folders.

Folders Created Through the My Reports Option

As each user logs on for the first time after the My Reports option is enabled, a new folder is created in the Users Folders folder. This new folder has the same name as the domain and logon name of the user signing in. The new folder is mapped to a folder called My Reports.

Let's discuss an example to make this clearer. Sally and José are two users in the Galactic domain. Shortly after the My Reports option is enabled, Sally accesses the Report Server using the Report Manager. A new folder is created in the Users Folders folder called Galactic Sally.

Sally is not assigned the System Administrator role, so she cannot see the Users Folders folder or the Galactic Sally folder inside of it. Instead, when Sally views her Home folder, she sees a folder called My Reports. Sally's My Reports folder is a mapping to the Galactic Sally folder.

When José accesses the Report Server using the Report Manager, a new folder is created in the Users Folders folder called Galactic José. José sees a folder called My Reports in his Home folder. José's My Reports folder is a mapping to the Galactic José folder.

José is assigned the System Administrator role. In addition to the My Reports folder, José can view the Users Folders folder. When José opens the Users Folders folder, he can see both the Galactic Sally and the Galactic José folders. In fact, José can open the Galactic Sally folder and view its contents.

Security and My Reports

Because the My Reports folder is for each user's personal reports, the users are granted more rights in the My Reports folder than they might be granted anywhere else on the site. On the Site Settings page, you decide which security role to assign to the user in their own My Reports folder. By default, users are assigned the My Reports role in their own My Reports folder.

A user can be granted broader rights in the My Reports folder, because they are the only one using the reports in this folder. No one else is going to set up caching and report history snapshots, for example, because no one else is going to use these reports. You want to be sure to assign the user to a role that has rights to publish reports; otherwise, each user will be unable to put reports in their own My Reports folder.

When to Enable the My Report Option

The My Reports option can be useful in two situations. First, if you have a number of individuals creating ad hoc reports for their own personal use, the My Reports folder provides a convenient spot for this to take place. If you do use the My Reports folder in this manner, you want to have some policies in place to ensure that each user's My Reports folder does not become an ad hoc dumping ground.

The second viable use of the My Reports folder is as a quality assurance (QA) testing area for report developers. The report developers can use their individual My Reports folders as a place to test a report in the server environment before it is deployed to a folder available to the users. This is convenient because the system administrator can navigate through the Users Folders folder to access the report, after it has passed QA testing, and move it to its production location. Of course, having a dedicated quality assurance server for this purpose is far better, but in situations where this is not feasible, the My Reports folder can be considered as an option.

Other Pages Accessed from the Site Settings Page

In addition to the configuration options and default values managed on the Site Settings page, the page itself serves as a menu to other pages. These pages enable you to manage the security configuration and other site-wide settings. The following is a brief discussion of each area managed from the Site Settings page.

Site-Wide Security

The Configure Site-Wide Security page lets you assign Windows users and Windows groups to system-level roles. These system-level roles provide users with the rights to view and modify settings for the Report Server, such as those found on the Site Settings page. System Administrator and System User are the two predefined system-level roles.

For more information on system-level roles and system-level tasks, see the "Security" section of Chapter 10.

Item-Level Role Definition

The Configure Item-Level Role Definitions page enables you to modify the item-level roles. The predefined item-level roles are Browser, Content Manager, Publisher, and My Reports. You can edit the tasks assigned to these roles or create new roles. If you look at this screen, you see it also includes the View Report security role we defined in Chapter 10.

Take great care before modifying predefined roles. This makes it difficult for anyone else to work with your Reporting Services installation. Rather than modifying a predefined item-level role, copy the predefined role to a new name, make your modifications to this newly created role, and then use the new role to assign rights to users and groups.

For more information on item-level roles and item-level tasks, see the "Security" section of Chapter 10.

System-Level Role Definition

The System-Level Role Definition page lets you modify the system-level roles. System Administrator and System User are the predefined system-level roles. You can edit the tasks assigned to these roles or create new roles.

Take great care before modifying predefined roles. This makes it difficult for anyone else to work with your Reporting Services installation. Rather than modifying a predefined system-level role, copy the predefined role to a new name, make your modifications to this newly created role, and then use the new role to assign rights to users and groups.

For more information on system-level roles and system-level tasks, see the "Security" section of Chapter 10.

Shared Schedules

Each time you had an option to create a schedule for a feature, such as report cache expiration or execution snapshot creation, it was accompanied by a choice to use a shared schedule. A *shared schedule* lets you use a single schedule definition in multiple places. A shared schedule is created using the same page used to create all the other schedules we have been looking at in this chapter.

Shared schedules are beneficial for situations where a number of events should use the same timing. For example, suppose you have ten reports that utilize execution snapshots, all pulling data from a data warehouse. That data warehouse is updated once a week. It makes sense to create one shared schedule that can be used to run the execution snapshots for all these reports.

Not only does this save the time that would otherwise be necessary to create the schedule ten times, but it also makes it easier if the timing of the data warehouse update is changed and the execution snapshot schedule must be changed. If you are using a shared schedule, you only need to make this change once, in the shared location. Without the shared schedule, you would be forced to make this change ten times.

Manage Jobs

Scheduled items in Reporting Services use the SQL Agent to handle their operation. When you create a schedule for a task, such as creating an execution snapshot, you are creating a job in the SQL Agent. When one or more of these jobs are executing, they can be managed on the Manage Jobs page. You can use the Manage Jobs page to view the status of executing jobs and to cancel a job that is not executing properly.

NOTE

Jobs appear on the Manage Jobs page only when they are executing on the server. In fact, a job must be running for more than 30 seconds before it appears on this page.

A Sense of Style

We do not have access to the source code of the Report Manager pages, so we cannot make changes to the way they function. However, because these pages are ultimately HTML pages sent to a browser, we can make changes to the way the pages look. This is done through a cascading style sheet (CSS).

The ReportingServices Style Sheet

The look of the Report Manager is controlled by the ReportingServices.css cascading style sheet. The default location for this file is

```
C:\Program Files\Microsoft SQL Server\MSSQL.3\Reporting Services\
                              ReportManager\Styles\ReportingServices.css
```

(There is also a cascading style sheet in this folder that controls the look of the web parts used to display reports in SharePoint.)

Let's take a look at the steps necessary to make a change to the cascading style sheet.

Modifying the ReportingServices Style Sheet

The following procedure changes the fonts for both the name displayed at the top of the Report Manager pages and the text showing the current folder.

1. Make a backup copy of the ReportingServices.css file.
2. Open the ReportingServices.css file in Notepad.
3. Locate the entry for msrs-lowertitle.
4. Change the font-size entry from medium to small to decrease the size of the current folder text.
5. Locate the entry for msrs-uppertitle.
6. Change the font-size entry from x-small to large to increase the size of the name.
7. Add the following text immediately below the font-size entry:

    ```
    font-weight:bold;
    ```
8. Save your changes to the ReportingServices.css file and exit Notepad.

> **NOTE**
>
> *You need to remove any cached copies of the ReportingServices.css file from your browser before the changes to this style sheet can take effect.*

9. Open the Report Manager in your browser, if it is not already open. Or, if it is already open, navigate to a new folder in the Report Manager. You see the name at the top of the page now appears in large, bold text and the text showing the current folder is smaller.

Building On

In this chapter, you learned ways to deliver reports and control their execution from within the Report Manager. In the next chapter, we look at ways to customize report delivery by building on to Reporting Services. These techniques enable you to integrate Reporting Services reports with your own websites and custom applications.

Extending Outside the Box: Customizing Reporting Services

IN THIS CHAPTER:

U p to this point, we have been using Reporting Services just as it comes out of the box (or off the installation CD, if you want to get technical). All our management of Reporting Services features and all our report execution have been through the Report Manager. Reporting Services and the Report Manager do, after all, provide a feature-rich environment in their default configuration.

One of the best features of Reporting Services, however, is the capability to extend it beyond its basic operation. In this chapter, we do just that. You learn ways to execute reports without using the Report Manager interface. You look at ways to manage Reporting Services without using the Report Manager interface. Finally, you work through an example showing how to change the security mechanism used by Reporting Services.

All of this gives you a brief taste of what Reporting Services can do when you start extending outside the box.

Using Reporting Services Without the Report Manager

The Report Manager provides a nice interface for finding and executing reports. However, the Report Manager is not always the best way to deliver a report to your users. Perhaps the user is browsing your website or using a custom application and needs to view a report. In these situations, it does not make sense to force the user to jump to Report Manager and begin navigating folders. We want to deliver the report to the user right where they are. In this section, we explore several ways to do just that.

URL Access

One way to execute a report without using Report Manager is through URL access. URL access allows a browser or a program capable of issuing HTTP requests to specify a URL and receive a report in the HTML report viewer. This URL can be built into a standard HTML anchor tag to allow a report to be displayed with one mouse click.

Basic URL Access

The basic URL used to access a report has two parts. The first part is the URL of the Report Server web service. In a default installation, this is

```
http://{computername}/ReportServer
```

where {computername} is the name of the computer hosting the Report Server. This is followed by a question mark and the path through the Reporting Services virtual folders to the report you want to execute. The Home folder is the root of this path, but it's not included in the path itself. The path must begin with a forward slash (/).

Let's try an example. We can execute the Invoice-Batch Number Report for the Axelburg office. This report is in the Axelburg folder inside the Galactic Delivery Services folder.

NOTE

In the examples used throughout the rest of this chapter, we assume Reporting Services is installed on your computer. The localhost name is used to access IIS information on this computer. If you have Reporting Services installed on a different computer, substitute the name of that computer in place of localhost in the following examples.

1. Start Internet Explorer.
2. Enter the following URL in the address bar:

   ```
   http://localhost/ReportServer?/Galactic Delivery Services/Axelburg/
                                       Invoice-Batch Number Report
   ```

3. Click Go. The Invoice-Batch Number Report appears in the browser inside the Report Viewer.

NOTE

When your URL is submitted, it is URL encoded. Some of the characters in your URL may be replaced by other characters or by hexadecimal strings such as %20. This ensures the URL can be interpreted correctly when it is sent to the web server.

As with Report Manager, Windows Integrated security is being used when a user executes a report through URL access. The user must have rights to execute the report; otherwise, an error results. However, because the user is not browsing through the folder structure to get to the report, the user does not need to have any rights to the folder containing the report. You can use this fact to hide a report from nonadministrative users who are browsing through folders in the Report Manager, while still making the report accessible to someone using URL access.

In addition to executing reports, you can also view the contents of folders, resources, and shared data sources. Try the following:

1. Enter this URL in the address bar:

   ```
   http://localhost/ReportServer?/Galactic Delivery Services
   ```

2. Click Go. The contents of the Galactic Delivery Services folder appears.

3. Click the link for the 2006 Conference folder. The contents of the 2006 Conference folder appears, as shown in Figure 12-1.

Command Parameters

Look at the URL in the address bar. You see something has been added to the URL, namely &rs:Command=ListChildren. This is called a *command parameter*. It tells Reporting Services what to do with the item pointed to by the URL. The four possible values for the command parameter are listed in Table 12-1.

Looking at this table, you quickly realize that only one command parameter value applies to each type of item you can encounter in the Reporting Services virtual folders. Attempting to use a command parameter with the wrong type of item results in an error. If you do not include the command parameter, Reporting Services simply performs the one and only command that applies to the type of item you are targeting in your URL. Because specifying the command parameter is completely unnecessary, one can only assume this was put in place to allow for future growth.

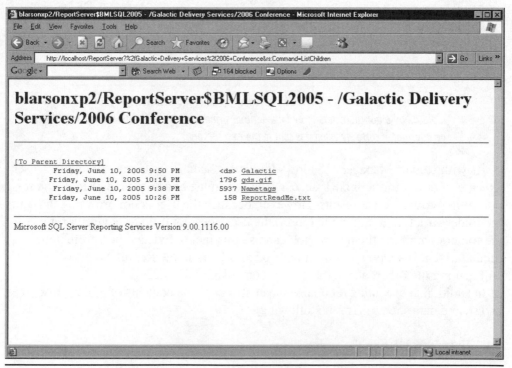

Figure 12-1 *Browsing folder contents using URL access*

Command Parameter	Applies To	Result
GetDataSourceContents	Data Source	Displays the data source definition as an XML structure.
GetResourceContents	Resource Item	Displays the contents of the resource item in the browser.
ListChildren	Folder	Lists the contents of the folder with links to each content item.
Render	Report	Displays the report in the Report Viewer.

Table 12-1 *Values for the Command Parameter*

Passing Parameters

When you executed the Invoice-Batch Number Report through URL access, you received the default values for the start date and end date. You can change these dates in the Report Viewer, but only after waiting for the report to execute with the default values. It would be much better to get exactly what you want the first time around.

Fortunately, you have a way to do just that. You can pass the values for report parameters as part of the URL. On the URL, include an ampersand (&) followed by the name of the report parameter, an equals sign, and the parameter value.

Try the following:

1. Enter the following URL in the address bar:

   ```
   http://localhost/ReportServer?/Galactic Delivery Services/Axelburg/
        Invoice-Batch Number Report&StartDate=11/1/2005&EndDate=11/30/2005
   ```

2. Click Go. The Invoice-Batch Number Report appears with data for November 2005.

It is possible to hide parameters from interactive report users, while still allowing values to be passed to those parameters through the URL or web service access. This is done through the Hide option for each parameter. Let's try the following:

1. Open the Report Manager and navigate to the /Galactic Delivery Services/ Axelburg folder.
2. Click Show Details.
3. Click the icon in the Edit column next to the Invoice-Batch Number Report.
4. Click Parameters on the left side of the screen. The Parameter Management page appears.
5. Check the Has Default check box in the StartDate row
6. Enter **11/1/2005** as the default value in the StartDate row.

7. Check the Hide check box in the StartDate row.

8. Click Apply.

9. Select the View tab. Notice the Start Date prompt no longer appears in the parameter area.

10. Enter the following URL in the address bar:

```
http://localhost/ReportServer?/Galactic Delivery Services/Axelburg/
     Invoice-Batch Number Report&StartDate=12/1/2005&EndDate=12/31/2005
```

11. Click Go. The Invoice-Batch Number Report appears with data for December 2005.

Even though Start Date parameter does not appear in the parameters area, we can still specify a value for it other than the default value. The Hide check box is not checked for the City parameter, so a value cannot be specified for this parameter in the URL. The following URL is going to fail:

```
http://localhost/ReportServer?/Galactic Delivery Services/Axelburg/
     Invoice-Batch Number Report&City=Utonal&EndDate=12/31/2005
```

Controlling the Report Viewer

In addition to specifying report parameters in the URL, you can also include parameters to control the format of the response from Reporting Services. You can specify which rendering format should be used for the report. Rather than using the Export drop-down list in the Report Viewer to export the report to a particular format, you can have it delivered in that format straight from Reporting Services.

Give this a try:

1. Enter the following URL in the address bar:

```
http://localhost/ReportServer?/Galactic Delivery Services/
                        2006 Conference/Nametags&rs:Format=PDF
```

2. Click Go.

3. If you are prompted whether to open or save the file, click Open.

4. The Nametags report appears in PDF format in Adobe Acrobat Reader.

5. Close Adobe Acrobat Reader. The valid format parameters are as follows:

   ▶ CSV

   ▶ EXCEL

   ▶ HTML3.2

   ▶ HTML4.0

- ▶ HTMLOWC
- ▶ IMAGE
- ▶ MHTML
- ▶ NULL
- ▶ PDF
- ▶ XML

In addition to the rs:Command and rs:Format parameters, several other Report Server parameters use the rs: prefix. Table 12-2 shows these.

Device information parameters can also be passed as part of the URL. These *device information parameters* are specific to the format being used to render the report. Because they are rendering format-specific, device information parameters can also be thought of as renderer control parameters. Therefore, they use an rc: prefix.

Let's look at a couple of examples using device information parameters. When you receive a report rendered as HTML, you also receive the Report Viewer controls. This may not always be desirable. Several device information parameters enable you to specify what portion of the Report Viewer interface you want visible. For example:

1. Enter the following URL in the address bar:

```
http://localhost/ReportServer?/Galactic Delivery Services/Axelburg/
    Invoice-Batch Number Report&StartDate=11/1/2005&EndDate=11/30/2005
    &rc:Parameters=false
```

Parameter	Valid Values	Function
rs:ClearSession	True False	When true, this parameter prevents a report from being pinned in cache by forcing the report to be rerendered.
rs:ParameterLanguage	a valid culture identifier such as "en-us"	Used to specify a language for the parameters passed in the URL that is different from the browser's language setting. This defaults to the browser's language setting when it is not specified.
rs:SessionID	a unique session identifier	Used to maintain session state when the Report Server has been configured not to use session cookies.
rs:Snapshot	the data and time of a valid snapshot for the specified report	Used to render the requested report from a history snapshot.

Table 12-2   *Report Server (rs) URL Parameters and Their Possible Values*

2. Click Go. The Invoice-Batch Number Report appears with data for November 2005. The parameter portion of the Report Viewer is invisible, so the user cannot change the parameter values.

You can get rid of the entire Report Viewer interface as follows:

1. Enter the following URL in the address bar:

```
http://localhost/ReportServer?/Galactic Delivery Services/Axelburg/
    Invoice-Batch Number Report&StartDate=11/1/2005&EndDate=11/30/2005
    &rc:Toolbar=false
```

2. Click Go. The Invoice-Batch Number Report appears with data for November 2005.

3. Expand the 445 row heading and the Axelburg column heading.

Even when we expand the row and column headings, causing a new page to be sent from the Report Server, the Report Viewer does not reappear.

Table 12-3 shows the device information parameters for the CSV format.

Table 12-4 shows the device information parameters for the Excel format.

The device information parameters for the HTML formats are shown in Table 12-5.

Table 12-6 shows the device information parameters for the image format.

Table 12-7 shows the device information parameters for the MHTML format.

Setting	Valid Values	Function
rc:Encoding	ASCII UTF-7 UTF-8 Unicode	The character encoding scheme to use. The default is Unicode.
rc:Extension		The file extension for the file. The default is **.CSV**.
rc:FieldDelimiter		The field delimiter to use in the file. The default is a comma.
rc:NoHeader	True False	If true, no header is written with the data in the file. The default is false.
rc:Qualifier		The string qualifier to put around fields that contain the field delimiter. The default is a quotation mark.
rc:RecordDelimiter		The record delimiter to use in the file. The default is a carriage return and linefeed.
rc:SuppressLineBreaks	True False	If true, line breaks in the data are not included in the file. The default is false.

Table 12-3 *CSV Format Device Information (rc) URL Parameters and Their Possible Values*

Setting	Valid Values	Function
rc:OmitDocumentMap	True False	If true, the document map for the rendered report is not included in the Excel file. The default is false.
rc:OmitFormulas	True False	If true, formulas are not included in the Excel file. The default is false.
rc:RemoveSpace	An integer or decimal followed by "in" (the abbreviation for inches)	When this parameter is included, rows and columns that do not contain data and are smaller than the size specified are not included in the Excel file. This parameter is used to exclude extra rows or columns that do not contain report items. The default is 0.125in.
rc:SimplePageHeader	True False	If true, the report page header is placed in the Excel page header. Otherwise, the report page header is placed in the first row of the worksheet. The default value is false.

Table 12-4   *Excel Format Device Information (rc) URL Parameters and Their Possible Values*

Setting	Valid Values	Function
rc:BookmarkID	{BookmarkID}	Jumps to the specified Bookmark ID in the report.
rc:DocMap	True False	Specifies whether the document map is shown.
rc:DocMapID	{DocMapID}	Jumps to the specified Document Map ID.
rc:EndFind	{PageNumber}	The last report page to be searched when executing a Find from the URL (*see* FindString).
rc:FallbackPage	{PageNumber}	The report page to go to if the Find is unsuccessful or a jump to a Document Map ID fails.
rc:FindString	{TextToFind}	Searches for this text in the report and jumps to its first location.
rc:HTMLFragment	True False	When this is set to true, the report is returned as a table rather than a complete HTML page. This table can then be placed inside your own HTML page. The default value is false.
rc:JavaScript	True False	If true, JavaScript is supported in the rendered report.

Table 12-5   *HTML Format Device Information (rc) URL Parameters and Their Possible Values* (continued)

Setting	Valid Values	Function
rc:LinkTarget	{TargetWindowName} _blank _self _parent _top	Specifies the target window to use for any links in the report.
rc:Parameters	True False	Specifies whether to show the parameters section of the Report Viewer.
rc:ReplacementRoot		The path used to prefix any hyperlinks created in the report.
rc:Section	{PageNumber}	The page number of the report to render.
rc:StartFind	{PageNumber}	The first report page to be searched when executing a Find from the URL (*see* FindString).
rc:StreamRoot	{URL}	The path used to prefix the value of the src attribute of any IMG tags in an HTML rendering of the report.
rc:StyleSheet		The name of a cascading style sheet in the Report Server Styles folder to be applied to the Report Viewer. The name should not include the .css extension. The default location of the Styles folder is C:\Program Files\Microsoft SQL Server\MSSQL.3\Reporting Services\ReportServer\Styles. The default value is HTMLViewer.
rc:StyleStream	True False	If true, styles and scripts are created as separate streams rather than in the document. The default is false.
rc:Toolbar	True False	Specifies whether the Report Viewer toolbar is visible.
rc:Type		The shortname of the browser type as defined in browsercap.ini.
rc:Zoom	Page Width Whole Page 500 200 150 100 75 50 25 10	The zoom percentage to use when displaying the report.

Table 12-5   *HTML Format Device Information (rc) URL Parameters and Their Possible Values*

Setting	Valid Values	Function
rc:ColorDepth	1 4 8 24 32	The color depth of the image created. The default is 24. This is only valid for the TIFF image type.
rc:Columns		The number of columns to use when creating the image.
rc:ColumnSpacing		The column spacing to use when creating the image
rc:DpiX		The number of dots per inch in the x-direction. The default is 96.
rc:DpiY		The number of dots per inch in the y-direction. The default is 96.
rc:EndPage		The last page to render. The default value is the value for the StartPage parameter.
rc:MarginBottom	An integer or decimal followed by "in" (the abbreviation for inches)	The bottom margin to use when creating the image.
rc:MarginLeft	An integer or decimal followed by "in" (the abbreviation for inches)	The left margin to use when creating the image.
rc:MarginRight	An integer or decimal followed by "in" (the abbreviation for inches)	The right margin to use when creating the image.
rc:MarginTop	An integer or decimal followed by "in" (the abbreviation for inches)	The top margin to use when creating the image.
rc:OutputFormat	BMP EMF GIF JPEG PNG TIFF	The graphics format to create.
rc:PageHeight	An integer or decimal followed by "in" (the abbreviation for inches)	The page height to use when creating the image.
rc:PageWidth	An integer or decimal followed by "in" (the abbreviation for inches)	The page width to use when creating the image.
rc:StartPage		The first page to render. A value of 0 causes all pages to be rendered. The default value is 1.

Table 12-6   *Image Format Device Information (rc) URL Parameters and Their Possible Values*

Setting	Valid Values	Function
rc:JavaScript	True False	If true, JavaScript is supported in the rendered report.
rc:MHTMLFragment	True False	When this is set to true, the report is returned as a table rather than a complete HTML page. This table can then be placed inside your own HTML page. The default value is false.

Table 12-7 *MHTML Format Device Information (rc) URL Parameters and Their Possible Values*

The PDF format device information parameters are shown in Table 12-8.

Table 12-9 shows the device information parameters for the XML format.

Finally, you can specify the user name and password for data sources that prompt for credentials each time the report is run. This is done using the dsu and dsp prefixes.

Setting	Valid Values	Function
rc:Columns		The number of columns to use when creating the PDF file.
rc:ColumnSpacing		The column spacing to use when creating the PDF file.
rc:EndPage		The last page to render. The default value is the value for the StartPage parameter.
rc:MarginBottom	An integer or decimal followed by "in" (the abbreviation for inches)	The bottom margin to use when creating the PDF file.
rc:MarginLeft	An integer or decimal followed by "in" (the abbreviation for inches)	The left margin to use when creating the PDF file.
rc:MarginRight	An integer or decimal followed by "in" (the abbreviation for inches)	The right margin to use when creating the PDF file.
rc:MarginTop	An integer or decimal followed by "in" (the abbreviation for inches)	The top margin to use when creating the PDF file.
rc:PageHeight	An integer or decimal followed by "in" (the abbreviation for inches)	The page height to use when creating the PDF file.
rc:PageWidth	An integer or decimal followed by "in" (the abbreviation for inches)	The page width to use when creating the PDF file.
rc:StartPage		The first page to render. A value of 0 causes all pages to be rendered. The default value is 1.

Table 12-8 *PDF Format Device Information (rc) URL Parameters and Their Possible Values*

Setting	Valid Values	Function
rc:Encoding	ASCII UTF-8 Unicode	The character encoding scheme to use. The default is UTF-8.
rc:FileExtension		The file extension for the XML file. The default is **.XML**.
rc:Indented	True False	If true, the XML file is indented. The default is false.
rc:MIMEType		The MIME type of the XML file.
rc:OmitSchema	True False	If true, the schema name and XSD are not included in the XML file. The default is false.
rc:Schema	True False	If true, the XSL schema definition (XSD) is rendered in the XML file. Otherwise, the report itself is rendered in the XML file. The default is false.
UseFormattedValues	True False	If true, the formatted value of each text box is included in the XML file. Otherwise, the unformatted value of each text box is included.
XSLT		The path in the Report Server namespace of an XSLT document to apply to the XML file. The XSLT must be a published resource on the Report Server and it must be accessed through the Report Server itself.

Table 12-9   *XML Format Device Information (rc) URL Parameters and Their Possible Values*

For example, to specify credentials for a data source called GalacticPrompt, you would add the following to the end of the URL:

```
dsu:GalacticPrompt=MyDBUser&dsp:GalacticPrompt=DBPassword
```

where MyDBUser is a valid database login and DBPassword is the password for that login.

URL Access Using an HTTP Post

The previous examples demonstrate the use of URL access using the HTTP Get method. This method has several limitations. First, all the parameter values are exposed in the URL itself. Second, the number of characters you can have in a URL has a limit.

You can get around these limitations and still use URL access by employing the HTTP Post method. The *HTTP Post method* passes parameters as fields in an HTML form, so they are not exposed in the URL. Also, the HTTP Post is not subject to the same length restrictions as the HTTP Get.

The following HTML page uses the HTTP Post to request the Transport Monitor Report for Transport Number 1305 in the HTML 4.0, TIFF image, or Excel format:

```
<HTML>
<Head>
<title>
Reporting Services URL Post Demo
</title>
</Head>
<Body>
<FORM id="frmRender" action="http://localhost/ReportServer?
            /Galactic Delivery Services/Chapter 08/TransportMonitor"
            method="post" target="_self">
<H3>Transport Monitor Report</H3><br>
<b>For Transport 1305</b><br><br>
Render the Transportation Monitor Report in the following format:<br>
<Select ID="rs:Format" NAME="rs:Format" size=1>
<Option Value="HTML4.0">HTML 4.0</Option>
<Option VALUE="IMAGE">TIFF Image</Option>
<Option VALUE="EXCEL">Excel FIle</Option>
</Select>
<Input type="hidden" name="TransportNumber" value="1305">
<br><br>
<INPUT type="submit" value="Render Report">
</FORM>
</Body>
</HTML>
```

Web Service Access

In addition to URL access, you can also access reports by using the web service interface. This is the same interface used by the Report Manager web application to interact with Reporting Services. This means anything you can do in Report Manager, you can also do through the web service interface.

The web service interface provides additional functionality not available through URL access. For example, the web service interface enables you to specify a set of credentials to use when executing a report. This allows your custom application to use a set of hard-coded credentials to access reports through the web service interface. This can be a big benefit in situations where you want Reporting Services reports to be exposed on an Internet or extranet site where each user does not have a domain account.

Using a Web Service Call to Execute a Report

This example takes you through the steps necessary to execute a report using the web service interface. In this example, you build a web application that acts as a front end for the Axelburg Invoice-Batch Number Report.

NOTE

Some basic knowledge of ASP.NET programming is assumed in the following discussion.

Creating a Project and a Web Reference   First, you need to create an ASP.NET project with a reference to the Reporting Services web service.

1. Start up Visual Studio 2005. (This example will also work in earlier versions of Visual Studio .NET.)
2. Create a new project.
3. Select Visual Basic in the Project Types area.
4. Select ASP.NET Web Application from the Templates area.
5. Enter **http://localhost/AxelburgFrontEnd** for Location.
6. Click OK.
7. When the new project has been created, right-click the project folder for this new project in the Solution Explorer and select Add Web Reference from the Context menu. The Add Web Reference dialog box appears.
8. Select the link for Web Services on the Local Machine.

NOTE

Again, if Reporting Services is not on your computer, do not use this link. Instead, look for the web service on the computer where Reporting Services is installed.

9. When the list of web services on the local machine appears, click the link for ReportExecution2005.
10. When the Reporting Service description appears in the dialog box, click Add Reference.

To use a web service, you need to create code that knows how to send data to and retrieve data from that web service. Fortunately, this code is generated for you by Visual Studio through the process of creating a web reference. Once the web reference is in place, you can call the methods of the web service the same way you call the methods of a local .NET assembly.

When you clicked the link for Web Services on the Local Machine, a URL beginning with http://localhost was used to locate the web services on the local machine. Because of this, the Reporting Services web service uses localhost.ReportingService as its namespace.

Creating the Web Form   Now, we need to create the web form that is going to serve as our user interface.

1. Change the name of WebForm1.aspx to **ReportFrontEnd.aspx**.
2. Place three labels, two calendar controls, and a button on the web form, as shown in Figure 12-2.
3. Change the Text property of each label as shown.
4. Change the ID property of the left calendar control to **calStartDate**.

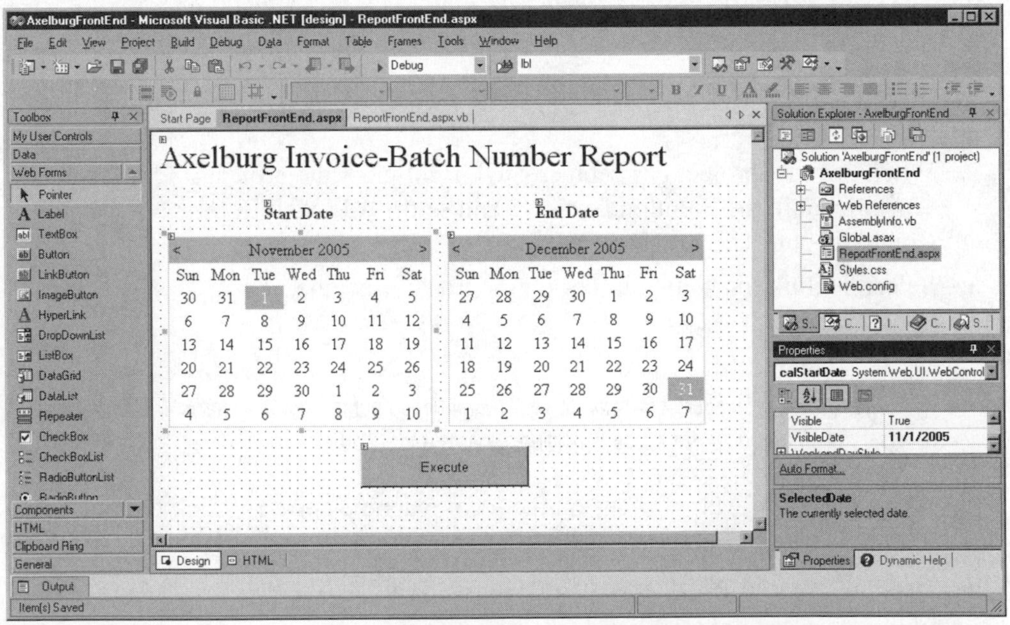

Figure 12-2   *The Axelburg Invoice-Batch Number Report front end*

5. Set the SelectedDate property and the VisibleDate property of calStartDate to **November 1, 2005**.

6. Change the ID property of the right calendar control to **calEndDate**.

7. Set the SelectedDate property and the VisibleDate property of calEndDate to **December 31, 2005**.

8. Change the ID property of the button to **cmdExecute**.

9. Change the Text property of the button to **Execute**.

10. Double-click the cmdExecute button to open the code window.

11. Enter the following code for cmdExecute_Click.

```
Private Sub cmdExecute_Click(ByVal sender As System.Object, _
                            ByVal e As System.EventArgs) _
                            Handles cmdExecute.Click
    Dim report As Byte() = Nothing

    ' Create an instance of the Reporting Services
    ' Web Reference.
    Dim rs As localhost.ReportExecutionService _
                    = New localhost.ReportExecutionService

    ' Create the credentials that will be used when accessing
    ' Reporting Services. This must be a logon that has rights
    ' to the Axelburg Invoice-Batch Number report.
    ' *** Replace "LoginName", "Password", and "Domain" with
    '     the appropriate values. ***
    rs.Credentials = New _
            System.Net.NetworkCredential("LoginName", _
        "Password", "Domain")
            rs.PreAuthenticate = True

    ' The Reporting Services virtual path to the report.
    Dim reportPath As String = _
    "/Galactic Delivery Services/Axelburg/Invoice-Batch Number Report"

    ' The rendering format for the report.
    Dim format As String = "HTML4.0"

    ' The devInfo string tells the report viewer
    ' how to display with the report.
    Dim devInfo As String = _
        "<DeviceInfo>" + _
        "<Toolbar>False</Toolbar>" + _
        "<Parameters>False</Parameters>" + _
        "<DocMap>True</DocMap>" + _
        "<Zoom>100</Zoom>" + _
        "</DeviceInfo>"

    ' Create an array of the values for the report parameters
    Dim parameters(1) As localhost.ParameterValue
    Dim paramValue As localhost.ParameterValue _
                        = New localhost.ParameterValue
```

```vb
paramValue.Name = "StartDate"
paramValue.Value = calStartDate.SelectedDate
parameters(0) = paramValue
paramValue = New localhost.ParameterValue
paramValue.Name = "EndDate"
paramValue.Value = calEndDate.SelectedDate
parameters(1) = paramValue

' Create variables for the remainder of the parameters
Dim historyID As String = Nothing
Dim credentials() As localhost.DataSourceCredentials = Nothing
Dim showHideToggle As String = Nothing
Dim encoding As String
Dim mimeType As String
Dim warnings() As localhost.Warning = Nothing
Dim reportHistoryParameters() As _
                    localhost.ParameterValue = Nothing
Dim streamIDs() As String = Nothing

Dim execInfo As New localhost.ExecutionInfo
Dim execHeader As New localhost.ExecutionHeader
rs.ExecutionHeaderValue = execHeader

execInfo = rs.LoadReport(reportPath, historyID)
rs.SetExecutionParameters(parameters, "en-us")

Try
    ' Execute the report.
    report = rs.Render(format,
        devInfo, "", mimeType, "", warnings, streamIDs)

    ' Flush any pending response.
    Response.Clear()

    ' Set the HTTP headers for a PDF response.
    HttpContext.Current.Response.ClearHeaders()
    HttpContext.Current.Response.ClearContent()
    HttpContext.Current.Response.ContentType = "text/html"
    ' filename is the default filename displayed
    ' if the user does a save as.
    HttpContext.Current.Response.AppendHeader( _
        "Content-Disposition", _
        "filename=""Invoice-BatchNumber.HTM""")

    ' Send the byte array containing the report
    ' as a binary response.
    HttpContext.Current.Response.BinaryWrite(report)
    HttpContext.Current.Response.End()
Catch ex As Exception
    If ex.Message <> "Thread was being aborted." then
        HttpContext.Current.Response.ClearHeaders()
        HttpContext.Current.Response.ClearContent()
        HttpContext.Current.Response.ContentType = "text/html"
```

```
                    HttpContext.Current.Response.Write( _
                        "<HTML><BODY><H1>Error</H1><br><br>" & _
                                     ex.Message & "</BODY></HTML>")
                    HttpContext.Current.Response.End()
                End If
        End Try
    End Sub
```

12. Click Save All in the toolbar.

13. Select Debug | Start from the Main menu. This executes your program.

14. When the browser window appears with the web application front-end page, click Execute. The report appears using the dates selected on the front-end page.

15. Switch back to Visual Studio and select Debug | Stop Debugging from the Main menu.

You can refer to the comments in the code sample for information on the purpose of each section of code. For additional information and additional examples, refer to Appendix B and the accompanying RSWebServiceSample program.

NOTE

The items in the DeviceInfo XML structure are the same rendering-specific, device information settings as those documented in the "URL Access" section of this chapter. Use the parameter name, minus the rc: prefix as the element name.

Managing Reporting Services Through Web Services

In addition to executing reports through the web service interface, you can also manage Reporting Services using the web services. If you choose, you can write an application that completely replaces the Report Manager web application for controlling Reporting Services. Refer to Appendix B for more information on management capabilities of the web service interface.

The Report Viewer Control

The Report Server web service gives you a tremendous amount of control over report access. However, the web service simply provides our applications with a stream that contains the report. It is up to our applications to provide an appropriate method for viewing the content of that report stream.

The Report Viewer control in Visual Studio 2005 takes things one step further. Not only does it provide access to the reports, but it also provides a means to view them.

In fact, the Report Viewer can even free you from the tether to the Report Server altogether. The Report Viewer control can be used in both Windows forms and web forms.

Displaying a Report from a Report Server

We first use the Report Viewer control to access a report on the Report Server. In this example, you build a Windows application that uses the Report Viewer to display the Axelburg Invoice-Batch Number Report. For this application to function properly, it must have access to the Report Server whenever a report is executed.

NOTE

The web service example in the previous section works in any version of Visual Studio .NET. The Report Viewer examples in this section require Visual Studio 2005.

Creating a Project and an Instance of the Report Viewer   First, you need to create a Windows application project in Visual Studio 2005.

1. Start up Visual Studio 2005.
2. Create a new project.
3. Select Visual Basic | Windows in the Project Types area.
4. Select Windows Application from the Templates area.
5. Enter **AxelburgRVFrontEnd** for Name. Select an appropriate Location for this project.
6. Click OK. A Windows application project with a Windows form, called Form1, is created.
7. Expand Form1 so it adequately displays the report.
8. Select the Toolbox window.
9. Locate the Data section of the Toolbox and, if it is not already expanded, expand it.
10. Drag the Report Viewer control from the Toolbox and drop it on Form1. See Figure 12-3.
11. Click the Dock in Parent Container link in the ReportViewer Tasks dialog box.

NOTE

If you plan to put other controls on the same form with the Report Viewer, do not dock the viewer in the parent container.

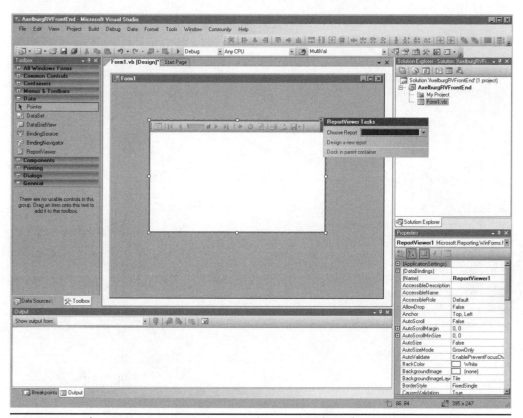

Figure 12-3   *Placing a Report Viewer control on a Windows form*

Configuring the Report Viewer   Now we need to point the Report Viewer at a report. You need to make several selections from the ReportViewer Tasks dialog box. If this dialog box is invisible, click the small black triangle in the upper-right corner of the Report Viewer control as shown in Figure 12-4.

1. In the ReportViewer Tasks dialog box, select <Server Report> from the Choose Report drop-down list.

2. Enter **http://{ReportServer}/ReportServer** for Report Server URL where {ReportServer} is the name of the server hosting Reporting Services.

3. Enter **/Galactic Delivery Services/Axelburg/Invoice-Batch Number Report** for Report Path.

4. Click Save All in the toolbar.

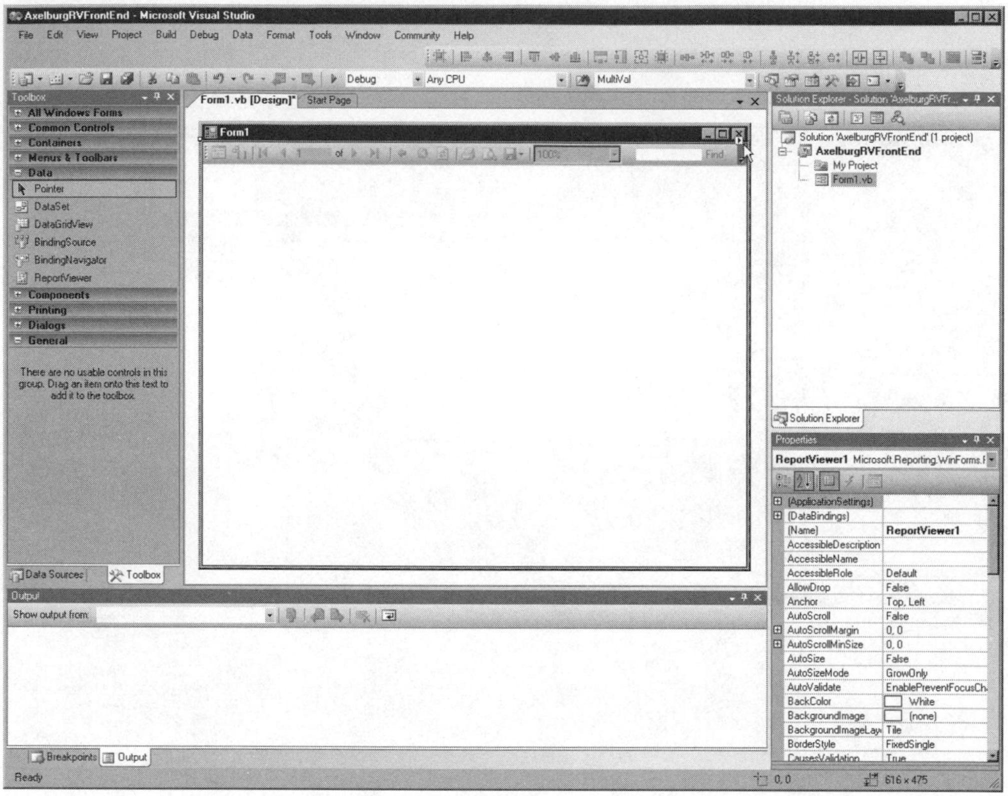

Figure 12-4   *Opening the ReportViewer Tasks dialog box*

5. Select Debug | Start Debugging from the Main menu. Form1 executes and displays the Invoice-Batch Number Report from the Report Server. If the report requires any parameters, the parameter entry area is displayed as shown in Figure 12-5.

6. Enter or select **11/01/2005** for the Start Date.

7. Enter or select **12/31/2005** for the End Date.

8. Click View Report. The report appears. Note the interactive features, such as drill-down work in the Report Viewer control as shown in Figure 12-6.

NOTE

You can use theServerReport:ReportServerUrl and ServerReport:ReportPath properties of the Report Viewer control to programmatically change the report that the Report Viewer displays. In this way, a single Report Viewer control can display different reports depending on user selection.

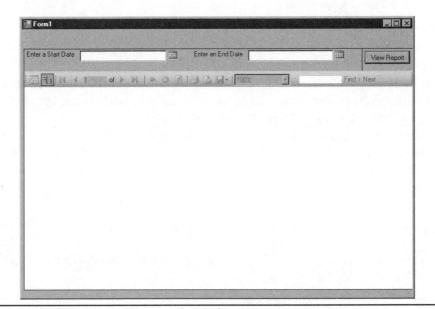

Figure 12-5   *The Report Viewer control with the parameter entry area*

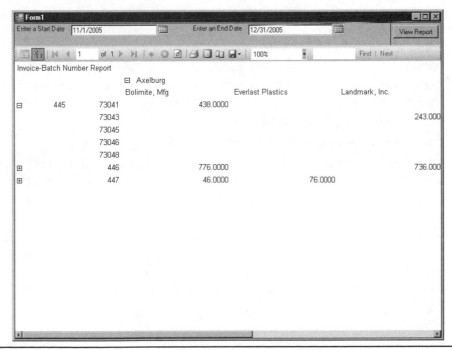

Figure 12-6   *The Report Viewer displaying a report with drilldown*

Displaying a Local Report in the Report Viewer

So far, all the methods of accessing reports we looked at in this chapter have required a Report Server. The Report Server provides a number of advantages for managing reports, including centralized control for updating report definitions and maintaining security. However, in some situations, it is impractical or undesirable for all installations of an application to pull reports from a Report Server.

The Report Viewer control provides an alternative. In addition to displaying reports rendered by a Report Server, the Report Viewer can also render reports contained within the Visual Studio project. In this example, we create a simple report right in the Visual Studio project, and then display it with the Report Viewer.

Creating a Local Report   We begin by creating a report in the Visual Studio project.

1. Close Form1 containing the report to return to Visual Studio 2005, if you have not already done so.

2. Open the ReportViewer Tasks dialog box.

3. Click the Design a New Report link. A new item, called Report1.rdlc, is created in the project.

4. As with reports created previously, the first step in designing a local report is to define the data source. Click the Add New Data Source link in the Data Sources window. The Data Source Configuration Wizard dialog box appears.

5. As you can see in the dialog box, we can use information from a database, from a web service, or from an object in our application as a data source for the report. Make sure Database is selected and click Next. The Choose Your Data Connection page of the wizard appears.

6. Click New Connection. The Add Connection dialog box appears.

7. Create a connection to the Galactic database. Use SQL Server authentication with GalacticReporting as the user and gds as the password. Test the connection to make sure you configured it correctly. When the connection passes the test, click OK.

8. The wizard warns you that sensitive information, namely the password, is being included in the connection string. Select the radio button next to "Yes, include sensitive data in the connection string" and click Next. The Save the Connection String to the Application Configuration File page of the wizard appears.

9. In most cases, it makes sense to store the connection information in the configuration file to make maintenance easier. Leave the default setting of Yes and click Next. The Choose Your Database Objects page appears.

10. Expand the stored procedures node and place a check next to stp_EmployeeList. Enter **EmployeeList** for the DataSet name.

11. Click Finish to complete the wizard. A typed dataset is created by the wizard for use with the report. The objects for the typed dataset appear just under the report layout area.

12. Select the Toolbox window and place a text box at the top of the report layout area. This text box is the title of the report. Enter **Employee List** as the content of the text box and format it appropriately for a report title.

13. Add a table to the report layout.

14. Select the Data Sources window. Expand the EmployeeList | stp_EmployeeList entry to see the fields in the dataset. Drag the fields into the detail line of the table. Format the column headings appropriately.

15. Your report layout should appear similar to the layout shown in Figure 12-7.

16. Click Save All in the toolbar.

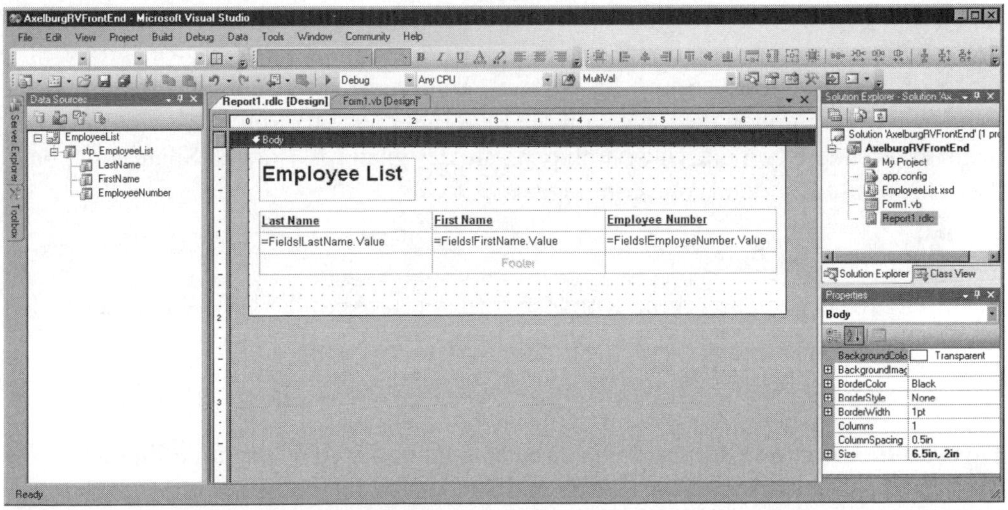

Figure 12-7   *Layout of the local report*

Point the Report Viewer at the Local Report Now, we point the Report Viewer at the new local report.

1. Click the Form1.vb [Design] tab in the layout area of Visual Studio 2005.
2. Open the ReportViewer Tasks dialog box.
3. Select AxelburgRVFrontEnd.Report1.rdlc from the Choose Report drop-down list.
4. Click Save All in the toolbar.
5. Select Debug | Start Debugging from the Main menu. Form1 executes and displays the local report. The local report you just created shows a list of all Galactic employees.
6. Close Form1 when you finish viewing this report.

When you compile the AxelburgRVFrontEnd project, the Report1.rdlc report definition is compiled as an embedded resource in the executable. Therefore, the data source is the only thing needed for the report to be rendered. The report always goes along with the application.

SharePoint Web Parts

We looked at a number of ways to integrate Reporting Services reports with applications, but we have one additional method yet to cover. Reporting Services provides a pair of web parts for use with SharePoint. The Report Explorer web part enables users to browse through the folders on the Report Server. The Report Viewer web part displays a rendered report. These web parts are designed for use with SharePoint, but they can be used as standalone components.

Installing the Web Parts

The SharePoint web parts come with Reporting Services in the RSWebParts.cab file ready for installation. The default location of this file is

```
C:\Program Files\Microsoft SQL Server\90\Tools\Reporting Services\SharePoint
```

This cab file should be installed using the Stsadm utility. The Stsadm utility unpacks the web parts, installs them in the appropriate location, and creates entries in the SafeControls section of the web.config file for the SharePoint virtual server. Use the following command line to complete the installation using default locations:

```
C:\Program Files\Common Files\Microsoft Shared\web server extensions\
        60\BIN\STSADM.EXE -o addwppack -filename
        "C:\Program Files\Microsoft SQL Server\80\Tools\
        Reporting Services\SharePoint\RSWebParts.cab"
```

NOTE

If you use the globalinstall switch with the Stsadm utility to install the web parts in the global assembly cache, you need to use the strong name for the assembly in place of the friendly name in the web.config file for the SharePoint virtual server.

Adding the Web Parts

Now that the web parts are installed, they need to be added to a web part page using the SharePoint window. Use the following steps:

1. Access the SharePoint site and click Create on the SharePoint toolbar.
2. Scroll down the page to the Web Pages section and click Web Part Page.
3. Type a name for the web part page and select a layout template.
4. Enter the location where your web part page is to be saved. The web part page appears.
5. Click Create at the bottom of the page.
6. Click Modify Shared Page. Point to Add Web Parts, and then click Browse.
7. Select the name of the gallery where you installed the Reporting Services web parts.
8. Select either Report Explorer or the Report Viewer from the list of web parts, and then drag it to an area of the web part page.

When both the Report Explorer and Report Viewer web parts are placed on the same web part page, you can connect them together. This enables the user to browse to a report in the Report Explorer web part, and then view the report in the Report Viewer web part. If the two web parts are not connected, selecting a report in the Report Explorer causes it to display in a new page. Use the following steps to connect the two web parts:

1. Click Modify Shared Web Part.
2. On the Report Explorer toolbar menu, click the down arrow, point to Connections, point to Show Report In, and then click Report Viewer.
3. Click OK.

Reporting Services Utilities

In addition to URL access, the web service interface, Report Viewer and SharePoint web parts, you can also interact with Reporting Services through several command-line utility programs. Like the other methods, these command-line utilities let you manage Reporting Services. These utilities enable you to control Reporting Services, as well as the encryption keys and encrypted values. The most capable of the utilities, the RS utility, lets you script and automate nearly any Reporting Service activity.

Each utility program is briefly described here. For more information, you can execute any of the utility programs followed by /? to view a listing of the valid parameters.

CAUTION

Even though the parameter listing for each utility program uses a dash before the parameter character (as in −a), you may need to enter a forward slash (as in /a) for the utility program to function properly.

The RSKeyMgmt Utility

The *RSKeyMgmt utility* is used to administer the encryption key used by Reporting Services. You can use the RSKeyMgmt utility to back up the encryption key. You can also use RSKeyMgmt to delete encrypted data in case of a problem.

When Reporting Services is installed, sensitive information stored in the configuration files, such as logon credentials, is encrypted for security. Also, any user names and passwords stored in reports or shared data sources are also encrypted. The encryption key used to decrypt the information is stored in the Report Catalog (ReportServer) database. Making certain changes can cause problems with the Reporting Services installation. These changes include the following:

▶ Modifying the user account used by the Reporting Services web service

▶ Modifying the name of the SQL Server used to store the Report Catalog

▶ Modifying the name of the computer hosting Reporting Services

A backup copy of the encryption key made with the RSKeyMgmt utility helps recover your Reporting Services installation in these situations.

The backup copy of the encryption key is protected by a password. You specify this password as a parameter to the RSKeyMgmt utility when you create the backup. You must have this password when you use the backup copy of the key.

Creating a Backup of the Report Server Encryption Key   To make a backup of the Report Server encryption key, do the following:

1. Insert a disk in the Report Server's floppy drive.
2. Open a command window.
3. Enter the following at the command prompt, where {password} is the password used to protect the encryption key:

   ```
   rskeymgmt /e /f a:\rsdbkey.txt /p {password}
   ```

4. Press ENTER.
5. When the backup process is complete, store the disk in a safe location.

Recovering a Reporting Services Installation   If your Reporting Services installation becomes disabled because of one of the situations described previously and you have a backup of the encryption key, follow this procedure:

1. Insert the disk containing the backup of your encryption code into the Report Server's floppy drive.
2. Open a command window.
3. Enter the following at the command prompt, where {password} is the password used to protect the encryption key:

   ```
   rskeymgmt /a /f a:\rsdbkey.txt /p {password}
   ```

4. Press ENTER.

If your Reporting Services installation becomes disabled because of one of the situations described previously and you do not have a backup of the encryption key, follow this procedure:

1. Open a command window.
2. Enter the following at the command prompt:

   ```
   rskeymgmt /d
   ```

3. Press ENTER.
4. Use the RSConfig utility to specify the connection information to the Report Catalog.
5. Reenter the user names and passwords for all reports and shared data sources stored on this Report Server that use stored credentials.

The RSConfig Utility

The *RSConfig utility* is used to change the credentials used by Reporting Services to access the Report Catalog (ReportServer) database. These credentials are encrypted in the configuration file, so they cannot be edited directly.

The following example changes the credentials used to access the Report Catalog on a SQL Server called RSServer to use a SQL Server logon called RSCatLogon with a password of rscat37:

```
rsconfig /c /s RSServer /d ReportServer /a Sql /u RSCatLogon
                                                    /p rscat37
```

NOTE

The Report Server Configuration Manager, discussed in Chapter 2, can be used to perform the same functions as the RSKeyMgmt and RSConfig utility programs. The Configuration Manager provides a graphical user interface, which you may find preferable to the command-line interface of the other utility programs.

The RSReportServer.Config File

The RSConfig utility (as well as the Reporting Services Configuration Tool) modifies information stored in the RSReportServer.config file. Some of the information in this file, such as logon credentials, is encrypted for security purposes. This information must be edited using the utility program. Other configuration information in this file is in plain text and can be edited with Notepad or another text editor. You need to stop and restart the Reporting Services Windows service for these changes to take effect.

CAUTION

Always make a backup copy of the RSReportServer.config file before editing. The Reporting Services Windows service cannot restart if this configuration file is invalid.

The default location of this file is

```
C:\Program Files\Microsoft SQL Server\MSSQL.3\Reporting Services\ReportServer
```

Table 12-10 shows the values immediately under the Configuration element in the RSReportServer.config file. The settings are shown in the order they occur in the file.

Setting	Valid Values	Function
Report Server Database Connection Information	(Encrypted—use the RSConfig utility or the Reporting Services Configuration Tool to modify)	This is the information required by Reporting Services to access the ReportServer database. This includes DSN, LogonUser, LogonDomain, and LogonCred.
ConnectionType	Default Impersonate	The type of credentials being used by Reporting Services to access the ReportServer database.
InstanceID		The identifier for the Reporting Services instance. This is tied to a SQL Server instance.
InstallationID		A GUID to identify this Reporting Services installation.
SecureConnectionLevel	0 to 3	The degree of security for the web service connection. 0—All requests processed. 1—Requests made over insecure connections and passing sensitive information, such as credentials, are rejected. 2—All rendered reports and web service calls require a secure connection. 3—All calls made to the Reporting Services SOAP API require a secure connection.
InstanceName		The name for the Reporting Services instance. This is tied to a SQL Server instance.
ProcessRecycleOptions	0 or 1	If 0, ASP.NET worker process is recycled when severe errors occur.
CleanupCycleMinutes		The number of minutes after which old sessions and expired snapshots are removed from the ReportServer databases. A value of 0 disables the cleanup process. The default is 10.
SQLCommandTimeoutSeconds		This setting is not used.

Table 12-10   *RSReportServer.config Configuration Elements* (continued)

Setting	Valid Values	Function
MaxActiveReqForOneUser		The maximum number of simultaneous, in-progress connections a single user can have open. This setting is intended to thwart a denial of service (DoS) attack. A value of 0 indicates no limit. The default is 20.
DatabaseQueryTimeout		The number of seconds before a connection to the ReportServer database times out. A value of 0 results in no timeout. The default is 120.
RunningRequestsScavengerCycle		The number of seconds before orphaned and expired requests are canceled. The default is 60.
RunningRequestsDbCycle		The frequency, in seconds, at which the Manage Jobs page is updated and the running jobs are checked to determine if they have exceeded the report execution timeout. The default is 60.
RunningRequestAge		The number of seconds after which a running job's status is changed from new to running. The default is 30.
MaxScheduleWait		The number of seconds Reporting Services waits for a schedule to be updated by the SQL Server Agent when a next run time is requested. The default is 5.
DisplayErrorLink	True False	If true, a link to the Microsoft Help and Support site is displayed when an error occurs. The default is true.
WebServiceUseFileShareStorage	True False	If true, the Reporting Services web service stores cached reports and temporary snapshots on the file system rather than in the ReportServerTempDB database. The default is false.

Table 12-10   *RSReportServer.config Configuration Elements* (continued)

Setting	Valid Values	Function
WatsonFlags		Specifies the type of dump sent with error reporting to Microsoft. 0x0430 — Full dump 0x0428 — Minidump 0x0002 — No dump The default is 0x0428.
WatsonDumpOnExceptions		Do not change this setting.
WatsonDumpExcludeIfContainsExceptions		Do not change this setting.

Table 12-10   *RSReportServer.config Configuration Elements*

Table 12-11 shows the values in the Service section of the RSReportServer.config file. The settings are shown in the order they occur in the file.

The next sections of the RSReportServer.config file deal with extensions to the Report Server for delivery, rendering, data processing, semantic query processing,

Setting	Valid Values	Function
IsSchedulingService	True False	If true, a thread is dedicated to making sure the schedules in the ReportServer database match the schedules in the SQL Server Agent. The default is true.
IsNotificationService	True False	If true, a thread is dedicated to polling the notification table in the ReportServer database to determine if there are any pending notifications. The default is true.
IsEventService	True False	If true, Reporting Services processes events in the event queue. The default is true.
PollingInterval		The number of seconds between polls of the event table. The default is 10.
WindowsServiceUseFileShareStorage	True False	If true, the Report Server Windows service stores cached reports and temporary snapshots on the file system rather than in the ReportServerTempDB database. The default is false.

Table 12-11   *RSReportServer.config Service Elements* (continued)

Setting	Valid Values	Function
FileShareStorageLocation		The path to the folder where cached reports and temporary snapshots are stored, if they are being stored on the file system. A UNC path can be used, but it is not recommended. The default is C:\Program Files\Microsoft SQL Server\MSSQL.3\Reporting Services\RSTempFiles.
MemoryLimit		The percent of available memory that may be used by Reporting Services before requests are rejected. The default is 60.
RecycleTime		The number of minutes for the recycling of the Report Server application domain. After this interval has elapsed, all new requests are sent to a new instance of the Reporting Services application domain. The default is 720.
MaximumMemoryLimit		The Report Server application domain is recycled when it reaches this percentage of available memory used. The default is 720.
MaxAppDomainUnloadTime		The number of minutes the Report Server application domain is allowed to upload during a recycle operation. The default is 30.
MaxQueueThreads		The maximum number of threads dedicated to polling the event table in the ReportServer database. The default is 0.
UrlRoot		The URL root used by delivery extensions to create the URL for accessing items stored on the Report Server.
UnattendedExecutionAccount		The credentials for the Execution Account. See Chapter 2 for more information. These credentials are encrypted and should be set using the Reporting Services Configuration Tool.
PolicyLevel		The security policy configuration file for the Report Server.
WebServiceAccount		The credentials used to run the Report Server web services. Also used to confirm the identity of the Report Server web service when doing data encryption.
IsWindowsServiceEnabled	True False	If true, the Report Server Windows service is enabled. This is set by the SQL Server Surface Area Configuration Tool. The default is true.
IsWebServiceEnabled	True False	If true, the Report Server web service is enabled. This is set by the SQL Server Surface Area Configuration Tool. The default is true.

Table 12-11   *RSReportServer.config Service Elements*

custom security, and event processing. These extensions are beyond the scope of this book, with the exception of the custom security extension, which is covered in the later section "Issues with Custom Security."

The RS Utility

The *RS utility* is used to execute script that can interact with Reporting Services. The scripting language supported by the RS utility is Visual Basic .NET. This scripting language supports the complete web service interface to Reporting Services.

The RS utility automatically creates a reference to the web service interface. This predefined reference, called rs, means you do not need to instantiate the web service interface; it is simply ready to go. All the Reporting Services classes and data types are also available.

The following sample code lists the contents of the Galactic Delivery Services virtual folder:

1. Enter the following into Notepad or some other text editor:

```
Public Sub Main()
    Dim items() As CatalogItem
    items = rs.ListChildren("/Galactic Delivery Services", False)

    Dim item As CatalogItem
    For Each item In items
        Console.WriteLine(item.Name)
    Next item
End Sub
```

2. Save this to a file called rstest.rss in a convenient folder on the Report Server.

3. Open a command window.

4. Change to the folder where you stored the rstest.rss file.

5. Enter the following at the command prompt, where {userID} is a logon with administrative rights on the Report Server and {password} is the password for that logon:

```
rs /i rstest.rss /s http://localhost/ReportServer
                    /u {userID} /p {password}
```

6. Press ENTER. A list of the folders in the Galactic Delivery Services folder appears in the command window.

Using the RS Utility to Manage System Properties

In Chapter 11, we looked at the Site Settings page in the Report Manager. This page enables you to make configuration changes to Reporting Services system properties. In addition to the settings exposed on the Site Settings page, Reporting Services has a number of other configuration options. Table 12-12 lists all these Reporting Services system properties.

Property	Valid Values	Function
EnableClientPrinting	True False	If true, users may download the ActiveX object and use client-side printing. The default is true.
EnableExecutionLogging	True False	If true, the execution of each report is recorded in a log table. The default is true.
EnableIntegratedSecurity	True False	If true, integrated security may be used in data sources. The default is true.
EnableMyReports	True False	If true, a MyReports folder is created for each Report Server user. The default is false.
EnableReportDesignClientDownload	True False	If true, a user with appropriate rights may use the Edit link in the Report Definition section of the report properties to download a copy of the report definition. The default is true.
ExecutionLogDaysKept	0 to 2,147,483,647	The number of days of log information kept in the report execution log. A value of 0 means an unlimited number of days are kept in the log. The default is 60.
ExternalImagesTimeout		The maximum number of seconds the Report Server attempts to retrieve an external image. The default is 600.
MyReportsRole	{Security Role}	The security role to assign to each user with their MyReports folder. The default is **My Reports**.
SessionTimeout	An integer value	The number of seconds a session remains active without any activity. The default is 600.

Table 12-12   *Reporting Services System Properties* (continued)

Property	Valid Values	Function
SiteName	A string up to 8,000 characters in length	The title displayed at the top of the Report Manager pages. The default is **Microsoft Report Server**.
SnapshotCompression	All None SQL	If All, report snapshots are compressed when stored in all locations, including both the Report Server database and the file system. If None, report snapshots are not compressed. If SQL, report snapshots are only compressed when stored in the Report Server database. The default is **SQL**.
SystemReportTimeout	−1 to 2,147,483,647	The maximum number of minutes a given report may execute. This value can be overridden for an individual report. A value of −1 means reports may execute for an unlimited amount of time. The default is 5.
SystemSnapshotLimit	−1 to 2,147,483,647	The maximum number of snapshots that can be saved for a given report. A value of −1 means there is no limit.
UseSessionCookies	True False	If true, the Report Server uses session cookies to track each session. If false, the rs:SessionID Report Server parameter must be used to pass the session ID. The default is true.

Table 12-12   *Reporting Services System Properties*

CAUTION

Using integrated security with a report exposes your SQL Server to a security risk. If a user with administration rights on the SQL Server executes a report with integrated security, that report then has administration rights on the server. A malicious query built into such a report could harm your SQL Server when it is run with integrated security. This risk can be mitigated by using a careful QA testing process before each report is deployed to the Report Server. If this is impossible and you want to eliminate the risk of this type of attack, set the EnableIntegratedSecurity system property to false.

One of the easiest ways to query and set the system properties that are unavailable on the Site Settings page is through the RS utility. The following script prints all the system properties and their current values:

```
Public Sub Main()
     Dim SSRSProperties() As [Property]
     Dim SSRSProperty As [Property]

     SSRSProperties = rs.GetSystemProperties(Nothing)
     For Each SSRSProperty In SSRSProperties
          Console.WriteLine(SSRSProperty.Name & " - " & SSRSProperty.Value)
     Next item
End Sub
```

This script sets the SystemReportTimeout property to ten minutes:

```
Public Sub Main()
     Dim SSRSProperties(0) As [Property]
     Dim SSRSProperty As New [Property]

     SSRSProperty.Name = "SystemReportTimeout"
     SSRSProperty.Value = 600
     SSRSProperties(0) = SSRSProperty

     rs.SetSystemProperties(SSRSProperties)
End Sub
```

Log Files

Along with the Reporting Services utilities, the logs created by Reporting Services can be helpful for managing and troubleshooting. These logs are text files that can be viewed with Notepad or any other text editor. In a default installation, the log files created by Reporting Services are stored in the following folder:

```
C:\Program Files\Microsoft SQL Server\MSSQL\
                                   Reporting Services\LogFiles
```

Four different types of log files are created, as listed in the following table.

File Name	Created By
ReportServer_{timestamp}.log	Report Server Engine
ReportServerService_{timestamp}.log ReportServerService_main_{timestamp}.log	Report Server Windows Service
ReportServerWebApp_{timestamp}.log	Report Manager

In addition to these log files is an ExecutionLog table in the Report Catalog (ReportServer) database. A record is created in this table each time a report is executed. The date and time of the execution, as well as the user name of the logged on user, are recorded. Unfortunately, the report being executed is identified by a globally unique identifier (GUID) rather than by the report name. Fortunately, Microsoft provides an Integration Services package for converting the information in the ExecutionLog table into something far more useable, including report names.

For more information on the Execution Log and the conversion Integration Services package, view "execution logs [Reporting Services]" in the index of SQL Server Books Online. (SQL Server Books Online is available in your Program menu under Microsoft SQL Server | Documentation and Tutorials | SQL Server Books Online.)

NOTE
Report Execution Logging must be turned on to use the logging features.

Custom Security

Another way to customize Reporting Services is through its security extension. By default, Reporting Services uses Windows integrated security. As you have seen, this means a user must have valid credentials (a user name and password) for either a local logon on the Report Server or for a domain logon on the domain containing the Report Server.

There are times, however, when creating Windows credentials for each Reporting Services user is not desirable or even feasible. You may want to expose reports on an Internet site or an extranet site. You may want to use the Report Manager as part of a web application that makes use of a different security model, such as forms authentication. In these situations, you can consider using the Reporting Services security extension to implement a security mechanism for the Report Manager and the Report Server web service that better fits your needs. As noted in Chapter 2, the Enterprise Edition of Reporting Services is required to use the Reporting Services security extension.

Authentication and Authorization

Before we discuss the security extension, let's look at the way security functions in Reporting Services. Security in Reporting Services has two parts: authentication and authorization. *Authentication* determines whether or not you can come in. *Authorization* determines what you can do once you are inside.

Authentication

Think of security like a trip to an amusement park as shown in Figure 12-8. If you are a big amusement park fan like me (I can't get enough of those roller coasters!), you probably purchase the multiday pass. Because the pass can only be used by the person who originally purchased it, you must prove you are the rightful owner of that pass when you get to the main gate. You may even have to show a picture ID to prove you are who you say you are.

This is the process of authentication. You must prove you have the appropriate credentials to gain access. At the amusement park gate, you need two things to gain entrance: a pass and some type of identification to prove you have the right to use that pass. The same is true for authentication in the computer world. First, you need some type of pass that has rights to get you in the gate. This usually takes the form of a user name, or more accurately, a user account identified by a user name. You must have a valid user account to log on.

Second, you must have some way to prove you are the rightful owner of that user account. This is often done by specifying a password along with the user name. In areas where security needs to be tighter, this proof of ownership might take the form of an electronic card or a thumbprint scan.

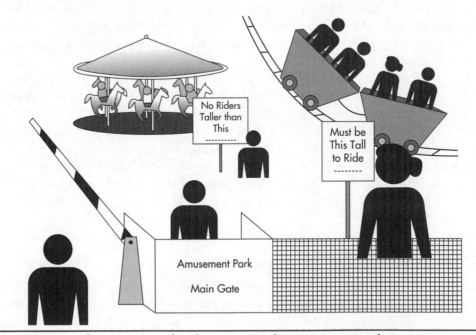

Figure 12-8   *Authentication and authorization at the amusement park*

In the default setup for Reporting Services, we are essentially outsourcing the main gate operations. Windows takes care of authenticating the user for us. If Windows says the user is okay, they must be okay. As you will see in a moment, when we implement custom security, we take back this job of authentication for ourselves.

Persisting Authentication

Because we are dealing with web interfaces—the Report Manager web application and the Report Server web service—we have one more authentication issue to deal with. Each time a user makes a request through either of these interfaces, the authentication has to be done again. This is just the nature of the HTTP requests we use with both web applications and web services. It is a bit like having to come in through the main gate of the amusement park every time you want to go on a different ride.

When we are using Windows authentication, the authentication process is completely transparent to the users. Because of this, having to redo the authentication each time a user requests a different Report Manager screen or executes a different report is not a big deal. However, if you create a logon screen as part of your custom security, this will be a different story. No user wants to reenter their user name and password each time they execute a report or navigate from one folder to another.

What we need is some way to remember we have already authenticated a particular user. We need the electronic equivalent of the ultraviolet-light-sensitive hand stamp used at the amusement park for exit and reentry. In computer terms, we need to *persist* the authentication.

For the custom security extension created in the section "Creating a Custom Security Extension," we use a browser cookie to persist the authentication. If the cookie is not present in an HTTP request, the logon screen is displayed. This should happen only at the beginning of a user session. Once we authenticate the user, we can send the cookie information to the user's browser and instruct it to create a cookie. The browser sends this cookie along with all subsequent HTTP requests made to Reporting Services. If the cookie is present, the logon information is taken from the cookie and the user does not see the logon screen.

Authorization

Let's return to our amusement park analogy. You passed through the main gate and are ready to ride that killer coaster. However, some limitations exist on just who can go on each ride. You must be taller than a certain height to go on the wild rides. You must be shorter than a certain height to go on the kiddie rides.

This is the process of authorization. You must prove you have rights to perform a certain activity before you can do that activity. At the amusement park, you must prove to the ride operator that you are taller or shorter than the height marking painted on the sign. If your head does not come above the line, you do not have the right to perform the activity of riding the roller coaster.

As you saw in Chapter 11, Reporting Services uses role-based authorization. Your logon account is assigned to a certain role for each folder, report, or resource. This role includes rights to perform certain activities on that item. Being assigned to the Browser role for a report means you are authorized to view that report.

The role assignments are stored in the Report Catalog within Reporting Services. When using the default security setup, Reporting Services checks the role assignments in the Report Catalog each time you try to perform a task. It determines from these role assignments whether or not you are authorized to perform that task, and then either lets you proceed or brings the process to a screeching halt.

When we implement custom security, you must perform this authorization check yourself. Fortunately, Reporting Services enables you to continue to use the role information stored in the Report Catalog. Therefore, if you want, you can still use the screens in the Report Manager to create and edit role assignments, and you can have those changes stored in the Report Catalog. Your custom security implementation can then use the information in the Report Catalog to determine authorization. If this does not fit your needs, you can create your own method for determining what a user is authorized to do.

Issues with Custom Security

Before you see how to create and deploy a custom security extension, we need to discuss several issues related to custom security. Changing the security mechanism for an enterprise application should not be done lightly. Before implementing a custom security extension, make sure you cannot fulfill your business needs without it, and then look at each of the following issues.

Tried and True

Windows integrated security is the default security model for Reporting Services and is, in fact, the only security model that comes with the product. Reporting Services was designed with Windows integrated security in mind. Therefore, it is the only thoroughly tested security model and the only one proven to provide a secure environment.

If you implement your own custom security extension, you are taking the responsibility of creating a secure environment on your own shoulders. You are responsible for the design, testing, and implementation of an environment that ensures the proper security for your Report Server. Remember, a custom security extension includes both authentication and authorization. Not only do you need to keep out those people who are not allowed to enter your Report Server environment, but you also have to restrict the activities of those users you do let in.

All or Nothing

When you implement a custom security extension, you completely replace the security mechanism on a Reporting Services installation. You cannot use your custom security extension for some users and the default behavior for others. This is an all-or-nothing proposition. Once you replace the default security mechanism, *all* authentication and *all* authorization comes through your custom code.

Validate All User Input

Care should be taken to validate all user input to prevent problems. This is especially true when you are creating a security interface. You should take steps to ensure that your custom security extension is not vulnerable to invalid characters and buffer overruns as a means of gaining unauthorized entry.

In addition to serving as the means for a security attack, special characters can also cause a problem if you are using the MyReports feature. As discussed in Chapter 11, when the MyReports feature is enabled, a virtual user folder is created from the user name of each Reporting Services user. The MyReports folder is then mapped to the appropriate user folder as each user logs on. User names containing any of the following characters can cause problems with these virtual user folders:

```
: ? ; @ & = + $ , \ * > < | . " / '
```

Using the Secure Sockets Layer

Anytime you are transmitting authentication information, you should use Secure Sockets Layer (SSL) to protect that transmission. When you use SSL, your data is encrypted before it is transmitted between the client and host computers. This helps prevent any interception or tampering with the authentication information while your data is in transit.

To use SSL, simply use https:// rather than http:// at the beginning of your URL. In addition, there is an SSL setting in the web application file and an SSL setting in the Internet Information Services management utility. These settings can be used to require all users to utilize an SSL connection when accessing the Reporting Services web application and web service.

Changing Security Models

Changing security models on your Reporting Services installation is not something to be done lightly. Any role assignments you created under a previous security model are removed when you change to a new model. Only the default system administration rights are present.

Changing back from a custom security extension to the default Windows integrated security, although possible, is not generally recommended. If you do so, you may experience errors when accessing items that had security roles assigned to them under your custom security extension. In addition, if you cannot successfully change back to Windows integrated security, you must reinstall Reporting Services.

Creating a Custom Security Extension

To demonstrate custom security in Reporting Services, we need to create our own code for both authentication and authorization. This code takes the form of several custom classes that implement Reporting Services interfaces. In addition, we create an override for some of the methods in the web service wrapper class to implement the cookie processing and persist our authentication.

If the previous paragraph sounds like Greek to you, then the custom security extension is probably not for you. You need a firm grasp of object-oriented programming (OOP) to understand the code samples in this section. Don't feel bad if OOP is not your thing—many people lead happy and productive lives without knowing how to implement an interface or override a constructor!

We are going to look at a sample security extension that implements forms security for Reporting Services. *Forms security* enables you to present the user with a form on which they can enter their user name and password. You can then validate that user name and password against a database table or other data store where you are maintaining a list of valid user credentials. This sample can help you become familiar with the workings of a security extension in Reporting Services. The sample is based on Microsoft's Forms Authentication Sample for Reporting Services. The original sample was written in C#. I have translated it into Visual Basic for consistency with the other examples in this book. Some revisions were also made to better fit with the Galactic Delivery Services examples.

CAUTION

The code provided here is merely a sample to aid in your understanding of the custom security extension. It is not intended to be used in a production environment. Discuss any intended security changes with your organization's security manager, system administrator, or network administrator before proceeding.

Preparing the Sample Code

The forms security sample consists of a single solution called FormsSecurity. This solution contains two projects—the FormsSecurity project and the StoreRSLogon project. The *FormsSecurity project* contains all the classes that implement the security extension along with the logon screens. The *StoreRSLogon project* contains code for a Windows application that enables you to assign user names and passwords to employees of Galactic Delivery Services.

First, three things need to be taken care of before we are ready to look through this sample code, so complete the following steps:

1. Download the FormsSecurity solution files and copy them to a test computer that contains both Reporting Services and Visual Studio 2005 with Visual Basic .NET.

2. Open the FormsSecurity solution.

3. Add a reference in the FormsSecurity project to the file:

   Microsoft.ReportingServices.Interfaces.dll

   The default location for this file is

   ```
   C:\Program Files\Microsoft SQL Server\MSSQL\Reporting Services\
                                               ReportServer\bin
   ```

NOTE

In this example, it is assumed you are using a copy of Visual Studio 2005 that is running on your Report Server.

4. Add a web reference to the ReportService web service on this computer. Name this web reference **RSWebService**. (Use the computer name rather than localhost when adding this reference. Testing has shown some unexpected results when using localhost for the web reference while building a custom security extension.)

5. Select Save All in the toolbar.

The AuthenticationExtension Class

The AuthenticationExtension class implements a Reporting Services interface called IAuthenticationExtension. The *AuthenticationExtension class*, along with a second class called CheckAuthentication, handles the authentication responsibilities. Some of the code from the AuthenticationExtension class is listed here (see the downloaded sample code for a complete listing):

```
Imports System
Imports System.Data
Imports System.Data.SqlClient
Imports System.Security.Principal
Imports System.Web
Imports Microsoft.ReportingServices.Interfaces
```

```vb
Namespace MSSQLRS.FormsSecurity
Public Class AuthenticationExtension : Implements _
                                        IAuthenticationExtension


    ' This function determines whether a user logon is valid.
    Public Function LogonUser(ByVal userName As String, _
                              ByVal password As String, _
                              ByVal authority As String) _
        As Boolean Implements IAuthenticationExtension.LogonUser
      Return CheckAuthentication.VerifyPassword(userName, password)
    End Function


    ' GetUserInfo is required by the implementation of
    ' IAuthenticationExtension.
    ' The Report Server calls the GetUserInfo method for each request to
    ' retrieve the current user identity.
    Public Sub GetUserInfo(ByRef userIdentity As IIdentity, _
              ByRef userId As IntPtr) _
              Implements IAuthenticationExtension.GetUserInfo
      ' If the current user identity is not null,
      ' set the userIdentity parameter to that of the current user.
      If (Not (HttpContext.Current Is Nothing)) And _
         (Not (HttpContext.Current.User.Identity Is Nothing)) Then
        userIdentity = HttpContext.Current.User.Identity
      Else
        userIdentity = Nothing
      End If

      userId = IntPtr.Zero
    End Sub


    ' This function is called by the Report Server when it sets
    ' security on an item. The function calls VerifyUser to make
    ' sure this is a valid user name.
    Public Function _
              IsValidPrincipalName(ByVal principalName As String) _
              As Boolean Implements _
              IAuthenticationExtension.IsValidPrincipalName
      Return VerifyUser(principalName)
    End Function


    ' Look up the user name in the database to make sure it is valid.
    Public Shared Function VerifyUser(ByVal userName As String) _
              As Boolean
```

```
Dim isValid As Boolean = False
Dim conn As SqlConnection = New SqlConnection(ConnectionString)
Dim cmd As SqlCommand = New SqlCommand("stp_LookupUser", conn)
Dim sqlParam As SqlParameter
Dim reader As SqlDataReader

' Look up the user name in the Employee table
' in the Galactic database.
cmd.CommandType = CommandType.StoredProcedure
sqlParam = cmd.Parameters.Add("@UserName", SqlDbType.VarChar, 255)
sqlParam.Value = username

Try
   conn.Open()
   reader = cmd.ExecuteReader

   ' If a row was returned, the user is valid.
   If reader.Read() Then
     isValid = True
   End If
Catch ex As Exception
   Throw New Exception("Exception verifying password. " & _
                                            ex.Message)
Finally
   conn.Close()
End Try

   Return isValid
  End Function
End Class
End Namespace
```

GetUserInfo Method   The *GetUserInfo method* of the AuthenticationExtension class is called by Reporting Services to determine the identity of the current user. This method reads the user's credentials that are being persisted in the cookie. Going back to our amusement park analogy, the GetUserInfo method puts our user's hand under the ultraviolet light to see if it has been stamped.

If GetUserInfo does not find a cookie with credential information, it returns an empty identity. When this occurs, the user is redirected to the logon page. The user then supplies the credentials and the authorization process can continue. If everything is working correctly, this should only occur once, at the beginning of the session.

Remember, GetUserInfo is simply extracting the credentials from the cookie. It is not determining the validity of those credentials. That is left to the LogonUser method.

LogonUser Method   Once you have the credentials, either from the cookie or from the logon page, they must be verified. Reporting Services calls the LogonUser method to do this verification. In our implementation, *LogonUser* calls the VerifyPassword method in the CheckAuthentication class.

VerifyPassword looks up the user name in the Employee table of the Galactic database. It encrypts the password supplied as part of the user's credentials and compares it with the encrypted password stored in the Employee table. If the two encrypted passwords match, the logon is valid. The result of this password match is returned to the LogonUser method, and then returned to Reporting Services.

IsValidPrincipalName and VerifyUser Methods · The *IsValidPrincipalName* and *VerifyUser* methods are used to determine whether a user name is valid. The IsValidPrincipalName method simply calls the VerifyUser method to perform this task. The VerifyUser method looks for the user name in the Employee table of the Galactic database. If the user name is found in the table, it is valid.

The VerifyUser method is called by a method in the AuthorizationExtension class. This is done to validate the user name in a configuration file. The IsValidPrincipal-Name method is called from Reporting Services whenever you create a new role assignment. This is done to validate the user name entered for that role assignment, before the assignment is saved in the Report Catalog.

The AuthorizationExtension Class

The *AuthorizationExtension* class implements a Reporting Services interface called IAuthorizationExtension. The AuthorizationExtension class handles the authorization responsibilities. Some of the code from the AuthorizationExtension class is listed here (see the downloaded sample code for a complete listing):

```
Imports System
Imports System.IO
Imports System.Collections
Imports System.Collections.Specialized
Imports System.Globalization
Imports System.Runtime.Serialization
Imports System.Runtime.Serialization.Formatters.Binary
Imports Microsoft.ReportingServices.Interfaces
Imports System.Xml
```

```
Namespace MSSQLRS.FormsSecurity
Public Class AuthorizationExtension : Implements _
                                      IAuthorizationExtension

  Private Shared m_adminUserName As String

  Public Function CheckAccess(ByVal userName As String, _
                   ByVal userToken As IntPtr, _
                   ByVal secDesc() As Byte, _
                   ByVal requiredOperation As FolderOperation) _
        As Boolean Implements IAuthorizationExtension.CheckAccess
    Dim acl As AceCollection
    Dim ace As AceStruct
    Dim aclOperation As FolderOperation

    ' If the user is the administrator, allow unrestricted access.
    ' Because SQL Server defaults to case-insensitive, we have to
    ' perform a case insensitive comparison.
    If String.Compare(userName, m_adminUserName, True, _
                      CultureInfo.CurrentCulture) = 0 Then
      Return True
    End If

    acl = DeserializeACL(secDesc)
    For Each ace In acl
      ' First check to see if the user has an access control
      ' entry for the item.
      If String.Compare(userName, ace.PrincipalName, True, _
                        CultureInfo.CurrentCulture) = 0 Then
        ' If an entry is found, return true if the given
        ' required operation is contained in the ACE structure
        For Each aclOperation In ace.FolderOperations
          If aclOperation = requiredOperation Then
            Return True
          End If
        Next
      End If
    Next

    Return False
  End Function
```

```vb
' Overload for an array of folder operations
Public Function CheckAccess(ByVal userName As String, _
                ByVal userToken As IntPtr, _
                ByVal secDesc() As Byte, _
                ByVal requiredOperations As FolderOperation()) _
        As Boolean Implements IAuthorizationExtension.CheckAccess

    Dim operation As FolderOperation

    For Each operation In requiredOperations
        If Not CheckAccess(userName, userToken, secDesc, operation) Then
            Return False
        End If
    Next

    Return True
End Function

' This subroutine implements SetConfiguration as required
' by IExtension
Public Sub SetConfiguration(ByVal configuration As String) _
            Implements IAuthorizationExtension.SetConfiguration
    ' Retrieve the admin user and password from the config settings
    ' and verify it.
    Dim doc As XmlDocument = New XmlDocument
    Dim child As XmlNode

    doc.LoadXml(configuration)

    If doc.DocumentElement.Name = "AdminConfiguration" Then
        For Each child In doc.DocumentElement.ChildNodes
            If child.Name = "UserName" Then
                m_adminUserName = child.InnerText
            Else
                Throw New Exception("Unrecognized configuration element.")
            End If
        Next

        If _
    MSSQLRS.FormsSecurity.AuthenticationExtension.VerifyUser( _
                                        m_adminUserName) _
                                        = False Then
```

```
      Throw New Exception("An attempt was made to load an " & _
  "Administrative user for the Report Server that is not valid.")
      End If
    Else
      Throw New Exception("Error loading config data.")
    End If
  End Sub

End Class
End Namespace
```

SetConfiguration Method   The *SetConfiguration* method reads a section of XML from the RSReportServer.config file. This XML information specifies the user name of the administrative user. This user name is stored in the m_adminUserName property of the AuthorizationExtension class.

The CheckAccess methods give this user all rights to all items. This ensures at least one user has rights to administer Reporting Services. This is necessary because, when you initially switch to your custom security extension, no role assignments exist for any of the items in Reporting Services.

CheckAccess Methods   The AuthorizationExtension class has several *CheckAccess* methods, which are overloaded based on the last parameter, requiredOperation. The correct method is called, depending on which type of access is being checked.

For example, if the user is trying to delete a folder, the CheckAccess method is called with a requiredOperation parameter of type FolderOperation. The version of CheckAccess that checks rights on folder operations is executed. If the user is using the check boxes on the Report Manager View Details page to delete several folders at once, the CheckAccess method is called with a requiredOperation parameter that is an array of the FolderOperation type. The version of CheckAccess that checks rights on an array of folder operations is executed.

Only two of the CheckAccess methods—the method for a folder operation and the method for an array of folder operations—are printed here. The CheckAccess methods for reports, resources, and other types of report items are similar to the CheckAccess methods shown here for folder operations. You can refer to the source code to view the other overloads of the CheckAccess methods.

The CheckAccess method is called by Reporting Services to verify the user's right to perform operations. It may be called once if the user is performing a specific operation. In other cases, the CheckAccess method may be called many times during the painting of a single screen. For example, if the user is viewing the Home folder, the CheckAccess method must be called for each item in the Home folder to determine if the user has rights to view that item.

The CheckAccess method first determines if the current user is the administrative user. If they are, the CheckAccess method returns true, indicating this user has rights to do whatever operation is being requested. The operation is then completed by Reporting Services.

If this is not the administrative user, the CheckAccess method walks through the security descriptor collection until it finds an entry for this particular user. It then walks through a second collection, which contains the rights assigned to this user. If it finds the rights to the requested operation, it returns true, allowing the operation to be completed. If it does not find the rights to the requested operation, it returns false, causing the operation to be aborted.

Deploying a Custom Security Extension

This section contains a process for deploying a custom security extension on a Report Server. If you want to complete this process solely for educational purposes, you should do so on a test installation of Reporting Services. That way, if anything goes wrong, either in deploying the custom security extension or in reverting back to Windows integrated security, you can reinstall Reporting Services without harming a production environment.

This process should not be tested on a production installation of Reporting Services with the intent to revert to Windows integrated security at its conclusion. As stated earlier, changing to a custom security extension, and then changing back to Windows integrated security, is not generally recommended. You have been warned. Don't come crying to me if you screw up your production server!

Preparation

CAUTION

Create a backup of all configuration files as directed in the following procedure. Without these backups, you may be unable to return to a working environment if the custom security extension fails.

To create a backup for all configuration files, follow these steps:

1. Add the reference and the web reference as instructed in the section "Preparing the Sample Code."

2. Create a folder called RSSecurityBackup on the Report Server. This folder can be anywhere it will not be accidentally deleted. This folder will hold a backup copy of your Reporting Services configuration files for backing up your custom security extension.

3. In the RSSecurityBackup folder, create a folder called ReportServer and a folder called ReportManager.

4. Copy the following files from the Reporting Services\ReportManager folder to the RSSecurityBackup\ReportManager folder:

```
rsmgrpolicy.config
RSWebApplication.config
Web.config
```

The default location for the Reporting Services\ReportManager folder is

```
C:\Program Files\Microsoft SQL Server\MSSQL\Reporting Services\
                                                  ReportManager
```

5. Copy the following files from the Reporting Services\ReportServer folder to the RSSecurityBackup\ReportServer folder:

```
RSReportServer.config
rssrvpolicy.config
Web.config
```

The default location for the Reporting Services\ReportServer folder is

```
C:\Program Files\Microsoft SQL Server\MSSQL\Reporting Services\
                                                  ReportServer
```

Compiling and Deploying the Custom Security Assembly and Logon Pages

Now that you have created backup copies of your Reporting Services configuration files, you can compile and deploy the custom security assembly and the logon pages.

1. Open the FormsSecurity solution in Visual Studio 2005.

2. Select Build | Build Solution from the Main menu to build the assembly and the executable in this solution.

3. Copy the resulting MSSQLRS.FormsSecurity.dll assembly and the MSSQLRS .FormsSecurity.pdb debug database to the ReportManager\bin folder. The default location for this folder is

```
C:\Program Files\Microsoft SQL Server\MSSQL\Reporting Services\
                                                  ReportManager\bin
```

4. Copy the same MSSQLRS.FormsSecurity.dll assembly and the MSSQLRS .FormsSecurity.pdb debug database to the ReportServer\bin folder. The default location for this folder is

```
C:\Program Files\Microsoft SQL Server\MSSQL\Reporting Services\
                                                  ReportServer\bin
```

5. Copy the UILogon.aspx file to the ReportManager\Pages folder. The default location for this folder is

```
C:\Program Files\Microsoft SQL Server\MSSQL\Reporting Services\
                                            ReportManager\Pages
```

6. Copy the Logon.aspx file to the ReportServer folder. The default location for this folder is

```
C:\Program Files\Microsoft SQL Server\MSSQL\Reporting Services\
                                                ReportServer
```

Modifying the Reporting Services Configuration

In addition to placing the assembly and the logon pages in the appropriate location, you need to modify several Reporting Services configuration files and the IIS configuration to enable your custom security extension.

1. You begin by modifying three Report Manager configuration files. These three files can all be found in the following folder:

```
C:\Program Files\Microsoft SQL Server\MSSQL\Reporting Services\
                                                ReportManager
```

2. Open the rsmgrpolicy.config file in a text editor, such as Notepad. This file contains the code access security configuration for the Report Manager.

3. Find the code group for the MyComputer zone. Change the permission set from Execution to FullTrust, as shown here:

```
<CodeGroup
        class="FirstMatchCodeGroup"
        version="1"
        PermissionSetName="FullTrust"
        Description="This code group grants MyComputer code Execution
                                                    permission. ">
    <IMembershipCondition
        class="ZoneMembershipCondition"
        version="1"
        Zone="MyComputer" />
```

This change is necessary to allow the custom security extension to access the database and to look up user information.

CAUTION

As with all XML documents, the config files are case-sensitive. Pay close attention to the case of each entry you make in these configuration files.

4. Save your changes.

5. Open the RSWebApplication.config file in your text editor. This file contains custom configuration information for the Report Manager web application.

6. Find the <UI> entry and add the following, replacing {computername} with the name of your Report Server computer:

```
<UI>
 <CustomAuthenticationUI>
        <loginUrl>/Pages/UILogon.aspx</loginUrl>
        <UseSSL>False</UseSSL>
 </CustomAuthenticationUI>
 <ReportServerUrl>http://{computername}/ReportServer</ReportServerUrl>
</UI>
```

This entry tells the Report Manager where to redirect a user who has not been authenticated. If you have SSL available on this server, change the <UseSSL> setting from False to True.

7. Save your changes.

8. Open the Web.config file in your text editor. This file contains the standard configuration information for the Report Manager web application.

9. Locate the <identity impersonate="true"/> entry. Change this entry to "false", as shown:

```
<identity impersonate="false"/>
```

10. Save your changes.

11. Next, you modify three Report Server configuration files. These three files can all be found in the following folder:

```
C:\Program Files\Microsoft SQL Server\MSSQL\Reporting Services\
                                              ReportServer
```

12. Open the RSReportServer.config file in your text editor. This file contains custom configuration information for the Report Server web service.

13. Find the <Security> and <Authentication> entries and modify them as shown:

```
<Security>
        <Extension Name="Forms"
                Type="MSSQLRS.FormsSecurity.AuthorizationExtension,
                                        MSSQLRS.FormsSecurity">
                <Configuration>
                        <AdminConfiguration>
                                <UserName>Stanley</UserName>
                        </AdminConfiguration>
                </Configuration>
        </Extension>
</Security>
```

```
<Authentication>
        <Extension Name="Forms"
                   Type="MSSQLRS.FormsSecurity.AuthenticationExtension,
                         MSSQLRS.FormsSecurity"/>
</Authentication>
```

These entries tell the Report Server web service what classes to use for
authentication and authorization and which assembly contains those classes.
The <Configuration> entry here contains the configuration information read
by the SetConfiguration method, as discussed previously. Stanley is the
administrative user.

14. Save your changes.

15. Open the rssrvpolicy.config file in your text editor. This file contains the code
    access security configuration for the Report Server.

16. Add a code group for the custom security assembly, as shown here:

```
<CodeGroup
        class="UnionCodeGroup"
        version="1"
        PermissionSetName="FullTrust">
    <IMembershipCondition
            class="UrlMembershipCondition"
            version="1"
            Url="$CodeGen$/*"
    />
</CodeGroup>
<CodeGroup
        class="UnionCodeGroup"
        version="1"
        Name="SecurityExtensionCodeGroup"
        Description="Code group for the sample security extension"
        PermissionSetName="FullTrust">
    <IMembershipCondition
            class="UrlMembershipCondition"
            version="1"
            Url="C:\Program Files\Microsoft SQL Server\MSSQL\Reporting
                 Services\ReportServer\bin\MSSQLRS.FormsSecurity.dll"
    />
</CodeGroup>
```

This code group uses URL membership to assign Full Trust rights to the custom
security assembly. If Reporting Services is not installed in the default location,
change the URL path as necessary.

17. Save your changes.

18. Open the Web.config file in your text editor. This file contains the standard
    configuration information for the Report Server web service.

19. Locate the <identity impersonate="true"/> entry. Change this entry to "false", as shown:

```
<identity impersonate="false"/>
```

20. Locate the <authentication mode="Windows" /> entry. Replace it with the following:

```
<authentication mode="Forms">
  <forms loginUrl="logon.aspx" name="sqlAuthCookie" timeout="60"
                                      path="/"></forms>
</authentication>
```

21. Add the following <authorization> entry immediately below the <authentication> entry:

```
<authorization>
  <deny users="?" />
</authorization>
```

22. Save your changes and close your text editor.

23. From the Administrative Tools area of the Control Panel, start the Internet Information Services management console.

24. Navigate to the entry for the Reports virtual directory. This virtual directory should be located under Default Web Site.

25. Right-click the Reports virtual directory and select Properties from the Context menu. The Reports Properties dialog box appears.

26. Select the Directory Security tab.

27. Click Edit in the Anonymous Access and Authentication Control area. The Authentication Methods dialog box appears.

28. Check the Anonymous Access check box.

29. Click OK to exit the Authentication Methods dialog box.

30. Click OK to exit the Reports Properties dialog box.

31. Right-click the ReportServer virtual directory and select Properties from the Context menu. The ReportServer Properties dialog box appears.

32. Select the Directory Security tab.

33. Click Edit in the Anonymous Access and Authentication Control area. The Authentication Methods dialog box appears.

34. Check the Anonymous Access check box.

35. Click OK to exit the Authentication Methods dialog box.

36. Click OK to exit the ReportServer Properties dialog box.

37. Close the Internet Information Services management console.

Reporting Services is now configured to use the custom security extension.

Restarting IIS

Anytime you make a change to the Reporting Services configuration files or to the custom security assembly, you need to restart IIS for these changes to take effect. Do not restart IIS if you have users in the middle of online sessions on your IIS server. You can restart IIS by using the following procedure:

1. Open a command window.
2. Type **iisreset** at the command prompt and press ENTER. The iisreset utility stops and restarts IIS.
3. Once IIS has restarted, close the command window.

Using the Custom Security Extension

To test the custom security extension, simply open your browser and go to the Report Manager. Rather than seeing the Report Manager, you see the logon page. Enter a user name and password, and then click Logon to log on to Reporting Services.

Two logons are set up in the Employee table of the Galactic database:

User Name	Password	Administrative User
Stanley	SR	Yes
Ellen	EH	No

The logon for Ellen does not have any security role assignments. Use the Stanley administrative logon to assign security roles to the Ellen logon.

NOTE

For the cookie to function properly, you need to access the Report Manager using the computer name rather than using localhost.

Creating Logons

You can create additional nonadministrative logons using the StoreRSLogon application. You created this executable when you built the FormsSecurity solution. To create a new logon, do the following:

1. Run StoreRSLogon.exe.
2. Select a Galactic Delivery Services employee from the Employee drop-down list.

3. Enter a user name and password for this employee.

4. Click Save to save these credentials in the Employee table of the Galactic database. The password is stored in the Employee table as an encrypted value.

5. Exit the StoreRSLogon program.

Debugging the Custom Security Assembly

In some cases, the custom security code does not work perfectly on the first try. Hard to believe, but true. You have two tools to help you in this situation: the log files and the Visual Studio debugger.

The *log files* are helpful because they record any exceptions that might occur. Because we deployed the debug database file (PDB) along with the assembly file (DLL), the log file even contains the method name and line number where the exception occurred. If an exception occurs, check the most recent log file for the Report Server, the Report Manager web application, and the Report Server web services.

You can also use the Visual Studio debugger to set breakpoints and step through the custom assembly code. Debugging should only be done on a test or development server, never on a production server. To use the debugger, do the following:

1. Start Visual Studio 2005 and open the FormsSecurity solution.

2. Open Internet Explorer and navigate to the Report Manager. The logon page appears. Do not log on yet.

3. Return to Visual Studio and set the desired breakpoints in your code.

4. Select Debug | Processes from the Main menu. The Processes dialog box appears.

5. From the list of processes, select the aspnet_wp.exe process (or the w3wp.exe process if you are using IIS 6.0), and then click Attach. The Attach to Process dialog box appears.

6. Check the Common Language Runtime and Native check boxes.

7. Click OK to exit the Attach to Process dialog box.

8. Click Close to exit the Processes dialog box.

9. Switch to Internet Explorer, enter the user name and password, and click Logon.

10. When one of your breakpoints is encountered, the debugger stops execution and changes focus to Visual Studio.

11. You can now view variables and step through the code as you do with any other Visual Basic program.

12. When you complete your debugging session, click Stop Debugging in Visual Studio, and then close Internet Explorer.

Changing Back to Windows Integrated Security

If your custom security extension does not function properly or, if despite all the warnings, you want to change from your custom security extension back to Windows integrated security, use the following procedure:

1. Remove all role assignments you created using the forms security user names.

2. Copy all the files in the RSSecurityBackup\ReportManager folder to the ReportManager folder. Replace the existing files. The default location of the ReportManager folder is

    ```
    C:\Program Files\Microsoft SQL Server\MSSQL\Reporting Services\
                                                      ReportManager
    ```

3. Copy all the files in the RSSecurityBackup\ReportServer folder to the ReportServer folder. Replace the existing files. The default location of the ReportServer folder is

    ```
    C:\Program Files\Microsoft SQL Server\MSSQL\Reporting Services\
                                                       ReportServer
    ```

4. Use the Internet Information Services management console to remove Anonymous access from both the Reports and the ReportServer virtual directories.

5. Use the iisreset utility program to restart IIS.

Other Extensions

In addition to the custom security extension, Reporting Services offers other APIs that enable you to extend its default functionality. You can develop your own data access extensions, rendering extensions, and delivery extensions. Examples showing how to utilize some of these extensions are included with Reporting Services. A number of third-party developers are using these APIs to create some capable add-ons for Reporting Services.

Best Practices

Before finishing, let's consider a few items that can make Reporting Services more efficient and easier to manage. These best practices are general rules of thumb that help things run smoother in most Reporting Services installations. As with all rules of thumb, exceptions always exist. However, as you create your Reporting Services installation and the business practices to go with it, consider these practices and the benefits that go with them.

Report-Authoring Practices

The following practices can make your report-authoring process more efficient and more consistent. A standard look and feel is usually desirable as users move from one report to the next. The ability to be responsive to your users and create reports in a timely manner is always a plus.

Use Report Templates

A number of tasks in report authoring can be repetitive, such as placing the company name and logo at the top of the page and placing the page number and date of execution at the bottom. Rather than wasting time creating these items afresh on each report, use one or more report templates. The report templates enable you to start your report layout with these redundant items already present.

In addition, the report templates let you provide a common look and feel to your reports. Templates can help ensure that certain style elements, such as a logo image or a page number in a certain location, are always present. The templates can help to enforce this common look and feel across a number of report authors.

Use Visual SourceSafe

Because the report-authoring environment for Reporting Services is also a development environment, seamless support for Visual SourceSafe is built right in. Use it! It takes very little additional time and effort to store your reports in Visual SourceSafe.

Visual SourceSafe has two advantages. First, no one has to wonder who has the latest source code for a report. This is especially important when modifying and then deploying reports to the Report Server. You do not want to have a report author deploy an old version of a report on top of a newer version. Second, Visual Source-Safe provides versioning of your report source code. If you decide you don't like the latest changes to a report, you can roll back to an older version. If an older version of an RDL file is pulled off of the Report Server on top of your newer version, Visual SourceSafe can save the day.

Use Shared Data Sources

Shared data sources can help cut down on management headaches. They centralize the storage of database credentials. If a database is moved to a new server, fewer places exist to change the connection information. If the database logon credentials are changed, fewer locations must be modified.

Shared data sources also facilitate the use of production and development database servers. Report development can be done using a shared data source pointing to the development database server. A shared data source with the same name can exist on the production Report Server pointing to the production database server. With the Overwrite

Data Sources option turned off, the shared data source from the development environment does not overwrite the shared data source in the production environment. Instead, the report goes seamlessly from querying development data in the development environment to querying production data in the production environment. Isn't that the way it's supposed to work?

Use Views and Stored Procedures

Give your report authors rights to query views and execute stored procedures. Avoid giving them rights to the underlying tables. Having them operate with views and stored procedures makes it easier to enforce security and maintain privacy. It also prevents accidental data modifications and deletions.

Use Navigation Features

Take advantage of the document map, bookmark, drilldown, and drillthrough capabilities to make your reports more usable. These navigation features make it easier for your users to find the information they are looking for. *Drilldown* and *drillthrough* make it possible to hide complex detail until your user specifically requests it. Finally, drillthrough allows several reports to be linked together into a working unit.

   Remember, the goal of reporting is to convey information to the end user. This is done best when a user can quickly navigate to desired information and follow the data intuitively from one level of detail to another or from one report to another. The Reporting Services navigation features make this possible.

Report Deployment Practices

The practices listed here can help you move reports from the development environment to the production Report Server. You need to make sure there is some level of control over which reports can access your production data. You also need to control who can do what on your production Report Server.

Create a Backup of the Encryption Key

This tip is not a report deployment practice, but it does help protect all the reports and shared data sources you have deployed to the Report Server. Occasionally, the key used to encrypt all the sensitive information stored on the Report Server becomes corrupt. When this happens, all that sensitive information is no longer accessible. The report credentials stored with each shared data source can no longer be decrypted and used. Worse yet, the credentials stored in the RSReportServer.config file cannot be decrypted, so the Report Server Windows service can no longer connect to the Report Catalog. In short, everything comes to a screeching halt.

If you do not have a backup copy of the encryption key, the only way to recover from this situation is to create a new encryption key and then reenter all the credential information. That is why the encryption key backup can be so important. With an encryption key backup, recovery from a corrupt key is trivial!

Review Reports Before Deploying

It is generally a good idea to have reports reviewed before they are put into production. This is especially true if you have nondevelopers creating their own reports. You need to make sure efficient queries are being used to extract the data, so an undue burden is not placed on the database server. You also need some level of assurance the information the report claims to present is the information being pulled from the database.

Use Linked Reports

Rather than deploying duplicate copies of the same report to your Report Server, use linked reports. Each linked report can have its own default parameters and its own security. At the same time, updates to that report are done in one centralized location. This helps prevent the confusion that can arise from having multiple versions of the same report running in the production environment at the same time.

Use Folders and Descriptions to Organize Reports

If your Reporting Services installation is as successful as we all hope, soon tens or even hundreds of reports will reside on your Report Server. With this number of reports, organizing the reports properly to aid both the end users and the administrators is important. Otherwise, both the users and the administrators can become frustrated.

Organize your reports into logical groupings in folders. Use the tree structure of the folders to create a multiple-level structure. You should create enough folders so no folder contains too many reports, but not so many folders that the structure becomes cumbersome.

Use meaningful report names and add informational descriptions to each report. Remember, both the report name and the description are searchable in Report Manager. Then make sure your users know how to use this search function.

Assign Security at the Folder Level

Make your security role assignments at the folder level. Let the reports inherit their security from the folders they reside in. Assigning individual security roles to individual reports is cumbersome and easily leads to errors. Your security practices should be relatively easy to implement; otherwise, they will not be followed.

Assign Security to Domain Groups

By the same token, it makes more sense to assign roles to domain groups than try to assign roles to each individual user. Just as with assigning security at the report level, making assignments at the user level causes things to become very complex very rapidly. The simpler security policy is usually better, because it is the one more likely to be followed.

Assign Only the Rights Needed

Only give each user the rights they need to complete their required tasks. Assigning broad rights rather than narrow is easier, but this can lead to security breaches and problems managing the Report Server. Take the time to create custom security roles that provide users with only those rights they need. Then use these custom roles as you are granting access to domain groups. The additional time taken during setup is more than made up for in the time saved not having to clean up after users who were doing things they shouldn't have been able to do in the first place.

Hide Items

Keep the folders looking as clean and uncluttered as possible. Use "Hide in list view" to hide items the user does not need to interact with. This might include shared data sources or subreports. If the user should not click on an item, then the user has no reason to see it in the folder.

Remember, however, this is not a security measure. The user can easily click on Show Details to reveal any of these hidden items. Security rights provide security; "Hide in list view" is a means of keeping things neat.

Deploy Supporting Items to the Report Server

The Report Server has the capability to store and serve supporting information. Documentation for your reports should be created as HTML pages, Word documents, PDF documents, Excel spreadsheets, and even PowerPoint presentations. These items can then be deployed to the Report Server right in the folders with the reports. This makes it easier for your users to understand the content and appropriate use of each report.

Use Caching and Snapshots

Use caching and snapshots to reduce the load on your Report Server and increase performance. Set up scheduled snapshots to execute long-running reports during off-hours. Believe me, users will not care if their data is eight hours old when they can get their reports back in seconds!

Where Do We Go from Here?

As Reporting Services matures over the next year or two, little doubt exists that it will remain an exciting product. With this new version of Reporting Services in SQL Server 2005, and third parties releasing alternative report-authoring environments and Reporting Services extensions, it is safe to say Reporting Services will continue to be in the news for some time to come. Based on the interest seen in the past year and a half, it also looks like Reporting Services is going to have a rapidly growing user community.

It may be difficult to say exactly where Reporting Services is going from here, but all the signs point in a positive direction. It might be easier to answer the question, Where does my business information go from here? With a tool as capable, flexible, and extensible as Reporting Services, the answer is, Anywhere you need it to go!

Appendixes

Report Item Reference

Report Objects

The first section of this appendix lists the report objects available in Reporting Services. These include the layout areas, the data regions, and the remaining report items. This section describes each object, including whether the object has its own custom properties dialog box, and lists all the properties for that object. Properties can be set in the Properties window or in the custom properties dialog box. The font of each property lets you know if the property can be set in the Properties window, the custom properties dialog box, or both. (See the following key.)

Layout Areas

KEY:

Property in Properties Window Only

Property in Properties Window and Custom Properties Dialog Box

Property in Custom Properties Dialog Box Only

Body

Description: The layout area containing the bulk of the report content
Custom Properties Dialog Box: No (The Columns and ColumnSpacing properties can be found in the custom properties dialog box for the report.)
Properties: BackgroundColor, BackgroundImage, BorderColor, BorderStyle, BorderWidth, **Columns**, **ColumnSpacing**, Size
Notes: If the Size: Width of the Body item added to the Margins: Left and Margins: Right of the Report item is wider than the PageSize: Width of the Report item, your report will span multiple pages horizontally.

Page Footer

Description: The layout area repeated at the bottom of each page. Can be enabled and disabled in the Report Properties dialog box or on the Report menu.
Custom Properties Dialog Box: No (The PrintOnFirstPage and PrintOn-LastPage properties can be found in the custom properties dialog box for the report.)
Properties: BackgroundColor, BackgroundImage, BorderColor, BorderStyle, BorderWidth, **PrintOnFirstPage**, **PrintOnLastPage**, Size
Notes: You cannot include field values in the Page Footer.

Page Header

Description: The layout area repeated at the top of each page. Can be enabled and disabled in the Report Properties dialog box or on the Report menu.
Custom Properties Dialog Box: No (The PrintOnFirstPage and PrintOn-LastPage properties can be found in the custom properties dialog box for the report.)
Properties: BackgroundColor, BackgroundImage, BorderColor, BorderStyle, BorderWidth, **PrintOnFirstPage**, **PrintOnLastPage**, Size
Notes: You cannot include field values in the Page Header.

Report

Description: The report is not a layout area itself but, rather, it is a container for the other layout areas.
Custom Properties Dialog Box: Yes
Properties: Author, **AutoRefresh**, **Classes**, *CustomCode*, **DataElementName**, **DataElementStyle**, **DataSchema**, **DataTransform**, **Description**, Description-LocID, **DrawGrid**, **EmbeddedImages**, **GridSpacing**, InteractiveSize, Language, **Margins**, **PageSize**, **References**, **ReportParameters**, **SnapToGrid**
Notes: If the Size: Width of the Body item added to the Margins: Left and Margins: Right of the Report item is wider than the PageSize: Width of the Report item, your report will span multiple pages horizontally.

Data Regions

KEY:
Property in Properties Window Only
Property in Properties Window and Custom Properties Dialog Box
Property in Custom Properties Dialog Box Only

Chart

Description: A business graphic such as a line graph or a pie chart. The chart is the only data region that cannot contain other report items.
Custom Properties Dialog Box: Yes
Properties: BackgroundColor, BackgroundImage, Bookmark, BorderColor, BorderStyle, BorderWidth, Calendar, *ChartAreaBorderAndLineStyle, ChartAreaFillStyle, Clustered*, Color, *Cylinder*, DataElementName,

DataElementOutput, **DataSetName**, Direction, *DisplayChartWith3-DVisualEffect, DisplayLegendInsidePlotArea*, **Filters**, Font, Format, *HorizontalRotation*, Label, LabelLocID, Language, *LegendBorderAndLine Style, LegendFillStyle, LegendFontStyle, LegendLayout, LegendPosition*, LineHeight, Location, **Name**, NoRows, NumeralLanguage, NumeralVariant, *Orthographic*, Padding, PageBreakAtEnd, PageBreakAtStart, **Palette**, Parent, *Perspective, PlotAreaBorderAndLineStyle, PlotAreaFillStyle*, PointWidth, *Shading, ShowLegend*, Size, **Subtype**, TextAlign, TextDecoration, *Title, TitleFontStyle*, ToolTip, ToolTipLocID, **Type**, UnicodeBiDi, VerticalAlign, *VerticalRotation*, Visibility, *WallThickness*, WritingMode, *X-AxisFormatting, Y-AxisFormatting*

Chart Category Group

Description: Controls the category groupings on the chart. These usually form the x-axis of the chart.
Custom Properties Dialog Box: Yes
Properties: *DataElementCollection, DataElementName, DataElementOutput, Filters, Group On, Label, Name, Parent Group, Sorting*

Chart Series Group

Description: Controls the series groupings on the chart. The series comes into play when there is more than one data point for each category grouping.
Custom Properties Dialog Box: Yes
Properties: *DataElementCollection, DataElementName, DataElementOutput, Filters, Group On, Label, Name, Parent Group, Sorting*

Chart Value

Description: Controls the values placed on the chart
Custom Properties Dialog Box: Yes
Properties: *Action, Angle, DataElementName, DataElementOutput, DataLabel, Format, JumpToBookmark, JumpToReport, JumpToReportParameters, JumpToURL, LabelFontStyle, MarkerSize, MarkerType, PlotDataAsLine, Position, SeriesLabel, ShowMarkers, ShowPointLabels, Value*

List

Description: A freeform layout area that can be tied to a dataset
Custom Properties Dialog Box: Yes

Properties: BackgroundColor, BackgroundImage, **Bookmark**, BorderColor, BorderStyle, BorderWidth, Calendar, Color, **DataElementName**, **DataElementOutput**, **DataInstanceElementOutput**, **DataInstanceName**, **DataSetName**, Direction, **Filters**, Font, Format, **Grouping**, **KeepTogether**, **Label**, LabelLocID, Language, LineHeight, Location, **Name**, NoRows, NumeralLanguage, NumeralVariant, Padding, **PageBreakAtEnd**, **PageBreakAtStart**, Parent, Size, *Sorting*, TextAlign, TextDecoration, **ToolTip**, ToolTipLogID, UnicodeBiDi, VerticalAlign, **Visibility**, WritingMode

List Details Group

Description: Grouping at the detail level in a list
Custom Properties Dialog Box: Yes
Properties: *DataElementCollection, DataElementName, DataElementOutput, Filters, Group On, Label, Name*, PageBreakAtStart, PageBreakAtEnd, *Parent Group, Visibility*

Matrix

Description: A pivot table for viewing row and column data
Custom Properties Dialog Box: Yes
Properties: BackgroundColor, BackgroundImage, **Bookmark**, BorderColor, BorderStyle, BorderWidth, Calendar, **CellDataElementName**, **CellDataElementOutput**, Color, **DataElementName**, **DataElementOutput**, **DataSetName**, Direction, **Filters**, Font, Format, **GroupsBeforeRowHeaders**, **KeepTogether**, **Label**, LabelLocID, Language, **LayoutDirection**, LineHeight, Location, **Name**, NoRows, NumeralLanguage, NumeralVariant, Padding, **PageBreakAtEnd**, **PageBreakAtStart**, Parent, Size, TextAlign, TextDecoration, **ToolTip**, ToolTipLocID, UnicodeBiDi, VerticalAlign, **Visibility**, WritingMode

Matrix Column

Description: Defines the appearance of a column in a matrix
Custom Properties Dialog Box: No
Properties: BackgroundColor, BackgroundImage, BorderColor, BorderStyle, BorderWidth, Calendar, Color, Direction, Font, Format, Language, LineHeight, NumeralLanguage, NumeralVariant, Padding, TextAlign, TextDecoration, UnicodeBiDi, VerticalAlign, Width, WritingMode

Matrix Column Group

Description: Defines the data that makes up each column in a matrix
Custom Properties Dialog Box: Yes
Properties: *DataElementCollection, DataElementName, DataElementOutput, Filters, FixedHeader, GroupOn, Label, Name, ParentGroup, Sorting, Visibility*

Matrix Row

Description: Defines the appearance of a row in a matrix
Custom Properties Dialog Box: No
Properties: BackgroundColor, BackgroundImage, BorderColor, BorderStyle, BorderWidth, Calendar, Color, Direction, Font, Format, Height, Language, LineHeight, NumeralLanguage, NumeralVariant, Padding, TextAlign, TextDecoration, UnicodeBiDi, VerticalAlign, WritingMode

Matrix Row Group

Description: Defines the data that makes up each row in a matrix
Custom Properties Dialog Box: Yes
Properties: *DataElementCollection, DataElementName, DataElementOutput, Filters, FixedHeader, GroupOn, Label, Name*, PageBreakAtEnd, PageBreakAtStart, *ParentGroup, Sorting, Visibility*

Matrix Subtotal

Description: Defines the formatting for a subtotal cell in a matrix
Custom Properties Dialog Box: No
Properties: BackgroundColor, BackgroundImage, BorderColor, BorderStyle, BorderWidth, Calendar, Color, DataElementName, DataElementOutput, Direction, Font, Format, Language, LineHeight, NumeralLanguage, NumeralVariant, Padding, Position, TextAlign, TextDecoration, UnicodeBiDi, VerticalAlign, WritingMode

Table

Description: A table for viewing columnar data
Custom Properties Dialog Box: Yes
Properties: BackgroundColor, BackgroundImage, **Bookmark**, BorderColor, BorderStyle, BorderWidth, Calendar, Color, **DataElementName**, **DataElementOutput**, **DataSetName**, **DetailDataCollectionName**, **DetailDataElementName**, **DetailDataElementOutput**, Direction, **Filters**, **FixedHeader**, Font, Format, **KeepTogether**, **Label**, LabelLocID,

Language, LineHeight, Location, **Name**, NoRows, NumeralLanguage,
NumeralVariant, Padding, **PageBreakAtEnd**, **PageBreakAtStart**, Parent,
RepeatFooterOnNewPage, **RepeatHeaderOnNewPage**, Size, *Sorting*,
TextAlign, TextDecoration, **ToolTip**, ToolTipLocID, UnicodeBiDi,
VerticalAlign, **Visibility**, WritingMode

Table Column

Description: Defines the appearance of a column in a table
Custom Properties Dialog Box: No
Properties: BackgroundColor, BackgroundImage, BorderColor, BorderStyle,
BorderWidth, Calendar, Color, Direction, FixedHeader, Font, Format,
Language, LineHeight, NumeralLanguage, NumeralVariant, Padding,
TextAlign, TextDecoration, UnicodeBiDi, VerticalAlign, Visibility, Width,
WritingMode

Table Details Group

Description: Grouping at the detail level in a table
Custom Properties Dialog Box: Yes
Properties: *DataElementCollection, DataElementName, DataElementOutput,
Filters, GroupOn, Label, Name*, PageBreakAtEnd, PageBreakAtStart, *Parent-
Group, Visibility*

Table Group

Description: Defines the data that makes up a group in the table
Custom Properties Dialog Box: Yes
Properties: *DataElementCollection, DataElementName, DataElementOutput,
Filters, GroupOn, IncludeGroupFooter, IncludeGroupHeader, Label, Name,
PageBreakAtEnd, PageBreakAtStart, ParentGroup, RepeatFooterOnNewPage,
RepeatHeaderOnNewPage, Sorting, Visibility*

Table Row

Description: Defines the appearance of a row in a table
Custom Properties Dialog Box: No
Properties: BackgroundColor, BackgroundImage, BorderColor, BorderStyle,
BorderWidth, Calendar, Color, Direction, Font, Format, Grouping, Grouping/
Sorting, Height, Language, LineHeight, NumeralLanguage, NumeralVariant,
Padding, TextAlign, TextDecoration, UnicodeBiDi, VerticalAlign, Visibility,
WritingMode

Notes: The Grouping property appears for the detail table row. The Grouping/Sorting property appears for the other types of table rows. The Grouping/Sorting property displays the correct information, but it displays it in the Details Grouping dialog box rather than the Grouping and Sorting Properties dialog box. (This is a bug.) The RepeatOnNewPage property does not appear for a detail table row.

Report Items

KEY:

Property in Properties Window Only

Property in Properties Window and Custom Properties Dialog Box

Property in Custom Properties Dialog Box Only

Image

Description: Places a graphic on the report

Custom Properties Dialog Box: Yes

Properties: Action, **Bookmark**, BorderColor, BorderStyle, BorderWidth, **JumpToBookmark**, **JumpToReport**, **JumpToReportParameters**, **JumpToURL**, **Label**, LabelLocID, Location, MIMEType, **Name**, Padding, Parent, **RepeatWith**, Size, Sizing, Source, **ToolTip**, ToolTipLocID, Value, **Visibility**

Line

Description: Places a line on the report

Custom Properties Dialog Box: Yes

Properties: Bookmark, EndPoint, **Label**, LabelLocID, LineColor, LineStyle, LineWidth, Location, **Name**, Parent, **RepeatWith, Visibility**

Rectangle

Description: Places a rectangle on the report

Custom Properties Dialog Box: Yes

Properties: BackgroundColor, BackgroundImage, **Bookmark**, BorderColor, BorderStyle, BorderWidth, **DataElementName**, **DataElementOutput**, **Label**, LabelLocID, LinkToChild, Location, **Name**, **PageBreakAtEnd**, **PageBreakAtStart**, Parent, **RepeatWith**, Size, **ToolTip**, ToolTipLocID, **Visibility**

Subreport

Description: Inserts one report into another
Custom Properties Dialog Box: Yes
Properties: Bookmark, BorderColor, BorderStyle, BorderWidth, Calendar, Color, **DataElementName**, **DataElementOutput**, Direction, Font, Format, **Label**, LabelLocID, Language, LineHeight, Location, MergeTransactions, **Name**, NoRows, NumeralLanguage, NumeralVariant, Padding, **Parameters**, Parent, **ReportName**, Size, TextAlign, TextDecoration, **ToolTip**, ToolTip-LocID, UnicodeBiDi, VerticalAlign, **Visibility**, WritingMode

Text Box

Description: Places a text box on the report
Custom Properties Dialog Box: Yes
Properties: Action, BackgroundColor, BackgroundImage, **Bookmark**, BorderColor, BorderStyle, BorderWidth, Calendar, **CanGrow**, **CanShrink**, Color, **DataElementName**, **DataElementOutput**, **DataElementStyle**, **Direction**, **Font**, **Format**, **HideDuplicates**, **InitialToggleState**, **JumpTo-Bookmark**, **JumpToReport**, **JumpToReportParameters**, **JumpToURL**, **Label**, LabelLocID, Language, **LineHeight**, Location, **Name**, Numeral-Language, NumeralVariant, **Padding**, Parent, **RepeatWith**, Size, TextAlign, **TextDecoration**, **ToolTip**, ToolTipLocID, UnicodeBiDi, UserSort, **Value**, ValueLocID, VerticalAlign, **Visibility**, **WritingMode**

Property Reference

This section describes the properties of the report objects. The property is listed only once, even if it is a property of several objects. If the property can be set in a custom properties dialog box, the explanation notes the tab where this property appears.

Some properties serve as a summary of several properties in the Properties window. BackgroundImage and BorderColor are two examples of these summary properties. A plus (+) sign to the left of a property in the Properties window tells you it is a summary property and has several detail properties beneath it. Click the plus sign to expand the summary property, so you can view and change the value of the detail properties.

In this section, the **Detail Properties:** entry signals this property is a summary property, which contains several detail properties. The detail properties are explained in the **Notes:** entry for the summary property.

Properties

Action

Description: Specifies which type of hyperlink action this item will execute.
When to Use: The report item is to cause the Report Viewer to navigate to a bookmark in this report, to another report, or to a website.
Notes: Linking to a bookmark or to another report works only in the Report Viewer or in the HTML and MHTML rendering formats. Linking to a website works only in the Report Viewer and the HTML, MHTML, PDF, and Excel rendering formats.
Property Of: Chart Value, Image, Text Box
Custom Properties Dialog Box Location: Navigation tab (Action tab for a chart value)

Angle

Description: Adjusts the angle of the point labels on a chart.
When to Use: A chart is to include labels on each data point, and the labels need to be rotated to an orientation other than horizontal.
Notes: Rotating data point labels to a 90-degree angle or a –90-degree angle helps fit more information in a tight space.
Property Of: Chart Value
Custom Properties Dialog Box Location: Edit Chart Value dialog box— Point Labels tab

Author

Description: Records the author of the report.
When to Use: The author's name is to be stored with the report.
Property Of: Report
Custom Properties Dialog Box Location: Report Properties—General tab

AutoRefresh

Description: Sets the number of seconds for the report to automatically reexecute when being displayed in the Report Viewer.
When to Use: The report shows constantly changing information and is viewed in the Report Viewer.

Notes: AutoRefresh only works in the Report Viewer in Report Manager. AutoRefresh does not work on the Visual Studio Preview tab or in any of the export formats.
Property Of: Report
Custom Properties Dialog Box Location: Report Properties—General tab

BackgroundColor

Description: Sets the fill color for the item.
When to Use: An item is to have its own fill color.
Property Of: Body, Chart, List, Matrix, Matrix Column, Matrix Row, Matrix Subtotal, Page Header, Page Footer, Rectangle, Table, Table Column, Table Row, Text Box

BackgroundImage

Description: Selects a graphic to fill the background of an item.
When to Use: An item is to have its own fill from a graphic.
Notes: The Source detail property specifies whether the image is embedded, external, in a database, or from a URL. The Value detail property contains the name of the image. The MIMEType detail property contains the MIME type of the image. The BackgroundRepeat detail property specifies how the image is repeated, if it does not fill the entire report object.
Property Of: Body, Chart, List, Matrix, Matrix Column, Matrix Row, Matrix Subtotal, Page Header, Page Footer, Rectangle, Table, Table Column, Table Row, Text Box
Detail Properties: Source, Value, MIMEType, BackgroundRepeat

Bookmark

Description: Creates a named bookmark in a report.
When to Use: A Chart Value, Image, or Text Box is to serve as a hyperlink to this report item.
Notes: The Bookmark serves as the target for a hyperlink jump within the same report. Clicking a Chart Value, Image, or Text Box whose JumpToBookmark property matches this report item's Bookmark property causes the Report Viewer to jump to this report item. Bookmarks work only in the HTML and MHTML rendering formats.
Property Of: Chart, Image, Line, List, Matrix, Rectangle, Subreport, Table, Text Box
Custom Properties Dialog Box Location: Navigation tab

BorderColor

Description: The color of the border around the outside of the report item
When to Use: A non-black border is to be around this report item.
Notes: The value in the Default detail property is used as the value for the Left, Right, Top, and Bottom detail properties, unless a value is specified for the detail property itself. The Left, Right, Top, and Bottom detail properties control the color for the individual sides of the report object.
Property Of: Body, Chart, Image, List, Matrix, Matrix Column, Matrix Row, Matrix Subtotal, Page Header, Page Footer, Rectangle, Subreport, Table, Table Column, Table Row, Text Box
Detail Properties: Default, Left, Right, Top, Bottom

BorderStyle

Description: The style (none, solid, dotted, dashed, and so forth) of the border around the outside of the report item
When to Use: A border is to be around this report item.
Notes: A border is displayed only when the BorderStyle property is set to a value other than None. Some of the more complex border styles, such as double and groove, are not clearly visible unless the corresponding BorderWidth property is set to a value larger than 1 point. The value in the Default detail property is used as the value for the Left, Right, Top, and Bottom detail properties, unless a value is specified for the detail property itself. The Left, Right, Top, and Bottom detail properties control the style for the individual sides of the report object.
Property Of: Body, Chart, Image, List, Matrix, Matrix Column, Matrix Row, Matrix Subtotal, Page Header, Page Footer, Rectangle, Subreport, Table, Table Column, Table Row, Text Box
Detail Properties: Default, Left, Right, Top, Bottom

BorderWidth

Description: The width of the border around the outside of the report item
When to Use: A border is to be around this report item with a width other than 1 point.
Notes: The value in the Default detail property is used as the value for the Left, Right, Top, and Bottom detail properties, unless a value is specified for the detail property itself. The Left, Right, Top, and Bottom detail properties control the width for the individual sides of the report object.

Property Of: Body, Chart, Image, List, Matrix, Matrix Column, Matrix Row, Matrix Subtotal, Page Header, Page Footer, Rectangle, Subreport, Table, Table Column, Table Row, Text Box
Detail Properties: Default, Left, Right, Top, Bottom

Calendar

Description: The calendar to use when dealing with date values in this report item
When to Use: A calendar other than the Gregorian calendar is to be used with date values in this report item.
Property Of: Chart, List, Matrix, Matrix Column, Matrix Row, Matrix Subtotal, Subreport, Table, Table Column, Table Row, Text Box

CanGrow

Description: Specifies whether a text box can grow vertically to display the entire contents of the Value property.
When to Use: The expected length of the Value property contents is not known or may vary.
Notes: Text boxes can grow in the vertical direction, but not in the horizontal direction.
Property Of: Text Box
Custom Properties Dialog Box Location: Text Box Properties—Format tab

CanShrink

Description: Specifies whether a text box can shrink vertically to remove any blank lines after the content of the Value property is displayed.
When to Use: The expected length of the Value property contents is not known or may vary.
Property Of: Text Box
Custom Properties Dialog Box Location: Text Box Properties—Format tab

CellDataElementName

Description: The name to be used for the element or attribute used to identify the cell data when exporting to the XML-rendering format.
When to Use: The report is to be exported using the XML-rendering format.
Property Of: Matrix
Custom Properties Dialog Box Location: Matrix Properties—Data Output tab

CellDataElementOutput

Description: Specifies whether the cell data is output when exporting to the XML-rendering format.
When to Use: The report is to be exported using the XML-rendering format.
Property Of: Matrix
Custom Properties Dialog Box Location: Matrix Properties—Data Output tab

ChartAreaBorderAndLineStyle

Description: The format of the line surrounding the entire chart item
When to Use: A line is to be around the entire chart item.
Notes: The Style detail property controls the style, the Width detail property controls the width, and the Color detail property controls the color of the line.
Property Of: Chart
Custom Properties Dialog Box Location: Chart Properties—General tab
Detail Properties: Style, Width, Color

ChartAreaFillStyle

Description: The fill behind the entire chart area
When to Use: The Chart item is to have its own fill color.
Notes: The fill can be a single color or a two-color gradient. The Color detail property contains the color of the area or is the first color in a two-color gradient when the Gradient detail property is true. The Gradient detail property specifies whether this is a single-color fill (false) or a two-color gradient (true). The EndColor detail property contains the second color in a two-color gradient.
Property Of: Chart
Custom Properties Dialog Box Location: Chart Properties—General tab
Detail Properties: Color, Gradient, End Color

Classes

Description: The classes (assemblies) referenced by this report, which include nonshared properties or methods.
When to Use: Nonshared properties or methods from an assembly are to be referenced by one or more expressions in the report.
Notes: The ClassName detail property contains a list of classes, contained in external assemblies, referenced by this report. The InstanceName detail property contains the name of an object (or instance) created from this class.

Property Of: Report
Custom Properties Dialog Box Location: Report Properties—References tab
Detail Properties: ClassName, InstanceName

Clustered

Description: Specifies that a series in a 3-D chart is to be shown front-to-back, rather than side-to-side.
When to Use: Depth is to be added to a 3-D chart to aid analysis or to add interest.
Property Of: Chart
Custom Properties Dialog Box Location: Chart Properties—3-D Effect tab

Color

Description: The foreground color
When to Use: A foreground color other than black is to be used.
Property Of: Chart, List, Matrix, Matrix Column, Matrix Row, Matrix Subtotal, Subreport, Table, Table Column, Table Row, Text Box

Columns

Description: The number of columns in the report body
When to Use: The report body is to have multiple columns.
Property Of: Body

ColumnSpacing

Description: The amount of space between multiple columns
When to Use: The report body is to have multiple columns with a separation other than 0.5 inch.
Property Of: Body

CustomCode

Description: Visual Basic functions and subroutines to be embedded in the report
When to Use: The report requires Visual Basic code too complex to put in a property value.
Property Of: Report

Cylinder

Description: Specifies that bars and columns in a 3-D chart are to be cylinders, rather than rectangular solids.
When to Use: Interest and variety is to be added to a 3-D chart.
Property Of: Chart
Custom Properties Dialog Box Location: Chart Properties—3-D Effect tab

DataElementCollection

Description: The name of the element to contain all instances of this group when exporting to the XML-rendering format.
When to Use: This group is to be included when exporting to the XML-rendering format.
Property Of: Chart Category Group, Chart Series Group, List Details Group, Matrix Column Group, Matrix Row Group, Table Details Group, Table Group
Custom Properties Dialog Box Location: Data Output tab

DataElementName

Description: The name to use for the element or attribute when exporting to the XML-rendering format.
When to Use: The report is to be exported using the XML-rendering format.
Property Of: Chart, Chart Category Group, Chart Series Group, Chart Value, List, List Details Group, Matrix, Matrix Column Group, Matrix Row Group, Matrix Subtotal, Rectangle, Report, Subreport, Table, Table Details Group, Table Group, Text Box
Custom Properties Dialog Box Location: Data Output tab

DataElementOutput

Description: Specifies whether this item is output when exporting to the XML-rendering format
When to Use: The report is to be exported using the XML-rendering format.
Property Of: Chart, Chart Category Group, Chart Series Group, Chart Value, List, List Details Group, Matrix, Matrix Column Group, Matrix Row Group, Matrix Subtotal, Rectangle, Subreport, Table, Table Details Group, Table Group, Text Box
Custom Properties Dialog Box Location: Data Output tab

DataElementStyle

Description: Specifies whether this item is output as an element or an attribute when exporting to the XML-rendering format

When to Use: The report is to be exported using the XML-rendering format.

Property Of: Report, Text Box

Custom Properties Dialog Box Location: Data Output tab

DataInstanceElementOutput

Description: Specifies whether the list instances are output when exporting to the XML-rendering format.

When to Use: The report is to be exported using the XML-rendering format.

Property Of: List

Custom Properties Dialog Box Location: List Properties—Data Output tab

DataInstanceName

Description: The name to use for the element when exporting to the XML-rendering format

When to Use: The report is to be exported using the XML-rendering format.

Property Of: List

Custom Properties Dialog Box Location: List Properties—Data Output tab

DataLabel

Description: The label to be used for data points on the chart.

When to Use: The data points on the chart are to be labeled.

Property Of: Chart Value

Custom Properties Dialog Box Location: Edit Chart Value—Point Labels tab

DataSchema

Description: The schema name used when exporting to the XML-rendering format.

When to Use: The report is to be exported using the XML-rendering format.

Property Of: Report

Custom Properties Dialog Box Location: Report Properties—Data Output tab

DataSetName

Description: The name of the dataset to be used with the data region.

When to Use: A dataset is to be used with a data region.

Property Of: Chart, List, Matrix, Table
Custom Properties Dialog Box Location: General tab (For chart, it is on the Data tab.)

DataTransform

Description: The name of a transform (XSLT document) to be applied after the report has been exported using the XML-rendering format.
When to Use: The XML document created by the export is to be transformed into another document format.
Property Of: Report
Custom Properties Dialog Box Location: Report Properties—Data Output tab

Description

Description: The description of the report
When to Use: The report's description is to be stored with the report.
Property Of: Report
Custom Properties Dialog Box Location: Report Properties—General tab

DescriptionLocID

Description: The localization identifier (language and culture, for example: "en-us") for a description property
When to Use: The report's description has been localized.
Property Of: Report

DetailDataCollectionName

Description: The name of the element to contain all instances of this group when exporting to the XML-rendering format.
When to Use: This group is to be included when exporting to the XML-rendering format.
Property Of: Table
Custom Properties Dialog Box Location: Table Properties—Data Output tab

DetailDataElementName

Description: The name to be used for the element or attribute used to identify the detail data when exporting to the XML-rendering format.
When to Use: The report is to be exported using the XML-rendering format.
Property Of: Table
Custom Properties Dialog Box Location: Table Properties—Data Output tab

DetailDataElementOutput

Description: Specifies whether this item is output when exporting to the XML-rendering format.
When to Use: The report is to be exported using the XML-rendering format.
Property Of: Table
Custom Properties Dialog Box Location: Table Properties—Data Output tab

Direction

Description: The writing direction to use with this item, either left-to-right or right-to-left.
When to Use: A character set that is written right-to-left is being used in this item.
Property Of: Chart, List, Matrix, Matrix Column, Matrix Row, Matrix Subtotal, Subreport, Table, Table Column, Table Row, Text Box
Custom Properties Dialog Box Location: Text Box Properties, Advanced—Format tab (for text box)

DisplayChartWith3-DVisualEffect

Description: Specifies whether to make a chart 3-D.
When to Use: Readability or interest is to be added by making a chart three-dimensional.
Property Of: Chart
Custom Properties Dialog Box Location: Chart Properties—3-D Effect tab

DisplayLegendInsidePlotArea

Description: Specifies whether to display the chart legend inside the chart-plotting area.
When to Use: Space can be saved by placing the chart's legend in an unused portion of the plotting area.
Property Of: Chart
Custom Properties Dialog Box Location: Chart Properties—Legend tab

DrawGrid

Description: Specifies whether the layout grid is shown on the Layout tab.
When to Use: The layout grid dots are not wanted on the Layout tab.
Property Of: Report
Custom Properties Dialog Box Location: Report Properties—General tab

EmbeddedImages

Description: The collection of graphics embedded in the report
When to Use: Images are to be embedded in the report.
Property Of: Report

EndPoint

Description: The coordinates of the end of the line
When to Use: A line is to be positioned on the report.
Notes: The Horizontal and Vertical detail properties specify the location of the end of the line.
Property Of: Line
Detail Properties: Horizontal, Vertical

Filters

Description: One or more expressions to exclude certain records from the dataset
When to Use: The dataset contains records not desired in the data region, and these records cannot or should not be removed by the dataset query.
Notes: The detail properties combine to build a set of filter expressions. Only records in the dataset that satisfy this set of filter expressions are included in the data region or grouping.
Property Of: Chart, Chart Category Group, Chart Series Group, List, List Details Group, Matrix, Matrix Column Group, Matrix Row Group, Table, Table Details Group, Table Group
Custom Properties Dialog Box Location: Filters tab
Detail Properties: Expression, Operator, Value, And/Or

FixedHeader

Description: Flag to freeze a group header on the screen during scrolling
When to Use: The group header should not scroll off the screen.
Property Of: Matrix Column Group, Table, TableColumn

Font

Description: The specification of the font to be used to render text within this item
When to Use: A font other than Normal, Arial, 10 point is desired.
Notes: The FontStyle detail property specifies whether the font is normal or italicized. The FontFamily detail property contains the name of the font.

The FontSize detail property specifies the size of the font in points. The FontWeight detail property specifies the thickness of the font and is used to create bold text. (Underlining is controlled by the TextDecoration property.)
Property Of: Chart, List, Matrix, Matrix Column, Matrix Row, Matrix Subtotal, Subreport, Table, Table Column, Table Row, Text Box
Detail Properties: FontStyle, FontFamily, FontSize, FontWeight

Format

Description: A formatting string to control the appearance of a value
When to Use: An appearance other than the default appearance of a value is required for better readability.
Property Of: Chart, Chart Value, List, Matrix, Matrix Column, Matrix Row, Matrix Subtotal, Subreport, Table, Table Column, Table Row, Text Box
Custom Properties Dialog Box Location: Text Box Properties—Format tab (for text box) or Edit Chart Value—Point Labels tab (for chart value)

GridSpacing

Description: The distance between layout grid points
When to Use: A distance other than 0.125 inch is desired between grid points.
Property Of: Report
Custom Properties Dialog Box Location: Report Properties—General tab

Grouping

Description: The grouping information for the detail level of the data region
When to Use: The detail level of this data region is to be a group.
Property Of: List, Table Row
Notes: This property displays the Detail Grouping dialog box.

Grouping/Sorting

Description: The grouping and sorting information for a header-level or footer-level table row
When to Use: Data is to be grouped or sorted.
Property Of: Table Row
Notes: This property displays the Detail Grouping dialog box. (This is the correct dialog box with the correct information, but it has a misleading title. The information in the dialog box applies to the group this table row belongs to. It is not the information for the detail level as the title would suggest.)

GroupOn

Description: The grouping expression
When to Use: Data is to be grouped when displayed by this data region.
Property Of: Chart Category Group, Chart Series Group, List Details Group, Matrix Column Group, Matrix Row Group, Table Details Group, Table Group
Custom Properties Dialog Box Location: General tab

GroupsBeforeRowHeaders

Description: The number of columns to appear to the left of the row headers (reverse this if you're using a right-to-left matrix)
When to Use: The row headers are to appear in the matrix, rather than to the left (or right) of it.
Property Of: Matrix
Custom Properties Dialog Box Location: Matrix Properties—General tab

Height

Description: The height of the row
When to Use: The row height is to be modified.
Property Of: Matrix Row, Table Row

HideDuplicates

Description: Specifies whether to hide duplicate values when the text box is repeated in a table column
When to Use: The value in the text box is to act as a group header, even though it is within the table detail rather than the group header.
Property Of: Text Box
Custom Properties Dialog Box Location: Table Properties—General tab

HorizontalRotation

Description: The horizontal rotation applied to a 3-D chart
When to Use: The horizontal rotation must be adjusted to provide the user with the optimum view of the chart data.
Property Of: Chart
Custom Properties Dialog Box Location: Chart Properties—3-D Effect tab

IncludeGroupFooter

Description: Specifies whether a footer row is to be included for this group
When to Use: Totals or other concluding information is to be displayed at the end of the table group.
Property Of: Table Group
Custom Properties Dialog Box Location: Grouping and Sorting Properties—General tab

IncludeGroupHeader

Description: Specifies whether a header row is to be included for this group
When to Use: Headers or other introductory information is to be displayed at the beginning of the table group.
Property Of: Table Group
Custom Properties Dialog Box Location: Grouping and Sorting Properties—General tab

InitialToggleState

Description: The initial state of the toggle graphic associated with this text box
When to Use: This text box is being used to control the visibility of another report item.
Property Of: Text Box
Custom Properties Dialog Box Location: Text Box Properties—Visibility tab

InteractiveSize

Description: The default page size of the report when it is viewed in an interactive renderer
When to Use: The page size of the report should be different when viewed in an interactive renderer than when viewed in a printed or fixed-page format.
Property Of: Report

JumpToBookmark

Description: The name of the bookmark to which this report item is to hyperlink
When to Use: This report item is to cause the Report Viewer to navigate to a bookmark in this report.
Notes: Linking to a bookmark works only in the Report Viewer or in the HTML- and MHTML-rendering formats.

Property Of: Chart Value, Image, Text Box
Custom Properties Dialog Box Location: Navigation tab (Action tab for a chart value)

JumpToReport

Description: The name of the report to which this report item is to hyperlink
When to Use: This report item is to cause the Report Viewer to navigate to another report.
Notes: Linking to another report works only in the Report Viewer or in the HTML- and MHTML-rendering formats.
Property Of: Chart Value, Image, Text Box
Custom Properties Dialog Box Location: Navigation tab (Action tab for a chart value)

JumpToReportParameters

Description: The parameters required by the report to which the item is to hyperlink
When to Use: This report item is to cause the Report Viewer to navigate to another report, and the target report requires report parameters.
Notes: The Parameter Name detail property contains a list of parameters for the hyperlinked report. The Parameter Value detail property contains a list of values to be assigned to each of those parameters.
Property Of: Chart Value, Image, Text Box
Custom Properties Dialog Box Location: Navigation tab (Action tab for a chart value)
Detail Properties: Parameter Name, Parameter Value

JumpToURL

Description: The URL to which this report item is to hyperlink
When to Use: This report item is to cause the Report Viewer to navigate to a website.
Notes: Linking to a website works only in the Report Viewer and the HTML-, MHTML-, PDF-, and Excel-rendering formats.
Property Of: Chart Value, Image, Text Box
Custom Properties Dialog Box Location: Navigation tab (Action tab for a chart value)

KeepTogether

Description: Specifies whether to attempt to keep this data region on one page
When to Use: The data region is to be kept on one page for better readability and analysis.
Property Of: List, Matrix, Table
Custom Properties Dialog Box Location: General tab

Label

Description: The document map label for this item
When to Use: The report is to include a document map, and this item is to be linked to one item in the document map.
Notes: The document map works only in the Report Viewer and in the PDF- and Excel-rendering formats.
Property Of: Chart, Chart Category Group, Chart Series Group, Image, Line, List, List Details Group, Matrix, Matrix Column Group, Matrix Row Group, Rectangle, Subreport, Table, Table Details Group, Table Group, Text Box
Custom Properties Dialog Box Location: General tab or Navigation tab

LabelFontStyle

Description: The font style of a chart point label
When to Use: The chart values are to have their own textual labels.
Notes: The FontFamily detail property contains the name of the font. The FontSize detail property specifies the size of the font in points. The FontStyle detail property specifies whether the font is normal or italicized. The FontWeight detail property specifies the thickness of the font and is used to create bold text. The Color detail property specifies the color of the type. The TextDecoration detail property specifies whether the text is underlined, lined through, or overlined.
Property Of: Chart Value
Custom Properties Dialog Box Location: Edit Chart Value—Point Labels tab
Detail Properties: FontFamily, FontSize, FontStyle, FontWeight, Color, TextDecoration

LabelLocID

Description: The localization identifier (language and culture, for example: "en-us") for a document map label

When to Use: The document map label has been localized.
Property Of: Chart, Image, Line, List, Matrix, Rectangle, Subreport, Table, Text Box

Language

Description: The language being used to display values within this report item
When to Use: The language being used is something other than the default language on the computer.
Property Of: Chart, List, Matrix, Matrix Column, Matrix Row, Matrix Subtotal, Report, Subreport, Table, Table Column, Table Row, Text Box

LayoutDirection

Description: The direction in which matrix columns are built, either left-to-right or right-to-left
When to Use: A matrix must be built from right-to-left.
Property Of: Matrix
Custom Properties Dialog Box Location: Matrix Properties—General tab

LegendBorderAndLineStyle

Description: The border and line style for the chart legend
When to Use: The chart legend is to have a nondefault border.
Notes: The Style detail property controls the style of the line. The Width detail property controls the width of the line. The Color detail property controls the color of the line.
Property Of: Chart
Custom Properties Dialog Box Location: Chart Properties—Legend tab
Detail Properties: Style, Width, Color

LegendFillStyle

Description: The fill style for the chart legend
When to Use: The chart legend is to have its own fill style.
Notes: The fill can be a single color or a two-color gradient. The Color detail property contains the color of the area or is the first color in a two-color gradient when the Gradient detail property is true. The Gradient detail property specifies whether this is a single-color fill (false) or a two-color gradient (true). The EndColor detail property contains the second color in a two-color gradient.
Property Of: Chart
Custom Properties Dialog Box Location: Chart Properties—Legend tab
Detail Properties: Color, Gradient, End Color

LegendFontStyle

Description: The font style for the chart legend
When to Use: The chart legend is to have a nondefault font style.
Notes: The FontFamily detail property contains the name of the font. The FontSize detail property specifies the size of the font in points. The FontStyle detail property specifies whether the font is normal or italicized. The FontWeight detail property specifies the thickness of the font and is used to create bold text. The Color detail property specifies the color of the type. The TextDecoration detail property specifies whether the text is underlined, lined through, or overlined.
Property Of: Chart
Custom Properties Dialog Box Location: Chart Properties—Legend tab
Detail Properties: FontFamily, FontSize, FontStyle, FontWeight, Color, TextDecoration

LegendLayout

Description: Specifies whether the chart legend is laid out in columns, rows, or as a table
When to Use: The chart legend is to have a nondefault layout for better readability.
Property Of: Chart
Custom Properties Dialog Box Location: Chart Properties—Legend tab

LegendPosition

Description: The position of the chart legend relative to the plot area
When to Use: The chart legend is to have a nonstandard position.
Property Of: Chart
Custom Properties Dialog Box Location: Chart Properties—Legend tab

LineColor

Description: The color of the line
When to Use: The line is to have a color other than black.
Property Of: Line

LineHeight

Description: The height of a line of text within this report item
When to Use: The report item is to use a nonstandard line height.
Property Of: Chart, List, Matrix, Matrix Column, Matrix Row, Matrix Subtotal, Subreport, Table, Table Column, Table Row, Text Box

LineStyle

Description: The style of the line (solid, dashed, dotted, and so forth)
When to Use: The line is to have a style other than solid.
Property Of: Line

LineWidth

Description: The width of the line in points
When to Use: The line is to have a width other than 1 point.
Property Of: Line

LinkToChild

Description: The report item within the rectangle that will be the ultimate target of a document map entry that points to the rectangle
When to Use: A rectangle containing several report items is the target of a document map entry.
Property Of: Rectangle

Location

Description: The location of the report item within the layout area
When to Use: Every time an item is placed in a layout area.
Notes: The Left and Top detail properties specify the position of the upper-left corner of the report item in the layout area.
Property Of: Chart, Image, Line, List, Matrix, Rectangle, Subreport, Table, Text Box
Detail Properties: Left, Top

Margins

Description: The size of the margins on the report page
When to Use: The margins are to be something other than 1 inch.
Notes: If the body width plus the left and right margins are greater than the report page width, the report will span more than one page horizontally. The Left, Right, Top, and Bottom detail properties specify the size of each margin in inches.
Property Of: Report
Custom Properties Dialog Box Location: Report Properties—Layout tab
Detail Properties: Left, Right, Top, Bottom

MarkerSize

Description: The size of the marker placed for each data value on a chart
When to Use: Each data value is to be highlighted with a shape to mark its position.
Property Of: Chart Value
Custom Properties Dialog Box Location: Edit Chart Value—Appearance tab

MarkerType

Description: The shape used to mark each data value on a chart
When to Use: Each data value is to be highlighted with a shape to mark its position.
Property Of: Chart Value
Custom Properties Dialog Box Location: Edit Chart Value—Appearance tab

MergeTransactions

Description: Combines any transactions from a subreport with the transactions of the parent report
When to Use: The queries in both the parent report and the subreport initiate data modifications that should be committed only if both are successful.
Notes: Both reports must use the same data source.
Property Of: Subreport

MIMEType

Description: The MIME type of the graphic used to populate the image item
When to Use: The MIME type must be selected only when using an external image source such as a database. The MIME type is automatically detected for embedded images.
Property Of: Image

Name

Description: The name of the report item
When to Use: The report item will be referenced by another item in the report (for example, to control visibility).
Notes: Report item names must be unique within a report.
Property Of: Chart, Chart Category Group, Chart Series Group, Image, Line, List, List Details Group, Matrix, Matrix Column Group, Matrix Row Group, Rectangle, Subreport, Table, Table Details Group, Table Group, Text Box
Custom Properties Dialog Box Location: General tab

NoRows

Description: The message displayed in place of a data region when that data region's dataset contains no rows
When to Use: A data region's dataset may be empty.
Property Of: Chart, List, Matrix, Subreport, Table

NumeralLanguage

Description: The language to use when applying formatting to numeric output
When to Use: The numeral language is to be something other than the default for the computer.
Property Of: Chart, List, Matrix, Matrix Column, Matrix Row, Matrix Subtotal, Subreport, Table, Table Column, Table Row, Text Box

NumeralVariant

Description: The variant of the numeral language to use when applying formatting to numeric output
When to Use: The numeral language variant is to be something other than the default for the computer.
Property Of: Chart, List, Matrix, Matrix Column, Matrix Row, Matrix Subtotal, Subreport, Table, Table Column, Table Row, Text Box

Orthographic

Description: Specifies whether to present a 3-D chart as an orthographic projection
When to Use: An orthographic projection of a 3-D chart is to be used to provide the best view for analysis.
Notes: An orthographic projection represents the three dimensions as perpendicular to one another. The Perspective property is ignored when the Orthographic property is selected.
Property Of: Chart
Custom Properties Dialog Box Location: Chart Properties—3-D Effect tab

Padding

Description: The amount of empty space left around the sides of an item
When to Use: The amount of empty space is to be changed to improve the report's presentation and readability.
Notes: The Left, Right, Top, and Bottom detail properties specify in points the white space on each side of the report item.

Property Of: Chart, Image, List, Matrix, Matrix Column, Matrix Row, Matrix Subtotal, Subreport, Table, Table Column, Table Row, Text Box
Custom Properties Dialog Box Location: Advanced Text Box Properties—Format tab (only for text box)
Detail Properties: Left, Right, Top, Bottom

PageBreakAtEnd

Description: Specifies whether a forced page break is to be inserted at the end of this report item
When to Use: A page break is to be forced to meet report-formatting needs.
Property Of: Chart, List, List Details Group, Matrix, Matrix Row Grouping, Rectangle, Table, Table Details Group, Table Group
Custom Properties Dialog Box Location: General tab

PageBreakAtStart

Description: Specifies whether a forced page break is to be inserted at the beginning of this report item
When to Use: A page break is to be forced to meet report-formatting needs.
Property Of: Chart, List, List Details Group, Matrix, Matrix Row Grouping, Rectangle, Table, Table Details Group, Table Group
Custom Properties Dialog Box Location: General tab

PageSize

Description: The size of the report page
When to Use: The report will be printed or exported to the PDF- or TIFF-rendering formats.
Notes: The Width detail property specifies the width of the report in inches. The Height detail property specifies the height of the report in inches.
Property Of: Report
Custom Properties Dialog Box Location: Report Properties—Layout tab
Detail Properties: Width, Height

Palette

Description: The color scheme to use for a chart
When to Use: A nondefault set of colors is to be used when creating a chart.
Property Of: Chart
Custom Properties Dialog Box Location: Chart Properties—General tab

Parameters

Description: The parameter values to be passed to a subreport
When to Use: The subreport is to receive values from the parent report to control the subreport's content.
Notes: The Parameter Name detail property contains a list of parameters for the selected subreport. The Parameter Value detail property contains a list of values to be assigned to each of those parameters.
Property Of: Subreport
Custom Properties Dialog Box Location: Subreport Properties—Parameters tab
Detail Properties: Parameter Name, Parameter Value

Parent

Description: The report item that contains this item
When to Use: This is a read-only property controlled by the item's location on the report layout.
Property Of: Chart, Image, Line, List, Matrix, Rectangle, Subreport, Table, Text Box

Parent Group

Description: The group that contains this group
When to Use: This is a read-only property maintained automatically by the group hierarchy.
Property Of: Chart Category Group, Chart Series Group, List Details Group, Matrix Column Group, Matrix Row Group, Table Details Group, Table Group
Custom Properties Dialog Box Location: General tab

Perspective

Description: The amount of perspective applied to a 3-D chart
When to Use: The default perspective of a 3-D chart is to be changed to improve readability or interest.
Property Of: Chart
Custom Properties Dialog Box Location: Chart Properties—3-D Effect tab

PlotAreaBorderAndLineStyle

Description: The format of the line surrounding the chart's plot area
When to Use: The format of the chart's plot area is to be changed from the 1-point, solid, black line.

Notes: The Style detail property controls the style of the line. The Width detail property controls the width of the line. The Color detail property controls the color of the line.
Property Of: Chart
Custom Properties Dialog Box Location: Chart Properties—General tab
Detail Properties: Style, Width, Color

PlotAreaFillStyle

Description: The fill behind the chart's plotting area
When to Use: The chart's plotting area is to have a fill color other than light gray.
Notes: The fill can be a single-color or a two-color gradient. The Color detail property contains the color of the area or is the first color in a two-color gradient when the Gradient detail property is true. The Gradient detail property specifies whether this is a single-color fill (false) or a two-color gradient (true). The EndColor detail property contains the second color in a two-color gradient.
Property Of: Chart
Custom Properties Dialog Box Location: Chart Properties—General tab
Detail Properties: Color, Gradient, End Color

PlotDataAsLine

Description: Specifies whether the chart data is to be represented by a line
When to Use: The chart data is to be represented by a line.
Property Of: Chart Value
Custom Properties Dialog Box Location: Edit Chart Value—Appearance tab

PointWidth

Description: Specifies the width, in points, of the column on a column chart or a bar on a bar chart
When to Use: The default width of the column or bar must be modified.
Property Of: Chart

Position

Description: The position of the chart value labels or the matrix subtotal
When to Use: The chart value label is to be placed in a position other than directly above the data point, or the matrix subtotal is to be placed above or before the detail, rather than below or after it.

Property Of: Chart Value, Matrix Subtotal
Custom Properties Dialog Box Location: Edit Chart Value—Point Labels tab. (This property does not appear in a custom properties dialog box for a Matrix Subtotal.)

PrintOnFirstPage

Description: Specifies whether the page header or page footer should print on the first page of the report
When to Use: The report contains a page header or footer that is not to be printed on the first page of the report.
Property Of: Page Header, Page Footer
Custom Properties Dialog Box Location: Report Properties—General tab

PrintOnLastPage

Description: Specifies whether the page header or page footer should print on the last page of the report.
When to Use: The report contains a page header or footer that is not to be printed on the last page of the report.
Property Of: Page Header, Page Footer
Custom Properties Dialog Box Location: Report Properties—General tab

References

Description: The custom assemblies referenced by the report
When to Use: A report expression is to make use of a property or method in a custom assembly.
Notes: The AssemblyName detail property contains a list of assemblies that are referenced by the report.
Property Of: Report
Custom Properties Dialog Box Location: Report Properties—References tab
Detail Properties: AssemblyName

RepeatFooterOnNewPage

Description: Specifies whether a footer should be repeated on each new page spanned by the table
When to Use: A table or table group contains a footer that is to be repeated on every page spanned by the table.
Property Of: Table, Table Group
Custom Properties Dialog Box Location: General tab

RepeatHeaderOnNewPage

Description: Specifies whether a header should be repeated on each new page spanned by the table

When to Use: A table or table group contains a header that is to be repeated on every page spanned by the table.

Property Of: Table, Table Group

Custom Properties Dialog Box Location: General tab

RepeatOnNewPage

Description: This table row should repeat on each page of the report

When to Use: One or more table rows should repeat on each page of the report for better report clarity.

Property Of: Table Row (Not a property of a detail table row)

RepeatWith

Description: The data region this report item should repeat with across multiple pages

When to Use: This report item is part of a heading that is to be repeated with a data region that spans multiple pages.

Property Of: Image, Line, Rectangle, Text Box

Custom Properties Dialog Box Location: General tab

ReportName

Description: The name of the report to be displayed in this subreport item

When to Use: The report name is always required when using a subreport item.

Property Of: Subreport

Custom Properties Dialog Box Location: Subreport Properties—General tab

ReportParameters

Description: The parameters used by this report

When to Use: User input is to be used in determining the content of this report.

Notes: The AllowNullValue detail property specifies whether each parameter can have a null value. The AllowBlankValue detail property specifies whether each parameter can have a blank value. The AvailableValues detail property contains a list of the valid values for each property, either as a list of constants or as a reference to a dataset. The DataType detail property specifies the data type of each parameter. The DefaultValues detail property contains a default value for each property, either as a constant value or as a reference to a dataset.

The Name detail property contains the name of each property. The Prompt detail property contains the prompt string for each property.

Property Of: Report

Custom Properties Dialog Box Location: Report Parameters

Detail Properties: AllowNullValue, AllowBlankValue, AvailableValues, DataType, DefaultValues, Name, Prompt

SeriesLabel

Description: A portion of the label applied to the series on the chart

When to Use: The series label is to include information from the data value.

Notes: The series label is made up of the expression specified in the series grouping concatenated with the expression specified with the chart value.

Property Of: Chart Value

Custom Properties Dialog Box Location: Edit Chart Value—Values tab

Shading

Description: The type of shading used in a 3-D chart

When to Use: Shading other than simple shading is to be used with a 3-D chart to increase readability or enhance interest.

Property Of: Chart

Custom Properties Dialog Box Location: Chart Properties—3-D Effect tab

ShowLegend

Description: Specifies whether to show the chart legend

When to Use: The chart is to include a data series that must be identified by the legend.

Property Of: Chart

Custom Properties Dialog Box Location: Chart Properties—Legend tab

ShowMarkers

Description: Specifies whether to place a marker for each data value on a chart

When to Use: Each data value on a chart is to be highlighted with a shape to mark its position.

Property Of: Chart Value

Custom Properties Dialog Box Location: Edit Chart Value—Appearance tab

ShowPointLabels

Description: Specifies whether to label each data value on a chart
When to Use: Each data value on a chart is to be labeled to improve readability or analysis.
Property Of: Chart Value
Custom Properties Dialog Box Location: Edit Chart Values—Point Labels tab

Size

Description: The size of the report item
When to Use: Every time an item is placed in a layout area
Notes: The Width detail property contains the width of the report object in inches. The Height detail property contains the height of the report object in inches.
Property Of: Body, Chart, Image, List, Matrix, Page Header, Page Footer, Rectangle, Subreport, Table, Text Box
Detail Properties: Width, Height

Sizing

Description: The technique used to size a graphic within an image report item
When to Use: The graphic is to be sized using a technique other than the fit technique.
Notes: The *AutoSize* technique changes the size of the image report item, so the graphic completely fills it at its normal size. The *Fit* technique stretches the graphic to fit the dimensions of the image report item. The *FitProportional* technique shrinks or magnifies the graphic to fit the image report item, but retains its proportions of height to width. The *Clip* technique displays as much of the graphic, at its normal size, as will fit within the image report item; the remainder is clipped off.
Property Of: Image

SnapToGrid

Description: Specifies whether report-item corner points are aligned with the grid when they are placed on the report layout
When to Use: The report layout is not to be constrained by the grid.
Property Of: Report
Custom Properties Dialog Box Location: Report Properties—General tab

Sorting

Description: The expression used to order the dataset or data grouping
When to Use: The dataset or data grouping is to be presented in a sort order that is not provided by the dataset query.
Notes: The Expression detail property contains a list of expressions used to sort the contents of the data region or grouping. The Direction detail property specifies whether each sort is in ascending order or descending order.
Property Of: Chart Category Group, Chart Series Group, List, Matrix Column Group, Matrix Row Group, Table, Table Group
Custom Properties Dialog Box Location: Sorting tab
Detail Properties: Expression, Direction

Source

Description: The source of the graphic
When to Use: A source must be specified for each image report item.
Notes: A Database image is extracted from a binary large object (BLOB). An Embedded image is stored in the report itself. An External image is stored in the report project and deployed to the Report Manager with the report.
Property Of: Image
Custom Properties Dialog Box Location: Image Wizard

Subtype

Description: The specific type of chart
When to Use: A chart subtype must be specified for all chart types except a bubble chart.
Property Of: Chart
Custom Properties Dialog Box Location: Chart Properties—General tab

TextAlign

Description: The horizontal position of the text within a report item
When to Use: The text is to be centered or right-justified.
Property Of: Chart, List, Matrix, Matrix Column, Matrix Row, Matrix Subtotal, Subreport, Table, Table Column, Table Row, Text Box

TextDecoration

Description: The decoration (underline, overline, or line through) applied to the text
When to Use: The text is to be underlined, overlined, or struck through.

Property Of: Chart, List, Matrix, Matrix Column, Matrix Row, Matrix
Subtotal, Subreport, Table, Table Column, Table Row, Text Box
Custom Properties Dialog Box Location: Text Box Properties—Font tab
(only for text box)

Title

Description: The title of the chart
When to Use: The chart is to be given a title to provide better understanding
of the data it contains.
Property Of: Chart
Custom Properties Dialog Box Location: Chart Properties—General tab

TitleFontStyle

Description: The font style of the chart title
When to Use: The chart is to have a title.
Notes: The *FontFamily* detail property contains the name of the font. The
FontSize detail property specifies the size of the font in points. The *FontStyle*
detail property specifies whether the font is normal or italicized. The *FontWeight*
detail property specifies the thickness of the font and is used to create bold text.
The *Color* detail property specifies the color of the type. The *TextDecoration*
detail property specifies whether the text is underlined, lined through, or
overlined.
Property Of: Chart
Custom Properties Dialog Box Location: Chart Properties—General tab
Detail Properties: FontFamily, FontSize, FontStyle, FontWeight, Color,
TextDecoration

ToolTip

Description: The tool tip displayed for this report item
When to Use: The user is to be provided with additional information
concerning a report item when interacting with the report.
Property Of: Chart, Image, List, Matrix, Rectangle, Subreport, Table, Text Box
Custom Properties Dialog Box Location: General tab

ToolTipLocID

Description: The localization identifier (language and culture, for example:
"en-us") for a ToolTip
When to Use: The ToolTip has been localized.
Property Of: Chart, Image, List, Matrix, Rectangle, Subreport, Table, Text Box

Type

Description: The general type of chart
When to Use: A general chart type must be specified for all charts.
Property Of: Chart
Custom Properties Dialog Box Location: Chart Properties—General tab

UnicodeBiDi

Description: The technique used for handling text rendered right-to-left embedded in a line of text rendered left-to-right or vice versa
When to Use: Multiple languages are to be included in the same text box, with one language rendered left-to-right and the other rendered right-to-left.
Property Of: Chart, List, Matrix, Matrix Column, Matrix Row, Matrix Subtotal, Subreport, Table, Table Column, Table Row, Text Box

UserSort

Description: The properties to facilitate a dynamic sort within the report
When to Use: The report is to include dynamic sorting.
Notes: The SortExpression detail property contains the expression which will be used for sorting. The SortExpressionScope detail property specifies the scope to which the sort is applied. The SortTarget detail property specifies the data region object, grouping, or data set to which the sort is applied.
Property Of: Text Box
Detail Properties: SortExpression, SortExpressionScope, SortTarget

Value

Description: Chart Value—An expression to determine the values to be charted; Image—The name of the graphic to be placed in the image item; Text Box—The text to be displayed in the text box.
When to Use: A value is required for a chart value, an image, or a text box.
Property Of: Chart Value, Image, Text Box
Custom Properties Dialog Box Location: Chart Value: Edit Chart Value—Values tab; Image: Image Wizard; Text Box: Text Box Properties—General tab

ValueLocID

Description: The localization identifier (language and culture, for example: "en-us") for a value
When to Use: The value has been localized.
Property Of: Text Box

VerticalAlign

Description: The vertical position of the text within a report item
When to Use: The text is to be located in the middle or at the bottom.
Property Of: Chart, List, Matrix, Matrix Column, Matrix Row, Matrix Subtotal, Subreport, Table, Table Column, Table Row, Text Box

VerticalRotation

Description: The vertical rotation applied to a 3-D chart
When to Use: The vertical rotation must be adjusted to provide the user with the optimum view of the chart data.
Property Of: Chart
Custom Properties Dialog Box Location: Chart Properties—3-D Effect tab

Visibility

Description: Specifies whether a report item is visible on the report
When to Use: The report item is not to be visible on the report, or the report item's visibility is to be toggled by another report item.
Notes: The Hidden detail property specifies whether this report item is visible or hidden. The ToggleItem detail property is a reference to another report item that will toggle the visibility of this report item.
Property Of: Chart, Image, Line, List, List Details Group, Matrix, Matrix Column Group, Matrix Row Group, Rectangle, Subreport, Table, Table Column, Table Details Group, Table Group, Table Row, Text Box
Custom Properties Dialog Box Location: Visibility tab
Detail Properties: Hidden, ToggleItem

WallThickness

Description: The thickness of the walls surrounding a 3-D chart
When to Use: The thickness of the walls surrounding a 3-D chart is to be adjusted to create the most pleasing chart representation.
Property Of: Chart
Custom Properties Dialog Box Location: Chart Properties—3-D Effect tab

Width

Description: The width of a column
When to Use: The column width is to be adjusted to the appropriate size for the data it contains.
Property Of: Matrix Column, Table Column

WritingMode

Description: Indicates whether the text is written left-to-right/top-to-bottom or top-to-bottom/right-to-left

When to Use: A character set that is written top-to-bottom/right-to-left is to be used.

Property Of: Chart, List, Matrix, Matrix Column, Matrix Row, Matrix Subtotal, Subreport, Table, Table Column, Table Row, Text Box

X-AxisFormatting

Description: The formatting for the x-axis of a chart

When to Use: A chart type with an x-axis is to be rendered.

Notes: The detail properties control the look of each aspect of the x-axis.

Property Of: Chart

Custom Properties Dialog Box Location: Chart Properties——x-axis tab

Detail Properties: CrossAt, FormatCode, FormatCodeStyle, InterlacedStrips, LogarithmicScale, MajorGridlines, MajorGridlinesInterval, MajorGridlinesStyle, MajorTickMark, MinorGridlines, MinorGridlinesInterval, MinorGridlinesStyle, MinorTickMark, NumericOrTime-scaleValues, Reversed, ScaleMaximum, ScaleMinimum, ShowLabels, SideMargins, Title, TitleAlign, TitleStyle

Y-AxisFormatting

Description: The formatting for the y-axis of a chart

When to Use: A chart type with a y-axis is to be rendered.

Notes: The detail properties control the look of each aspect of the y-axis.

Property Of: Chart

Custom Properties Dialog Box Location: Chart Properties——y-axis tab

Detail Properties: CrossAt, FormatCode, FormatCodeStyle, Interlaced Strips, Logarithmic Scale, MajorGridlines, MajorGridlinesInterval, Major-GridlinesStyle, MajorTickMark, MinorGridlines, MinorGridlinesInterval, MinorGridlinesStyle, MinorTickMark, Reversed, ScaleMaximum, Scale-Minimum, ShowLabels, SideMargins, Title, TitleAlign, TitleStyle

Web Service
Interface Reference

IN THIS CHAPTER:

Reporting Services Web Service

Reporting Services Web Service

Creating a Web Reference

To use a web service, you need to create code that knows how to send data to and retrieve data from that web service. Fortunately, this code is generated for you by Visual Studio through the process of creating a web reference. Once the web reference is in place, you can call the methods of the web service the same way you call the methods of a local .NET assembly.

Two web service interfaces are provided for Reporting Services: the ReportService2005 web service and the ReportExecution2005 web service. The ReportService2005 web service enables you to manage Reporting Services. The ReportExecution2005 web service lets you execute reports.

Here are the steps for creating a web reference:

1. In your Visual Basic .NET or C# project (not a Report project), right-click the project entry in the Solution Explorer and select Add Web Reference from the Context menu. The Add Web Reference dialog box appears.
2. Select the link for Web Services on the Local Machine.
3. When the list of web services on the local machine appears, click the link for ReportService2005 or ReportExecution2005.
4. When the "ReportingService2005" Description or "ReportExecutionService" Description appears in the dialog box, click Add Reference.

When you click the link for Web Services on the Local Machine, a URL beginning with http://localhost is used to locate the web services on the local machine. Because of this, the ReportService2005 web service uses localhost. ReportService2005 as its namespace and the ReportExecution2005 web service uses localhost.ReportExecution2005 as its namespace.

Credentials

Most ReportService2005 and ReportExecution2005 methods require logon credentials to be authenticated prior to their execution. This is accomplished by creating a network credential object and assigning it to the Credentials property of the web service object.

In the following code, a logon is accomplished prior to the execution of the ListChildren method. The *ListChildren method* returns an array with one element for each report item found in the specified folder (the Home folder in this example). The array only contains those items the specified credentials have the right to view.

```
Dim rs As localhost.ReportingService2005
Dim LogonCredentials As System.Net.NetworkCredential
Dim items As localhost.CatalogItem()

rs = New localhost.ReportingService
LogonCredentials = New _
    System.Net.NetworkCredential("LogonName", "Password", "Domain")
rs.Credentials = LogonCredential
rs.PreAuthenticate = True

items = rs.ListChildren("/", False)
```

Of course, if you were to use this sample code, you would need to replace LogonName, Password, and Domain with the appropriate logon name, password, and domain name for a valid domain logon. Also, this code sample assumes you created a web reference to the ReportService2005 web service called ReportingService2005, as described in the previous section.

When the PreAuthenticate property is true, the credentials are sent with the first web service request. When the PreAuthenticate property is false, the credentials are not sent to the server until the server issues an authentication challenge. In other words, when the PreAuthenticate property is false, the credentials are not sent to the server until the server requires a login. Setting the PreAuthenticate property to true can save one roundtrip between the server and the client, but as long as you have the Credentials property initialized to a valid logon, either setting for the PreAuthenticate property (true or false) works.

Code Sample

Unfortunately, space restrictions prevent the inclusion of code samples for each of the ReportService2005 and ReportExecution2005 web service properties, methods, and classes. A sample program incorporating all these items is available for download from the web page for this book. Go to http://www.osborne.com and locate the book's page using the ISBN 0072262397.

ReportExecution2005 Properties

The ReportExecution2005 class inherits from the HttpWebClientProtocol class, the SoapHttpClientProtocol class, and the WebClientProtocol class. The following public properties are defined in the ReportExecution2005 class itself.

ExecutionHeaderValue

Description: This property holds information about the state of the current Report Server session. This state information is contained in an Execution-Header object. The ExecutionHeader inherits from the SoapHeader object.

ServerInfoHeaderValue

Description: This property holds information about the current version of the Report Server.

ReportExecution2005 Methods

The ReportExecution2005 class inherits from the HttpWebClientProtocol class, the SoapHttpClientProtocol class, and the WebClientProtocol class. The following public methods are defined in the ReportExecution2005 class itself.

GetDocumentMap

Description: This method returns a representation of the document map for the execution. This method returns a DocumentMapNode object.
Parameters: None

GetExecutionInfo

Description: This method returns information about the report execution. This method returns an ExecutionInfo object.
Parameters: None

GetRenderResource

Description: This method gets a resource for the specified rendering extension. This method returns a byte array containing a base-64 encoding of the requested resource.

Parameters:

Name	Type	Description
Format	String	The rendering extension format (for example, PDF or XML).
DeviceInfo	String	A device-specific setting for the specified rendering format.
MimeType	String	The MIME type of the resource. (This parameter must be called ByRef.)

ListRenderingExtensions

Description: This method lists the rendering extension formats available on this Report Server. This method returns an array of Extension objects.
Parameters: None

ListSecureMethods

Description: This method lists the ReportExecution2005 web service methods that require a secure connection. This method returns an array of strings containing the method names.
Parameters: None

LoadDrillthroughTarget

Description: This method creates a report execution from a drillthrough from the current execution to a new report. This method returns an ExecutionInfo object.
Parameters:

Name	Type	Description
DrillthroughID	String	The ID of the item that is the target of the drillthrough.

LoadReport

Description: This method creates a new execution from a report on the Report Server. This method returns an ExecutionInfo object.
Parameters:

Name	Type	Description
Report	String	The folder path and name of the report to load.
HistoryID	String	The ID of the history snapshot from which to render the report. (Set this to Nothing if the report should not be rendered from a history snapshot.)

LoadReportDefinition

Description: This method creates a report execution from a report definition supplied by the client. This method returns an ExecutionInfo object.

Parameters:

Name	Type	Description
Definition	Array of Bytes	The Report Definition Language (RDL) defining the new report in base-64 binary.
Warnings	Array of Warning Objects	A list of warnings generated when the report definition was loaded. (This parameter must be called ByRef.)

Logoff

Description: This method logs off the current user making requests of the ReportExecution2005 web service. This method must be called using an HTTPS (SSL) request. This method does not return a value.

Parameters: None

LogonUser

Description: This method logs a user on to the ReportExecution2005 web service. This method does not return a value.

Parameters:

Name	Type	Description
UserName	String	The user name to use for the log on.
Password	String	The password to use for the log on.
Authority	String	The authority to use when authenticating this user. This parameter is optional.

NavigateBookmark

Description: This method navigates to a specified bookmark. This method returns an integer that corresponds to the bookmark ID. This method returns zero if the specified bookmark ID is invalid or is not found.

Parameters:

Name	Type	Description
BookmarkID	String	The ID of the bookmark to navigate to.
UniqueName	String	The unique name of the report item pointed to by the bookmark. (This parameter must be called ByRef.)

NavigateDocumentMap

Description: This method navigates to a specified document map entry. This method returns an integer that corresponds to the document map ID. This method returns zero if the specified document map ID is invalid or is not found.

Parameters:

Name	Type	Description
DocMapID	String	The ID of the document map entry to navigate to.

Render

Description: This method renders the specified report. This method returns a byte array containing the rendered report.

Parameters:

Name	Type	Description
Format	String	The rendering format to be used.
DeviceInfo	String	An XML structure to control the behavior of the renderer.
MimeType	String	The MIME type of the rendered report. (This parameter must be called ByRef.)
Encoding	String	The encoding used for the contents of the report. (This parameter must be called ByRef.)
Warnings	An Array of Warning Objects	An array containing any warnings that resulted from the rendering of the report. (This parameter must be called ByRef.)
StreamIDs	String	A stream identifier used by the RenderStream method. This is used to render an external resource such as an image. (This parameter must be called ByRef.)

RenderStream

Description: This method obtains the contents of an external resource used by a rendered report. This method returns a byte array containing the external resource.

Parameters:

Name	Type	Description
Format	String	The rendering format to be used.
StreamID	String	The ID of the stream for the main report.

Name	Type	Description
Encoding	String	The encoding used for the contents of the report. (This parameter must be called ByRef.)
MimeType	String	The MIME type of the rendered report. (This parameter must be called ByRef.)

ResetExecution

Description: This method resets the current execution. This method returns an ExecutionInfo object.

Parameters: None

SetExecutionCredentials

Description: This method sets the credentials associated with the current execution. This method returns an ExecutionInfo object.

Parameters:

Name	Type	Description
Credentials	Array of DataSourceCredentails Objects	The credentials to set.

SetExecutionParameters

Description: This method sets the parameter property for the current execution. This method returns an ExecutionInfo object.

Parameters:

Name	Type	Description
Parameters	An Array of ReportParameter Objects	An array of information on report parameter properties.
ParameterLanguage	String	The language and culture identifier for the parameter (for example, "en-us").

Sort

Description: This method applies or removes a sort based on user action. This method returns an integer providing the page number where the item indicated by the ReportItem parameter now falls.

Parameters:

Name	Type	Description
SortItem	String	The ID of the item.
Direction	SortDirectionEnum	The direction of the sort. Valid values are Ascending, Descending, and None.
Clear	Boolean	True if all other sorts on this item should be cleared.
ReportItem	String	The ID of the item on the page being used to position the view. (This parameter must be called ByRef.)
NumPages	Integer	The new total number of pages after the sort.

ToggleItem

Description: This method toggles the show/hide property of a report item. This method returns a Boolean that is true if the item is found.

Parameters:

Name	Type	Description
ToggleID	String	ID of the report item to toggle.

ReportService2005 Properties

The ReportService2005 class inherits from the HttpWebClientProtocol class, the SoapHttpClientProtocol class, and the WebClientProtocol class. The following public properties are either inherited properties used in the code samples in this book or properties defined in the ReportService2005 class itself.

BatchHeaderValue

Description: This property is used to hold a unique, system-generated batch ID. This batch ID serves to group multiple method calls from the ReportService2005 web service into a single batch. The batch ID is created by calling the CreateBatch method. The batch is committed by calling the ExecuteBatch method. The batch is rolled back by calling the CancelBatch method.

Credentials

Description: This property is used to hold the logon credentials used by the client application to authenticate on the ReportService2005 web service. Most ReportService2005 methods require authentication before they execute.

ItemNamespaceHeaderValue

Description: This property determines how items are retrieved with the GetProperties method. Items can be retrieved by passing an item identifier or the full path of the item.

PreAuthenticate

Description: When the PreAuthenticate property is true, the credentials are sent with the first web service request. When the PreAuthenticate property is false, the credentials are not sent to the server until the server issues an authentication challenge.

ServerInfoHeaderValue

Description: This property holds information about the current version of the Report Server.

ReportService2005 Methods

The ReportService2005 class inherits from the HttpWebClientProtocol class, the SoapHttpClientProtocol class, and the WebClientProtocol class. The following public methods are defined in the ReportService2005 class itself.

CancelBatch

Description: This method cancels the current batch of ReportService2005 method calls. The current batch is specified by the BatchHeader object and must be assigned to the BatchHeaderValue property of the ReportingService object. If the batch is cancelled, none of the method calls in the batch are executed.

This method does not return a value.

Parameters: None

CancelJob

Description: This method cancels an executing job. This method returns true if the job was cancelled; otherwise, it returns false.

Parameters:

Name	Type	Description
JobID	String	The ID of the job to cancel.

CreateBatch

Description: This method creates a batch ID that can be used to group ReportService2005 method calls into a batch. If an error occurs in one of the method calls in the batch, all previous operations performed by the batch are rolled back and subsequent operations are not attempted. This is useful when you have one ReportingService method call that depends on the successful completion of a prior ReportingService method call. For instance, you may call the CreateFolder method to create a new folder, and then call the CreateReport method to create a report in your new folder. You do not want to attempt to create the report if the folder cannot be created.

This method returns a batch ID string. This batch ID must be assigned to the batchID property of a BatchHeader object. The BatchHeader object must be assigned to the BatchHeaderValue property of the ReportService2005 object. The methods in the batch are not executed until the ExecuteBatch method is called to commit the batch.

Parameters: None

CreateDataDrivenSubscription

Description: This method creates a data-driven subscription for a report. This method returns a string containing the subscription ID.

Parameters:

Name	Type	Description
Report	String	The folder path and name of the report to which to subscribe.
ExtensionSettings	ExtensionSettings Object	An object containing the settings for the delivery extension (for example, e-mail delivery) used by this subscription.
DataRetrievalPlan	DataRetrievalPlan Object	An object containing the information necessary to connect to and retrieve the data used for the data-driven subscription.
Description	String	The description of this subscription.
EventType	String	Either TimedSubscription for a subscription triggered by a schedule or SnapshotUpdated for a subscription triggered by the updating of a snapshot.
MatchData	String	Information used to implement the event type.
Parameters	An Array of ParameterValue OrFieldReference Objects	An array of the values used for the report's parameters.

CreateDataSource

Description: This method creates a new shared data source. This method does not return a value.

Parameters:

Name	Type	Description
DataSource	String	The name of the data source.
Overwrite	Boolean	True if this data source should overwrite an existing data source; otherwise, false.
Parent	String	The path to the folder where the shared data source is created.
Definition	DataSourceDefinition Object	An object containing the connection information for the shared data source.
Properties	An Array of Property Objects	An array of property settings for the shared data source.

CreateFolder

Description: This method creates a new Reporting Services folder in the specified folder. This method does not return a value.

Parameters:

Name	Type	Description
Folder	String	The name of the new folder.
Parent	String	The path to the folder where the new folder is created.
Properties	An Array of Property Objects	An array of property settings for the folder.

CreateLinkedReport

Description: This method creates a new linked report in the specified folder. This method does not return a value.

Parameters:

Name	Type	Description
Report	String	The name of the new linked report.
Parent	String	The path to the folder where the new linked report is created.
Link	String	The folder path and name of the report to which the new linked report should be linked.
Properties	An Array of Property Objects	An array of property settings for the new linked report.

CreateModel

Description: This method creates a model for use with the Report Builder. This method returns an array of Warning objects.

Parameters:

Name	Type	Description
Model	String	The name of the new model.
Parent	String	The path to the folder where the new model is created.
Definition	An Array of Bytes	The model definition of this model.
Properties	An Array of Property Objects	The properties of this model.

CreateReport

Description: This method creates a new report in the specified folder. This method returns an array of Warning objects.

Parameters:

Name	Type	Description
Report	String	The name of the new report.
Parent	String	The path to the folder where the new report is created.
Overwrite	Boolean	True if an existing report with the same name in the same folder is to be replaced with the new report; otherwise, false.
Definition	An Array of Bytes	The Report Definition Language (RDL) defining the new report in base-64 binary.
Properties	An Array of Property Objects	An array of property settings for the report.

CreateReportHistorySnapshot

Description: This method creates a history snapshot of a specified report. The snapshot is created immediately, not at a scheduled time. This method call fails if report history is not enabled for the specified report.

This method returns a string representing the data and time at which the history snapshot was created.

Parameters:

Name	Type	Description
Report	String	The Reporting Services folder and the name of the report from which the history snapshot is created.
Warnings	An Array of Warning Objects	An array of warning messages generated when creating this report history snapshot. (This parameter must be called ByRef.)

CreateResource

Description: This method creates a new resource entry in the specified folder. This method does not return a value.

Parameters:

Name	Type	Description
Resource	String	The name of the new resource.
Parent	String	The path to the folder where the new resource is created.
Overwrite	Boolean	True if an existing resource with the same name in the same folder is to be replaced with the new resource; otherwise, false.
Contents	An Array of Bytes	The contents of the resource in base-64 binary.
MimeType	String	The MIME type of the resource (260 characters maximum).
Properties	An Array of Property Objects	An array of property settings for the resource.

CreateRole

Description: This method creates a new Reporting Services security role. This method does not return a value.

Parameters:

Name	Type	Description
Name	String	The name of the new role.
Description	String	The description of the new role.
Tasks	An Array of Task Objects	An array of Reporting Services tasks that may be executed by this role.

CreateSchedule

Description: This method creates a new shared schedule. This method returns a string containing the schedule ID.

Parameters:

Name	Type	Description
Name	String	The name of the schedule.
ScheduleDefinition	ScheduleDefinition Object	An object containing the information necessary to define a schedule.

CreateSubscription

Description: This method creates a new subscription for a report. This method returns a string containing the subscription ID.

Parameters:

Name	Type	Description
Report	String	The folder path and name of the report to which to subscribe.
ExtensionSettings	ExtensionSettings Object	An object containing the settings for the delivery extension (for example, e-mail delivery) used by this subscription.
Description	String	The description of this subscription.
EventType	String	Either TimedSubscription for a subscription triggered by a schedule or SnapshotUpdated for a subscription triggered by the updating of a snapshot.
MatchData	String	Information used to implement the event type.
Parameters	An Array of ParameterValue Objects	An array of the values used for the report's parameters.

DeleteItem

Description: This method removes an item from a Reporting Services folder. This can be a report, a resource, a shared data source, or a Reporting Services folder. If a report is deleted, any subscriptions and snapshots associated with that report are also deleted. This method does not return a value.

You cannot use this method to delete the My Reports folder or the Users folders created when the My Reports option is enabled.

Parameters:

Name	Type	Description
Item	String	The folder path and name of the item to be deleted.

DeleteReportHistorySnapshot

Description: This method removes a specified history snapshot. This method does not return a value.

Parameters:

Name	Type	Description
Report	String	The folder path and name of the report from which the history snapshot is to be deleted.
HistoryID	String	The ID of the history snapshot to delete.

DeleteRole

Description: This method removes a Reporting Services security role. This also removes all security assignments involving the deleted security role. This method does not return a value.

Parameters:

Name	Type	Description
Name	String	The name of the security role to delete.

DeleteSchedule

Description: This method removes a shared schedule. In addition, any snapshots or subscriptions using this schedule are also deleted. This method does not return a value.

Parameters:

Name	Type	Description
ScheduleID	String	The schedule ID of the schedule to delete.

DeleteSubscription

Description: This method removes a subscription from a report and it does not return a value.

Parameters:

Name	Type	Description
SubscriptionID	String	The subscription ID of the subscription to delete.

DisableDataSource

Description: This method disables a shared data source. Any reports and data-driven subscriptions that use this shared data source will not execute. This method does not return a value.

Parameters:

Name	Type	Description
DataSource	String	The folder path and name of the shared data source to be disabled.

EnableDataSource

Description: This method enables a shared data source and it does not return a value.

Parameters:

Name	Type	Description
DataSource	String	The folder path and name of the shared data source to be enabled.

ExecuteBatch

Description: This method executes all method calls associated with the current batch. (See the CreateBatch method.) The method calls in the batch are not executed until the ExecuteBatch method is called. This method does not return a value.

Parameters: None

FindItems

Description: This method finds reports, resources, shared data sources, and folders whose name or description satisfies the search conditions. The contents of the specified folder and all the folders contained within that folder are searched. This method returns an array of CatalogItem objects that satisfy the search conditions.

Parameters:

Name	Type	Description
Folder	String	The folder path and name of the folder that serves as the root of the search.
BooleanOperator	BooleanOperatorEnum	Either AND if all the search conditions must be true; otherwise, OR if only one of the search conditions must be true.
Conditions	An Array of SearchCondition Objects	An array containing the search conditions.

FireEvent

Description: This method triggers a Reporting Services event. You can use the ListEvents method to get an array of valid events and their parameters. This method does not return a value.

Parameters:

Name	Type	Description
EventType	String	The name of the event.
EventData	String	The values for the parameters associated with this event.

FlushCache

Description: This method clears any cached copies of the specified report. This includes cached copies created both by caching and by execution snapshots. It does not clear history snapshots. This method does not return a value.

Parameters:

Name	Type	Description
Report	String	The folder path and name of the report whose cache is to be flushed.

GetCacheOptions

Description: This method checks whether there is a cached copy of the specified report. If a cached copy of the report exists, the expiration time or the scheduled expiration information for the cached copy is returned in the Item parameter. This method returns a Boolean, which is true if caching is enabled for the report; otherwise, it returns false.

Parameters:

Name	Type	Description
Report	String	The folder path and name of the report whose cache options are to be checked.
Item	ExpirationDefinition Object	An object containing the expiration information for the cached copy of the report. (This parameter must be called ByRef.)

GetDataDrivenSubscriptionProperties

Description: This method gets information from the specified data-driven subscription. The data-driven subscription information is returned in several reference parameters. This method returns a string containing the ID of the owner of the specified data-driven subscription.

Parameters:

Name	Type	Description
DataDrivenSubscriptionID	String	The data-driven subscription ID of the data-driven subscription whose information is to be returned.
ExtensionSettings	ExtensionSettings Object	An object containing the extension settings. (This parameter must be called ByRef.)
DataRetrievalPlan	DataRetrievalPlan Object	An object containing the data source and query used to select data for the data-driven subscription. (This parameter must be called ByRef.)
Description	String	The description of the data-driven subscription. (This parameter must be called ByRef.)
Active	ActiveState Object	An object containing the active state of the data-driven subscription. (This parameter must be called ByRef.)
Status	String	The status of the data-driven subscription. (This parameter must be called ByRef.)
EventType	String	The event type associated with the data-driven subscription. (This parameter must be called ByRef.)
MatchData	String	The parameter data for the event type associated with the data-driven subscription. (This parameter must be called ByRef.)
Parameters	An Array of ParameterValueOrFieldReference Objects	An array of parameter information for the report associated with the data-driven subscription. (This parameter must be called ByRef.)

GetDataSourceContents

Description: This method gets the information for the specified shared data source. This method returns a DataSourceDefinition object containing the information for the shared data source.

Parameters:

Name	Type	Description
DataSource	String	The folder path and name of the shared data source whose information is to be returned

GetExecutionOptions

Description: This method gets the execution options for the specified report. This method returns an ExecutionSettingEnum value of either Live, indicating the report is to be executed, or Snapshot, indicating the report is to be rendered from a history snapshot.

Parameters:

Name	Type	Description
Report	String	The folder path and name of the report whose execution option is to be returned.
Item	ScheduleDefinitionOrReference Object	An object containing a schedule definition or a reference to a shared schedule. (This parameter must be called ByRef.)

GetExtensionSettings

Description: This method gets the parameter information for the specified delivery extension. This method returns an array of ExtensionParameter objects containing the parameter information.

Parameters:

Name	Type	Description
Extension	String	The name of the delivery extension.

GetItemDataSourcePrompts

Description: This method gets the prompt strings for all the data sources tied to the specified item. This method returns an array of DataSourcePrompt objects.

Parameters:

Name	Type	Description
Item	String	The folder path and name of the item whose data source prompts are to be returned.

GetItemDataSources

Description: This method gets the data sources tied to the specified item. This method returns an array of DataSource objects.

Parameters:

Name	Type	Description
Item	String	The folder path and name of the item whose data sources are to be returned.

GetItemType

Description: This method gets the type of the specified Reporting Services item. This method returns an ItemTypeEnum value, as shown here:

Value	Description
Unknown	Invalid Item Path or Item of Unknown Type.
Folder	This item is a folder.
Report	This item is a report.
Resource	This item is a resource.
LinkedReport	This item is a linked report.
DataSource	This item is a shared data source.
Model	This item is a report model.

Parameters:

Name	Type	Description
Item	String	The folder path and name of the item whose type is to be returned.

GetModelDefinition

Description: This method gets the definition of the specified model. This method returns an array of bytes.

Parameters:

Name	Type	Description
Model	String	The folder path and name of the model whose definition is to be returned.

GetModelItemPermissions

Description: This method gets the permissions associated with the specified model item. This method returns an array of strings.

Parameters:

Name	Type	Description
Model	String	The folder path and name of the model that contains the item whose permissions are to be returned.
ModelItemID	String	The ID of the model item whose permissions are to be returned. If omitted, the permissions of the model root are returned.

GetModelItemPolicies

Description: This method gets the Reporting Services security policies associated with the specified model item. This method returns an array of Policy objects.

Parameters:

Name	Type	Description
Model	String	The folder path and name of the model that contains the item whose policies are to be returned.
ModelItemID	String	The ID of the model item whose policies are to be returned. If omitted, the policies of the model root are returned.
InheritParent	Boolean	True if the policies are inherited from the parent folder; otherwise, false. (This parameter must be called ByRef.)

GetPermissions

Description: This method gets the tasks that may be executed on the specified Reporting Services item by the logon credentials currently being used to access the ReportService2005 web service. This method returns an array of strings, with each string containing the name of one task the logon credentials have permission to execute.

Parameters:

Name	Type	Description
Item	String	The folder path and the name of the item whose permissions are to be returned.

GetPolicies

Description: This method gets the Reporting Services security policies associated with the specified Reporting Services item and returns an array of Policy objects.

Parameters:

Name	Type	Description
Item	String	The folder path and the name of the item whose policies are to be returned.
InheritParent	Boolean	True if the policies are inherited from the parent folder; otherwise, false. (This parameter must be called ByRef.)

GetProperties

Description: This method gets the values of each specified property of the Reporting Services item and returns an array of Property objects.

Parameters:

Name	Type	Description
Item	String	The folder path and the name of the item whose properties are to be returned.
Properties	An Array of Property Objects	An array of the properties whose values you want returned.

GetRenderResource

Description: This method gets a resource for the specified rendering extension. This method returns a byte array containing a base-64 encoding of the requested resource.

Parameters:

Name	Type	Description
Format	String	The rendering extension format (for example, PDF or XML).
DeviceInfo	String	A device-specific setting for the specified rendering format.
MimeType	String	The MIME type of the resource. (This parameter must be called ByRef.)

GetReportDefinition

Description: This method gets the definition for the specified report and returns a byte array with the report definition as a base-64-encoded RDL structure.

Parameters:

Name	Type	Description
Report	String	The folder path and name of the report whose definition is to be returned.

GetReportHistoryLimit

Description: This method gets the maximum number of history snapshots that may be saved for the specified report. This method returns an integer representing the history snapshot limit.

Parameters:

Name	Type	Description
Report	String	The folder path and name of the report whose snapshot history limit is to be returned.
IsSystem	Boolean	True if the report history snapshot limit comes from the system limit; otherwise, false. (This parameter must be called ByRef.)
SystemLimit	Integer	The system limit for report history snapshots. (This parameter must be called ByRef.)

GetReportHistoryOptions

Description: This method gets the report history snapshot options and properties for the specified report. This method returns a Boolean value that is true if a history snapshot is enabled and, otherwise, is false.

Parameters:

Name	Type	Description
Report	String	The folder path and name of the report whose snapshot history options are to be returned.
KeepExecutionSnapshots	Boolean	True if a history snapshot is enabled; otherwise, false. (This parameter must be called ByRef.)
Item	ScheduleDefinitionOrReference Object	An object that contains information about a schedule definition or a reference to a shared schedule used to create the history snapshot. (This parameter must be called ByRef.)

GetReportLink

Description: This method gets the name of the report to which the specified linked report is tied. This method returns a string containing the folder path and the name of the report.

Parameters:

Name	Type	Description
Report	String	The folder path and name of the linked report whose underlying report is to be returned.

GetReportParameters

Description: This method gets the report parameter properties for the specified report. This method returns an array of ReportParameter objects.
Parameters:

Name	Type	Description
Report	String	The folder path and name of the report whose parameter properties are to be returned.
HistoryID	String	Set this parameter to a history ID to retrieve the parameters for a history snapshot; otherwise, set it to Nothing (Null for C#).
ForRendering	Boolean	Set this parameter to true to return the parameter properties used during the creation of the specified history snapshot; otherwise, set it to false.
Values	An Array of ParameterValue Objects	An array of the values to be validated for the report.
Credentials	An Array of DataSourceCredentials Objects	An array specifying data source credentials to be used when validating parameters.

GetResourceContents

Description: This method gets the contents of a Reporting Services resource and returns a byte array containing the base-64-encoded contents of the resource.
Parameters:

Name	Type	Description
Resource	String	The folder path and name of the resource whose contents are to be returned.
MimeType	String	The MIME type of the resource. (This parameter must be called ByRef.)

GetRoleProperties

Description: This method gets a description of the specified role, along with the tasks this role is able to complete. This method returns an array of Task objects.

Parameters:

Name	Type	Description
Name	String	The name of the role whose description and tasks are to be returned.
Description	String	The description of the role. (This parameter must be called ByRef.)

GetScheduleProperties

Description: This method gets the properties of the specified shared schedule. This method returns a Schedule object.

Parameters:

Name	Type	Description
ScheduleID	String	The schedule ID of the schedule to be returned.

GetSubscriptionProperties

Description: This method gets the properties of the specified subscription. This method returns a string containing the ID of the owner of this subscription.

Parameters:

Name	Type	Description
SubscriptionID	String	The subscription ID of the subscription whose properties are to be returned.
ExtensionSettings	An ExtensionSettings Object	An object containing the settings for the delivery extension associated with this subscription. (This parameter must be called ByRef.)
Description	String	The description of the subscription. (This parameter must be called ByRef.)
Active	An ActiveState Object	An object containing the active state of the subscription. (This parameter must be called ByRef.)
Status	String	The status of the subscription. (This parameter must be called ByRef.)

Name	Type	Description
EventType	String	Either TimedSubscription for a subscription triggered by a schedule or SnapshotUpdated for a subscription triggered by the updating of a snapshot. (This parameter must be called ByRef.)
MatchData	String	Information used to implement the event type. (This parameter must be called ByRef.)
Parameters	An Array of ParameterValue Objects	An array of the values used for the report's parameters. (This parameter must be called ByRef.)

GetSystemPermissions

Description: This method gets the system permissions assigned to the logon credentials currently being used to access the ReportService2005 web service. This method returns an array of strings that contain the system permissions.
Parameters: None

GetSystemPolicies

Description: This method gets the system policy for this Reporting Services installation. This method returns an array of Policy objects.
Parameters: None

GetSystemProperties

Description: This method gets the value of each specified system property. This method returns an array of Property objects.
Parameters:

Name	Type	Description
Properties	An Array of Property Objects	An array of properties and their values.

GetUserModel

Description: This method gets the semantic portion of a model for which the current user has access permission. This method returns an array of bytes.
Parameters:

Name	Type	Description
Model	String	The folder path and name of the model whose user model is to be retrieved.
Perspective	String	The ID of the perspective whose user model is to be retrieved.

InheritModelItemParentSecurity

Description: This method sets the mode to inherit its security from its parent. As a result, any policies assigned specifically for this model are deleted. This method does not return a value.

Parameters:

Name	Type	Description
Model	String	The folder path and name of the model that contains the item whose policies are to be inherited.
ModelItemID	String	The ID of the model item whose policies are to be inherited.

InheritParentSecurity

Description: This method sets the Reporting Services item to inherit its security from its parent folder. As a result, any role assignments made specifically for this item are deleted. This method does not return a value.

Parameters:

Name	Type	Description
Item	String	The folder path and name of the item whose security is to be inherited.

ListChildren

Description: This method lists all the Reporting Services items that are children of the specified folder. The list includes only those items that the logon credentials currently being used to access the ReportService2005 web service have a right to view. This method returns an array of CatalogItem objects.

Parameters:

Name	Type	Description
Item	String	The folder path and name of the folder whose children are to be listed.
Recursive	Boolean	True if the list should recurse down the folder tree; otherwise, false.

ListDependentItems

Description: This method lists all the Reporting Services items dependent on the specified item. This method returns an array of CatalogItem objects.

Parameters:

Name	Type	Description
Item	String	The folder path and name of the folder whose dependants are to be listed.

ListEvents

Description: This method lists the events supported by this Reporting Services installation and returns an array of Event objects.
Parameters: None

ListExtensions

Description: This method lists the extensions of the specified type defined for this Reporting Services installation. It returns an array of Extension objects.
Parameters:

Name	Type	Description
ExtensionType	ExtensionTypeEnum	Either Delivery for delivery extensions, Render for rendering extensions, Data for data access extensions, or All for all of the above.

ListJobs

Description: This method lists the jobs currently running on this Reporting Services installation and returns an array of Job objects.
Parameters: None

ListModelDrillthroughReports

Description: This method lists the reports tied to a specific entity in a model. It also returns an array of ModelDrillthroughReport objects.
Parameters:

Name	Type	Description
Model	String	The folder path and name of the model that contains the item whose drillthrough reports are to be listed.
ModelItemID	String	The ID of the model item whose drillthrough reports are to be listed.

ListModelItemChildren

Description: This method lists all the children of the specified model item. This method returns an array of ModelItem objects.
Parameters:

Name	Type	Description
Model	String	The folder path and name of the model that contains the item whose children are to be listed.
ModelItemID	String	The ID of the model item whose children are to be listed. If omitted, the children of the model root of the model are listed.
Recursive	Boolean	True if the list should recurse through the model tree; otherwise, false.

ListModelPerspective

Description: This method lists the perspectives of the specified model and it returns an array of ModelCatalogItem objects.
Parameters:

Name	Type	Description
Model	String	The folder path and name of the model whose perspectives are to be listed.

ListReportHistory

Description: This method lists the history snapshots and their properties for the specified report. It also returns an array of ReportHistorySnapshot objects.
Parameters:

Name	Type	Description
Report	String	The folder path and name of the report whose history snapshots are to be listed.

ListRoles

Description: This method lists the roles defined for this Reporting Services installation. This method returns an array of Role objects.
Parameters:

Name	Type	Description
SecurityScope	SecurityScopeEnum	The security scope of the roles to be listed. Valid values are All, Catalog, Model, and System.

ListScheduledReports

Description: This method lists the reports using the specified shared schedule and returns an array of CatalogItem objects.
Parameters:

Name	Type	Description
ScheduleID	String	The schedule ID of the shared schedule whose reports are to be listed.

ListSchedules

Description: This method lists all the shared schedules and returns an array of Schedule objects.
Parameters: None

ListSecureMethods

Description: This method lists all the ReportService2005 web service methods that require a secure connection. This method returns an array of strings containing the method names.
Parameters: None

ListSubscriptions

Description: This method lists the subscriptions a specified user has created for a specified report. It also returns an array of Subscription objects.
Parameters:

Name	Type	Description
Report	String	The folder path and name of the report whose subscriptions are to be listed.
Owner	String	The name of the owner whose subscriptions are to be retrieved.

ListSubscriptionsUsingDataSource

Description: This method lists the subscriptions using the specified shared data source and returns an array of Subscription objects.
Parameters:

Name	Type	Description
DataSource	String	The folder path and name of the shared data source whose subscriptions are to be listed.

ListTasks

Description: This method lists the tasks defined for this Reporting Services installation and returns an array of Task objects.

Parameters:

Name	Type	Description
SecurityScope	SecurityScopeEnum	The security scope of the tasks to be listed. Valid values are All, Catalog, Model, and System.

Logoff

Description: This method logs off the current user making requests of the ReportService2005 web service. It must be called using an https (SSL) request. This method does not return a value.

Parameters: None

LogonUser

Description: This method logs a user on to the Report Server web service. It does not return a value. An authentication cookie is passed back in the header of the https request.

Parameters:

Name	Type	Description
UserName	String	The user name to use for the log on.
Password	String	The password to use for the log on.
Authority	String	The authority to use when authenticating this user. This parameter is optional.

MoveItem

Description: This method moves the specified Reporting Services item to the specified folder path. It does not return a value.

Parameters:

Name	Type	Description
Item	String	The folder path and name of the item to be moved.
Target	String	The folder path to which this item is to be moved.

PauseSchedule

Description: This method pauses the execution of the specified schedule. It does not return a value.

Parameters:

Name	Type	Description
ScheduleID	String	The ID of the schedule to pause.

PrepareQuery

Description: This method determines the fields to be returned by the specified query running against the specified data source. This information can be used by the CreateDataDrivenSubscription and SetDataDrivenSubscriptionProperties methods. This method returns a DataSetDefinition object.

Parameters:

Name	Type	Description
DataSource	DataSource Object	An object containing the data source information.
DataSet	DataSetDefinition Object	An object containing the query to return the fields for the data-driven subscription.
Changed	Boolean	True if the dataset passed in the DataSet parameter is different from the dataset returned in the DataSetDefinition object; otherwise, false. (This parameter must be called ByRef.)

RemoveAllModelItemPolicies

Description: This method deletes all policies associated with the items in the specified model. It does not return a value.

Parameters:

Name	Type	Description
Model	String	The folder path and name of the model.

ResumeSchedule

Description: This method resumes a schedule that has been paused. It does not return a value.

Parameters:

Name	Type	Description
ScheduleID	String	The ID of the schedule to resume.

SetCacheOptions

Description: This method sets the caching options for the specified report. It does not return a value.

Parameters:

Name	Type	Description
Report	String	The folder path and name of the report whose caching options are to be set.
CacheReport	Boolean	True if each execution of the report is to be cached; otherwise, false.
Item	ExpirationDefinition Object	An object containing information telling when the cached report is to expire.

SetDataDrivenSubscriptionProperties

Description: This method sets the properties of a data-driven subscription. It does not return a value.

Parameters:

Name	Type	Description
DataDrivenSubscriptionID	String	The ID of the data-driven subscription whose properties are to be set.
ExtensionSettings	ExtensionSettings Object	An object containing the settings for the delivery extension (for example, e-mail delivery) used by this subscription.
DataRetrievalPlan	DataRetrievalPlan Object	An object containing the information necessary to connect to and retrieve the data used for the data-driven subscription.
Description	String	The description of this subscription.
EventType	String	Either TimedSubscription for a subscription triggered by a schedule or SnapshotUpdated for a subscription triggered by the updating of a snapshot.
MatchData	String	Information used to implement the event type.
Parameters	An Array of ParameterValue OrFieldReference Objects	An array of the values used for the report's parameters.

SetDataSourceContents

Description: This method sets the properties of a shared data source. It does not return a value.
Parameters:

Name	Type	Description
DataSource	String	The name of the data source.
Definition	DataSourceDefinition Object	An object containing the connection information for the shared data source.

SetExecutionOptions

Description: This method sets the execution options (either Live or Snapshot) of the specified report. It does not return a value.
Parameters:

Name	Type	Description
Report	String	The folder path and name of the report whose execution option is to be set.
ExecutionSetting	ExecutionSettingEnum	Either Live if the report is to be executed from the data sources or Snapshot if the report is to come from an execution snapshot.
Item	ScheduleDefinitionOrReference Object	An object containing the information for a schedule or a reference to a shared schedule. This schedule is used to create the execution snapshot and is valid only if the ExecutionSetting is Snapshot.

SetItemDataSources

Description: This method sets the properties for data sources associated with the specified item. It does not return a value.
Parameters:

Name	Type	Description
Item	String	The folder path and name of the item for which the data source properties are to be set.
DataSources	An Array of DataSource Objects	An array of data sources and their properties.

SetModelDefinition

Description: This method sets the model definition of the specified model. This method returns an array of Warning objects containing any warning messages that may result from this operation.

Parameters:

Name	Type	Description
Model	String	The folder path and name of the model for which the model definition is to be set.
Definition	An Array of Bytes	A byte array containing the model definition in base-64 binary.

SetModelDrillthroughReports

Description: This method associates a set of drill-through reports with the specified model. It does not return a value.

Parameters:

Name	Type	Description
Model	String	The folder path and name of the model.
ModelItemID	String	The ID of the model item.
Reports	Array of ModelDrillthroughReport Objects	The drillthrough reports to set for the model item.

SetModelItemPolicies

Description: This method sets the security policies for the specified model item. It does not return a value.

Parameters:

Name	Type	Description
Model	String	The folder path and name of the model.
ModelItemID	String	The ID of the model item.
Policies	An Array of Policy Objects	An array of security policy information.

SetPolicies

Description: This method sets the security policies for the specified report. It does not return a value.

Parameters:

Name	Type	Description
Item	String	The folder path and name of the Reporting Services item for which the security policies are to be set.
Policies	An Array of Policy Objects	An array of security policy information.

SetProperties

Description: This method sets the properties of the specified Reporting Services item. This method does not return a value.

Parameters:

Name	Type	Description
Item	String	The folder path and name of the Reporting Services item for which the properties are to be set.
Properties	An Array of Property Objects	An array of properties and their values.

SetReportDefinition

Description: This method sets the report definition of the specified report. It returns an array of Warning objects containing any warning messages that may result from this operation.

Parameters:

Name	Type	Description
Report	String	The folder path and name of the report for which the report definition is to be set.
Definition	An Array of Bytes	A byte array containing the Report Definition Language (RDL) in base-64 binary.

SetReportHistoryLimit

Description: This method sets the limit for the number of history snapshots that may be saved for the specified report. It does not return a value.

Parameters:

Name	Type	Description
Report	String	The folder path and name of the report for which the history snapshot limit is to be set.

Name	Type	Description
UseSystem	Boolean	True if the system default history snapshot limit is to be used with this report; otherwise, false.
HistoryLimit	Integer	The limit for the number of history snapshots saved for this report.

SetReportHistoryOptions

Description: This method sets the options specifying when a history snapshot is created for the specified report. This method does not return a value.

Parameters:

Name	Type	Description
Report	String	The folder path and name of the report for which the history snapshot options are to be set.
EnableManualSnapshotCreation	Boolean	True if snapshots can be created using the CreateReportHistorySnapshot method; otherwise, false.
KeepExecutionSnapshots	Boolean	True if execution snapshots are saved as history snapshots; otherwise, false.
Item	ScheduleDefinitionOrReference Object	An object containing the information for a schedule or a reference to a shared schedule. This schedule is used to create the history snapshot.

SetReportLink

Description: This method sets the report to which the specified linked report should be linked. It does not return any value.

Parameters:

Name	Type	Description
Report	String	The folder path and name of the linked report.
Link	String	The folder path and name of the report to which this should be linked.

SetReportParameters

Description: This method sets the parameter property for the specified report. It does not return a value.

Parameters:

Name	Type	Description
Report	String	The folder path and name of the report whose parameter property should be set.
Parameters	An Array of ReportParameter Objects	An array of information on report parameter properties.

SetResourceContents

Description: This method sets the contents of a Reporting Services resource. It does not return a value.

Parameters:

Name	Type	Description
Resource	String	The folder path and name of the resource whose contents are to be set.
Contents	An Array of Bytes	The contents of the resource in base-64 binary.
MimeType	String	The MIME type of the resource. This is optional and is returned through an out parameter.

SetRoleProperties

Description: This method sets the properties of a security role. This method does not return a value.

Parameters:

Name	Type	Description
Name	String	The folder path and name of the security role whose properties are to be set.
Description	String	The description of the security role.
Tasks	An Array of Task Objects	An array of Reporting Services tasks that may be executed by this role.

SetScheduleProperties

Description: This method sets the properties of a shared schedule. It does not return a value.

Parameters:

Name	Type	Description
Name	String	The name of the shared schedule.
ScheduleID	String	The ID of the shared schedule whose properties are to be set.
ScheduleDefinition	ScheduleDefinition Object	An object containing the information necessary to define a schedule.

SetSubscriptionProperties

Description: This method sets the properties of a subscription. It does not return a value.

Parameters:

Name	Type	Description
SubscriptionID	String	The ID of the subscription whose properties are to be set.
ExtensionSettings	ExtensionSettings Object	An object containing the settings for the delivery extension (for example, e-mail delivery) used by this subscription.
Description	String	The description of this subscription.
EventType	String	Either TimedSubscription for a subscription triggered by a schedule or SnapshotUpdated for a subscription triggered by the updating of a snapshot.
MatchData	String	Information used to implement the event type.
Parameters	An Array of ParameterValue Objects	An array of the values used for the report's parameters.

SetSystemPolicies

Description: This method sets the system policies for this Reporting Services installation. It does not return a value.

Parameters:

Name	Type	Description
Policies	An Array of Policy Objects	An array of the values used to set the system policies.

SetSystemProperties

Description: This method sets the specified system properties. It does not return a value.

Parameters:

Name	Type	Description
Properties	An Array of Property Objects	An array of properties and their values.

UpdateReportExecutionSnapshot

Description: This method updates the report execution snapshot for the specified report. It does not return a value.

Parameters:

Name	Type	Description
Report	String	The folder path and name of the report whose execution snapshot is to be updated.

ValidateExtensionSettings

Description: This method validates the settings for a Reporting Services extension and returns an array of ExtensionParameter objects.

Parameters:

Name	Type	Description
Extension	String	The name of the extension.
ParameterValues	An Array of ParameterValueOrFieldReference Objects	An array of parameter values to be validated.

ReportService2005 and ReportExecution2005 Web Service Classes

The Namespace for Reporting Services Web Service Classes

The namespace for Reporting Services web service classes is the same as the namespace used for web services themselves. If the ReportService2005 web service has a namespace of

```
localhost.ReportService
```

then the namespace for each web service class associated with the ReportService2005 web service would be

```
localhost.{ClassName}
```

where {ClassName} is the name of one of the classes. The description for each class will tell you whether it is a class of the ReportService2005 web service or the ReportExecution2005 web service.

The "Specified" Properties

Many of the properties for these classes have a corresponding property of the same name, with "Specified" on the end. These properties are used to let any code using the class know if a value was specified for this property or if it was left with no value specified. In most cases, these "specified" properties are added to correspond to class properties with data types of Boolean, date, and others that cannot easily represent an empty state.

For example, the DataSourceDefinition class has a property named Enabled. When this property is set to true, the data source is enabled. When this property is set to false, the data source is disabled. If you do not specify a value for this property, it defaults to false and the data source is disabled. To prevent this from happening, a property called EnabledSpecified of type Boolean has been added to the Data-SourceDefinition class. This additional property lets the code using this class know whether the value for the Enabled property should be used because it was specified by the user or if it should be ignored because it was not specified.

As the developer, you must make sure these "specified" properties are set properly. Any time you provide a value for a property with a corresponding "specified" property, you need to set that "specified" property to true. If you do not take care of this in your code, these property values will be ignored by the methods using these classes.

In some cases, "specified" properties were added for read-only class properties. This seems to make no sense because you cannot specify a value for a read-only property. Nevertheless, there they are. In these cases, the "specified" properties can be safely ignored.

ActiveState

Description: An object of the ActiveState class type is returned by the GetSubscriptionProperties method to provide information on various error conditions that may be present in a specified subscription. In addition to the properties listed here, this class includes a "specified" property for each of the properties shown. These "specified" properties can be ignored. This is a class of the ReportService2005 web service.

Properties:

Property	Type	Description
DeliveryExtensionRemoved	Boolean	True if the delivery extension used by the subscription has been removed; otherwise, false. (Read-only.)
InvalidParameterValue	Boolean	True if a parameter value saved with a subscription is invalid; otherwise, false. (Read-only.)
MissingParameterValue	Boolean	True if a required parameter value is not saved with a subscription; otherwise, false. (Read-only.)
SharedDataSourceRemoved	Boolean	True if a shared data source used with a subscription has been removed; otherwise, false. (Read-only.)
UnknownReportParameter	Boolean	True if a parameter name saved with a subscription is not recognized as a parameter for this report; otherwise, false. (Read-only.)

BatchHeader

Description: This class contains the Batch ID for a batch of web-service method calls. This is a class of the ReportService2005 web service.
Properties:

Property	Type	Description
BatchID	String	The identifier for a batch.

CatalogItem

Description: This class contains information about a single item in the Report Catalog. This may be a Reporting Services folder, a report, a shared data source, or a resource. This is a class of the ReportService2005 web service.
Properties:

Property	Type	Description
CreatedBy	String	The name of the user who created the item. (Read-only.)
CreationDate	Date	The date and time the item was created. (Read-only.)
CreationDateSpecified	Boolean	True if a value for CreationDate is specified; otherwise, false.
Description	String	The description of the item.
ExecutionDate	Date	The date and time a report item was last executed. (Valid only for report items.) (Read-only.)
ExecutionDateSpecified	Boolean	True if a value for ExecutionDate is specified; otherwise, false.
Hidden	Boolean	True if the item is hidden; otherwise, false.

Property	Type	Description
HiddenSpecified	Boolean	True if a value for Hidden is specified; otherwise, false.
ID	String	The ID of the item. (Read-only.)
MimeType	String	The MIME type of a resource item. (Valid only for resource items.) (Read-only.)
ModifiedBy	String	The name of the user who last modified the item. (Read-only.)
ModifiedDate	Date	The date and time the item was last modified. (Read-only.)
ModifiedDateSpecified	Boolean	True if a value for ModifiedDate is specified; otherwise, false.
Name	String	The name of the item.
Path	String	The folder path to the item. (Read-only.)
Size	Integer	The size of the item in bytes. (Read-only.)
SizeSpecified	Boolean	True if a value for Size is specified; otherwise, false.
Type	ItemTypeEnum	The type of the item. Valid values are Unknown, Folder, Report, Resource, LinkedReport, and Datasource. (Read-only.)
VirtualPath	String	The virtual path to the item. This is populated only when viewing items under the MyReports folder. (Read-only.)

DailyRecurrence

Description: This class contains the time that must elapse, in days, before a schedule recurs. This class inherits from RecurrencePattern. This is a class of the ReportService2005 web service.
Properties:

Property	Type	Description
DaysInterval	Integer	The number of days before a schedule recurs.

DataRetrievalPlan

Description: This class is used to define the data to be selected for a data-driven subscription. This is a class of the ReportService2005 web service.
Properties:

Property	Type	Description
DataSet	DataSetDefinition	Defines the dataset to use with the data-driven subscription.
Item	DataSourceDefinitionOrReference	Defines the data source to use with the data-driven subscription.

DataSetDefinition

Description: This class contains the information necessary to define a dataset. This is a class of the ReportService2005 web service.

Properties:

Property	Type	Description
AccentSensitivity	SensitivityEnum	True if this dataset is sensitive to accents. False if this dataset is not sensitive to accents. Auto if the sensitivity setting should be determined from the data provider.
AccentSensitivitySpecified	Boolean	True if a value for AccentSensitivity is specified; otherwise, false.
CaseSensitivity	SensitivityEnum	True if this dataset is case-sensitive. False if this dataset is not case-sensitive. Auto if the sensitivity setting should be determined from the data provider.
CaseSensitivitySpecified	Boolean	True if a value for CaseSensitivity is specified; otherwise, false.
Collation	String	The locale used when sorting the data in the dataset. (Uses the SQL Server collation codes.)
Fields	An Array of Field Objects	An array containing the field information.
KanatypeSensitivity	SensitivityEnum	True if this dataset is kanatype-sensitive. False if this dataset is not kanatype-sensitive. Auto if the sensitivity setting should be determined from the data provider. (This is used only for some Japanese character sets.)
KanatypeSensitivitySpecified	Boolean	True if a value for KanatypeSensitivity has been specified; otherwise, false.
Name	String	The name of the dataset.
Query	QueryDefinition Object	An object containing the query used to retrieve the data.
WidthSensitivity	SensitivityEnum	True if this dataset is width-sensitive. False if this dataset is not width-sensitive. Auto if the sensitivity setting should be determined from the data provider.
WidthSensitivitySpecified	Boolean	True if a value for WidthSensitivity is specified; otherwise, false.

DataSource

Description: This class contains either a reference to a shared data source or an object with the information necessary to define a data source. This is a class of the ReportService2005 web service.

Properties:

Property	Type	Description
Item	A DataSourceReference Object or a DataSourceDefinition Object	If the data source is referencing a shared data source, this is a DataSourceReference object; otherwise, this is a DataSourceDefinition object.
Name	String	The name of the data source.

DataSourceCredentials

Description: This class contains the credentials used to access a data source. This is a class of the ReportExecution2005 and ReportService2005 web service.

Properties:

Property	Type	Description
DataSourceName	String	The name of the data source that uses these credentials.
Password	String	The password used to connect to the data source.
UserName	String	The user name used to connect to the data source.

DataSourceDefinition

Description: This class contains the information necessary to define a data source. This class inherits from DataSourceDefinitionOrReference. This is a class of the ReportService2005 web service.

Properties:

Property	Type	Description
ConnectString	String	The connection string.
CredentialRetrieval	CredentialRetrievalEnum	Prompt if the user is to be prompted for credentials when accessing this data source. Store if the credentials are stored in the data source definition. Integrated if Windows Authentication is to be used to access the data source. None if no credentials are required.
Enabled	Boolean	True if the data source is enabled; otherwise, false.

Property	Type	Description
EnabledSpecified	Boolean	True if a value for Enabled is specified; otherwise, false.
Extension	String	The name of the data source extension. Valid values include SQL, OLEDB, ODBC, and a custom extension.
ImpersonateUser	Boolean	True if the Report Server is to impersonate the user after a connection has been made to the data source; otherwise, false.
ImpersonateUserSpecified	Boolean	True if a value for ImpersonateUser is specified; otherwise, false.
Password	String	The password when the credentials are stored in the data source definition.
Prompt	String	The message used when prompting the user for credentials.
UseOriginalConnectString	Boolean	True if the data source should revert to the original connection string; otherwise, false.
UserName	String	The user name when the credentials are stored in the data source definition.
WindowsCredentials	Boolean	True if the stored credentials are Windows credentials. False if the stored credentials are database credentials.

DataSourceDefinitionOrReference

Description: This class serves as a parent class. Any class that inherits from the DataSourceDefinitionOrReference class can be used where a Data SourceDefinitionOrReference type object is required. This is a class of the ReportService2005 web service.

Classes Inheriting from This Class:

Class Name	Description
DataSourceDefinition	Used when a data source definition is to be specified.
DataSourceReference	Used when a reference to a shared data source is to be specified.

DataSourcePrompt

Description: This class contains information about the message displayed to the user when prompting for data source credentials. This is a class of the ReportExecution2005 and ReportService2005 web service.

Properties:

Property	Type	Description
DataSourceID	String	The unique ID of a data source.
Name	String	The name of the data source.
Prompt	String	The prompt message.

DataSourceReference

Description: This class contains a reference to a shared data source. This class inherits from DataSourceDefinitionOrReference. This is a class of the ReportService2005 web service.

Properties:

Property	Type	Description
Reference	String	The folder path and name of the shared data source.

DaysOfWeekSelector

Description: This class contains information for the days of the week on which a schedule runs. This is a class of the ReportService2005 web service.

Properties:

Property	Type	Description
Friday	Boolean	True if the schedule is to run on Friday; otherwise, false.
Monday	Boolean	True if the schedule is to run on Monday; otherwise, false.
Saturday	Boolean	True if the schedule is to run on Saturday; otherwise, false.
Sunday	Boolean	True if the schedule is to run on Sunday; otherwise, false.
Thursday	Boolean	True if the schedule is to run on Thursday; otherwise, false.
Tuesday	Boolean	True if the schedule is to run on Tuesday; otherwise, false.
Wednesday	Boolean	True if the schedule is to run on Wednesday; otherwise, false.

DocumentMapNode

Description: This class contains the definition of a single node in a document map. This is a class of the ReportExecution2005 web service.

Properties:

Property	Type	Description
Children	Array of DocumentMapNode Objects	The children of the document map node.
Label	String	The label of the document map node.
UniqueName	String	The unique name of the report item or grouping pointed to by this document map node.

ExecutionInfo

Description: This class describes the state of the current report execution. This is a class of the ReportExecution2005 web service.

Properties:

Property	Type	Description
AllowQueryExecution	Boolean	True if the user can provide values for the parameters used in the query.
CredentialsRequired	Boolean	True if the report requires credentials to be supplied.
DataSourcePrompts	Array of DataSourcePrompt Objects	The prompt strings for each data source used by the report.
ExecutionDateTime	DateTime	The date and time the snapshot associated with the execution was created.
ExecutionID	String	The unique identifier of this report execution.
ExpirationDateTime	DateTime	The date and time this execution expires.
HasDocumentMap	Boolean	True if the report has a document map.
HasSnapshot	Boolean	True if data has been retrieved and processed for the report.
HistoryID	String	Contains the history ID of the report, if the report is from a report history snapshot.
NeedsProcessing	Boolean	True if the snapshot for this execution needs to be created or reprocessed.
NumPages	Integer	The number of logical pages, including soft page breaks, in the report.
Parameters	Array of ReportParameter	The parameters for the execution.
ParametersRequired	Boolean	True if the report requires parameter values.
ReportPath	String	The folder path to the report on the Report Server.

ExpirationDefinition

Description: This class serves as a parent class. Any class that inherits from the ExpirationDefinition class can be used where an ExpirationDefinition type object is required. This is a class of the ReportService2005 web service.
Classes Inheriting from This Class:

Class Name	Description
ScheduleExpiration	Used when a date and time are to be specified for the expiration.
TimeExpiration	Used when an elapsed time, in minutes, should be specified for the expiration.

Extension

Description: This class represents a Reporting Services extension. This is a class of the ReportExecution2005 web service and ReportService2005 web service.
Properties:

Property	Type	Description
ExtensionType	ExtensionTypeEnum	Delivery for a delivery extension, Render for a rendering extension, Data for a data-processing extension, or All to represent all extension types. (Read-only.)
LocalizedName	String	The localized name of the extension for display to the user. (Read-only.)
Name	String	The name of the extension. (Read-only.)
Visible	Boolean	True if the extension is visible to the user interface; otherwise, false.

ExtensionParameter

Description: This class contains information about a setting for a delivery extension. This is a class of the ReportService2005 web service.
Properties:

Property	Type	Description
DisplayName	String	The name of the extension parameter.
Encrypted	Boolean	True if the Value property should be encrypted; otherwise, false. (Read-only.)
Error	String	An error message describing a problem with the value specified for this extension parameter. (Read-only.)
IsPassword	Boolean	True if the value for this parameter should not be returned in SOAP responses (this prevents passwords from being sent in clear text); otherwise, false. (Read-only.)
Name	String	The name of the device information setting. (Read-only.)

ReadOnly	Boolean	True if this extension parameter is read-only; otherwise, false. (Read-only.)
Required	Boolean	True if this extension parameter is required; otherwise, false. (Read-only.)
RequiredSpecified	Boolean	True if a value for Required is specified; otherwise, false.
ValidValues	An Array of ValidValue Objects	An array of valid values for this extension parameter.
Value	String	The value of this extension parameter.

ExtensionSettings

Description: This class contains information for a delivery extension. This is a class of the ReportService2005 web service.

Properties:

Property	Type	Description
Extension	Extension Object	An object representing a Reporting Services extension.
ParameterValues	An Array of ParameterValueOfFieldReference Objects	An array of parameter values for this extension.

Field

Description: This class contains information for a field within a dataset. This is a class of the ReportService2005 web service.

Properties:

Property	Type	Description
Alias	String	The alias of a field in a report.
Name	String	The name of a field in a query.

ItemNamespaceHeader

Description: This is used to determine how property information is retrieved with GetProperty. It inherits from SoapHeader. The following property is not inherited, but it is defined in the ItemNamespaceHeader class. This is a class of the ReportService2005 web service.

Properties:

Property	Type	Description
ItemNamespace	ItemNamespaceEnum	The method used for retrieving properties. Valid values are GUIDBased and PathBased.

MinuteRecurrence

Description: This class contains the time that must elapse, in minutes, before a schedule recurs. This class inherits from RecurrencePattern. This is a class of the ReportService2005 web service.

Properties:

Property	Type	Description
MinutesInterval	Integer	The number of minutes before a schedule recurs.

ModelCatalogItem

Description: This class contains information about a model. This is a class of the ReportService2005 web service.

Properties:

Property	Type	Description
Description	String	The description of a model catalog item.
Model	String	The folder path and name of the model catalog item.
Perspectives	Array of ModelPerspective Objects	The perspectives of the model catalog item.

ModelDrillthroughReport

Description: This class contains information about a model drillthrough report. This is a class of the ReportService2005 web service.

Properties:

Property	Type	Description
Path	String	The full path and name of the drillthrough report.
Type	ModelDrillthroughTypeEnum	The type of the data presented by the drillthrough report. Valid values are Detail and List.

ModelItem

Description: This class contains a semantic definition of a model item. This is a class of the ReportService2005 web service.

Properties:

Property	Type	Description
Description	String	The description of a model item.
ID	String	The ID of a model item.

Property	Type	Description
ModelItems	Array of ModelItem Objects	The children of a model item.
Name	String	The name of the model item.
Type	ModelItemTypeEnum	The type of the model item. Valid values are Attribute, Entity, Entity Folder, Field Folder, Model, and Role.

ModelPerspective

Description: This class contains information about a model perspective. This is a class of the ReportService2005 web service.
Properties:

Property	Type	Description
Description	String	The description of a perspective.
ID	String	The ID of a perspective.
Name	String	The name of a perspective.

MonthlyDOWRecurrence

Description: This class contains the days of the week, the weeks of the month, and the months of the year on which a schedule runs. This class inherits from RecurrencePattern. This is a class of the ReportService2005 web service.
Properties:

Property	Type	Description
DaysOfWeek	DaysOfWeekSelector Object	An object that determines the days of the week on which the schedule runs.
MonthsOfYear	MonthsOfYearSelector	An object that determines the months of the year on which the schedule runs.
WhichWeek	WeekNumberEnum	FirstWeek if the schedule is to run the first week of the month, SecondWeek if the schedule is to run the second week of the month, ThirdWeek if the schedule is to run the third week of the month, FourthWeek if the schedule is to run the fourth week of the month, or LastWeek if the schedule is to run the last week of the month.
WhichWeekSpecified	Boolean	True if a value for WhichWeek has been specified; otherwise, false.

MonthlyRecurrence

Description: This class contains the days of the month and the months of the year on which a schedule runs. This class inherits from RecurrencePattern. This is a class of the ReportService2005 web service.
Properties:

Property	Type	Description
Days	String	The days of the month on which the schedule recurs.
MonthsOfYear	MonthsOfYearSelector	An object that determines the months of the year on which the schedule recurs.

MonthsOfYearSelector

Description: This class contains information on the months of the year in which a schedule runs. This is a class of the ReportService2005 web service.
Properties:

Property	Type	Description
April	Boolean	True if the schedule is to run in April; otherwise, false.
August	Boolean	True if the schedule is to run in August; otherwise, false.
December	Boolean	True if the schedule is to run in December; otherwise, false.
February	Boolean	True if the schedule is to run in February; otherwise, false.
January	Boolean	True if the schedule is to run in January; otherwise, false.
July	Boolean	True if the schedule is to run in July; otherwise, false.
June	Boolean	True if the schedule is to run in June; otherwise, false.
March	Boolean	True if the schedule is to run in March; otherwise, false.
May	Boolean	True if the schedule is to run in May; otherwise, false.
November	Boolean	True if the schedule is to run in November; otherwise, false.
October	Boolean	True if the schedule is to run in October; otherwise, false.
September	Boolean	True if the schedule is to run in September; otherwise, false.

NoSchedule

Description: This class is used when no schedule is associated with an execution snapshot or a history snapshot. This class inherits from Schedule DefinitionOrReference. It does not contain any properties. This is a class of the ReportService2005 web service.

ParameterFieldReference

Description: This class represents a field in a dataset used to supply the value for a parameter. This class inherits from ParameterValueOrFieldReference. This is a class of the ReportService2005 web service.
Properties:

Property	Type	Description
FieldAlias	String	The alias of a field.
ParameterName	String	The name of a field.

ParameterValue

Description: This class represents the actual value for a parameter. This class inherits from ParameterValueOrFieldReference. This is a class of the ReportExecution2005 web service and the ReportService2005 web service.
Properties:

Property	Type	Description
Label	String	The label used for this parameter.
Name	String	The name of the parameter.
Value	String	The value of the parameter.

ParameterValueOrFieldReference

Description: This class serves as a parent class. Any class that inherits from the ParameterValueOrFieldReference class can be used where a ParameterValueOrFieldReference type object is required. This is a class of the ReportExecution2005 and the ReportService2005 web service.
Classes Inheriting from This Class:

Class Name	Description
ParameterFieldReference	Used when a reference to a field is to be specified.
ParameterValue	Used when a parameter value is to be specified.

Policy

Description: This class represents a domain user or domain group and the security roles assigned to that user or group. This is a class of the ReportService2005 web service.

Properties:

Property	Type	Description
GroupUserName	String	The name of a domain user or domain group.
Roles	An Array of Role Objects	An array of security roles.

Property

Description: This class represents a property of a Reporting Services item. This is a class of the ReportService2005 web service.
Properties:

Property	Type	Description
Name	String	The name of the property.
Value	String	The value of the property.

QueryDefinition

Description: This class contains information to define a query used for a dataset or a data-driven subscription. This is a class of the ReportService2005 web service.
Properties:

Property	Type	Description
CommandText	String	The query text (usually a SELECT statement).
CommandType	String	The type of query supplied in the CommandText property. (For data-driven subscriptions, this always has a value of Text.)
Timeout	Integer	The number of seconds the query may execute before it times out.
TimeoutSpecified	Boolean	True if a value for Timeout has been specified; otherwise, false.

RecurrencePattern

Description: This class serves as a parent class. Any class that inherits from the RecurrencePattern class can be used where a RecurrencePattern type object is required. This is a class of the ReportService2005 web service.
Classes Inheriting from This Class:

Class Name	Description
MinuteRecurrence	Used when the schedule is to recur in minutes.
DailyRecurrence	Used when the schedule is to recur on a daily basis.

Class Name	Description
WeeklyRecurrence	Used when the schedule is to occur on certain days of the week and to recur on a weekly basis.
MonthlyRecurrence	Used when the schedule is to occur on certain days of the month and certain months of the year.
MonthlyDOWRecurrence	Used when the recurrence is to occur on a day of the week, week of the month, and month of the year.

ReportHistorySnapshot

Description: This class contains information defining a history snapshot. This is a class of the ReportService2005 web service.

Properties:

Property	Type	Description
CreationDate	Date	The date and time the history snapshot was created. (Read-only.)
HistoryID	String	The ID of the history snapshot. (Read-only.)
Size	Integer	The size (in bytes) of the history snapshot. (Read-only.)

ReportParameter

Description: This class contains information about a report parameter. This is a class of the ReportExecution2005 web service and the ReportService2005 web service. Properties vary between the two web services.

Properties:

Property	Type	Description
AllowBlank	Boolean	True if this report parameter can be empty; otherwise, false. (Read-only.)
AllowBlankSpecified	Boolean	True if a value for AllowBlank was specified; otherwise, false.
DefaultValues	String	The default value of the report parameter.
DefaultValuesQueryBased	Boolean	True if the default value comes from a query; otherwise, false. (Read-only.)
DefaultValuesQueryBasedSpecified	Boolean	True if a value for DefaultValuesQueryBased is specified; otherwise, false.

Property	Type	Description
Dependencies	An Array of Strings	An array showing which other report parameters are depended on by the query used to provide the default value and the query used to provide valid values. Used only if the default value or the valid values come from a parameterized query. (Read-only.)
ErrorMessage	String	Any error messages describing errors with this report parameter.
MultiValue	Boolean	True if the parameter can be a multivalued parameter. (Read-only.)
MultiValueSpecified	Boolean	True if a value for MultiValue is specified; otherwise, false.
Name	String	The name of the parameter. (Read-only.)
Nullable	Boolean	True if the report parameter may be null; otherwise, false.
NullableSpecified	Boolean	True if a value for Nullable is specified; otherwise, false.
Prompt	String	The message displayed to the user when prompting for a value for this parameter.
PromptUser	Boolean	True if the user is to be prompted for this report parameter; otherwise, false.
PromptUserSpecified	Boolean	True if a value for PromptUser has been specified; otherwise, false.
QueryParameter	Boolean	True if this parameter is used in a data source query; otherwise, false. (Read-only.)
QueryParameterSpecified	Boolean	True if a value for QueryParameter is specified; otherwise, false.
State		HasValidValue if the report parameter has a valid value, MissingValidValue if a valid value for the report parameter does not exist, HasOutstandingDependencies if other report parameters depended on by this report parameter are not yet specified, or DynamicValuesUnavailable if no values were returned by a query designated to provide the list of valid values. (Read-only.)

Property	Type	Description
StateSpecified	Boolean	True if a value for State is specified; otherwise, false.
Type		Boolean if type boolean, DateTime if type datetime, Float if type float, Integer if type integer, or String if type string. (Read-only.)
TypeSpecified	Boolean	True if a value for Type is specified; otherwise, false.
ValidValues	An Array of ValidValue Objects	An array of the valid values for this report parameter.
ValidValuesQueryBased	Boolean	True if the valid values come from a query; otherwise, false.
ValidValuesQueryBased Specified	Boolean	True if a value for ValidValuesQueryBased is specified; otherwise, false.

Role

Description: This class contains information about a security role. This is a class of the ReportService2005 web service.
Properties:

Property	Type	Description
Description	String	The description of the role.
Name	String	The name of the role.

Schedule

Description: This class contains information about a schedule. This is a class of the ReportService2005 web service.
Properties:

Property	Type	Description
Creator	String	The name of the user who created the schedule. (Read-only.)
Definition	ScheduleDefinition Object	The definition of the schedule.
Description	String	The description of the schedule.
LastRunTime	Date	The date and time the schedule was last run. (Read-only.)

Property	Type	Description
LastRunTimeSpecified	Boolean	True if a value for LastRunTime is specified; otherwise, false.
Name	String	The name of the schedule.
NextRunTime	Date	The date and time the schedule will run next. (Read-only.)
NextRunTimeSpecified	Boolean	True if a value for NextRunTime is specified; otherwise, false.
ReferencesPresent	Boolean	True if this is a shared schedule and it is referenced by reports and subscriptions.
ScheduleID	String	The ID of the schedule. (Read-only.)
State	ScheduleStateEnum	Running if one or more reports associated with this schedule are currently running, Ready if one or more reports associated with this schedule are ready to run, Paused if the schedule is paused, Expired if the end date for this schedule has passed, Failing if an error has occurred and the schedule has failed.

ScheduleDefinition

Description: This class contains information for defining a schedule. This class inherits from ScheduleDefinitionOrReference. This is a class of the ReportService2005 web service.

Properties:

Property	Type	Description
EndDate	Date	The end date and time for the schedule.
EndDateSpecified	Boolean	True if a value for EndDate has been specified; otherwise, false.
Item	RecurrencePattern Object	An object containing information about when the schedule should run.
StartDateTime	Date	The start date and time for the schedule.

ScheduleDefinitionOrReference

Description: This class serves as a parent class. Any class that inherits from the ScheduleDefinitionOrReference class can be used where a ScheduleDefinitionOrReference type object is required. This is a class of the ReportService2005 web service.

Classes Inheriting from This Class:

Class Name	Description
NoSchedule	Used when no schedule is to be specified.
ScheduleDefinition	Used when a schedule definition is to be specified.
ScheduleReference	Used when a reference to a shared schedule is to be specified.

ScheduleExpiration

Description: This class defines when a cached copy of a report should expire. This class inherits from ExpirationDefinition. This is a class of the ReportService2005 web service.

Properties:

Property	Type	Description
Item	ScheduleDefinitionOrReference Object	Either a schedule definition or a reference to a shared schedule.

ScheduleReference

Description: This class contains a reference to a shared schedule. This class inherits from ScheduleDefinitionOrReference. This is a class of the ReportService2005 web service.

Properties:

Property	Type	Description
Definition	ScheduleDefinition Object	The definition of the schedule.
ScheduleID	String	The ID of the shared schedule.

SearchCondition

Description: This class provides information on a search within the Report Catalog. This is a class of the ReportService2005 web service.

Properties:

Property	Type	Description
Condition	ConditionEnum	Contains if the search must match only a portion of the property's value to be considered a match, Equals if the search must match all the property's value to be considered a match.
ConditionSpecified	Boolean	True if a value for Condition has been specified; otherwise, false.

Property	Type	Description
Name	String	The name of the property being searched.
Value	String	The value to find.

ServerInfoHeader

Description: This class contains information on the current version of the Report Server. This is a class of the ReportExecution2005 web service and the ReportService2005 web service.

Properties:

Property	Type	Description
ReportServerEdition	String	A read-only property containing the edition of the Report Server.
ReportServerVersion	String	A read-only property containing the version of the Report Server.
ReportServerVersionNumber	String	A read-only property containing the version number of the Report Server.

Subscription

Description: This class contains information to define a subscription. This is a class of the ReportService2005 web service.

Properties:

Property	Type	Description
Active	ActiveState Object	The active state of the subscription. (Read-only.)
DeliverySettings	ExtensionSettings Object	The settings specific to the delivery extension.
Description	String	A description of the format and the delivery method.
EventType	String	The type of event that triggers the subscription.
IsDataDriven	Boolean	True if the subscription is data-driven; otherwise, false.
LastExecuted	Date	The date and time the subscription was last executed. (Read-only.)
LastExecutedSpecified	Boolean	True if a value for LastExecuted is specified; otherwise, false.
ModifiedBy	String	The name of the user who last modified the subscription. (Read-only.)
ModifiedDate	Date	The date and time of the last modification to the subscription. (Read-only.)

Property	Type	Description
Owner	String	The user name of the owner of the subscription. (Read-only.)
Path	String	The full path and name of the report associated with the subscription.
Report	String	The name of the report associated with the subscription.
Status	String	The status of the subscription. (Read-only.)
SubscriptionID	String	The ID of the subscription.
VirtualPath	String	The virtual path to the report associated with the subscription. This is populated only if the associated report is under the MyReports folder.

Task

Description: This class contains information about a Reporting Services task. This is a class of the ReportService2005 web service.

Properties:

Property	Type	Description
Description	String	The description of this task. (Read-only.)
Name	String	The name of this task. (Read-only.)
TaskID	String	The ID for this task. (Read-only.)

TimeExpiration

Description: This class contains the time that must elapse, in minutes, before a cached copy of a report expires. This class inherits from ExpirationDefinition. This is a class of the ReportService2005 web service.

Properties:

Property	Type	Description
Minutes	Integer	The number of minutes before expiration.

ValidValue

Description: This class contains information on a valid value for an extension parameter or a report parameter. This is a class of the ReportExecution2005 web service and the ReportService2005 web service.

Properties:

Property	Type	Description
Label	String	The label for the valid value.
Value	String	The valid value for the setting.

Warning

Description: This class contains information on a warning message or an error message. This is a class of the ReportExecution2005 web service and the ReportService2005 web service.

Properties:

Property	Type	Description
Code	String	The error or warning code. (Read-only.)
Message	String	The error or warning message. (Read-only.)
ObjectName	String	The name of the object associated with the warning or error. (Read-only.)
ObjectType	String	The type of the object associated with the warning or error. (Read-only.)
Severity	String	Warning if this is a warning, Error if this is an error.

WeeklyRecurrence

Description: This class contains the days of the week on which a schedule runs and the number of weeks to elapse before each recurrence. This class inherits from RecurrencePattern. This is a class of the ReportService2005 web service.

Properties:

Property	Type	Description
DaysOfWeek	DaysOfWeekSelector Object	An object that determines the days of the week on which the schedule runs.
WeeksInterval	Integer	The number of weeks before a schedule runs again.
WeeksIntervalSpecified	Boolean	True if a value for WeeksInterval is specified; otherwise, false.

APPENDIX

C

Report Definition Language Reference

IN THIS APPENDIX:

Report Definition Language

Report Definition Language

The Report Definition Language (RDL) is an XML structure defined by Microsoft for storing Reporting Services reports. RDL is an element-centric XML structure. That is to say, RDL primarily uses elements to store information, rather than attributes.

The two types of elements within RDL are parent elements and property elements. *Parent elements* contain other elements, whereas *property elements* define a property of the parent element. The name of the property is the same as the name of the element. The value of the property is the contents of the element. For example, if the LeftMargin property of the report is set to one inch, the element containing that property would look like this:

```
<LeftMargin>1in</LeftMargin>
```

Property elements do not contain other elements.

Default Values

To keep the RDL files from becoming unwieldy, properties set to a default value are not included in the RDL file. For example, the default value for the PageHeight property of a report is 11 inches. If the PageHeight of a report is set to 11 inches, the RDL file for that report will not contain a PageHeight element. The programs that read (or consume) the RDL file need to know these default values and fill them in automatically.

RDL Structure

> **NOTE**
>
> In the following illustrations, the single arrows indicate a one-to-zero-or-one relation between the parent element and the child element. For example, the Report element may contain zero or one PageHeader elements. The arrows with shading indicate a one-to-zero-or-many relation between the parent element and the child elements. For example, the DataSources element may contain zero or many DataSource elements.

Report

The entire report definition is contained within the Report element. The structure of
the parent elements within the Report element is shown here:

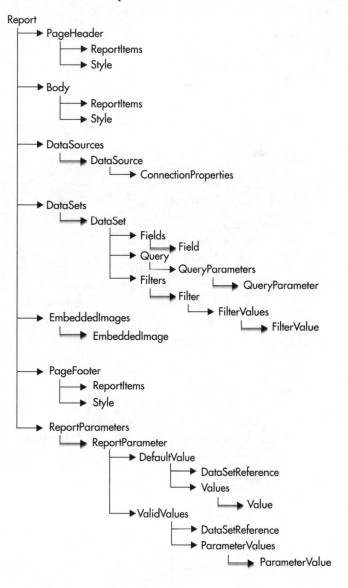

ReportItems

The report layout is made up of report items. As you saw in the previous illustration, report items can be placed in the PageHeader, the Body, and the PageFooter elements. The structure of the parent elements within the ReportItems element is shown here:

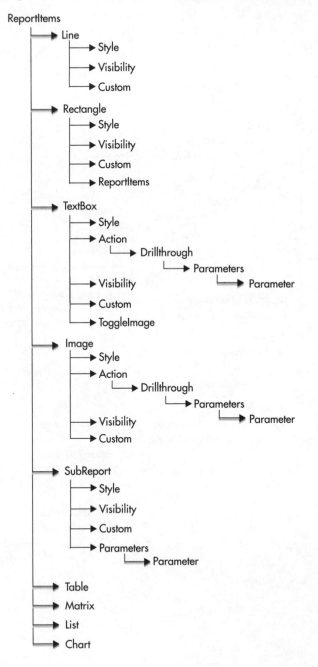

The structure of each of the data regions is shown in the following sections.

Table

The structure of the parent elements within the Table element is shown here:

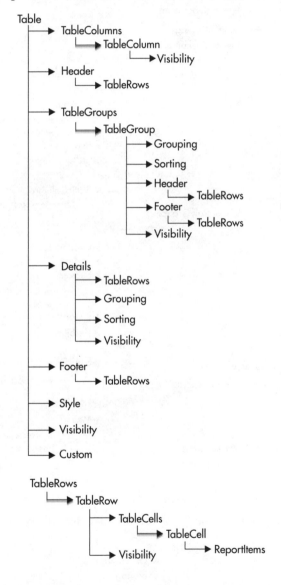

Matrix

The structure of the parent elements within the Matrix element is shown here:

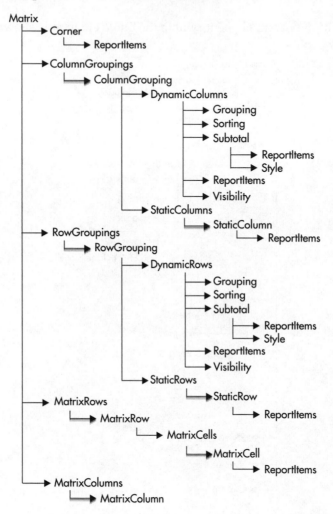

List

The structure of the parent elements within the List element is shown here:

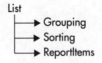

Chart

The structure of the parent elements—Chart, Axis, and ChartSeries—within the Chart element is shown here and on the following page:

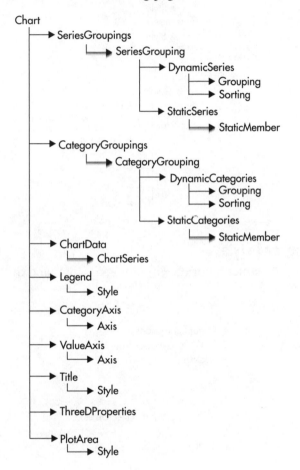

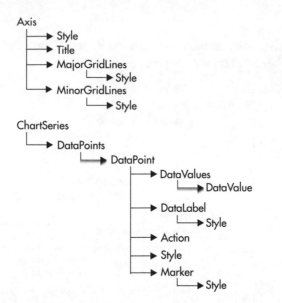

Grouping, Sorting, and Style

Last, but not least, the structure of the Grouping, Sorting, and Style elements is shown here:

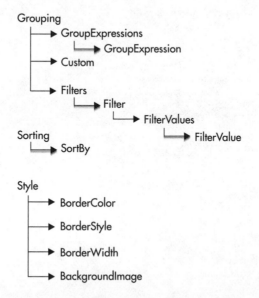

These items are used within a number of the other elements.

Ad Hoc Reporting

IN THIS CHAPTER:
The Report Model
Creating Reports with the Report Builder
Give It a Try

Three previous sections of this book were aimed at report authors creating reports to be used over and over again. These types of reports are often referred to, rather ignominiously, as "canned" reports. While not a glamorous moniker, it is rather fitting. These reports are prepared ahead of time, packaged, and stored for later execution by the user.

At times, however, rather than opening a can, cooking from scratch is more appropriate. A user may need some information on short notice, so a report author has no time to create a report. An analyst may need a bit of data for a one-time analysis, so a report development effort is hard to justify. In cases such as these, it would be beneficial to have a way for a knowledgeable user to quickly create a report or explore the data to find the desired information.

Fortunately, SQL Server 2005 Reporting Services provides such a mechanism with Report Models and the Report Builder. Report Models provide an easy-to-understand view of the database structure. The Report Builder provides a straightforward and readily available tool for creating reports. Together, they offer the means for users to quickly and easily gain access to the information they need.

The Report Model

One of the biggest hurdles for nondatabase professionals to overcome when creating reports is the creation of the dataset. Unless data is being pulled from a ready-made view or stored procedure, dataset creation is going to involve the creation of a SQL SELECT statement with all the INNER JOINs and WHERE clauses that go along with it. For those who want to get the full benefits of the Reporting Services environment, becoming conversant in the SQL dialect is worthwhile. For others who would rather spend time on analyzing data than learning the ins and outs of the GROUP BY, and who would rather concentrate on aiding their organizations than becoming intimate with UNION queries, there is the Report Model.

The *Report Model* provides a nontechnical user with a view of database content without requiring an intimate knowledge of relational theory and practice. It hides all the complexity of primary keys and foreign key constraints. In other words, the Report Model hides the technical nature of the database and enables the users to concern themselves with the data.

Once created, the Report Model serves as the basis for report creation with the Report Builder. First, we need to have one or more Report Models built over the top of our database. Once these are created and deployed to the Report Server, then we can turn a select number of users loose to create ad hoc reports and do data analysis on the fly.

Creating a Report Model

The following sections walk through the creation of a Report Model for the Galactic database. This model is then used to construct ad hoc reports with the Report Builder in the second part of this appendix. Like reports, Report Models are created in Visual Studio 2005 or the Business Intelligence Development Studio, and then deployed to a Report Server to be used. Unlike reports, Report Models can have security rights assigned to different pieces of their structure to provide the fine-grained security often required in ad hoc reporting situations.

We use the Report Model Wizard to create the Report Model, and then do some manual tweaking to make it more usable. We deploy the Report Model to the Report Server. Finally, we look at the method for setting security within the model itself.

NOTE

Before defining a Report Model from a relational database, it is important that the database exhibit good design and implementation practices. Tables should have explicitly declared primary keys. Also, all foreign keys should be maintained by foreign key constraints.

Create a Report Model Project in the Business Intelligence Development Studio

Follow these steps to create a Report Model project in Visual Studio 2005 or the Business Intelligence Development Studio.

1. Start up Visual Studio 2005 or the Business Intelligence Development Studio and create a new project.
2. Select Report Model Project in the Templates area of the New Project dialog box. (See Figure D-1).
3. Type **GDS Model** for the Name and select the MSSQLRS folder for the location.
4. Click OK to continue.

Create a Data Source

As with reports, Report Models require a data source to provide the information and credentials for connecting to a database. The following steps enable us to create a data source in the Report Model project.

1. Right-click the Data Sources folder in the Solution Explorer window and select Add New Data Source from the Context menu. The Data Source Wizard dialog box appears.
2. Click Next. The Select How to Define the Connection page appears.

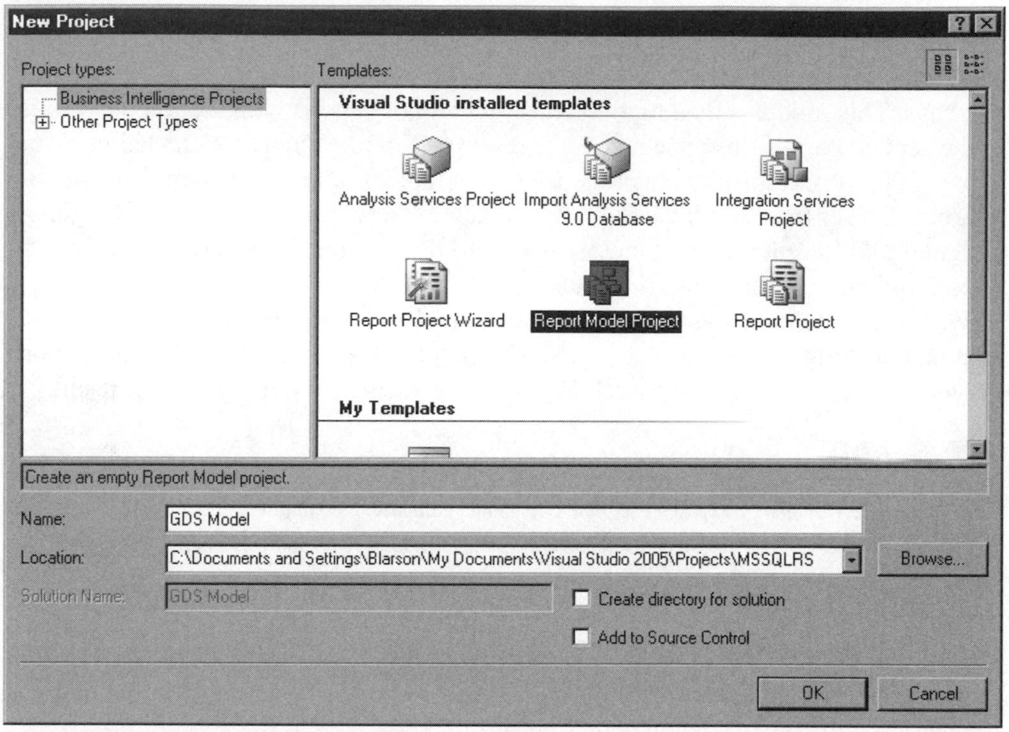

Figure D-1   *Creating a Report Model project*

3. If a connection to the Galactic database already exists in the Data Connections list, select this connection and go to Step 12. If there is no connection, click New. The Connection Manager dialog box appears.

4. Type the name of the Microsoft SQL Server database server hosting the Galactic database or select it from the drop-down list. If the Galactic database is hosted by the computer you are currently working on, you may type **(local)** for the server name.

5. Click the Use SQL Server Authentication radio button.

6. Type **GalacticReporting** for the user name.

7. Type **gds** for the password.

8. Click the Save My Password check box.

9. Select Galactic from the Select or Enter a Database Name drop-down list.

10. Click Test Connection. If a Test Connection Succeeded message appears, click OK. If an error message appears, make sure the name of your database server, the user name, the password, and the database were entered properly. If your test connection still does not succeed, make sure you have correctly installed the Galactic database.

11. Click OK. You return to the Data Source Wizard dialog box.

12. Click Next. The Completing the Wizard page appears.

13. Make sure the Data source name is **Galactic**. Click Finish.

Create a Data Source View

In addition to the data source, the Report Model also requires a data source view. The *data source view* is simply a selected subset of the tables from the data source itself. In many cases, we do not want our model to include data from all the tables in the database. Some tables might be used for logging or a temporary holding place for other operations. The data source view enables us to exclude these types of tables from the Report Model.

The following steps create a data source view for the tables in the Galactic database.

1. Right-click the Data Source Views folder in the Solution Explorer window and select Add New Data Source View from the Context menu. The Data Source View Wizard dialog box appears.

2. Click Next. The Select a Data Source page appears.

3. Select the Galactic data source and click Next. The Select Tables and Views page appears.

4. Move all the tables *except* the dtproperties, TransMonitorI, TransMonitorQ, and TransportMonitor into the Included objects list. Do *not* include any of the views in the Included objects list. The dtproperties table is a system table, so it should not be included. The other three tables are used for temporary processing and do not hold any meaningful data for ad hoc reporting.

5. Click Next. The Completing the Wizard page appears.

6. Make sure the Data source view name is **Galactic**. Click Finish.

Create a Report Model

With the preliminaries done, the following steps utilize the Report Model Wizard to create the Report Model.

1. Right-click the Report Models folder in the Solution Explorer window and select Add New Report Model from the Context menu. The Report Model Wizard appears.

2. Click Next. The Select Data Source View page appears.

3. Select the Galactic data source view and click Next. The Select Report Model Generation Rules page appears. See Figure D-2. This page enables you to select the rules to apply during the first pass and the second pass through the tables in the data source view. The default settings work for most data models, so we will leave the default settings. You can also select the language to use when creating your data model. The figures here use a data model generated in English.

4. Click Next. The Collect Model Statistics page appears.

5. The data model generation process uses the database statistics in the data source view. To create a data model that best reflects the current database and how it is used, we recommend you select the Update Statistics Before Generating radio button. Therefore, leave the Update Model Statistics Before Generating radio button selected. Click Next. The Completing the Wizard page appears.

6. Make sure the report model name is Galactic. Click Run. The wizard creates the model.

7. The wizard page shows the actions taken during each pass of the model generation process. See Figure D-3. When the process is complete, click Finish.

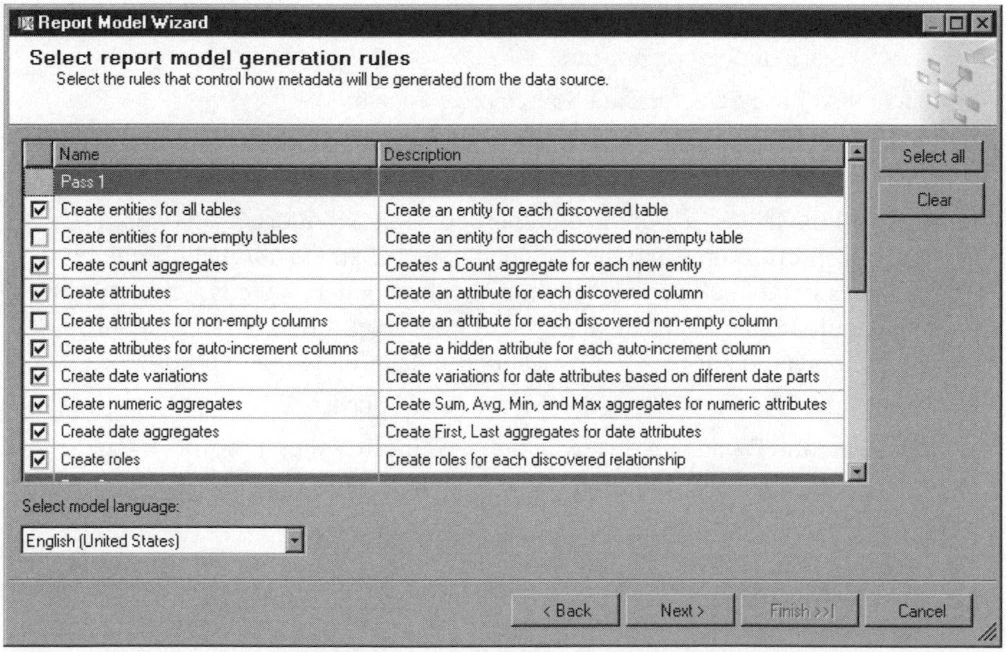

Figure D-2   *The Select Report Model Generation Rules page of the Report Model Wizard*

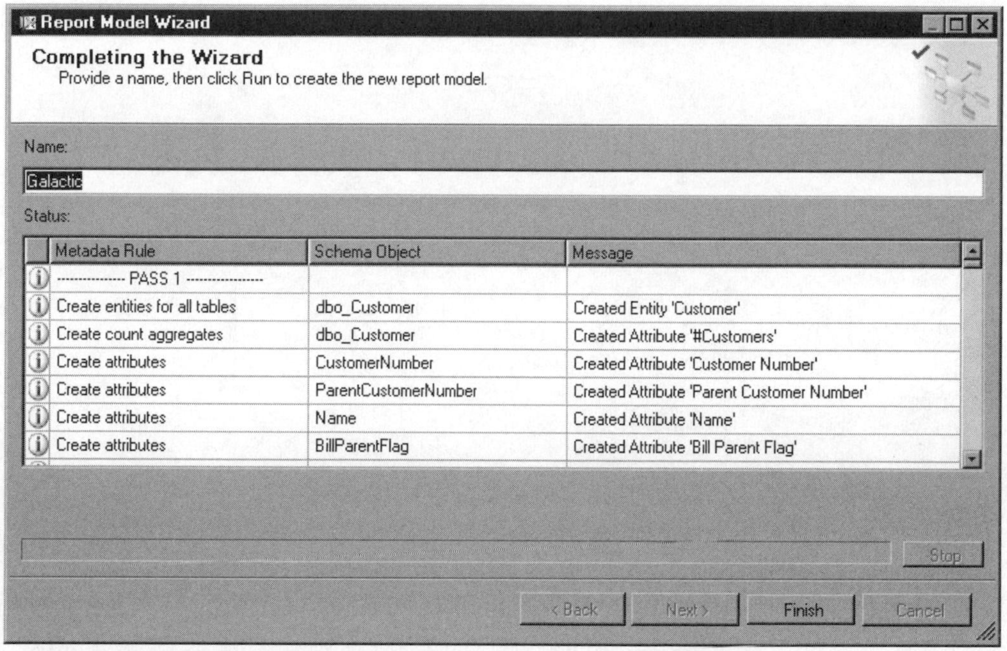

Figure D-3   *The Report Model Wizard creating the report model*

8. You may receive a message stating the data source view file has been modified outside of the editor and asking if you want it reloaded. If this message appears, click Yes.

The Report Data Model Parts and Pieces

Let's first take a look at the model that resulted from the wizard. Double-click the Galactic.smdl file entry in the Solution Explorer window to open it, if it is not already open. The model appears as shown in Figure D-4. You can see each of the tables in the Galactic database has become an entity in the model. An *entity* is simply a set of things, events, or concepts of interest to us in the data world. Each individual thing, event, or concept is an instance of an entity.

The fields from our database become attributes of our entities as shown in Figure D-5. *Attributes* are bits of information about each instance of an entity—the name of a particular company, the address of a particular employee. Attributes may also be referred to as *fields*. The field, or set of fields, that uniquely identifies a particular instance of an entity is called the *identifying field*. This is the primary key from the database.

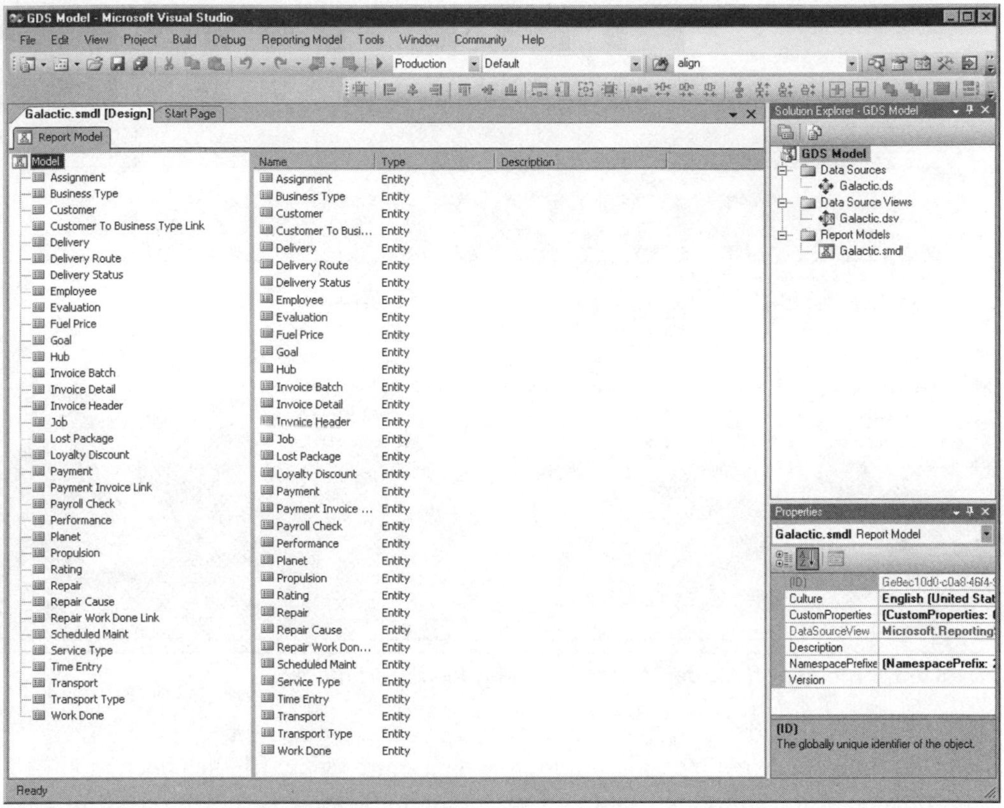

Figure D-4 *Entities in the Galactic Report Model*

The attribute type is identified in Figure D-5 by the icon to the left of each attribute name. The # notes a numeric attribute. The *a* notes an alphanumeric attribute. The calendar identifies a date/time attribute. The check box identifies a bit or Boolean attribute. Numeric attributes also include sum, average, minimum, and maximum aggregates. Date/time attributes also include the date parts of day, month, year, and quarter, along with aggregates for the first and last date.

NOTE

The Report Model contains some attributes that provide a count of the number of instances of an entity. For example, Figure D-5 shows an attribute called #Customers, which provides a count of the number of customer entities. Do not confuse the # icon, which indicates the attribute type with the # that is used at the beginning of the attribute name.

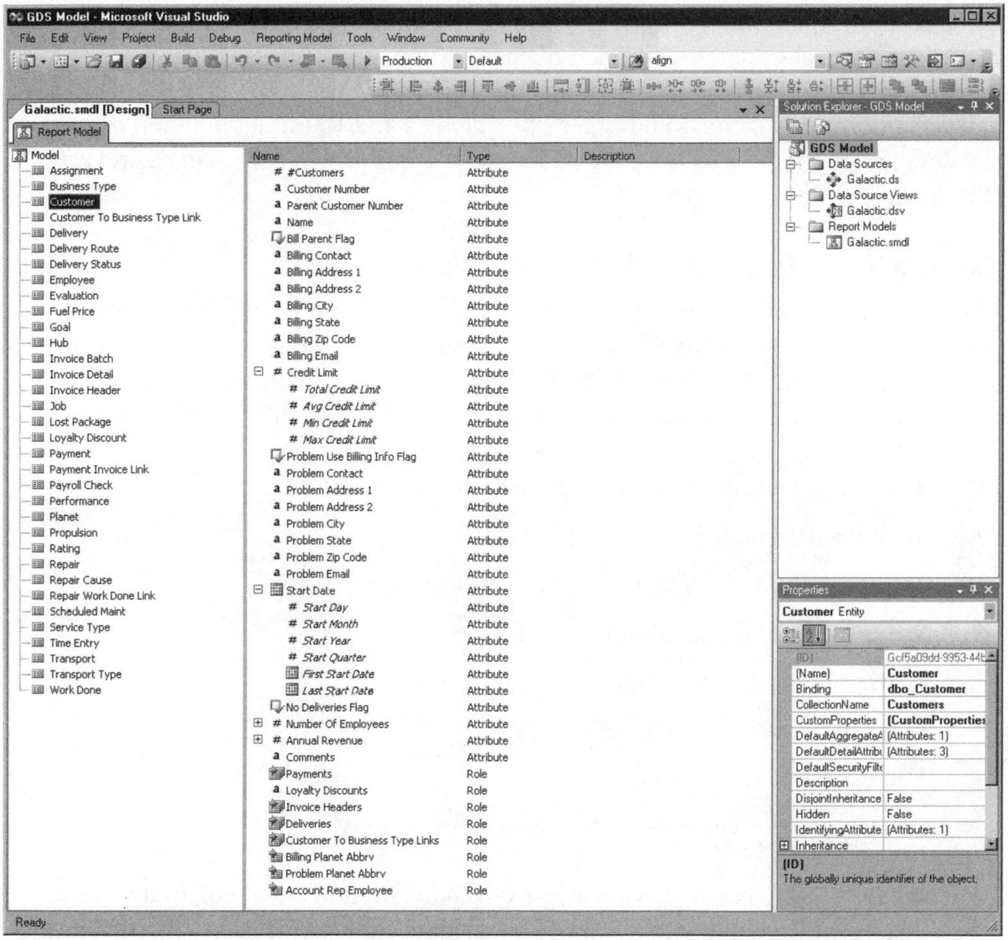

Figure D-5   *Attributes and roles of the Customer entity in the Galactic Report Model*

Finally, in the model, entities can have various roles. *Roles* are created by the foreign key constraints in the database. The roles link one entity to other entities in the model. A role can be a one-to-many, many-to-one, or one-to-one relationship. For example, in Figure D-5, a customer may have many invoice headers associated with it. This is a one-to-many relationship. On the other hand, an Account Rep Employee is an account representative for many customers. From the customer entity's point of view, this is a many-to-one relationship. Finally, a customer may have no more than one loyalty discount. This is a one-to-one relationship. Note the differing icons associated with each of these types of relationship.

Anyone familiar with entity relationship diagrams (ERD) immediately recognizes this terminology. A database designer often creates an ERD first, and then designs the database from the ERD. We are now working this same process in the reverse direction.

Cleaning Up the Report Model

Creating the Report Model using the Report Model Wizard is only half the battle. The wizard does a great job of creating the model for us. However, a number of refinements still need to be made to the model by hand to get it ready for the users.

Here are the tasks that must be accomplished to clean up the Report Model:

► Remove any numeric aggregates that don't make sense

► Remove attributes that should not be present

► Rename entities with cryptic names

► Use folders to organize entities, attributes, and roles

► Rearrange the entity, attribute, and role order

► Manually create calculated attributes

► Add descriptions

► Create perspectives coinciding with business areas

This appendix does not provide step-by-step instructions to clean up the entire Galactic Report Model. Instead, it provides a single example of each of these cleanup tasks using the Galactic Report Model. Of course, these cleanup tasks should be applied exhaustively to your own production models.

Remove Any Numeric Aggregates That Don't Make Sense   As stated earlier, the Report Model Wizard creates aggregates for all numeric attributes. In the case of a numeric identifying field, such as the Invoice Number, these aggregates are complete nonsense and should be removed from the model. We do not want a user using the average of the invoice numbers when they think they are getting the average of the invoice amounts! Let's keep our users out of trouble and remove these aggregates that simply don't add up.

1. Select the Invoice Header entity.
2. Select the Total Invoice Number, Avg Invoice Number, Min Invoice Number, and Max Invoice Number attributes.

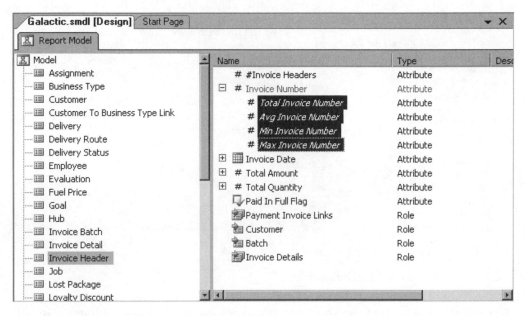

3. Press DELETE.
4. Click OK to confirm the deletion.

Remove Attributes That Should Not Be Present   Spotting numeric aggregates that don't make sense is a fairly easy exercise. Finding other attributes that do not belong is a bit harder. After all, each of these attributes comes from a database field and, if the information in a particular field is not useful, what is it doing in the database in the first place? Still, there may be fields in the database for system tasks, housekeeping chores, or security purposes, which should not be available to end users.

The Galactic Report Model provides an example in the Employee entity. There are fields to hold a user name and the pieces necessary for password encryption. Nothing good can come from having these exposed to prying eyes!

1. Select the Employee entity.
2. Select the User Name, Password Hash, and Password Salt attributes.

3. Press DELETE.

4. Click OK to confirm the deletion.

Rename Entities with Cryptic Names   The whole reason for the Report Model is to make it easy for users to create ad hoc reports without having to know the technical ins and outs of the database. Therefore, we want to make sure our entities, attributes, and roles have names that are obvious to the users. Any names that include acronyms and abbreviations that are not well known to the users should be changed.

I will give myself a pat on the back here and state that the names used in the Galactic database are pretty self-explanatory, so the entity, attribute, and role names in the model are, as well. This is an endorsement for good database design. However, here is one example of a name generated by the wizard that could be improved on.

1. Select the Employee entity.

2. Right-click the Account Rep Employee role and select Rename from the Context menu.

3. Type **Accounts for this Account Rep** as the new name and press ENTER.

Use Folders to Organize Entities, Attributes, and Roles   We can create folders to help organize our entities and attributes. Not only can these folders help us with organization, but we can also assign specific security roles to these folders. Entities and attributes that should have more restricted access, therefore, should be put in their own folders.

We put the entities related to the employee evaluations in a separate folder to make it easier to assign security later. We put the contact-related attributes in separate folders in the Customer entity to keep things more organized.

1. Select Model in the left-hand pane.
2. Right-click in the right-hand pane and select New | Folder from the Context menu.

3. Rename the new folder **Employee Evaluation**.
4. Select the Evaluation, Goal, Performance, and Rating entities in the right-hand pane.
5. Drag these entities to the Employee Evaluation folder and drop them there.
6. Select the Customer entity.
7. Make sure no attribute or role is selected, and then right-click and select New | Folder from the Context menu.
8. Rename the new folder **Billing Contact Info**.
9. Select all the billing contact–related attributes in the right-hand pane.
10. Drag these to the Billing Contact Info folder and drop them there.
11. Make sure no attribute or role is selected, and then right-click and select New | Folder from the Context menu.
12. Rename the new folder **Problem Contact Info**.
13. Select all the problem contact–related attributes in the right-hand pane.
14. Drag these to the Problem Contact Info folder and drop them there.

Rearrange the Entity, Attribute, and Role Order Entities and attributes can be arranged in any desired order in the model. By default, entities appear in the model in alphabetical order, while attributes and roles appear in the order in which the fields and foreign key relationships are encountered in the database. This may not be the most appropriate order.

You may want to group your entities together into related groups. This is a bit difficult in the Galactic model because so many entities are interrelated. Instead, let's keep the entities arranged alphabetically. However, several of the items we moved around are not in alphabetical order, so we still have some rearranging to do. In the Delivery entity, it might make more sense to have the Pickup Date Time attribute right before the pickup contact and address information. The same is true with the Delivery Date Time.

1. Select the Delivery entity.
2. Right-click the Pickup Date Time attribute and select Move Up from the Context menu.
3. Repeat Step 2 until the Pickup Date Time attribute is immediately above the Pickup Contact attribute.
4. Use the same process to put the Delivery Date Time attribute immediately above the Delivery Contact attribute.

Manually Create Calculated Attributes   The Report Model Wizard created some calculated attributes containing counts, aggregates, and date parts. Some additional calculated attributes may be helpful. These calculated attributes could contain arithmetic calculations or even string concatenations. We look at an example of each of these.

1. Select the Delivery entity.
2. Right-click and select New | Expression from the Context menu. The Define Formula dialog box appears.
3. In the Entities list, select Service Type.
4. Drag the Cost field from the Fields list to the Formula area.
5. Click the minus (−) button.
6. In the Entities list, select Delivery.
7. Drag the Discount field from the Fields list and drop it after the minus sign in the Formula Area.
8. Click OK.
9. Rename the NewExpression attribute you just created to **Net Cost**.
10. In the Properties window, set the Nullable property of the Net Cost attribute to True.
11. Select the Employee entity.
12. Right-click and select New | Expression from the Context menu. The Define Formula dialog box appears.

13. Drag the First Name field from the Fields list to the Formula area.
14. Click the ampersand (&) button.
15. Type " " and click the ampersand button.
16. Drag the Middle Initial field from the Fields list and drop it after the ampersand.
17. Click the ampersand button.
18. Type " " and click the ampersand button.
19. Drag the Last Name field from the Fields list and drop it after the ampersand.
20. Click OK.
21. Rename the NewExpression attribute you just created to **Full Name**.
22. In the Properties window, set the Nullable property of the Full Name attribute to True.

Add Descriptions   Perhaps the most helpful thing you can do during this entire cleanup process is to add descriptions to each entity, attribute, role, and folder. These descriptions are displayed to the users when they hover the mouse over an item during report creation. The descriptions enable you to provide a detailed explanation of each item. These detailed descriptions can insure the users are selecting the correct items and getting exactly the information they are looking for. We are only entering one description as an example here. In your production Report Model, descriptions should be entered for all entities, attributes, roles, and folders.

1. Select the Employee entity.
2. Select the Full Name attribute you just created.
3. In the Properties window, enter **The first name, middle initial, and last name of the employee.** for the Description property of the Full Name attribute.

Create Perspectives Coinciding with Business Areas   *Perspectives* hide some of the complexity of the complete data model by grouping entities into logical units. Perspectives organize entities into sets that are likely to be used together by a given set of ad hoc report users. As you have seen, entity folders can also be used to group entities, but with two major differences. More on those differences in a moment.

Let's consider the groupings first used to introduce the Galactic database in Chapter 3. The tables were presented in four diagrams, each relating to a different functional area of Galactic Delivery Services: Accounting Information, Package Tracking, Personnel Information, and Transport Maintenance. We use these four groupings to create four perspectives in the Report Model.

Someone working in the accounting department is most likely to run reports from the tables in the Accounting Information diagram. Conversely, someone in the package tracking area will have little interest in the Accounting tables, but will primarily report from the Package Tracking tables. Both of these people are interested in the content of the Customer table, however. This means both want the Customer table to show up in their perspective. Fortunately, an entity can appear in multiple perspectives.

This, then, is the first difference between perspectives and entity folders. A single entity can show up in multiple perspectives, but it can only reside in one entity folder. The second difference between perspectives and entity folders is security roles can be assigned to entity folders, but they cannot be assigned to perspectives.

Let's create our four perspectives.

1. Select Model in the left-hand pane.

2. Right-click and select New | Perspective from the Context menu.

3. Click Clear All.

4. Select the following entities:

    BusinessType
    Customer
    Customer To Business Type Link
    Invoice Batch
    Invoice Detail
    Invoice Header
    Loyalty Discount
    Payment
    Payment Invoice Link

NOTE

Other entities related to the entities you select are implicitly checked and marked with a dark gray checkmark in a light gray check box. Explicitly check all of the entities listed here, so they are marked with a black checkmark in a white check box. After you make all the explicit selections, leave the implicit selections as they are.

5. Click OK.

6. Rename the new perspective to **Accounting Information**.

7. Right-click on Model in the left-hand pane and select New | Perspective from the Context menu.

8. Click Clear All.

9. Select the following entities:

   Customer
   Delivery
   Hub
   Lost Package
   Planet
   Service Type
   Transport

10. Click OK.

11. Rename the new perspective to **Package Tracking**.

12. Right-click on Model in the left-hand pane and select New | Perspective from the Context menu.

13. Click Clear All.

14. Select the following entities:

    Assignment
    Employee
    Evaluation (Remember, this is located in the Employee Evaluation folder)
    Goal (Remember, this is located in the Employee Evaluation folder)
    Job
    Payroll Check
    Performance (Remember, this is located in the Employee Evaluation folder)
    Rating (Remember, this is located in the Employee Evaluation folder)
    Time Entry

15. Click OK.

16. Rename the new perspective to **Personnel Information**.

17. Right-click on Model in the left-hand pane and select New | Perspective from the Context menu.

18. Click Clear All.

19. Select the following entities:

    Fuel Price
    Propulsion
    Repair
    Repair Cause
    Repair Work Done Link
    Scheduled Maint
    Transport
    Transport Type
    Work Done

20. Click OK.

21. Rename the new perspective to **Transport Maintenance**.

22. Click Save All in the toolbar.

Deploy the Model

Once you have the Report Model looking the way it should, it can be deployed to the Report Server. This is done in a manner similar to the process for deploying reports.

1. Right-click the entry for the GDS Model Project in the Solution Explorer window and select Properties from the Context menu. The GDS Model Property Pages dialog box appears.

2. Enter **/Galactic Delivery Services/Shared Reports** for the TargetDataSourceFolder. This causes the Report Model to use the Galactic shared data source that already exists in this folder.

3. Enter **/Galactic Delivery Services/Models** for the TargetModelFolder. This creates a new folder to contain the Report Model itself.

4. Enter **http://{ReportServer}/ReportServer** for the TargetServerURL where {ReportServer} is the name of the Report Server.

5. Click OK to exit the dialog box.

6. Right-click the entry for the GDS Model Project and select Deploy from the Context menu. The model deploys to the server. You receive one warning stating that the shared data source cannot be deployed because it already exists.

Secure the Model

The number of people who have access to the Report Model for ad hoc reporting is probably larger than the number of people who have access to the database for report authoring. This wider audience and increased exposure makes security doubly important. Personal information such as Social Security numbers, pay rates, and employee's health care information must be protected. In addition, important financial information, which should not be widely disbursed, may be in the data.

Let's first take a look at the Report Model using the Report Manager. Open Report Manager and browse to the /Galactic Delivery Services/Models folder where the model was deployed. As you can see in Figure D-6, the entry in the folder for the Galactic model looks much like the entries we have seen for reports and shared data sources. Clicking on the Galactic model opens the Properties tab for the model.

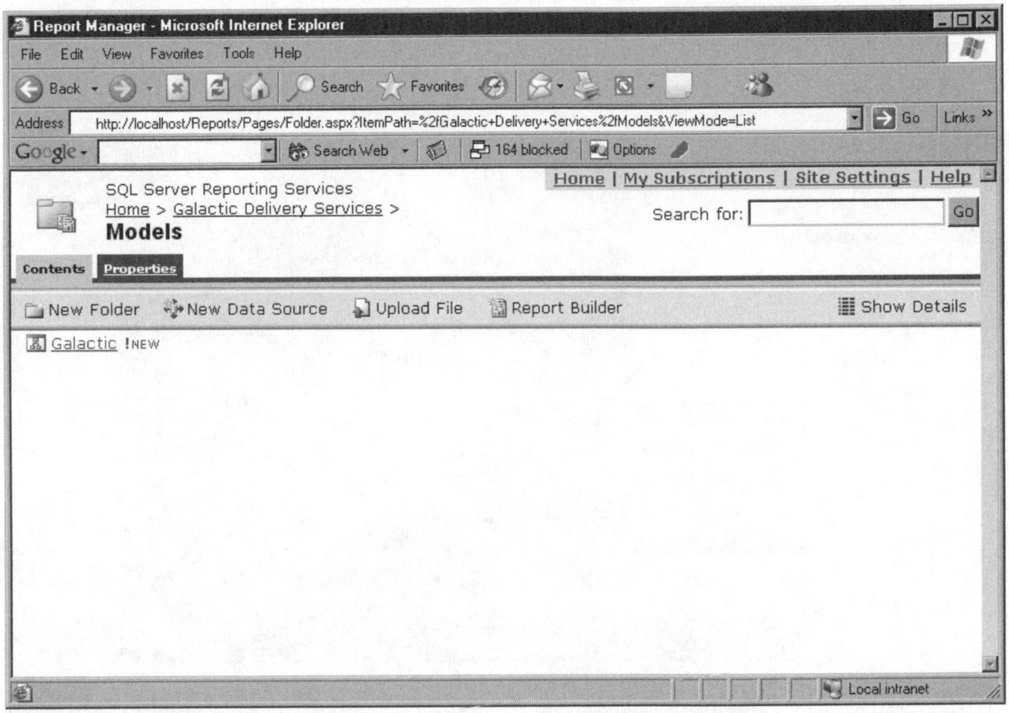

Figure D-6   *The Galactic Report Model deployed to the Report Server*

The General page, the Data Sources page, and the Security page on the Properties tab for the Report Model look and function almost identical to their counterparts for a report. This means you can use the Report Manager to make security role assignments on the Report Model as a whole. The Report Manager does not let you make security role assignments for individual parts of the model.

The SQL Server Management Studio provides you with more flexibility. Open the SQL Server Management Studio and connect to the Report Server. Navigate through the folders until you come to the entry for the Galactic Report Model. Now, double-click the entry for Galactic to open the Model Properties dialog box. This is shown in Figure D-7.

The pages of the Report Model Properties dialog box in the SQL Server Management Studio mirror the property pages available in the Report Manager. The one exception is the Model Item Security page shown in Figure D-8. This page enables you to assign specific security roles to individual items within the model.

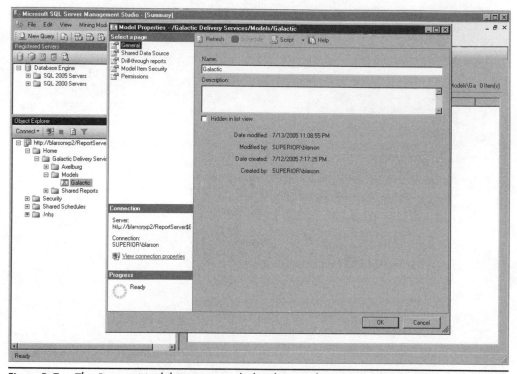

Figure D-7   *The Report Model Properties dialog box in the SQL Server Management Studio*

Check Secure Individual Model Items Independently for This Model to allow security roles to be assigned within the model. Next, create independent security entries for the root (Galactic) folder of the model. You must create at least one independent security entry for the root folder before you can create entries for model items and child folders.

Next, navigate to an item within the model that should have its own security assignment. For example, the Employee Evaluation folder in our model should have different security role assignments than the rest of the model. You can select the Employee Evaluation folder within the model and click Use These Roles for Each Group or User Account. This breaks the security roles this model folder would otherwise inherit and enables you to set your own. You can then use the Add Group or User button to add a security role assignment to a user or a group.

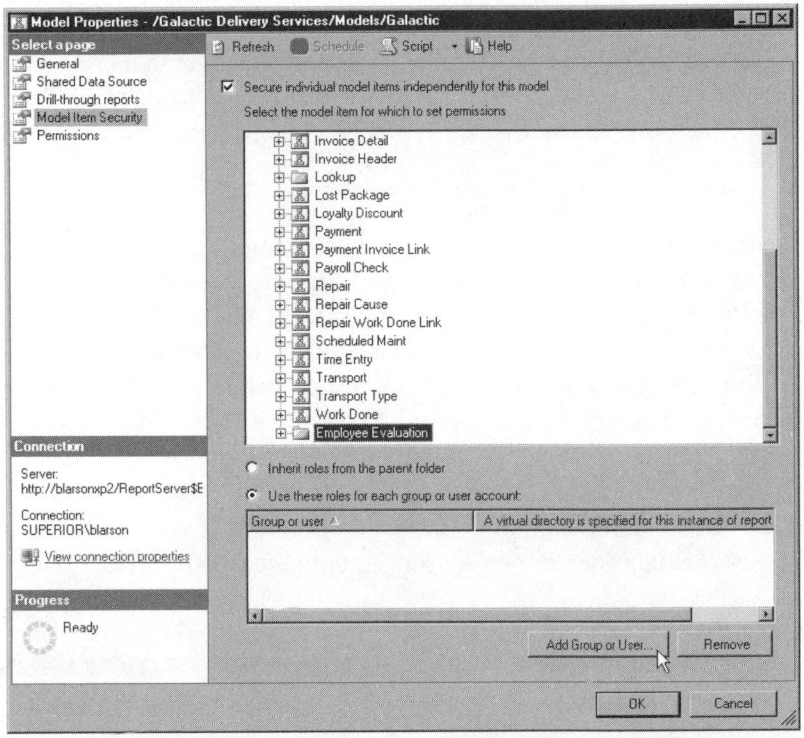

Figure D-8   *The Model Item Security page of the Report Model Properties dialog box*

Creating Reports with the Report Builder

Now that a Report Model is in place on the server, users can create reports based on that model using the Report Builder. Three types of report layouts are available in the Report Builder: the table report, the matrix report, and the chart. We look at brief examples of all three reports but, first, let's go over some of the basics.

Report Builder Basics

The Report Builder is a special type of Windows program known as a *ClickOnce application*, which is installed on your computer by following a link or clicking a button on a web form. The application is launched in the same way.

Launching the Report Builder Application

You launch the Report Builder by bringing up Report Manager in a browser, and then clicking the Report Builder button in the toolbar. You can also launch the Report Builder without first going to the Report Manager. This is done using the following URL:

```
http://{ReportServer}/ReportServer/ReportBuilder/ReportBuilder.application
```

where {ReportServer} is the name of your report server.

The Microsoft Report Builder launches and begins creating a new report. The Task pane is displayed on the right side of the screen. You must select a data source for the report. See Figure D-9. Instead of basing your report on the entire Report Model, you can select a perspective from within the model. As you learned earlier, a perspective is a subset of the information in the model. Usually, a perspective coincides with a particular job or work area within an organization.

If a plus sign is to the left of the model, then the model contains one or more perspectives. Click the plus sign to view the perspectives. If you select one of these perspectives as the data source for your report, only the entities in that perspective

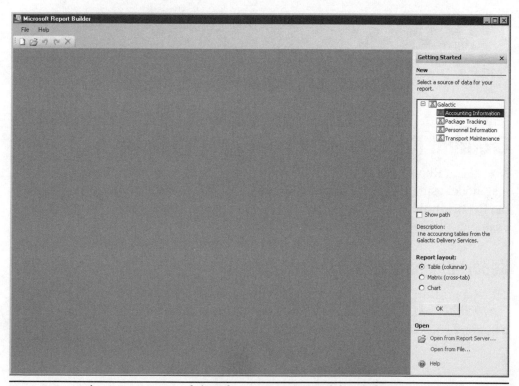

Figure D-9   *Selecting a source of data from a Report Model with four perspectives*

are available to your report. Because perspectives reduce the number of entities you have to look through to find the data you need on your report, it is usually a good idea to choose a perspective rather than using the entire Report Model.

You must also select a report layout. The Task pane shows the three types of report layouts available in Report Builder. The *table report* creates a report with rows and columns. This is the most familiar report layout. In a table report, the columns are predefined by the report layout and we will not know the number of rows until the data is selected at run time.

The *matrix report* creates a report containing what is known as either a crosstab or a pivot table. We do not know how many columns or rows will be in the matrix in advance, because it uses data selected at run time to define both. The matrix report can be somewhat confusing the first time you encounter it, but an example usually helps. If you are fuzzy on how a matrix works, be sure to check out the sample matrix report.

The *chart* creates a business graphic from the data. This can be a line graph, a bar chart, or a pie chart, among other things. While you can create a basic chart with a few mouse clicks, the chart report itself has a large number of options that enable you to format the chart just the way you want it.

If you are creating a new report, select the Report Model or the perspective that should serve as the data source along with the report layout and click OK. If you want to edit an existing report, click the Open button in the toolbar. You can then navigate the Report Server folder structure to find the Report Builder report you want to edit. You cannot use the Report Builder to edit reports that were created or edited using the Report Designer in Visual Studio 2005 or the Business Intelligence Development Studio.

Entities, Roles, and Fields

Reports are created in the Report Builder using entities, roles, and fields. Entities are simply the objects or processes our data know something about. Employees, Customers, and Deliveries are all examples of entities in the Galactic Report Model used in these examples. A single report may contain information from a single entity or from several related entities. Entities can be grouped together in entity folders within the Report Model or perspective to help keep things organized.

Roles show us how one entity relates to another entity. For example, a delivery is related to a customer through its role as a delivery of a package for that customer. An employee is related to a customer through the employee's role as an account representative for that customer. A delivery hub is related to a delivery through its role as a stop on a delivery route.

Roles enable us to show information from multiple entities together on a single report in a meaningful manner. This may seem a bit confusing as you read about it but, remember, the roles are already defined for you by the Report Model. If the model has been created properly, you should find they are natural to the way you think about your business processes. Information from different entities should combine on your reports just as you expect, without having to get caught up in the technical structure behind the relationships.

The information about the entities is stored in fields. A field is simply one bit of information: a first name, an invoice number, a hiring date. Fields are what we place on our reports to spit out these bits of information.

The Entities List

Once a Report Model is selected for your data source, or an existing report is chosen for editing, the main Report Builder opens. When creating a new report with the Accounting Information perspective chosen as the source, the Report Builder appears similar to Figure D-10. Let's take a look at each of the windows that make up this screen.

The *Entities list*, in the upper-left corner, shows the entities and entity folders in the selected Report Model or perspective. All the data in a Report Builder report

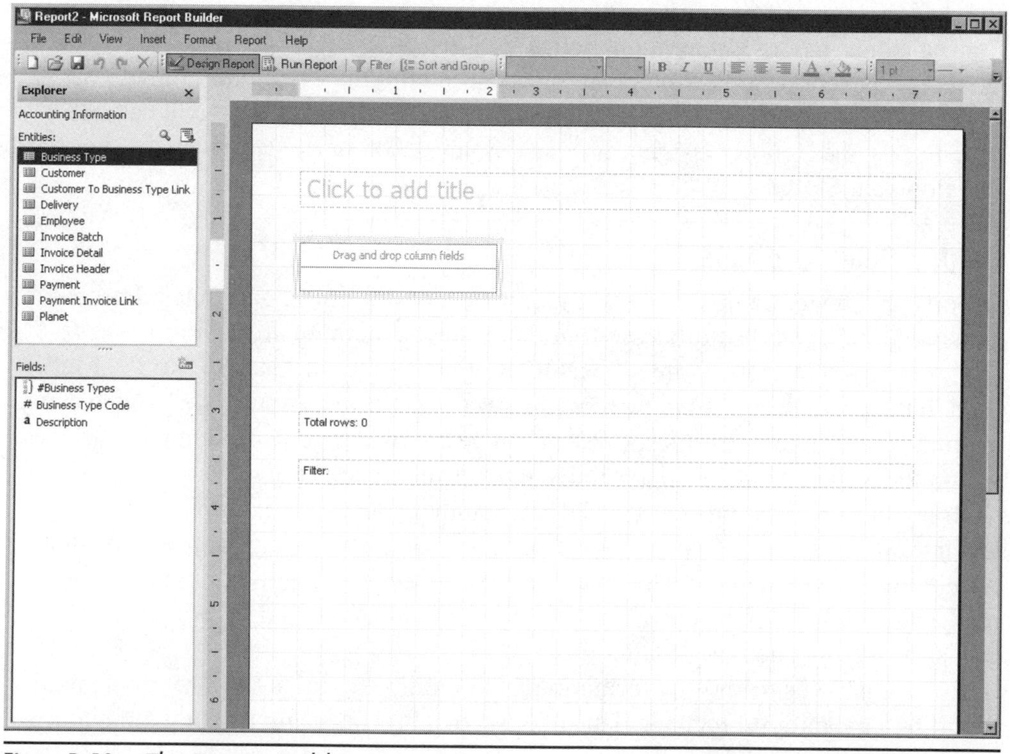

Figure D-10   *The Report Builder screen*

comes from the entities displayed in this window. Once an entity has been selected and placed on the report, the Entities list shows that entity along with its roles.

The Fields List

The *Fields list*, in the lower-left corner, shows the fields available for the selected entity. Some of these fields contain information coming directly from the database, while others contain information calculated by the report. The icon to the left of the field identifies the type of data being stored in the field. A pound sign (#) indicates a field contains numeric data. A small letter *a* indicates a field containing alphanumeric data. A check box indicates a field that contains yes or no, true or false data. A calendar indicates a date and time. A grouping of three yellow boxes indicates a calculated field that combines values from a number of items into one value, for example, the sum of all invoice amounts for a customer.

You can create your own calculated fields by clicking the new field button at the upper-right corner of the Fields list. This displays the Define Formula dialog box shown in Figure D-11. Use this dialog box to define your calculated field. You can

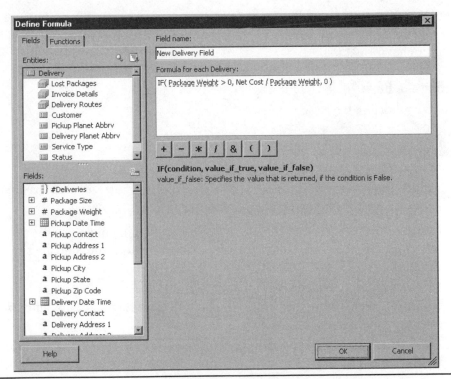

Figure D-11   *The Define Formula dialog box*

create expressions by dragging existing fields on to the Formula area. The fields values can be combined using the arithmetic and string operator buttons below the Formula area. You can also use the Functions tab to reference a large number of functions that can be used in your expressions. Once you click OK to create the calculated field, it is displayed in the Fields list of the Report Builder.

Clickthrough Reports

As discussed earlier, entities are related through roles in our data model. Sometimes it can be helpful, as you are analyzing your data, to follow these role relationships through your data. The Report Builder enables you to do this by using clickthrough reports.

Clickthrough reports are automatically created when you click on a role relationship to move from one entity to another. The clickthrough reports are defined on the fly according to the data in the model for the entity being reported on. Each clickthrough report can lead to other clickthrough reports. Using clickthrough reports, you can continue to follow your data wherever it may lead to perform in-depth analysis.

Creating a Table Layout Report

We begin by creating a table layout report showing customers and their deliveries. We create the basic report, modify the report to show monthly information, and then add additional formatting.

Creating the Basic Table Layout Report

We start by creating the basic report.

1. Open a browser and bring up the Report Manager using the following URL:

   `http://{ReportServer}/Reports`

   where {ReportServer} is the name of your Reporting Services Report Server.
2. Click the Report Builder button in the Report Manager toolbar.
3. Click the appropriate responses to any security warning dialog boxes that may appear to allow the Report Builder application to be downloaded and installed.
4. Make sure the Galactic Report Model is selected as a source of data for your report. Also, make sure the Table (columnar) Report Layout radio button is selected. Click OK.
5. Double-click the Click to Add Title text box on the report layout. Enter **Customer Deliveries**.

6. Click Customer in the Entities list. Drag Customer and drop it on the Drag and Drop Column Fields area of the report layout. A grouping is created for Customer with three columns: Name, Customer Number, and Billing Contact.

7. The string of *X*s in each column is the template for the data. It shows you how wide and in what format the data will appear. The data in the Customer Number column is much narrower than the heading. To save space, let's make this a two-line heading. Position the mouse pointer so you can drag the Customer Number column narrower as shown in Figure D-12. Drag the column just narrow enough so the Customer Number heading wraps to two lines.

8. Now, drag the headings row tall enough to accommodate the two-line heading.

9. The Customer Number is helpful in our report, but Billing Contact is not necessary. Right-click the Billing Contact column and select Delete from the Context menu. The Billing Contact column will be removed from the report.

10. Next, you want to use the date of pickup to identify each delivery. If you are familiar with the Report Model, you can use the Entities list and the Fields list to find the appropriate field. If you are not familiar with the Report Model, you may need some assistance. Click the magnifying glass in the upper-right corner of the Explorer pane to get that assistance. The Search dialog appears.

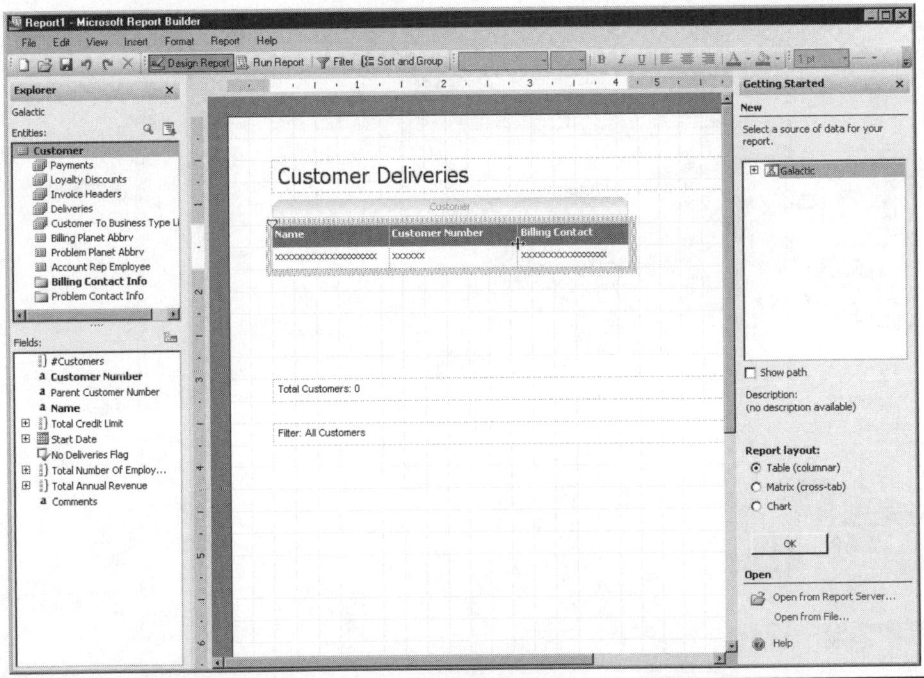

Figure D-12   *Narrowing a column in the Report Builder*

11. Enter **delivery date** for the Search text. Select Entire Data Source to search the entire Report Model rather than the current item only. (The current item would be the Customer entity, because that was the last entity placed on the report.) Click Find.

12. You see a list of all fields in the Report Model that contain "delivery date." Note, the search is not case-sensitive. Scroll down until you find the Delivery Date Time field with a location of Customer/Deliveries in the Search Result. (Make sure you select the Delivery Date Time field from the correct location!) Select this item and click OK. You jump to the Delivery Date Time field in the Fields list.

13. Click the Delivery Date Time field and drag it onto the report layout, over the top of the Customer Number column. You see a blue insert bar as shown in Figure D-13. Drop the field to create a new column at the location of the insert bar.

14. There is a template for the content of the Delivery Date Time column. It shows the date portion will be displayed, but the time portion will not. With a package delivery, both the date and time are important. To change this formatting, right-click on the Delivery Date Time and select Format from the Context menu. The Format dialog box appears.

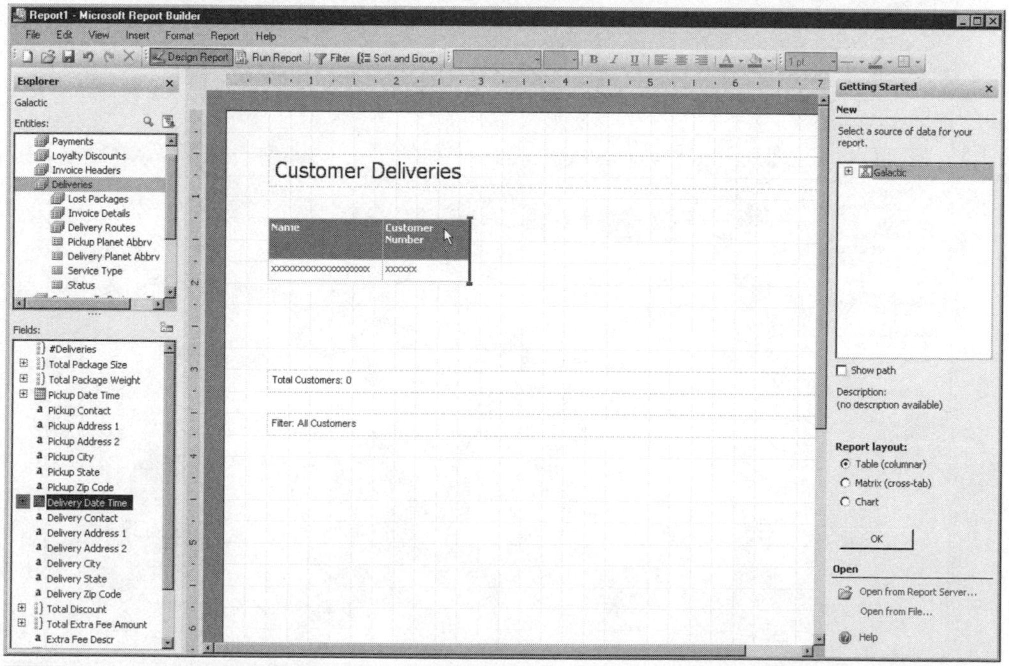

Figure D-13   *Adding a column to the report*

15. Select the Number tab. (Why this is called Number when it contains other formatting options as well is beyond me.)

16. You can see a number of available formats for the Delivery Date Time. Select a format that contains both the date and the time. Click OK to return to the report layout.

17. Expand the Delivery Date Time column, so the template and the heading do not wrap.

18. Now let's add the cost of each delivery. The cost is in the Service Type entity, because cost is based on the type of service used. In the Entities list, click Service Type. The Fields list now shows the fields for the Service Type entity. Select Total Cost and drag-and-drop it on the report layout. Note, as you drag the Total Cost field over the existing layout, you could put it in between any of the existing columns. For this layout, drop it on the right side. Your report layout should appear as shown in Figure D-14.

19. Let's preview the report and see what we have so far. Click Run Report in the Report Builder toolbar. The report should appear as shown in Figure D-15.

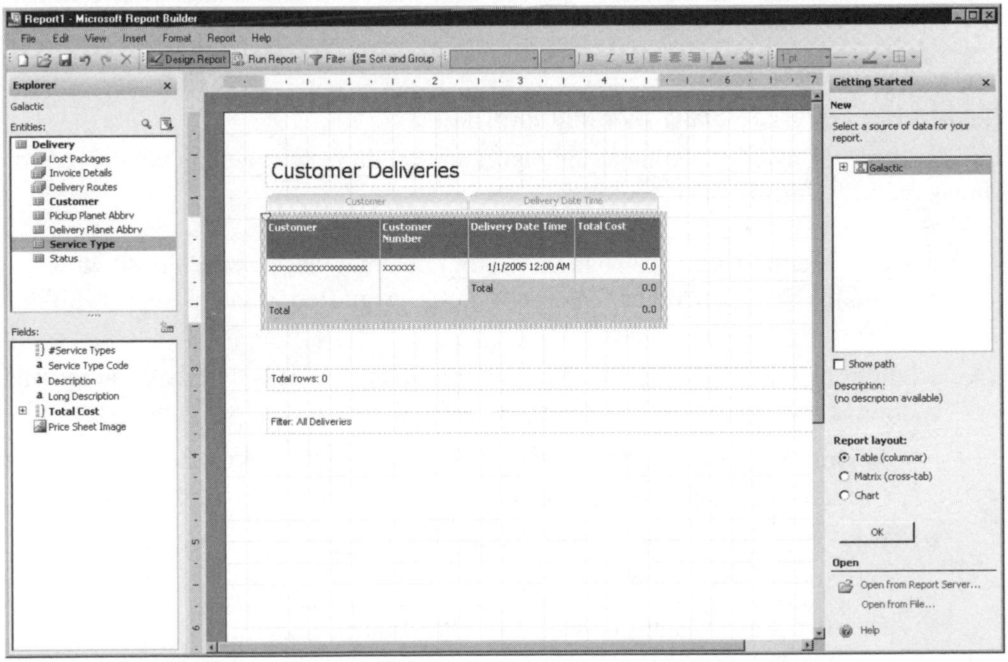

Figure D-14   *The table report layout*

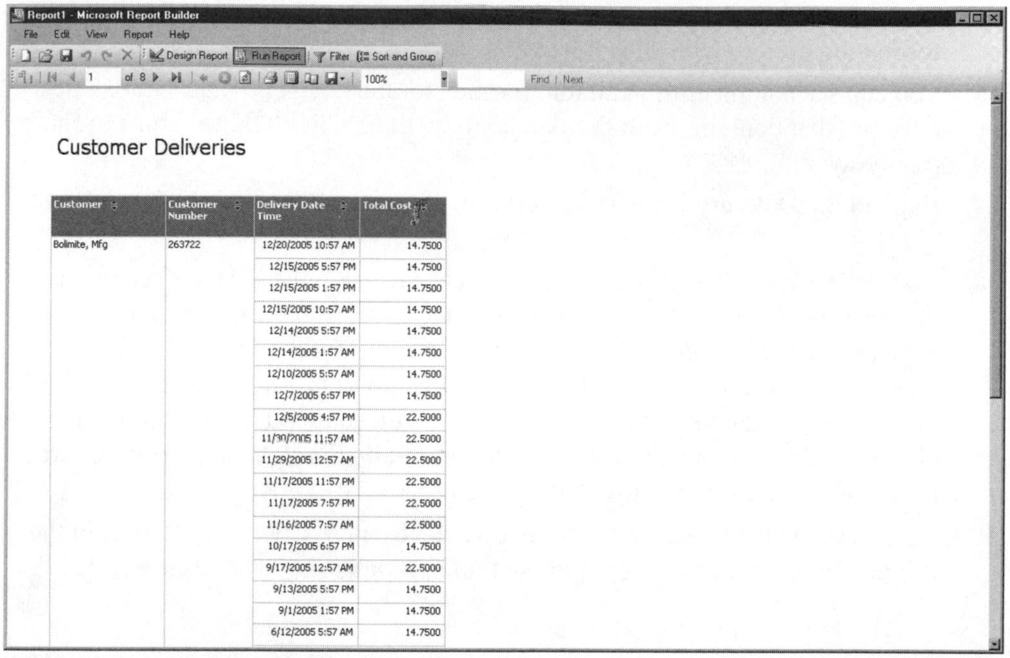

Figure D-15 *The table report preview*

Modify the Report to Show Monthly Information

Let's add some basic formatting to the report and modify our grouping, so the report shows monthly information.

1. You can see the Total Cost column has four decimal places, which is not how we usually like to see dollar amounts. Click Design Report in the Report Builder toolbar to return to the report layout.

2. Right-click the template in the Cost column on the report layout. Take a moment to look at the options available in the Context menu shown in Figure D-16.

   ▶ **Format**   Displays the Format dialog to modify the colors, borders, and formatting of the column content.

   ▶ **Edit Formula**   Displays the Define Formula dialog box to modify the content of the column.

   ▶ **Delete**   Removes this column from the report.

   ▶ **Show Subtotal**   Unchecking this option removes all the subtotaling from the report.

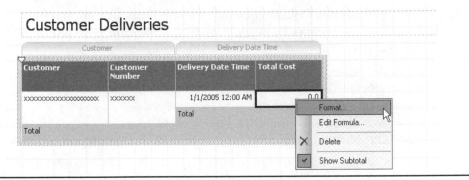

Figure D-16   *The column Context menu*

3. Select Format from the Context menu. The Format dialog box appears.

4. Select the format that includes the dollar sign and click OK.

5. Repeat this for each field in the Total Cost column. You can use SHIFT to select and change the format of both remaining fields at the same time.

6. Looking at the cost for every delivery is a bit overwhelming for the user. Instead, let's look at the cost for each month. To do this, you need a field that contains the year and month from the Delivery Date Time field. Select Delivery in the Entities list, and then click the New Field button above the Fields list. The Define Formula dialog box appears.

7. Enter **Delivery Month** for Field Name.

8. Select the Functions tab and expand the Conversion entry. Double-click the TEXT function. This function converts a numeric or date value to text.

9. Select the Fields tab. Expand the Delivery Date Time entry in the Fields list. Double-click the Delivery Date Time Year field, which is the third entry under Delivery Date Time. Notice this field was placed inside the TEXT function. The formula takes the year portion of the Delivery Date Time and converts it from a number to text.

10. Press END to move the cursor to the end of the formula. Click the ampersand button.

11. Select the Functions tab and expand the Text entry. (This is the Text entry with the folder icon, not the TEXT entry with the *fx* icon.) Double-click the RIGHT function. This function returns the rightmost characters of a string.

12. Replace the highlighted text with " " and click the ampersand button.

13. Double-click the TEXT function. The TEXT function is nested inside the RIGHT function. Functions may be nested up to seven levels deep.

14. Select the Fields tab. Double-click the Delivery Date Time Month field. This is the second entry under Delivery Date Time. This field is placed inside of the TEXT function.

15. Replace the yellow-highlighted word "length" with **2**. This second part of the formula appends the month number, as a string, after the year. The RIGHT function adds a space before single-digit month numbers, so they sort properly with the two-digit month numbers. When complete, your formula should match the formula shown in Figure D-17.

16. Click OK to exit the Define Formula dialog box. The new Delivery Month calculated field appears at the top of the Fields list.

17. Drag the Delivery Month field from the Fields list and drop it to the left of the Delivery Date Time field in the report layout.

18. Right-click the Delivery Date Time column in the report layout and select Delete from the Context menu. Now the Total Cost column is part of the Delivery Month group. The report layout appears as shown in Figure D-18.

19. Click Run Report to preview the report.

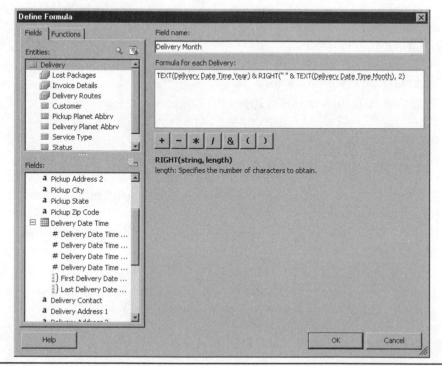

Figure D-17 *The Delivery Month field formula*

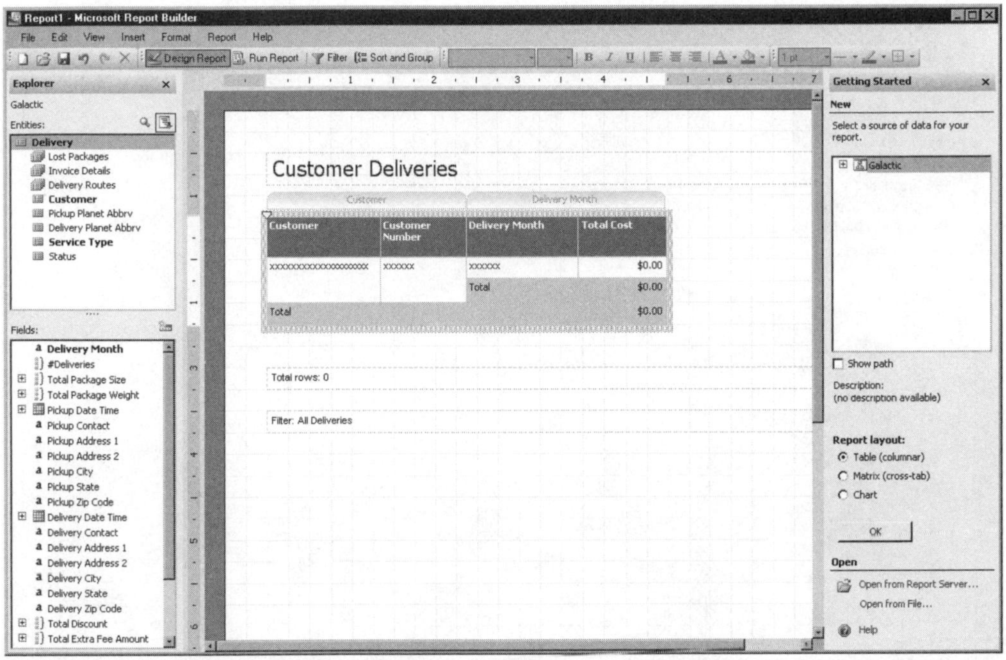

Figure D-18   *The table report layout with monthly information*

Add More Formatting

Now, let's add more formatting, filtering, and sorting.

1. Note, there are entries from both 2004 and 2005. Let's look at only 2005 deliveries. Click Design Report in the Report Builder toolbar to return to the report layout.

2. Click Filter in the Report Builder toolbar. The Filter Data dialog box appears.

3. Select Delivery in the Entities list of the Filter Data dialog box, and then expand Delivery Date Time in the Fields list. Double-click Delivery Date Time Year in the Fields list of the Filter Data dialog box. Enter **2005** for the Equals value. (See Figure D-19.)

4. While we are filtering, let's also limit the report to only those deliveries made to the city of Axelburg. Double-click the Delivery City field in the Fields list of the Filter Data dialog box.

5. Notice how the Report Builder creates a drop-down list of all unique values in the Delivery City field. Select Axelburg from this drop-down list.

6. The Filter Data dialog box should appear as shown in Figure D-19.

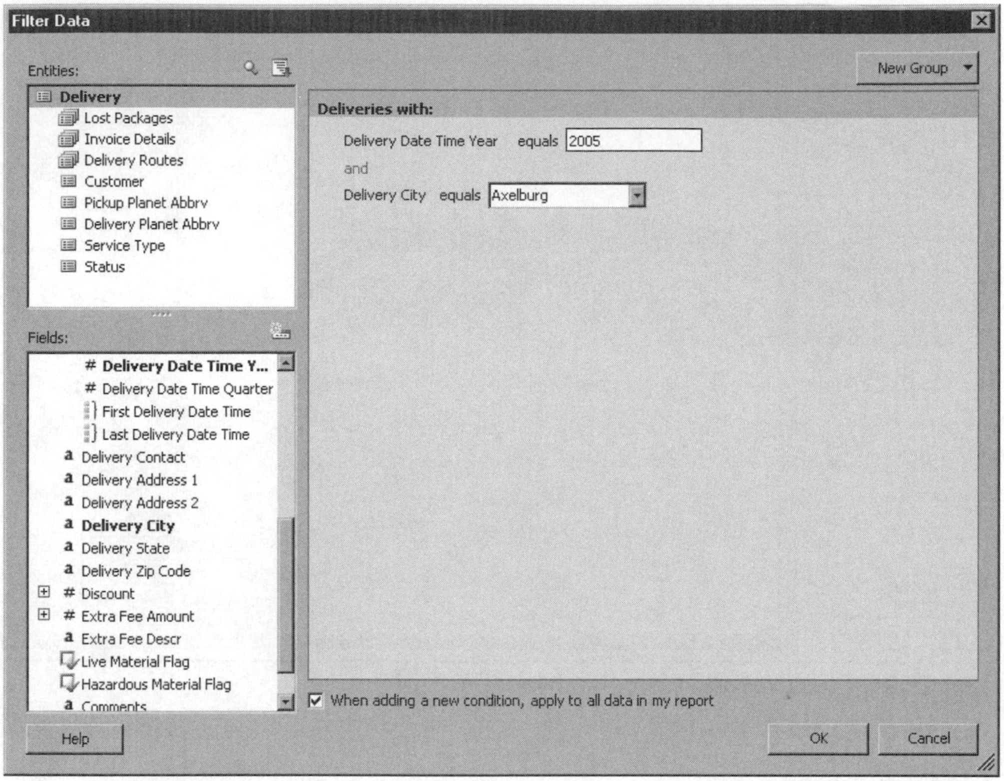

Figure D-19   *The Filter Data dialog box*

7. Click OK to exit the Filter Data dialog box.

8. Let's also change the sort order, so we can see the most recent month first. Click Sort and Group in the Report Builder toolbar. The Sort dialog box appears.

9. Select the Delivery Month group in the Select Group list. Pick Delivery Month from the Sort By drop-down list and select Descending for this sort. The dialog box should appear as shown in Figure D-20.

10. Click OK to exit the Sort dialog box.

11. Click Run Report to preview the report. Note, there are now only entries for 2005 and the months are in descending order.

12. Click Design Report. We'll try one more modification. Suppose, now that we have seen the information in this report, we want to analyze not only which companies are sending packages to Axelburg, but also where those packages

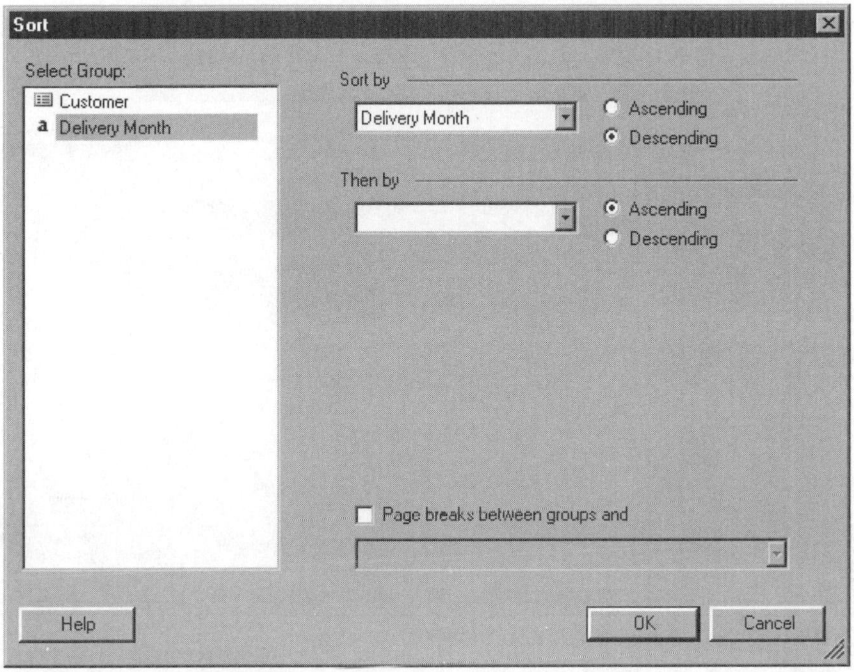

Figure D-20   *The Sort dialog box*

are originating from. We need to look at the location of each company. We use
the city from the billing address to make that determination.

13. Select Customer in the Entities list, and then select the Billing Contact Info folder
     under Customer in the Entities list.

14. Click the Billing City field in the Fields list and drag it to the *left* of the Customer
     column in the report layout. A new grouping is created for Billing City. Your report
     layout should appear as shown in Figure D-21.

15. Click Run Report. The report should appear similar to Figure D-22.

Clickthrough Reports and Saving the Report Builder Report

You have seen how the Report Builder enables us to quickly build a table report.
You have also seen how you can enhance that report to gain more information as you
conduct your ad hoc analysis. Beyond this, exploring related information during ad
hoc analysis is often helpful. Further, once you have a report that works well, you
may want to share that report with others.

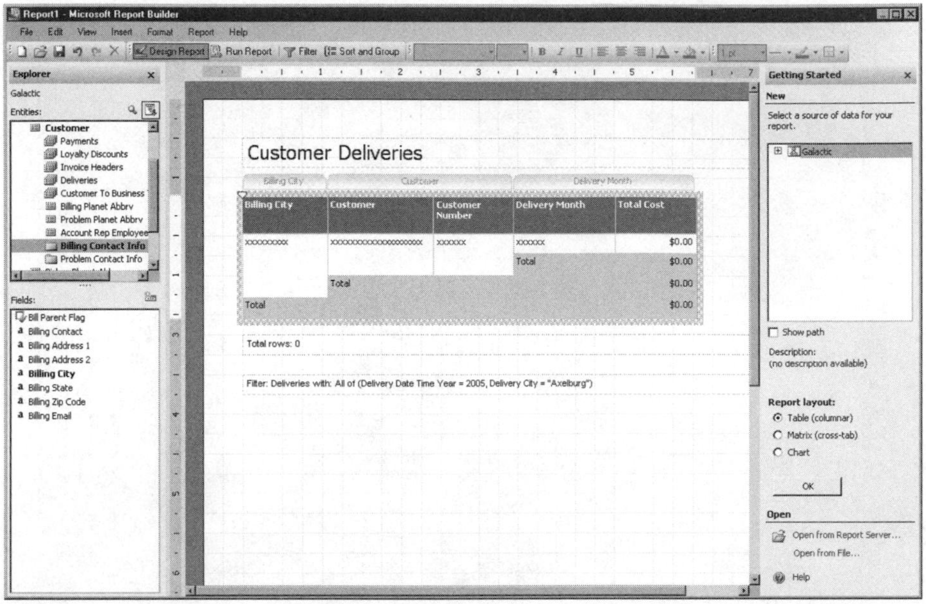

Figure D-21 *The completed table report layout*

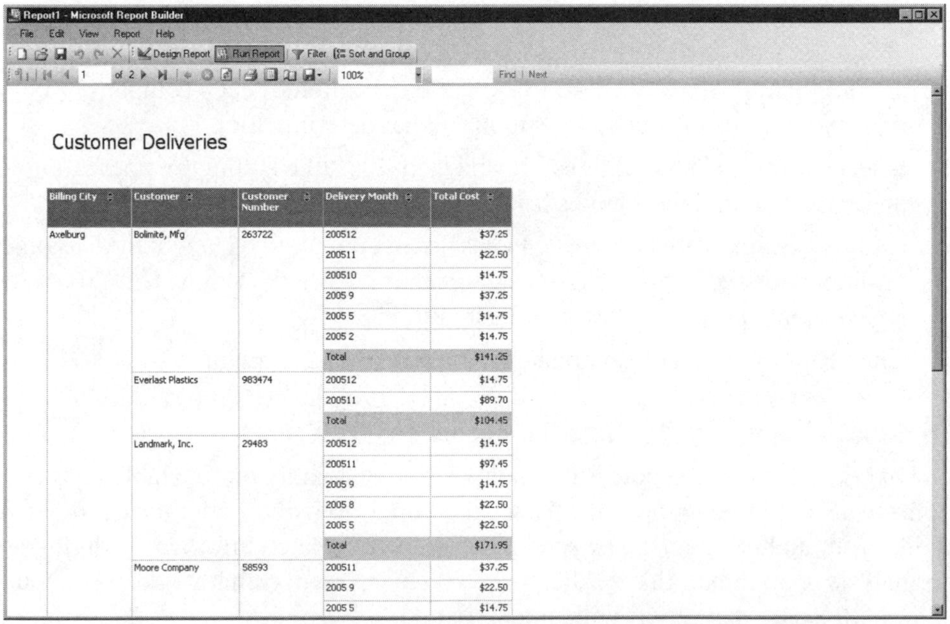

Figure D-22 *The completed table report preview*

Let's look at how to do both of these tasks.

1. Click Run Report, if the report is not running.

2. Hover the mouse pointer over Landmark, Inc. on Page 1 of the report. The mouse pointer changes from an arrow to a hand. This indicates a clickable link is at this location in the report.

3. Go ahead and click this link. A report showing information about the customer, Landmark, Inc., appears. This is a clickthrough report. This report did not exist before you clicked the link. Instead, it was built on the fly when you asked for it.

4. Click the 2 across from # Invoice Headers. A clickthrough report showing the two invoice headers appears.

5. Click the 10 under # Invoice Details. A clickthrough report showing the ten invoice detail lines for this invoice appears.

6. Click the 7 under Line Number. A clickthrough report showing the information from invoice detail line 7 appears. As long as there is related information, you can continue to navigate to new reports using the clickthrough links.

7. Click the Back to Parent Report arrow in the Report Viewer toolbar to navigate back through the clickthrough reports. The back arrow is shown in Figure D-23. Continue going back until you get to the original Customer Deliveries table report.

8. Click Save in the Report Builder toolbar. The Save As Report dialog box appears. The Save Report dialog box always starts at the Report Server Home folder.

9. Double-click Galactic Delivery Services in the list of folders. Double-click Shared Reports. Enter **Customer Table Report** for Name, and then click Save. (To open an existing Report Builder report, click Open on the Report Builder toolbar.)

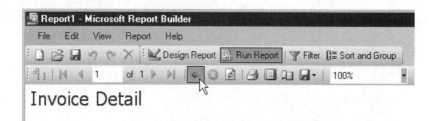

Figure D-23   *The Back to Parent Report arrow in the Report Viewer*

10. Return to the Report Manager running in your browser and navigate to the Shared Reports folder. An entry for the Customer Table Report is in the Shared Reports folder. This entry was created when you saved the report. In fact, the only way to save a Report Builder report is to place it in a folder on the Report Server.

11. Click the entry for the Customer Table Report to run the report. You see it looks exactly the same as when you ran the report in the Report Builder. You can even click on items to jump to clickthrough reports.

Once you have a report in the Report Manager, you can save the report definition to a file in your file system and edit it in a report project with Visual Studio 2005. This makes it possible for an ad hoc report to serve as a starting point for the authoring of a standard report. To do this, click the Properties tab while you are viewing the Customer Table Report in the Report Manager. The Edit link under Report Definition enables you to save this report definition to a file. See Chapter 10 for more information.

If you do edit a Report Builder report in Visual Studio 2005, you may have to modify the data source and query used in the dataset of the report. Once these changes have been made, the report cannot be edited in the Report Builder. You may be able to make some minor formatting, without previewing the report in Visual Studio, save the report back to the Report Manager, and still edit the report in the Report Builder.

Creating a Matrix Layout Report

Next, we look at a Report Builder report that functions a bit differently. This is the matrix layout report. As mentioned earlier, a matrix layout report is the same as what other tools call a pivot table or crosstab report. Let's see how it works.

Creating the Basic Matrix Report

1. Return to the Report Builder, if you are not already there. Click Design Report, if the previous report is still being run.

2. Click New in the Report Builder toolbar.

3. We use one of the perspectives from the data model for this report. Expand the Galactic Report Model entry in the Task pane and select the Package Tracking perspective.

4. Select Matrix (cross-tab) for the report layout in the Task pane.

5. Click OK in the Task pane.

6. Double-click the Click to Add Title text box.

7. Enter **Deliveries by Customer by Service Type** into this text box as the report title.

8. Select Customer in the Entities list.

9. Drag the Name field from the Fields list and drop it on the Drag and Drop Row Groups area of the report layout.

10. In the Entities list, select Deliveries. Also in the Entities list, select Service Type under Deliveries.

11. Drag the Description field from the Fields list and drop it on the Drag and Drop Column Groups area of the report layout.

12. Drag the #Deliveries field from the Fields list and drop it on the Drag and Drop Totals area of the report layout.

13. Click Run Report. Just that quickly, you have a report showing the number of deliveries of each type for each customer.

Adding Groupings to the Matrix

Let's add more grouping levels to the matrix.

1. Click Design Report.

2. Drag the Pickup City field from the Fields list and drop it to the left of Customer in the matrix. This creates a grouping on the pickup city.

3. Click Run Report. Note how the report now has a row grouping for each Pickup City. You can expand a Pickup City to see the row groupings for the Customers within that Pickup City.

4. Click Design Report.

5. Because this report grows horizontally, it should use a landscape page layout. Right-click somewhere on the page layout area that is not occupied by a report item. Select Page Setup from the Context menu. The Page Setup menu appears.

6. Select Landscape and click OK.

7. Expand Pickup Date Time in the Fields list. Drag the Pickup Date Time Year field from the Fields list and drop it below the Service Type (#Deliveries) column heading as shown in Figure D-24. This creates a column grouping for each year with columns within each year for each Service Type.

8. Click Run Report. Note the new column grouping.

9. Click Save in the Report Builder toolbar. The Save As Report dialog box appears.

10. Double-click Galactic Delivery Services in the list of folders. Double-click Shared Reports. Enter **Deliveries by Customer by Service Type Report** for Name. Click Save. This report is now available in the Shared Reports folder on the Report Server.

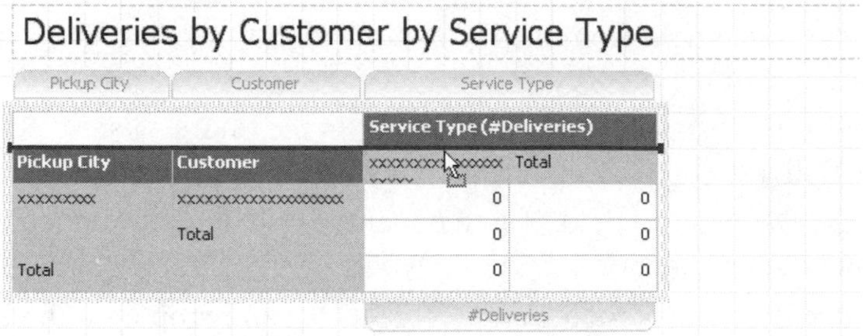

Figure D-24 *Adding a new column grouping to the matrix*

Creating a Chart Layout Report

Finally, we look at a Report Builder report that creates a business chart.

Creating the Chart Layout Report

1. Return to the Report Builder, if you are not already there. Click Design Report, if the previous report is still being run.

2. Click New in the Report Builder toolbar.

3. Select the Galactic Report Model in the Task pane.

4. Select Chart for Report layout in the Task pane. Click OK in the Task pane.

5. Right-click somewhere on the page layout area that is not occupied by a report item. Select Page Setup from the Context menu. The Page Setup menu appears.

6. Select Landscape and click OK.

7. Charts like lots of space. Click the chart. Click the sizing handle on the right side of the chart and drag the chart as wide as the page. This is shown in Figure D-25.

8. Select the text box containing the word "Filter:" and drag this text box down to the bottom of the page.

9. Click the chart. Click the sizing handle on the bottom of the chart and drag the bottom of the chart, so it is just above the Filter text box.

10. Select Customer in the Entities list. Drag the Name field from the Fields list and drop it on Drag and Drop Category Fields.

11. Select Deliveries in the Entities list. Drag the #Deliveries field from the Fields list and drop it on Drag and Drop Data Value Fields.

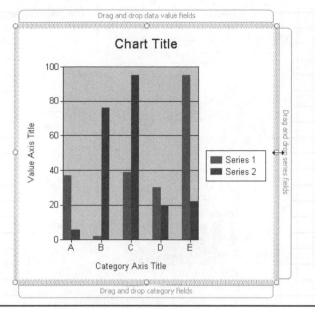

Figure D-25   *Expanding the chart report item*

12.   Expand the Pickup Date Time field in the Fields list. Drag the Pickup Date Time Year field from the Fields list and drop it on Drag and Drop Series Fields.

13.   Right-click the chart and select Chart Options from the Context menu. The Chart Options dialog box appears.

14.   The Chart Type tab of the dialog box enables us to change the type of chart being used to display the data. We use the default chart type, the Column chart. Select the Titles tab.

15.   Enter **Deliveries by Customer by Year** for Chart Title. Enter **Customers** for Category Title. This is the label on the *X* axis of the chart. Enter **Number of Deliveries** for Value Title. This is the label on the *Y* axis of the chart.

16.   Select the 3-D Effect tab.

17.   Check the Display Chart with 3-D Visual Effect check box. Also, check the Orthographic check box.

18.   Click OK to exit the Chart Options dialog box.

19.   Click Run Report. Your report should appear as shown in Figure D-26.

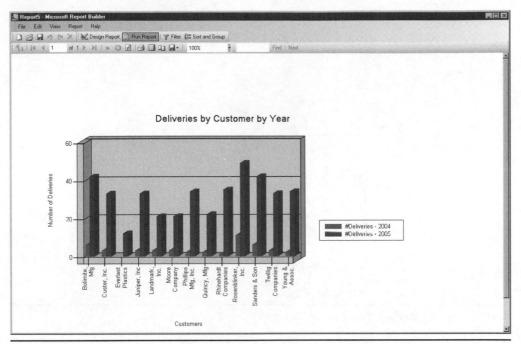

Figure D-26   *The chart report preview*

20. Click Save in the Report Builder toolbar. The Save As Report dialog box appears.

21. Double-click Galactic Delivery Services in the list of folders. Double-click Shared Reports. Enter **Deliveries by Customer by Year Chart** for Name. Click Save. This report is now available in the Shared Reports folder on the Report Server.

Give It a Try

As with most skills, the best way to become proficient at creating ad hoc reports with the Report Builder is to do it. Use the model built on the Galactic database to practice your data analysis. Better yet, have one or more models created from your own organization's data and jump right in.

Remember, you can't break anything, so give it a try.

Index